Managing Your Company Cars

3rd edition

Colin Tourick

Eyelevel Books

Comments on **Managing Your Company Cars** by leaders in UK vehicle management and leasing

"With constant pressure to cut costs and a rapidly changing legislative and tax environment, the modern fleet manager faces more challenges than ever. Colin has produced a very timely update of this essential fleet management handbook"

John Lewis
Chief Executive
British Vehicle Rental and Leasing Association

Every profession should have a reference book; if you're in fleet management, this is it!

James Langley,
Chairman,
Training & Education Committee,
Institute of Car Fleet Management

Fleet management can be a complex and sometimes confusing occupation. Colin's book unravels the mystery, providing a compendium of fleet best practice. Essential reading for any professional fleet decision maker.

Stephen Briers, Editor, Fleet News

You will be hard pressed to find a company car issue which is not covered somewhere in this book – it's a positive mine of knowledge and best practice compiled by an undoubted expert.

Professor Peter Cooke
Head of the Centre for Automotive Management
University of Buckingham Business School

A concise, insightful and invaluable resource. If Fleet Management is your religion, then this book is your bible!

Keith Cook
Financial Controller
Computacenter

The much-awaited third edition of Managing Your Company Cars is indispensible in the fast-moving fleet industry. Colin has devised a way of minimising the obsolescent of an all-encompassing text book such as this, which surely adds to its being a vital part of any fleet manager's portfolio.

Brian Rogerson
Managing Editor
Asset Finance International

Professor Tourick is brilliant at this: simplifying complex business car management issues into easily understood English. Whether you are a fleet manager with a 100 vehicles, or a small business with 10 cars, this latest book is invaluable.

Ralph Morton
Editor
BusinessCarManager.co.uk

If you're running, financing, managing, servicing or selling business cars or vans, you need this book close to hand - it's an invaluable reference point for all fleets.

Steve Moody
Editor
Fleet World

Managing Your Company Cars
3rd edition

Colin Tourick

Managing Your Company Cars 3rd edition
Colin Tourick

© Colin Tourick 2011

Published by:

Eyelevel Books
Worcester

www.eyelevelbooks.co.uk

Printed in Great Britain by
Ashford Colour Press, Gosport

ISBN 9781902528328

The information contained in this book is of a general nature believed to be correct at the time of writing.

Readers of this book will work for many different types of organisation, domestic and overseas, tax payers and non-taxpayers, VAT-registered and not, creditworthy and not, government bodies, clubs, trade bodies, trusts and with large fleets or small fleets. Advice that works in one situation may be wholly inappropriate for another. So please use this book to point you in the right direction, for general principles rather than advice that will definitely work for you. There is no substitute for professional advice that is tailored to your individual needs.

Neither the author nor publisher can take any responsibility for any loss, cost or expense arising from use of this book, whether arising from errors or omissions, from subsequent changes to the information or for any other reason. While we have taken great care over the details in the book and the information is believed to be correct, we cannot be responsible for any inaccuracies.

The views expressed in this book are those of the author and may not necessarily be shared by the sponsor.

For Hilary Davis

Always an inspiration

A NOTE FROM KEITH ALLEN, MANAGING DIRECTOR, ALD AUTOMOTIVE (UK)

As the operational leasing and fleet management division of Société Générale the ALD Automotive group is the second largest vehicle leasing operation in Europe and manages over 877,000 vehicles across 37 countries worldwide.

Established in the UK in 1958, ALD Automotive has over 50 years experience in providing vehicle funding and ancillary support services and today manages a fleet of almost 70,000 vehicles for major corporates, SMEs and personal consumers. A lot of miles have been driven and a lot of changes have taken place since writing our first lease agreement – a Ford Prefect De Luxe saloon for a doctor in Bristol!

Back then, when there were fewer than 5 million cars on the road and cars were owned by less than a third of UK households, company cars were very much a rarity. Today, however, one million new company cars are acquired every year and, beyond this, an estimated 8 million drivers use their own cars on business, otherwise known as the 'grey fleet'.

Whilst it's not surprising that we've seen huge changes over a span of 50 years, the pace of change in the last decade has been phenomenal. Fleet funding and management decision making has become ever more complex or, at least, the options now available to businesses and to their drivers have become ever more varied. As a result, ALD Automotive has evolved considerably, immersing itself in understanding the key issues of the day and building up a wealth of experience and expertise to help guide our customers through the maze of factors impacting on them. Companies need to know about the ever evolving tax and legislative landscape within which their fleets operate, and the wide ranging influences encountered daily whether it be with 'cash for cars', accident management, driver training, telematics, e-commerce, outsourcing, insurance, fuel management or pan European leasing, etc.

Whilst ALD Automotive has helped its customers in a consultative role for over 50 years, as an additional support to gain a better understanding of the key issues we are delighted to be working in association with Professor Colin Tourick in the production of the 3rd edition of **Managing Your Company Cars**.

Colin is a man whose industry knowledge over the last 30 years is respected by everyone within the fleet industry and we hope you will find this book and the companion book **Company Car and Van Tax** to be useful reference guides that help you to manage your fleet.

Keith Allen, Managing Director,
ALD Automotive (UK)

www.aldautomotive.co.uk

AUTHOR'S FOREWORD

When I look at the extraordinarily wide range of functions carried out by the people in the contract hire, vehicle leasing and fleet management industries and the qualifications these people possess, I can only conclude that running a car fleet is a very complex thing to do.

It was while thinking about this that I started looking for a book that explained what the industry does and how it does it. I wanted such a book for staff training, particularly for newcomers to the industry. I also hoped it would be useful reading for students on the BVRLA Professional Development Programme, particularly the MBA course. I was surprised to see that, while the individual elements of vehicle finance and management were covered by a variety of books, nothing existed that covered them all in one place.

I decided to start to write a book to fill this gap and set to work whilst on holiday, sitting under a palm tree. An early decision was to write it as if I was talking to a fleet manager.

As I started writing I was amazed at how many topics come under the heading of 'vehicle management'. I found myself writing about the industry's products, legislation, purchasing, maintenance, disposal, rental calculations, interest, personal contracts, lease v buy, international leasing, fleet policy, vans, in-house leasing companies, fleet and tax administration, fleet management software, journey planning, telematics, taxation (of many types), the environment, developments in engine technology, alternative fuels, government grants – it seemed the list was endless. After two days I had a list of more than 300 bullet points.

Several months later, having spent goodness knows how many evenings and weekends on the project, I was able to fill in the many gaps and finish what proved to be the first draft of the first edition.

I was pleased with the response to the 1st edition and wrote the 2nd edition in 2005.

It has been seven years since the 2nd edition of this book was published. I had been meaning to produce a 3rd edition for some time but it's a massive undertaking – about 250 hours' work – so I kept on putting it off.

I decided instead to produce two books of interviews with fleet experts instead under the title Managing Your Company Cars: Expert Opinion. But I always knew I would eventually return to this book and was delighted when ALD Automotive offered to support the publication.

Seven years is a long time in the fleet sector. Once again I had to read through thousands of pages of legislation and research materials before I could start updating the book. We have seen changes in lease accounting, market practices and of course a lot of legislation – tax, consumer credit, consumer rights, engine emissions, continuous insurance enforcement, money laundering, driving offences, etc. The 2nd edition did not contain any reference to the grey fleet because this expression did not exist at that time and did not mention salary sacrifice.

This new edition includes two chapters of interviews with experts from ALD Automotive. I think these chapters add a great deal to the book.

I have significantly beefed up the information about company vans, to the point that I was thinking of renaming it Managing Your Company Cars and Vans (or maybe Managing Your Company Vehicles). In the event I decided to stick with the original name to show continuity with the earlier editions.

I am delighted that KPMG have been kind enough to double-check and recommend changes to the tax chapter.

Tax is the one issue that has always caused a problem for the publisher. It is such an essential fleet topic and any fleet manager will rightly expect to be able to find the answers to all of their tax questions in this book. The problem, of course, is that this book is not updated annually so the tax chapter gets out of date very quickly. This in turn tends to make the book age rather quickly.

I have finally solved that problem by producing two manuscripts.

- **Company Car and Van Tax**, a brand new publication that sets out the tax rules in detail.
- Chapter 17 of the book you are now reading, which explains the tax rules and concepts without referring to any particular year's rules or tax rates.

ALD Automotive has kindly agreed to sponsor both books.

Those two manuscripts are very similar. Chapter 17 of this book will give you a broad understanding of the employer's and employee's tax positions but if you want to see the tax rates and examples for a specific year you'll need a copy of Company Car and Van Tax.

As ever, you can't put together a book like this without help. I must thank:

- the BVRLA and FLA who once again were kind enough to supply material for inclusion
- ALD Automotive and KMPG for their support
- David Yates and all the team at ALD Automotive for their valuable input
- Marc van Eck and Stéphane Renie at ALD International for their chapter
- David Chandler, James Reardon and Stuart Bremner at KPMG for their hard work in reviewing the tax chapter
- Richard Freeman for help with research; and
- Jon Moore of Eyelevel Books for pulling it all together.

Colin Tourick
London
October 2011

www.tourick.com
Colin Tourick & Associates Limited
@ColinTourick

CONTENTS

INTRODUCTION

This book is written for fleet managers, that is, people who manage business vehicles.

'Fleet manager' may not be your job title. You may be an accountant, company secretary, purchasing manager, human resource manager or transport manager, or you may work in a department run by one of these people. You may be a managing director, finance director, commercial director, HR director or operations director or indeed hold any one of a wide range of board positions.

If you are responsible for some aspect of running your company's vehicle fleet – purchasing vehicles, approving and paying maintenance invoices, selling vehicles, arranging finance, dealing with a contract hire company, obtaining finance quotes, renewing motor insurance, or, indeed, anything whatsoever to do with company vehicles - this book is for you.

The book covers company cars, vans and light commercial vehicles weighing up to 3.5 tonnes. It excludes heavy goods vehicles above this weight because different operational and licensing rules apply to these vehicles. However, many of the principles in this book will apply to heavier vehicles too.

To make it more readable and less wordy I have tried wherever possible to use the word 'you' and to avoid using 'the fleet manager', 'the borrower', 'the lessee', 'your company', 'your business' or 'the client'.

Several types of fleet organisation can deliver the same service, so there are many places where it would have been correct to write 'the contract hire company, leasing company, fleet management company or funder'. For example,

> 'You should be able to obtain car benefit tax information from a contract hire company, leasing company or fleet management company'.

I have tried to avoid this, generally using 'the lessor' or 'the supplier'.

There is a brief section on how car leasing and contract hire companies run their businesses, to give you an insight into the issues that affect these companies and perhaps to explain why they do some of the things they do.

If you are responsible for a car fleet and you are new to fleet management, don't worry, you are not alone.

There are over a million businesses running fewer than five vehicles, 50,000 running 5-25 vehicles, 10,000 running 26-100 vehicles and 5,000 running over 100 vehicles.

Number of vehicles	Number of businesses (approx)
>5	>1,000,000
5-25	50,000
26-100	10,000
>100	5,000

By and large the issues confronting managers of large fleets are the same as the issues you have to deal with. The difference is just a matter of scale. There is a great deal of help available to you; from organisations, magazines, publications, professional advisers and consultants.

I would welcome feedback, particularly if you feel that something is ambiguous or inaccurate.

If I have omitted something you consider important, please let me know so that this can be included in any future edition.

HOW TO USE THIS BOOK

One of the most difficult aspects of writing this book has been dealing with the interrelationships between the various topics. For example, when covering any of the financial products, it would be quite reasonable to touch on corporation tax, income tax, VAT, off balance sheet finance, SSAP21, FRS5, IAS17, various risks and a plethora of operational issues.

I have tried to solve this problem by touching lightly on all of the relevant issues within each section and using footnotes to draw your attention to the sections where you can find more in-depth information.

If you are looking for a particular topic and cannot see it listed in the table of contents, please look through the index.

Each chapter finishes with some revision exercises. Some of the larger sub-chapters also have these. You will find the answers in the main text of the chapter.

The book contains many website addresses that you can use to obtain further information. Organisations change their websites frequently so an address that works correctly today may well not work tomorrow. However, this does not necessarily mean that the target document is no longer available; it may have been moved elsewhere on their website.

For example, the book refers the reader to this page on the Department for Transport website. dft.gov.uk/topics/sustainable/olev/plug-in-car-grant/. That page was available as at the date of publication. If it is not available when you come to search, please try to remove sections of the web address and search again. First search on dft.gov.uk/topics/sustainable/olev/ and then dft.gov.uk/topics/sustainable. If you do not find the result you want, remove everything except for the main part of the web address (i.e. dft.gov.uk) and then use the Search function on the site to look for the document you require.

Different readers of this book will have different interests. On the following pages is a guide to help you to find the chapters and sections that you may wish to read first.

ABOUT THE AUTHOR

Colin Tourick MSc FCA FCCA MICFM is a management consultant specialising in vehicle leasing and management.

Colin's fleet career started in 1980 when he was the first accountant at LeasePlan UK, and he then spent five years in big ticket leasing in the City of London financing aircraft, ships and property. He was general manager of Fleet Motor Management, director of Commercial Union Vehicle Finance and corporate finance director of BNP Paribas lease group. For six years he was managing director of CitiCapital Fleet.

For nine years he has been a fleet management consultant working for some of the world's largest banks, motor manufacturers and vehicle leasing companies.

Colin has served as chairman of the BVRLA Training Committee, a member of the BVRLA Leasing and Fleet Management Committee and a member of the Finance & Leasing Association's motor finance management committee. He is a chartered accountant, a certified accountant and a member of the Institute of Car Fleet Management. He has a Master of Science degree in Accounting and Finance from London School of Economics and is a Visiting Professor at the Centre for Automotive Management at University of Buckingham Business School.

He is a frequent commentator, writer and speaker on fleet industry issues. His particular interests are reducing fleet management costs and building successful vehicle management businesses.

Further information is available from www.tourick.com.

1 VEHICLE FINANCE, INSURANCE AND MANAGEMENT PRODUCTS

1.1 OUTRIGHT PURCHASE

1.1.1 BACKGROUND

Traditionally, when companies needed vehicles, they simply went out and bought them. Despite the growing popularity of other methods of acquisition and particularly contract hire, outright purchase is still the favoured acquisition method for around half of business vehicles in the UK.

No review of vehicle finance products can commence before we consider this important method of vehicle finance.

1.1.2 ADVANTAGES

Companies choose to buy their own vehicles for a variety of reasons. For many, it is simply the approach they have always adopted. Some are suspicious about involving a third party in the process ('Surely it must cost more? They have to make a profit too'). Others buy their vehicles because they like the idea of 'ownership' and all that this implies, including the ability to place an asset on their balance sheets and have complete control of when they sell it. Some like the idea of keeping the full sale proceeds. And there are those who like having a close working relationship with a local car dealer who will look after them and their vehicles should anything go wrong.

1.1.3 DISADVANTAGES

The move away from outright purchase has been taking place, slowly but steadily, for decades. It was hastened by changes to the VAT regulations in 1995 which allowed leasing companies to recover VAT on the purchase of new cars. This saving was not available to most other businesses buying cars for their own use, so the net cost of leasing a car fell relative to buying outright, which tipped the economic argument more heavily towards leasing.

In the absence of special arrangements made with a fleet management company, if you buy your own cars you will be fully exposed to movements in the used vehicles market when you come to sell. In other words, you take the residual value risk.[1]

---

1   See 5.12.

Unless your fleet is very large, when you buy your own cars you will not get the same levels of dealer and manufacturer discounts (called 'volume related bonuses') that leasing companies can attract. These can be significant.[2]

When you buy a vehicle you have to show it as an asset ('capitalise it') on the balance sheet of your business. If yours is a private company this may be of no consequence to you. However, directors of quoted companies are keen to present their financial statements in the most favourable light possible to their shareholders and City analysts. This ensures that the market price of their shares stays high. Analysts use a number of tools to measure the relative profitability of a company compared with others in the same market segment, including return on assets.[3]

However we are rapidly moving towards a situation where many companies will be required to capitalise almost all assets on their balances sheets, regardless of whether they buy them or lease them.[4]

If you buy your vehicles you normally have to go out and find them and negotiate the deals. Many companies find this to be an administrative headache. Some avoid this by using products such as contract hire; others have arrangements with fleet management companies to buy vehicles for them.

Outright purchase may tie up the working capital your company needs for its normal day-to-day trading activity.[5]

The most popular forms of vehicle finance require you to make fixed repayments. Most UK companies use their overdrafts or bank loans as their main form of working capital. These are variable rate forms of borrowing so if you use your overdraft to buy your cars you will be exposed to the vagaries of market interest rate movements.[6]

1.2 CONTRACT HIRE

1.2.1 FEATURES

Contract hire has been the most popular funding product with UK fleets for many years. More than a million cars are currently leased on contract hire, accounting for about half of the company cars in the UK.

Contract hire is one of several different types of lease that we will mention here, so it's worthwhile pausing for a moment to ask the question: what is a lease?

---

2   See 5.1.2.

3   See 8.2.

4   See 8.6.

5   See 1.16.

6   See 6.3.8.

Leasing is not defined in legislation. It is a contract for the hiring (or bailment) of goods or equipment.

Bailment is a long-established legal concept under which a person parts with possession of something under an agreement that says that he will recover it at a future date. There is a substantial body of law in this area, which the courts will apply in the event that the contract is silent on a particular issue.

1.2.2 LESSEE

The lease agreement will refer to the Lessee, the Client or the Hirer.[7] Some leasing companies have moved to 'plain English' contracts, in which the client is simply referred to as 'you'. Whatever wording is used, the lessee is the person who is granted the use of the vehicle for the period of the lease, subject to payment of rentals and meeting the other contractual obligations.

1.2.3 LESSOR

The lease agreement will refer to the Lessor, the Owner, the Company, us or we. This means the party granting the lease to another party, the lessee. The lessor may be a contract hire company, bank, finance company, leasing company or motor dealership that leases vehicles.

In many cases the lessor may not be the owner of the vehicle. It may be an intermediary (a small contract hire company or broker) using a finance company's vehicles and acting as their undisclosed agent.

It is always worthwhile asking whether the lessor is the owner of the vehicle because if something goes wrong with the lessor's business you may find yourself dealing with an organisation that you have not heard of before.

Anyone can set up a leasing company in the UK. UK lessors don't have to comply with any special regulations though if they want to do business with consumers they must be licensed under the Consumer Credit Act.[8] The Financial Services Authority regulates those leasing companies that are owned by banks or that sell insurance products.[9]

In a lease, the owner remains the owner and grants possession and use of the goods to the hirer or lessee, in exchange for a rental. Some of the language that we use in vehicle or equipment finance comes from the property world, where leasing is well established. Examples include 'term', 'rental' and 'peppercorn rental'.

'Contract hire' is a British vehicle leasing industry expression. The equivalent product elsewhere in the English-speaking world would be called an operating lease or a closed-end lease.

---

7   If the first letter of a word in a contract is shown in Upper Case, it will be defined elsewhere in the contract.

8   See Chapter 4.

9   See 19.6.8.

Under contract hire, the supplier leases a vehicle to you for a fixed period and mileage in return for a fixed rental. At the end of the lease, so long the vehicle has not been driven more than the agreed mileage and is in fair condition, you simply return it without further cost.

In calculating the rental the supplier will make an assumption as to the likely sale proceeds of the vehicle at the end of the lease (the 'residual value' or 'RV'). If the vehicle sells for more or less than this estimate, the supplier will make a profit or loss respectively. Normally, you will have no financial interest in this profit or loss. Through this mechanism the supplier is said to take the 'residual value risk' in the vehicle.[10]

As you don't pay the residual value, one way of viewing contract hire is to say that you are only paying for what you use – the diminution in the market value of the vehicle during the period when you are using it – rather than the whole price of the car. In other words, you are paying for the depreciation (plus of course interest).

There are two types of contract hire, 'maintenance-inclusive' and 'maintenance-exclusive'. If it includes maintenance, the supplier will normally pay for all standard servicing and maintenance work arising during the lease period.

The contract may limit the number of tyres the supplier will replace at its expense during the lease. It will invariably say that the supplier will pay for the vehicle excise duty (the 'tax disc') every year.

Practically all contract hire arrangements exclude motor insurance, although other insurances are sometimes offered including credit payment insurance, payment accident protection, mechanical breakdown insurance, early termination protection and gap insurance.[11]

The agreement will not cover work or expenses that arise if the vehicle is damaged, neglected or wilfully mistreated. Examples include 'kerbed' tyres and wheels, engines being allowed to run dry, diesel fuel being pumped into petrol-engined cars, dented doors, broken mirrors and deep scratches. If the supplier chooses to pay for these items it will do so as a service to you and will recharge you the cost, although some suppliers will bear these costs up to a limit set out in the contract.

Where maintenance is included in the contract, the rental will include an amount to cover the supplier's estimate of the cost of maintaining the vehicle. If the estimate is too low, the supplier will make a loss; if too high, it will make a profit. Through this mechanism it is said that the supplier takes the 'maintenance risk' in the vehicle.[12]

It is important to realise that with contract hire you are buying more than just a financial product: you are getting a service and you will wish to satisfy yourself as to the ability of the supplier to deliver a service that meets your needs.

---

10   See 5.12.

11   See 1.22.

12   See 5.13.

1.2.4 LEASE PERIOD

You can normally choose whatever lease period you require, though many contract hire companies will refuse to lease you a vehicle for less than twelve months or more than five years.

During the 1970s it was normal for companies to replace their vehicles after two years. In the 1980s and 1990s the average lease period increased and three years became the norm. The recession of the early 1990s prompted companies to look again at cost reduction and many extended their replacement cycle to four years. More than 50% of all fleet vehicles are now replaced every three years and more than 33% every four years and it is unlikely that we will go back to three years being the norm.

Some fleet managers feel that 80,000 or 100,000 miles should be the ceiling for business car use as cars become less reliable, more expensive to maintain and are less attractive to used car buyers beyond this point. So these fleet managers will choose a shorter lease period for high-mileage drivers.

1.2.5 RENTALS

Almost all contract hire rentals are fixed, that is, they do not vary with changes in market interest rates. As your rentals are fixed you do not have any interest rate risk. This is one of the attractions of contract hire; it provides you with the certainty that your rentals will remain fixed for three or four years regardless of any movement in market interest rates.[13]

You will also have the certainty of knowing that your service costs are fixed and you are not exposed to the vagaries of the used car market.

1.2.6 CONTRACT MILEAGE

If you lease a vehicle on contract hire, the quotation and agreement (or the schedule to the agreement) will set out the maximum vehicle mileage allowed during the lease period.

The leasing company will have based their rental calculation on this mileage. Obviously, if the vehicle is only likely to cover a low mileage its true depreciation (the loss of market value) and maintenance costs will be lower than those of a similar vehicle covering more miles, so you will pay a lower rental.

If the agreed contract mileage is exceeded, you will have to pay an excess mileage charge. This allows the supplier to recover the additional depreciation and maintenance costs it incurs when excess miles are driven. The excess mileage charge will be an amount in pence per mile and will be set out on the contract or schedule.

It has become fashionable to call excess mileage charges 'penalties' but this is an unfair expression. All that these charges should do is to ensure that you pay for the mileage actually covered by the vehicle.

---

13   See 6.3.8.

If you lease several vehicles from one supplier, pooled mileage will normally be included in the agreement.[14] This allows any under-mileage driven by one car to be credited against over-mileage in another, thus reducing the net excess mileage charge.

1.2.7 EXCLUDED CARS – EXOTICS

There are now more than six thousand makes and models of vehicle available on contract hire but some contract hire companies will refuse to lease certain vehicles. These include 'exotic vehicles', that is, extremely expensive cars where it is difficult to set residual values and maintenance budgets and where there are relatively few examples on the road.

You will also find it difficult to obtain contract hire on unusual imported vehicles or grey imports[15] and probably impossible on kit cars.

1.2.8 CONTRACT HIRE QUOTES

The written quote from the contract hire company will typically split the rental between finance and maintenance elements.

The rental includes the supplier's estimate of the depreciation of the vehicle (the cost less the residual value), vehicle excise duty, the likely cost of servicing and maintenance and (if you have requested this) an allowance for the cost of a replacement vehicle when the primary vehicle is off the road.

As the supplier is taking the residual value risk, you might expect it to charge a premium for doing so. In practice, however, few companies make such charges, as competitive pressure always means that rentals have to be as low as possible or you will take your business elsewhere. Similarly, it would be logical for the supplier to charge a premium for taking the maintenance risk but in practice this is seldom seen.

You can expect your quotes to show the carbon dioxide output of the vehicle, so that you can see whether you will get full corporation tax relief of the lease rental[16] and your driver can calculate how much car benefit tax they will have to pay on their company car.[17]

Most contract hire quotes expire after thirty days. Normally the quote will include a clause allowing the supplier to recalculate the rental if the manufacturer's list price has changed before you place your order. It was once common for quotes to contain a similar protection against interest rate rises but this is less common nowadays.

---

14   See 2.6.1.

15   See 5.1.6.

16   See 17.1.3.

17   See 17.2.1.

If you receive a quote that is acceptable to you, it is probably a good idea to accept it promptly. Otherwise there is the danger that the manufacturer will increase the price and the rental will have to be increased. This can lead to disappointment if the driver then discovers that the revised rental exceeds their allowed limit.

Most suppliers now offer quotes online. Some ask you to register and give them some information about your organisation so that they can decide the appropriate rental to charge; a lower rental if you have a large fleet and are creditworthy, a higher one if you have only a small business with a small fleet. There is more competition for bigger clients and this drives down prices, whereas smaller clients have to pay the 'rack rent' (to borrow another expression from the property rental market).

Some contract hire companies and comparison sites offer web-based quotations without 'pre-qualifying' you, but generally speaking you will get a lower rental from a company that knows something about you.

If you have an established relationship with a contract hire company you will be offered the use of their web-based quoting system. Rather than phoning several times to ask for quotes as you refine your choice of vehicle, you just click away until you have chosen the vehicle and rental that suits you.

Contract hire isn't all about price. You are buying a service and should choose a supplier according to the balance you require between service and price.[18]

1.2.9 EARLY TERMINATION

You may decide to terminate a contract hire agreement before the contracted end-date; for example, if the vehicle has been written-off in an accident or stolen, or if the driver has left your employment.

All contract hire companies will allow you to terminate your lease early; indeed, where this arises because the vehicle has been lost or stolen, it is difficult to think of anything else that could be done.

The supplier entered into the lease expecting that you would keep the vehicle until the contractual end-date. They calculated their rentals and arranged their own funding on this basis.[19] They also expected to get capital allowances for the full term of the lease.[20]

On early termination they have to clear their books, recover any extra costs to be borne in keeping their own funding in place until the end of the lease, recover any adverse effects of disrupting their capital allowance flows and (perhaps) recover some element of the profit they had hoped to make had the contract run to maturity.

---

18   See 19.5 Selecting a fleet company.

19   See 19.4.8.

20   See 17.1.2.

With all finance agreements, although you make equal monthly repayments the amount outstanding does not decline in equal monthly amounts. This is because finance agreements are annuities.[21]

Many contract hire agreements are silent on what happens in the event of an early termination. This can lead to misunderstandings and disputes when early terminations occur, so it is far better to agree this in writing with the contract hire company up front.

There are several methods of calculating a contract hire early termination settlement figure. They include:

THE PERCENTAGE OF FUTURE RENTALS METHOD

This may be defined in a simple formula that says something like:

- If you terminate in the first 12 months we will charge you 60% of all future rentals.
- If you terminate in the second 12 months we will charge you 50% of all future rentals and
- If you terminate thereafter we will charge you 40% of all future rentals.

There is no consistent way of calculating this figure in the market and individual suppliers will have their own way of calculating this charge.

When entering into the lease the supplier will have no idea whether you might ask to early terminate the lease, or how much the vehicle will be worth (or how much the insurance settlement will be) at that time. Hence a 'percentage of outstanding rentals' settlement policy is risky for the supplier and can cause them to make a loss.

Nonetheless, many contract hire companies offer this arrangement as it gives you certainty and removes the need for discussion, debate and possible disagreement at a later date.

ACTUAL COST METHOD

Under this method, the lessor will take the balance outstanding in its books, including any arrears of rental, add any costs or fees it has paid to recover or sell the vehicle, deduct the sale proceeds of the vehicle and charge you the difference. Normally, for the sake of simplicity, capital allowance or other tax matters are ignored.

This is a particularly simple way to calculate an early termination settlement and can be a feature of 'open-book' contract hire arrangements.[22]

The actual cost method is often the cheapest method of early termination available to you. For this reason it is usually only offered to large, creditworthy businesses with large fleets, where there is strong competitive pressure and the contract hire company is keen to preserve the relationship.

---

21 See 6.5.1.

22 See 1.14.

SLIDING SCALE ACCORDING TO THE TIMING OF THE EARLY TERMINATION

This is a refinement of the percentage of outstanding rentals method.

At the start of the agreement the supplier will provide you with a chart showing the amount that will be payable, month by month, in the event of early termination. An example is shown below.

This schedule assumes a £12,000 capital cost, a 3+33 rental profile[23] on a thirty-six month lease and a £4,000 residual value. As this is a contract hire agreement the vehicle will be returned to the supplier on termination.

Termination during month number	Amount payable £
1	4,900.69
2	4,752.19
3	4,603.68
4	4,455.17
5	4,306.67
6	4,158.16
7	4,009.66
8	3,861.15
9	3,712.65
10	3,564.14
11	3,415.63
12	3,267.13
13	2,494.90
14	2,376.09
15	2,257.29
16	2,138.48
17	2,019.68
18	1,900.87
19	1,782.07
20	1,663.27
21	1,544.46
22	1,425.66
23	1,306.85
24	1,188.05
25	801.93
26	712.83
27	623.72
28	534.62
29	445.52
30	356.41
31	267.31
32	178.21
33	89.10
34-36	Nil

Note that nothing needs to be paid if you terminate during months 34, 35 or 36, as no rentals are due in those months.

Termination schedules such as this are less common in the vehicle leasing market but are often seen with other forms of equipment leasing, particularly 'big ticket' leases involving large amounts.

OTHER EARLY TERMINATION ISSUES

Whatever early termination method is used, the amount you are charged will include any arrears, interest on arrears, costs, fees or expenses that the supplier incurs in recovering and selling the vehicle.

If the agreement is regulated by the Consumer Credit Act you have the right to hand it back after half the payments have been made.[24]

Whilst it may be your policy to take all vehicles on lease for, say, three years, there may well be occasions when you know in advance that you are likely to need a particular vehicle for a shorter period. For example, if you need it for an overseas visitor who is in the UK for a fixed period or to someone who plans to retire in 18 months.

In these situations you will usually save money if you enter into the lease for the shorter period at the outset. If you think it likely that you may later wish to extend the lease, speak to your leasing company before entering into the lease to discuss whether and on what terms they will be prepared to extend it. While the rentals that you pay will be more expensive initially, this arrangement will normally work out cheaper than entering into a three-year lease and early terminating after 18 months.

The message is simple: don't enter a lease knowing it is likely that you will have to break it early; enter into it for the period you expect you will need the vehicle.

You may have to terminate a lease early because a driver has left your employment. So long as you have a use for the vehicle you will find that it is almost always cheaper for you to redeploy it within your business rather than hand it back and pay an early settlement charge.

If you expect to have a high incidence of early termination, perhaps because you are in an industry with high staff turnover, you should consider taking ex-lease or used cars for some staff to avoid early termination costs. Another option would be to lease cars for short periods. A number of leasing companies and specialist suppliers will offer you a 'flexi-lease' for anything between 3 and 12 months. Alternatively you could use pool cars.

---

23 The equivalent of three months' rental is paid on day one. This is followed by 33 further rentals, commencing one month after the start of the agreement. This is described further in 6.2.

24 See 4.7.

Depending on your fleet size, some manufacturers and contract hire companies may be able to provide you with long-term demonstration vehicles. While generally these are only provided to allow you to test the vehicle in real-life use, it is a fact that many companies use long-term demonstrators as a tool to reduce vehicle costs and create a more flexible fleet.

1.2.10 EXTENSIONS

Leasing companies are usually happy to allow you to extend a lease at the end of the contract period. However, there are some circumstances when they may not permit an extension. For example:

- If you are in default of your payment or other obligations. Here they may not feel inclined to do anything that will prolong their relationship with you.
- If the vehicle has already cost a lot to maintain and costs are likely to mount. They will be concerned that the additional rentals you pay might be dwarfed by the extra running costs, particularly if a major service is due soon.
- If the value of the vehicle in the used vehicle market has fallen or is likely to fall sharply, the supplier may wish to dispose of it as quickly as possible to avoid any further loss.
- If you want to keep the vehicle until a month when the used vehicle market is traditionally sluggish – December, for example – the supplier will fear that they will make a loss if they allow this.

There are two methods of extending a contract – formal extension and informal extension.

INFORMAL EXTENSION

Where you want to keep a vehicle for a short period, perhaps for up to three or four months, the supplier will normally allow you to do so.

With informal extension the rental is normally kept at the same level and they don't ask you to sign a new contract.

However, if you simply keep hold of the vehicle against the supplier's wishes you may well find they increase the rental after the contracted end-date.

FORMAL EXTENSION

If you want to retain the vehicle for a longer period, the supplier may agree to grant a formal extension. An agreement will be drawn up, commencing on the end date of the original contract and showing the new end date.

In the past, formal extensions were arranged at reduced rentals, reflecting the fact that the monthly depreciation of a three-year old car is that much lower than its monthly depreciation in the first three years. However, depending on the state of the used car market you may well find that your leasing company asks you to paying the same rental, or even an increased rental, during the extension period.

1.2.11 ACCESSORIES

The contract hire agreement will refer to accessories fitted to the vehicle after delivery. This clause may simply deny you the right to attach an accessory. Alternatively, it may allow you to do so if the accessory is removed at your expense at the end of the lease without damaging the vehicle. Often the agreement will say that any accessories added to the vehicle become the supplier's property.

In practice, most contract hire companies are willing to allow accessories to be added post-delivery if they can be sure that these will not detract from the value of the vehicle or affect its safety or efficiency.

The advice here is simple; if you wish to add an accessory after delivery, speak to the contract hire company first.

1.2.12 COLLECTION AND INSPECTION

At the end of the lease period the contract hire company will contact you to arrange vehicle collection. Most will collect from any address to suit you, for example, from your fleet department, head office, a regional office or the driver's home.

When the vehicle is collected the collection agent will complete a report for both parties to sign, confirming that the vehicle has been handed over and whether there has been any damage to the vehicle.

It is in both parties' interests that this report should be as accurate as possible to avoid later disputes about the condition of the vehicle.

As part of offering a good customer service, many contract hire companies will deliver the driver's new vehicle and collect their ex-lease vehicle at the same time. This is 'key-for-key exchange' and it has obvious advantages for everyone. The disadvantage is that the driver, in his excitement over the arrival of his new vehicle, may sign a form that confirms that there is damage to the old vehicle without realising that he has done so or fully realising the consequences. He may not even have noticed the physical damage to the old vehicle. Some days or weeks later the supplier will send you a bill for the damage and before you know it there will be a dispute. In some cases the car will have been sold already so it will not be available for you to inspect.

In many ways, the ideal approach to collection is for the fleet manager – or someone else in your company who is familiar with vehicles – to inspect all vehicles at the end of the lease and to sign the collection report.

Bear in mind that if the car is dirty, the light is poor or the weather is bad it may be difficult for the condition of the vehicle to be assessed accurately.

1.2.13   FAIR WEAR AND TEAR

The contract hire agreement will say the supplier is responsible for the maintenance and repair of the vehicle, and the replacement of tyres, etc arising from normal use. It will also say that the vehicle has to be returned to the supplier at the end of the lease in good condition 'fair wear and tear for the age and mileage excepted'.

Which leaves us with the question; what is the dividing line between fair wear and tear and unfair damage?

Fortunately, the BVRLA[25] has produced Fair Wear and Tear Guides for use by the industry and clients. There are three guides; for cars, light commercial vehicles and heavy goods vehicles. Extracts of the first two are shown below, and all three are available from the BVRLA.

The BVRLA Fair Wear And Tear Guide for drivers of leased and financed cars[26] is shown in pages 15 to 30.

The BVRLA Fair Wear And Tear Guide for drivers and operators of contract hired and leased light commercial vehicles under 3.5 tonnes gvw and minibuses from 9 to 17 seats [27] is shown starting on page 31.

---

25   British Vehicle Rental and Leasing Association. See 19.6.3.
26   All BVRLA material in this book is reproduced by kind permission of the BVRLA
27   © BVRLA

the aim of this guide

The aim of the BVRLA Fair Wear and Tear Guide is to provide an industry-wide, accepted standard that defines fair wear and tear on passenger vehicles when they are returned to a BVRLA Member at the end of a contract or finance agreement. This guide covers all passenger vehicles including multiple passenger vehicles (MPVs) with up to eight seats.

Fair wear and tear occurs when normal usage causes deterioration to a vehicle. It is not to be confused with damage which occurs as a result of a specific event or series of events such as impact, inappropriate stowing of items, harsh-treatment, negligent acts or omissions. This guide not only provides guidance on the industry standard for fair wear and tear but also promotes best practice in vehicle maintenance and upkeep that will prevent unacceptable wear and tear from occurring.

the fair wear and tear standard

This guide defines the industry standard at return for every aspect of the vehicle's condition. For ease of reference, the condition of the vehicle is considered under the following headings:

❑ General appearance, documentation, keys

❑ Paintwork, vehicle body, bumpers and trim

❑ Windows and glass

❑ Tyres and wheels

❑ Mechanical condition

❑ Vehicle interior

❑ Equipment and controls

advice to the driver

This guide also contains advice to the driver with details of maintenance routines and preventative action necessary to keep the vehicle in acceptable condition and minimise de-hire charges at end of lease. Dependent on the circumstances of the driver, some duties and responsibilities covering risk assessment of the vehicle's use in the context of work-related driving may be set out by employers and these should be referred to also.

Taken together, each section provides a comprehensive view of the necessary vehicle upkeep and the resulting vehicle condition.

Drivers and fleet operators will benefit from a robust maintenance system and good practices in fleet management because they promote compliance and road safety, lower operating costs and reduce the likelihood of incurring de-hire charges on the vehicle's return.

Also included is a pull-out section that will help drivers appraise their vehicle prior to return. It illustrates typical forms of acceptable wear and tear (green framed boxes) and unacceptable wear and tear (red framed boxes).

acceptable

Scratches up to 25mm are acceptable

a

not acceptable

Scratches over 25mm are not acceptable

b

the industry fair wear and tear standard for leased and financed cars

the fair wear and tear standard

GENERAL APPEARANCE, DOCUMENTATION, KEYS

this is acceptable

this is unacceptable

The service book must be date-stamped by the authorised repairer.

1

A full set of keys, including master and spares, should be available at return. 4

All documentation must be in the vehicle on return.

2

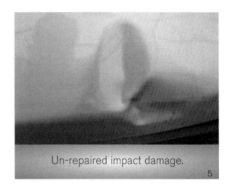

Un-repaired impact damage.

5

The interior of the vehicle must be valeted and cleared of rubbish.

3

Inspection is difficult if the exterior is not clean.

6

the fair wear and tear standard

PAINTWORK, BODY, BUMPERS AND TRIM

this is acceptable

this is unacceptable

Small areas of chipping are acceptable if
there is no corrosion present.
7

Adhesive residue following removal of
company badges and logos.
10

Scratches up to 25mm are acceptable except
8 where primer or bare metal is showing.

Dents and abrasions as a result of impact.
11

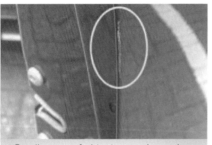

Small areas of chipping on door edges
are acceptable.
9

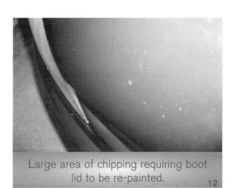

Large area of chipping requiring boot
lid to be re-painted.
12

the fair wear and tear standard

this is acceptable

this is unacceptable

Scratch does not interfere with driver line of sight.
13

Windscreen chip.
16

Light scratch on passenger window.
14

Damaged door mirror.
17

Damage to lens has not broken glass - no water ingress.
15

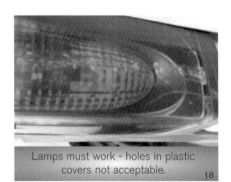

Lamps must work - holes in plastic covers not acceptable.
18

the fair wear and tear standard

TYRES AND WHEELS

this is acceptable

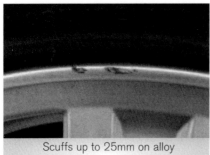

Scuffs up to 25mm on alloy wheels are acceptable.

19

Tyres must meet minimum UK legal requirements.

20

Surface deterioration on alloy wheel.

21

this is unacceptable

Wheel damage due to kerbing.

22

Hole in wheel trim.

23

There must be no damage to side wall of tyre.

24

the fair wear and tear standard

this is acceptable

this is unacceptable

Light staining to driver seat area.
25

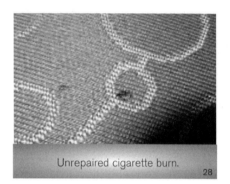

Unrepaired cigarette burn.
28

Controls and mechanisms for raising the
26 hood must be intact and operational.

All original equipment must be present
and operate correctly.
29

Interior fittings e.g. rear view mirrors
27 must be present and intact.

Torn covering and trim in boot area.
30

at a glance summary of the BVRLA
fair wear and tear standard

the standard

❏ **General**
The vehicle must meet MOT standards and have been serviced according to the manufacturer's servicing schedule. The stamped service book must be available for inspection. All other vehicle documents must be intact and available. A full set of keys must be returned as originally supplied. The vehicle should be sufficiently clean to allow a detailed inspection.

acceptable

Vehicle must be clean to allow for inspection.

not acceptable

Abrasions longer than 25mm are not acceptable.

the standard

❏ **Paint, Body, Bumpers and Trim**
There should be no rust or corrosion on any painted area e.g. painted bumpers, body panels and door mirrors. Relative to the vehicle's age and mileage, the following is acceptable: scratches up to 25mm. dents up to 10mm (provided no more than two per panel and the paint surface is not broken), small areas of chipping (including door edges).

acceptable

Scratches up to 25mm are acceptable.

not acceptable

Scratches over 25mm are not acceptable.

the standard

❏ **Windows and Glass**
On the windscreen, light scratching is acceptable if it is not interfering with the driver's line of sight. Chips, holes and cracks are not acceptable. Lights must work. Missing, cracked or damaged door mirrors are not acceptable.

acceptable

Retractable door mirrors must work.

not acceptable

Broken lens cover.

Please use this summary to appraise your vehicle against the BVRLA fair wear and tear standard prior to its return to the leasing company. For more information, you should consult the full detailed guidelines published in the BVRLA Fair Wear and Tear Guide. To avoid end of contract charges, you can arrange to correct unacceptable areas of damage before the vehicle is returned. Check the terms of your contract. Always point out any uncorrected wear or damage when the vehicle is collected to avoid problems later.

the standard

❐ **Tyres and Wheels**
All tyres must meet minimum UK legal requirements and comply with manufacturers' recommendations of tyre type, size and speed rating. Scuffs up to 25mm on wheel trims and alloy wheels are acceptable. There must be no damage to sidewalls or tread.

the standard

❐ **Vehicle Interior**
Upholstery must be clean and odourless with no visible burns, tears or staining. All seats originally supplied must be present. Fittings and accessories must be present and intact. Holes and other damage left by the removal of accessories such as car telephones must be neatly repaired.

the standard

❐ **Tools, Equipment and Accessories**
All original equipment, accessories and controls must be present, intact and operate correctly. A full set of keys, including master and spares should be available at return.

acceptable

Regular tyre pressure checks are essential.

acceptable

Soiling due to normal wear and tear.

acceptable

All original accessories and controls must be present and operative.

not acceptable

Wheel trim damage due to kerbing is not acceptable.

not acceptable

Paint and other heavy soiling.

not acceptable

Any holes left when items like phones are removed are unacceptable.

summary of **fair wear and tear** standard

remember pull-out pages

❐ On collection, the vehicle must be in a safe and roadworthy condition with all appropriate keys, equipment, accessories and documentation available.

❐ Your leasing company will arrange collection of the vehicle at the end of your agreement. All readily apparent damage and wear, irrespective of liability, will be documented when the vehicle is collected. You will be given the opportunity to agree with the condition of the vehicle at the point of collection. Your leasing company will then be able to carry out a full assessment of your vehicle to calculate what end of rental charges, if any, are payable.

❐ If you cannot be present during the collection of the vehicle or if other conditions e.g. poor weather, prevent the vehicle from being inspected, your leasing company will issue you with a written condition report of the vehicle and advise you of any charges that may subsequently become due, together with summary details of how any charges are calculated.

❐ Ensure all your personal effects are removed from the vehicle e.g. sunglasses, music CDs from the player/multi-stacker.

❐ Remove your house-key from the vehicle key fob.

❐ CDs for satellite navigation should be left in the vehicle and, for security reasons, you should delete any personal information from the navigation database e.g. home address, post code etc.

❐ The vehicle's number plate should be intact and the characters making up the registration mark must be of the specified size and font set out in Road Vehicles (Display of Registration Marks) Regulations 2001.

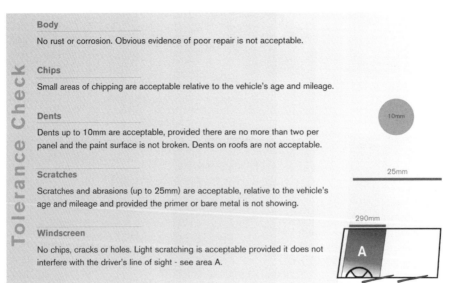

Tolerance Check

Body
No rust or corrosion. Obvious evidence of poor repair is not acceptable.

Chips
Small areas of chipping are acceptable relative to the vehicle's age and mileage.

Dents
Dents up to 10mm are acceptable, provided there are no more than two per panel and the paint surface is not broken. Dents on roofs are not acceptable.

10mm

Scratches
Scratches and abrasions (up to 25mm) are acceptable, relative to the vehicle's age and mileage and provided the primer or bare metal is not showing.

25mm

290mm

Windscreen
No chips, cracks or holes. Light scratching is acceptable provided it does not interfere with the driver's line of sight - see area A.

A

the fair wear and tear standard

The vehicle must be returned in a safe, legal and reliable mechanical condition, capable of passing an MOT test. All electronic safety features and devices to help the driver e.g. parking sensors, adaptive cruise controls, etc. must be in working order.

GENERAL

maintenance and servicing
The vehicle must have been serviced according to the manufacturer's servicing schedule. The service book must be date-stamped by the authorised repairer so that it can be inspected. In addition, all necessary maintenance and repairs must be carried out by an authorised agent and where the leasing company is not responsible for such items, a proper record must be kept and be available for inspection on the vehicle's return.

documentation
All vehicle documentation including the V5C (where appropriate), MOT, operation manual, service book and any other documents relating to vehicle equipment, must be intact and available. All documents must be in the vehicle on its return - including details of all audio equipment security codes.

Any odometer alterations must have been reported to the leasing company. Unauthorised odometer changes are not acceptable.

appearance
The vehicle's exterior should be sufficiently clean to allow a detailed inspection. The inside should have been valeted, cleared of rubbish and the ashtrays emptied.

vehicle keys
A full set of keys including the master key, spares and locking wheel-nut keys, should be returned if originally supplied. If a remote locking system is fitted, the appropriate remote controls should be available and functioning.

PAINTWORK, BODY, BUMPERS AND TRIM

There should be no rust or corrosion on any painted area including painted bumpers, body moulding and mirrors. Obvious evidence of poor repair is not acceptable.

chips
Small areas of chipping, including door edge chipping, are acceptable relative to the vehicle's age and mileage. If the areas of chipping require the entire panel to be re-painted, the damage is not acceptable. .

dents
Dents (up to 10mm) are acceptable provided there are no more than two (2) per panel and the paint surface is not broken. Dents on the roof are not acceptable.

scratches
Scratches and abrasions (up to 25mm) are acceptable, relative to the vehicle's age and mileage, and provided the primer or bare metal is not showing.

moulding, wheel arch trims
Scuffs and scratches are acceptable provided the moulding or trim is not broken, cracked or deformed.

badges and labels
Badges, labels or advertising fitted to the bodywork or glass of the vehicle should be removed unless originally fitted with the agreement of the leasing company and any damage caused by their attachment or removal must be made good. Any difference in

the fair wear and tear standard

paintwork colour noted following the removal of advertising, labelling or logos is not acceptable.

soft top convertibles
Convertible roofs must be fully operative and free from rips and tears. The rear window must not be cracked or creased. Accessories originally supplied, e.g. tonneau cover, must be present and in good condition.

tow bars
A tow bar, if fitted, must be in good, rust-free condition with electrical connections working properly. A ball cover must be in place.

WINDOWS, GLASS, DOOR MIRRORS AND LIGHTS

windows/windscreens
Light scratching is acceptable provided it does not interfere with the driver's line of sight and any heating elements still work properly. Chips, cracks or holes are not acceptable

door mirrors
Missing, cracked or damaged door mirrors are not acceptable. If adjustable and/or heated door mirrors, they must work correctly.

lights and lenses
All lights must work. Minor scuff marks or scratches are acceptable. Holes or cracks in the glass or plastic covers of lamp units are not acceptable.

TYRES AND WHEELS

tyre wear and damage
All tyres, including the spare, must meet minimum UK legal requirements and comply with the vehicle manufacturer's

recommendations of tyre type, size and speed rating for the vehicle. There must be no damage to sidewalls or tread.

wheels and wheel trims
Dents and holes on steel rims and the main body of the wheel, are not acceptable. Scuffs up to 25mm on the outside edge of wheel trims and on alloy wheels are acceptable. The spare wheel, (including 'spacesaver') jack and other tools (including emergency tyre inflation canister) must be intact, stowed properly and in good working order.

MECHANICAL CONDITION

The vehicle must meet current MOT standard. The following items are not acceptable fair wear and tear because the driver has neglected to service the vehicle and/or failed to action warnings from the vehicle management system;

❐ **brakes:** grooved brake discs or drums caused by excessive wear or metal to metal contact from worn out disc pads

❐ **engine:** seized or damaged due to running vehicle with insufficient coolant, oil or with broken internal components

❐ **manual transmission:** clutch slipping, noisy clutch or gearbox, excessively worn or ineffective synchromesh

❐ **automatic transmission:** noisy gearbox or torque converter, abrupt gear changes, loose gear linkage

vehicle underside
Any significant impact damage to the vehicle's underside is not acceptable. Catalytic converters not working because of obvious abuse or damage are not acceptable.

advice to the driver

If yours is a company car, your company may outline the preventative vehicle maintenance and safety measures that you need to undertake on a daily or weekly basis. You should check your company driver policy, to ensure you comply. If you are personally leasing the vehicle, you should consult the vehicle supplier. Vehicle manufacturers invest a good deal of time and effort in the preparation of vehicle operation manuals, so we recommend you always have the manual to hand and consult it often.

GENERAL

maintenance and servicing
Regular maintenance and servicing should be carried out by accredited servicing outlets which adhere to standards set by regulatory bodies and/or members of a recognised trade body. The vehicle service record must be stamped at each service. Any defects or damage that occur during normal vehicle usage should be rectified promptly. In certain circumstances, you will have to wait until authority for the repair has been given by the leasing company.

documentation
Always keep the V5C registration document in a safe place (not in the car) if you are the registered keeper - the vehicle cannot be re-licensed without producing the V5C or the V11 renewal notice. Keep all other documentation relating to the car, including service history, MOT certificate (see page 17), key codes, radio codes, etc. in a safe place, too. Store the vehicle's operation manual in the protective wallet provided and keep it in the glove-box.

When you are returning the vehicle, you should make sure that your service and maintenance record is as comprehensive and as up to date as possible. If you don't provide the full information, you can expect to incur a de-hire charge at end of contract as trade buyers will mark down the price they are willing to pay or choose a car that has a full set of documents.

appearance
Regular cleaning of both the interior and exterior ensures the vehicle looks good. Polishing the vehicle exterior around four times a year will help reduce the effects of any stone-chip damage, limit the effects of air-borne contamination (e.g. bird-droppings, etc), remove traffic grime and make routine washing easier.

vehicle keys
Spare keys should be identified and tagged. You can expect to be charged for replacement keys if they are not returned with the vehicle at end of contract. Always make sure that vehicle keys are kept safely with the spare key stored in a different place. Car thieves often target the keys as the easiest means of stealing vehicles because manufacturers achieve very high levels of vehicle security. Never leave keys in a conspicuous place in the house and certainly never in the hallway in reach of the letter box.

personal number plates
You should liaise with your leasing company 10 to 12 weeks in advance to ensure your personal number plate is transferred to your new vehicle.

security system
All security systems fitted after manufacture should meet the appropriate Thatcham standard and be fitted according to a recognised standard, e.g. Vehicle Systems Installation Board (VSIB).

advice to the driver

PAINTWORK, BODY, BUMPERS AND TRIM

chips, dents, scratches
It is recommended that any damage is repaired as soon as possible after it occurs. This is particularly important when the paintwork is damaged and likely to cause corrosion.

All work must be completed to a professional standard by repairers who provide full warranty on their work. Your leasing company will advise you and will authorise repairs if you have a full maintenance contract. For small areas of damage, a SMART (small and medium area repair technique) repair may be appropriate. See page 18 of this Guide.

badges and labels
Advertising should never be painted directly onto the vehicle without the leasing company's written permission. Any advertising, labelling or logos should be fitted so that they can be easily removed without damaging or deteriorating any part of the bodywork of the vehicle.

soft top convertibles
Drivers should familiarise themselves with the operation of the hood, including any buttons and fasteners. Drivers should always wash convertible cars by hand - they must not be taken through an automatic car wash, and care must be exercised when raising or lowering the hood so as not to scratch or damage the rear window.

tow bars
The leasing company's permission must be obtained before fitting a tow bar. All such equipment must be fitted in accordance with the manufacturer's fitting instructions and guidelines.

WINDOWS AND GLASS
WINDSCREEN AND WINDOWS
All vehicle glass should be kept clean not only for safety reasons, but also to enable any damage to be identified quickly and repairs put in hand. Any damage in the driver's direct line of sight, or affecting any heating elements, should be repaired immediately. Cracks and bulls-eye damage can easily be smart-repaired to prevent further damage.

door mirrors
Door mirrors should be kept clean and replaced if damaged - obtain approval from the leasing company if necessary.

lights and lenses
Lamps and lenses should be kept clean and replaced if damaged - obtain approval from the leasing company if necessary.

TYRES AND WHEELS

tyre wear and damage
Tyre pressures should be kept at manufacturer's recommended pressures in order to avoid damage and undue wear. Under-inflation will cause excess wear on the edges of the tyre, while over inflation will cause excess wear in the centre of the tyre tread. As part of company risk management procedures, employers often advise drivers on the frequency with which tyre pressures should be checked. Employers may require documentary evidence that these checks are made.

wheels and wheel trims
Care should be taken when parking and manoeuvring so as to avoid damage, especially to alloy wheels as these are easy to damage and expensive to replace. However, if damage does occur, it should be repaired, or the wheel/wheel trim replaced - subject to the appropriate approval if applicable.

advice to the driver

MECHANICAL CONDITION

servicing and maintenance
The vehicle must be maintained and serviced according to the manufacturer's guidelines. It is important to keep the vehicle in good mechanical condition by keeping all fluids topped up and by immediately investigating any poor running symptoms or unusual mechanical noises. Drivers should follow the manufacturers' recommendations regarding fuel and fuel blends because using some fuel and fuel blends can invalidate the vehicle's warranty and cause long-term damage to its fuel system. Drivers should ensure that oil and coolant levels are checked regularly and are maintained at correct levels between services. In the context of road-related, driver risk management, employers may advise drivers on the frequency with which oil levels should be checked. Employers may require a written log to be completed.

vehicle underside
Any suspected impact damage should be investigated and dealt with professionally, as soon as possible.

catalytic converter and emissions
Catalytic converter failure is preventable through using the correct fuel, regular servicing and maintenance, immediately investigating any poor running symptoms and not towing or bump-starting the vehicle.

VEHICLE INTERIOR

passenger area, seats and trim
The interior of the vehicle should be kept clean. Any stains should be removed with a suitable, proprietary cleaner as soon as practicable to avoid long term damage. Regular smoking in the car leaves an unpleasant residual smell, causes staining and should be avoided.

door aperture, boot and luggage area
It is recommended that heavy items are always firmly secured and positioned centrally within the load area in order to minimise the effect on the vehicle's handling and to avoid damage. Carpets and the load area should always be protected from excessive soiling. Heavy items or inappropriate loads should never be carried on the seats.

GENERAL EQUIPMENT AND CONTROLS
All general equipment, controls and accessories should be present and fully functional. If stolen or lost, they must be replaced with equipment of similar standard and specification.

in car entertainment equipment, telephones and navigation systems
The driver should always operate these systems with care, ensuring no damage occurs to the dash, control knobs, etc. If a replacement is required, due to theft, for example, it must be of similar standard and specification.

glossary

☐ **Abrasion**   Multiple scratches in the material surface.

☐ **Chip**   Removal of the surface material (glass or paintwork) in a concise area.

☐ **Dent**   Deformation of the surface structure usually caused by impact damage.

☐ **Light scratch** A scratch with no raised edges - can be polished out using smart repair techniques.

☐ **Scratch**   A single line mark or score in the material surface.

☐ **Scuff**   Light scraping of top surface not penetrating base material.

☐ **Smart Repair**   Small and Medium Area Repair Technique - a cost effective way of repairing chips, dents and scratches.

☐ **VSIB**   The Vehicle Systems Installation Board is the national regulatory and accreditation body for vehicle systems Installers and their installations.

Note from page 14:

If you have lost the MOT certificate and you want to check the vehicle's current MOT status, you can request this information by contacting the Vehicle Operator & Services Agency MOT Enquiry Service on 0870 33 00 444 or online at www.motinfo.gov.uk.   You will need to quote the reference no. on the V5C log book or from the previous test certificate.

THE BVRLA FAIR WEAR AND TEAR GUIDE FOR DRIVERS AND OPERATORS OF CONTRACT HIRED AND LEASED LIGHT COMMERCIAL VEHICLES UNDER 3.5 TONNES GVW AND MINIBUSES FROM 9 TO 17 SEATS.

the aim of this guide

The aim of the BVRLA's Fair Wear and Tear Guide is to provide an industry-wide, accepted standard that defines fair wear and tear on light commercial vehicles up to 3.5t GVW and on minibuses with between 9-17 seats when they are returned to a BVRLA Member at the end of a contract or finance agreement.

Fair wear and tear occurs when normal usage causes deterioration to the vehicle. It is not to be confused with damage which occurs as a result of a specific event or series of events such as impact, inappropriate stowing of items, harsh-treatment, negligent acts or omissions. This guide not only provides guidance on the industry standard for fair wear and tear but also promotes best practice in vehicle maintenance and upkeep that will prevent unacceptable wear and tear from occurring.

the fair wear and tear standard

This guide defines the industry standard at return for every aspect of the vehicle's condition. Commercial vehicles are 'working' vehicles and as such, some areas of the vehicle will be subject to far higher wear and tear than others. For ease of reference in deciding acceptability, the vehicle has been divided into zones as described on Page 4. The degree of wear and tear acceptable in each zone is also defined.

advice to driver/fleet operator

This guide contains advice to the driver and fleet operator about details of maintenance routines and preventative action necessary to keep the vehicle in acceptable condition and thus minimise de-hire charges at end of lease. Dependent on the circumstances of the driver, some duties and responsibilities covering risk assessment of the vehicle's use in the context of work-related driving may be set out by employers and these should be referred to also.

Taken together, each section provides a comprehensive view of the necessary vehicle upkeep and the resulting vehicle condition. Drivers and fleet operators will benefit from a robust maintenance system and good practices in fleet management because they promote compliance and road safety, lower operating costs and reduce the likelihood of incurring de-hire charges on the vehicle's return.

Also included is a pull-out section that will help drivers and fleet operators appraise their vehicle prior to vehicle return. It illustrates typical forms of acceptable fair wear and tear (green framed boxes) and unacceptable fair wear and tear (red framed boxes).

BLUE ZONE:	non-working surface
acceptable	not acceptable

Scratches up to 25mm are acceptable.

a

Multiple heavy scratches and dents are not acceptable.

b

the zones

LCVs and minibuses are working vehicles and their condition at end of contract must allow for wear and tear appropriate to their usage. For ease of definition, we have divided a vehicle into three main areas;

BLUE ZONE:

An area designated a Blue Zone is not a working surface. Only light wear and tear is acceptable. Paintwork must be intact. Any chips, dings or scratches must fall within the tolerances listed in the table below. There must be no deviation to the original shape of the vehicle outside these tolerances.

Throughout this guide reference has been made to the fair wear and tear standard and of what that consists. The table below shows what is acceptable within a Blue Zone.

defining tolerances: size		the standard number allowed as FW&T	
chips	less than 8mm in diameter	4 per panel 8 on a bonnet	6 per door edge 10 per front grille
dings	less than 12mm in diameter		2 per panel
scratches/abrasions	less than 25mm in length		4 per panel

YELLOW ZONE:

An area designated a Yellow Zone is a working surface. Heavy wear and tear is acceptable. Any chips, dents or scratches falling within the tolerances listed in the table below are acceptable. Paint can be absent from surfaces. There must be no deviation to the original shape of the vehicle outside these tolerances.

Throughout this guide reference has been made to the fair wear and tear standard and of what that consists. The table below shows what is acceptable within a Yellow Zone.

defining tolerances: size		the standard number allowed as FW&T
chips	any size	all
dents	less than 12mm in diameter	2 per panel
scratches/abrasions	any length	all

MAGENTA ZONE:

The Cab Interior Zone describes the interior passenger cabin, including driver and passenger areas, seats etc. Wear and tear is acceptable but there must be no rips, holes, heavy scratches, burns, deposits or deformation to any component.

the zones

These images below represent typical light goods vehicles with:
working surfaces - YELLOW ZONE
non-working surfaces - BLUE ZONE

Car Derived Vans (CDV),
Panel Vans, Boxes and
Lutons
(GRP and Glass Fibre)

Manufacturer Built Pick-Up
(integrated body at point of
manufacture)

Coach Built (body separate
from cab), Dropsides,
Tippers, Flat Beds and
Beaver Tails

the industry fair wear and tear standard for light commercial vehicles under 3.5t and minibuses

5

exterior body   BLUE ZONE

An area designated a Blue Zone is not a working surface. Only light wear and tear is acceptable. Paintwork must be intact. Any chips, dings or scratches must fall within the tolerances listed on page 4.

this is acceptable

Single scratch under 25mm in length.
1

No more than 4 non-rusted scratches through to the metal.
2

A maximum of 6 non-rusted door edge chips per door.
3

A maximum of 8 non-rusted stone chips on a bonnet or 4 per panel.
4

No more than 2 isolated dings less than 12mm per panel.
5

Use of correct colour matchstick to touch up chips prior to the metal rusting.
6

BLUE ZONE   exterior **body**

An area designated a Blue Zone is not a working surface. Only light wear and tear is acceptable. Paintwork must be intact. Any chips, dings or scratches must fall within the tolerances listed on page 4.

this is unacceptable

Paint removed to base metal on non-working surface.

7

Multiple heavy scratches and dents on non-working surface.

8

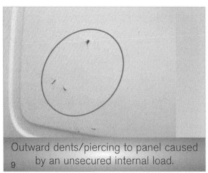

Outward dents/piercing to panel caused by an unsecured internal load.

9

Chips over 8mm should not be allowed to blister and rust.

10

Unrepaired damage made by a key or key fob.

11

Impact damage must be professionally repaired.

12

the industry fair wear and tear standard for light commercial vehicles under 3.5t and minibuses

exterior body   BLUE ZONE

An area designated a Blue Zone is not a working surface. Only light wear and tear is acceptable. Paintwork must be intact. Any chips, dings or scratches must fall within the tolerances listed on page 4.

this is acceptable

Approved roof rack system fitted with the permission of the rental company.
13

Roof rack correctly fitted with anti-rust mounting clamps and pads.
14

All fittings should be sealed against water penetration, preventing rust.
15

Drilled holes should be treated against water penetration and rusting.
16

No more than 10 stone chips and some light scuffing to metal grille area.
17

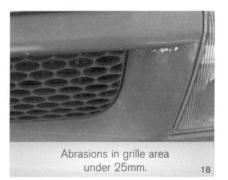

Abrasions in grille area under 25mm.
18

BLUE ZONE
exterior **body**

An area designated a Blue Zone is not a working surface. Only light wear and tear is acceptable. Paintwork must be intact. Any chips, dings or scratches must fall within the tolerances listed on page 4.

this is unacceptable

Roof rack has been incorrectly fitted and not fit for purpose.
19

Damaged gutter rails due to metal-on-metal contact and overloading.
20

Roof beacon fitted with inadequate water proof fixings.
21

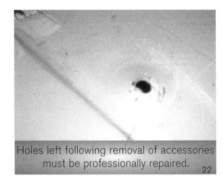

Holes left following removal of accessories must be professionally repaired.
22

Missing or broken grille.
23

Grilles must be properly fixed and secured.
24

exterior body   YELLOW ZONE

An area designated a Yellow Zone is a working surface.
Any chips, dents or scratches falling within the tolerances listed in the table on page 4 are acceptable.
Paint can be absent from surfaces.

this is acceptable

Removal of paint in some areas due to
25   stone chips/wear and tear.

Heavy scuffing to the tailgate,
a working surface.   26

Corrosion to lightboard and mudguard
27   acceptable (no deviation to metal).

Tailgate abrasions.
28

Light deposits and heavy abrasions to
29   rear passenger access area.

Removal of paint in access areas
e.g. door bottoms or sills.   30

the industry fair wear and tear standard for light commercial vehicles under 3.5t and minibuses

YELLOW ZONE

exterior **body**

An area designated a Yellow Zone is a working surface.
Any chips, dents or scratches falling within the tolerances listed in the table on page 4 are acceptable.
Paint can be absent from surfaces.

this is unacceptable

Impact damage causing deformation to metal and broken light cluster.
31

Side panel damaged by incorrect working practices.
32

Collision or impact damage causing holes in floor.
33

Heavy deposits of cement, tarmac, etc. on tipper floor.
34

Damaged tailgate.
Deviation from original shape.
35

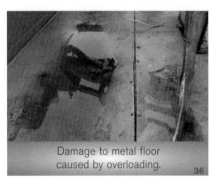

Damage to metal floor caused by overloading.
36

the industry fair wear and tear standard for light commercial vehicles under 3.5t and minibuses

11

interior body   YELLOW ZONE

An area designated a Yellow Zone is a working surface.
Any chips, dents or scratches falling within the tolerances listed in the table on page 4 are acceptable.
Paint can be absent from surfaces.

this is acceptable

Removal of paint and multiple scratches
37   to a loading area.

Removal of paint and multiple scratches
to a loading area due to wear.   38

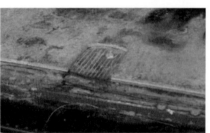

Removal of paint and no deviation
39   to metal in load area.

Removal of paint due to heavy wear and
tear with no deviation to metal.   40

Removal of paint within a passenger
41   carrying area of a minibus.

Light scuffing and soiling to passenger area.
42

summary of **fair wear and tear** standard

appraisal tips pull out pages

remember:

☐ Carry out the appraisal of the vehicle 10 - 12 weeks before the vehicle is due for return. This will allow you to arrange to have any unacceptable wear and tear rectified.

☐ It is important to appraise the vehicle as honestly as you can - be objective. Ask a friend or colleague to help you.

☐ Choose a time and place with good light. This is how the leasing company will examine your vehicle. Appraisals carried out in poor light invariably miss some faults.

☐ Before appraising the vehicle, make sure that it has been washed and is thoroughly clean but remember to allow time for it to dry. Water on the paintwork can mask faults.

☐ Walk all the way around the vehicle and examine closely each panel including the roof, bonnet, doors, and body for significant damage. Observe where the light is reflected differently from dents and scratches.

☐ Crouch or kneel down at the front and rear of the vehicle and look along each side. This will help you pick up scratches and dents that may otherwise be difficult to spot.

☐ Inspect lamps, lenses, windows and mirrors for chips, cracks and holes.

☐ Check the tyres (including spare) for damage. Check that the wear on the tread across each tyre is even. Inspect wheels and wheel trims (if fitted) for deterioration.

☐ Clean and valet the interior.

☐ Check upholstered areas for odours, tears, burns, stains and wear.

☐ Inspect all controls, including audio equipment and accessories – they should be present and fully functional.

vehicle condition report

Use this checklist to appraise your vehicle before it is due for return.

Vehicle Appraisal Form

MANHEIM Auctions

CUSTOMER:	Driver of vehicle: Yes ☐ No ☐
Inspector's Name	Contact No:
Location of Vehicle	

Time:	Date:	ITEMS OUTSIDE OF FAIR WEAR & TEAR AND REQUIRING ATTENTION:

RegNo:	1.
Make:	2.
Model:	3.
Style:	4.
Extras:	5.
	6.

CAB INTERIOR & SEATS
1.
2.
3.

Man/Auto	Fuel Type:
Chassis No:	
Colour:	
Mileage:	

1.
2.
3.
4.
5.
6.

ACCESSORIES:
Radio/CD

Service Book ☐	Spare Wheel ☐ L ☐ I
Side Door(s) ☐	P.A.S. ☐
No. of Keys ☐	Remote Fobs ☐
Tax ☐	Exp Date:

LOAD AREA (INTERIOR)
1.
2.

ROOF
1.

SIGNAGE:
CREW VAN/MINIBUS INTERIOR & SEATS
1.
2.
3.

Painted ☐	Stickers ☐
Silver-backed ☐	Glue Residue ☐

INSPECTION CONDITIONS:
Vehicle Valeted?   Yes ☐   No ☐

1.
2.
3.
4.
5.
6.

WEATHER	LIGHTING
Sunny ☐	Artificial ☐
Overcast ☐	Daylight ☐
Raining ☐	Dusk ☐
Hailstone ☐	Night ☐
Ice ☐	
Snow ☐	
Storm ☐	

1.
2.
3.
4.
5.
6.

TYRES:
LEGAL / ILLEGAL   Please mark on illustration ➜

At the end of the contract period this vehicle will undergo a detailed damage and condition assessment in a controlled inspection environment. Any damage that falls outside the BVRLA Fair Wear and Tear Guidelines (ie is deemed unfair wear and tear) will be recorded, the repair(s) costed and a re-chargeable as per the terms of the contract.

BVRLA

summary of **fair wear and tear** standard

appraisal tips pull out pages

fair wear and tear **tolerance check**

Please use this summary to appraise your vehicle against the BVRLA fair wear and tear standard prior to its return to the leasing company. For more information, you should consult the full detailed guidelines published in BVRLA's Fair Wear and Tear publication.

To avoid end of contract charges, you can arrange to correct unacceptable areas of damage before the vehicle is returned. Check the terms of your contract. Always point out any uncorrected wear or damage when the vehicle is collected to avoid problems later.

BLUE ZONE: non -working area

Throughout this guide reference has been made to the fair wear and tear standard and of what that consists. The table below shows what is acceptable within a Blue Zone.

defining tolerances:	size	the standard number allowed as FW&T	
chips	less than 8mm in diameter	4 per panel 8 on a bonnet	6 per door edge 10 per front grille
dings	less than 12mm in diameter		2 per panel
scratches/abrasions	less than 25mm in length		4 per panel

YELLOW ZONE: working area

Throughout this guide reference has been made to the fair wear and tear standard and of what that consists. The table below shows what is acceptable within a Yellow Zone.

defining tolerances:	size	the standard number allowed as FW&T
chips	any size	all
dents	less than 12mm in diameter	2 per panel
scratches/abrasions	any length	all

MAGENTA ZONE: cab interior

The Cab Interior Zone describes the interior passenger cabin, including driver and passenger areas, seats etc. Wear and tear is acceptable but there must be no rips, holes, heavy scratches, burns, deposits or deformation to any component.

summary of **fair wear and tear** standard

appraisal tips pull out pages

vehicle collection **tips**

☐ On collection, the vehicle must be in a safe and roadworthy condition with all appropriate keys, equipment, accessories and documentation available.

☐ Your leasing company will arrange collection of the vehicle at the end of your agreement, or you may be required to return it to a specified location. All readily apparent damage and wear, irrespective of liability, will be documented and you will be given the opportunity to agree with the condition of the vehicle at that point. The leasing company will then be able to carry out a full assessment of the vehicle and calculate if any de-hire charges are payable.

☐ If you cannot be present during the collection of the vehicle, or if other conditions, e.g. poor weather, prevent the condition of the vehicle to be documented, your leasing company will issue you with a written condition report of the vehicle and advise you of any charges that may subsequently become due, together with summary details of how any charges are calculated.

☐ Ensure all personal effects and business materials are removed from the vehicle.

☐ Remove all keys from the key fob that don't belong to the vehicle.

☐ Any CDs for satellite navigation should be left in the vehicle. Any driver's home address information should be deleted.

YELLOW ZONE   interior **body**

An area designated a Yellow Zone is a working surface.
Any chips, dents or scratches falling within the tolerances listed in the table on page 4 are acceptable.
Paint can be absent from surfaces.

this is unacceptable

Damage to the semi bulkhead caused by an unsecured load.

43

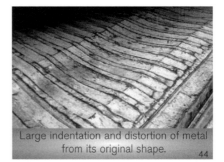

Large indentation and distortion of metal from its original shape.

44

Damage to wheel arch caused by an unsecured load.

45

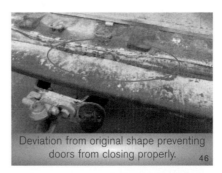

Deviation from original shape preventing doors from closing properly.

46

Damage to door lining through abuse or unsecured load.

47

Distortion from original shape though excessive wear or abuse.

48

exterior body   YELLOW ZONE

An area designated a Yellow Zone is a working surface.
Any chips, dents or scratches falling within the tolerances listed in the table on page 4 are acceptable.
Paint can be absent from surfaces.

this is acceptable

Scuffs of any length on plastic bumpers.
49

Heavy wear on rear bumper designed
to be used as loading area.
50

this is unacceptable

A cracked bumper caused by impact
or collision.
51

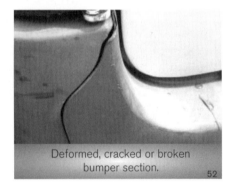

Deformed, cracked or broken
bumper section.
52

MAGENTA ZONE

cab **interior** including Minibuses

Dashboard, fascia, doors interior trim, headlining and floorcovering.
The Cab Interior Zone describes the interior passenger cabin. Wear and tear, no rips, holes, burns, stains, deposits, deep scratches or deviation from its original shape.

this is acceptable

Light staining and discolouring of fabric.
53

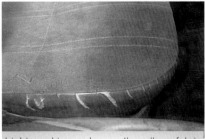

Light cracking and some threadbare fabric through wear.
54

this is unacceptable

Seats removed and not replaced.
55

Heavy soiling and stains of seats.
56

Rips, tears or burns on seats.
57

Burns and heavy deposits on seats.
58

the industry fair wear and tear standard for light commercial vehicles under 3.5t and minibuses

15

cab interior including Minibuses   MAGENTA ZONE

Dashboard, fascia, doors interior trim, headlining and floorcovering.
The Cab Interior Zone describes the interior passenger cabin. Wear and tear, no rips, holes, burns, stains, deposits, deep scratches or deviation from its original shape.

this is acceptable

Wear on steering wheel.
59

Soiling, non-permanent damage or light scratches to glove box.
60

Scratches caused by light scuffing from footwear on interior trim/door.
61

Light scratches to centre console and wear to gear stick gaiter.
62

Light soiling and wear due to normal use.
63

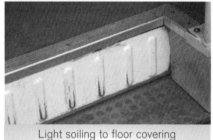

Light soiling to floor covering and removal of paint on step.
64

MAGENTA ZONE

cab **interior** including Minibuses

Dashboard, fascia, doors interior trim, headlining and floorcovering.
The Cab Interior Zone describes the interior passenger cabin. Wear and tear, no rips, holes, burns,
stains, deposits, deep scratches or deviation from its original shape.

this is unacceptable

Holes left when items like mobile phones are removed.
65

Burn marks and damage to console.
66

Heavy staining and scoring to dashboard.
67

Cracks and deformation caused by impact damage and neglect.
68

Seatbelts damaged (i.e. not retracting).
69

Broken dashboard and/or knobs and/or radio missing.
70

cab interior including Minibuses   **MAGENTA ZONE**

Dashboard, fascia, doors interior trim, headlining and floorcovering.
The Cab Interior Zone describes the interior passenger cabin. Wear and tear, no rips, holes, burns, stains, deposits, deep scratches or deviation from its original shape.

this is acceptable

Light discolouration to roof and visors.
71

Greasy handmarks and non permanent staining on visor.
72

Light damage caused by everyday use.
73

Heavy scratches and removal of paint to access areas.
74

Minibus side access area with heavy wear.
75

Heavy abrasions and removal of paint to access areas/ramp on minibus.
76

MAGENTA ZONE   cab **interior** including Minibuses

Dashboard, fascia, doors interior trim, headlining and floorcovering.
The Cab Interior Zone describes the interior passenger cabin. Wear and tear, no rips, holes, burns,
stains, deposits, deep scratches or deviation from its original shape.

this is unacceptable

Rips, tears and burns in
headlinings and trim.
77

Heavy deposits and soiling.
78

Water damage to headlining.
79

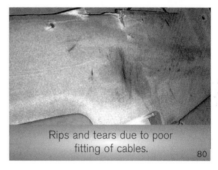

Rips and tears due to poor
fitting of cables.
80

Allowing the floor covering to become
81 unsafe with large holes in the mat.

There must be no deposits of tarmac,
paint or concrete in cabin.
82

defining wear and tear

badges and labels
Badges, labels or advertising fitted to the bodywork or glass of the vehicle should be removed unless originally fitted with the agreement of the leasing company and any damage caused by their attachment or removal must be made good. Any difference in paintwork colour noted following the removal of advertising, labelling or logos is not acceptable.

roof racks, tow bars
Roof racks must be fit for purpose and meet the manufacturer's specification where applicable. Holes may be drilled provided rust prevention and water proofing measures are taken and there is no distortion to the panels or gutter rails.
Tow bars, if fitted, must be in good, rust-free condition with electrical connections working properly.

lamps and lenses
All lamps must work. Minor scuff marks or scratches are acceptable. Holes or cracks in the glass or plastic covers of lamp units are not acceptable.

windows/windscreens
Some light scratching and/or isolated stone chips are acceptable provided they do not interfere with the driver's line of sight (MOT regulations apply) and the heating elements still work properly. Chips, cracks or holes are not acceptable

tyre wear and damage
All tyres, including the spare, must meet minimum UK legal requirements and comply with the vehicle manufacturer's recommendations of tyre type, size and speed rating for the vehicle. They must be of an equivalent standard to those fitted to the vehicle at the time of commencement of the hire. There must be no damage to sidewalls or tread.

wheels and wheel trims
Dents and holes on steel rims and the main body of the wheel are not acceptable. The spare wheel, jack and other wheel tools, if supplied, with the vehicle must be returned intact with the vehicle, stowed properly and in good working order.

passenger area, seats and trim
The interior upholstery and trim must be clean, odourless and with no visible burns, tears or staining. All seats originally supplied must be present. Wear and soiling through normal use is acceptable. Interior fittings such as seat belts, rear view mirrors, courtesy lights, sun visors, door bins etc. must be present and intact.

in-vehicle entertainment equipment, telephones and navigation systems
All original equipment, accessories and controls (including satellite navigation CDs) must be present and operate correctly. If accessories such as mobile telephones and other non-standard equipment have been wired-in or mounted on the dashboard, any holes or other damage must be neatly repaired when they are removed.

aerials
Aerials must be undamaged and functioning.

accessories
All accessories provide with the vehicle at the commencement of lease, such as, tool kits, towing pins, roof racks, first aid kits, fire extinguishers etc. must be returned in good working order with the vehicle or replaced with items of similar standard and specification.

roller shutters
Scratches to the paintwork on roller shutters are acceptable when caused through normal usage. Damage caused through impact, or by movement of the load is not acceptable. Shutters should be closed and secured at all times when the vehicle is moving.

tail-lifts and other vehicle-mounted equipment
Paint deterioration on tail-lift platforms is acceptable. Platforms and runners must operate satisfactorily and be free of impact damage and distortion. Current, valid statutory certificates must be available.

advice to the **driver/fleet operator**

If yours is a company vehicle, your company may outline the preventative vehicle maintenance and safety checks that you need to undertake on a daily and weekly basis. You should check your company driver policy to ensure that you comply. The vehicle leasing company is also an excellent source of advice and assistance on all aspects of the vehicle's operation. If you are personally leasing the vehicle, you should consult the vehicle supplier.

general
We have said previously in this guide that light goods vehicles and minibuses are 'working' vehicles. It makes sense therefore for drivers and fleet operators to work with their leasing company to ensure that all vehicles supplied have the appropriate specification for the job that's to be carried out. If the intended use of the vehicle should change during the period of hire, the leasing company should be informed.

maintenance and servicing
Regular maintenance and best practice in fleet management will help prevent unacceptable wear and tear from occurring. A robust maintenance regime will include vehicle inspection, adhering to manufacturers' recommended service intervals, daily checks and scheduled repairs. These ensure the vehicle is not only safe and roadworthy but will also achieve lower operating costs.

Whether carried out in-house, out sourced or by the leasing company, regular maintenance and servicing should be carried out by accredited servicing outlets which adhere to standards set by regulatory bodies and/or members of a recognised trade association. The service record must be stamped at each service.

It is recommended that any defects or damage that occurs during normal vehicle usage should be rectified promptly and/or notified to the leasing company. All work must be completed to a professional standard by repairers who provide full warranty on their work. Your leasing company will advise you and will authorise repairs if it is responsible for the maintenance of the vehicle. For small areas of damage, a SMART (small and medium area repair technique) repair may be appropriate.

advice to the driver/fleet operator cont.

The leasing company will expect you to regularly report the mileage reading of the vehicle and any mechanical or other fault that requires rectification or which may result in the deterioration in the vehicle's mechanical, electrical and bodywork condition.

operation of the vehicle

Ensure that drivers are qualified and competent to drive the vehicle, are familiar with its equipment and have received full training on operating special equipment like tail-lifts.

The vehicle should not be overloaded and goods should be stored safely and securely within the vehicle at all times. The vehicle should not be used for the conveyance of noxious or toxic substances, un-refrigerated foodstuffs, fish, offal or any other pungent smelling goods without prior approval from the leasing company.

Seek permission from the leasing company before any alterations to the vehicle are made, drilling holes to fit beacon lights or mobile phones, for example. Holes and other damage left following the removal of such accessories should be filled with suitable blanking grommets, or otherwise professionally repaired.

Always seek permission from the leasing company before taking the vehicle abroad and request the appropriate documentation e.g. VE103, Vehicle on Hire Certificate.

The BVRLA produces a best practice guide covering all aspects of renting and leasing commercial vehicles. The BVRLA Guide to Renting and Leasing Commercial Vehicles helps all parties to be clear about the do's and don'ts of renting and leasing commercial

vehicles. It is available to BVRLA Members and their customers from the BVRLA's website www.bvrla.co.uk.

drivers

Drivers should receive proper induction regarding company vehicle policy and procedures. A good company policy will have clear rules on reporting accidents, clearly communicated and irrespective of who owns the vehicle they are driving.

Drivers should be encouraged to perform their own routine daily safety check of tyres, oil, water and screen wash in between scheduled inspections.

Regular cleaning of both the interior and exterior ensures the vehicle always looks good and presents a professional image. Floor mats and other areas of heavy wear should be regularly replaced.

glossary of **terms**

❑ **Burr** Raised edge around scratch.

❑ **Car Derived Van (CDV)** Van based on a car.

❑ **Chassis Cabs** LCV cab with open chassis and no body attached i.e. Luton, tipper, etc.

❑ **Dent** Deformation of the original structure.

❑ **Ding** Small dent that hasn't broken paintwork e.g. minor carpark damage.

❑ **Grommet** Small piece of rubber to fill drill hole, preventing ingress of water etc.

❑ **Heavy abrasions** Heavy scratch to bare metal.

❑ **Heavy staining** Deposits which render material texture smooth.

❑ **Impact damage** Dents or damage causing deformation of panels.

❑ **Light staining** Discolouring of material which does not change the texture. Normal wear and tear that can be cleaned.

❑ **Outward dents** Raised dent on external bodywork usually caused by insecure loads piercing bodywork from the inside.

❑ **Scuffs** Light scratches or marks usually on plastic bumpers.

❑ **Glasonite Reinforced Panels (GRP)** Sheet material used in construction of Luton and box bodies.

1.2.14 INSURANCE

All contract hire agreements require that you take out comprehensive insurance on the vehicle.[28] The supplier will normally ask for proof that insurance is in place and that the premiums have been paid.

1.2.15 ROADSIDE ASSISTANCE

If you have selected a maintenance-inclusive arrangement this will normally include membership of a roadside assistance service. This may be just a basic service that attempts to repair the vehicle at the roadside and tows it to a garage if a roadside repair cannot be effected. Alternatively it may be a more comprehensive package including get-you-home and at-home cover. Some of the better packages include European travel assistance too.

1.2.16 REPLACEMENT VEHICLE

Contract hire agreements can provide you with a replacement vehicle (sometimes called a 'relief vehicle') if your vehicle is off the road.

The agreement will specify:

- The circumstances in which the replacement will be provided (if the main vehicle is off the road after an accident, or servicing or both).
- The delay before it will be provided (12, 24, 36, 48 hours) at no cost.
- The period for which it can be used (7, 14, 28 days etc).
- The maximum number of days during the term of the lease for which replacement vehicles will be supplied.[29]

If you need a replacement vehicle and this is included in your contract, you don't have to wait for the 'delay' period to expire. Every leasing company will be happy to deliver a replacement vehicle immediately. You will pay for the initial period (12, 24, 36, 48 hours) and the leasing company will cover the cost thereafter.

1.2.17 TYRES

If you enter into a maintenance-inclusive contract hire agreement, the leasing company will pay for the replacement of worn tyres during the term of the agreement. It is likely that the contract will limit the number of tyres replaced and will not cover tyres that have been damaged by bad driving.

Generally speaking the number of tyres provided should cover normal driving over the lease period and mileage. You may wish to enquire into the driving habits of any driver who requires more than this number of tyres during the term of an agreement.

If you need an unlimited number of tyres, some contract hire companies will include this in the contract for a slightly higher rental.

---

28   See 1.21.3.
29   See 5.6.

On the continent some leasing arrangements include the supply and seasonal swapping over of winter tyres. This is unusual in the UK though some suppliers are considering it.

1.2.18 Client default

The contract hire agreement assumes that the supplier will allow you to enjoy quiet possession[30] of the vehicle. Your obligation is to pay your rentals when due and to meet the other obligations shown in the lease. If you fail to comply with any of these obligations, you will be in default of the terms of the agreement.[31]

1.2.19 VAT disallowance 50% of rental if any private use

As with all types of lease, if you wish to use the vehicle for private use, 50% of the VAT on the lease rental will be disallowed as input tax. This only applies to the finance element of the rental, not any maintenance element.

The contract hire quote will show the net cost to you after this disallowance.[32]

The 50% lease rental disallowance is meant to reflect HMRC's view that the average company car has 50% private use. The BVRLA is currently[33] trying to persuade HMRC that the 50% recoverable figure is too low and should be increased to 70%.

1.2.20 Corporation tax deductibility of contract hire rentals

If you lease a vehicle on contract hire you can offset the whole or a part of the rental against your corporation tax (or income tax) liability.[34]

1.2.21 Used vehicle contract hire

Whilst the majority of the vehicles on contract hire in the UK are supplied when new, a small number of companies offer used vehicles too.

There are advantages to both parties. You get a vehicle at a lower rental than you would pay for the equivalent new vehicle.

The lessor has a lower risk in the vehicle, which will not suffer the huge depreciation that normally happens when a new vehicle is driven out of the showroom door. So the difference between the value of the vehicle and the amount outstanding in the lessor's books will be lower if you were to stop paying and they had to repossess it.

However, practical issues have hampered the development of the used vehicle contract hire market. If a dealer has a used vehicle on his forecourt, you see it, like

---

30 See 2.3.3.
31 See 2.3.4.
32 See 17.1.4.
33 October 2011.
34 See 17.1.3.

it and decide to take it on contract hire from the dealer's contract hire company, so things are very straightforward. The salesperson gives you a quote based on their knowledge of the vehicle, you sign the contract and they hands over the keys.

If you decide you want to lease a used vehicle from a leasing company that is not part of a dealership, things get a bit more difficult.

- ■ You phone them for a quote.

- ■ They probably have to go and find a suitable vehicle, unless they happen to have an ex-lease vehicle in stock that meets your needs.

- ■ You will want to inspect it to see if it is of satisfactory condition.

- ■ Then they will want to inspect it to establish a maintenance budget and a residual value.

There is a lot of expense for the supplier here (sourcing, transportation, inspection) even before you have seen the vehicle and if you then reject it they have no way to recover this cost.

It can also be quite difficult for the supplier to source vehicles with the required specification and mileage.

For these practical reasons relatively few used vehicles are leased on contract hire. Nonetheless, a few companies specialise in it. They have cracked the supply problem, usually by forging relationships with used vehicle vendors, many of whom sell ex-rental or manufacturer demonstration vehicles.

One final point needs to be borne in mind. Most employees prefer not to be given a second-hand car as their company car.

1.2.22   CONTRACT HIRE ADVANTAGES

Contract hire offers you a comprehensive solution that includes:

- ■ Supply of the vehicle (no need for you to go out and find it).

- ■ Low interest rates built into the rental (often lower than you would get if you searched the market for credit).

- ■ The benefit of big fleet purchasing power.

- ■ Payment of all routine maintenance and servicing bills (no need to scrutinise maintenance bills or negotiate with garages).

- ■ Automatic annual vehicle excise duty renewal.

- ■ An off-balance sheet finance product[35] (currently, though see 8.6).

- ■ No residual value risk.[36]

- ■ No maintenance cost risk.[37]

---

35   See 8.1.

36   See 5.12.

37   See 5.13.

The success of the product has been its simplicity. You get a vehicle for an agreed term and mileage and just hand it back at the end of the lease. So long as the agreed mileage has not been exceeded and the vehicle is undamaged, that's all that needs to happen.

The contract hire market is highly competitive. If you wish you can simply shop around on a car-by-car basis to find the lowest quote and take cars from a variety of suppliers. In fact, many smaller organisations do just that.

1.2.23 CONTRACT HIRE DISADVANTAGES

With contract hire you are using a professional to supply and manage your vehicles and are buying a bundled package that includes finance. In buying this package you are giving away an element of control of the vehicle. You will feel this most acutely if you decide to early terminate the lease or if the mileage you drive exceeds the contract mileage. If you need to be able to change your vehicles at short notice or you are in a high staff-turnover business, you may find that the early termination charges become burdensome.

If you own your own vehicles you can do as you wish. For some, this is crucial.

Whilst early termination charges can be annoying it's worthwhile mentioning that these are largely designed to compensate the leasing company for the loss they suffer when they dispose of the vehicle earlier than planned. If you were to buy the vehicle outright rather than lease it, you would suffer this loss too. The only difference is that you wouldn't receive an invoice for the early termination but would still have to write off the loss as additional depreciation in your books.

1.2.24 SHOULD YOU USE CONTRACT HIRE?

CONTRACT HIRE AND TAXATION

You should seriously consider using contract hire if your business is making taxable profits and you believe that the advantages listed above outweigh the disadvantages for your business.

You should use a discounted cash flow (DCF) approach to compare the cash flows arising from the different methods of funding vehicles and select the method that minimises your costs.[38]

Taxation should be part of this analysis.[39]

The tax rules change from 1 April 2009 for limited companies and 6 April 2009 for sole traders and partnerships.

The old rules are ignored in this book because most vehicles leased before that date have now been de-fleeted. Cars acquired or leased under the old rules are 'grandfathered' for tax purposes; i.e. they will continue to be taxed under those rules for 5 years.

---

38   See 7.1.
39   See 17.1.3.

The new rules are much simpler and apply to company cars, taxis, hire cars and cars leased to the disabled. If the CO_2 emissions of one of these vehicles are less than 160g/km the full rental is tax-deductible. Otherwise 15% is disallowed.

Contract hire and VAT

VAT is chargeable on all lease rentals but not on hire purchase or conditional sale payments. A contract hire company can recover the input VAT they pay when they buy a vehicle to lease to you. However, they cannot recover this on a vehicle they sell to you under, for example, hire purchase or conditional sale.

Most businesses are able to recover input VAT through their VAT returns. However, businesses that sell goods or services that are exempt from VAT cannot recover all of this input VAT. These businesses are said to be wholly or partially exempt.[40]

And some companies aren't registered for VAT at all.

Because of these different treatments, you need to consider VAT when evaluating your choice of vehicle financing method.

Other service issues

When you take a vehicle on contract hire, the leasing company does far more than just supply finance. It sources, buys, maintains, administers and disposes of the vehicle and takes residual value and maintenance cost risk.

The relationship you forge with your contract hire company is normally quite close and involves quite a lot of day-to-day interaction. You are effectively outsourcing part of your administration to a third party and you need to be happy that they have the ability to meet your needs and add value to your business.

---

40   See 17.1.4.

Different contract hire companies offer different types and levels of service. At one extreme a team of people may have been designated to manage your account on a day-to-day basis. The other extreme is a 'no-frills' approach: 'Here is our price, deal with us via the internet only, don't expect us to speak to you or meet you'.

Both methods are valid and there are variations within these two extremes. The key is to find the organisation that will work the way that you want. They may not offer the lowest price on a particular day but over time you are more likely to be happy with them. 'You get what you pay for' applies here.

1.2.25 Exercises

What is meant by 'outright purchase?'

List the disadvantages of outright purchase.

Define 'bailment'.

What is a residual value?

What is residual value risk and who takes it in a contract hire agreement?

Explain what is meant by 'excess mileage'.

What cars might you find it hard to obtain on contract hire?

What would you expect to be included in a contract hire quote?

Do all contract hire companies allow you to early terminate a lease?

Why may early termination charges seem high?

List the early termination methods that are available in the market.

How can you avoid or minimise early termination charges?

When might a contract hire company refuse to allow you to extend the lease of a vehicle on contract hire?

What are the two methods of extending a contract hire agreement?

How might you agree what is and what is not, fair wear and tear on a leased vehicle?

In what circumstances might you need a replacement vehicle?

What are the advantages and disadvantages of contract hire?

1.3 OPERATING LEASE

1.3.1   FEATURES

There is no legal definition of an operating lease.

The accounting standard SSAP21 says that a finance lease is one that transfers 'substantially all of the risks and rewards of ownership to the lessee' and then says that every other type of lease is an operating lease.[41]

It follows therefore that an operating lease is one where the lessor retains these risks. In practice, it is best to think of an operating lease as a simple rental agreement. You pay a rental for a period of time and then hand the asset back to the lessor. In order to recover their investment, either they will have to lease it to another party or they will have to sell it.

So, for example, if you hire a sanding machine from a hire shop for the weekend, the lease that you enter into will be an operating lease (even though it may be called a rental agreement or hire agreement). Vehicle contract hire and daily hire agreements are operating leases, although it is worthwhile mentioning that for some people the expression 'contract hire' automatically includes maintenance, whereas an operating lease does not have this automatic association.

With an operating lease the supplier takes the residual value risk in the vehicle, so you do not have to show it on your balance sheet.

1.3.2   ADVANTAGES

All of the advantages shown under contract hire apply to an operating lease.

1.3.3   DISADVANTAGES

All of the disadvantages shown under contract hire apply to an operating lease.

1.4 SALE AND LEASE BACK

This is the name for the transaction where you sell your vehicles to a lessor, then continue to use them under the terms of a leasing agreement, often contract hire.

There are a variety of reasons why you may wish to do this.

You may wish to raise cash, remove residual value risk, reduce your administration or remove the vehicles from your balance sheet. Or perhaps you have decided to

---

41   See 8.1.2.

use contract hire for the first time and you sell the existing fleet to the contract hire company and immediately start to enjoy the service advantages, rather than waiting up to three years until the whole fleet has been replaced piecemeal.

Sale and lease back is often called 'purchase and lease back' or simply 'leaseback'.

1.5 CONTRACT PURCHASE

1.5.1 FEATURES

Contract hire has been growing in popularity for decades. However, by the early 1980s it was apparent that it did not work for all businesses. Companies that were exempt or partially exempt for VAT purposes could not recover some or all of the VAT charged on the lease rentals. Many companies that used contract hire did not use it for their expensive vehicles because at that time there was a permanent corporation tax disallowance on rentals for 'expensive' cars.

The contract hire industry responded by creating a new product – contract purchase.

The concept was quite simple: by putting three agreements together a client could be given all of the advantages of contract hire without the VAT or corporation tax disadvantages. Those three agreements were:

1. A conditional sale or hire purchase agreement containing a lump-sum ('balloon') payment at the end of the contract[42]
2. A repurchase undertaking
3. A maintenance agreement

Under the conditional sale or hire purchase agreement the client agreed to buy the vehicle on deferred purchase terms (by paying instalments over a period of time).

The repurchase undertaking said that the contract hire company would, at the client's option, buy the vehicle back at the end of the contract for a pre-agreed fixed price.

The maintenance agreement covered the standard maintenance items normally found in a maintenance-inclusive contract hire agreement.

As the finance agreement was a purchase-type agreement, no VAT was chargeable on the payments and the permanent tax disallowance on lease rentals did not apply. The maintenance agreement was separate so it was clear that the client could recover VAT on the maintenance payments.

It is fair to say that this arrangement attracted the early attention of HM Revenue and Customs, as it denied Customs the VAT it might otherwise have expected to

---

42 See 6.4.

receive. There were a number of well-publicised cases where contract hire companies had to withdraw contract purchase agreements that were challenged by Customs and to reissue them after consultation with legal counsel.

In 1995 there was a change in the VAT rules and leasing companies were allowed to recover VAT on the vehicles they bought to lease to clients. Most other businesses remained unable to recover this input VAT. This change in the law led to a general reduction in contract hire rentals. This tilted the equation in favour of leasing and contract hire, thus adding another variable into the analysis fleet managers had to make when deciding which financial product to use to acquire their vehicles.

The uncertainties of the early years of contract purchase are now long gone and it now an accepted form of vehicle finance. Most lessors now combine the three agreements – conditional sale (or hire purchase), maintenance and buy-back – into one document.

Contract purchase is widely used by companies but is also the basis of a very popular method of consumer motor finance called personal contract purchase.[43]

While contract purchase is similar in many respects to contract hire, there are key differences. As the product is legally a conditional sale or hire purchase agreement, under which you are buying the vehicle, contract purchase is an 'on balance sheet' product.

The repurchase price that the supplier agrees to pay represents their estimate of the likely future value of the vehicle. They take the risk of whether you will sell the vehicle back to them and the market price of the vehicle if you do so.

The pre-agreed price is usually called the guaranteed repurchase price, the guaranteed minimum purchase value or the guaranteed minimum future value (GMFV).

Contract purchase represents less than 5% of the fleet finance market, reflecting the fact that it is a niche product.

1.5.2 ADVANTAGES OF CONTRACT PURCHASE

Contract purchase gives you the option to buy or return the vehicle as well as the tax advantages described above. It offers predictable costs and you pay VAT only on the maintenance element.

1.5.3 DISADVANTAGES OF CONTRACT PURCHASE

As with outright purchase, contract purchase is an 'on balance sheet' form of finance.[44]

1.5.4 WHEN TO USE CONTRACT PURCHASE

You might also use contract purchase if you like the idea of having an option to either buy the vehicle or hand it back to the supplier at the end of the contract.

---

43 See 1.18.1.
44 See 8.1.

1.6 FINANCE LEASE

1.6.1 FEATURES OF FINANCE LEASE

A finance lease is defined in SSAP21 as a lease that transfers 'substantially all of the risks and rewards of ownership of the asset to the lessee'. In plain English this means that it puts the lessee in much the same position as they would have been if they had bought the asset.

A finance lease is a financing device. It gives you an alternative way to obtain the use of a vehicle other than hire purchase, conditional sale or one of the other methods of vehicle purchase. It is also known as a 'full pay-out lease' or, in the United States, an 'open-ended' lease.

The general assumption with a finance lease is that there will be only one lessee. This distinguishes it from an operating lease, where the lessor either has to lease the vehicle to several parties in succession or to sell it before they recover their investment.

In a finance lease, the lessor will charge you rentals that are sufficient to repay their investment in full during the primary period of the lease; that is, to clear their books. You are committed to paying the rentals for at least this period. A finance lease is therefore said to be non-cancellable. This is rather odd, because almost all leasing companies will early terminate a finance lease as willingly as a contract hire agreement; nonetheless, finance leases are still considered by many to be non-cancellable.

The key difference between a finance lease and an operating lease (contract hire) is the treatment of the vehicle at the end of the lease. Depending on the wording of the finance lease agreement, one (or more) of the following will occur:

- You will sell the vehicle as the lessor's agent
- You will allow the lessor to recover the vehicle and sell it or
- You will elect to enter into a secondary lease period.

Whoever sells the vehicle, the lessor will retain a small proportion of the sale proceeds and you will retain the majority of the sale proceeds. These are normally given to you as a rebate of rentals.

It is worthwhile dwelling for a moment on how this normally works.

In a finance lease you have an obligation to pay all of the rentals, including the balloon rental. Once you have paid these the lessor will have recovered its full investment in the vehicle, covered its interest and other costs and made a profit. But it still owns the vehicle and the lease will stipulate very clearly that you cannot become the owner. To ensure that it does not then sell the vehicle, retain the sales proceeds and make a windfall profit, the lease will stipulate an amount of money that the lessor has to pass back to you once the vehicle has been sold. This payment will normally be described as a rebate of rentals, which makes it clear that, for tax purposes, the payment is a revenue (trading) item rather than a capital receipt of sales proceeds. Typically, the amount payable might be 95% of the sale proceeds of the vehicle.

Technically, the lessor has to:

1. Invoice you for the balloon rental
2. Receive this from you
3. Sell the vehicle
4. Receive the sales proceeds
5. Raise a credit note to you for 95% of the sales proceeds and then
6. Refund this to you.

In reality, many lessors do not collect the balloon payment but simply raise an invoice for this amount and a credit note for the rebate of rentals, and ask you to pay (or pay you) the difference.

A finance lease has two distinct phases. The first period is called the primary period and this is the initial non-cancellable period of the lease. It runs for the fixed period set out in the agreement, by the end of which the lessor will normally have no balance outstanding in its books relating to the lease.

The primary period is followed by the secondary period. This may last for an indefinite period of time. The lessor allows you to continue leasing the vehicle, perhaps for many years. The secondary period ends when either when the parties agree or when the vehicle is sold.

Vehicle finance leases often include a balloon rental payable at the end of the primary period. The amount of the balloon rental will be set out in the lease and will usually be equal to the estimated residual value of the vehicle at the end of the primary period. Hence the monthly amount payable under a finance lease will often be similar to the rentals in an operating lease or contract hire agreement (excluding maintenance in all cases).[45] The difference, of course, is that you are obliged to pay the balloon rental in the finance lease but have no such obligation in contract hire.

Normally, any secondary period rental will be very much smaller than the primary period rental, perhaps only a few per cent of the capital cost of the vehicle. This is often called a peppercorn rental, reflecting the fact that a peppercorn is an item of very little value. It is normally paid annually. This is a small additional amount of income for the lessor and therefore most welcome, particularly as they no longer have any investment in the vehicle. However its primary purpose is to provide an ongoing acknowledgement from you that the vehicle is still under lease and that you are not the owner. You cannot just sell it and retain the proceeds.

In a finance lease you bear the risk of obsolescence of the vehicle. You cannot hand it back mid-term if it no longer suits your requirements, unless you pay an early termination charge.

45   See 6.4 for an explanation of the mathematics at work here.

You will normally be responsible for the maintenance of the vehicle, though if required the lessor may add a maintenance package to the agreement (as in contract hire), or they may offer to pay for maintenance and recharge the cost to you as it is incurred.

The lessor's VAT treatment of finance leases is the same as for contract hire. They can recover the input VAT on the purchase of the vehicle and have to charge you output VAT on the rentals. You can recover this in full as input VAT so long as your business is not partially or wholly VAT-exempt.

However, your corporation tax treatment of the finance lease rentals can differ from that of an operating lease or contract hire. A government order called SP3/91 sets out to ensure that you do not get accelerated corporation tax relief by paying uneven rentals, for example, large initial rentals. Instead, if uneven rentals are payable, you can only claim corporation tax relief on the rentals on a straight-line basis, taken evenly over the life of the lease.[46]

For leases written by companies on or after 1 April 2009 (or 5 April 2009 for partnerships and sole traders), the rental is fully tax deductible for cars emitting less than 160g/km of CO_2. Otherwise 15% of the rental is disallowed.

As you are bearing the residual value risk on the vehicle, it has to be shown on your balance sheet.[47] This was not the case before SSAP21 was introduced.

Normally, finance leases are offered as fixed interest rate products. The rentals remain fixed throughout the life of the lease and you are not exposed to the risk of interest rates changing during this time. Some financiers offer variable interest rate finance leases too.[48]

Most vehicle lessees do not like finance leases. They consider that finance leases have few advantages over contract hire. Hence finance leasing represents around just 1% of the business vehicle finance market.

1.6.2 ADVANTAGES OF FINANCE LEASE

Finance leases allow the lessor to recover input VAT on the purchase price of a vehicle, thus reducing the starting point for calculating the finance lease rentals you will be charged. They offer you the flexibility to retain the use of the vehicle at the end of the lease for a modest annual outlay.

1.6.3 DISADVANTAGES OF FINANCE LEASE

The vehicles must be shown on your balance sheet and you have to take the residual value risk.

---

46 See 17.1.3.

47 See 8.4.2.

48 See 6.3.7.

1.7 HIRE PURCHASE

1.7.1 FEATURES OF HIRE PURCHASE

Hire purchase is defined in SSAP 21 as 'a contract for the hire of an asset that contains a provision giving the hirer an option to acquire legal title to the asset upon the fulfilment of certain conditions stated in the contract'.

Note the use of the word 'hire'. The contract is essentially a hire agreement. You only become the owner of the vehicle if you opt to acquire legal title (ownership) at the end of the agreement. It is not unusual to see hire purchase described as 'lease with option to purchase'.

However, for most people, hire purchase is simply a method of buying a vehicle on deferred payment terms and for this reason the word 'buyer' is normally used to describe the client, rather than 'hirer', and the payments are usually called 'instalments' or 'payments' rather than 'rentals'.

The agreement will give you the option to buy the vehicle for a nominal 'bargain' amount. You pay this to take title to the vehicle but need not do so if you do not wish to. If you prefer, you could simply pay the instalments and walk away. Unlike conditional sale, the option to buy is just that – an option – and not a contractual obligation. Normally, you will pay the option amount and take title.

Typically, the hire purchase payment profile[49] will be one payment followed by 35 or 47 equal monthly instalments starting one month after commencement of the agreement. A deposit may also be required.

A hire purchase agreement is a financing agreement and you have all of the risks and rewards of ownership from the date of delivery, including residual value risk. Therefore, for accounting purposes the vehicle has to be shown as an asset on your balance sheet, and there will be a corresponding liability representing the balance due to the funder. This is the same accounting treatment that would apply if you financed a vehicle on a loan or a finance lease.[50]

In nearly all hire purchase transactions you expect to become the owner. The tax regime recognises this and treats hire purchase as a deferred purchase agreement rather than a hire agreement. Hence for corporation tax purposes the vehicle is deemed to belong to you from delivery, so you can claim capital allowances as if you had paid for it in full on delivery. The lease rental tax disallowance rules do not apply to hire purchase payments.[51]

For VAT purposes the 'supply' is deemed to have happened at the time of delivery. The funder charges output tax on the sale and you account for input tax on the

---

49   See 6.2.

50   See 8.4.3.

51   See 17.1.3.

purchase. The instalments are not subject to VAT, unlike rental or leasing arrangements.[52]

Vehicle hire purchase is widely available from contract hire companies, finance companies and banks.

It is suitable for borrowers who want to buy vehicles using deferred payments.

1.7.2 ADVANTAGES OF HIRE PURCHASE

Hire purchase is a simple method of finance.

You can obtain capital allowances from the date of delivery. It does not suffer a partial lease rental tax disallowance.

1.7.3 DISADVANTAGES OF HIRE PURCHASE

It is an on balance sheet form of finance and you retain the residual value risk.

1.8 LEASE PURCHASE

1.8.1 FEATURES

A lease purchase agreement is exactly the same as a hire purchase agreement but with a balloon instalment payable at the end of the contract. This makes the regular monthly instalments similar to those payable under a finance lease agreement incorporating a balloon payment, or payable under maintenance-exclusive contract hire.

Lease purchase is a contradiction in terms; it is not a lease, simply a method of deferred purchase.

Generally, the expression 'hire purchase' is seen in both commercial and consumer transactions, while 'lease purchase' is reserved for commercial transactions.

1.8.2 ADVANTAGES OF LEASE PURCHASE

These are the same as for hire purchase but with the advantage of lower monthly instalments.

A final balloon instalment is payable. If this has been estimated accurately to equal the market value of the vehicle at the end of the lease, the sale proceeds of the vehicle will cover the balloon payment so you will not be left out of pocket at the end of the contract.

1.8.3 DISADVANTAGES OF LEASE PURCHASE

These are the same as for hire purchase.

---

52   See 17.1.4.

1.9 CONDITIONAL SALE

1.9.1 FEATURES

Conditional sale allows you to buy a vehicle, subject to meeting all the conditions of the agreement. Unlike hire purchase, with conditional sale you are contractually committed to become the owner of the vehicle once all of the payments have been made.

The funder keeps title in the vehicle as security until all of the payments have been made, then title automatically passes to you. As both parties intend from day one that title will pass, you are called the buyer rather than the lessee.

A conditional sale agreement is non-cancellable. There is no need for an 'option-to-purchase' fee to be paid, as title passes automatically when the last payment is made.

1.9.2 ADVANTAGES OF CONDITIONAL SALE

Conditional sale has all of the advantages of hire purchase. It is agreed in advance that you will complete the purchase of the vehicle.

1.9.3 DISADVANTAGES OF CONDITIONAL SALE

The only disadvantage of conditional sale is that it compels you to complete the purchase of the vehicle. When conditional sale is the basis for a contract purchase agreement, this disadvantage is overcome by using a separate agreement that allows the funder to take back the vehicle at the end of the contract for a pre-agreed price.

1.10 CREDIT SALE

This is yet another form of finance that is very similar to hire purchase or conditional sale. However, under a credit sale arrangement, the title to the vehicle passes to the customer at the start of the agreement, rather than the end. As this involves the funder giving up the security of ownership of the asset, credit sale has not been a common form of finance.

Nonetheless, we have seen more credit sale deals as employee car ownership schemes (ECOS) have grown in popularity. See 3.7.

The car benefit tax in kind rules do not only apply if title in the vehicle transfers to the employee, so by using credit sale agreements in these schemes, ownership transfers to the employee on day one and car benefit tax is avoided.

EXERCISES

What is an operating lease?

If you rent a large garden mower for the weekend, is this a lease? If so, what type?

What are the advantages of an operating lease?

What is a sale and lease back?

Why was contract purchase developed?

What are the three key components of a contract purchase agreement?

Define 'finance lease'.

What is the source of this definition?

What is the Rule of 78?

How is hire purchase accounted for in the buyer's books?

How does conditional sale differ from lease purchase?

What are the advantages of conditional sale?

Why has credit sale grown in popularity?

1.11 FLEET MANAGEMENT

A true story: a friend of mine was stopped at passport control on returning to the UK from a holiday abroad. The customs officer told my friend that he was delighted to see 'Fleet Manager' listed in my friend's passport under 'Occupation', as he too had once been in the Royal Navy.

This story highlights the fact that 'fleet management' has several meanings. It can be used to describe:

- What fleet managers do
- What a fleet management company does in totality
- The fee-based services provided to you by a fleet management or contract hire company involving cars that you own; for example purchasing, maintenance control, disposal and administration
- The outsourcing of vehicle management functions to a fleet management company

1.11.1 THE FLEET MANAGEMENT CONTRACT

The contract you enter into with a fleet management company is likely to cover the following topics:

- The services to be provided

  These may include:

  - Vehicle purchase
  - Maintenance control
  - Invoice checking
  - Vehicle excise duty renewal
  - Vehicle disposal
  - Accident management
  - Provision of replacement vehicles
  - Breakdown cover arrangements
  - Management reporting
  - Dealing with parking and speeding fines

    and more.

  In a well-drafted agreement, these will be defined in detail.

- How vehicles are to be added to or removed from the managed fleet.
- The procedure and liability for paying fines and fixed penalty charges.
- How the agreement will be terminated
- Confidentiality undertakings
- The schedule of fees

  - This can be either a long list of the fees to be charged for specific events or one monthly fixed charge to cover a package of services.

- The fee payment arrangements.

  - Fees are usually paid by direct debit a fixed number of days after delivery of the monthly invoice.

There is often a lot of interaction between a fleet management company and its client and it is important to set out very clearly who will do what.

The great advantage of using a fleet management service is that it gives you access to the supplier's expertise and economies of scale. Fleet management and contract hire companies manage thousands of vehicles, so they have the expertise and contacts to buy vehicles and services efficiently and cost-effectively. They can also arrange for vehicles to be maintained to the right standard while only authorising necessary work, dispose of vehicles effectively and for the right price and deal with all of the day-to-day administrative matters that arise in the management of a fleet. They are set up to do this; experts handle each part of the process.

The fleet management company can take the residual value and maintenance risks or you can, or you can agree a 'risks and rewards sharing' arrangement whereby they share profits and losses with you.[53]

Even if you wish to take residual value risk, it may be worthwhile offering the supplier an incentive to achieve the highest disposal price. If you offer them a share of any sale proceeds received in excess of, say, CAP Clean plus a certain percentage, this can work well for you both.

When you engage a fleet management company to buy things for you it is important to know how they are making their money. Discounts and rebates for volume purchases are a feature of the automotive market like all others, and it may be that they charge you a small fee but retain the discounts they are achieving.

If you use their payment card to pay for service, maintenance and repair items, they may be taking a merchant fee of up to 5% from the garage.

It is for you to decide whether there is anything wrong with this. After all, if they are buying vehicles and maintenance services for you at prices that are the same as you could get yourself, and you are incurring a fee that is less than you would have to pay to run the fleet in-house, you may feel happy to allow them to keep the discounts.

In this situation many fleet managers would want either to have a share (if not all) of those discounts or to be charged a very low fee indeed. At the very least, it is worthwhile building a right of audit into your contract so you can look at their books should you wish to check that they really are passing back the discounts that they have earned on your account. No reputable fleet management company will deny you that right.

If your contract says that the fleet management company is your purchase agent they are legally required to give you full details of all of the transactions they enter into on your behalf.

1.11.2 WHO USES FLEET MANAGEMENT?

Fleet management is suitable for a wide variety of businesses. Large fleets needing a tailor-made service are major users of fleet management services. Medium size businesses wishing to outsource administrative functions are another big user group. Cash-rich companies that purchase their own vehicles often use fleet management as a form of administrative support.

Smaller companies have tended to buy contract hire rather than fleet management.

A word of caution; suppliers can offer you lots of fleet management services and will tailor them to your needs. However, you might not need a tailor-made solution: as with all other areas, made-to-measure is usually much cheaper than tailor-made. If it works for everyone else do you really need to ask them to bend their standard service to meet your needs? An off-the-shelf product could save a great deal of time and money for both parties. Using the supplier's standard service should also reduce the risk that they will make mistakes.

53 See 1.14.

1.12 CONTRACT MANAGEMENT

Contract management is a service that provides the fixed-cost advantages of contract hire but without the need to have the vehicle funded externally.

You buy a maintenance package that lists all of the services that will be supplied. Typically this includes all of the standard and non-standard maintenance expenditure that would normally be included in a maintenance-inclusive contract hire agreement. The contract may also include road tax renewal and provision of a replacement vehicle.

The advantage of contract management is that you pay just one fixed monthly cost and the supplier takes the risk on the actual level of costs.

Contract management is useful if you want fixed running costs, while funding your own cars or buying them on a deferred purchase method such as hire purchase.

1.13 OUTSOURCING

1.13.1 FEATURES

This is one of the most widely used terms in the vehicle management market – and everyone has their own understanding of what it means.

At its simplest, outsourcing means passing to a third party some functions that you previously carried out in-house.

It is normally carried out for a flat monthly fee per vehicle.

There are many fleet-related functions that you can successfully outsource to a contract hire or fleet management company. For example, vehicle purchasing, maintenance, parking fine administration, fuel management, vehicle disposal, driver contact, accident management and query handling.

At a minimum it involves using a third party's services, having dedicated support staff allocated to your account and receiving detailed – and probably tailored – reporting so that you can monitor what is happening.

If you have a large fleet, the outsourcing arrangement may include the use of 'implants' or 'outplants'.[54]

An implant is a member of the supplier's (the fleet management company's or contract hire company's) staff who works at a desk in your office and manages the day-to-day functions of the contract.

---

54 I used the word 'inplant' in the first edition, as this is the general spelling of this word. However, this word does not appear in any dictionary, so I have changed it to implant, here. Interesting to note that the word 'outplant' is not in the dictionary either, but I have included it here as it is a common expression in the industry.

An outplant is a member of your staff who works in the supplier's office, managing the day-to-day functions of the contract.

In many senses contract hire is also outsourcing, in that it encompasses many of the fleet administration and management functions that you would otherwise carry out yourself.

1.13.2 ADVANTAGES OF OUTSOURCING

Outsourcing can offer many advantages.

It can reduce your costs, increase efficiency and be more flexible than in-house solutions. It may offer fixed costs and risk management. If yours is a small organisation it can give you access to better systems and purchasing power and allow you to focus on your core business.

1.13.3 DISADVANTAGES OF OUTSOURCING

Unless implemented carefully, outsourcing can involve a loss of control. For example, if you outsource the authorisation of maintenance expenditure, someone other than you will be deciding how to spend your money. They may be more knowledgeable than you, buy more cheaply than you and may act in your best interests – but they are still spending your money and when the invoices start rolling in you may feel you are losing control.

As discussed in 1.11 above, you need to understand how the supplier earns their income. You may have bought a package of services from them at what you consider to be a great price but you need to understand whether they are supplementing this with rebates and discounts they have earned by spending your money.

1.14 OPEN-BOOK LEASING

1.14.1 FEATURES

One of the problems of any bundled product such as contract hire is that it can leave you with the suspicion that it might be cheaper for you to unbundle the elements and buy them all separately.

You may believe that the contract hire company is, somehow, making huge profits on the deal. These suspicions will be fuelled by occasional press comment on how much profit contract hire companies make on residual values.

It is true that they can make profits when times are good but they also make losses – sometimes devastating ones – when times are bad.

Many clients are keen to look behind their contract hire rental to see how it is calculated.

In order to create competitive advantage, some contract hire companies may be willing to give you a share of any profit they make in maintaining or selling your vehicles. There are several ways these schemes can operate but they all involve the supplier sending you initial information about how your rentals have been calculated and then sending you reports showing the financial performance of the lease. We can group all of these schemes together under the heading 'open-book leasing'.

There are lots of different permutations available. Some suppliers will offer you a proportion of any profit they make on selling or maintaining your vehicles, perhaps 25%. Sometimes the percentages are different; for example, 25% of maintenance profit and 50% of used vehicle sale profit.

Normally open-book leasing is only offered if you have at least 10 or 15 vehicles that will come off lease in a given period. This allows losses on some vehicles to be netted off against profits on others so that you only get the net profit, if any. The calculation period is usually twelve months but for a big fleet it could be six or three months, to avoid building up big balances.

At the extreme there are products that give you all of the profit and where the supplier takes all of the losses.

"OK, tell you what, how's this for a deal? We'll lease this car to you for £400 per month. Nice competitive rental, I'm sure you'll agree.

"And we'll do all of the standard servicing and maintenance, provide you with membership of a roadside assistance club, pay for your tax discs, etc.

"We'll give you an open quotation so that you can see how much we expect it to cost us to buy the car and provide all these services and how much we expect to sell the car for.

"At the end of the lease, we'll sell the car and send you a report showing how much it really cost us to run. And tell you what, if we've made a profit we'll pay it back to you and if we've made a loss we'll swallow that and it won't cost you another penny. It's heads you win, tails we lose.

"We couldn't be fairer than that now, could we?"

It's an appealing prospect and it works for many organisations. Many thousands of vehicles are financed through open-book schemes in the UK.

1.14.2   ADVANTAGES OF OPEN-BOOK LEASING

LESSOR ADVANTAGES

Heads you win, tails they lose. It makes wonder – how can they do it?

If you ask them the question, you will be told that it works for the leasing company because it normally gets them win sole supplier status and that their clients like the service so much that they tend to stick with one supplier for the long term. In other words, it ensures client loyalty.

There is definitely something in this. Most fleet companies spend a great deal of time and money trying to wrest clients away from each other, so a product that saves this cost must give them a real benefit.

They will also tell you their open-book clients tend to look after their cars better because this product gives the client a vested interest in the return condition of the vehicle. To some extent this is true, too.

LESSEE ADVANTAGES

Open-book deals can be very valuable to lessees. They can give you cheaper motoring and a good, close, long term relationship with a trusted supplier who will come to understand your business and will therefore hopefully be able to anticipate your needs.

They work particularly well for organisations that have large fleets and have negotiated volume rebates directly with manufacturers on the cars they use.

1.14.3   DISADVANTAGES OF OPEN-BOOK LEASING

THE RISK TO THE LESSEE

Many clients are wary of these schemes, believing the money the fleet company pays back to them was their own money in the first place. Hence they can end up feeling they were overcharged from the outset and gave the fleet company an interest-free loan for the period of the lease.

It is very important to read the fine print in these deals, to see what is and what is not included in the calculation of profit and loss. It is definitely worthwhile asking the fleet company this question:

"In calculating the profit or loss on the open-book scheme, will you take into account all bonuses, discounts and rebates that you receive from suppliers, dealers and manufacturers on the cars that you supply to me, and give me the right to audit your books to check that you have done this?"

If the answer is no, you would probably be better off looking for another supplier that will answer yes.

Alternatively, you could opt for contract hire, perhaps using two suppliers. Contract hire companies have to build all discounts and rebates into their rentals in order to be competitive. They are normally duty bound to build volume related bonuses[55] into their rentals to comply with their contractual obligations with the manufacturer. So you automatically get these advantages when you take a vehicle on contract hire.

---

55   See 5.1.2.

1.15 LOANS

1.15.1 FEATURES OF LOANS

Many companies use loans to finance their vehicles. Loans from banks and finance companies are available with a wide variety of periods, payment profiles and interest rates.

They are usually unsecured: that is, the lender cannot repossess and sell the vehicle if the borrower stops paying. So unless your business has high financial strength the interest rates will be high to compensate for the fact that the lender lacks security.

An exception to this is where the lender holds a debenture or charge.

A debenture is a registered security that gives the lender fixed and floating charges over specific assets owned by the borrower.

A charge is a mortgage over property, a right you give a lender/lessor to deal with your assets in the event of your default. It is registered at Companies House and on your company's register of charges.[56] Charges provide the lender with security, that is, rights in your assets. These assets may be tangible, for example vehicles, plant or equipment. Alternatively they may be intangible, for example monies you are due to receive at a future date from your debtors. The lender can take possession of the specified assets, control them and sell them if you do not meet your obligations under the loan agreement to which the charge relates.

Charges can be fixed, in which case they list the specific assets to which they relate, for instance a house or car. Or they can be floating, in which case they give the lender security over a general class of assets over which you have title, the nature of which changes over time (for example, debtors).

If the lender has a fixed charge over an asset, any sale of the asset may be ineffective, and even if it is effective the buyer buys the asset subject to the charge.

A floating charge becomes fixed when the borrower or hirer defaults on their obligations.

It is worthwhile stopping here to look at the meaning of the word 'title'. It means the absolute ownership of an asset (for example, a property[57] or a vehicle).

Title vests in you immediately if you purchase a vehicle outright or take it on credit sale.

If you take it on conditional sale it will vest in you at the end of the contract.

---

56 Where the asset is an interest in land, the charge must be registered at the Land Registry.

57 The Crown is the ultimate owner of all of the land in this country, even freehold land. Don't worry about this too much. It's been several hundred years since the monarch has willfully repossessed property from landowners and Buckingham Palace has no immediate plans to do so.

If you take it on contract purchase it will vest in you at the end of the contract, if the underlying legal contract is a conditional sale agreement.

You have an option to obtain title under hire purchase or lease purchase agreements but need not do so if you do not wish to.

You never get title under contract hire, daily hire, operating lease or finance lease agreements.

A loan that is not secured on assets is said to be unsecured.

1.15.2 ADVANTAGES OF LOANS

Loans are very widely available. They can be obtained at fixed or variable interest rates and for short or long periods. You can use a loan to finance one asset or a group of assets of different types. They are simple to administer and do not require you to get involved in the complexities of lease accounting. Variable rate loans can often be repaid without penalty. Loan interest is normally deductible as a business expense for corporation tax purposes.

If you have title to a vehicle, or if you may obtain title under the agreement, you can claim capital allowances.

1.15.3 DISADVANTAGES OF LOANS

Vehicles financed on loans have to be disclosed ('capitalised') on your balance sheet.[58] Unlike a leasing company, if you borrow money to buy a car you will not be able to recover any input tax on the purchase of the vehicle.

Many companies use loans and overdrafts interchangeably.

Variable rate, short term loans have many of the features of overdrafts. See 1.16.3 before using your overdraft to finance your vehicles.

1.16 BANK OVERDRAFT

1.16.1 FEATURES OF BANK OVERDRAFTS

The bank overdraft is the most widely used form of business finance in the UK. Most companies, including most cash-rich ones, have an overdraft facility.

The operation of an overdraft could not be simpler. You agree an overdraft limit with your bank manager and then you deposit funds and draw cheques in the normal course of your business. Once every month or quarter you are charged interest on the amount of the overdraft that you have used, for the number of days you have used it.

An overdraft is normally secured by a debenture.

---

58   See 8.1.2.

It is always provided as a variable rate interest product, and the interest rate is quoted as a margin over the base rate of the bank that supplies it.

It is worthwhile reiterating this point; each bank has its own base rate. There are hundreds of banks in the UK. While the major banks tend to keep their base rates in line, some smaller or foreign banks have higher base rates than the major UK clearing banks.

1.16.2 ADVANTAGES OF BANK OVERDRAFTS

Bank overdrafts are cheap to set up and, as you only pay for what you use, they are cheap to use.

1.16.3 DISADVANTAGE OF BANK OVERDRAFTS

There is a limit to the amount of overdraft facility that your company will be able to obtain from its bank.

Overdrafts are a type of working capital. That is, they provide you with cash to finance the trade cycle between buying goods and services to make your product and being paid by your customer. If you use your overdraft to finance long term assets, such as vehicles, you will drain your company of its working capital.

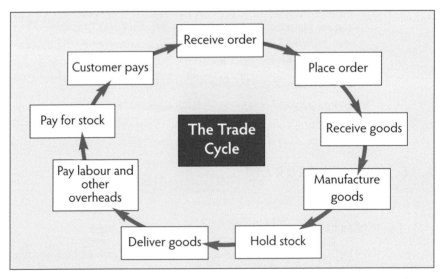

Conventional business thinking is that you should use short term money (loans, other short term borrowings, overdrafts) to finance the trade cycle and other short-held assets. You should use longer term borrowing (leases, hire purchase, long term loans) to finance the acquisition of longer term assets (vehicles, plant and equipment, etc). Very long term assets, such as property, should be financed on very long term borrowings, such as mortgages or by issuing share capital.

It is a truism, but companies don't collapse because they make losses. They collapse because they don't have the money to pay the wages at the end of the month. If you borrow money for the correct period, your company will not become starved for cash in the short term simply through having used up its short term funds to buy long term assets.

Most contract hire, finance lease or hire purchase arrangements are offered at fixed rentals or repayments. That is, the payments do not change, regardless of movements in market interest rates.

Most overdrafts are offered as variable rate products. If you finance your vehicles for three years at fixed rates you will have fixed your outgoings over that period. Finance them on overdraft for three years and you will be exposed to interest rate changes during that time. If rates rise the actual cost of financing the vehicle may end up being much more than you had planned.

1.17 SELECTING BETWEEN DIFFERENT METHODS OF FLEET FUNDING

1.17.1 CHOOSING THE BEST METHOD FOR YOU

As we have seen, there are many different methods of vehicle finance available to businesses in the market today. As each business is different and has different priorities, internal resources, tax positions and so on, there is no one product that is going to be right for all businesses.

To determine the best way to fund your fleet you should consider:

- The overall cost of each method to your business, using discounted cash flow techniques to make these costs comparable[59]
- The balance sheet effect[60]
- The corporation tax effect[61]
- Any relevant VAT issues[62]
- The employee car benefit tax issues[63]
- The amount of flexibility you need
- Relevant human resource issues[64]
- Risk management[65]
- Internal administrative issues

Most of these are discussed elsewhere in this book.

---

59 See 7.1.
60 See 8.4.
61 See 17.1.
62 See 17.1.4.
63 See 17.2.
64 See 3.5.
65 See 5.12 and 5.13.

Such an exercise will allow you to focus on the products that work best for you. Bear in mind that for many businesses several methods may be appropriate to cover different classes of vehicle or groups of employees.

1.17.2 IF YOUR COMPANY IS CASH RICH

'Cash-rich' companies have strong cash balances in the bank and have no need to borrow. Many never consider leasing because they see it as a form of borrowing.

However, leasing can be attractive to these businesses. It allows them to lease vehicles at a capital cost based on a pre-VAT price, because, unlike most other businesses, leasing companies can recover the input VAT when buying vehicles. This is not possible for most UK businesses.[66]

Leasing also takes away the residual value risk.[67]

Contract hire is currently[68] an off-balance sheet product and this may be an important factor for some cash-rich companies.[69]

And finally, many cash-rich companies use fleet management products (purchasing, maintenance control, disposal, administration, etc) to outsource non-core activities and get the benefit of fleet discounts and expertise.

---

66 See 17.14.

67 See 5.12.

68 See 8.6.

69 See 8.4.1.

1.18 PERSONAL FINANCE PRODUCTS

1.18.1 PERSONAL CONTRACT PURCHASE (PCP)

FEATURES

Personal contract purchase is a method of finance that allows a consumer (a private individual, sole trader or partnership) to buy a vehicle on deferred payment terms and that gives them a series of options at the end of the agreement.

PCPs are based on either conditional sale or hire purchase agreements, both of which are long-standing legal structures. Regardless of which underlying agreement is used, the normal arrangement is that the client (the buyer) agrees to buy the vehicle and to make payments over a period of time. At the end of that period they have three choices:

■ Make the final payment and keep the vehicle

■ Hand back the vehicle and have no further obligation

■ Use the equity in the vehicle (the difference between the amount still owed and the market value of the vehicle) as a deposit for another vehicle

A feature of contract purchase agreements is the guaranteed minimum future value (GMFV). This is an undertaking by the funder to buy the vehicle back at the end of the contract at a pre-agreed price. This is a very valuable option as it allows the buyer to decide whether it is worthwhile or not to retain the vehicle.

Normally, if the vehicle is worth more than the GMFV the buyer will opt to retain it. If less, he will hand it back and allow the funder to take any loss. Some funders add an amount to the balloon payment to protect them against the risk of loss should the client return a vehicle at the end of the agreement.

The Consumer Credit Act requires the Annual Percentage Rate of interest, (APR) to be stated prominently on consumer credit quotations and some adverts.[70]

Some PCP agreements offer maintenance options similar to those provided to companies in maintenance-inclusive contract hire agreements.

Most PCPs are sold by motor dealers, using the finance facilities provided by car manufacturers' captive finance houses, though a number of leasing companies offer PCPs too.

ADVANTAGES OF PCP

PCPs are a widely available form of personal finance. As the funder has title in the vehicle the consumer can be offered a lower interest rate than if the lending was unsecured.

---

70   See 4.3.

The purchase option can be valuable to the client.

Rather than just providing finance and leaving the client to find the vehicle, suppliers of PCPs invariably supply the vehicle,

The monthly cost of a PCP will be significantly less than loan or hire purchase payments, because you are not paying for the residual value of the car, just the depreciation.

If you wish you can just hand back the car at the end of the contract. There is no need to sell it unless you want to.

A PCP can work well for employees who take a cash option under a cash-for-car scheme, because it allows them to spread the cost of a vehicle over a number of years.

The supplier takes the depreciation risk.

DISADVANTAGES OF PCP

There are few disadvantages with PCPs. However, from time to time there has been some adverse publicity surrounding the GMFV.

Customers who buy vehicles using PCPs expect that the vehicles will be worth at least the amount of the GMFV. When used vehicle values have fallen sharply (as they did in 2008), consumers have discovered that their vehicles are worth much less at the end of the contract than they had expected. So it was not worthwhile for them to pay the balloon payments and take ownership of the vehicles. Instead, they elected to return the vehicles to the funders. This made sense for the customers because they pushed the losses onto the leasing companies. However some customers then realised that they had paid a deposit and monthly payments for their vehicles, handed the vehicles back and now had neither the vehicle nor a deposit to put down on another vehicle.

For some reason, the occasional press reports on this topic cast the funders in a poor light and sometimes refer to 'negative equity' in the vehicle. In fact, the funders lose heavily but this is rarely mentioned.

If a customer is worried about the possibility of 'losing' their deposit in this way they should seek a funder willing to offer them a 1+35 or 1+47 payment profile; i.e. payment of just one rental in advance.

Generally, PCPs are bought as a modern alternative to hire purchase, against which they offer clear advantages to the customer.

1.18.2 PERSONAL CONTRACT HIRE (PCH)

FEATURES

Personal contract hire is a consumer product with all of the features and benefits of corporate contract hire.

The underlying contract is a regulated hire agreement (a simple rental or operating lease agreement).[71] The client agrees to pay the rentals and gets the right to use the vehicle for a period of time. At the end of that period the vehicle is simply handed back to the lessor. There is no option to own the vehicle at the end of the contract.

As this is a hire agreement the lessor has to charge VAT on the rentals, which most consumers are unable to recover. However, the lessor can recover in full the input VAT paid on the purchase of the vehicle, so this mitigates the effect of the additional VAT the hirer has to pay compared with, for example, PCP. In other words, the hirer has to pay VAT on the rentals under PCH, but the rentals are lower anyway as the leasing company can recover the input VAT on the initial purchase price.

The Consumer Credit Act does not require APRs to be quoted on rental-type agreements, so no APRs are quoted on PCH deals.

This can make it slightly harder for a consumer to compare two different rates.

For example, if you are quoted £395 per month on a 3+33 rental profile[72] and another lessor is prepared to supply the vehicle for £400 on a 1+35 basis, which is cheaper? A discounted cash flow exercise would reveal the answer. DCF is discussed in more detail in 7.1. Here is an example of the discounted cash flow calculation the consumer would have to do, unless they had a financial calculator to hand. How many consumers can do these, particularly while standing in a dealer's showroom?

The first table (shown on page 86) shows the 1+35 rental of £400 per month:

This shows that the interest rate required to repay £16,208.50 down to a residual value of £5,000 after 36 months with a 1+35 rental pattern is 10% p.a.

For example: in month 1, £15,808.50 x 10% ÷12 = £131.74

The second table (shown on page 87) shows the 3+33 rental of £395 per month.

The interest rate required to reduce £16,208.50 to a residual value of £5,000 after 36 months, with a 3+33 rental pattern, is 10.154%% p.a.

Therefore, even though the repayments at £395 per month are £5 lower, the interest rate is higher

This is despite the fact that the total repayments and total interest payable are lower on the 3+33 deal.

Hence the 1+35 deal at £400 per month is cheaper than the 3+33 deal at £395 per month.

---

71 See 4.1.
72 See 6.2.

	Opening balance	Rental	Sub-total	Interest	Closing balance
1	16,208.50	400.00	15,808.50	131.74	15,940.23
2	15,940.23	400.00	15,540.23	129.50	15,669.74
3	15,669.74	400.00	15,269.74	127.25	15,396.98
4	15,396.98	400.00	14,996.98	124.97	15,121.96
5	15,121.96	400.00	14,721.96	122.68	14,844.64
6	14,844.64	400.00	14,444.64	120.37	14,565.01
7	14,565.01	400.00	14,165.01	118.04	14,283.06
8	14,283.06	400.00	13,883.06	115.69	13,998.75
9	13,998.75	400.00	13,598.75	113.32	13,712.07
10	13,712.07	400.00	13,312.07	110.93	13,423.00
11	13,423.00	400.00	13,023.00	108.53	13,131.53
12	13,131.53	400.00	12,731.53	106.10	12,837.63
13	12,837.63	400.00	12,437.63	103.65	12,541.27
14	12,541.27	400.00	12,141.27	101.18	12,242.45
15	12,242.45	400.00	11,842.45	98.69	11,941.14
16	11,941.14	400.00	11,541.14	96.18	11,637.31
17	11,637.31	400.00	11,237.31	93.64	11,330.96
18	11,330.96	400.00	10,930.96	91.09	11,022.05
19	11,022.05	400.00	10,622.05	88.52	10,710.57
20	10,710.57	400.00	10,310.57	85.92	10,396.49
21	10,396.49	400.00	9,996.49	83.30	10,079.79
22	10,079.79	400.00	9,679.79	80.66	9,760.46
23	9,760.46	400.00	9,360.46	78.00	9,438.46
24	9,438.46	400.00	9,038.46	75.32	9,113.78
25	9,113.78	400.00	8,713.78	72.61	8,786.40
26	8,786.40	400.00	8,386.40	69.89	8,456.28
27	8,456.28	400.00	8,056.28	67.14	8,123.42
28	8,123.42	400.00	7,723.42	64.36	7,787.78
29	7,787.78	400.00	7,387.78	61.56	7,449.34
30	7,449.34	400.00	7,049.34	58.74	7,108.09
31	7,108.09	400.00	6,708.09	55.90	6,763.99
32	6,763.99	400.00	6,363.99	53.03	6,417.02
33	6,417.02	400.00	6,017.02	50.14	6,067.16
34	6,067.16	400.00	5,667.16	47.23	5,714.39
35	5,714.39	400.00	5,314.39	44.29	5,358.68
36	5,358.68	400.00	4,958.68	41.32	5,000.00
		14,400.00		**3,191.50**	

	Opening balance	Rental	Sub-total	Interest	Closing balance
1	16,208.50	1,185.00	15,023.50	127.13	15,150.62
2	15,150.62	395.00	14,755.62	124.86	14,880.48
3	14,880.48	395.00	14,485.48	122.57	14,608.05
4	14,608.05	395.00	14,213.05	120.27	14,333.32
5	14,333.32	395.00	13,938.32	117.94	14,056.26
6	14,056.26	395.00	13,661.26	115.60	13,776.86
7	13,776.86	395.00	13,381.86	113.23	13,495.10
8	13,495.10	395.00	13,100.10	110.85	13,210.95
9	13,210.95	395.00	12,815.95	108.45	12,924.39
10	12,924.39	395.00	12,529.39	106.02	12,635.41
11	12,635.41	395.00	12,240.41	103.58	12,343.99
12	12,343.99	395.00	11,948.99	101.11	12,050.10
13	12,050.10	395.00	11,655.10	98.62	11,753.72
14	11,753.72	395.00	11,358.72	96.11	11,454.84
15	11,454.84	395.00	11,059.84	93.59	11,153.42
16	11,153.42	395.00	10,758.42	91.04	10,849.46
17	10,849.46	395.00	10,454.46	88.46	10,542.92
18	10,542.92	395.00	10,147.92	85.87	10,233.79
19	10,233.79	395.00	9,838.79	83.25	9,922.04
20	9,922.04	395.00	9,527.04	80.62	9,607.66
21	9,607.66	395.00	9,212.66	77.96	9,290.61
22	9,290.61	395.00	8,895.61	75.27	8,970.89
23	8,970.89	395.00	8,575.89	72.57	8,648.45
24	8,648.45	395.00	8,253.45	69.84	8,323.29
25	8,323.29	395.00	7,928.29	67.09	7,995.38
26	7,995.38	395.00	7,600.38	64.31	7,664.69
27	7,664.69	395.00	7,269.69	61.51	7,331.21
28	7,331.21	395.00	6,936.21	58.69	6,994.90
29	6,994.90	395.00	6,599.90	55.85	6,655.75
30	6,655.75	395.00	6,260.75	52.98	6,313.72
31	6,313.72	395.00	5,918.72	50.08	5,968.81
32	5,968.81	395.00	5,573.81	47.16	5,620.97
33	5,620.97	395.00	5,225.97	44.22	5,270.19
34	5,270.19	395.00	4,875.19	41.25	4,916.44
35	4,916.44	-	4,916.44	41.60	4,958.05
36	4,958.05	-	4,958.05	41.95	5,000.00
		14,220.00		**3,011.50**	

ADVANTAGES OF PCH

The benefit of PCH to the customer is that they simply pay a rental and then hand back the vehicle at the end of the agreement. So long as they do not drive more than the agreed mileage and they hand back the vehicle in reasonable condition, there is no more to pay. PCH is therefore a simple 'pay for use' product.

DISADVANTAGES OF PCH

There are few disadvantages to PCH. After all, who can object to paying for the use of a vehicle and handing it back after use? The disadvantages become apparent, however, when comparing PCH to the main alternative, PCP.

With PCH the customer has no opportunity to own the vehicle at the end of the lease. There is no option to purchase. So they can be left with the feeling that they have paid a lot and have nothing to show for it, particularly if they sold their previous vehicle and used the proceeds as the deposit for the PCH deal.

While this is perhaps an irrational customer response – after all, they have got what they paid for – the ability to own the vehicle at the end of the contract is very important for many people.

Historically, demand for PCH has been low, despite a big push by some manufacturers. Demand has risen slightly in recent years but it still seems that in the UK, unlike the USA, consumers prefer to own things rather than to lease them.

1.18.3   PERSONAL LOANS

FEATURES

Many consumers take out personal loans to buy cars. These are available from many banks and finance companies. The borrower agrees to make a series of payments over a period of time. The interest rate may be fixed but it is more likely to vary with bank base rate or finance house base rate.

Occasionally, personal loans are offered as part of an employer-sponsored cash-for-car scheme,[73] in place of personal contract hire or personal contract purchase. Generally personal loans are only offered where the employer is a financial institution able to offer loans in its normal course of business.

ADVANTAGES OF PERSONAL LOANS

Personal loans are simple finance agreements that offer the borrower an amount of money that is repayable over a period of time. As the loan is not linked to the vehicle in any way – that is, the vehicle is not provided as security for the loan and the lender does not manage or own the vehicle – the loan can be taken out for any period regardless of how long the borrower intends to keep the vehicle. In addition, the loan can stay in place even if the borrower decides to sell the vehicle and buy another one.

So loans offer flexibility to the borrower.

---

73   See Chapter 3.

DISADVANTAGES OF PERSONAL LOANS

The main disadvantage of using a personal loan to buy a vehicle is the cost. Personal loans are unsecured so they tend to be expensive. The lender has a more onerous task in recovering his advance in the event of default than would be the case with hire purchase or a lease, where they can just repossess the vehicle.[74]

In addition, compared with personal contract purchase, the buyer does not get an option to hand back the vehicle at the end of the agreement. The absence of this option makes loans less attractive to most borrowers than PCP.

1.18.4 EMPLOYEE CAR OWNERSHIP SCHEMES

These arrangements have been developed in response to increasing levels of car benefit tax. They are a financial product so are listed here for completeness but are covered in more detail in 3.7.

1.18.5 EXERCISES

What is the difference between lease purchase and conditional sale?

What type of lease is a lease purchase?

What is credit sale?

Explain the different meanings of the expression 'fleet management'.

What might be included in a fleet management contract?

What types of business use fleet management?

What risks can contract management take from you?

What are the advantages of outsourcing?

What are the disadvantages of open-book leasing?

What are the different types of charge?

What are the advantages of loans?

What are the disadvantages of bank overdrafts?

What is the difference between a PCP and a PCH?

Why are personal loans often more expensive than PCPs?

---

74 Subject to the one-third rule. See 4.8.

1.19 ACCIDENT MANAGEMENT

1.19.1 FEATURES

When one of your drivers has an accident there can be a great deal of administration involved in processing the claim and getting the vehicle back on the road. Specialised knowledge is necessary during this process, knowledge you may not have in-house. An accident management service takes all of the work away from you and puts it into the hands of specialists.

Accident management is also known as *insurance claims management* or *incident management*. You can buy this service from many contract hire, fleet management or accident management companies.

The best accident management services take over from the moment of impact and handle the whole process until the claim has been finalised.

They:

■ Arrange to remove the damaged vehicle from the road

■ Inspect the damage

■ Obtain quotes for repair

■ Accept the best quote

■ Inspect the completed work

■ Pay the repairer

■ Handle claims paperwork

■ Provide a replacement vehicle or courtesy car while your vehicle is off the road and

■ Handle correspondence with the other side's insurer.

If you have an accident and it is not your fault, some of your expenses may have to be recovered from the other party or their insurer. These could include legal fees, your insurance excess and any out of pocket expenses that were not covered by your insurance. Therefore *uninsured loss recovery* is normally offered as part of the accident management service.

The main emphasis of an accident management service is to get your driver back on the road as quickly as possible.

Accident management is normally a fee-based service.

The supplier normally controls costs by using a network of approved repairers.

Some accident management companies charge very low fees and earn the bulk of their income by taking a percentage of the cost of the repair work and car hire charges that they pay on your behalf. You may feel that there is nothing wrong with this approach. Indeed, you may prefer to pay a nominal amount for your vehicles to be covered by the accident management service and to then pay a premium over the actual repair costs when your vehicles are involved in accidents.

The problem with this is that it gives the supplier a conflict of interest. Rather than trying to minimise the cost of the work for you benefit or your insurer's benefit, they have an incentive to incur even higher charges to boost their income.

The key point here is to know how your supplier plans to earn his income from you.

1.19.2 ADVANTAGES OF ACCIDENT MANAGEMENT

Professional accident management takes away a substantial administrative task and puts it into the hands of specialists. You benefit from nationally agreed repair labour rates and the supply of a courtesy vehicle, and you will receive regular management reports to keep you up-to-date with what is happening with each claim.

Whoever is to blame for the accident, it is usually a relief for the driver to hand over control to an expert who is emotionally detached from the distress of the accident.

The better accident management companies will only place your vehicle in the hands of repairers meeting their standards for quality, equipment level, skill and training.

1.19.3 HUMAN ASPECTS OF ACCIDENTS

Every accident requires a lot of administration and sorting out. However, before dealing with the car there is an altogether more important asset that needs to be considered – the driver.

If one of your drivers has been involved in an accident they may be:

- Injured
- Upset
- Annoyed

■ Traumatised

■ Confused

■ Disorientated

■ Feeling guilty

■ Angry

Make sure that the driver is ok and that their needs have been taken care of before you get them involved in the administration.

Establish the 'human facts'. It may be that the driver has done no more than scraped the car whilst driving out of the office car park. At the other extreme it might be that they have been in an accident where someone has been killed or seriously injured, perhaps a loved one.

You may be the first person they have spoken to and the accident may have happened only a few minutes ago.

The employee may need hospitalisation, the attention of a doctor or nurse, counselling or time off.

If you have a human resources manager, make them aware that one of your employees has been involved in an accident. Advise the employee's manager too.

1.19.4   CREDIT HIRE

This is a good point at which to mention credit hire. Credit hire companies will supply you with hire cars when your cars are off the road and being repaired. They enter into contracts with accident management companies and businesses with large vehicle fleets. Most insurance policies give you the right to a courtesy car when your car is off the road and you have claimed under the policy. Having supplied a hire vehicle, the credit hire company reclaims their hire charges from your insurer.

The credit hire industry grew rapidly in the 1990s. It is probably fair to say that insurers were not impressed with credit hire companies. Insurers already had their own vehicle hire arrangements and were unhappy to receive bills from third parties when they had no control of the hiring or – crucially – the cost. In many cases the credit hire companies billed the insurers more than they would have paid through their own hire car suppliers.

The insurers refused to pay, saying that they were not responsible for the costs of a third party unless they engaged them directly. This led to court cases, which led to appeals and eventually a House of Lords decision that absolved the insurers from the need to pay the credit hire companies unless they had engaged them.

A number of credit hire companies suffered major losses through being unable to recover large amounts billed to insurers.

Credit hire is now an established part of the fleet management market with the bigger credit hire companies providing cars for several hundred thousand rental days each year.

Nonetheless, this has proved to be quite a volatile sector of the market and a number of credit hire businesses have had financial issues.

So the old adage is still true; make sure you know whom you are doing business with. It would not be helpful if you discovered that the credit hire company that supplies your replacement vehicles has suddenly and unexpectedly gone out of business, so check their financial reports.

The insurance industry has drawn up a set of drawn up a set of general terms of agreement that a credit sale company can agree to subscribe to, and which will then regulate the way they do business together. This document, the Association of British Insurers General Terms of Agreement between Subscribing Insurers and Credit Hire Organisations ("the GTA"). Is published by the ABI and can be downloaded from their website.[75]

1.20 DRIVER TRAINING

1.20.1 FEATURES

We all have to be trained and to pass a driving test before being allowed to drive. Then we tear up our L-plates and are let out onto the roads, never to be tested again. Over time we can pick up bad driving habits.

Many enlightened employers have come to realise that their drivers need ongoing training if they are to be expected to drive safely for the company and to look after themselves and other road users.

This has given rise to the growth of specialist companies offering training to drivers of fleet vehicles.

All driver training organisations employ instructors who are approved by the Driving Standards Agency.[76] Their proficiency is tested regularly.

The Driving Standards Agency (DSA) operates a register of driving instructors specialising in training fleet drivers. Only Approved Driving Instructors are allowed onto the register and then only once they have undergone DSA accredited training or passed a DSA examination.

Driver training organisations can offer you courses to suit all needs and budgets. The 'standard' fleet driver course focuses on defensive driving, sometimes also called 'advanced driving'. The idea here is that, while other drivers may drive badly, so long as you drive well you can minimise the possibility of accidents.

---

75 apps.abi.org.uk/tphire

76 Driving Standards Agency, The Axis Building, 112 Upper Parliament Street, Nottingham, NG1 6LP Phone 0300 200 1122.

They can provide a classroom-based training session for all of your drivers in one morning, providing insights into the reasons why accidents happen and making your drivers think about their own driving styles.

They also run one-to-one on-the-road training sessions where a qualified driving instructor will spend perhaps half a day with each participant or a whole day with two participants. This may start with the instructor giving a demonstration drive, and pointing out the steps he is taking to ensure the journey is as safe as possible without compromising the need to arrive at the destination as quickly as possible. Your driver then takes over the wheel and continues the drive. The instructor will point out the good aspects of their driving and those that could benefit from being changed.

One course assesses not just the driver's skill but also the level of risk they when driving. It is aimed at people who drive long distances for their companies. The training organisation suggests that the course should be used in recruitment before a driver has joined the organisation, to weed out potentially dangerous drivers. This is an excellent idea.

Also available are skid training, motorway driving courses, off-road courses, post-accident counselling and courses tailored to your specific needs.

Many firms only think of training their drivers after an accident. This is definitely a case of closing the stable door after the horse has bolted and experts in this field advise against this approach. They believe that it is best not to intimidate drivers by making it obvious that they belong to a high risk group. Instead they suggest that it is better to mix low, medium and high risk drivers together in a varied training programme so as not to alienate the high risk drivers.

They also advise against the 'Train All Drivers' approach, believing instead that all drivers must be properly assessed according to their individual needs so that they can receive training tailored to their requirements.

A better approach is to send all drivers for training or to send them in groups according to the level of risk they will be exposed to. For example, groups of high mileage drivers or those with poor accident records might be the first to receive training.

Directors are likely to find themselves in the dock if their drivers do not behave on the road.[77] Bad, dangerous, negligent or aggressive driving by your employees is hard for you to control: after all, you are not the one driving the car at the time of an accident.

Driver training courses can offer an excellent line of defence for your business. They reduce the risk of accidents and demonstrate your company's commitment to safe driving. They work best if used as just one element of the company's risk management programme, not the sole measure.[78]

1.20.2   ADVANTAGES OF DRIVER TRAINING

The insurance industry and the driver training industry have statistics that show that trained drivers have significantly fewer accidents. This leads to lower repair bills, less vehicle downtime and reduced driver stress.

In past years insurance companies were prepared to offer discounted motor insurance to clients whose drivers were trained. In a hardening insurance market these discounts are generally no longer available though it is still worthwhile asking your insurer if they offer these. If they do not, you may still be able to get a reduction in the increase in your annual premiums if you can show that you have introduced a comprehensive driver training programme.

1.20.3   DISADVANTAGES OF DRIVER TRAINING

Driver training is one of those 'motherhood and apple pie' issues – how can anyone possibly say that there is anything wrong with something that is patently so good?

Many industry experts believe that every driver of a company vehicle should be required to attend a driver training course before they are allowed to drive on business.

However, there are a number of different suppliers of driver training and some are more experienced than others. So shop around, not just on price but also on the type and style of courses available, and try to find one that will work best for your organisation.

---

77   Directors who are concerned about the risk of claims being made against them personally for actions that they take while at work, can consider taking out directors' and officers' insurance cover. While this will not help the director who is sent to prison, at least it will cover the cost of legal fees and fines that the court may impose.

78   See Chapter 13.

Ask your contract hire or fleet management company for suggestions. They may well be able to introduce you to their preferred driver-training supplier, one they have vetted and recommended to other clients in the past.

1.20.4   HOW AM I DRIVING?

Over the years many commercial vehicle fleets have marked their vehicles with a notice saying something to the effect that 'If this vehicle is being driven badly, please call such-and-such a phone number'.

This process has been updated with the arrival of the 'How am I driving?' and 'Well driven?' schemes. A sticker with a freephone number is attached to the rear of your vehicles inviting other motorists to let you know how they are being driven.[79]

The system makes your drivers aware that they could be reported.

These schemes can be a valuable tool in your driver safety armoury. If you start receiving a number of calls about one driver, it will pinpoint where action is required.

The system involves a registration fee (under £20 per vehicle per year) and a small fee payable for each phone call received.

1.21 MOTOR INSURANCE

Your business may operate one car or many hundreds, so this section deals first with insurance if you have only a few cars, and 1.21.19 sets out the differences if you have a bigger fleet.

1.21.1   INSURANCE DOCUMENTATION

When you take out motor insurance the insurer will issue three documents:

a) Certificate of insurance

This confirms that insurance is in place and is required by the Road Traffic Act. As the certificate has a statutory status, the insurer retains legal title to the document and will ask you to return it if cover ceases for any reason.

b) Insurance policy document

This sets out the full terms and conditions of the policy

c) Cover note

This acts as a temporary certificate of insurance and policy, covering the period from the commencement of cover until the date when you receive the policy document and certificate of insurance.

---

79   I will ignore the implicit suggestion here that the driver of the car behind should pick up the phone or write down the phone number.

1.21.2 TYPES OF MOTOR INSURANCE COVER

There are three main classes of insurance policy:

- third party
- third party fire and theft
- comprehensive.

THIRD PARTY

If you wish to drive a motor vehicle you must take out insurance covering damage to other vehicles or injury to others that may arise from the use of the vehicle – third party cover.

Most types of insurance are bought as a matter of choice but there are about a dozen areas where insurance is required by law, and third party motor insurance is one of these.

This type of policy insures the motorist (or the insured, perhaps the motorist's employer) against their liability for the death of the driver, the passengers or third parties, or liability for damage to their property, arising from the use of the vehicle. It also covers the liability of passengers for any accidents they may cause.

It is illegal under the Road Traffic Act to drive without third party cover.

THIRD PARTY, FIRE AND THEFT

You can buy this if you prefer to take the full risk of damage to your own vehicle whilst being covered for fire and theft as well as the legal minimum of third party cover.

It costs less than comprehensive cover but does not cover you for any damage your drivers may accidentally cause to your vehicles.

Two main groups choose this cover:

- drivers of older vehicles who cannot afford comprehensive cover and are willing to bear the cost of any damage that they may cause to their own vehicles and
- business fleets that wish to self-insure this risk.[80]

If your vehicle is stolen this insurance will cover you for your loss, subject to any excess.[81] However, the insurer's definition of theft will not include theft of the vehicle arising through fraud. If you sell the vehicle to a fraudster and only later realise that you have parted with it without receiving proper payment, the insurer will not pay out. So when you sell a used vehicle it is important to be careful.

If you sell via an auction the auction house will not allow the vehicle to be driven away unless the buyer has paid cash or bought the vehicle on a pre-approved credit account. In the latter case, the auction house takes the credit risk of non-payment by the buyer.

---

80 See 1.21.20.

81 See 1.21.5.

If you sell your vehicle direct to a buyer you are advised to take cash or a banker's draft, or to wait until the buyer's cheque has cleared, before you hand over the vehicle.

It is worthwhile noting that from time to time batches of bankers' drafts are stolen, forged and used to buy vehicles. If you are uncertain about where a banker's draft has come from, you should present it at the bank on which it is drawn before giving up possession of the vehicle.

If you lease a vehicle, the lessor will insist that you take out comprehensive cover. If you plan to take only third party, fire and theft cover you should discuss this first with the lessor.

If you rent a vehicle on daily hire and choose the rental company's insurance and collision damage waiver cover, you will have little or no liability for any accidental damage to the vehicle.

Comprehensive

In addition to the cover provided by third party, fire and theft insurance, comprehensive cover includes the cost of accidental damage to your own vehicle.

Most comprehensive policies pay medical expenses in the event of an accident and benefits in the event of serious injury. They may also cover the loss of personal effects from the vehicle. Once again, in the event of a claim, there will usually be an excess that will be deducted from any claim.

Comprehensive policies often provide useful extra benefits, such as cover for loss of keys.

Issues to consider with motor insurance

If you have leased a vehicle the lessor will often require that you advise your insurers of the lessor's interest in the vehicle and ask them to note this on the insurance policy.

In this way the lessor ensures they receive the value of any insurance claim if the vehicle is written off in an accident. They are also kept notified of any other claims.

Theft prevention

One car is stolen in the UK every minute so it makes sense to try to reduce the risk that yours will be next. In recent years there has been a significant improvement in the quality of vehicle security that manufacturers build into their cars. This has been helped to some extent by the annual BVRLA Security Award, which showcases those vehicles with the best security.

Alarms and immobilisers, whether fitted by the manufacturer or retrofitted, are a sensible investment.

The Thatcham Motor Industry Repair Centre is recognised by British insurance companies as the pre-eminent approval organisation for alarms and immobilisers.[82]

They carry out an annual test of car security features and rank vehicles using a star rating.

You can usually get a discount on your insurance premium if you use a Thatcham-approved system.

See www.thatcham.org.

1.21.3 Classes of cover

From more than a century of experience, insurers know that different types of motoring create different risks. The sales representative who spends four hours a day driving between appointments spends more time in his car than the retired person who rarely drives further than the local shops or the golf course.

There are four broad classes of cover:

- social domestic and pleasure
- driving to and from work
- business use
- driving for hire and reward.

Strictly speaking 'driving to and from work' is not a class or cover in its own right; it is an add-on to social domestic and pleasure cover.

You should always be honest with the insurer when declaring the type of cover required. It is tempting to request only 'social domestic and pleasure' cover including driving to and from work, when you plan to drive daily for work as well as to and from work.

This becomes much more important if you pay mileage allowances to drivers who use their own cars for business mileage[83] or if you offer employees a cash-for-car scheme[84] There is a danger here that you might leave them to organise their own insurance. If they don't insure their cars for business use they risk being uninsured. The insurer will reject a claim if there is an at-work accident.

It is estimated that 40% of drivers who use their own cars for work do not have insurance for this purpose. Could this include some of your drivers?

1.21.4 Total loss

Your insurer will declare your vehicle a total loss if the vehicle has been stolen and remains unrecovered after 30 days or if it has been damaged beyond economic repair.

---

82   They also test seats for whiplash prevention, provide most of the data that insurers use when setting insurance group and test crash repair parts.

83   The 'grey fleet'. See 12.10.

84   See chapter 3.

This begs the question – at what point is a vehicle deemed to be damaged beyond economic repair?

Different insurers have varying views on this but typically they will declare a vehicle a total loss if it will cost more than 50%-60% of the list price to reinstate to its previous condition.

Most insurers will replace a nearly-new vehicle with a new one if it is declared a total loss. Otherwise they will offer an amount to compensate you for the loss. This amount they will pay will represent their estimate of the current market value of the used vehicle and, as we know, there are many 'used values', including auction price (which varies according to the car's condition), private sale price and retail price when the car is sold with a warranty.

SO WHAT IS THE AMOUNT OF YOUR LOSS?

Let's say you lost a car that you knew, had looked after and that was unlikely to give you any immediate problems. You might reasonably feel that the only way to get a similar vehicle would be to buy it from a dealer with a warranty. Hence you might feel you have lost the full retail value of the vehicle.

The insurer might feel that all that you lost was the value you could have obtained had you decided to sell the car to a retail dealer, who would then mark it up and sell it for full retail price with a warranty.

Insurance is a contract of indemnity; it is meant to put you back into the position you were in before the car was lost. Therefore you should be able to argue that you need the retail price that a dealer would charge you for a car of similar make, model, age and condition to the one that was lost.

Most leasing companies will give you an assessment of the market value of your car to help in your discussions with the insurer.

You might have to negotiate the price with your insurer. It will help your case if you can provide evidence to support your argument, for example, a copy of the relevant page from a trade price guide or a relevant classified or dealer advert. It will also help if you can supply the full maintenance history of the vehicle, showing that it has been properly maintained. If the car is a prestige marque and the maintenance history shows that the manufacturer's approved service agent routinely serviced the car, this will enhance its used value.

If you take a car on a lease or contract hire agreement you will be responsible for insuring it for its full replacement cost. If you choose to self-insure and the car is a total loss, you will be responsible for repaying the lessor.

If you insure and have a problem obtaining a pay-out from your insurer, this is your problem not the lessors. You have to repay the lessor even if you have not received the proceeds from the insurer.

Lease agreements deal with this in a variety of ways. All leases end as soon as the vehicle is stolen. Most give you full responsibility for immediately paying the lessor a lump sum, often called a 'termination sum', to clear their books and contribute to their costs. You can then keep all of the proceeds of the insurance pay out. In practice, many lessors will allow you to carry on making lease payments for a month or two until the insurance proceeds arrive, then pay a reduced termination sum.

1.21.5 INSURANCE EXCESSES

An insurance excess is the amount the insurer will deduct from each claim. It is common in most types of insurance. It reduces the insurer's risk by a small amount but more importantly, it stops them having to deal with lots of small claims. This minimises their administration and helps them control their costs.

You can reduce your insurance premium by accepting a higher level of excess.

However, if you lease your vehicles and have a high excess on your motor insurance policy, the lessor will have something to say about this. They take some comfort from the fact that your vehicles are insured. If the excess is set very high they will have to rely on you rather than your insurer to pay them in the event of a total loss. Therefore if you self-insure the lessor bears the extra risk that you will not have the funds to make this payment, and they will need to be satisfied in advance that your financial strength is adequate for this purpose.

1.21.6 INSURANCE WHEN DRIVING ABROAD

If you are driving abroad it is important to understand how your insurance works. The rules vary depending on whether you are driving in a European Union country.

At the time of writing the member states of the EU are

Austria	Belgium	Bulgaria
Czech Republic	Cyprus (Greek section)	Denmark
Estonia	Finland	France
Germany	Greece	Hungary
Ireland	Italy	Latvia
Lithuania	Luxembourg	Malta
Poland	Portugal	Romania
Slovakia	Slovenia	Spain
Sweden	The Netherlands	United Kingdom

Every UK insurance policy automatically provides the minimum level of cover required to drive in any EU country, at no extra cost. The key word here is 'minimum'; in most cases your UK motor insurance policy only provides third party cover when you drive abroad.

In addition, the policy will normally provide the minimum level of cover required in Croatia, Gibraltar, Liechtenstein, Monaco, Norway, and Switzerland. However, it is quite possible that your insurer will not extend the third party cover to include all of these countries, so it's important that you check the policy before you set off.

So far we have been discussing only the minimum level of cover. If you have comprehensive cover in the UK you are likely to want that when driving overseas too. To achieve this you need to ask your insurer to extend your cover.

If you drive a vehicle abroad you are advised to carry your certificate of insurance with you.

A Green Card is a document that provides evidence you have the minimum level of cover necessary to drive in the country you are visiting. It is issued for free by your insurer (though your broker may charge a handling fee) and is recognised internationally. There is no need to obtain and carry a Green Card in an EU country or in Andorra, Croatia, Iceland, The Netherlands, Norway or Switzerland

If you are driving to one of the following countries, you must carry a Green Card: Albania, Belarus, Bosnia and Herzegovina, Former Yugoslav Republic of Macedonia (FYROM), Islamic Republic of Iran, Israel, Moldova, Morocco, Russia, Serbia and Montenegro, Tunisia, Turkey, Ukraine.

As local rules change from time to time this information may have changed since the date of writing so it is important to check with your insurer before setting out.

If you wish to take a leased vehicle abroad you will need to obtain a VE103 from your leasing company. [85]

1.21.7 PREMIUMS

Where an individual driver is offered motor insurance, the premium is based on:

- the driver (age, driving record)
- the car (age, mileage, engine size, value)
- where the car is kept (on the street, in a garage)
- what it is used for (commuting, carrying samples, carrying hazardous materials)
- where the driver lives
- the type of insurance required.

If the car is changed part way through the premium year, the insurer should be notified as it may be necessary to amend the policy. A new certificate has to be issued.

Motoring convictions will add to the cost and if you have more than three points the cost will rise sharply.

It is difficult for motorists with speeding convictions to get motor insurance at normal rates; insurers load their premiums by 15%-60%.

Drivers with drink-driving convictions can find it difficult to get cover at all. Some insurers will only offer them third party fire and theft cover.

---

85   See 2.4.5. VE103 – Vehicle on Hire certificate for overseas travel

It normally costs less to comprehensively insure an older car than a late car. Cars over four years old typically cost 15%-20% less to insure.

Insurance claims are usually higher in value and frequency in urban areas so premiums are therefore more expensive. On the edges of urban areas two neighbours living opposite each other can be quoted substantially different premiums if they are in different postal areas.

Young inexperienced drivers (especially men under age 26) or drivers in high-risk professions (based on the insurer's claims experience) may find it difficult to obtain affordable insurance, particularly if they plan to drive high-performance cars.

Some motor insurers also modify premiums based on your marital status and whether you are a smoker.

The insurance company will determine its risk and the premium by considering the information you provide, so the information you give them must be complete and accurate. Insurance is a contract uberrima fide – utmost good faith – where it is implied that you will volunteer all necessary information to enable the insurer to assess its risk. If you have not been sufficiently open in providing information the insurer may cancel the cover or refuse to pay out in the event of a claim.

You can obtain motor insurance direct from an insurance company or via a broker. The Financial Services Authority has licensed hundreds of insurance companies to offer motor insurance in the UK. Many of these do not actively trade in the market. Nonetheless, if you are shopping around for motor insurance you still have a very wide choice and can probably get quotes from up to 100 insurers and Lloyd's syndicates. Many offer fleet cover.

If your requirement is unusually complex or you are in a high-risk category, it makes sense to use a broker. They will earn commission from the transaction which ultimately you will pay through the premium but they could save you time and money.

Many insurers give discounts when tracking devices are fitted to vehicles. These systems have been responsible for the recovery of thousands of stolen vehicles and have saved the insurance industry tens of millions of pounds.

Many insurers will charge a higher premium, or require a higher excess, if the vehicle is normally left overnight on the road rather than in a garage.

1.21.8 NO-CLAIMS BONUS

If you have not made a claim for some time you can qualify for a discount on your motor insurance premium. This is the no-claims bonus or discount. It applies only where you have not made a claim, rather than where you made a claim for an incident that was not your fault. So it's a no-claim bonus, not a no-blame bonus.

Typically the no-claims bonus will be 30% to 60% or more for one to four years of claim-free motoring. Normally it is only available on private policies, not fleet policies.

Drivers moving to cash-for-car may find they are not entitled to no-claims bonuses. Employers may be able to resolve this problem by making an arrangement with the company's insurers, particularly if all of the employees are moving to an employee car ownership scheme.[86]

1.21.9   PROTECTED NO-CLAIMS BONUS

For an extra premium, perhaps 15% more, your insurer may be willing to allow you up to three claims in a period (of one, two, or more years) without loss of no-claims bonus.

For the no-claims bonus to be of value, you are advised to try to ensure that the insurer has a full obligation to offer you cover in future years. If they can choose to decline cover at renewal, the protected no-claims bonus will be of little value to you.

Historically, motor insurance cover was arranged annually. However, some motor insurers now offer three-year policies where the premium is fixed for the whole period. These policies can be particularly valuable to drivers taking cash allowances and entering into personal contract purchase or credit sale arrangements. The insurer protects itself by raising the excess every time a claim is made.

Some car manufacturers now give one or more years' free insurance on selected new models. These deals tend to be available to private buyers only.

1.21.10   INSURANCE GROUPS

Each make and model of vehicle is assigned an insurance group number from 1 to 50. (The old system of groups running from 1-20 is being phased out). The grouping system is recommended by the Association of British Insurers but is not mandatory for its members. Different insurers can use their own grouping systems and not all insurers are members of the Association.

The grouping system takes into account the cost and power of the vehicle, how long it takes to repair, the cost of parts, any security features and the fact that more powerful vehicles tend to be the subject of more insurance claims than less powerful ones.

If Thatcham has assessed a vehicle's security features[87] the vehicle's insurance grouping will show a suffix. This shows whether the vehicle's security features meet the minimum standards expected by Thatcham from a car in that group.

---

86   See 3.7.

87   See Theft Prevention 1.21.2.

The suffixes are:

Suffix	Meaning
A	Meets security requirement
D	Does not meet security requirement for this group so rating has been increased
E	Exceeds security requirement for this group so the rating has been reduced
P	Provisional – Data for the group was incomplete when the vehicle was launched
U	Unacceptable
G	Imported vehicle

1.21.11 THE INSURANCE POLICY

The policy may cover only the named drivers or it may extend cover to any qualified person over a certain age who is driving with the insured's permission. Most policies cover the insured when driving other cars but only on a third party basis, even if the primary car is insured comprehensively. If you plan to drive someone else's car on a regular basis the owner should consider extending their comprehensive insurance to include you as an additional named driver. That way, if you damage the car, the cost will be covered.

1.21.12 POLICY EXCLUSIONS

Most policies exclude claims arising from radiation, war terrorism.

Damage caused in riots of the sort we saw in the UK in 2011 is usually covered in comprehensive policies but not in third party policies.

You should advise your insurer if your business involves work carried out 'airside' at airports, as many policies specifically exclude losses arising from use of a vehicle airside.

1.21.13 LOSS MITIGATION

As with all forms of insurance, you are obliged to take all reasonable steps to mitigate any loss that may occur.

All policies require your car to be maintained in roadworthy condition. Generally speaking, 'roadworthy' includes keeping the car in the condition required by law and as recommended by the manufacturer. The manufacturer, of course, recommends that servicing be carried out at the prescribed intervals. So you risk being treated as uninsured if you fail to service the car when due and an accident occurs then as a result of a component failure that would have been picked up during a standard service.

1.21.14   UNINSURED LOSS RECOVERY

If you are not responsible for a claim you can use an uninsured loss recovery company to recover your excess and any losses or out-of-pocket expenses. Many insurance policies include an uninsured loss recovery service, often handled by an independent specialist company.

1.21.15   MAKING A CLAIM

Call the insurer. They will guide you. Many have 24 hour help lines.

1.21.16   WHAT IF THE OTHER DRIVER IS UNINSURED?

It's a nightmare scenario. You are stopped at traffic lights when a car hits you from behind. No one is hurt but you notice that the other driver is very young. It transpires that he is driving his father's car, is uninsured and has no driving licence.

You cannot claim on his insurance – he doesn't have any. And he doesn't have any money either. You have a choice: claim on your policy and lose your no-claims bonus or pay for the repair without making a claim. And if you have only third party fire and theft cover you have no choice at all – you have to pay for it yourself.

The insurance industry has long recognised that this situation causes problems that are not of the policyholder's making. Fortunately, they have a solution, The Motor Insurers' Bureau.

The Motor Insurers' Bureau (MIB) will pay for third party property and personal injury claims where the motorist who was at fault had no insurance.

If the offending motorist cannot be found, the MIB will only pay for personal injury.

The bureau is funded by a levy paid by all motor insurers.

See www.mib.org.uk.

You can also obtain the booklet *Victims of Uninsured and Untraced Drivers*, from the Department for Transport. Website www.dft.gov.uk

If you are injured because of the criminal actions of another motorist, you can claim compensation under the Criminal Injuries Compensation Scheme, even if the offender has not been caught.

You can download a guide to the scheme from the Ministry of Justice website[88] or get a paper copy from the Criminal Injuries Compensation Authority. See www.cica.gov.uk.

The directgov website contains useful advice if you are the victim of a crime.[89]

---

88   www.justice.gov.uk/downloads/guidance/compensation-schemes/cica/how-to-apply/

89   www.direct.gov.uk/en/CrimeJusticeAndTheLaw/VictimsOfCrime/DG_181641

1.21.17 Getting repairs done

If you do not have comprehensive insurance cover, you have to arrange and pay for your own repairs or get the other driver to pay them for you.

To get another driver to pay for damage to your car you should:

- Tell your insurer that you are making a claim against the other driver.
- Write to the other driver (or the owner of their car, if the driver was not the owner) stating that you hold them responsible for the damage and setting out your claim.
- Ask them to advise their insurers.
- Write to their insurers, setting out the name, address and insurance certificate number (if available) of their client.
- Send them a repair estimate.

The other driver should confirm to their insurer that they were to blame for the accident. If this does not happen, you may need to pursue a legal claim through the courts for your loss. Without an independent witness, this may be difficult.

If you have comprehensive cover your insurer will normally direct you to a particular repairer or may allow you the freedom to select your own. Using their repairer may speed up the process. It will also make it more likely that you will be offered the use of a courtesy car while yours is being repaired. Many insurers require their repairers to provide these. If they don't, you may like to consider using a credit hire service.[90]

If you obtain an estimate, send this to the insurer to authorise the work.

Most insurers have special arrangements with windscreen suppliers to speed up the normal process. The insurer will give you a helpline phone number and the supplier will come promptly to repair or replace the damaged glass. The accident report form will follow later for you to complete. The insurer will have negotiated preferential pricing with the windscreen supplier so if you do not use their supplier they may levy a surcharge.

Once any window or damage repair has been completed you will have to pay your insurance excess to the repairer. This is because the insurer will only pay them the amount of your claim, less the excess.

If you are registered for VAT your insurer will not pay the input VAT arising on any repair costs. The repairer will ask you to pay this amount when the repair work has been completed. You can reclaim this amount as input tax on your VAT return.

However, if you are not registered for VAT your loss includes the VAT on the repair so the insurer will pay this.

When thinking about repairs you should bear in mind that as motor manufacturers are using more advanced processes and materials, some repairers are finding it difficult to stay up-to-date. According to their trade body, the Vehicle Builders and

Repairers Association, some repairers are only capable of cosmetic repairs rather than full structural repairs.

Ideally you want your vehicles to be repaired by a business that has all the relevant manufacturer data, is up-to-date on repair methods and has invested in tools and staff training. It is worthwhile asking the repair company about these things before handing over your vehicle for repair.

1.21.18   INSURANCE PREMIUM FINANCE

Most insurers will offer you the option to pay your premium over a period of time, usually 10 or 12 months. Interest is charged in these arrangements so you should consider whether to use the insurer's arrangements or other sources of finance (for example, your bank overdraft) to spread the cost of the premium.

1.21.19   FLEET INSURANCE

BACKGROUND

If you have more than five vehicles, you will normally be eligible for fleet motor insurance cover.

Fleet insurance differs from single-vehicle insurance in several important ways.

The premiums are established by reference to the claims history of your fleet. Once established, the same premium is payable on all of the vehicles in the fleet.

A claim on one vehicle will affect your overall claims experience and will be reflected in the following years' premiums.

Your policy will be renewed annually, regardless of the dates on which vehicles join or leave the fleet.

Fleet insurance policies are designed to reduce administration for both you and the insurer compared with having lots of individual policies.

Many insurers will offer lower premiums – perhaps 25% less – if you limit your insurance cover to named drivers only.

Motorists no longer have to produce their insurance certificate at a police station after an accident because the police have direct access to the Motor Insurance Database, a central register of all insurance policies.[91]

If you are a private motorist your insurance company will provide the relevant details to the Motor Insurance Database.

If you have a business policy you have to do this for your fleet. Your insurer will normally tell you what to do but if they do not do so the onus is on you to find out. As a general rule, if you insure two or more vehicles and they are collectively insured on one policy, you must give details direct to the Motor Insurance Database unless your insurer has confirmed that they will be doing so.

---

91   See 16.16.

You can obtain more information about the database from www.mib.org.uk. This shows the various ways that you can supply information to the database.

FLEET INSURANCE POLICIES AND THE MARKET

The fleet insurance market is as mature and competitive as the private motor insurance market. The cost of claims has risen and it has been tough for insurers to make big profits in this market.

There has been constant pressure on fleet insurers to increase their premiums, which has only been moderated by the fact that the market is so competitive. The number of insurers offering fleet cover has reduced. Insurers are now saying that premiums will have to rise in the next few years as the cost of claims is rising sharply.

Notwithstanding the fact that the market is tough, or perhaps because of it, insurers are very keen to attract and retain your business. Some fleet insurers have started offering three-year policies and some will give you a partial refund of your premium if your claims are less than a percentage (perhaps 75%) of the premiums paid.

Some fleet insurance policies include roadside assistance membership.

When a leased car is written off as a total loss, the lease settlement figure will normally exceed the insurance settlement figure and you will have to pay the lessor the difference. In response to this problem some motor insurance policies now cover not just the used value of the car but the total amount due to the finance or leasing company. So these policies combine traditional motor cover and gap insurance[92] in one package.

INSURANCE BROKERS

Most fleet insurance is bought through brokers. Most brokers provide an excellent service to their clients and add value in many areas. However, it is worthwhile asking your broker how he does business.

Is he placing the risk with an underwriting syndicate at Lloyd's? If so, does he have direct access to that syndicate or does he have to go through a Lloyd's broker? If the latter, an extra layer of commission is being paid.

Does the broker have expertise in risk management? If not, it may be that he is doing little for you other than shopping around, effecting an introduction and handling the paperwork.

FLEET INSURANCE AND CASH-FOR-CAR

Insurers know there is an opportunity for them to lose business when companies opt for cash-for-car schemes so many now provide fleet policies to cover cars owned by employees who have opted out of company cars.[93]

---

92 See 1.22.6.

93 See also 3.4.

Fierce competition in the private motor insurance market, especially since the arrival of the 'direct insurers' and comparison websites, has driven down the cost of private motor insurance so that it is now much cheaper than fleet cover.

If you own a small fleet you may be tempted to ask your employees to arrange cover in their own names rather than have a company insurance policy. You should resist this temptation, for several reasons:

If your employee or a third party is seriously injured when your employee is driving for business under a business policy, the policy protects your business against any claims. However, if the employee is the insured party – in other words, if they only have private motor insurance – you have no such protection and are exposed to the full cost of any claim by the employee or the third party. This applies even if the driver was insured to drive the car for business purposes.

If the employee leaves the company and a new one joins, the old employee will have taken the no-claims bonus with them. The new employee may have to start building up their own no-claims bonus from scratch.

If the employee leaves and you find that the car is damaged, your company cannot claim on the insurance for the cost of repair, as it is not the insured party.

Dealing with drivers

Around 60% of companies charge their employees if they cause an accident in a company vehicle. 25% charge the employee for every incident, the remainder charge only if the driver has been responsible for more than one accident in a twelve-month period.

The amounts vary but most charge an amount equal to the excess on the insurance policy.

If you wish to levy a charge when your drivers cause an accident, it is important to set this out in a written company policy and to make sure all drivers are aware of this.

Advice to drivers in the event of an accident

You will wish to give your drivers guidance on what to do in the event of an accident.

Your insurer will provide a written procedure that you can customise to your own company's situation. Alternatively, you can use the following wording as a starting point.

This procedure should be included in a booklet or notice in the car so that it will be available immediately in the event of an accident:

PROCEDURE IN THE EVENT OF AN ACCIDENT:

In the event of an accident you must ensure that no one has been hurt. If there has been an injury, call an ambulance and the police.

If anyone is injured the police will check your insurance cover – they have direct access to the details of every UK motor insurance policy. If they can't find details of your insurance you will have to produce your insurance certificate at a police station within seven days. You can get a copy of the certificate from [insert name, department and extension number]

Complete our accident report form. It is located in the driver handbook.

If you have killed or injured a horse, donkey, bull, cow, sheep or dog, or damaged roadside property, you must notify the police within 24 hours.

Do not admit liability for the accident, even if you think you may have been wholly or partially to blame.

Make a note of what happened as soon as possible. If you do not have a camera on your phone or in the vehicle, return to the scene of the accident with a camera as soon as possible and take photographs that show the scene all important angles.

If the other driver(s) is (are) are carrying their certificate of insurance, ask to see this and note the details on our accident report form. If they do not have their certificate to hand, ask for the name of their insurer or, failing this, their broker.

Send our completed accident report form to [name of person and department] within 24 hours of the accident, as we have to advise our insurers promptly. You must do this even if there is no need for us to make a claim. It is a condition of our policy.

You are required by law to give your name and address to the other driver.

If our insurance company asks for their own accident report form to be completed, we will obtain this and send it to you.

The accident report form is a standard form that you should devise, with boxes for the driver to fill in.

Here is a list of the most important items of information that need to be recorded on the form. You may wish to add items to this list that are important to you:[94]

- your driver's name
- the registration number, make and model of their vehicle
- if your driver was injured, the details of their injury
- name, address and telephone number of the other driver(s)

---

94   For example, employee number, branch, job title, how many years they have had a driving licence, how many hours they had been driving on the day of the accident before the accident occurred. You can use this information to collate accident statistics.

■ the registration number(s) of their vehicle(s)

■ their vehicle type(s)

■ details of damage to any vehicle

■ if any driver is not the owner of the vehicle they were driving; the name, address and telephone number of the owner

■ if someone is injured; their name, address, telephone number and the name of the hospital they were taken to

■ witnesses' names, addresses and telephone numbers

■ name and number of any police officer attending

■ if there are any independent witnesses, their names, addresses and phone numbers

■ details of the other driver's insurance company, the policyholder's name, address and phone number

■ details of the other driver's insurance cover and insurance certificate number

1.21.20   SELF-INSURING

Insurance works by spreading the risk over lots of insured parties. The premiums paid by all of the parties are calculated to cover all claims that may arise and leave the insurer with a profit.[95]

If you have a large fleet you may be better off paying for the cost of damage to your own vehicles as it arises, rather than asking an insurer to pay this for you. You will save that part of the insurance premium that covers damage to your own vehicles.

This is self-insurance. It is common for large organisations to self-insure many risks in their businesses, not just motoring risks. However, by law you cannot self-insure third party risks.

It is a little surprising that more companies do not self-insure their comprehensive motoring risks. If you have a fleet of more than, say, 50 vehicles, you should find that it is worth considering. Once you get to more than 200 vehicles the financial case for self-insuring usually becomes compelling, unless your fleet has a particularly poor accident history. The premiums you save should be ample to cover the damage costs you will incur.

Of course, this exposes you to the full cost of damage that your drivers do to your vehicles and therefore gives you a very direct interest in how your drivers behave on the road. Compare this with the normal situation where the insurer takes the immediate pain of the cost of any damage and you only incur extra costs if your

---

95   It is interesting to note that many insurers pay out more on motor insurance than they collect in premiums. Only by earning interest or investment income on the premiums can they hope to make a profit. In many years even this is not enough, particularly when the stock market tumbles and interest rates are low.

premiums rise in future years. That is not much of an incentive for you to do anything about the original issue, which is that one of your drivers may have been responsible for causing an accident.

If self-insurance is combined with driver training and a scheme to reward them for good driving and penalise them for having accidents, you end up with a virtuous circle that should keep accidents down, keep costs low, keep you and your company protected against involuntary manslaughter claims and make the roads a safer place.

Rather than self-insuring you may prefer to look at other ways to reduce your motor insurance bills.

One approach is to have a comprehensive insurance policy with a large excess. For example, you might not claim the first £5,000 of loss per claim. Alternatively, you might choose to bear the first £50,000 of claims in a year.

You can obtain some quotes and look at your claims history as the first step in deciding whether such an approach has any merit.

Another approach is to set up an off-shore captive insurance company. This allows you to fund your own risks and can confer valuable tax benefits. This is a complex area requiring specialist advice. As most fleets would not consider this option it is beyond the scope of this book.

If you decide to look at alternatives to comprehensive cover, bear in mind that there are some downsides. If you do not have comprehensive cover you will have to handle some aspects of your own claims and repairs. You can sub-contract some functions but will have to pay for this service. Your insurer will be getting large discounts on parts and labour costs, and these economies of scale will not be available to you unless you sub-contract them to a third party accident management company.[96]

SELF-INSURING RENTAL CARS

If you rent vehicles you can choose to insure the vehicle via the rental company or you can insure using your own fleet policy.

The rental company will permit you to use your own insurance but will want to ensure the car is properly insured from the moment it comes off cover with their own insurer until the moment it goes back on cover with their insurer.

This may be slightly different from the period of hire, given that some hirers like to drop off their car outside the rental company's office before opening hours and pop the keys through the door. If the car is then stolen before the rental office opens up there's a risk that the car will not have been insured under either party's policy.

---

96   See 1.19.

The rental company will also want to ensure that they can recharge the cost of any damage to either you or your insurer.

HAZARDOUS WASTE

If your vehicle is declared a total loss after a major accident, the insurance company will handle the disposal of the vehicle. If you self-insure and the vehicle is a total loss, you will have to dispose of the vehicle.

The Hazardous Waste Act[97] classifies end-of-life vehicles as hazardous waste. You must ensure that written-off vehicles are disposed of in a way that is consistent with the provisions of the Act and you are not allowed to delegate this obligation. The best way to deal with this is to use a disposal company that is licensed under the Act.

1.21.21 INSURANCE INDEMNITY FORM

If you rent a car and you wish to use your own motor insurance cover, the daily hire company will insist that you complete an insurance indemnity form, in which you undertake to keep the vehicle comprehensively covered for its full replacement value and to ensure that any driver holds a valid driving licence.

By signing the form you agree to indemnify the rental company against any loss, expense etc that arises should they suffer a loss through a breach of your undertakings.

1.21.22 COMPLAINTS AGAINST INSURANCE COMPANIES

Your policy will set out what happens in the event of a dispute with your insurance company.

If you cannot resolve the complaint with the insurer a further avenue is open to you – you can apply to the Financial Ombudsman Service.

This body was set up by parliament to resolve disputes between consumers (and small businesses with turnover under €2,000,000) and providers of the following financial services: consumer credit, banking, insurance, mortgages, credit cards and store cards, loans and credit, pensions, savings and investments, hire purchase and pawn broking, money transfer, financial advice and stocks, shares, unit trusts and bonds. The ombudsman will take up your complaint as a last resort before you go to court. The judgement is binding on the insurer but not on you. You can still take the case to court if the decision goes against you. It costs nothing to submit a complaint to the ombudsman.

Website: www.financial-ombudsman.org.uk.

---

97   www.legislation.gov.uk/uksi/2005/894/contents/made
98   See 16.2

1.21.23 CONTINUOUS INSURANCE ENFORCEMENT

In 2011 it became a legal requirement for vehicles to be insured at all times, even when a vehicle is kept off the road, unless it has been the subject of a Statutory Off Road Notification (SORN).[98]

The DVLA now carries out automatic cross-reference checks with the Motor Insurance Database that is maintained by the Motor Insurers' Bureau[99] to see which cars are uninsured. If a car is registered with the DVLA but is shown as uninsured on the database, the registered keeper will be sent a letter requiring them to insure the vehicle or face a fixed penalty notice and the risk the vehicle will be clamped or seized, and disposed of. If the vehicle has not been insured after a month the DVLA will send a £100 fixed penalty notice at which point the vehicle becomes liable to clamping or seizure.

If the £100 is not paid the registered keeper will be prosecuted where on conviction they can be fined up to £1,000.

This new law marks the government's desire to deal with the hundreds of thousands of uninsured cars on the road. The police already seize nearly 200,000 uninsured cars every year, but this new law will mean these vehicles will no longer have to be caught on the road.

It is essential that fleet managers ensure that all of their vehicles are registered with the Motor Insurers' Bureau.

1.21.24 EXERCISES

What is 'Thatcham'?

What are the four classes of motor insurance?

What is a total loss?

What is insurance excess?

How can you obtain third party motor insurance to drive on the Continent?

How do insurers determine your motor insurance premium?

What is a no-claims bonus?

What is loss mitigation and why is it important?

What happens if you have an accident and the other driver is uninsured?

In what ways does fleet cover differ from normal motor insurance?

What items should be on the driver's accident checklist?

What is self-insurance?

What is an insurance indemnity form?

---

99   See 1.21.16

1.22 OTHER INSURANCES

1.22.1 KEYMAN INSURANCE

FEATURES

This insurance covers you in the event that a key person in your business has an accident or is ill and unable to work. The insurer will pay the rentals or repayments that fall due under your finance agreement. This type of policy is best suited to smaller businesses where the loss of one person could have a major impact on the income or success of the business.

Benefits under a keyman policy are normally paid thirty days after the death or incapacity of the insured, although longer periods of deferral are available at reduced premiums.

The policy will contain limitations. For example, the insurer will not pay any arrears under the finance agreement. It is important to note that the amount of the cover reduces during the life of such a policy. If you only have two rentals left to pay under your finance agreement your maximum benefit will be only those two rentals.

Insurance brokers normally sell keyman insurance as a stand-alone policy. However, a number of fleet finance and leasing companies also offer it as a product linked to a vehicle finance agreement, so it protects the payments due under the agreement.

ISSUES WITH KEYMAN INSURANCE

While a number of fleet companies offer this product, take-up is low because most clients believe it is of limited value. There are few businesses where a lease rental is such a material expense that the business needs to cover its cost in the event of the incapacity of the driver. In most cases, if the incapacity would cause such harm to the business, it would be better to take out a bigger personal accident or life policy covering much more than just the finance payments on the vehicle.

1.22.2 CREDIT PAYMENT INSURANCE

FEATURES

Credit payment insurance is similar to keyman insurance. Benefits become payable if the insured person becomes unable to work through accident, sickness or unemployment. Unlike keyman insurance, which gives benefit to the employer, credit payment insurance provides the benefit to the private individual or sole trader.

Fleet companies offer this cover to clients taking personal contract purchase or personal contract hire.

On the death of the insured, the policy normally repays the balance due on the finance agreement. In the event of unemployment or disability the policy will cover the monthly repayments for a pre-set period.

The policy will contain a number of exclusions. These are likely to include unemployment caused by the resignation or misconduct of the insured or the insured volunteering for redundancy.

ISSUES WITH CREDIT PAYMENT INSURANCE

Credit payment insurance is sold widely to private individuals and small businesses when they buy vehicle finance products. These clients get peace of mind from knowing that their finance payments will be met in the event that a major life event makes it difficult or impossible for them to make the payments.

For many people the cost of a car is their second largest expenditure after the cost of their house, so being sure that they can meet the repayments is a major concern.

As with all insurances, it is worthwhile shopping around for cover. The premium is only a small part of the purchasing decision. The benefits, incidents covered, exclusions and deferral periods are all important.

1.22.3 PAYMENT ACCIDENT PROTECTION INSURANCE

FEATURES

Payment accident protection insurance covers you in the event that your vehicle is off the road for repairs after an accident. It is designed to ease the financial loss that can arise if you are unable to use your vehicle. While the vehicle is being repaired the insurer pays the weekly equivalent of your monthly lease or finance agreement payment.

Normally the vehicle will have to be in the garage for more than seven days before payments commence. Payments are not made if the vehicle is declared a total loss.

ISSUES WITH PAYMENT ACCIDENT PROTECTION INSURANCE

It is very unusual for a modern vehicle to be off the road for more than a week, awaiting parts or specialist repair. Therefore this insurance covers you against quite a remote risk. In addition, most comprehensive motor insurance policies will provide you with a replacement vehicle while yours is off the road being repaired.

Nonetheless, if having a vehicle off the road for a long period could have a high cost to your business, you may well feel that the premium is worth paying. A good example might be where a light commercial vehicle has been specially fitted out to meet your business needs and another vehicle would not be able to do the same job.

This cover is likely to be of interest to smaller businesses where the loss of a specific vehicle for a long period would cause significant business disruption.

1.22.4 MECHANICAL BREAKDOWN INSURANCE

FEATURES

Mechanical breakdown insurance covers the cost of parts and labour if your vehicle suffers a mechanical or electrical component failure. Normally the insurer will expect you to take the vehicle to a garage nominated by the insurer to have the work carried out. The work will then be authorised and paid for by the insurer.

This insurance therefore covers unforeseeable costs.

The policy will set out a number of exclusions including frost or accident damage and the cost of normal servicing. Cover does not apply where the vehicle has been written off as a total loss. The policy will stipulate that the vehicle has to have been properly serviced and the MoT has to be up to date.

This cover is sometimes given free when you buy a used car. If you sell a used car to a member of your staff or the public you may wish to add this insurance as it costs little and gives peace of mind to you and the buyer. Indeed, it may help to clinch the sale.

ISSUES

Mechanical breakdown insurance is likely to be of interest to smaller businesses wishing to reduce the risk that their vehicles will suffer a higher than normal incidence of mechanical breakdown and associated costs.

If it is offered free when you buy a used car, take it.

1.22.5 EARLY TERMINATION PROTECTION INSURANCE

FEATURES

Early termination protection insurance covers you for the cost of early termination if you have to hand back a leased vehicle due to unforeseen circumstances beyond your control.

The amount paid will represent the loss the lessor makes when it has to sell the vehicle without having received an adequate number of rentals to cover market depreciation – in other words, the difference between the capital cost and sale proceeds of the vehicle.

The policy will normally cover the driver's unexpected death, retirement through ill health or pregnancy, or their being required to surrender their licence on medical grounds. Some policies cover you[100] if you make the driver redundant.

The premium is normally paid in a single instalment per vehicle on delivery. This allows the insurer to collect the full premium for the full risk that they are taking. If they charged you monthly instead, their premium income would cease on early termination of the lease. This would be unreasonable given that their risk of loss is greatest in the first year when the vehicle suffers its greatest loss of market value.

---

100 In this book, 'you' are assumed to be a fleet manager or a person responsible for the vehicles your business operates.

Typically, if the driver resigns you will be allowed to change the driver who is covered by the policy. The policy will normally exclude the employee's suicide, retirement or dismissal, or their departure due to alcohol or drug abuse.

ISSUES

Early termination protection insurance can offer you valuable protection against the so-called 'penalties' associated with the early termination of vehicle leases. Many lessees feel penalised when required to make early settlement payments that arise through circumstances beyond their control and this cover obviates the need for these payments.

Some organisations with large fleets consider that their risk of unforeseen early termination is so well diversified that the cost to protect this risk will exceed the likely benefit. If you have fewer than, say, thirty vehicles, you may feel you do not have enough spread of risk, so this type of cover may work well for you.

1.22.6   GAP INSURANCE

FEATURES

When you lease a vehicle or buy it under a financing arrangement, the reduction of the balance outstanding in the leasing company's books happens more slowly than the reduction in the market price of the vehicle. This is because used vehicles depreciate faster in the first year after registration than in the second, more in the second than the third, and so on. Indeed, the greatest reduction in market value occurs when the vehicle is driven out of the showroom.

In order for the balance in the lessor's books to reduce at the same speed as market value, your rentals or finance payments would have to be higher in the early part of the contract and lower later on. Most lessees and borrowers are not keen on this idea, so they pay equal monthly or quarterly payments, perhaps with a single large initial payment.

This arrangement works well until the car is written off in an accident. Your motor insurance company indemnifies you for the loss of the vehicle and will only pay out its market value. However, the balance outstanding in the lessor's books will be greater than this amount. Hence there is a 'gap', and gap insurance fills this.

Gap insurance covers you if the vehicle is declared a total loss through accident, fire or theft, and it pays for the financial shortfall between the insurance payout and settlement amount you are required to pay the lessor.

The chart below shows the likely level of loss a lessor would incur in the event of the total loss of a vehicle costing £10,000, financed over three years on a 3+33 basis,[101] with a 40% residual value or balloon payment. The rentals are £216.06 per month. It assumes that the lessor uses the pre-tax actuarial accounting method.[102] The interest rate implicit in the lease is 9% pre-tax.

---

101 See 6.2.1.

102 Pre-tax actuarial is one of the accounting methods approved for use by lessors under SSAP21. See 8.1.2 and 8.5.

Month	Balance in the lessor's books	Market value of the vehicle	Gap to be covered
	£	£	£
On delivery	10,000.00	10,000.00	0.00
1	9,421.97	9,100.00	321.97
2	9,274.96	8,933.00	341.96
3	9,126.85	8,766.00	360.85
4	8,977.62	8,599.00	378.62
5	8,827.28	8,432.00	395.28
6	8,675.81	8,265.00	410.81
7	8,523.20	8,098.00	425.20
8	8,369.45	7,931.00	438.45
9	8,214.54	7,764.00	450.54
10	8,058.48	7,597.00	461.48
11	7,901.24	7,430.00	471.24
12	7,742.82	7,250.00	492.82
13	7,583.22	7,063.00	520.22
14	7,422.41	6,876.00	546.41
15	7,260.41	6,689.00	571.41
16	7,097.18	6,502.00	595.18
17	6,932.74	6,315.00	617.74
18	6,767.06	6,128.00	639.06
19	6,600.13	5,941.00	659.13
20	6,431.96	5,754.00	677.96
21	6,262.52	5,567.00	695.52
22	6,091.82	5,380.00	711.82
23	5,919.83	5,193.00	726.83
24	5,746.55	5,000.00	746.55
25	5,571.97	4,917.00	654.97
26	5,396.09	4,834.00	562.09
27	5,218.88	4,751.00	467.88
28	5,040.35	4,668.00	372.35
29	4,860.47	4,585.00	275.47
30	4,679.25	4,502.00	177.25
31	4,496.67	4,419.00	77.67
32	4,312.72	4,336.00	-23.28
33	4,127.39	4,253.00	-125.61
34	3,940.67	4,170.00	-229.33
35	3,970.22	4,087.00	-116.78
36	4,000.00	4,000.00	0.00

It is worthwhile plotting this on a graph that shows this from the lessor's point of view:

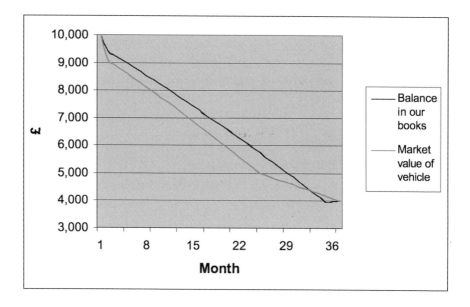

The strange-looking situation in months 32 to 36 is not an error. It reflects the 3+33 rental profile: by the time you have made the last month's payment the contract still has three months to run. During this time interest will continue to accrue on the balance in the lessor's books, until the end of the contract when they sell the car (or you pay the balloon payment). Only at that point is the outstanding balance in the lessor's books cleared.

The premium on gap insurance is payable in a lump sum at the commencement of the contract. It cannot be paid in monthly payments, as these would stop if the vehicle was declared a total loss and the insurer would not collect its full premium.

There are normally a number of exclusions on gap insurance. For example, it doesn't cover arrears of finance or lease payments or any excess deducted by the insurer when paying the total loss claim.

ADVANTAGES

Gap insurance offers smaller fleets a valuable protection against the expense of the early settlement of a finance agreement arising on the total loss of a vehicle.

It is not suitable for larger fleets, as they already have a good spread of risk and can self-insure this risk effectively.

ISSUES

As with all forms of insurance, you are buying peace of mind. If you have a large number of total loss incidents the premium may seem small, if not it will seem expensive. Ultimately, whether or not to buy this cover is a risk-reward decision that every business must evaluate for itself.

One point worth bearing in mind is that gap insurance premiums are often quoted as a flat amount regardless of the value of the vehicles or the speed at which they depreciate. If most of your vehicles are expensive and fast-depreciating, a low flat-rate premium will offer good value for money. On the other hand, if they are inexpensive and slowly-depreciating, the same premium may be a waste of money.

1.22.7   EXERCISES

What is keyman insurance?

What type of company will most benefit from it?

Why is take-up low and what might be a better form of insurance to cover these risks?

How does credit payment insurance differ from keyman insurance?

When is benefit payable under credit payment insurance?

What is covered by personal accident protection insurance?

Why might you prefer not to take it?

You are thinking about selling a used car to a member of the public. What insurance might you offer with it?

Why is early termination protection insurance necessary?

What does it cover?

How does it differ from gap insurance?

1.23 CAR CLUBS

Car clubs are arrangements whereby an agency owns a pool of cars that members can hire for an hour, a day etc. The cars are parked in special parking bays in cities and towns for use by local residents. In some cases this can remove the need to own a car. In others it can mean that a family will have just one car, plus membership of a car club, rather than having two family cars.

The thinking here is that most family cars stand idle for nearly twenty-four hours a day, so if cars can be removed from the roads, it will save money and reduce congestion.

Car clubs could be of interest to a fleet manager with staff who live and work in major cities. Often the best way to move around a city is by public transport but there are also occasions when only a car will do. A company car can in fact be a liability in a city, where it is often a problem to find a parking space. In this situation it may well be viable for the employer to join a car club so that their staff have access to cars when required and can forget about them at other times.

1.24 CAR SHARING[103]

For many employers, car parking is a scarce resource. A Department for Transport study concluded that the average annual cost of each parking space was £400. Building additional parking capacity can be as expensive as £10,000 per space for multi-storey parking. Some organisations need to lease off-site parking and provide a shuttle bus service – another costly solution.

In most organisations, staff generally travel in from a similar catchment area and work comparable hours, so it makes sense to encourage them to share journeys to work. It saves them money and saves the employer needing to provide so much parking space – a definite win-win.

The other big saving is in carbon emissions. One journey rather than two means a halving of emissions. Many organisations don't measure business travel and commuting when calculating their carbon output,

Car sharing by colleagues need not stop at commuting. Many organisations have employees making similar journeys, whether between offices, to visit key suppliers or clients, or to airports for international travel. These journeys are typically taken without any consideration of efficiency, so several colleagues could drive, or book private cars, to travel nearly identical routes.

Employers can encourage their staff to share journeys by making available an online tool to allow employees to list their upcoming journeys, creating the opportunity to match with colleagues with similar plans.

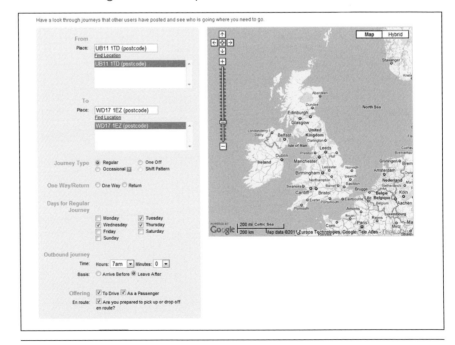

103 This section has been contributed by carbon heroes. www.carbonheroes.com

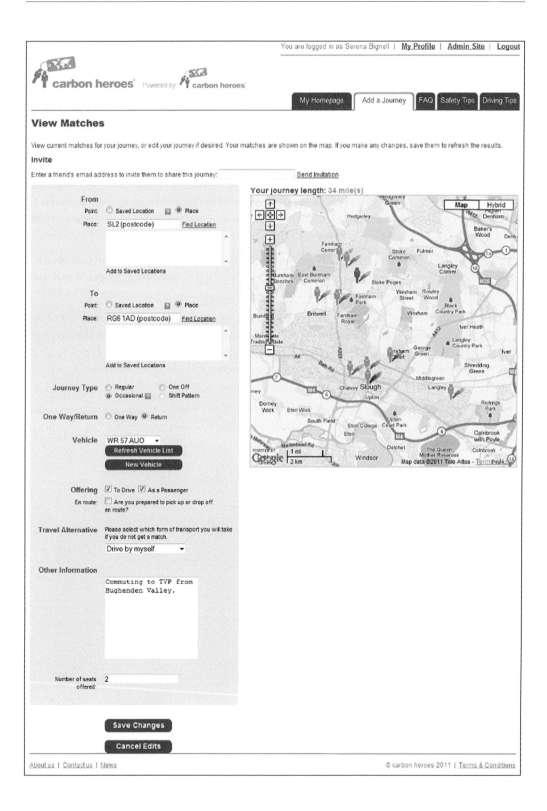

HM Revenue and Customs permits an additional allowance of 5 pence per mile to be paid for each passenger carried on business travel. This creates an incentive for employees to share journeys.

Research by the National Business Travel Network (www.nbtn.org.uk) demonstrates that a well-managed travel plan, which should include a car sharing scheme, can reduce employee turnover and also staff absenteeism. In more general terms sharing the commute to work can be made more pleasant when shared and business trips become less stressful.

When managed poorly, a company car sharing scheme can be perceived as an imposition from management, restricting employees' travel choices. When managed well, such a scheme can be seen as saving employees' costs and making work a more sociable place.

2 STANDARD LEASE CONTRACT

In some cultures it is considered to be the height of bad taste to ask for a written contract to be signed when entering into an agreement. This is because it implies a lack of trust between the parties and, so the argument goes, if we cannot trust each other why should we do business?

In the UK we don't think that way. We expect to enter into a written contract whenever we do business with another party. And with good reason too. In contractual matters, when there is a dispute between two parties, UK law seeks to establish precisely what was agreed. The intentions of the parties are largely irrelevant; it is the wording of the agreement that is the key when determining what was agreed. Without a written contract, it is very difficult to prove this.

So when you enter into a leasing or motor finance agreement you will always be offered a contract to sign.

Every agreement will be different so it is not possible to deal here with everything that may come up. Therefore, the limited ambition of this chapter is to point out some of the issues that you are likely to find in most vehicle leasing or finance agreements.

2.1 SINGLE-VEHICLE AGREEMENTS

If you have a small fleet, or if you are entering into an agreement regulated by the Consumer Credit Act[104], you will be invited to sign a document setting out all of the terms of the agreement including details of the vehicle and the rentals.

It will usually say that the agreement is the whole agreement between the parties. If it does not contain the full details agreed with the salesman, you should point this out before signing or those details will not become part of the agreement and you won't be able to rely on the things the salesman said.

Single vehicle agreements are usually presented using 'no-carbon-required' paper so that both parties get an identical copy of the signed agreement. This is important for regulated agreements where, by law, the customer must receive an identical copy of the agreement to the one held by the lessor/lender.

---

104 See 4.6.

2.2 MASTER AGREEMENT AND SCHEDULE

When many vehicles are to be financed, perhaps over a period of time, you will normally be asked to sign a master agreement. This will contain all of the terms and conditions of the finance or lease agreement that are to remain unchanged as each vehicle is financed.

When the time comes for a new vehicle to be financed, you will be asked to sign a schedule to the master agreement. This will be a brief document – probably just one page – showing only the information that is specific to that vehicle such as the rental/repayment, start date, end date, registration number, vehicle identification number ('VIN number'), etc.

Once signed, the schedule forms part of the master agreement.

2.3 FEATURES OF STANDARD LEASE CONTRACTS

This is a list of typical clauses that you might expect to find in a lease agreement:

2.3.1 HOW RENTALS CAN BE MODIFIED

There can be many reasons why a lessor might want to be able to modify the rentals during the course of the agreement.

The most common will be when the list price of the vehicle changes between the date the contract is signed (in anticipation of delivery some time later) and the date the vehicle is delivered.

It is not uncommon for prices to be 'protected' by dealers or manufacturers, so that price changes do not affect the prices of vehicles already ordered. But price protection is not universal and sometimes prices change without warning, so the lessor needs to be able to alter the rentals before delivery to reflect this.

2.3.2 MISUSE OF THE VEHICLE

The contract will normally refer to misuse of the vehicle. Unless specifically negotiated and included, lease agreements will deny you the right to use a vehicle for racing, off-roading or for carrying fare-paying passengers. You will be in breach of contract if you allow any of these to happen and the contract will make you responsible for any costs or losses that arise.

2.3.3 QUIET POSSESSION

The contract may say that the lessor will allow you uninterrupted use of the vehicle – 'quiet possession' – and will not interfere with your use of it so long as you meet your obligations under the agreement. Even if the contract does not say this you have this right automatically by law – it is an implied term of any lease agreement.

However, if you fail to comply with any of your obligations you will be in default of the terms of the agreement.

2.3.4 EVENTS OF DEFAULT

If you fail to meet your obligations or you carry out some actions that are not allowed under the agreement, you will be deemed to be 'in default' of your obligations.

The list of 'events of default' in a lease can be very long. Typically, it will include the following:

- If you fail to pay rentals or other amounts when due or within a fixed period (perhaps 14 days) of the due date
- If you fail to insure the vehicle comprehensively
- If there is a material change in your circumstances that is likely to be disadvantageous to the lessor, in their reasonable opinion
- If you attempt to sell, charge, pledge or mortgage the vehicle
- If you remove it from the United Kingdom without the lessor's written consent
- If you breach any term of the agreement that is capable of being remedied, then fail to remedy the breach within, say, 14 days of receiving the lessor's notice requiring you to remedy it
- If you enter into (or propose to enter into) any arrangement with your creditors for the satisfaction of your debts under insolvency legislation
- If you wind up or attempt to wind up your business
- If you fail to meet your obligations under any other finance agreements
- If any distress is executed by a third party ('distress' here could refer to the situation where HM Revenue and Customs takes possession of one of your assets for non-payment of tax or VAT)
- If you cease or threaten to cease carrying out business
- If you transfer or dispose of a substantial part of your assets
- If you admit that you are unable to meet your debts as they fall due

The lessor will want these clauses to be worded in their favour to allow them to act promptly to protect themselves if something goes wrong with your business that could adversely affect their position.

Many leases split events of default into different categories depending on the severity of the default and allow the lessor different remedies for each category.

So, for example, non-payment of a recharged parking fine might give the lessor the right to terminate the agreement after they have given you notice of their intention to terminate and you have failed to make the payment within the specified time.

At the other extreme, the convening of a creditors' meeting to consider the appointment of a liquidator or receiver may be in the category that immediately brings the contract to a close and gives the lessor rights of repossession that they can use immediately.

Other examples of immediate automatic termination, requiring no action on behalf of the lessor, may include the bankruptcy or death of a sole trader or partner.

2.3.5 CONSEQUENCES OF DEFAULT

The contract will set out the consequences if you are in default of your obligations under the agreement. These will normally include allowing the lessor to recover ('repossess') the vehicle, to enter into your premises to do so if necessary and to charge interest on late payment at a default rate.

TERMINATION SUM

The contract will set out how the lessor will calculate the sum payable by you on default. This amount, often called the 'termination sum', is designed to guarantee that the lessor will cover the balance outstanding in his books on termination. It will include the following elements:

- Any loss, costs or expenses the lessor incurs in repossessing or collecting the vehicle, including court and legal costs
- All arrears of rental
- Any other amounts you are required to have paid under the contract up to the date of termination
- All future rentals that would have been payable had the lease continued to the normal end date.

These will be subject to a discount for early payment. This discount is often expressed as an annual interest rate, for example 5% per annum. This does not mean that the amount payable will be the future rentals less 5%. The 'per annum' part here is important, as it is a discounted cash flow[105] concept that means that the rental payable in twenty-four months' time will be discounted more heavily than the rental payable in 12 months' time.

As a simple example, if an annual rental of £100 is payable in 12 months' time, it will be discounted by 5%, so £95 will be payable.

The same rental payable in twenty-four months' time will be discounted by $(1.05^2 -1)$ x 100, that is, 10.25%. So £95 x 89.75%, that is £85.26, will be payable for the rental due in month twenty-four. And so on, for all future rentals.

Interest will be due on any of the above items if you pay them after the normal due date.

The rate of interest the lessor charges you on late payment may be higher than their regular rate of interest but it cannot be a randomly determined figure designed to penalise you. In legal terminology, the lessor can charge 'liquidated damages' but not a 'penalty'. The courts will not enforce a penalty and will strike it out if the matter comes to court.

Liquidated damages are an amount representing the lender's reasonable estimate of their additional cost once you have gone into default.

105 See 7.1.

Usually, you will be required to pay the termination sum within a short period and the lessor will refund an amount equal to the net proceeds he receives from the sale of the vehicle. In practice, however, where the lessor recovers and sells the vehicle promptly, you will only be charged the termination sum less the net sale proceeds of the vehicle.

On termination of the agreement you will no longer be said to be 'in legal possession' of the vehicle with the consent of the owner.

2.3.6   TAX VARIATION CLAUSES

In large transactions it is normal to see a tax variation clause, giving the lessor the right to alter the rentals (even retrospectively or after the lease has ended) in the event of tax changes.

When they calculate their lease rentals and enter into leases, lessors assume they will get certain tax benefits including capital allowances and interest relief on borrowing costs.[106] If the tax rules change during the lease, the lessor's return changes. In extremis, a lessor could find that they have made a loss on a contract solely because of changes in tax regulations.

A tax variation clause will allow the lessor to charge you more, even after the lease has ended, so that they still earn the 'net of tax return' they planned to earn when they entered into the lease. These clauses are almost always seen in master leases but are sometimes left out of single-vehicle leases.

You may feel that the lessor's tax concerns have little to do with you but this may be one of the clauses you will have most difficulty trying to alter. The lessor may take the view that they are already taking a risk on the maintenance cost and residual value of the vehicle as well as on the likelihood you will make the agreed payments. However, they may feel that taking the full burden of the risk of an adverse tax change is a risk too far.

Some lessors do not include these clauses. If yours does, and they are unwilling to remove it and this is a major issue for you, you might decide to look for a new lessor. A different strategy, however, would be to point out to the lessor that any tax change is as likely to benefit them as it is to disadvantage them and therefore you would be willing to retain the clause but wish to make it a mutual clause. So if the changes disadvantage them you will accept extra charges; if they benefit them they will reduce your payments.

Tax variation is a complex area. If your contract has a tax variation clause, mutual or not, you would be well advised to ask in advance to see an example of the calculation showing how the lessor would change your rentals. This calculation will normally take the form of a 'lease evaluation' print-out produced using a discounted cash flow program.

---

106 See 17.1.2.

There have been long, protracted, expensive court cases fought over tax variation clauses. It is important to make sure that you understand what the clause means if it appears in your agreement.

2.3.7 APPLICABLE LAW

The contract will stipulate whether the agreement is to be governed by the law in England and Wales, or that in Scotland, or by the law in some other jurisdiction. Scottish law differs in some regards from English and Welsh law in financial contracts. For example, in Scotland there is a requirement for contracts to be witnessed by two parties.

2.3.8 ARBITRATION

If you have a disagreement with your lessor you can try to resolve it amicably. The next step might be to make a complaint to the appropriate trade body, perhaps the British Vehicle Rental and Leasing Association or the Finance & Leasing Association (FLA).[107] After that you could take the dispute to court. However, the Arbitration Act 1996 provides an alternative way to resolve disputes – arbitration.

Many lease agreements allow disputes to be resolved by arbitration, often stating that the President of the BVRLA shall appoint the arbitrator. The Act covers only England and Wales: Scotland has its own procedures that are not covered in this book.

Arbitration involves you and the lessor agreeing to refer the dispute to an independent third party. The arbitrator looks at the evidence, hears the cases of the parties (who can be represented by lawyers if they wish) and makes a judgement that is binding on both parties – you cannot back out of the process and ignore the judgement if it goes against you.

Normally the costs of the arbitration will be borne by the 'loser'. However, if party A makes an offer to settle the dispute which party B rejects, and B subsequently wins the case but is awarded less than A's original offer, B will have to pay any costs arising after the offer was made.[108]

Generally, arbitration is a cheaper and quicker method of dispute resolution than going to court. The arbitrator will normally be an expert in the matter under dispute, unlike a court judge.

2.3.9 DIRECT DEBIT

Most contracts nowadays require payments to be made by direct debit. You sign a direct debit mandate to authorise the lessor to collect monies from your bank account without your further involvement. If they take the wrong amount your bank is contractually bound to refund this to you on demand. Hence the direct debiting

107 See 19.3.

108 Shall we run over that again?

system is safe for the lessee. It allows the lessor to automate their collection procedures and reduced their administration.

As lease and motor finance agreements are financial contracts, where time of payment is of the essence and where you are undertaking to pay on time, there is little reason why you should not be willing to pay on the agreed date. However, many lessees are tempted to delay the payment of their lease rentals in the same way as they delay payments to other suppliers, in order to stretch their working capital.

All finance payments are calculated on the assumption that you will pay on the due date. Pay late and you risk running up large interest charges, the suspension of maintenance services (for maintenance-inclusive contracts) or the repossession of the vehicles.

Most lessors will be reluctant to move from their insistence on direct debit payment for all but the largest clients. If you insist on paying by cheque on receipt of an invoice, you may find that the lessor loses interest in supplying you.

2.3.10 BALANCING RIGHTS

It is worthwhile mentioning that even though the standard agreement you are asked to sign may be pre-printed, it may still be negotiable. If your business is big or important enough to the lessor, you may be surprised at how much you can get them to change their standard terms. If there is something in there which is unacceptable to you, stand your ground and ask for it to be changed. And if they won't change it, there may be others out there in the market that will offer you what you want.

You will find that the agreement gives the lessor a long list of absolute rights. For example, they will want the absolute right to regard non-payment as an event of default, allowing them to terminate the agreement and repossess the vehicles. However the contract should balance the lessor's rights with those you might reasonably require.

So, for example, if the contract gives them the right to declare you are in default for doing (or not doing) something, it is reasonable for you to insist that it should also give you a period of notice in which to remedy the default.

As a fleet manager negotiating a lease, you will want these clauses watered down as much as possible to ensure that, should your company's trading situation get tough, you do not find the contract hire company arriving to repossess your vehicles.

Often, the compromise between these conflicting positions comes from the insertion of the word 'reasonable'.

So, for example, rather than accepting the lessor's clause:

> 'If, in the opinion of the lessor, there shall have been a material change in the financial situation of the lessee which may prejudice its ability to meet its obligations under this lease, then…'

You can try to replace it with:

'If, in the *reasonable* opinion of the lessor...' etc

If you can get the lessor to agree to this change, you will have taken from them the absolute right to decide when to act and replaced it with a right they can only use if they are being reasonable. If you feel that they are being unreasonable, you can challenge their reasonableness in court.

2.4 NON-STANDARD SERVICES

The rental you pay the contract hire company assumes you will use the vehicle until the contractual end date and then return it. However, during the life of the agreement you may need to ask the lessor to perform services that are not mentioned in the contract. Most contract hire companies will accommodate any reasonable request, though some will make a charge for these.

If you know in advance that you are likely to use any of the items in 2.4.1 to 2.4.5 below, it is advisable to specify them in the contract:

2.4.1 RESCHEDULING CONTRACTS

Take this scenario. You agree to enter into a three-year lease on a vehicle that will cover 60,000 miles. Half way through the lease you realise that it is only likely to cover 40,000 miles. The lessor expected to pay for servicing, repairs and tyres for 60,000 miles and to have to sell a 60,000-mile car after three years. By reducing the mileage you have given them an advantage. In theory, you are now paying too much for the lease rentals. What can you do?

Most leasing companies will allow you to reschedule the contract and reduce the rentals.

If you discover at some later stage in the agreement that the vehicle will only travel a total of 35,000 miles, they will probably reduce the rentals again at your request. However, they will not be too keen if you keep on asking for the rentals to be changed and at a certain point they will begin to talk of charging you for this service. They will not charge a lot, perhaps £75, but this means you will think twice about asking for further changes.

The better contract hire companies will proactively advise you if your vehicles are running at well under or over the contracted mileage. They will be keen for you to reschedule so as not to build up nasty shocks for either party at the end of the contract.

2.4.2 NOVATION

A novation is a legal agreement entered into between three parties that relates to an earlier contract between two of them. In a fleet context, novations often arise when an employee resigns and wishes to take their company car with them to a new employer who is willing to take over the lease. There are advantages to this arrangement; the old employer avoids an early termination charge and the new employer inherits a shorter lease.

In the novation agreement the three parties essentially agree to restart the lease as if one of the original parties was never involved in the contract and the new party had been in their place from the start of the original contract. All three parties sign the novation agreement.

Another common use for novations is where an employee moves jobs between two divisions of the same group and the old division wishes to be absolved from all responsibility for the lease and the vehicle.

All three parties have to agree to the novation. Most lessors will permit a novation to take place if they are satisfied about the creditworthiness of the new party with whom they are to have a contractual relationship.

Most lessors will levy a charge for novations: £100 is not uncommon.

2.4.3 ASSIGNMENT

Vehicle finance agreements often contain a clause denying you the right to assign any part of the agreement without the consent of the leasing company. The same clause often gives the leasing company the right to assign their rights should they so wish.

An assignment is a legal transfer of rights between two parties.

Take this situation. Your contract hire supplier tells you that its business has been sold to someone else. The owners may have sold the ordinary shares of the company or they may just have assigned the vehicles and lease contracts to the buyer. There has been a lot of consolidation in the vehicle leasing market in recent years, so this has happened to thousands of leases.

In English law, unless the contract says otherwise, a party to an agreement is allowed to assign its rights under the contract to a third party without the consent of the person with whom they originally contracted. For the assignment to be completed the person who wants to transfer away their rights (the assignor) and the person to whom they want to transfer them (the assignee) enter into an agreement (an assignment) and then notify the other party to the contract.

You may receive a notice of assignment and an accompanying letter inviting you to confirm that in future you will deal only with the assignee. It does not matter if you disagree with the assignment and refuse to sign the confirmation; you are still bound by the assignment.

Only rights can be assigned, not obligations.

If you don't like the idea that your contract with a contract hire company could end up being sold on to someone else, you could try to remove their right to do this, though in today's marketplace you might find this difficult.

2.4.4 NON-STANDARD REPORTING

All contract hire companies provide reports to their clients. At their most basic, these will include lists of vehicles soon to come off lease or soon to require an MoT.

Some suppliers will routinely produce exception reports to show you vehicles that are running at particularly high or low mileages compared with the original contract mileages.

Given that the contract hire company holds a great deal of information about your vehicles and drivers, they can produce special reports that are particularly useful to you, either routinely or on an ad hoc basis. Contract hire companies are normally happy to accommodate requests of this type, although there will come a point where they say that the requirement is so far outside their normal activities, or will require the use of so much of their internal resource, that they want you to pay for these.

Tailor-made reporting is labour intensive for the supplier, so they will levy a charge so that you are not being cross-subsidised by their other clients with less demanding requirements.

2.4.5 VE103 – VEHICLE ON HIRE CERTIFICATE FOR OVERSEAS TRAVEL

If you wish to take a leased vehicle abroad you have to obtain a certificate confirming the owner has consented.[109]

A letter from the owner is insufficient for this purpose. A special VE103 certificate is required. Only a handful of bodies in the UK (including the BVRLA – which issues a version of the VE103 called the VE103B) can issue these. The leasing company has to buy VE103s from an issuing body to give to you.

Many contract hire companies levy a small charge for this service. The better companies also provide a booklet giving the driver advice and information on driving abroad.

The history of the VE103 is quite interesting. In 1961 the United Nations adopted a resolution designed to make it more difficult for stolen hire cars to be moved across borders. Members were required to introduce a system to prove that a hirer had the owner's permission when taking a hire car abroad. The UK government introduced the VE103 to meet the requirements of this resolution.

---

109 See 16.5.

2.5 UPLIFT FOR UNAUTHORISED EXTENSION

At the end of the lease period, your contract hire agreement will require that you return the vehicle to the leasing company. Normally collection will be arranged from a location to suit your needs.

If you would like to keep the vehicle for an extra period, the contract hire company can often accommodate this.

The better companies will write to you several months before the vehicle is due to come off lease and let you know whether they would be willing to extend the contract or if they require you to return it.

You might ask, 'Why should they be willing to extend the agreement? Surely they want it back to sell so they can lease us a new vehicle for another three or four years? '

The answer is that normally they will be happy for you to continue to keep the vehicle for a period, as part of their normal culture of fitting in with the needs of their clients. You will continue to pay rentals to them, after all.

So, if this is the case, why do they insist on some vehicles being returned on the pre-agreed end-of-contract date?

There can be a number of reasons.

- The vehicle could have been expensive to maintain and they might be worried about incurring further large expense if it stays on lease.
- They might be worried you will hand the vehicle back at a time when the used vehicle market is known to be slow; for example, August or December. They will prefer to get it back on time to sell it in a buoyant month to get the best price.
- If your payment history has been less than perfect, they may want to get the vehicle back and say goodbye to you as soon as possible.

Problems arise if the contract hire company insists that the vehicle must be returned on the contracted end-date and you do not cooperate with their collection department in returning the vehicle. What happens then?

In general, they will continue to charge you rentals, perhaps with an uplift to help them feel more comfortable with the fact that you are still using the vehicle. The message they are sending you here is simple: they are not happy you have breached the agreement by continuing to use the vehicle without their consent but as they do not feel inclined to forcibly repossess the vehicle the next best thing they can do is to charge you extra to cover their additional costs and risk – and maybe to discourage you from doing it again.

2.6 CONTRACTUAL CONCESSIONS

There are a number of negotiation areas where you might be able to persuade your leasing company to alter their standard contract for your benefit.

If you do a particularly good deal with a lessor and get a stream of concessions at no cost, they may make a loss on their dealings with you. In the long run, you want a relationship with a lessor to be mutually beneficial so that they will be prepared to invest time and effort in helping you to achieve optimum management of your fleet. If you are at the bottom of their list of revenue-producing clients, this will not serve either of you.

2.6.1 POOLED MILEAGE

Pooled mileage is a common contractual concession.

Rather than charging you for excess mileage at the agreed rate (pence per mile) and giving no credit for under-mileage, the mileages of all your vehicles that have terminated in a 'pooling period' will be aggregated and compared with the aggregate of the contractual mileages for these vehicles.

If there is a net excess you will be charged for this or possibly allowed to carry ("roll") the excess miles forward into the next pooling period.

If there is a net credit (because you have driven below the contracted aggregate mileage) you will be allowed to carry this forward to the next pooling period, or possibly receive a refund.

Different contract hire companies offer different pooling calculation methods. Some give credit for under-mileage at the same pence per mile figure as they charge for over-mileage. Others give less credit for under-mileage: they argue that if one vehicle has travelled 5,000 miles in excess of the contract mileage and another has travelled 5,000 miles below the contract mileage, the reduction in sale proceeds on the high-mileage vehicle will be greater than the increase in sale proceeds on the low mileage vehicle.

The other reason is that maintenance costs tend to increase with time and mileage, so the extra miles are likely to cost relatively more in servicing and repair costs.

An example may help here:

> You lease four identical cars from a contract hire company. The leases all end on 30 September 2012, the contractual end date of the leases. By this date all four cars are due to have travelled 60,000 miles. The contract says the excess mileage charge is 16p per mile.

(See tables on page 138.)

Scenario one: no mileage pooling

Vehicle Reg:	Actual termination mileage
AA59ABC	63,000
AA59ABD	73,000
AA59ABE	54,000
AA59ABF	46,000

Vehicle Reg:	Excess miles	Excess mileage charge @ 16p per mile
	Miles	*£*
AA59ABC	3,000	480
AA59ABD	13,000	2,080
AA59ABE		
AA59ABF		
You receive an invoice for	£2,560	

Scenario two: mileage pooling

Vehicle Reg:	Excess/(shortfall) miles	Excess mileage charge @ 16p per mile
	Miles	*£*
AA59ABC	3,000	480
AA59ABD	13,000	2,080
AA59ABE	-6,000	-960
AA59ABF	-14,000	-2,240
You have a credit of	£640	

Scenario three: excess and shortfall mileages charged and credited at different rates

Vehicle Reg:	Excess/(shortfall) miles	Excess mileage charge @ 16p per mile	Shortfall mileage credit @ 12p per mile
	Miles	*£*	*£*
AA59ABC	3,000	480	
AA59ABD	13,000	2,080	
AA59ABE	-6,000		-720
AA59ABF	-14,000		-1,680
		2,560	-2,400
You will be invoiced	£160		

Your contract will set out whether it is the mileage charges or the actual mileage travelled that will be pooled. In this example the mileage charges were pooled rather than the miles travelled.

Pooling periods may be of any length but quarterly, six-monthly and annual are quite common. Annual pooling probably works best for smaller fleets and quarterly pooling for larger fleets, where many vehicles will come off lease in a given quarter.

2.6.2   EARLY TERMINATION CHARGES

Rather than allow the contract to be silent on the issue of early termination charges, you should include these in the agreement.

The simplest method is for an early settlement amount to be based on the rentals payable and the timing of the early termination during the lease.

For example, the agreement may stipulate:

- 18 months' rentals are payable for early termination in the first 12 months of the contract

- 12 months' rentals are payable for early termination during months 13-24 and

- Six rentals are payable for early termination thereafter.

This arrangement protects the contract hire company against the cost of the extra depreciation suffered by the vehicle in the early period of the lease.

Another method is to attach a schedule to the master lease agreement, setting out the percentage of the capital cost of the vehicle that is payable for early termination in every month of the contract.

A third possibility is to attach a calculation to each lease schedule, showing, for that specific vehicle, the early termination charge payable during each month of the contract.[110]

These three methods are easy for both parties to understand. Whichever method is chosen, the lessor will try to err on the side of caution in establishing the amount payable so as to minimise the risk that they will make a loss on early termination, particularly on vehicles that have suffered high levels of maintenance expenditure.

Rather than using one of these formulae, some lessors calculate early terminations using an actual cost method, also called a 'no-profit, no-loss' or 'breakeven' method.

Here the lessor calculates the balance they need in order to clear the lease from their books and this becomes the early termination amount. If you wish to use this method it is important that your agreement should specify how the calculations will be done. This is not as straightforward as it may appear because tax issues need to be considered to arrive at the true amount required by the lessor to break even.

In some cases a formula based on the number of rentals payable in future can give you a lower early termination charge than the actual cost method.

---

110 See 1.2.9.

2.6.3   FAIR WEAR AND TEAR

In requiring you to return the vehicle to the lessor in good condition, 'fair wear and tear excepted', the agreement leaves a great deal open to interpretation.

BVRLA members are encouraged to comply with the *Fair Wear and Tear Guide*.[111] However, while this publication may reduce misunderstandings, it cannot say whether you should be charged £50, £90 or £175 for a particular scratch.

To avoid disputes over small amounts of damage, some lessors insert a damage recharge waiver into their agreements. There are several ways in which this can work but the normal way is to set a level (perhaps £100) below which you will not be charged for damage to the vehicle (a 'damage waiver' limit). Damage above this amount is then charged to you in full.

It is definitely worthwhile shopping around to find the contract hire company that will give you the highest level of damage recharge costs, particularly if your current supplier charges for damage on a large number of the cars you return. Some contract hire companies are making a point of not charging unless the damage cost is rather high; £250 or even more.

2.7 CREDIT TERMS

A contract hire agreement is a finance agreement and the lessor's raw ingredient is money. The lessor has to pay for this money on a day-to-day basis.

You might be tempted to try to negotiate credit terms of 60 or 90 days for the payment of lease rentals, in the same way that you negotiate credit terms from suppliers of other services. It is very unusual for such requests to be granted by lessors but where they are, the lessor simply recalculates the rentals to take account of the payment delay.

Often there is no discussion of credit terms until the client starts to take extended credit periods that have not been agreed. If several suppliers are quoting for every car and the client is choosing the cheapest quote car by car, matters get complicated. If some of the suppliers do not realise the client expects to take a long credit period and they do not price for this, they will win the business only then to become embroiled in a long-running dispute over payment of rentals.

---

111 See 1.2.13.

112 Example assumes £12,000 vehicle, £4,000 residual value, 3+33 payment profile, 9.5% p.a. cost of funds, 2.5% p.a. margin.

An example may help to give a feel for the numbers involved.

> Say a normal monthly rental for vehicle X is £297.01, assuming payment is made monthly on the due date. If nothing else changes, the rental for the same vehicle needs to increase to £299.98 or £302.98 if the lessee is to have 30 or 60 days' credit respectively and the lessor is still to make the same return as on the original rental.

These may not seem great differences but they can account for 35% of the lessor's gross profit margin. How many other businesses can lose such an amount simply by allowing 60 days' credit to a client?

2.8 SOLE SUPPLY

Sole supply is the name of the arrangement where you agree to place all of your vehicle finance and management requirements with one supplier, perhaps a contract hire company.

There are many advantages to having a sole supply agreement. It means having only one point of contact to meet all your needs and you can develop a good working partnership with that organisation.[113] They then have the incentive to deliver a high quality proactive service and to anticipate your needs because if they fail to do so you can take away the whole of your business at once.

In contract hire, sole supply allows all of your vehicles to be grouped together for pooled mileage purposes. This is not possible if they are spread over several suppliers. This arrangement can provide you with real advantages. With two contract hire suppliers, you could find you have a large excess mileage position with one of them (which you have to pay) and a large under-mileage position with the other (without the ability to get any benefit from this). Another advantage is that sole supply gives you one set of reports to review; there is no need for you to consolidate information from several sources.

The main disadvantage of sole supply is that you may lose out on the benefits of competitive pricing. Suppliers always offer keener prices if they know they are in a competitive position, car by car.

However you can always spot check your supplier's prices against their competitors' from time to time, to keep them on their toes.

The alternatives to sole supply are dual-supply or multi-supply - having two or more suppliers.

---

113 See 2.9.

2.9 PARTNERSHIP SOURCING

The word 'partnership' in 2.8 above was used in the marketing sense that the word has acquired over the years – *working closely together* – rather than in the strict legal sense of owning a business together and sharing the profits.

Partnership Sourcing is a government-backed initiative to encourage customers and suppliers to work closely together for mutual benefit rather than employing an adversarial stance.

The Department of Business Innovation and Skills and the Confederation of British Industry run Partnership Sourcing Limited to drive forward this initiative.

Several contract hire companies have adopted the principles of the Partnership Sourcing initiative. By working with one of these you are more likely to get a tailor-made solution to your fleet needs, from a company committed to finding ways to constantly improve the way it serves you.

You can get more information from Partnership Sourcing Ltd, 4 Grosvenor Gardens, London, SW1 0DH. Phone: +44 (0)20 7824 1800. www.pslcbi.com.

2.10 EXERCISES

What is a master agreement?

In which ways might a lease provide for a rental to be modified?

What is a tax variation clause?

List eight events of default.

How might you try to water down a lessor's rights in a lease?

What is a termination sum?

How might it be calculated?

What is novation?

How does it differ from assignment?

What might happen if you wish to retain the use of a car at the end of a contract hire agreement?

What is a contractual concession?

How does pooled mileage work?

Why might your lease contain different mileage rates for over-mileage and under-mileage?

How might you be charged for early termination?

What is the normal basis for calculating damage recharges?

What are the advantages to you of sole supply?

3 CASH-FOR-CAR

3.1 CONCEPT

In concept, this is very simple: your employee gives up their company car and the company pays them more salary.

Increasing levels of car benefit tax in recent years have clearly disadvantaged many company car drivers. For some, the company car no longer represents good value because the tax they pay exceeds the cost they would incur if they simply took extra salary from their employer and acquired their own car. At the same time, some employers believe the administration of a company car fleet is an unnecessary burden. This often occurs in fleets with a high proportion of perk cars where there is no direct business benefit in having company cars, other than as a recruitment and retention tool.

In the mid-1990s American businesses operating in the UK, particularly in financial services, led a move away from company cars. They simply added an amount to their employees' salaries to compensate for the withdrawal of the car. The perk car culture is less well established in the USA than in the UK and these companies had always questioned whether they should be providing company cars. Rising levels of car benefit tax gave them the opportunity to withdraw this benefit.

When your employee takes extra salary in lieu of a company car, they fall outside the benefit-in-kind income tax regime. This saves you having to pay employer's Class 1A National Insurance contributions.[114]

Some of your employees will still need a vehicle in order to carry out their jobs. They will have to provide this themselves, using their increased salary to do so. In addition, you will have to pay them a mileage allowance for each business mile they drive.

There is some evidence that employers who have withdrawn company cars have experienced problems recruiting new staff.

---

114 See 17.1.5.

3.2 FEATURES

You can choose between several different cash-for-car arrangements.

Many employers have given their staff the option to have a car or take extra salary. Employees like to have a cash option available to them, even when they don't take it up.

A few employers have downgraded the value of the car on offer and simultaneously given their employees a cash offer to opt out of the company car. The message here is clear: 'If you want the company to provide you with a car it will do so but it will be a lower grade car than you have been used to. On the other hand, if you opt out of a company car you can take this money and get the car you really want.'

Some employers have introduced employer-sponsored personal contract purchase schemes, in which they introduce their staff to a leasing company that provides fully maintained cars.

Some have introduced employee car ownership schemes (ECOs).[115]

Some employers have stopped providing cars altogether, paid extra salary and left the employees to get on with it.

Quite often, cash-for-car schemes can generate significant savings. You need to decide who will benefit from these.

- Will the company keep the full savings? If so, you may find it hard to encourage employees to opt out of the company car.

- Will the savings be shared between the company and the employees? If so, how much will each party receive?

- Will all the savings be passed to the employees? This will encourage take-up but will not be ideal for the shareholders.

It makes sense to work with a leasing company to introduce a cash-for-car scheme. You are not going to give an employee a lump sum of thousands of pounds to buy a car. Instead, you will pay them a monthly allowance and they need a way to convert that allowance into mobility. A lease or personal contract purchase agreement allows them to do this.

If you set up such a scheme with a leasing company you can influence the deal your employees receive. In return, you may be asked to deduct the lease payments from the employees' net pay and pass these direct to the leasing company.

---

115 See 3.7.

3.3 TAX ISSUES WITH CASH-FOR-CAR

The tax rules relating to company cars are set out in Chapter 17.

Given the choice between cash or car, an employee has to decide which to take. They have to calculate their cash receipts and payments (including tax) under both scenarios. You may wish to follow the example of many employers and help your drivers to understand these calculations or do the calculations for them.

As an employer, you have to be sure that moving to a cash option is the best move for your business.

The calculations for both you and employee are complicated. Doing the sums and explaining them to a single driver is time-consuming but for a large group it is awesome. Employees have had to learn a new language. In the past few years and consultants have earned a great deal introducing these schemes to companies.

Another problem has been that, technically, car benefit charges on company cars are designed to give HM Revenue and Customs a simple method of calculating the benefit that an employee receives when they are given a company car. If employees are offered cash instead of a car, HM Revenue and Customs has the right to tax them on the value of the cash offered, even if they decide to keep the company car.

There is a danger that a badly set up cash-for-car scheme will fail to remove the car benefit tax charge from the employee. Several schemes have failed to pass HM Revenue and Customs' tests.

You should be wary of giving the funder a guarantee that you will meet your employees' payment obligations under PCP or PCH arrangements if the employees fail to do so. If you guarantee these obligations it may trigger a tax liability. However, HM Revenue and Customs has approved employee car ownership schemes[116] that feature employers' guarantees.

If your employee fails to make his or her payments under a finance arrangement, and your business pays this for them, this will be a taxable benefit.

In all cases, you are strongly advised to clear the scheme with HM Revenue and Customs.

If an employee is given cash instead of a car, there will be no car benefit tax to pay on a company car. If the employer pays a high level of mileage allowance to the employee for using his own car, a high business mileage driver can potentially make a tax saving compared with taking a company car, particularly if he drives a car emitting high levels of carbon dioxide.

---

116 ECO Schemes. See 3.7.

NATIONAL INSURANCE AND CASH-FOR-CAR

If you offer a cash allowance instead of a company car, you will save the cost of the Class 1A National Insurance contributions you would otherwise have to pay.

Any cash allowance you pay to an employee in lieu of his company car will be fully taxable in the hands of the employee at their marginal rate of tax.

You will pay Class 1 employer's National Insurance contributions on the cash allowance.

The employee will pay Class 1 NIC on the cash allowance.

MILEAGE ALLOWANCES AND CASH-FOR-CAR

You will need to pay a mileage allowance to the employee who uses his or her private vehicle on company business.

The allowance can be any amount you agree with the employee. So long as this is not above the level of HM Revenue and Customs Approved Mileage Allowance Payments (AMAP)[117] the employee will not have a tax liability on these payments. If the mileage rate paid is less than the AMAP, the employee will be able to claim the shortfall as an additional amount of tax relief in their tax return.

If the payment exceeds the AMAP levels, the excess over the AMAP level will be taxable at the employee's marginal rate.

If you wish to adopt a cash-for-car scheme, it makes sense to pay the employee the full amount of the AMAP (on which they pay no tax or National Insurance contributions) and a lower level of cash allowance (on which they pay tax and possibly Class 1 National Insurance, and on which the employer pays Class 1A National Insurance).

This could be better than paying a higher cash allowance and a lower mileage rate.

If you wish you may give employees interest-free loans of up to £5,000 to help them buy their own vehicles. There is no income tax charge on this benefit so long as the loan is fully repayable, and it is indeed repaid and not written-off. This loan can be used as a deposit towards a finance or lease agreement and it will therefore reduce the monthly payments the employee has to make to the funder/lessor. In practice, most employers prefer not to offer such a loan.

You need to give very careful consideration to setting up a cash-for-car scheme and also decide whether any savings should be kept by the company or shared with the employees.

In recent years we have seen the development of employee car ownership schemes[118] that move all employees en masse out of company cars and into cars they own themselves. These are designed to remove the car from the car benefit tax regime and provide the benefits of some of the tax savings mentioned above.

---

117 See 17.2.6.

118 See 3.7.

3.4 OPERATIONAL ISSUES

Selecting, test-driving, buying, maintaining, insuring, arranging roadside recovery and disposing of a car all involve an element of hassle.

With company cars the employer has the hassle, with many cash-for-car arrangements it is left with the employee.

As well as making complex calculations when implementing your cash-for-car scheme, you will have to make some important policy decisions.

In many company car schemes, employees are allowed to select a car from a list, according to their grade within the company. When introducing cash-for-car schemes, many employers have tried to replace these car bands with cash bands – "if you are at such-and-such a grade you are entitled to receive £400 per month instead of a company car".

They have come up against a major complication. If two employees are earning the same salary and doing the same job, and one drives a high level of business miles and one a low level, giving them the same cash allowance and the same mileage allowance will leave one substantially better off than the other. This means they will be unable to afford the same car. By and large, cash bands do not work well in cash-for-car schemes.

Another issue is that the scheme needs to set out what will happen if a driver changes job inside the organisation and therefore drives a greater or lesser mileage than was originally planned. Who will be responsible for any additional costs or get the benefit of the savings, the employer or the employee?

Motor insurance has proved problematic in some cash-for-car schemes. Employees do not build up any no-claims bonuses while driving the company's vehicles. Therefore, some employees who have opted for cash allowances have discovered that motor insurers have quoted very large premiums and have not recognised their years of accident- and claim-free motoring. The better cash-for-car schemes recognise this issue and include arrangements with the companies' insurers to continue to cover to those staff who move out of company cars. After all, the insurers still want the business and the risk has not changed.[119]

VEHICLE CHOICE AND CASH-FOR-CAR

Vehicle selection has been an issue in some schemes. Where cars are to be used in your business (for example, by salespeople) you might think it reasonable for you to be able to stipulate the type, age and quality of car that can be used by the employee on company business.

---

119 See also 1.21.19. FLEET INSURANCE AND CASH-FOR-CAR

There is a slight problem of course; the employee can reasonably say they should be able to spend their income on whatever they want.

In practice, many cash-for-car schemes limit the range of cars that employees can use on company business. Typical limitations have included: no convertibles, no sports cars, nothing over four years old and no two-door cars.

Many company car schemes are more prescriptive than this, so thousands of employees have enjoyed the newly-found freedom to choose from a much wider range of cars than they could have driven previously and many have selected quality used vehicles to stretch their cash allowance further.

Some schemes allow cash to be deducted from salary and paid by the employer directly to a leasing company. Leasing companies prefer this as it reduces their administration and gives them just one point of contact for payment.

However, for a cash-for-car scheme to work effectively, the employee needs to have a good idea of the level of business mileage they will drive – and many don't.

Calculating the cash allowance that you will pay the employee is complex. Many employers have started from the viewpoint they will pay a monthly allowance equal to the contract hire rental they had hitherto paid for the employee's car. In many cases, after this has been added to the employee's salary and taxed, the employee has not had enough left to lease a car.

If your employees use their own cars on company business, the cars must comply with health and safety legislation. The cars must be properly serviced and maintained, roadworthy and insured for business. These cars should be included in your health and safety assessments.[120]

If you wish to assist your employees to arrange their vehicle finance, perhaps on a personal contract purchase basis, you must consider whether you need to obtain a consumer credit licence from the Office of Fair Trading.

It is not difficult or expensive to obtain a CCA licence but many employers are reluctant to do so because it involves an extra piece of bureaucracy. However, if you introduce your employees to a lessor or lender for the purpose of obtaining consumer finance and you do not have a CCA licence, you will be breaking the law.

It is hard to get the Office of Fair Trading to be prescriptive about where the dividing line exists, beyond which you must obtain a licence. However, it seems that if you simply advertise a leasing company's PCP scheme on your staff notice board and invite staff to apply direct to the leasing company, you will not require a licence.

At the other extreme, if you handle all of the finance application process, passing the application forms and finance agreements to the staff for completion, getting them back, forwarding them to the leasing company and arranging for the agreements to be signed, you will be doing the same job as a broker and your business has to be licensed.

120 See Chapter 13.

Your leasing company may tell you that you do not need a CCA licence to introduce a PCP scheme but you should check the principles set out above and reach your own judgement on whether this advice is correct. If they advise you incorrectly it will be your company that is breaking the law, not theirs. If you are still in doubt you are advised to get a licence and comply with the legislation.[121]

3.5 HUMAN RESOURCES ISSUES

There is a great deal of disagreement on how employees can be encouraged to take up cash-for-car schemes. Some consultants insist that all employees can be pushed into them on the same day without any problems.

An employee's terms and conditions of employment are set out in their contract of employment. While this should be very obvious, it is remarkable how many management teams have ignored this simple fact when introducing a cash-for-car scheme. If your company's standard employment contract says you will provide the employee with such-and-such a car or its equivalent, you must do so. You cannot unilaterally withdraw this benefit.

If the contract says that you can withdraw or modify this benefit at your sole discretion, you are free to make whatever changes you wish, except that you may well have an exceptionally unhappy workforce if you impose a scheme on them.

To avoid staff dissatisfaction most employers have consulted their staff and tried to encourage them to relinquish their cars in favour of cash.

Faced with the withdrawal of their company vehicles, employees are rarely enthusiastic. Once their company cars are gone, many will have to enter into finance agreements to obtain their car, involving a commitment to pay thousands of pounds over a number of years.

In this situation employees find themselves having to think about a number of issues. If they have concerns about job security (for example, if the company has made people redundant recently, or if they have received adverse comments about their personal performance) they will be reluctant to enter into such an obligation. If they are planning to move home they may have concerns about their ability to raise a mortgage if they have to disclose several thousand pounds of additional indebtedness to potential lenders.

They will also be concerned about the financial aspects of the cash-for-car scheme. When the scheme is introduced, the employees may calculate that they benefit, or are at least not disadvantaged, by receiving a cash allowance and a mileage allowance. However, if they change jobs internally, perhaps to a role requiring them to drive fewer business miles, this may alter the economics of the cash allowance

121 See 4.2.

and make it less beneficial than if they had kept a company car. Maternity leave or illness may keep the driver off the road for several months but the lease payments on the car will still have to be made.

In some cash-for-car schemes the employer organises accident, sickness and redundancy insurance for the employees through an insurance company. It may seem strange for the employer to organise redundancy cover but it provides an important safety net that the employees may need to call on.

Salary is normally the starting point for calculating some employee benefits; particularly pension contributions (depending on whether a defined contribution or defined benefits pension scheme is in place). As a cash-for-car scheme involves adding a sum of money to the employees' salaries, most schemes specifically state that the cash allowance shall be excluded when calculating pension benefits.

Cash-for-car schemes can be good for companies that have flat grading structures as these schemes do away with overt status symbols.

3.6 ADVANTAGES AND DISADVANTAGES

Introduced correctly, cash-for-car schemes can be motivational.

They can allow the individual employee quite a lot of freedom in selecting their own vehicle. The schemes can save money for the employer and some save lot of administration.

Introduced incorrectly they can expose your drivers to financial risks and can have a demotivating effect.

They expose the company to health and safety risks that may be hard to control.

3.7 EMPLOYEE CAR OWNERSHIP SCHEMES (ECOS)

3.7.1 FEATURES

Employee car ownership schemes are employer-sponsored schemes that use credit sale agreements[122] to reduce the overall tax burden of providing cars to employees. Some organisations call these Employee Car Ownership Schemes, Employee Car Ownership Plans, Structured Leasing Schemes and Structured Car Purchase Schemes. HMRC generally calls them Employee Car Ownership Schemes.

By utilising credit sale agreements, title in the vehicle passes immediately to the employee at the inception of the agreement.

---

122 See 1.10.

Section 157 Income and Corporation Taxes Act 1988 reads as follows:

(1) Where in any year in the case of a person employed in director's or higher-paid employment, a car is made available (without any transfer of the property in it) either to himself or to others being members of his family or household, and

> *a) it is so made available by reason of his employment and it is in that year available for his or their private use; and*

> *b) the benefit of the car is not (apart from this section) chargeable to tax as the employee's income,*

> *there is to be treated as emoluments of the employment, and accordingly chargeable to income tax under Schedule E, an amount equal to whatever is the cash equivalent of that benefit in that year.*

So this piece of legislation says that if a car is made available to a director or higher-paid employee by reason of his employment he should pay income tax on the car benefit.

Now look again at the words in brackets "without any transfer of the property in it". These words mean that if there is a transfer of title in the car the employee is not subject to car benefit tax.

So if a scheme can be put together where title does pass to the employee, it will be outside the scope of car benefit tax. This does not mean that it will avoid taxation completely, just the company car benefit tax. This is the legal provision that has allowed ECO schemes to be established.

There are many hurdles to trip the unwary, however, and parts of any such scheme may cause other taxable benefits to arise.[123]

These schemes are complex to set up and require ongoing management and tax consultancy.

They can be very expensive too. Fleets with a few hundred vehicles are being asked to pay set-up consultancy fees of more than £100,000.

These schemes work by giving the employee a cash allowance and this needs to be amended if there is a change in:

- the driver's circumstances (e.g. their business and personal mileage)

- the rate of income tax they pay

- general rates of corporation tax or

- National Insurance contribution rates.

These schemes are generally unsuited to companies with high levels of staff turnover.

HM Revenue and Customs has been willing to check and pre-approve ECO schemes – a sensible precaution for any employer or supplier.

---

123 See 3.3.

These schemes are not 'tax evasion' and are perfectly acceptable to HMRC. They have even issued detailed instructions to tax inspectors on how to review these schemes[124] and a lengthy HMRC review concluded that no additional tax needs to be levied on properly-constituted ECO schemes.

You are strongly advised not to make any change to the scheme without going back to HM Revenue and Customs to get the changes approved.

There is a parallel to be drawn between an employee car ownership scheme and a final salary pension scheme. The employer takes on an open-ended risk on both.

ECOS represents perhaps 3% of the fleet market.

3.7.2   ADVANTAGES AND DISADVANTAGES

If correctly established, an employee car ownership scheme will allow an employee to have all of the advantages of a company car while their employer, and possibly also the employee, saves money.

The disadvantages are that these schemes are extremely costly to set up, require long term assistance and consultancy from external experts and require reworking every time there is a change in tax rates or rules.

If you are keen to explore these schemes, the message is the same as with any other major change: shop around, do your research, involve all interested parties within your business (purchasing, human resources, finance, legal) and only proceed when you are sure that it will not cause major problems to your business.

3.8 SALARY SACRIFICE SCHEMES

Let's consider what happens when a company leases its cars from a contract hire company. The supplier will almost definitely buy cars and other services at lower prices than the client would pay. Almost all leased cars are supplied new, and replaced every few years, so they are modern and fuel-efficient. The income tax system encourages drivers to choose low-CO_2 cars to save tax. The supplier administers all of the servicing, repairs and supplies the annual tax disk. This is an efficient, low cost and environmentally-friendly way for any company to obtain its cars.

Now let's consider an employee who doesn't have a company car but uses her own car for work. And claims a mile allowance for business mileage. Who ensures her car is regularly serviced and the MOT is up to date? Her employer has a statutory duty to ensure she is driving a safe car but who checks to ensure her car is insured (for business purposes) and is safe to be on the road?

---

124 www.hmrc.gov.uk/manuals/eimanual/eim31501.htm

The average UK car is 6.7 years old, and there's no particular reason to think that employees' own cars are any younger. Therefore these cars are generally less reliable, more likely to have breakdowns and have higher CO_2 emissions than leased cars.

Neither of these employees would be able to do their jobs without their cars. But clearly the lease car arrangement is superior for a whole range of reasons.

Over the past few years, the fleet industry has been promoting Salary Sacrifice as a solution to these issues. These schemes use tax benefits to encourage employees to stop driving their own cars for business mileage and to use leased vehicles instead.

Under these arrangements the employee agrees to forego part of their salary and their company gives them another benefit instead – the use of a leased company car.

By giving up part of their salary so their company saves the sacrificed salary and Class 1 national insurance (NIC). The company then pays for the car lease and Class 1A NIC. The employee also pays benefit in kind tax but this will be low if they choose a car with a relatively low level of CO_2. Taken together, significant amounts

of tax and NIC can be saved, though this is just one of the many advantages of salary sacrifice. The tax treatment of these schemes is described in more detail in 17.2.14

Rather than use the expression "salary sacrifice", some leasing companies have chosen unique brand names for their salary sacrifice products.

A properly set up salary sacrifice can deliver a number of benefits for a company:

- Income tax savings for their employees

- National insurance savings for both the employee and company

- A valuable recruitment and retention tool

- A reduction in their risks under health and safety and corporate manslaughter legislation.

- CO_2 emissions reductions

- Less chance the employee will call in to say their car won't start

- Assurance that employees are insured to drive for work

- An end to the practice whereby the employer pays more than necessary for work-related mileage

- Delivery of a valuable new employment benefit at no additional cost to the employer. Indeed, the employer can expect to save money

There are a number of steps you need to go through to set up a salary sacrifice scheme, including changing contracts of employment, modifying payroll systems, communicating with employees, promoting the scheme and so on.

These schemes don't have to be signed off by HM Revenue & Customs but it is definitely worthwhile seeking their clearance before introducing a scheme.

The lease for salary sacrifice vehicles will typically include all of the features the employer would normally specify on their other leased vehicle that are being driven by their company car drivers, e.g. servicing, maintenance, replacement tyres, repairs, UK emergency roadside recovery, accident management, annual road tax renewal, etc. Some schemes also include an annual check of the driver's licence.

Once the car has been delivered the employer deducts a monthly amount from the employee's gross salary to cover the cost of providing the vehicle. The employee can sacrifice as much salary they wish but this must not bring their gross salary below the national minimum wage, which from 1 October 2011 is £6.08 an hour (age 21 and over) and £4.98 an hour (age 18 to 20).

If the employee takes maternity, paternity, adoption or sick leave, the employer must legally continue to provide all employment benefits, including the salary sacrifice car.

Salary increases and pension contributions will need to be calculated based on the employee's pre-sacrifice salary (the 'notional salary'), rather than the new gross salary, so you will have to keep a record of employees' notional salaries, which may require a change to your HR and payroll systems.

If you are thinking of setting up a salary sacrifice scheme you should be prepared to commit some time and effort to getting it set up and off launched, though your leasing company will help with some aspects of this.

You will need to decide in advance how to deal with vehicle damage.

The leasing company will pay to replace worn tyres and exhausts but not if they have been damaged, and if a damaged car is returned at the end of the lease we also need to make a charge. Will you recharge these costs to the employee or will your company bear the cost?

You also need to consider what will happen when an employee leaves your company. The leasing company may wish to terminate the lease. Who will pay the early termination charges?

There are a number of risks involved in a salary sacrifice scheme:

- You invest time and effort in setting up the scheme and take-up is low

- The scheme is incorrectly set up so does not generate the expected tax and NIC benefits

- Future changes in income tax or NIC legislation, or HMRC practice, that adversely affect the economics of these schemes

- Early termination charges

- Damage recharge costs

- You don't handle the payroll issues correctly, e.g. the salary sacrifice, SSP, SMP, notional salary, paternity leave, etc.

Many of those risks can be mitigated by setting up the scheme properly. However, whilst current legislation allows salary sacrifice schemes to flourish, and there is no sign this is likely to change, no-one can be sure that this will not change at some time in the future.

THE ASTRA ZENECA CASE

A decision by the Court of Justice of the European Union[125] in July 2011 may affect some aspects of salary sacrifice schemes.

The case related to the VAT treatment of shopping vouchers that Astra Zeneca provided to employees as part its flexible employment benefits scheme. However, it appears that the judgement will also affect salary sacrifice schemes.

---

125 Case C-40/09.

In the past, HMRC has drawn a distinction between schemes where employees pay for goods and services by deduction from salary, and schemes where employees contractually agree to forego part of their salary and receive other benefits from their employer. HMRC treated the former scheme as a supply of goods and services and required the employer to account for output VAT on the transaction as it was a sale. In the latter case – salary sacrifice – HMRC did not treat the transaction as a sale so no output tax was payable.

The judgement in the Astra Zeneca case says that this distinction is incorrect; there is a supply of goods or services in both cases and therefore the employer needs to account for output tax on the consideration it receives – the deduction from salary.

As a result of this, with effect from 1 January 2012, employers will have to pay over output tax on salary sacrifice deductions.

The good news for fleet managers who operate car salary sacrifice schemes is that the HMRC guidance note[126] on the judgement says that employers should not account for output tax when cars are made available to employees. In other words, as far as the vehicle is concerned, no output VAT will be payable.

However at the time of writing it is unclear whether this applies solely to the car or if it also extends to the package of services that is normally supplied to employees in these schemes – maintenance, repairs, accident management, etc.

This judgement will only affect the VAT treatment of salary sacrifice schemes, not the affect on an employee's income tax liability.

---

126 Issued 28 July 2011: hwww.hmrc.gov.uk/briefs/vat/brief2811.htm

3.9 EXERCISES

What is cash-for-car?

Why was it introduced?

List five types of cash-for-car scheme.

What are the dangers in cash-for-car schemes?

How do the savings arise in cash-for-car schemes?

What is the AMAP?

Can an employee get tax relief on loan interest incurred in buying a car that he uses for business?

What human resource issues arise when introducing cash-for-car schemes?

What is an ECO scheme?

Why do these involve the use of a credit sale agreement?

4 CONSUMER CREDIT LEGISLATION

The Consumer Credit Act 1974 was a landmark piece of consumer protection legislation. It remains in force though it has been modified by the following legislation:

- Consumer Credit (Advertisements) Regulations 1989 which were then replaced by the Consumer Credit (Advertisements) Regulations 2004.
- Consumer Credit (Early Settlement) Regulations 2004
- Consumer Credit (Advertisements) Regulations 2010
- Consumer Credit Act 2006
- Regulations that came into force in 2010 when the UK adopted the provisions of the 2008 Consumer Credit Directive.
- The Consumer Credit (EU Directive) Regulations 2010 (SI No. 1010)
- The Consumer Credit (Total Charge for Credit) Regulations 2010 (SI No. 1011)
- The Consumer Credit (Disclosure of Information) Regulations 2010 (SI No. 1013)
- The Consumer Credit (Agreements) Regulations 2010 (SI No. 1014)
- The Consumer Credit (Advertisements) Regulations 2010 (SI No. 1970)
- The Consumer Credit (Amendment) Regulations 2010 (SI No. 1969)
- The Consumer Credit (Amendment) Regulations 2011 (SI No. 11)

You can find all of this legislation in full on the government's website.[127]

In this chapter when I refer to "the Act" I am referring to the 1974 Act and any subsequent amendments.

Consumer credit legislation is just one element of the UK's consumer protection regime. I am not sure the extent to which fleet managers will be interested in this area so I have concentrated my focus on the Consumer Credit Act. You should be aware however that at times you may also need to know about the following:

- OFT – Irresponsible Lending Guidance.
- Financial Services Authority principle of Treating Customers Fairly.
- Sale of Goods Act 1979
- Supply of Goods (Implied Terms) Act 1973

---

127 See www.legislation.gov.uk/all?title=consumer%20credit to commence search.

- Supply of Goods and Services Act 1982.
- Unfair Contract Terms Act 1977.
- The Unfair Terms in Consumer Contracts Regulations 1999.
- Consumer Protection from Unfair Trading Regulations 2008.

Consumer credit legislation is complex. This chapter only sets out a thumbnail sketch of the legislation and you are advised to take professional advice before embarking on any activity that involves consumer credit transactions.

4.1 BACKGROUND

The Consumer Credit Act sets out the rules that lenders, lessors and brokers must follow when doing business with consumers.

'Consumers' for the purpose of the Act are private individuals, sole traders and partnerships with no more than three partners. Limited liability companies are not protected by the Act.

Where agreements are governed by the Act they are called 'regulated agreements'.

The Act defines two types: – consumer credit and consumer hire.

'**Consumer credit**' transactions include loans, hire purchase, lease purchase, credit sale and personal contract purchase (PCP).

'**Consumer hire**' transactions include contract hire, finance lease, personal contract hire (PCH), operating lease and daily hire.

The Act applied to transactions up to £25,000, being the amount advanced for consumer credit transactions, or the total amount payable for consumer hire transactions. These limits were modified by the Consumer Credit (EU Directive) Regulations 2010 (CCD) which sets out to establish common rules for some aspects of consumer credit across the EU.

The CCD applies to any consumer credit agreement relating to the purchase of an asset, i.e. hire purchase, lease purchase, etc, but not to consumer hire agreements. This regulation became effective on 1 February 2011 though there were transitional arrangements and some companies implemented the rules earlier than this.

It applies to amounts financed up to £60,260, regardless of where they were signed, and gives the consumer the right to **withdraw** from a finance agreement within 14 days of signing the agreement. Once they have informed the lender, they have to pay the daily rate of interest set out on the finance agreement until they settle the finance balance which they must do within 30 days of giving notice.

The consumer also has a right to **cancel** agreements with amounts financed over £60,260 that were signed off trade premises or where there was no face-to-face contact between the retailer or lender and the customer.

High net worth customers can cancel their agreement if the balance financed on a regulated credit agreement exceeds £60,260 or the total rentals (including VAT) on a regulated hire agreement exceed £25,000. A high net worth customer is one who earns over £150,000 p.a. and/or who has net assets of at least £500,000 (excluding their home). A solicitor or chartered accountant must sign a statement confirming the customer's high net worth status.

The Consumer Credit Act is unlikely to affect most fleets except those operated by sole traders or small partnerships.

However, if you introduce your employees to a lender or contract hire company under a cash-for-car or ECO arrangement you may have to register under the Act.[128]

Lenders and lessors have to follow the strict rules of the Act before, during and at the end of the consumer finance contract. If they fail to do so their agreements will void and unenforceable, though a court has the power to make them enforceable.

The Consumer Credit Trade Association and the Office of Fair Trading both produce excellent publications covering all aspects of this legislation.

Websites:

Consumer Credit Trade Association: www.ccta.co.uk.

Office of Fair Trading: www.oft.gov.uk.[129]

4.2 LICENSING

4.2.1 WHO NEEDS A LICENCE?

Organisations must be licensed under the Act if they:

- ■ Sell goods or provide service on credit
- ■ Hire or lease out goods for more than three months
- ■ Lend money
- ■ Arrange credit for others
- ■ Offer hire purchase terms
- ■ Collect debts or purchase debts
- ■ Help people with debt problems
- ■ Advise people of, or help them find information on, their credit standing
- ■ Administer agreements without collecting debts

---

128 See 3.4.

129 You can search all of the UK government's services via www.direct.gov.uk

Even if you don't charge for your services or are non-profit making, or you don't do these activities all the time, you may still need a licence.

You are not likely to need a credit licence if you:

■ are only planning to accept credit cards issued by other businesses, or

■ only deal with limited companies.

Consumer credit licences can be obtained from the Office of Fair Trading and last for an indefinite period. The application process is quite simple.

When deciding whether to accept an application, the OFT will consider, among other things:

■ Whether the applicants are 'fit and proper persons'. For example, whether they have been convicted of deception or fraud, had a licence revoked in the past or engaged in improper behaviour. The OFT have issued guidance on how they decide whether an applicant passes this test.[130]

■ Whether the applicant has 'credit competence'. In other words, whether they are sufficiently knowledgeable and experienced to assess the creditworthiness of potential customers and the whether the business practices and procedures will be adequate to ensure the company operates lawfully.

4.2.2 DIFFERENT TYPES OF LICENCE

There are nine categories of licence:

■ consumer credit business

■ consumer hire business

■ credit brokerage

■ debt adjusting

■ debt counselling

■ debt collecting

■ debt administration

■ provision of credit information services (whether or not it includes or excludes credit repair and if on a commercial or non-commercial basis)

■ credit reference agency.

Businesses that want to 'canvass' for business 'off trade premises' require a special endorsement to their licences. However, this does not apply to consumer credit arranged in connection with the supply of goods or services

Credit brokerage means introducing a consumer to a financier. If an employer operates a PCP or ECO scheme they may require a CCA licence covering credit brokerage, though the OFT is clear that if you merely advertise other people's credit or hire, you don't need a licence.

---

130 www.oft.gov.uk/shared_oft/business_leaflets/credit_licences/oft969.pdf

Debt adjusting and counselling involve assisting a consumer in disputes with financiers.

Debt collecting is self-explanatory.

Licence holders are required to notify the OFT within 28 days if key details set out in the licence application have subsequently changed. The OFT can levy fines of up to £50,000 for failure to do so.

The Director General of Fair Trading has powers to revoke a licence if the licence-holder is found to have breached the terms of the Act or is lending irresponsibly. These are quite strong powers as it is not possible to trade in this market without a licence.

4.3 ANNUAL PERCENTAGE RATE (APR)

The Act introduced the concept of the Annual Percentage Rate of interest, or APR.

The APR is a standardised method for showing the interest rate in a loan or hire purchase transaction. It allows borrowers to compare different finance deals. The formula for the calculation is set out in the legislation and an example of the calculation is shown in 6.3.6.

It is only necessary to quote the APR on 'consumer credit' transactions, not on 'consumer hire' transactions. With a consumer hire agreement (that is, a lease or rental) it is assumed that the client will simply select between different lessors and deals by comparing the rentals quotes they are given.

It is important to note that the APR includes all fees and other charges the client may be required to pay. The lender cannot disguise a high interest rate by quoting a low APR then adding a fee.

When shown in an advert, the APR must be more prominent than any other interest rate and at least as prominent as information about the amount, number and frequency of any payments.

The introduction of the APR has ensured that advertising of interest rates does not mislead consumers. The worst example of this was the use of flat rates of interest.[131] These look low in a quote or advert and have misled many a borrower into believing they are obtaining finance at rates close to bank base rate, when in fact they are being charged double this rate.

---

131 See 6.3.2.

4.4 ADVERTISING AND THE SALES PROCESS

Consider this scenario:

> In conjunction with a contract hire company you introduce a PCP scheme for those of your staff who take a cash allowance rather than a car.
>
> Let us say you have read Section 3.4 above and decided you need a CCA licence. You apply for one and it is granted.
>
> You are pleased to have done a good deal for your staff – the Annual Percentage Rate of Interest (APR) of the PCP scheme is significantly lower than if your employees went to their banks to borrow the money to finance their cars. Flushed with pride for having done such a good deal, you pop a brief notice onto your staff notice board or intranet saying, "Cheap rate finance available to staff from ABC Contract Hire".

Marvellous – you have just broken the law.

According to the Act, an advert is any method used to inform potential borrowers that consumer credit facilities are available. Hence the notice on your staff notice board is an advert and has to comply with the detailed requirements of the Act.

The Act sets out what should appear in an advert.

Every advert needs to be in plain language so it can be understood and easy to read (or to hear if it is being broadcast). 'Small print' isn't allowed. It must show the name of the lender/lessor, as shown on the consumer credit licence.

If your advert sets out the repayment amount, other amounts payable (such as fees) or the total amount payable, it must also show the amount of credit being granted, any amount payable in advance, the amount of any payment, the timing of payments, the total amount payable and the postal address of the person or organisation providing the credit.

Your advert must include the 'representative APR' if it includes any information about any amounts payable (number, timing, amount), the total amount payable, any other charge or rate of charge, or if it states that low-price credit is available, offers a gift or incentive or intimates that it is suitable for people who might normally find it hard to get credit. Gifts are permitted but only if there are no circumstances in which the customer could be asked to return them.

The **'representative APR'** is defined as the maximum rate at which the lender/lessor reasonably expects to price two thirds of the business written as a result of the advert. It must be given more prominence than any other rate or piece of financial information on the advert and be at least 50% bigger than any other of the key information.

If you show a range of APRs, the lowest and highest must appear with equal prominence and the lower must be the rate at which you reasonably expect to write at least 10% of the business. You also need to show the representative APR.

All of this key credit information has to be shown together in one place and given equal prominence. Once again, it's not possible to put these key details into small print or require the potential customer to click through to another web-page to find more details.

The expression "Interest Free" can only be used where the total amount payable equals the price the customer would pay if they paid cash for the item.

It is not permitted to say the 'weekly equivalent' of any amount payable unless the payments are indeed to be made weekly; or that there is no deposit payable if there in fact are amounts payable in advance (e.g. fees); or if the loan has been 'pre-approved' unless that is indeed the case or the credit will be advanced without a credit check being made.

Wealthy people can opt out of the requirements of the Act by setting out a declaration saying they don't want it protection and stating their net worth, though some finance houses/lessors will not accept this.

The customer must be given a reasonable explanation of the agreement, which will need to include information about the consequences of default, and should have the opportunity to ask questions if they wish. All pre-contract information has to be provided early enough for the borrower/lessee to have time to study them in detail. If the lender decides not to proceed because they have received adverse information from a credit reference agency, this fact and the agency's details must be provided to the consumer. If the lender/lessor fails to provide this information they will only be able to enforce the agreement if they get a court order.

If the agreement has been entered into at a distance – for example, over the telephone or internet – the lender/lessor has to comply with the terms of the **Financial Services (Distance Marketing) Regulations 2004**, the full text of which is available on the government's website.[132] These say that before the agreement commences the borrower/hirer has to be sent a clear, understandable outline of the key features of the agreement, the full name and address of the lender/lessor, the total amount to be paid under the agreement, how payment should be made, and how the agreement can be ended. Once the consumer has received this they have 14 days during which they may cancel the agreement if they wish.

Consumers also have a more general set of rights under the Distance Selling Regulations 2000, which apply to the sale of all goods and services by business to individuals. Here again the consumer has the right to receive in writing; details about the supplier, the transaction, cancellation rights, the complaints procedure, after-sales service and guarantees and confirmation of their order. Delivery must take place within 30 days unless otherwise agreed and customers have 7 working days from delivery in which they are free to cancel to cancel the contract for any reason and receive a full refund. If the supplier fails to provide details of the 7 day 'cooling-off' period it is extended to three months.

---

132 www.legislation.gov.uk/uksi/2004/2095/contents/made

The Consumer Credit Agreements Regulations allow for the possibility that an agreement will be signed electronically by requiring that in this situation the lender/lessor will provide information in the signature box of the agreement setting out how the borrower/lessee can sign electronically. Whilst we are definitely in the electronic age we are not yet in an age where it is easy to prove that someone actually signed something unless they follow the old procedure of physically signing and asking someone to witness their signature. It is uncertain how lenders/lessors are going to be able to implement the idea of electronic signatures.

4.5 QUOTATIONS

If a consumer asks for details of the terms on which a lender or lessor is prepared to do consumer credit or hire business, they must be provided with this information unless they are a company, a minor or not resident in the UK.

The lender or lessor can refuse to issue a quote in the following situations:

■ If the full details of the quote are prominently displayed at the trade premises of a dealer or broker

■ If the lender/lessor has recently declined the consumer's finance application

■ If the consumer was given a similar quote from the lender/lessor within the last 28 days.

Quotes have to be delivered within a reasonable time and must be in writing.

Consumer credit (hire purchase, lease purchase, PCP) quotes must include:

■ the information set out under 'full adverts' above

■ details of any maintenance contract or insurance policy required

■ details of any excess mileage or other charges that may arise.

Consumer hire (personal contract hire, contract hire, daily hire, operating lease) quotes must include:

■ the name and address of the lessor

■ details of the vehicle

■ details of any guarantees required

■ details of the deposit

■ the period of hire

■ the frequency

■ the amount of rentals payable

■ any other amounts payable.

Consumer credit and consumer hire quotes must both show the period for which the quote is valid.

Credit brokers or other persons who are introducing lenders/lessors to potential borrowers/hirers must explain that they are an intermediary and whether they are independent or work solely for a limited number of creditors. Any fee payable to the intermediary by the debtor must be agreed in writing prior to the credit agreement commencing, and must be included in any APR calculation shown to the debtor.

4.6 THE AGREEMENT

Agreements governed by the Act are called regulated agreements. A regulated agreement must set out all of the terms of the deal, details of all of the amounts payable and a statement of the consumer's rights. It must also be legible, so printing the terms and conditions in small print in a pale colour is not acceptable.

The Act sets out a procedure for signing the agreement. If these have not been complied with the financier can only enforce the agreement by obtaining a court order.

The Act requires that the relationship between the lender/lessor and consumer should be fair. If a court finds unfairness in any part of the agreement or a related agreement, or in anything the lender/lessor has done, they have wide discretion to alter the agreement, order that the lender/lessor make payments to the consumer or reduce the burdens the agreement place on the consumer.

4.7 EARLY TERMINATION

A consumer has the right to partially or fully terminate a regulated credit agreement before the agreed contract end date. A consumer also has the right to terminate a hire agreement early. Once the consumer has confirmed their wish to early terminate the settlement will normally take place after 28 days, unless the agreement still has more than one year to run in which case it can take place a month later.

The financier has the right to terminate the agreement early if the borrower or hirer is in default.

The amount payable by the consumer on early termination must be calculated under the actuarial method.[133]

However, once the consumer has made at least half of the payments under a consumer credit agreement (other than a credit sale agreement) they have the right to notify the lender/lessor that they wish to terminate the agreement. Once they have received this written notice the lender/lessor is obliged to allow them to

---

133 See 6.5.1.

simply hand back the vehicle without any further obligation. This is known as voluntary termination.

Many consumers have exercised this right in recent years. This has cost the finance industry millions of pounds and remains one of the major unresolved problems the industry faces.

4.8 DEFAULT

The Act requires the lender/lessor to send a default notice to a consumer who is in default of the terms of a regulated agreement. They have 14 days to respond.

This notice must set out

- the nature of the breach
- what has to be done to remedy the breach
- the time limit for this
- the amount payable if the breach cannot be remedied, and
- the consequences of default.

If the contract is a conditional sale or hire purchase agreement (for example, a PCP agreement) and the consumer defaults on his obligations after making at least one third of the total payments due, the lender has to obtain a court order before he can repossess the vehicle.

When a lender or lessor sends an arrears or default notification to a consumer, it must include an information sheet produced by the OFT. These sheets are designed to help the customer understand their rights.

The lender is permitted to charge interest on late payments/default items, but only at simple interest.

If a borrower has used the credit to buy goods costing no more than £30,000, has borrowed no more than £30,260 and there is a problem with the goods or service, the borrower can ask the lender for redress.

4.9 OTHER ISSUES

If you have a complaint about any organisation that holds a consumer credit licence and are not happy with the way they have dealt with it, you can complain to the Financial Ombudsman Service (FOS).[134] See 1.21.22. You must allow at least eight weeks to pass after the licensed organisation received your complaint. The FOS has the power to award the complainant up to £100,000.

134 www.financial-ombudsman.org.uk

4.10 EXERCISES

What is an APR?

Who needs to be licensed under the CCA?

What are 'Consumers' for the purpose of the Act?

What are the transaction limits under the Act?

How might you be affected by the Act?

What are the nine categories of licence?

What is the difference between 'Consumer credit' and 'Consumer hire' transactions?

What is an APR?

You advertise 'Cheap rate finance available from ABC Contract Hire'. Is this legal?

What are the rules for early termination?

5 OPERATIONS

5.1 PURCHASING

If you don't have a fleet management arrangement or obtain your vehicles from a leasing company you have to decide how to go about acquiring your vehicles.

5.1.1 BUYING FROM DEALERS

Buying a vehicle should be a simple matter. You pop round to a dealer, take a test drive, select the specification, place your order and a few weeks later the vehicle arrives. This is how many, many smaller businesses buy their cars; they give the driver the authority to order a vehicle up to a certain price, then they leave them to select, find and order it.

There are, of course, disadvantages in this approach. Buying the occasional vehicle from a wide range of dealers means you are spreading your buying power around, rather than concentrating it.

Giving employees the authority to buy cars may not impress your auditors. You open the door to unscrupulous employees manipulating the transaction for personal gain. For example, selling their spouse's car as part of the deal and arranging a high trade-in price for that car at the cost of a lower discount on the new car.

A far better approach is to nominate one dealer for each make of vehicles and negotiate a standard discount off the manufacturer's list price.

Dealer discounts are far lower than they used to be. Not too long ago it was possible to obtain discounts approaching 20% from dealers. Those days ended in the 1990s when the starting point for calculating car benefit tax changed from engine size to list price. High list prices and high discount levels meant that drivers were paying tax on amounts that were higher than they needed to be. So manufacturers reduced their list prices and dealer margins, and dealers were unable to offer high discounts.

As a result there is now a much closer relationship between the price you pay to the dealer and the value on which the employee is taxed. Nonetheless, dealer discounts are still valuable and are normally be available on many cars; certainly all bread-and-butter fleet cars.

If you have a small fleet you can get the benefit of big fleet purchasing power by taking your cars on contract hire or asking a fleet management company to buy them for you.

5.1.2 VOLUME RELATED BONUSES

One of the unusual features of the motor industry is that fleet buyers can get three discounts; one from the dealer and two from the manufacturer.

The first type of manufacturer discount, normally called volume related bonuses or VRBs, is available to organisations that buy large numbers of vehicles, for example fleet management companies, contract hire companies and other organisations that have big vehicle fleets.

Normally, the level of VRB paid is determined by a series of thresholds: if you buy 25 units of a model, you may receive £200 per vehicle, if you buy 50 you may receive £500 and so on.

It is hard to generalise about these schemes. The amounts and thresholds vary by make and model and change from time to time.

All contract hire companies obtain dealer discounts and manufacturer VRBs and they generally reflect these in their contract hire rentals. If they left them out they would find it hard to be competitive.

In place of volume related bonuses, some manufacturers offer customer-specific 'support' targeted at individual customers. Once again, it is hard to generalise on the amounts that are available or the nature of the schemes, though it is fair to say that for the largest fleets, manufacturers will pay very large amounts to induce fleets to buy their product rather than someone else's.

Customer-specific support is available direct from the manufacturer and your contract hire or fleet management company will negotiate to obtain these on your behalf.

Manufacturers will not provide VRBs on parallel imports.[135]

Another type of manufacturer discount is normally only available to bulk buyers, which generally means leasing and fleet management companies. In return for a commitment to buy a certain number of cars in a short period, the manufacturer will provide additional 'tactical' support, which is a targeted discount that helps the manufacturer move large numbers of vehicles quickly.

5.1.3 ORDERING AND CANCELLATION

It is good practice to place your orders in writing, using your own standard order form. The form can contain signature boxes setting out details of your authorised signatories. By using your own standard form you reduce the chance of ordering the wrong vehicle.

---

135 See 5.1.6.

Nonetheless, on rare occasions, the wrong vehicle will arrive. If you can point to your order and show that the dealer did not deliver the correct car, you will not have a problem. However, if the dealer's order form was signed by the driver at the dealership and was not brought back to your office, you have a recipe for disaster.

If you decide to cancel an order you may be asked to pay a cancellation fee. A long chain of actions will have been put in motion to get you the car you require and the supplier will have gone to some expense.

If you cancel the order after the dealer has registered the vehicle, they may well be left with a vehicle built to your specification they cannot sell. Once it has been registered this becomes a used vehicle to anyone else they may sell it to.

The dealer can deregister the vehicle at the Driver and Vehicle Licensing Agency but this is a hassle and the DVLA can refuse to deregister a vehicle that has been delivered to a customer.

If you cancel an order that you have placed with a contract hire company, either the dealer or the contract hire company – or both – may charge a cancellation fee. Normally, no fee will be charged if you cancel before delivery because the price of the vehicle has increased.

The economic downturn has made manufacturers reluctant to hold large stocks, which means that order lead times have grown significantly since before the recession. The best way for your drivers to avoid disappointment is to order early.

5.1.4 BUYING NEARLY-NEW CARS

Most fleets buy only new cars.

There are various reasons for this:

- it is reassuring to have the full benefit of the manufacturer's warranty
- it is easy to find the car you are looking for
- there are no doubts about the history of the car
- you know you are the first owner
- the mileage will be negligible (and verifiably so), and
- the driver gets the nice warm feeling that comes from having a car from new.
- the driver gets exactly the specification they want

The big downside, of course, is that you pay a huge premium for a new vehicle. There are plenty of situations where a company could make do with a quality used car rather than having to buy a new one. Newly recruited or promoted employees, junior employees, staff on secondment, staff requiring a temporary car only, pool cars – in all of these situations a company could easily employ a used car rather than buy a new one.

A well-maintained twelve-month-old car is the same car as it was twelve months earlier. It has the same specification and performance, the same fuel consumption and carbon dioxide output – but it is 20-30% cheaper to buy.

You can buy a quality used vehicle at a dealer and it will come with the benefit of the dealer's warranty. Or perhaps even the manufacturer's warranty, depending on the age of the car. But if you buy from a dealer you will also be paying the dealer's mark-up.

If you buy a used car from a small dealer or a private individual you should check the provenance of the car.

There are two sources of useful information, the DVLA and HPI.

If you are unsure of the age and description of a car, you can use the DVLA's premium rate phone line (0906 185 8585) to check its first registration date and engine size.

You will also want to ensure that a finance company does not still own the car. The easiest way to do this is to check with the HPI database, maintained by Hire Purchase Information Limited.

This database exists to assist fraud detection. Finance companies register their interest in a vehicle. If a potential buyer or a finance company searches for a vehicle on the database, HPI reports if another party has already registered an interest. It then advises both parties and leaves them to sort it out.

Websites: www.hpicheck.com and www.hpi.co.uk.

The Finance and Leasing Association website also includes useful information under the heading *Don't fall victim to motor fraud!*[136]

While your financial director can make a compelling argument for using used cars on your fleet, your human resource director will have a different view. He or she will argue that a used car will be less appealing to your employees, will imply a loss of status and may affect staff motivation and recruitment.

5.1.5   BUYING USED AT AUCTION

If you buy a used car at an auction you will be buying at trade price and you can pick up some real bargains.

It's true that you need to know what you are doing if you buy at auction but if you follow some simple rules you can get all of the benefits of the low auction price whilst minimising your risk.

The first thing to understand is that there are many reasons why cars are sold at auction. Contract hire companies sell ex-lease cars at auction because of the speed and efficiency of the process. They are prepared to trade a lower price for a faster sale. Their cars are normally two to four years old, properly maintained and serviced and normally come with a full maintenance history.

Daily rental companies also sell their cars at auctions. They do so for the same reasons as contract hire companies but are normally selling much younger stock,

136 www.fla.org.uk/media/150611_fraud_checklist

almost always less than twelve months old. They get very large discounts from manufacturers and it pays them to take advantage of these discounts and turn over their fleets rapidly, rather than hold onto the cars for longer and run the risk of increased maintenance costs. In some cases they even sell before the first service is due.

Many companies sell their cars at auction because of the speed of the process. They are also attracted by the fact that they do not need to give a normal warranty if they sell a car at auction.

Whether the buyer has any comeback at all after the hammer has fallen depends on the way the seller has chosen to sell the vehicle. The different selling descriptions are shown in 5.5.2.

If they have decided to sell a vehicle *As Seen* you will have no comeback once the hammer falls.

However, if the vehicle has been described as having *No Major Mechanical Faults* or *Specified Faults*, you will have perhaps an hour to complain about any faults you have found.[137]

Daily hire and contract hire companies don't just sell their 'dog' cars at auction and keep the best for direct sale to the public. They sell a large cross-section of cars at auction because they like a quick clean sale that allows them to forget about the car once it is sold.

Historically, members of the general public would only auction their cars when they have been unable to sell them privately or unable to get a dealer to take them in part exchange. Most such cars are now probably now sold on eBay, so the average quality of cars sold by the public at auction has probably now lifted a little.

If you go to an auction to buy a vehicle it is a good idea to take with a motor engineer with experience of the make and model you are interested in. If you do not have such a person to hand, a conversation with the manager of the local garage could be helpful. If they get your servicing work they may be willing to lend you an engineer for a couple of hours. There may be a charge but it will be money well spent.

Each auction house offers a range of different types of sales, including sales for 'Top Cars' (executive cars), classic cars, sales by specific contract hire companies and general sales. You can find out what sales are coming up and what cars are available by looking at auction houses' websites.

When you go to an auction you need to have a good idea of what you are looking for and the price you want to pay. You will be lost without a copy of one of the published trade price guides, the small books the professional traders will be referring to.

---

137 These are BCA sale terms. They have different terms for online sales. Other auction houses may use different terms.

Two well-known suppliers of used car data are CAP Motor Research Limited (www.cap.co.uk) and Glass's Information Service Ltd (www.glass.co.uk).

CAP publishes the 'CAP Black Book to Used Car Prices' and Glass's publishes 'Glass's Used Car Price Guide'. Both are issued monthly and show the prices for used cars depending on their mileage and condition.

There are other guides, some available from newsagents, but motor traders do not use them.

CAP and Glass's can provide information either in book form or on electronic media, the latter being particularly useful if you are buying lots of cars as they allow you to enter the precise vehicle mileage to determine the value of the vehicle.

As these are the pre-eminent publications, we could have an interesting debate as to whether they report what's going on in the used car market or whether they drive the prices up or down.

In my view they have a significant influence on used car prices.

However, for the average fleet buyer this is probably an academic debate; on the day, in the auction hall, buyers will be trying to beat the 'book' prices and sellers will be trying to extract the highest price possible relative to book.

If you decide to bid for a particular car, you should set a limit at which you will stop bidding. Auctioneers are skilled at getting the best possible price.

If you buy at auction you have an obligation to pay for the vehicle when the hammer falls unless you have pre-agreed credit facilities with the auction house.

5.1.6   PERSONAL IMPORTS

These are advertised in the Sunday newspapers and in the back of motoring magazines. There are two broad classes of personal import – parallel and grey.

PARALLEL IMPORTS

Under European Union law you can buy a new car from any dealer in any EU country.

Within the EU, VAT is charged on most items at the time that you buy them, according to the rules of the country in which you have made the purchase.

When the VAT rules were being formulated, governments were keen to protect their tax revenues. They feared that if their citizens wanted to buy major items, they would shop around the EU for the cheapest VAT rate and import the items from there. This would deny VAT on the purchase to the country where the buyer lived and would move sales (and hence jobs) abroad.

To avoid this problem it was agreed that cars, yachts and light aircraft would have a special VAT regime: rather than VAT being payable in the country of purchase it would be payable in the country of use.

That should be the end of the matter, except that the rate of tax on cars in the EU varies widely. Manufacturers set different pre-tax prices in different countries to make sure their cars remain affordable. So bargains are there to be had if you have the time to seek them out.

A number of businesses have been set up to bring in cars from the Continent. Sadly, a number of these have gone bust and clients have lost their deposits or more.

There are some disadvantages to buying a parallel import. You can wait much longer for a right-hand drive car ordered from the Continent than from the UK. Unless you physically collect the car on the Continent, you will have to pay for delivery and customs clearance. You will also have to pay VAT on importation.

Most UK cars are now supplied with three-year warranties.[138] Typically, the first year is provided by the manufacturer, the next two by the dealer. If you buy from elsewhere in the EU you will find that you only get a one-year warranty.

Some buyers of parallel imports have reported unexpected problems when having vehicles serviced or repaired. Some have had difficulty getting parts. Others have discovered that the one-year warranty commences from the date that the vehicle is delivered by the Continental dealer to the collection agent. If it then takes weeks to get the vehicle to you, you have lost the benefit of part of your warranty.

Others have found that problems with paperwork have caused warranty repair delays.

When a car is delivered for servicing or repair the driver normally expects to be able to pick it up and drive it away that evening. When it is not available because the dealer is waiting for a phone call from the Continent confirming that the vehicle is under warranty, drivers get stranded, cars have to be rented and costs (and tempers) rise.

As these are EU-specification cars, there should be no problems on resale of the vehicle, but used car buyers are conservative and may well mark down the value of a parallel import simply because it is 'different'.

It is illegal for a manufacturer to obstruct you if you wish to buy a new car elsewhere in the EU or to make problems for you once the car is in the UK.

While the UK is outside the Eurozone, the relative attractiveness of parallel imports will always depend on the Sterling-Euro exchange rate.

So, should you buy parallel imports? You can make some good savings but against this there is a long list of disadvantages to be considered. Most contract hire companies will not buy, or finance, parallel imports.

GREY IMPORTS

With parallel imports it is possible to buy cars in the EU and make significant savings over UK prices. Which begs the question; if it is cheaper to buy on the Continent,

---

138 See 5.4.

might it not also be cheaper to buy cars elsewhere in the world and import them to the UK?

The answer is yes – these cars are called grey imports.

Most of the world drives on the right hand side of the road. The exceptions are former British possessions (India, Australia, etc) and, notably, Japan.

Cars are much cheaper in many of these countries and a big business has developed in recent years importing right-hand drive cars, particularly used cars, from these countries.

Many problems have been reported with grey imports. As some of them are not UK-specification vehicles some owners have had difficulty obtaining spare parts or insurance quotes.

Lessors are reluctant to buy them, as the law requires that they give the customer an implied warranty as to the merchantability of the vehicle. In many cases lessors have been unable to verify whether the car is fit to be driven on the UK highway. They have also had concerns about product safety under consumer protection legislation.

Finally and crucially, lessors have been worried about whether they were getting 'good title' (proper legal ownership) to the vehicle in the first place. When a vehicle has been first registered in Japan and the original registration and subsequent sale documents are in Japanese, life becomes difficult for lessors.

Sadly, there have been many thousands of well-documented cases of right-hand drive vehicles being stolen to order in Japan, transported on containers to the Middle East, fitted out with false papers and then shipped by traders to the UK for sale to unsuspecting buyers. This was the subject of a detailed BBC TV investigation.

Where a stolen vehicle is acquired the buyer cannot get good title. Many buyers of such vehicles, believing that they have got a bargain legitimately bought in Japan, have had their cars impounded by UK police. Buyers have recourse to the importer but this is of limited value if the importer cannot be found or has insufficient financial strength to repay the purchase price.

Because of these issues buyers of grey imports can expect problems selling these vehicles and insiders in the motor industry are wary of buying them.

Notwithstanding this, there are many thousands of British citizens who are absolutely delighted with their grey import vehicle.

If you choose to buy a grey import, do your research thoroughly. Check the UK model of the same vehicle and see how much it differs from the actual car you are interested in. If it is very different it may be hard to get spare parts. And make sure that you buy from a reputable dealer.

The British Independent Motor Traders Association (BIMTA) provides services for people buying imported vehicles, including a money back guarantee if the vehicle turns out to be stolen. Their website is www.bimta.com.

If you decide to import a vehicle personally you must notify HM Customs Central Processing Unit within seven days of bringing it into the country. You will have to provide them with the purchase invoice and Appendix D of form 728, available from HM Customs. They will determine the VAT payable and this must be paid within 30 days of your receipt of their notification. On payment, you will receive a customs clearance form 386. This must be sent to DVLA to register the vehicle.

5.1.7 BLOCK EXEMPTION

For decades, most manufacturers have used franchised dealers to sell cars in the UK. These are independent companies that obtain an exclusive right to market a manufacturer's cars in a limited geographic area.[139]

This arrangement gives the manufacturer the benefit of only dealing with a limited number of customers, which means they can focus training, support and marketing on their dealers.

The benefit for the dealers is that they can make their investment in the firm knowledge they will gain exclusive rights to sell the manufacturer's vehicles in their area.

Manufacturers claim this system benefits end user customers and consumers. Knowledgeable, manufacturer-trained people sell the cars. Engineers with specialist knowledge carry out the servicing. Safety recall work can be carried out efficiently.

The big disadvantage of this system is that it limits competition. Yet EU competition law is designed to maximise competition. So how is it possible for the franchised dealer system to exist?   The answer is to be found in Block Exemption.[140]

It is worthwhile looking at the history of this topic.

In 1985 motor manufacturers applied to the European Commission for permission to retain the long-standing franchised dealer system, arguing that it benefited consumers, particularly in the area of vehicle safety. They won their argument and were granted this exemption – block exemption – for ten years.

Block exemption allowed manufacturers to operate a selective and exclusive distribution system.

'Selective' means that they can select the dealers that sell their vehicles to the public.

'Exclusive' means that, once it has been granted a contract, the dealer can sell only that manufacturer's vehicles from its premises.

139 The word 'franchised', while commonly used, is probably incorrect to use here. No 'franchise' is given to the dealer to do anything in the name of the manufacturer; this is not the same as a fast-food outlet being able to trade in the name of the master franchise holder and to behave for all extents and purposes like they are the same company. Independent dealers simply enter into a contract with the manufacturer that allows them to buy and sell the manufacturer's vehicles. They trade in their own name and it is obvious to all that they are independent businesses.

140 While we call it 'block' exemption, perhaps it would be clearer to call it 'bloc' exemption, to make clear that the motor industry obtained the exemption 'en bloc'.

In practice manufacturers appoint dealers that are able to meet the quality standards they define. Block exemption allows manufacturers to refuse to sell vehicles to other dealers. Where they do appoint a dealer, they can insist the dealer provides the full product range and after sales service, operates primarily in their local area and sells that manufacturer's brand exclusively at the point of sale.

Block exemption applies to cars, light commercial vehicles and trucks – not motorcycles.

When the renewal of block exemption fell due in 1995, the European Commission felt uneasy about granting a further ten years' exemption and instead granted it for only seven years. It set two conditions for renewal; that manufacturers would keep the pre-tax price of the same vehicle across the EU within a 12% band and that they would not block or inhibit cross border sales of vehicles.

Over the ensuing seven years the EU decided that manufacturers had failed to meet either of these conditions.

To some extent it was always likely they would fail to meet the 12% price banding condition, as this requires altering prices whenever exchange rates move. In time this would mean selling vehicles at a profit in some countries and at a loss in others.

For several years there was considerable unease in the corridors of power in Brussels about the renewal of Block Exemption. Commentators said that the wide price differences across the EU provided evidence that competition was not working properly. The motor industry admitted there was a problem with the system but said it needed modification and improvement, not scrapping.

The European Commission instructed an external consultancy firm to report on the options for replacing the block exemption regime. Its report was published in December 2001 and set out the following options:

- free-for-all distribution by any organisation
- dealers being selected by manufacturers and granted exclusive territories without having to meet quality standards or targets (and being permitted to resell to other dealers)
- manufacturers appointing dealers based only on quality criteria
- manufacturers appointing dealers based on quality criteria and the dealers meeting minimum size and financial strength tests
- the existing system of dealers being allowed to sell (and prospect for sales) outside their allocated territory.

The Commission changed the block exemption system in 2002. These are the main features that were introduced, and still operate:

- manufacturers can decide between one of two distribution arrangements; either allocate exclusive territories to dealers as in the past, or supply any dealer meeting the manufacturer's quality and financial strength criteria.
- dealers are allowed to sell vehicles abroad.

- dealers are allowed to sell several manufacturers' vehicles from one site, so long as they display them separately.

- manufacturers can allow supermarkets and internet companies to sell their products.

- independent service and repair companies that meet the manufacturers' quality criteria are allowed to carry out scheduled servicing and maintenance work without invalidating the manufacturers' warranty. They need not be franchised dealers. Manufacturers are now obliged to provide all necessary technical information to allow these independent businesses to do this work.

- manufacturers are unable to limit the number of such independent servicing and repair companies in any area and these companies can work on vehicles produced by any number of manufacturers' should they so wish.

- a dealer can sub-contract service maintenance and repair work to a third party.

- the rules also contain provisions that will allow the EU to make new rules if their objectives are not achieved.

The legislation[141] was fully implemented on 1 October 2003.

It was renewed[142] largely unchanged in 2010 and reaffirmed a customer's right to choose where to go to get their car serviced. This regulation lasts until 2023.

However the commission didn't believe that block exemption was warranted for the sale of new cars and commercial vehicles so it extended existing regulations until 2013, when they will expire. Normal EU regulations[143] banning uncompetitive arrangements across all vertical markets will then take over.

The EU has confirmed that leasing companies will continue to enjoy the status of 'end users' under the legislation, so they don't have to tell the manufacturer the name of the end-user client who will be using the vehicle.

The current arrangement is designed to achieve pre-tax price harmonisation across the EU. The expression 'pre-tax' is important here. Manufacturers argue that most price distortions arise because of the different tax rates across the EU. The European Commission has no powers to direct countries to harmonise their tax rates, so all it can do is to take steps to bring pre-tax prices into line.

The Office of Fair Trading has discovered that most new cars are still being serviced at manufacturers' franchised dealers, notwithstanding the significant savings available from non-franchised outlets. The OFT believes this is because most car buyers wrongly believe their warranty will be invalidated if they use non-franchised suppliers.

A growing number of vehicle leasing and management companies now use non-franchised garages to carry out standard servicing and maintenance work.

---

141 Motor Vehicle Block Exemption Regulation
142 Motor Vehicle Block Exemption Regulation 461/2010
143 (EU) 330/2010

5.2 VEHICLE SPECIFICATION

One of the problems of allowing drivers to choose vehicles based on list price is that two vehicles with the same list price can have very different whole-life costs.

Whole-life costs will increase if you choose a vehicle specification that is unattractive to used buyers. It is hard to produce a definitive list of those items that make a difference to the used car price but these are some to be considered:

- power steering is essential on all fleet cars. It achieves better sale prices and is also much safer for your employees.
- air-conditioning is essential on large cars and is becoming important on medium-size cars.
- electric windows and metallic paint are essential on prestige cars.
- alloy wheels are essential on sporty cars.
- metallic paint looks better on most cars.

Without these, the resale value of a vehicle will be much reduced.

It was once thought that satellite navigation systems would be highly valued by buyers of used prestige cars. However, whilst it is clear that they like these systems it seems they're not prepared to pay more for them.

5.3 MAINTENANCE

5.3.1 BACKGROUND

If you have an arrangement with a contract hire or fleet management company the supplier can handle all service, maintenance and repair (SMR) issues for you and remove the administration and risk.[144]

Otherwise, you will have to arrange this yourself. Few fleets have their own servicing facilities so you will have to rely on local dealerships, fast-fits and repair shops to meet your needs.

In many small businesses the driver decides when their vehicle requires servicing or repair work. They then take it to a convenient servicing centre, get the work done, pay the bill and claim it back on their expenses.

There are many problems with this approach. The driver may forget to have their vehicle serviced or MoT tested on time or may pay too much for the work. The garage may say that a piece of work is necessary, or a part needs to be fitted, when an alternative, cheaper option could be available.[145]

---

144 See 5.3.7.

145 Sad to say, this does happen

There are no economies of scale here: the dealer might have offered you a discount if they knew they would be getting more than one car in for servicing or repair.

You have no control over the driver's actions: they may ask for work to be done simply because they feel it would be nice to have, rather than it being essential for the function or safety of the vehicle.

Many companies allow their drivers to buy their company cars when they are de-fleeted. There is a strong correlation between drivers buying their used cars and asking for additional work to be done to the car at the company's expense just before they buy it. All in all, giving your employees full control of the maintenance of their vehicles is unlikely to be in the best interests of your business.

The key elements of managing maintenance expenditure are:

■ pre- and post-event control

■ written maintenance policies

■ pre-agreed pricing structures

■ warranty claims.

5.3.2 PRE-EVENT CONTROL

Pre-event control is a management process whereby a qualified, authorised person receives a quote for servicing, maintenance or repair work and decides whether or not to accept it.

They need sufficient knowledge to be able to decide whether a piece of work is appropriate and necessary and whether the quote is reasonable.

To make the right decision they need access to the maintenance history of the vehicle.

Whether they accept or reject the quote, the details of this decision have to be recorded.

If they accept the quote they should issue an order number and record this on the maintenance record.

The maintenance record can be quite unsophisticated. In many cases, for a small fleet, it is sufficient to have a file where, for each vehicle, you simply log each event that happens to the car, showing the date, cost and details of the work. For a bigger fleet or where the needs of the business are more sophisticated, fleet software will be useful.[146]

5.3.3 POST-EVENT CONTROL

Post-event control involves checking suppliers' invoices against the maintenance record to ensure the work authorised has been correctly billed. If these tally, the invoice can be passed for payment. If they differ it should be returned to the supplier for amendment.

A surprisingly high percentage of invoices received by contract hire companies have to be rejected because they do not reflect the work that was authorised.

5.3.4 WRITTEN MAINTENANCE POLICY

A written maintenance policy is a simple set of rules issued to each driver, setting out what he or she should do if work needs to be done to their car. If the car is supplied on contract hire or subject to a fleet management arrangement, the supplier will include this information in the driver handbook they supply with the car.

In the absence of such an arrangement you can produce a similar document and issue it with the car.[147]

5.3.5 PRE-AGREED PRICING

Pre-agreed pricing can considerably reduce service, maintenance and repair costs. Discounts are there to be had in many areas of SMR but these should be pre-agreed to maximise the discount you obtain. Some servicing items, particularly those

---

146 See 16.8.
147 See 12.5.

supplied by fast-fits, are offered at an all-in list price (a 'menu' price). Otherwise the price you agree will normally be a flat discount off a published menu price.

Other items, such as repair work, are quoted on a 'parts plus labour' basis. Here the price will comprise three elements; the list price of the part, the hourly labour rate and the time to do the job. It should go without saying but you may get a great discount off the parts list price and the labour rate but unless you know how long a piece of work should take you are not controlling your costs effectively.

One valuable aspect of having a pre-agreed deal with a dealer is that you may be able to obtain the use of courtesy cars when your cars are being serviced.

5.3.6 WARRANTY CLAIMS

Manufacturing processes are now much better than in the past and a visit to a car factory is worthwhile if you want to see an object lesson in accuracy and quality. There are very few 'Monday morning' or 'Friday afternoon' cars nowadays – cars that always seem to be having problems.

It is not unusual to enjoy many years of motoring with a new car without any major problem arising. From time to time, however, components will fail and you will need to claim on the warranty.

Many new cars now come with three years' warranty. The first year is given by the manufacturer, and the following two years are normally given by the dealer.

The terms of the dealer warranty are normally identical to those of the manufacturer warranty but in the past they often tied the buyer into having their car serviced by the franchised dealer. The Office of Fair Trading has forced manufacturers to discontinue this practice. Hence non-franchised and fast-fits now advertise the fact that they can carry out warranty work.[148]

Warranties normally cover all component failure or manufacturing failure up to the full cost of rectification. They are usually limited to a maximum mileage.

The buyer of a used car enjoys the benefits of the warranty: it transfers with the car

Manufacturers usually warrant the body for corrosion for much longer than they warrant other parts of the vehicle, perhaps six to twelve years (though often less on vans than on cars). It is important to note that this cover normally refers to perforation of the body by rust (that is, rust creating a hole) rather than just the body panels showing rust marks.

Manufacturers' corrosion warranties are usually very specific. If your car's bodywork requires a repair during the warranty period, the corrosion warranty will be invalidated unless the anti-corrosion treatment has been restored.

A separate paintwork warranty may be given. This will cover the new vehicle against fading, peeling, etc, for perhaps three years.

Even once the manufacturer's (and dealer's, if any) warranty has expired, the manufacturer will usually entertain 'goodwill' claims (often called 'policy' claims).

148 See also 5.3.6.

They do so for a variety of reasons, not the least of which is they would otherwise run the risk of disgruntled customers running to the press and complaining publicly if a major and expensive failure occurred soon after the warranty expired. Hence you can normally recover a percentage of the cost of major a component failure for some time after the warranty period has ended.

This is not a haphazard process; most manufacturers have a schedule showing the percentage of the cost they will pay and how this reduces in the months after the warranty expires.

Some manufacturers now offer an extended warranty. You pay an additional premium and they cover the vehicle for four or five years and perhaps 120,000 miles. Whether these types of cover are worthwhile depends on their cost and your attitude to risk.

5.3.7 Outsourcing maintenance

One way to avoid almost every aspect of maintenance control is to obtain your vehicles on maintenance-inclusive contract hire or use a fleet management company. They employ teams of qualified maintenance controllers to carry out pre- and post-event control. These are generally time-served motor engineers who once worked at motor dealerships carrying out the repair work they are now authorising.[149]

The supplier will remind you when a service or MoT is due or overdue.

They know how long each piece of work should take and can minimise the hassle of maintaining your vehicles. Competition in this market being stiff, all of the benefits are passed back to you in a competitive rental.

You only pay extra for accidental damage or items that are not covered by the contract. For example, the cost of 'kerbed' tyres and wheels, damaged mirrors and broken aerials.

Most contract hire companies will carry out only essential safety-related work in the last few months of the contract. This is good fleet management practice for all fleets; otherwise you are wasting money.

5.3.8 Windscreens

Poorly maintained roads, low flying birds, materials falling from lorries and a myriad of other events can cause windscreens to break. Fortunately, laminated windscreens have been legally required for many years, so windscreen damage does not normally cause injury to the occupants of the vehicle. Nonetheless, windscreen damage is one of those problems that pop up from time to time to blight the poor fleet manager's life.

A whole industry has built up around the repair and replacement of windscreens, and mobile windscreen replacement vans are on call 24 hours a day. They offer an

---

149 So would it be fair to describe them as poachers turned gamekeepers? Maybe – this is how a lot of people in the industry describe them.

efficient service. These suppliers hold vast stocks of replacement units and in most cases your windscreen can be professionally replaced at an address to suit you within hours of the damage occurring.

What is not so widely known is that in many cases you do not need to replace a cracked windscreen. It can be repaired instead for less than half the cost of a replacement windscreen.

In order to be repairable, the damage to the windscreen must fall within the limits set out in the legislation. For this purpose the windscreen is split into two zones, A and B.

- Zone A is a 290mm wide area directly in front of the driver, with the boundary being the edge of the arc cleaned by the driver's windscreen wiper. Within Zone A it is OK to repair a crack no larger than 10mm in size.
- Zone B is the rest of the arc cleaned by the driver's windscreen wiper. Here it is OK to repair a crack no larger than 15mm in size.
- Zone C is the arc cleaned by the passenger's windscreen wiper, but not including anything within Zones A or B. Here it is OK to repair a crack no larger than 25mm in size.
- Zone D is any other part of the windscreen. Here it is OK to repair a crack no larger than 40mm in size.

If the crack is larger than this the windscreen has to be replaced.

The cost of repair may be less than the excess on your comprehensive motor insurance policy. In some cases the insurer will be happy to pay for the whole cost of a repair without deduction of the excess, as it saves them the cost of a replacement window.

A trained technician should carry out a windscreen repair. They will remove any dirt from the crack, then create a vacuum over the damaged area and inject resin to fill the crack. The repair is then dried using ultra violet light and polished so that it is invisible.

You should discourage drivers from putting washing up liquid in windscreen washer bottles. It leaves a residue of fatty acids that impedes vision.

In the not-too-distant future motor vehicles will come fitted with night-vision windscreens. This technology will superimpose an enhanced image of the road onto the windscreen, to help the driver see unlit or poorly lit objects on the road ahead.

5.3.9 FAST-FITS

This is the generic term for the retail workshops that specialise in fitting a range of vehicle parts, most notably tyres, brakes, batteries and shock absorbers. Less well known is that some of them can now do standard servicing on most cars.

Before asking them to do any major work, you should check that this will not invalidate the manufacturer's or dealer's warranty. It is unlikely to do so nowadays but it's worthwhile asking the question.

Many lessors and fleet management companies prefer to use fast-fits instead of conventional garages for this type of work. The service is usually provided while the driver waits, with no need for pre-booking.

These organisations carry huge stocks and the work can often be done by a mobile unit at the driver's office or home.

One of the reasons lessors like to buy from fast-fits is that prices tend to be lower than those charged by conventional garages. Partially this is because they buy in such large volumes but the main reason is that they are prepared to offer big discounts to fleets.

5.4 TYRES

THE TYRE FOR THE JOB

We all want the highest level of grip, tread life, durability and comfort from our tyres. We want them to look reasonably good and be fairly quiet on the road. We want them to drive as well on the motorway as on minor roads and just as well in summer as on winter ice and snow. And we don't want to pay too much for them either.

The bad news is that you cannot have all of these attributes in one tyre. Tyres represent a compromise, and manufacturers have to trade off one attribute against another when they design a tyre.

The manufacturer of your new car will have selected the tyres in consultation with the tyre manufacturer. The tyre they chose will represent the best option for the weight, style and power of your vehicle.

This is worthwhile bearing in mind when replacing tyres. It is best to replace a worn tyre with the same one as the manufacturer specified, even if it costs more. The expression 'You get what you pay for' applies here.

TYRE SAFETY AND THE LAW

The legal minimum tyre tread depth for cars and similar vehicles throughout the European Union is 1.6mm across a continuous band comprising the central 75% of the breadth of tread and the entire circumference of the tyre. There must be no tears, deep cuts, lumps, bulges or separation of the components of the tyre and no part of the underlying cords or ply should be visible.

For safety reasons many leasing and fleet management companies replace tyres when the tread depth reaches 2mm.

Temporary-use 'run-flat' tyres can be used if the vehicle speed does not exceed 50mph. These tyres must be supplied with clear instructions for use and state clearly that they are for temporary use only. They must be a different colour to normal tyres.

Surveys have consistently shown that a high proportion of cars are driven with dangerously worn tyre tread.

Most car tyres have tread wear indicators set at 1.6mm. These are six or more small ribs that can be found across the bottom of the main tread grooves. The tyre must be replaced when the tread surface has worn down to the ribs.

The law on driving with defective tyres is quite harsh. For all vehicles (other than goods vehicles and vehicles adapted to carry more than eight passengers) every offence carries a fine at level 4 of the standard scale set by statute, with discretionary disqualification and three penalty points. The Level 4 fine is currently £2,500. Each faulty tyre is considered as a separate offence. Having four faulty tyres can involve fines of up to £10,000.

It is illegal in the United Kingdom to mix radial ply and cross ply tyres on the same axle or to have radial ply tyres on the front axle and cross ply tyres on the rear axle. The only exception is when spare tyres are used in an emergency.

CHECKING TYRES

All tyres are worn down through normal use but you should check the pattern of wear to see if it reveals a cause that is not just mileage-related.

If the tyre is worn around the inner or outer edge, this can be caused by poor wheel alignment or suspension problems.

New tyres need to be balanced to ensure they are in correct alignment. Badly aligned tyres will cause tyres to wear more quickly than they should, which will lead to poor handling and vehicle vibration.

Tyres should always be inflated according to the manufacturer's recommendation. Inflation should be carried out when the tyres are cold as the pressure inside a tyre rises when it is hot. If the tyres are not inflated to the correct pressure the vehicle's handling, steering and braking will be affected, and this can easily lead to accidents.

All tyres have a series of codes on their sidewall, showing the maximum weight the tyre can carry, maximum speed, country of origin, size, type approval, etc.

To take a fictitious example, let us assume your tyre shows the following codes:

Great Tyres BB3 265/60R17 93W DOT 5692HTYI E41236598 Made in the UK

■ Great Tyres BB3 is the manufacturer and model name

■ 265 is the width of the tyre in mm

■ 60 is the ratio between the height and width

■ R shows this is a radial tyre

■ 17 is the diameter of the rim, in inches

■ 93 reflects the load capacity of the tyre, according to an index

■ W shows the speed rating of the tyre, according to this table:

TYRE SYMBOLS – side of tyre

SYMBOL GUIDE (NORMAL USE)		
SPEED SYMBOL	SPEED (kph)	SPEED (mph)
CAR		
S	180	111.8
T	190	118.1
U	200	124.3
H	210	130.5
V	240	149.1
W	270	167.8
Y	300	186.4
VR*	210+	130+
ZR*	240+	150+
WINTER/REINFORCED		
Q	160	99.4
R	170	105.6
VAN		
N	140	87
P	150	93.2
TRUCK		
J	100	62.1
K	110	68.4
L	120	74.6
M	130	80.8

> * Old designation
>
> * DOT denotes the tyre is type-approved by the US Department of Transport.
>
> * 5692HTYI is the manufacturer's batch number. E41236598 is the EU type approval number of the tyre.
>
> * The country of manufacture is always shown.

TYRESAFE

TyreSafe (formerly the Tyre Industry Council) is a not-for-profit organisation that promotes awareness of the importance of the dangers of defective, worn or illegal tyres. It comprises representatives from rubber manufacturers, tyre importers and retread tyre manufacturers. Its website contains valuable information on tyre safety: www.tyresafe.org.

Website: www.tyresafe.org

RETREADS

It is rare for retreaded tyres to be fitted to company cars but not at all uncommon for them to be fitted to commercial vehicles. In normal use the tread is the only part of a tyre to wear away and it makes economic and ecological sense to give a new lease of life to an otherwise good tyre by retreading it.

All retread tyres supplied in the UK must meet the requirements of BS AU 144e, the British Standard for retreaded tyres and must be marked with the Standard number. Certain foreign-made tyres may be supplied if they are of an equivalent standard.

The British Standard requires examination and inspection of retreaded tyres at all stages of production. Tyre debris, often seen at the side of motorways, does not necessarily come from retreaded tyres. Retreaded tyres are used extensively on aircraft and in motor racing.

Further information on retreads is available from the Retread Manufacturers Association.[150]

BUYING USED TYRES

There are many dangers in buying part-worn or 'second-hand' tyres. Their history is unknown; they may come from a vehicle involved in an accident or have been damaged by 'kerbing'. Repairs may not have been carried out properly, as required by British Standard BS AU 159e.

The Motor Vehicle Tyres (Safety) Regulations 1994 (as amended)[151] control the quality of part-worn tyres offered for sale. They have to have been properly examined internally and externally, and be marked with an EC approval mark, the

---

150 See 19.6.7.

151 See www.legislation.gov.uk/uksi/1994/3117/contents/made

load capacity, the maximum speed and the words 'PART-WORN' should be shown adjacent to the 'e' or 'E BS' marking in letters at least 4mm high.

The regulations make it illegal to sell a tyre with: an external cut exceeding the greater of 25mm long or 10% of the width of the tyre and deep enough to reach the ply or cord; any deterioration caused by partial failure of the structure; any ply or cord being visible; any unrepaired penetration damage; or having less than 2mm of tread anywhere on the tyre. Conviction could render the seller liable to six months imprisonment and a fine of up to £5,000.

Trading Standards officers have for a long time taken an interest in the illegal sale of part-worn tyres. They can provide information on this topic and will certainly be interested to hear from you if you suspect you have found someone selling tyres illegally. Trading Standards offices are regionalised so you will need to speak to your local office who you can find via the Trading Standards Institute website: www.tradingstandards.gov.uk

REPAIRED TYRES

There are some situations in which a punctured tyre can be repaired, and other situations where repair would be illegal.

If you take a damaged tyre to one of the national tyre companies they will tell you whether it can be legally repaired. If they repair it the work will comply with BS AU 159f, 1997: specification for repairs to tyres for motor vehicles used on the public highway. If you are uncertain whether the company is competent to carry out the repair legally, take it elsewhere for a second opinion or have a new tyre fitted.

The standard splits repairs into major and minor. Minor repairs are those carried out on the central 75% of the tyre tread. Major repairs are those carried out on the remaining (outer) 25% of the tyre tread and on the curved surface where the tread joins the sidewall. Both types of repair are legal but most tyre companies will not do a major repair because it is more complex.

It is illegal to repair a tyre with less than 1.6mm of tread remaining across the central 75% of the tread and that continues around the whole of the tyre; or if faulty repairs have already been carried out; where the tyre's overall structure has been damaged; or where the rubber is perishing, the internal cording is exposed or the beading has been damaged.

DISPOSAL OF TYRES

For most fleets, tyre disposal is a simple matter: when you have a new tyre fitted the supplier disposes of the old one. You don't have to worry about what they do with the old one because that's their business, not yours.

Right?

No, actually, that's wrong.

The EU Directive on Landfill bans the burying of whole or shredded tyres. And, crucially, you have to make sure that your tyre supplier takes this responsibility seriously. If they do not do so, you are responsible alongside them.[152]

It is extremely unlikely that a large national tyre supplier will fail in its duty to dispose of tyres legally. But many fleets use small local companies to maintain their cars, and enjoy the low prices this can bring. If you have any doubts you should check your supplier is using a registered collection agent to dispose of your tyres legally.

NEW EU REGULATIONS

The EU is introducing new rules[153] designed to improve tyre performance and provide more information for consumers. This is a long term project that will start in November 2011 which be part of UK law.

From that date tyres manufacturers have to provide the following information:

- How well the tyres grip in the wet – a scale of A (best) to G (worst)
- Their fuel efficiency – a scale of A (best) to G (worst) and
- The noise they make in use – in decibels.

The information must be available in any promotional material, on websites and on a label that must accompany the tyre at the point of sale.

The regulations apply to tyres for cars, 4x4s, vans and trucks but not to tyres designed for temporary use or some specialist tyres for classic vehicles.

5.5 DISPOSAL

5.5.1 BACKGROUND

If you obtain your vehicles on contract hire or have a fleet management arrangement, you will not have to worry about disposal. The supplier will handle this for you. In all other cases you will have direct exposure to the used car market.

The market operates in much the same way as any other market – the more you understand how it works, the better the price you will achieve.

Used car prices fluctuate according to a variety of macro and microeconomic factors. If the economy is doing badly, interest rates are high, jobs are less secure than they were and people have less money in their pockets to spend, used car prices will be relatively low. When the reverse applies used car prices will be higher.

On the supply side, if there is low supply of used cars into the market, prices will tend to rise.

---

152 See www.environment-agency.gov.uk for further information

153 EU Regulation (1222/2009)

Until mid 2007 demand had been high and the economy had been strong, so prices were relatively high. In the following eighteen months supply remained high but demand-side factors (economic downturn, buyer's concerns their jobs) made buyers wary about replacing their cars, despite falling interest rates, so used car prices fell sharply. And then in a remarkable turnaround used car prices began rising sharply again because they were in short supply.[154]

As a fleet manager you cannot do much about the state of the UK economy: when you need to sell cars you need to sell them, though when prices are low you might wish to consider extending your vehicle retention period for a few months or even a year.

When deciding what cars to put on your fleet, think about the typical used car buyer. He or she is operating on a budget. They cannot afford to buy a new car. They will be thinking about the same personal, status, fashion, practical and transport needs as buyers of new cars – they just have less to spend. They will want smaller cars because they are cheap to run or people carriers (MPVs) for family practicality.

If you are selling a significant number of large executive models you will not be selling the cars the average buyer wants to buy. The prices you achieve will reflect the fact that the used car market does not favour these models.

Most business cars enter the used car market when they are three years old. The market price for these will vary according to how long it has been since the model was introduced to the market, that is, how far it is through its life cycle. Most used cars sell for a premium for a year after introduction of the model to the used car market. Prices then flatten out for a few years. Then, towards end of model life cycle, they begin to decline. There is some evidence that this pattern can be predicted, manufacturer-by-manufacturer. That is, each manufacturer's models tend to follow the same pattern whereby they achieve a premium price, then have a stable price and finally a declining price. While this correlation may exist there is certainly no such correlation across different manufacturers in the same car size sector.

'Special editions', often launched by manufacturers to boost the sale of unpopular models nearing their replacement date, do not command a premium on resale. The colour of the car is important in the used car market. Used car buyers are a conservative lot. Cars that are brown or green will not sell as easily or achieve the same prices as cars that are red, grey, silver, black or dark blue.

It is interesting to note that most police forces now order silver cars, to make the cars more attractive to the used car market. Silver (and silver/grey) is the most fashionable colour in the UK (and indeed across the world). It accounted for 26% of new car sales in 2010, up from only 12% a decade earlier.[155]

---

154 See 5.12.4.

155 See www.smmt.co.uk/wp-content/uploads/SMMT-Motor-Industry-Facts-2011.pdf

Some believe it will soon become less fashionable, leading to a glut of old-looking used silver models and lower prices. Some manufacturers and paint suppliers believe that white with be the next 'in' colour, despite the fact that it shows all marks and looks dull after a few years. Until recently, a white upper medium sector car would sell for up to £500 less than a blue or silver model.

Blue appears to be a perennial favourite for new car buyers, accounting for 25% of sales in 2000 and still accounting for 23% in 2010.

Colours that sell well on small cars do not necessarily sell well on bigger cars. So, for example, a 'flat' (non-metallic) blue will be shunned on a big car but, if it is quite a bright blue, it will sell well on a smaller car. Similarly, a flat red looks acceptable on a smaller car. Generally speaking, the larger the car the more conservative the colour should be. A good colour can add 10% to the sale proceeds of a used car compared with a poor colour.

Unpopular colours seem to find their way into rental fleets, then quickly onto the used car market in volume, so prices fall.

The used car market values air-conditioning, electric windows, central locking and power steering.

If accessories have been removed leaving holes, or if tow bars have been fitted, the value will be marked down.

Used car prices fall in the month before the registration plate changes in March and September. This is because traders and dealers don't want to hold stocks of cars over the change date, only to find that they then look older to the buying public. Don't take delivery of a new car in February or August or you will be trying to sell it three years later in a quiet used car market. If you want to take a vehicle on contract hire in the last fortnight of February or August, you may well find that your contract hire company asks you to wait until the next month or charges a small premium for earlier delivery. There is a huge increase of supply into the used car market in March and September because of the large number of vehicles taken by dealers in part-exchange.

If you wish to sell a vehicle to a retail customer (perhaps a friend of the driver, or someone who will buy through the internet) it is a good idea to advertise it as early as possible, ideally before it becomes available. That way you can sell it as soon as it is replaced. The downside here is that it may be difficult to arrange a test-drive if your driver still needs the vehicle for work.

There are many ways to sell used vehicles and we will consider some of them here. Generally, the closer you can get to the retail buyer the higher the price achieved but selling to the retail buyer is also the slowest route and has most risk attached.

Remember that it takes up to six weeks for the DVLA to relicense a vehicle if the buyer does not have a V5C: before issuing a new one they check with the previous owner to ensure the car has not been stolen. If you dispose of a car without a V5C the dealer will have to hold the car in stock for this period before they can sell it.

During this time the car will depreciate for two further months and the buyer will have to pay for storage and other holding costs. This will be reflected in the reduced price they will be willing to pay for the car. Traders will mark down prices by up to £500 where the V5C is missing. So you should always make sure that the V5C is available when you sell a car.

5.5.2 AUCTIONS

Auctions are an efficient way to dispose of your vehicles. Generally they achieve the fastest sale at the lowest risk.

Many believe that the seller's risk ends when the hammer falls, but that will depend on the Selling Description they have chosen. Different auction houses adopt different selling descriptions. BCA uses the following terms:

- **no major mechanical faults** – vehicles sold under this description should not have any major faults in the engine, gearbox, clutch, brakes or transmission
- **specified faults** – the auctioneer will read out any particular defects notified by the seller.
- **sold as seen** (and with all its faults if any) – such vehicles are purchased as they are and with no warranties whatsoever by the seller.
- **on an engineer's report** – with the benefit of an engineer's report produced by BCA.

If the vehicle is described as having No Major Mechanical Faults or Specified Faults on the sales entry form, the purchaser has one hour after the end of the auction to complain to the BCA Branch Engineer about any mechanical defects that were not disclosed by the seller. The Branch Engineer will investigate the complaint and if it is justified the seller will be contacted with a view to negotiating an adjustment to the price to cover the cost of rectifying the fault. If the complaint is extremely serious, the branch engineer will cancel the sale.

The problem is that selling a car at auction will generally achieve the lowest prices, as most people who attend are traders who are buying for resale. They have buy stock so they can sell it but they always need to pay a low enough price to leave themselves with a margin on resale. Nonetheless, the speed and efficiency with which cars are sold at auction are impressive, and these can save you money and management time.

The auction house will advise you on valuation and setting a reserve price. All offer a collection and valeting service and will arrange prompt transfer of the sale proceeds to you. They can also for the car to be fully prepared for sale– anything from a 'smart repair'[156] to remove small dents, all the way up to comprehensive refurbishment and repair.

If possible it will be beneficial if you (or someone else who is also responsible for your fleet) can attend the auction in person to see the sale take place. This gives you

156 See 5.5.12.

a chance to see the condition of your vehicles and will help you set accurate reserve prices. By attending in person you can amend prices according to how the bidding is going on the day. If the weather is awful and only a few people have turned up to buy, you can decide there and then whether to lower your reserve prices or pull the cars out of the auction so they can be sold on another day. And if a car fails to attract the reserve price you can do a deal there and then with the final bidders.

You should discuss your sale with the auction house and take their advice on when to put your vehicles under the hammer. You want to sell your cars when the right type of buyer is in the auction hall. Auctions hold special sales targeted at different buyers.

It is probably not a good idea to tell anyone the estimated residual value you originally set on the vehicle. You may need to achieve this amount to clear your books and indeed potential bidders may actually ask you for this figure but it's not relevant to the market price and it's not in your interests to tell anyone.

Retail customers buy used vehicles from manufacturers' franchised dealers, used car supermarkets, small independent used vehicle showrooms and motor traders. Regardless of the type of operation, all dealers take in a large number of used cars in part exchange. In many cases, however, these are not of the right type or quality for them to sell on their forecourts so they have to sell them to traders or through auction houses.

Franchised dealers have had a hard time of it in recent years. They have faced pressure on margins on new vehicle sales while bigger fleets (including contract hire and fleet management companies) have kept tight control over the charges they can make for maintenance work. For many dealers, used car sales have represented one of the most profitable parts of their business. They need a ready supply of good quality stock to feed this business, so many will be happy to retail your vehicles.

Various arrangements can be made: they may simply buy your cars from you, take them on 'sale or return' or sell them for a share of the sales proceeds. One useful approach is to agree that they will display your vehicles for a fixed period of, say, 40 days. If they sell during this period they will pay you, say, 90% of the sale proceeds. If they fail to sell within 40 days they will immediately pay you CAP or Glass's Retail price less 12%. Alternatively you might agree they will retain 100% of any proceeds over a pre-agreed figure. These arrangements give them the incentive to sell the car quickly and at the best possible price.

If you arrange for a dealer to sell your vehicles you should agree the deal in writing at the outset. If the dealer sells as your agent, you will be responsible to the buyer if anything goes wrong with the vehicle. If the dealer sells as principal he has this risk.

5.5.3   PART-EXCHANGE

Part-exchange offers you an efficient way to dispose of a vehicle. You agree a purchase price for the new car and a disposal price for the old one, pay over the difference and enjoy key-for-key exchange on delivery.

Part-exchange is a good way to dispose of 'difficult' cars – those that have suffered damage, are old models or the wrong colour. The dealer will feel obliged to take the car and dispose of it as part of the price he has to pay for supplying you with a new car.

When part exchanging, it is important to ensure the net price you pay is reasonable. Consider the purchase price and the sale price separately and be happy that both are fair. Otherwise there is a risk the dealer might increase the used car price to satisfy your ego – your desire to get a great price for your car – and then reduce the discount on the new car below that which you could get elsewhere.

5.5.4   DEALER BUY-BACK

Occasionally, as part of the negotiation for the sale of a new car, a dealer may be willing to offer to buy it back at a future date. The buyback price will be expressed as an amount payable at a certain date and mileage.

You should take care with the wording of the agreement or you could create unexpected tax consequences. Tax legislation normally gives capital allowances to the person who is expected to become the ultimate owner of a vehicle. That's the reason why hire purchase works the way that it does; you are treated for tax purposes as the owner from the outset because it's extremely likely that you will become the owner at the end of the agreement.

So if you buy a car and have an agreement with the dealer that you will keep it for a few years then sell it back to them under a buy-back, you may find you have given away your right to any capital allowances.

5.5.5   DEALER PUT OPTION

If you want to avoid this problem you may wish to consider using a 'put option'. This is an agreement that gives you the right, but not the obligation, to require the dealer to buy the vehicle at a certain date and for a certain price. You will have no commitment to sell but the dealer will be obligated to buy.

While this resolves the possible capital allowance problem, in real life a dealer will be unhappy to give you a put option. It gives them the risk that you will use the put option if it gives you the highest price, or sell the vehicle elsewhere if you can get a better price. This puts them in the position of, at best, making a small profit and at worst making a large loss.

While a dealer buy-back will normally commit you to delivering up the vehicle, a put option gives you the opportunity to decide on the best course of action at the time. Hence it is more valuable for you than the dealer buyback.

The reverse of a put option is a 'call option'. Under this arrangement, one party has the right to demand that the other sells them something. They are uncommon in vehicle-related transactions and are mentioned here only for completeness.

5.5.6 DEALER SALES AGENCY

Rather than using a buy-back agreement a good approach may be to agree on day one that you will appoint the dealer as your sales agent and let him have any profits above a pre-determined amount.

In all cases you should ensure the agreement is crystal clear about what will happen if the vehicle is returned before or after the agreed date, with higher or lower mileage than planned or in below average condition.

5.5.7 DRIVER SALE

If you sell the car to the driver you can achieve a rapid sale at a price that is attractive to both parties. After all, the driver knows the car better than anyone else having driven it for some years and has an incentive to look after it if they know they will be given the opportunity to buy it.

In selling the car to the driver you will achieve a rapid sale with no disposal costs. So you can set a price that is higher than you would achieve at auction but lower than the driver would pay if they bought from a dealer. Both parties win.

When selling to an individual you have to give a warranty under Sale of Goods legislation. You can protect yourself by buying mechanical breakdown insurance and giving this to the driver with the car.

You are also legally required to ensure the vehicle is roadworthy, and that the brakes, steering, lights and tyres are in a legal condition. If you fail to do so you can be fined.

As an alternative to selling the car to the driver, you could sell it to another employee or to a friend or family member. The only disadvantage of selling to your employees arises when they start making a part-time business out of buying company vehicles and selling them on commercially. This is not only distracting from the work they should be doing, it becomes somewhat distasteful for you and other employees to see a commercial operation being carried out on former company assets. To avoid this, you can set up rules limiting the number of vehicles any employee can 'deal' in during any given period.

Unfortunately many drivers feel tempted to ask for work to be carried out on their cars before they buy them from the company. Some have dubbed this 'preconditioning', the tendency for a car to need extra work, new tyres, etc, in the few months before it is sold to the driver. Here again you can avoid this by setting out rules. The contract hire industry has a general rule that it will only pay for safety-related or legally-required work in the last three months of a contract. You could adopt such a policy for your own business.

5.5.8 RETAIL SALE

It is quite possible to set up a retail site for your used vehicles. A number of contract hire companies have set up such sites over the years and a number of companies definitely have fleets that are big enough to consider this.

To many fleets, this is the Holy Grail; achieving a sale to an end buyer at retail prices. This guarantees you the highest prices as your sale takes place at the end of the supply chain – there are no dealers or traders in the middle adding value and costs and taking a profit.

The main downside, of course, is the cost of setting up and maintaining the site. Having a site in a prime position will generate the highest turnover but by definition this will also be the most expensive location. Then there are the costs associated with moving vehicles to the site and preparing them for sale. The costs of marketing the vehicles – encouraging buyers to visit your site rather than going elsewhere – will also be considerable. These costs can be offset to some extent by the sale of add-on products at the point of sale, such as motor finance, insurance, extended warranties and so on. The retail site becomes a business in its own right, with its own risks and rewards, requiring specialist knowledge.

Most large fleets steer away from this option because they prefer to concentrate on their core business. Nonetheless, it could be a real option for some. Perhaps one day, experts in retailing used vehicles will offer an outsourcing service for larger fleets, setting up and running used vehicle sites on a consultancy basis?[157]

Even if you have your own retail site you will not be able to use it to sell all of your vehicles. Some will be unsuitable for retail sale; for example, because of their condition. Unfortunately, retail sale is the slowest method of sale. The car can sit on a retail site for weeks before it is sold and there is no guarantee it will ever sell. You will also have to make sure that you receive a cleared cheque or a banker's draft before parting with the vehicle. Otherwise you risk being left with no car and holding a worthless piece of paper.

While mechanical breakdown insurance is a good sales tool and may help avoid some costs if a vehicle breaks down after you have sold it, you still have to give a warranty to a retail buyer regarding the merchantability, fitness for purpose and description of the vehicle. Your risk remains quite high – you are still responsible if the car explodes when the customer drives it away.

5.5.9   NEWSPAPERS

The vast majority of businesses avoid selling through local newspapers because it is extremely time consuming to deal with inbound phone calls and show vehicles to potential purchasers. Here again, you have to give a warranty and retain the sale of goods risk.

5.5.10   INTERNET

The internet offers a good route for the sale of used vehicles and has grown into a major disposal route for corporate fleets. Retailing your cars delivers the highest price – but adds costs and risks

Currently, there are several organisations that can advertise used vehicles for sale on the internet, for a fee payable initially or on completion of a successful sale.

---

157 If you adopt this idea, please remember where to send the royalty cheque.

Geography is a limiting factor. If you have a potential buyer in Scotland but you are based in London you cannot afford to drive the vehicle up there in the hope that they will buy it. Internet sales work best if a picture of the actual vehicle can be posted on the site.

5.5.11 MONEY LAUNDERING

You might be wondering what possible connection there could be between this topic and the disposal of your vehicles. Unfortunately, there is a connection. Criminals need to find ways to exchange cash for other assets and the used car market provides a good place for them to do so.

The Money Laundering Regulations 2007 apply to financial institutions and professionals such as accountants and solicitors, but they also apply to anyone who regularly sells items for cash where the total payment exceeds €15,000, either as a single payment or a series of payments.

So if you routinely sell used cars to a dealer who pays cash, you may need to comply with the legislation.

To do so you need to:

- register with HMRC as 'High Value Dealer'
- keep proper records of all transactions
- have proper procedures in place to allow you to be able to prove the identity of the customer
- train your staff in these procedures
- and, if you suspect someone is trying to use your business to launder money, you are required to report them to the Serious and Organised Crime Agency (SOCA).

You can obtain more information on this topic from the HMRC website.[158]

5.5.12 PREPARATION PRIOR TO DISPOSAL

Regardless of how you choose to dispose of your vehicles you should give some thought to preparing them for sale.

If a vehicle is well-presented it will achieve a much better sale price than one that is poorly presented. A modest amount of money spent on preparing a vehicle is almost always repaid handsomely. Yet many fleets do not bother to prepare their vehicles prior to sale.

If a vehicle is in poor condition and requires a great deal of expenditure to bring it up to a reasonable condition, you may be tempted just to sell it 'as is' for a low price. However, no matter how bad the condition of the vehicle, it is always worthwhile to wash and vacuum the interior and maybe to put in an air freshener if it has been driven by a smoker. You may think the vehicle is awful but someone will buy it so it pays to present it well.

158 www.hmrc.gov.uk/mlr/getstarted/register/hvd.htm

There are several options available if you wish to improve vehicle presentation:

- ■ The lowest cost option is to have the vehicle washed and polished.
- ■ 'Smart' dent repairs can be a valuable way to enhance value at moderate cost. This is a special method of paintless dent removal. Skilled technicians gently manipulate panels back to their original shape. These repairs only work where the original paintwork is unbroken. The process does not involve repainting so it is a same day service as there is no need to wait for paint to dry between applications, as in traditional repairs. Smart repairs have become very popular.
- ■ You should only embark on expensive bodywork repairs after carefully considering the likely return on your investment.
- ■ Broken glass will reduce a car's price by perhaps £100. If you can get it repaired for less it may be worthwhile doing so.

If you use an auction, they will be able to prepare the vehicle for you.

5.5.13   EXERCISES

What are the disadvantages of selling your drivers their ex-company cars?

What is a VRB?

Why do dealers and contract hire companies charge cancellation fees?

Why might you consider taking nearly-new cars onto your fleet?

What types of companies sell cars at auction?

How should you decide what to pay for a car at auction?

What issues arise with parallel imports?

Are grey imports safe?

How do you get an imported car registered in the UK?

What is Block Exemption?

What are the rules?

What are the key elements in managing vehicle maintenance expenses?

What are pre- and post-event control?

What causes used vehicle prices to rise or fall?

What colours of used car sell well?

What are bad months in which to sell used cars?

What are the various ways to sell your ex-fleet cars?

What is a put option?

Why might you consider selling a car to the driver?

How might you best prepare a car for sale?

5.6 REPLACEMENT VEHICLE

A replacement vehicle is sometimes offered as part of a contract hire deal. You can view this as a form of insurance. If your car is off the road because of an accident or for repair, the contract hire company will provide a vehicle to cover.

You will normally be given options when you sign the agreement. For example, the contract may say the replacement vehicle will be provided after your car has been off the road for 24, 48 or 72 hours, in the event of an accident or repairs or both, with a time limit of 21, 30 or 45 days.

The contract hire company will normally obtain the replacement vehicle from a daily rental company. They are therefore taking the risk of your vehicles being off the road.

Some fleets consider that this is valuable insurance against unexpected events. Others prefer to decline this option and pay for daily hire cars as required, therefore effectively self-insuring this risk. As cars have become more reliable, fewer fleet managers have opted to include a replacement vehicle with their lease.

As with all insurance agreements, before opting to include a replacement vehicle you should weigh up the likely costs and benefits.

5.7 ROADSIDE ASSISTANCE

5.7.1 UK BREAKDOWN RECOVERY

Roadside assistance organisations will attend when your vehicle breaks down and they will try to get you started or towed to a garage.

For many years there were only two well-known providers but several players now compete in this market and this has created more price competition.

Services vary but all include the basic roadside assistance and towing service, which can be extended to cover breakdowns outside your home, transportation of the car and its occupants to the intended destination and hotel expenses.

As breakdowns are, by their very nature, unpredictable, you can view a roadside assistance service as a form of insurance. And, as with most insurances, you have the option to decide whether to buy insurance or self-insure.

Many fleets now adopt a hybrid approach; paying a roadside recovery company a small annual fee per vehicle and a second charge if they actually use the service.

Manufacturers often give away free roadside recovery with new cars, typically for twelve months. If you have breakdown recovery cover for your whole fleet – perhaps arranged by a contract hire or fleet management company – remember to take this into account so you do not pay twice.

5.7.2 INTERNATIONAL BREAKDOWN RECOVERY

A vehicle breakdown in this country is inconvenient but for many drivers a breakdown on the Continent would leave them asking 'What do I do now?' Therefore, many drivers feel that international assistance is essential because it gives them real peace of mind.

Most roadside assistance companies provide this cover, which can include payment for minor repairs, finding and collecting spare parts, emergency car hire, a replacement driver if your driver is taken ill and is unable to drive, payment of the cost of alternative travel arrangements and – that most valuable of facilities – a telephone helpline manned by English-speaking staff.

It is definitely worthwhile including repatriation of the vehicle in the cover. Otherwise, in an extreme case, the driver could have to wait around for some days until the car is repaired, or, even worse, return home while it is being repaired and then have to return to the Continent to pick it up.

International breakdown recovery cover is usually bought by the trip according to the number of days you plan to be away and the number of people travelling, though it is also possible to arrange annual cover.

Conventional travel insurance covers loss of baggage, illness, cancellation of ferry, etc and is usually offered as an add-on to an international breakdown recovery package.

5.8 FUEL MANAGEMENT

5.8.1 BACKGROUND

Fuel management is the process of minimising expenditure on fuel for your company's vehicles. It is achieved by ensuring you pay the lowest price possible, minimise fuel consumption and only pay for fuel used that has been used for legitimate purposes.

This is quite a tall order. Fortunately, tools exist to help you.

5.8.2 FUEL CARDS

Cost control is only achievable if you have information. Unfortunately, for many companies, fuel information is only available if they assemble lots of scraps of paper (petrol bills) and trying to make sense of what they say. Many thousands of UK companies have realised that this is a thankless task and that the first step to getting control of fuel expenditure is to use a fuel card.

Fuel cards are used much like credit cards. The driver presents the card at the petrol station, the cashier swipes it through a reader and the driver drives away without having to use their own cash or credit card.

The cards can be customised to ensure they are only used by a named driver or for a specific car or both. They can also be restricted to cover petrol only, petrol and oil, or a wider range of products. They ensure that your company does not pay for non-business items and that no fuel finds its way into private cars.

The cards can also be configured so that the mileage of the vehicle has to be entered at the point of sale. This is particularly valuable as it provides an excellent way for you to keep track of vehicle mileage so that routine services are not missed.

You receive one invoice (usually weekly, fortnightly or monthly) showing all fuel expenditure.

Additional reports are available – usually online – and it is through these that you take control of your fuel costs. These reports can show:

- Price paid per gallon/litre – allowing you to target those drivers who are spending more than they need
- The current mileage of each car – this can be the best tool available to you to ensure that cars are serviced at the correct time/mileage
- Mileage per gallon/litre for each vehicle – you can see which drivers are heavy on the accelerator pedal
- Exception reporting – showing where fuel consumption is varying from the norm
- Suspect transactions reporting – highlighting missing, dubious or inaccurate information
- Amounts of fuel bought, analysed by fuel company

The management information can be analysed by driver or by car.

Fuel card suppliers now offer e-billing to reduce the amount of paper even further.

Many businesses are attracted to fuel cards simply because they are an efficient way to collect all fuel expenses onto one invoice. Others find them a useful form of credit – there is no need to give staff cash advances for fuel and no need for staff to use up their personal credit card limits on company fuel.

Fuel cards work well when the company is paying for all of the driver's fuel, both business and private. The company gets one bill, pays it and that's that.

The cost control aspect of fuel management is important because car benefit taxation on private fuel can be very expensive for some employees.

If the company pays for private fuel for an employee the driver is taxed according to a charge based on the list price of the car and its engine emissions.[159] In addition, the employer pays Class 1A National Insurance contributions on the amount of these benefits (based on the same charge) and also has to pay VAT (either monthly, quarterly or annually) based on a scale of charges.[160]

Many companies have now abandoned providing free private fuel to their drivers because the tax cost to the driver has exceeded the benefit the drivers were getting. This has made a number of businesses think again about providing fuel cards. They have had to choose between either:

■ continuing to provide fuel cards and requiring the driver to submit a form analysing mileage between business and personal; or

■ discontinuing the use of fuel cards completely and requiring the driver to claim for business mileage driven.

The general view in the fleet industry is that fuel cards provide a really valuable management tool. Employees can submit a monthly form showing their total mileage and their business mileage (listed journey by journey). The company then pays the entire fuel card bill and deducts an amount from the employees' net salaries equal to the cost of the private fuel used. Each employee signs a form authorising this deduction to be made.

Fuel cards cost a small amount per vehicle per month and some fleets get them for free. The fuel card companies are amongst the biggest buyers of fuel and oil in the country. They pay slightly less than the pump price so they can afford to give free fuel cards to their larger clients because they get a rebate from the fuel company.

If you spend a large amount on fuel the fuel card company may be willing to give you a discount off the pump price too. It may not be huge, only a fraction of a penny per litre in most cases, but if you buy a lot of litres it can add up to quite a tidy sum every year. The information on your fuel card reports will capture all of the

159 See 17.2.8.
160 See 17.1.4.

expenditure by fuel brand so you can see how the rebate is calculated.

When you choose a fuel card supplier you will want it to have the widest possible coverage of the 8,900 or so garages in the UK. Sadly, there are few fuel card operators in the UK compared with, for example, the United States, where you can choose from dozens of suppliers. If you want a card that can be used on the Continent, there are fewer still. So, while in theory you can shop around, in practice you will be surprised how short your short-list will be.

Fuel cards are good but not perfect. If you want to ensure that your fuel is only going into your employee's company car, not their private car, you can have their company car registration number embossed on the card. Some garages will check to see if the number on the card corresponds with the vehicle registration number but many will not. In fact, at large motorway filling stations, it is doubtful whether the cashier would be able to see the registration number on the car even if they tried.

Similarly, if you want to record the odometer reading whenever the tank is filled you can require the mileage to be entered by the cashier. There is no incentive for the cashier to do this, and if the driver doesn't provide mileage details, the cashiers know they can just enter zero in the mileage field to complete the transaction.

Fuel cards are a valuable addition to the fleet manager's toolbox.

5.8.3 BUNKERING

When you buy fuel from a garage you are paying for many things; the fuel, the garage's overheads, their profit margin and a small amount to cover the losses they make when motorists drive off without paying.

Bunkering involves the bulk purchase of fuel delivered to your own storage facility to be pumped into your company's vehicles.

Once you have made the capital investment to set up the facility, you pay for the fuel at wholesale prices, cutting out the garage costs.

Clearly there are many issues to consider when deciding whether bunkering would make sense for your business.

Bunkering works best for organisations that have a large number of vehicles working within a small geographic area, particularly those that have to return to base most days such as service or delivery vehicles.

If you are interested in bunkering, you will have to select a suitable location in which to store the fuel tank (or tanks, if your vehicles operate on different fuels) and comply with strict safety rules.

5.9 DAILY HIRE

5 9.1 Features

Daily hire (vehicle rental) is a useful and cost-effective way to buy mobility for your staff. You get the car or van when you need it and someone else has to worry about depreciation, road tax and maintenance. Whether you need a car for a day, week or month, a lot of highly-competitive daily hire companies are waiting for your call.

It may be cheaper to use daily hire than allow your employees to use their own cars and claim mileage reimbursement. It may be safer, too, as daily hire cars rented from recognised companies are likely to be well maintained, something that you may not be able to say about your employees' own cars.[161]

Daily hire is the most visible part of the fleet industry. We are all used to seeing car rental company sites across the country and particularly at airports where several outlets can normally be found.

Some daily hire companies are manufacturer-owned, some have exclusive deals with specific manufacturers, while others will trawl the market for the best deal at the time, regardless of the manufacturer.

The daily hire market is very competitive. By shopping around you should get a good deal, with good volume discounts if you are likely to be a big user.

With so much choice around, how do you choose the right supplier?   As with all services, it's best not to choose solely on the basis of price. If you are going to rent a lot of vehicles, consider the quality of the supplier's administration, the web-tools they offer, the range of cars they can supply and the availability of one-way rentals.

You will also have to decide whether to choose a local company or one of the national networks.

The biggest names in car rental appear to be everywhere and you might be forgiven for thinking they make up the whole market. In fact, there are hundreds of smaller independent suppliers nationwide that can often offer a friendly, local, tailor-made service you might value more than a big brand name.

The national players have big networks and promote the fact that they have many branches around the country. In some cases these are owned by the 'brand' you are dealing with (the nationally recognisable name) but in many cases branches are operated by franchisees – independent companies that own the right to trade in the name of the brand owner in a particular area.

Normally that does not prove a problem but there have been occasional reports that some franchisees are less than happy to allow hirers to drop off cars at another franchisee's depot. It can take some time for them to get them back.

---

161 There are health and safety issues to consider. See Chapter 13.

A car rented from a reputable company will have been properly maintained and will be roadworthy. However, it might not be in perfect condition. Rental companies will routinely rent you a car showing bodywork damage and this will be marked on the vehicle condition report when you take delivery of the car. You (or the driver) will want to inspect the car on delivery and double-check the accuracy of the condition report in order to avoid problems later.

You should also check that the driver is insured to drive the vehicle, either covered by your motor insurance or insurance bought from the daily hire company.[162]

Generally, rental companies will deliver a car with a full tank of petrol and expect you to return it to them with a full tank. If the tank is not full they will charge to fill it up, usually at a price significantly in excess of normal pump prices.

Trading standards are investigating a fraud where a 'rental company' advertises a particularly cheap deal on the internet. The customer is told the vehicle will be delivered to them and that they have to prepay the rental in cash. Unsuspecting customers – enticed by the cheap deal – have handed over the cash only to find that the rental car and indeed the rental company don't exist. The message here is clear – only rent from a reputable company and don't pay by cash.

Let's say you need a new vehicle for your fleet. You or the driver identify a particular model that seems, on paper, to meet your requirements, but you are worried that it might not be ideal in practice.

In this situation many fleet managers would ask for a test drive then make their decision. Others will ask the dealer or manufacturer for the loan of a demonstration vehicle. Rather than using the vehicle for a few hours or days, why not rent one for a few weeks?   This will give you a much better chance to check out the vehicle in real life situations. It will not cost you that much and could help avoid an expensive mistake.

5.9.2 BVRLA KNOW WHAT YOU'RE RENTING GUIDE

The BVRLA has issued a couple of helpful publications on daily hire.

Top Tips for Rental Customers is available for free download from the BVRLA website[163] and includes sections on:

- why rent a car?
- booking a vehicle
- at the rental desk
- checking the vehicle
- during the rental
- returning the vehicle and
- top 10 tips for successful car rental

162 See 1.21.20 Self-insuring

163 www.bvrla.co.uk/Publications/Publications_full_listing.aspx

The BVRLA also produces *Know what you're renting*, a guide for hirers of light and commercial vehicles.

It is available from the BVRLA and an extract is shown here. Wording that only applies to heavy goods vehicles has been removed as these vehicles are outside the scope of this book.

The guide says:[164]

> The guide sets out what you as a customer can expect from a BVRLA Member and your responsibilities whilst in possession of the vehicle.
>
> It is the member's responsibility to ensure that:
>
> - The vehicle has undergone a satisfactory pre-rental check, any faults have been rectified and it has been valeted.
> - Servicing is up to date.
> - Any necessary mechanical repairs to the vehicle have been carried out.
> - No major body damage exists which might constitute a GV9 offence.
> - Where accessories including first aid kit, tool-kit, etc., are present, they are in good condition.
>
>   Members may provide spare wheels, however there is no legal obligation for them to do so. In the interests of safety Members often make the decision to ensure a breakdown service is provided to assist the customer rather than provide a spare wheel.
>
> - All legislation is complied with in respect of Vehicle Excise Duty, test certificates, periodic safety inspections and, in the case of HGVs, that the goods vehicle test certificate, the tachograph certificate, the speed limiter certificate and the last safety inspection report are available on request.
> - The customer is presented with a pre-rental inspection report detailing any damage present to bodywork, paintwork or vehicle interior for verification and signature of acceptance by the customer. The report should also confirm that the vehicle is in a roadworthy condition.
> - The customers' requests for necessary servicing and repair during the hire period are met with a prompt and positive response.
> - Details of the procedures to be followed in the event of breakdown or accident, including the phone number to use both during and outside working hours, are provided.
> - Make the contractual obligations of the customer clear, in easy to read and understandable language and provide a copy of the terms and conditions of the rental.
> - Provide information, preferably in the cab, on the weight (gross and axle) of the vehicle, its payload and dimensions. If the vehicle height exceeds three metres, there must be a notice in the cab, where the driver can read

it. Under The Road Vehicles (Construction and Use) (Amendment) Regulations 1997, certain vehicles and trailers over three metres in height must display a notice in the cab and be fitted with a warning device.

- Make the customer aware of the procedures for refuelling the vehicle at the end of the hire period and of any additional charges that could be incurred at the end of hire, for example, damage, road traffic offences, loss of use if the vehicle is impounded or off the road due to repairs being carried out, excessive cleaning is required or the correct hazardous waste certificate has not been obtained.

- Provide guidance on how to use ancillary equipment, for example, grabbers, tail lifts, refrigeration units, tippers, etc.

The customer has a responsibility to ensure that:

- Daily checks, relative to use, are carried out on all vehicle fluids, tyre pressures, wheel nuts, tyre tread depth and general vehicle condition.

- The vehicle is regularly cleaned.

- Driver(s) are qualified and competent to drive and operate the vehicle and are familiar with its equipment and maintenance, and are certified to carry out operational use with the vehicle where necessary.

The Member is advised of the following;

- The mileage of the vehicle on a monthly basis

- Any mechanical, electrical or other fault that requires rectification

- Any deterioration in the mechanical, electrical or body work condition of the vehicle

- Inform the Member of use of the vehicle and request permission before taking the vehicle abroad (if allowed to do so).

- The Member authorises all mechanical, electrical or body repairs prior to work being carried out.

- All replacement parts fitted to the vehicle are new and meet manufacturers' standards as per the original parts.

- The vehicle is presented for servicing and/or inspection when advised to do so by the Member.

- No alterations to the vehicle e.g., drilling holes to fit racks, telephones, radios etc, are carried out without prior written approval from the Member.

- When not being driven, the vehicle is made secure, parked in a safe location and the keys kept in a secure place.

- The Member's livery and stickers are not removed from the vehicle, without the written permission of the Member.

- The vehicle is not used for the conveyance of noxious or toxic substances, unrefrigerated foodstuffs, fish, offal or any other offensive or pungent smelling goods without prior written approval from the Member.

- No accessories in, or on, the vehicle are removed or exchanged.

- No signwriting or any form of livery is applied to the vehicle without the written permission of the Member.

- The vehicle is not overloaded and that goods are stored safely and securely within the vehicle at all times.

- Return the vehicle in a comparable state to when it was hired, subject to fair wear and tear.

- Members will use a fair wear and tear standard which will be available from them on request. In addition, the Association has fair wear and tear standards which may be adapted by the Member. Inform the Member, (if it is responsible for the O Licence inspection requirements on your behalf), of any changes which occur to the servicing/inspection requirements.

If you are responsible for insuring the vehicle while it is on rent, you must make sure the appropriate cover is in place and an insurance indemnity form (please see Annex 4) should be completed.

If the vehicle is involved in an accident you must not admit responsibility. You should get the names and addresses of everyone involved, including witnesses.

You should also:

- make the vehicle secure

- tell the police straight away if anyone is injured

- call the Member you rented the vehicle from immediately.

An accident report form must be filled in and sent to the Member as soon as practically possible.

5.9.3 Daily hire brokers

If you want to hire a car for a short period you might decide to approach one of the local or national car rental companies direct. Alternatively, you might decide to approach one of the organisations that operate as intermediaries between hirers and car hire companies, and ask them to arrange the car hire for you. There are a number of intermediaries or brokers in this market. Many leasing companies operate as daily hire brokers; they do so in order to provide a 'one-stop-shop' for their clients' mobility needs. There are also a number of brokers who are independent of the leasing companies.

There are clearly some advantages in using a broker. The most obvious one is price; the broker can shop around and find the cheapest price for you, saving you the need to do so. A less obvious advantage is that a broker can gain access to the combined rental fleets and branch networks of many car hire companies, so if you want a particular vehicle at a particular time and a particular place, they are more likely to be able to obtain this than any single daily hire company. To put this into perspective the largest UK daily hire company operates 50,000 vehicles from 300 branches but a broker can give you simultaneous access to many daily hire companies, more than 100,000 vehicles and more than 1,000 branches. So going via a broker can make good operational sense.

This comes at a cost, of course; the broker has to make a profit. Yet in many cases this profit will come from the discounts the broker has negotiated with the daily hire companies, which are based on the broker's huge order volumes and which would not be available to any but the largest organisations. So, in fact, going via a broker could save you money, though as in all areas of fleet you should shop around, compare prices and decide which option works best for you.

There isn't much margin for a broker in an individual car hire booking. After all, the average booking is only for a few days and the rental is not going to be a huge amount. Therefore the broker has to administer the booking in the most cost-effective way possible, which means that many of these companies use very slick IT systems that match the client's booking with the car hire company's vehicles whilst also finding the cheapest solution for you.

5.9.4   ISSUES WITH DAILY HIRE

The relationship between the daily hire industry and motor manufacturers is interesting.

It is well known that there is much more vehicle manufacturing capacity in the world than the market requires, yet manufacturers seem reluctant to close down factories. This may be because they want to be able to meet peak demand, or because of union issues or whatever. Perhaps it doesn't even matter. The key point is that we produce too many cars and vans so manufacturers have to come up with all manner of marketing strategies to encourage us to buy them.

The problem, of course, is that manufacturers only make new cars. By the time a car has sat around in a field for six months they still want to sell it to us as a new car. There would be good demand for that used car in the used car market – at an auction, say – but manufacturers would not dare to put zero mileage cars into public auctions in big numbers. If it became public knowledge that large numbers of 'very nearly new' cars were available at 'very nearly new' mileages and still within their warranty mileage, the public would flock in droves to buy them and the retail market would collapse.

Yet the manufacturers do something very similar to this – they sell these cars to daily hire companies at huge discounts. The only proviso is that the hire companies have to hold on to the cars for a minimum period, perhaps four or six months. At the end of that period they are allowed to sell them. And they do sell them, often for prices close to or more than they paid in the first place. This means the rental companies suffer little or no depreciation on the cars they sell.

Fortunately, most manufacturers limit the number of vehicles they will put into the market in this way, in order to protect residual values.

By moving large numbers of cars through the daily hire market you might say the manufacturers manage to produce second-hand cars. And this is why most of the vehicles available on hire from daily hire companies are new, low mileage models.

Is this arrangement fair? Yes, but there are losers.

Prices fall when large numbers of nearly new cars are dumped on the used car market in this way. If a six month old car sells for 72% of its list price, a nine month old car has to sell for less, as does a year-old car and so on, right the way down to the three-year old car you are going to sell from your fleet. In other words, the knock-on effect of this approach is that residuals fall.

There are many who think the situation would be improved if manufacturers could shorten their supply cycles so cars could be manufactured to order within days, not months. Then they would not need to keep fields full of cars or 'manufacture' used cars.

The issue of manufacturers making too many cars tends to come and go in cycles. During the downturn of 2009/10 manufacturers chose to cut production rather than filling up fields with cars and this eventually had a very positive effect on used car prices. Fleet managers, however, were complaining that they had to wait for four months to order new cars because the manufacturers had such little stock available. It is, in truth, very difficult for manufacturers to balance supply and demand so the symbiotic relationship they have developed with the rental sector has been good for them both.

5.10 PARKING FINES

It's quite simple really: you park illegally, the local authority pops a ticket on your windscreen and you pay it. In most cases, if you don't pay within a certain period or if they have to send you a reminder, the fine increases.

So the first thing to do is to ensure your company car rules set out clearly that it is the employee's responsibility to pay parking fines.

If you take vehicles on lease or contract hire, the parking fine notices will be sent to the registered keeper, normally the contract hire company. They will forward the bill to you to pay. You will then normally pass it to the driver to pay. Therefore, it may take some time from the date the contract hire company receives the notice until it gets into the hands of the driver. So the message to the driver should be clear; pay these fines promptly after the fixed penalty notice has been placed on your windscreen.

If a reminder is then sent to the contract hire company because the notice has not been paid, they will normally pay the bill and recharge it to you. By paying promptly they ensure that the matter does not get more serious. No one wants summonses to start arriving. They will recharge the payment to you and normally add an administration charge. These vary across contract hire companies but £25 is not uncommon.

Local councils are expected to issue parking fine notices within six months of the date of the offence. This is not a statutory provision but has been required since the case of Davies v Royal Borough of Kensington and Chelsea. In this case, held before the Parking Adjudicator, it was decided that it is unfair to the driver or owner if there has been a long delay in notification, because this makes it more difficult for the case to be defended.

New regulations governing parking enforcement by local authorities took effect in 2008, under powers in the Traffic Management Act 2004.

There are now 'lesser offences' and 'serious offences', and the maximum fines are:

	Serious offence	Lesser offence
Inside London	£130	£80
Outside London	£80	£50

A 50% discount applies for prompt payment and fines can now be imposed for double parking. Once the enforcement officer starts to write the penalty notice it can be served by post if it was not possible to put the ticket on the window. In most cases councils will not be allowed to use wheel clamping within 30 minutes of the offence taking place, but they can do so if the offence was caused by a persistent offender.

5.11 DRIVING OFFENCES

5.11.1 SPEEDING FINES AND TRAFFIC LIGHT OFFENCES

The bad news is that each year around 1.1 million motorists are prosecuted for speeding offences that are recorded on speed or traffic light cameras.[165]

The good news is that the proliferation of cameras across the country has reduced the number accidents on the roads; 100 lives a year according to the Department for Transport. Local authorities discovered that these cameras have the twin benefits of reducing accidents and giving a 500% return on investment in the first year. Hence they could not put them in fast enough.

Once your car has been snapped, the film is removed from the camera and processed. (Except in the case of the new digital cameras where the image is sent immediately to the central processing station).

165 Source: RAC Foundation

Within a few days, you will receive a letter asking for details of the driver of the vehicle. This is the Notice of Intended Prosecution.[166]

At one stage there was some suggestion that you need not provide details of the driver because it would breach your human rights to require you to incriminate someone. This issue was tested in court[167] and ultimately the Privy Council decided that there is no breach of human rights involved here. It is now an offence to fail to provide this information.[168]

If a company refuses to name the driver, it can be prosecuted for failing to disclose this information.

The normal procedure therefore is for the company to return the form giving information about the driver. The driver then receives a Notice of Intended Prosecution and in due course they are prosecuted.

If your cars are leased or on contract hire, the registered keeper will receive the Notice of Intended Prosecution and advise the authorities the vehicle is on lease to you.

There are different types of speed camera: DS2, Gatsos, SPECS, Speedcurb, Truvelo, Teletraffic.

Gatsos are the most common. Most of these photograph the rear of the vehicle after it has passed, though they can be configured to take front-facing photographs too. They use radar to measure vehicle speed.

SPECS cameras are often placed near road works on motorways. They look like a cluster of three lights and face the front of the approaching vehicles. They read the number plate of each vehicle when it enters or leaves the controlled section of road. Where a vehicle has been speeding the system sends digital photographs to the central station.

Truvelos face the rear of the vehicles and combine a digital infra red camera with sensors built into the road. The sensors detect the speed of the vehicle, then the camera takes the photograph without the use of film or flash.

DS2s employ three strips on or just under the surface of the road to measure speed, which is then relayed to enforcement officers in an adjacent car or van. Alternatively, in fully automatic mode, a photograph of the speeding car is taken and the registered keeper is sent a penalty notice in the post.

Speedcurb cameras tend to be used to monitor traffic light offences. They are usually rear-facing, in fixed positions and use strips on the road to measure speed, similar to the DS2s.

---

166 Road Traffic Act 1998 s172

167 Stott (Procurator Fiscal of Dunfermline) v Brown, a decision binding anywhere in the UK.

168 See 5.11.3, MS90, Failure to give information as to identity of driver etc

Teletraffic systems employ a laser gun that takes a video recording of a vehicle's speed and registration number. They work to a range of about one kilometer and have to be held by the operator.

5.11.2 Bus lane offences

Drivers can be prosecuted for driving in bus lanes without authority. Local authority officers or the police can stop them or they can be caught on camera. Many buses now carry on-board video cameras to catch bus lane offenders.

The current legislation covering bus lane offences imposes the liability on the owner of the vehicle, not on the driver.

This has caused problems because local authorities refused to accept representations from leasing companies to transfer liability to the driver. As owner of the vehicle the leasing companies had to pay up then try to recharge the cost to the lessee. The problem here was that the driver would not have had the opportunity to challenge the validity of the fine before it has been paid.

The leasing industry regards this as defective legislation. It becomes farcical when the police (who often hire rental cars) drive a car in a bus lane and get caught on a bus lane camera. The rental company receives the fixed penalty notice and try to pass it on to the police, who reply that they are exempt from such charges and leave the rental company to pay the fine! Both central and local government have recognised that this is farcical bit we still await legislation to rectify the situation.

Meanwhile the problem has been partially fixed through an agreement secured by the BVRLA. As it currently stands, a leasing company can transfer the liability to a hirer if the alleged bus lane offence was committed outside London. If it was committed inside London liability can only be transferred if the lease period exceeds six months. If the period is shorter supplier still has to pay the bill and attempt to recharge this to the hirer.

5.11.3 Conviction codes and points

Once convicted of a motoring offence, a driver will have his or her licence endorsed with details of the offence.

Each conviction carries a certain number of points, depending on the seriousness of the offence. Once twelve points have been accumulated, the driver is usually automatically banned from driving for a set period of time. This is called the 'totting-up' system.

Each offence is given a code and these are set out below. This list will help you to determine conviction histories when you inspect your drivers' licences.

Offence Code	Description	Points
AC10	Failing to stop after an accident	5-10
AC20	Failing to give particulars or to report an accident within twenty-four hours	5-10
AC30	Undefined accident offences	4-9
BA10	Driving while disqualified by order of court	6
BA30	Attempting to drive while disqualified by order of court	6
CD10	Driving without due care and attention	3-9
CD20	Driving without reasonable consideration for other road users	3-9
CD30	Driving without due care and attention or without reasonable consideration for other road users	3-9
CD40	Causing death through careless driving when unfit through drink	3-11
CD50	Causing death through careless driving when unfit through drugs	3-11
CD60	Causing death through careless driving with alcohol level above the limit	3-11
CD70	Causing death through careless driving then failing to supply a specimen for analysis	3-11
CD80	Causing death through careless or inconsiderate driving	3-11
CD90	Causing death by driving; unlicensed, disqualified or uninsured drivers	3-11
CU10	Using a vehicle with defective brakes	3
CU20	Causing or likely to cause danger by reason of use of unsuitable vehicle or using a vehicle with parts or accessories (excluding brakes, steering or tyres) in a dangerous condition.	3
CU30	Using a vehicle with defective tyre(s)	3
CU40	Using a vehicle with defective steering	3
CU50	Causing or likely to cause danger by reason of load or passengers	3
CU80	Using a mobile phone when driving a motor vehicle	3
DD40	Dangerous Driving	3-11
DD60	Manslaughter or culpable homicide while driving a vehicle	3-11
DD80	Causing death by dangerous driving	3-11
DD90	Furious driving	3-9
DR10	Driving or attempting to drive with alcohol level above limit	3-11
DR20	Driving or attempting to drive while unfit through drink	3-11
DR30	Driving or attempting to drive then failing to supply a specimen for analysis.	3-11
DR40	In charge of a vehicle when alcohol level above limit	10
DR50	In charge of a vehicle while unfit through drink	10
DR60	Failure to provide a specimen for analysis in circumstances other than driving	10
DR70	Failure to provide a specimen for breath test	4

DR80	Driving or attempting to drive when unfit through drugs	3-11
DR90	In charge of a vehicle when unfit through drugs	10
IN10	Using a vehicle uninsured against third party risks	6-8
LC20	Driving otherwise than in accordance with a licence	3-6
LC30	Driving after making a false declaration about fitness when applying for a licence	3-6
LC40	Driving a vehicle having failed to notify a disability	3-6
LC50	Driving after a licence has been revoked or refused on medical grounds	3-6
MS10	Leaving a vehicle in a dangerous position	3
MS20	Unlawful pillion riding	3
MS30	Play Street offences	2
MS40	Driving with uncorrected defective eyesight or refusing to submit to a test	3
MS50	Motor racing on the highway	3-11
MS60	Offences not covered by other codes	As appropriate
MS70	Driving with uncorrected defective eyesight	3
MS80	Refusing to submit to an eyesight test	3
MS90	Failure to give information as to identity of driver etc	6
MW10	Contravention of Special Roads Regulations (excluding speed limited)	3
PC10	Undefined Contravention of Pedestrian Crossing Regulations	3
PC20	Contravention of Pedestrian Crossing Regulations with moving vehicle	3
PC30	Contravention of Pedestrian Crossing Regulations with stationary vehicle	3
SP10	Exceeding goods vehicle speed limits	3-6
SP20	Exceeding speed limit for type of vehicle (excluding goods or passenger vehicles)	3-6
SP30	Exceeding statutory speed limit on a public road	3-6
SP40	Exceeding passenger vehicle speed limit	3-6
SP50	Exceeding speed limit on a motorway	3-6
SP60	Undefined speeding offence	3-6
TS10	Failing to comply with traffic light signals	3
TS20	Failing to comply with double white lines	3
TS30	Failing to comply with 'Stop' sign	3
TS40	Failing to comply with direction of a constable/warden	3
TS50	Failing to comply with traffic sign (excluding 'stop' signs, traffic lights or double white lines)	3
TS60	Failing to comply with a school crossing patrol sign	3
TS70	Undefined failure to comply with a traffic direction sign	3
TT99	Disqualified under the totting-up procedure	n/a

If a licence-holder is convicted of aiding, abetting, counselling or procuring the commission of an offence, their licence is marked with the same code as shown in the list above but the 0 is changed to 2, i.e. CD10 becomes CD12. If they cause or permit the offence, the 0 is replaced with a 4. If they incite the offence the 0 is replaced with a 6.

With so many more speeding cameras appearing on our roads, many more drivers are being disqualified from driving under the totting-up scheme. There is therefore more risk that some will drive while disqualified.

Whilst penalty points count towards the totting-up scheme for three years, endorsements can remain printed on a licence for longer:

Code	Years
AC	4
BA	4
CD10 – 30	4
CD40-70	11
CD80-90	4
CU	4
DD	4
DR10-30	11
DR40-70	4
DR80	11
DR90	4
IN	4
LC	4
MS	4
MW	4
PC	4
SP	4
TS	4
TT	4

Drivers who are convicted of an offence are required to send their licences to the DVLA to allow the endorsement to be marked on the licence. Until 2011 the DVLA allowed the driver up to a year to send in the licence, but they have now tightened up the rules so licences have to be submitted within 28 days of conviction. If DVLA don't receive the licence in this period they will revoke the licence and the driver will have to apply for a new one. Once a licence has been revoked it is not lawful to drive a vehicle on the public highway.

5.11.4 WHEEL CLAMPING ON PRIVATE LAND

The Protection of Freedoms Bill 2010-11 was making its way through parliament as this book was being written.[169] It contains regulations designed to stop the menace of private clampers.

The Bill will make it a criminal offence to immobilise a vehicle on private land without lawful authority from, for example, a local authority, the DVLA or the police.

5.11.5 DRINK DRIVING

There are an more than 90,000 prosecutions each year for drink-driving offences. Many of these drivers are company car drivers, and often they are 'at work' when they are caught.

You need to have a policy setting out what will happen if one of your drivers is banned from driving.

This should deal with:

■ Disciplinary sanctions, which may include loss of benefits, withdrawal of car, dismissal, etc

■ Business drivers; what should happen when an employee cannot do their job without being able to drive?

■ Whether the car may be retained by the employee for the sole use of their spouse/partner

■ Whether the employee should be compensated for the loss of the car (This is a contentious point. A perk driver who never uses the company car for work might reasonably argue that the car is part of their remuneration package, the drink-driving ban does not affect their ability to perform their duties and that therefore the company should not benefit financially because the employee made a mistake in his own time)

■ What should happen in cash-for-car situations where the employee gets a cash allowance?

■ What should happen if the employee is part of the employer's ECO[170] or Salary Sacrifice[171] scheme?

If you publish a well thought-out and fair policy your drivers will not be able to say that they did not know what would happen, and you will not have to negotiate with individual drivers once they have been caught drink-driving.

The current legal limit for driving while under the influence of alcohol is 80mg of alcohol per 100 ml of blood. One of the biggest problems with drink driving is that drivers are not sure how much they can drink without being over the limit. The

---

169 services.parliament.uk/bills/2010-11/protectionoffreedoms.html

170 See 3.7.

171 See 3.8.

government says that for most people this will be two units of alcohol, which is two small glasses of wine, one pint of regular-strength beer or two regular measures of spirits. On average it takes an hour for the body to dispose of one unit of alcohol. But these are only rough guides. It is possible to buy devices at pharmacies to measure the amount of alcohol in the blood but it is far better fleet management practice to advise your drivers not to touch alcohol for several hours before getting into a car. They should be reminded that alcohol remains in the blood stream for many hours and that first thing in the morning a driver can still be over the limit from the drinks he had the night before.

The penalties for drink or drug related offences are high:

Offence	Maximum Penalty
Causing death by careless driving under the influence of drink or drugs	14 years' imprisonment Unlimited fine Also – minimum 2 year ban Must pass extended driving test to regain licence
Attempting to drive whilst unfit to drive through drink or above the legal limit	6 months' imprisonment £5,000 fine Also – minimum 12 month ban
Being in charge of a vehicle whilst over the legal limit or unfit through drink	3 months' imprisonment £2,500 fine Driving ban
Failing to provide a specimen of breath, blood or urine	6 months' imprisonment £5,000 fine Also – minimum 12 month ban

If a driver's licence is endorsed for a drink-driving offence, the totting-up points[172] remain on their licence for 11 years.

The number of **drug-related driving offences** is significant. Unfortunately there are no statistics available showing how many of these are work-related. Government figures show that up to 90,000 people are banned from driving every year for driving under the influence of drink or drugs.

172 See 5.11.3.

5.11.6 PARKING OFFENCE CAMERAS

A number of London boroughs have installed kerbside cameras to catch vehicles that are parked illegally, including vans that have stopped to load or unload for just a few minutes.

The fines are £50 if paid within 14 days, £100 thereafter.

5.11.7 ON THE SPOT FINES, VEHICLE IMMOBILISATION AND SEIZURE

Since 2009 the police and VOSA have had new powers to levy on the spot fines, immobilise vehicles and seize them. The legislation was originally designed to sharpen up the enforcement regime for drivers of overseas-registered HGVs operating in the UK. However it is drawn more widely than this so can also be used against the driver of a company car or van who has a defective vehicle or is not properly licensed.

If the police or VOSA wish to penalise the driver they will check to see if he or she has a permanent UK address. If so they will issue an on the spot fine.

If they discover the driver does not have a permanent UK address they will ask for a deposit (the same amount as the on the spot fine), and if the driver cannot or will not pay the deposit the vehicle can be clamped or seized.

Further information is available on the Business Link website.[173]

5.11.8 CONGESTION CHARGING FINES

These are discussed in 11.4.4.

5.11.9 EXERCISES

How might you decide whether a replacement vehicle is a good form of insurance?

Why might you inadvertently pay twice for roadside assistance on a new car?

List the different types of restriction that can be placed on the use of a fuel card.

Many companies have now stopped paying for free private fuel. Should they also stop giving their employees fuel cards?

What happens when a contract hire company receives a parking fine for a car they have leased to you?

Why might it be safer to use daily hire than allow employees to use their own cars?

What criteria might you use to select a daily rental company?

What is the limit for driving when under the influence of alcohol, in mg per ml of blood?

---

173 www.businesslink.gov.uk/bdotg/action/detail?itemId=1082646557&type=
RESOURCES

5.12 RESIDUAL VALUE RISK

5.12.1 Background

Residual value risk is the risk in the price that a vehicle will achieve on resale.

As more than half of all company cars are acquired on contract hire, where the supplier takes the residual value risk, many fleet managers don't need to worry about RV risk.

However, if you buy your own vehicles, hold them for a period of time, then sell them on your own account, you are taking residual value risk and need to manage this risk.

The cost price of the vehicle minus the sale price equals its depreciation, so another way of expressing residual value risk is 'depreciation risk'.

We should draw a distinction between 'residual value' and 'estimated residual value'. Residual value is the price you achieve on sale of the vehicle. Estimated residual value (sometimes called forecast residual value) is an estimate of the likely sale proceeds of the vehicle, such estimate having been made when the vehicle was new. Quite often the expression 'residual value' is used to describe both situations and this can lead to confusion.

Contract hire companies assess residual values for a living. They have to; contract hire, the product demanded most often by British businesses, gives complete residual value protection to the client. The contract hire company takes this risk.

In assessing this risk and setting an estimated residual value, you should take into account all of the macro- and micro-economic factors that can affect the sale price of a car. We can divide these into supply and demand side issues.

5.12.2 Supply side issues

New vehicle supply numbers

The number of new vehicles entering the market today will determine the supply of used cars in the market in three years' time. As the supply of new vehicles was low from 2008 to 2010, the supply of used cars will be low in 2011 to 2014.

The willingness of owners to dispose of them

This used to be easy to measure as about half of all new vehicles were operated by companies and sold after thirty-six months. This is now rather less certain as many companies are now running vehicles for four years to reduce average costs.

Only twenty years ago it was normal for companies to keep vehicles for just two years.

Private owners are also extending ownership cycles, despite manufacturers' efforts to induce them to buy new cars.

THE SHORT-CYCLE MARKET

Manufacturers supply heavily discounted new vehicles to daily hire companies and large fleets – the short-cycle market. The number of vehicles currently entering the short-cycle market has a direct impact on the number of nearly-new cars that will become available over the next 12 months. If this is a large number this is likely to have a knock-on effect on the price of used cars in two and three years' time.

In estimating residual values you need to consider the likelihood of such deals continuing.

THE LIFE CYCLE OF THE VEHICLE

You need to consider whether a vehicle will still be a current model at the time of sale.

MANUFACTURERS' CONSUMER OFFERS

From time to time manufacturers use special offers to promote the sale of particular models. These offers are generally made on vehicles that are particularly attractive to the retail, as opposed to the fleet, buyer. Nonetheless, you should be aware of these deals as they depress the new price of the vehicle and therefore have a direct effect on the used price.

5.12.3   DEMAND SIDE ISSUES

THE ECONOMY

You will have to consider the general economic climate (gross domestic product, inflation, interest rates, employment, etc).

THE AMOUNT OF DISPOSABLE INCOME IN THE HANDS OF CONSUMERS

Private individuals buy the vast majority of used cars. While there has been a move towards companies buying used cars in the last few years, this is still not the norm. Where companies do buy used cars, the majority are less than twelve months old and the supply of these varies according to how many cars the manufacturers feed into the daily hire market.

Disposable income is a function of economic growth, employment, interest rates and the willingness of people to part with their savings.

TECHNOLOGICAL AND ENVIRONMENTAL CHANGES

Three years is long enough for technology, legislation or fashion to change and affect the attractiveness of a used vehicle to a buyer. Some changes can be foreseen and you can attempt to measure the likely effect on residual values. Most changes seem to have an adverse effect on the second-hand value of the 'old' model.

DEMOGRAPHIC TRENDS

Demographic trends in the UK population are likely to make some cars more popular than others. With an ageing population, smaller cars are likely to gain in popularity over big expensive ones.

CHANGES IN VEHICLE MODELS BY MANUFACTURERS

Old models look old and are not as attractive to the used car buyer. Product life cycles vary. By reading motoring publications you can usually ascertain whether a model change is likely to occur within the next year or two and, if so, whether it is going to be a facelift or a total replacement. However, it is not normally possible to get information on model changes planned for later than this.

THE AVAILABILITY OF SUBSTITUTES

The buyer of a three-year-old Ford Mondeo 2.0 next month will have an idea in mind of the amount they are prepared to spend. If, for reasons listed under 'supply' above, or for other reasons, the market price of these used Mondeos is high, they will switch to a different model or make of vehicle and the prices for those models will rise. The substitution effect is very real but is very hard to predict or measure.

PUBLICITY

Adverse publicity about a particular make or model of vehicle will affect its resale value.

Lancia, Skoda, Rover – these are names brands that got into difficulty when the press (and stand-up comedians) rounded on them and wouldn't let go.

Positive publicity tends to lift prices. Volkswagen has done a remarkably good job repositioning Skoda in the eyes of the public, which in turn has led to much better residual values.

THE PRICE OF SLIGHTLY OLDER/NEWER CARS

The prices of 12, 18 and 24 month old cars are strongly affected by manufacturers' efforts to maintain output and market share. As already discussed, at times some very large discounts are offered to daily rental companies to encourage them to take new vehicles for up to six months and then put them back into the used car market.[174]

The volumes are significant, though this tends to go in cycles. Each time a manufacturer has such a campaign it distorts the market for nearly new cars and this has a direct 'knock-on' effect on the prices of older cars.

A similar effect has been seen with the advent of 'solus' schemes, in which a manufacturer will offer big discounts to end-user companies that agree to buy only that manufacturer's vehicles. A common feature of these deals is that the customer replaces the vehicles after nine to twelve months.

If there is oversupply of nearly new cars, the prices of all of the older cars of the same model will fall.

---

174 See 5.9.4.

VEHICLE GUIDES

Having already said that current values are used as a starting place for future value projections, and given the fact that traders use published guides to determine the current market price of a used vehicle, it is obvious that the published guides are an important factor in this market.

Glass's Guide and CAP Black Book are monthly publications that take data from auctions and calculate average market values. Parker's Guide is available to consumers at stationers.

Every now and then one of these guides may report that, in its opinion, a certain vehicle is under or over-valued. The trade responds accordingly.

Prices shown in the guides reflect the average sale prices several weeks earlier. Supply can vary enormously in the intervening period, having a significant effect on the prices achieved. So these guides are correctly named: they can indeed only be 'guides'.

DISPOSAL METHODS

The price achieved in a private sale is usually significantly higher than the price achieved at auction.[175]

FASHION

Some vehicle colours hold their values well while others tend to devalue a vehicle. The used vehicle market has come to expect that some optional extras will be fitted to prestige marques so prices will be marked down if these extras are missing.[176]

5.12.4 THE PORTFOLIO EFFECT

If you have a large mixed fleet you will be cushioned against some market downturns by the portfolio effect – an over-estimate on one vehicle may be compensated for by an under-estimate on another.

It is no secret that contract hire companies routinely get their sums wrong when estimating residual values on individual cars. You need look no further than the wide range of estimated residual values they build into their quotes on individual vehicles to realise this. It is not unusual to see two contract hire companies quoting on the same new car with one estimating that the car will sell in three years for £750 more than the other.

Broadly speaking, they gain if the used car market rises unexpectedly and they lose if it falls unexpectedly.

175 See 5.5.2.
176 See 5.2.

There are two risks they do not accept, however:

■ The risk the vehicle will be returned having travelled more miles than agreed[177]

■ The risk that it will be returned in an unacceptable condition.[178]

It may seem a truism but one way contract hire companies can protect themselves from residual value risk is to get the highest possible price for the vehicle when it is sold. They do this by adopting all of the advice in section 5.5.

The volatility of the used car market can be shown from the following chart.[179]

CAP Motor Research holds vast amounts of used vehicle price data going back over many years and has produced this chart to show the performance of the used car market over the last 11 years.

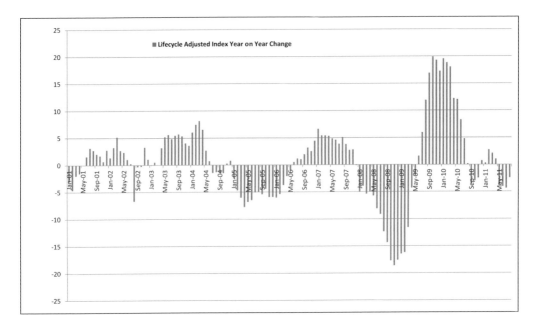

The chart plots depreciation in used car values year-on-year. Values are affected by the general state of the market and the age of a vehicle within its lifecycle, so the chart has been modified to neutralise the lifecycle effect.

Therefore this chart measures the true yearly depreciation in the market every month. The steeper the decline in the index, the more monthly values are depreciating.

Looking at the period 2008 to mid 2009 we can see how used car prices declined sharply as a result of the credit crunch, and how the market then came back strongly until mid-2010.

---

177 See 1.2.6.

178 See 1.2.13.

179 Kindly supplied by CAP Motor Research Limited

Contract hire companies tend to make residual value profits when the economy is strong, demand is high and used car supply was relatively low, and losses when the economy is weak, demand is weak and used car supply is relatively high.

The position from early 2008 to mid 2009 partially reflected this historic position. The downturn in the economy after three years of growth meant that there were far more used cars available than buyers who wished to buy them. Buyers were unsure of the future so tended to keep their cars longer. It is always possible to delay replacing a used car for a few months.

Lease extensions have always been a feature of this market. Leasing companies' clients extend their leases for many reasons; the driver hasn't got around to choosing a new car, the new car is on order and hasn't been delivered yet, and so on.

But in 2008 and 2009 the press was reporting a significant increase in the number of extensions, driven both by leasing companies wanting to put off the day when cars were returned and sold at a loss, and their clients keen not to take on new cars whilst there was so much uncertainty about the economy.

I carried out some research for the Vehicle Remarketing Association in summer of 2010 to try to measure how the recession had affected the top 25 leasing companies in the FN50[180] and their clients.

14 leasing companies responded, representing 67% of the total fleet of these top 25 companies. So the results are likely to be highly representative of the whole contract hire market and in turn the whole fleet market.

The respondents were distributed as follows:

Quartile of the FN25	Respondents (No. of companies)
1	4
2	5
3	3
4	2

These were the answers to the question "What proportion of your fleet went into extension before the recession, at the peak of the recession and now?

% of fleet that went into extension	Before the recession	At the peak of the recession	Summer 2010
Cars	15.7%	24.2%	19.6%
LCVs	31.9%	42.9%	24.3%
Total Fleet	18.3%	27.2%	20.6%

180 The top 50 contract hire companies as measured in the annual Fleet News survey. I've used FN25 to designate the top 25 of these.

These results confirmed that there had been a sharp increase in the number of leases that had been extended, for both cars and LCVs, but that it the level of extensions had since dropped back sharply. Indeed fewer LCV leases were being extending by summer 2010 than had been extending before the recession, though that is probably because such a large proportion had extended at the peak of the recession there were relatively few left to be extended.

These were the answers to the question: what was the average length of extension, in months?

Average extension length in months	Before the recession	At the peak of the recession	Summer 2010
Cars	6.1	8.8	7.6
LCVs	8.1	9.2	7.2
Total Fleet	6.6	8.9	7.5

This shows that the average extension period increased by around two months during the recession and had reduced by summer 2010. Once again it is interesting to look at LCVs, where the average extension length was shorter by the end of the recession than it had been immediately before the recession.

Contract hire companies setting residual values in 2005 and 2006 could not have expected the sharp downturn they experienced from 2008 to mid-2009 and as a result they made large RV losses.

The economy hadn't picked up noticeably by mid-2009 but by then used car buyers had waited long enough. They returned to the market and discovered that a lot of the cars they might have bought – relatively young ex-rental and demonstrator cars – were not available, because car manufacturers had stopped supplying such low-price and therefore low-margin cars to the market. Instead, they'd just cut manufacturing output. These buyers needed to buy something so this pushed up demand for ex-fleet cars and prices began to rise. This brought delight to contract hire companies, many of whom had previously made loss provisions against those cars and were now able to sell them at higher-than-expected prices, clear their books and reverse the provisions back into profit.

The relative stability of used car prices from mid-2010 to mid-2011 reflects the continuing uncertainty in the general economy. The used car market has found its equilibrium for now.

So long as there is not another economic downturn in 2012 or 2013, it is likely that used car prices will remain fairly strong. The reduction in new car sales from 2008 means there will be fewer 3 or 4 year old cars entering the used car market and this should move prices upwards. Time will tell.

Occasionally, some event will occur that is completely outside anyone's plans and this will have an effect on used car prices. An act of God (such as very bad weather) or a major national event that diverts the public's attention (such as a royal wedding) fits into this category.

If you acquire your company cars using your own funds (outright purchase), a sharp reduction in the used market price of one vehicle can often be offset by an increase in another. If there is a general downturn in the used car market as there was in 2008 and 2009, you could suffer a much bigger loss on disposal, though you might take steps to mitigate this by simply holding onto your cars for a further period in the hope that the market will recover.

However, if you are a contract hire company your options in this situation are limited. You receive back a torrent of used cars every month and there's little you can do with them other than sell them and take the loss. Residual value losses can devastate a contract hire company.

An example may be helpful here.

> XYZ Contract Hire Limited has 10,000 vehicles on lease. Its total assets are £100,000,000. These are financed through £10,000,000 in shareholders' funds (share capital and retained profits) and £90,000,000 of borrowings secured on the vehicle leases.
>
> These vehicles cost on average £14,000 each. The average estimated residual value of the vehicles is £5,600, (40% of the original cost). The portfolio has remained static over the last few years, so these estimated residual values represent £60,000,000 on the company's balance sheet.[181]
>
> The company makes residual value losses. Let us assume (taking a highly simplified view) that over a three-year period it sells all of these vehicles for an average of £4,600 each. So it loses £1,000 on 10,000 vehicles. That's £10,000,000. That represents the whole capital of the company. It has wiped out its capital.
>
> In the absence of an understanding parent company or very tolerant creditors (or both), the company will collapse.

An extreme example? Not particularly. Many contract hire companies have a gearing ratio (borrowings to equity) this high and a 40% estimated residual value after three years is not particularly high by recent standards.

As the used vehicle market is cyclical, it would make sense for contract hire companies to set aside residual value profits from the good times against the day when the market turns, so there are sufficient reserves in the company to ride out the storm.

---

181 If a car costs £14,000 and its residual is £6,000, half way through its life it will have a balance sheet value of approx. £10,000. XYZ's balance sheet therefore comprises, on average, 10,000 vehicles with an average balance sheet value of £10,000 = £100,000,000 and 10,000 residuals of average value £6,000 = £60,000,000.

It seems few contract hire companies do this. They prefer to believe they have made these profits through being wise and therefore pay away their profits through bonuses, dividends or making large investments, only then to find they have little to cushion them when the market turns.

5.12.5   HOW TO PROTECT AGAINST RESIDUAL VALUE RISK

If you acquire vehicles by outright purchase, hire purchase, lease purchase, finance lease, conditional sale or credit sale, you are fully exposed to residual value risk.

If you estimate that the residual value of a vehicle at disposal will be £5,000 and it sells for only £4,000, the loss (that is, the extra depreciation) is all yours.

You can shift this risk to another party by entering into a buy-back agreement or put-option with the dealer that supplied the cars, or, in some cases, with your funder.[182]

If you acquire your vehicles through contract hire, operating lease, daily hire or contract purchase, you have no residual risk – the lessor takes it all from you.

Like all forecasting, estimating residual values is part art, part science. And getting it wrong can be expensive.

If you wish to take your own residual value risk and need help in setting residuals, several trade and retail publications will provide you with information to help you arrive at your own estimated residual values. None is likely to be more reliable than the others. Like most estimates, historical performance is no guarantee of future performance.

You can buy insurance to cover residual value risk. Before doing so, you have to decide why you would wish to do so.

If your objective is to remove the full residual risk in the vehicle, you will find this cover is hard to obtain and can be very expensive. You will be putting the insurer in a position to take the full risks without giving them control of the vehicle maintenance or disposal, two essential tools for controlling the risk.

If your objective is solely to remove these assets from your balance sheet, the cover should be easier to obtain and less expensive. The insurer should be able to offer you a policy that removes some of your risk (enough to make your accountants happy) while keeping their risk manageable. The accounting standards SSAP21 and FRS 5 are important to consider when looking to remove assets from your balance sheet[183] and it seems that in the near future larger businesses will be unable to remove leased assets from their balance sheets.[184]

---

182 See 5.5.5.

183 See 8.1.2 and 8.1.3.

184 See 8.6.

5.12.6 GOOD PRACTICE IN SETTING RESIDUAL VALUES

If you are taking residual value risk you will wish to determine your own residual value estimates. Without doing so you will be unable to determine whole-life costs and therefore unable to decide which vehicles to put on your fleet.

This checklist sets out good and bad practice in estimating residual values.

WHEN ESTIMATING RESIDUAL VALUES

Good practice:

- Obtain information from manufacturers about vehicle supply numbers for each make/model
- Decide how likely it is that owners of a particular make and model of vehicle will dispose of them in two, three and four years' time
- Follow macro-economic developments (The Economist is an excellent source of information) and have an agreed company position on the likely strength of the UK economy in two, three and four years' time, and the amount of disposable income in the hands of private individuals
- Consider all of the technological, environmental and fashion issues likely to affect used car values in three years' time
- Monitor upcoming changes in vehicle models
- Consider how attractive a particular vehicle in your fleet will be to a used car buyer in three years' time, compared with other similar vehicles in its class. (The availability of substitutes)
- Monitor manufacturers' marketing activities, particularly heavy discounts to daily rental companies and rapid cycle schemes, and consider how they are likely to affect used car prices
- Consider whether your disposal method is consistently likely to produce *CAP Black Book* 'average', *CAP Black Book* 'Clean' or some other benchmark sale price. If you know your method of disposal consistently produces 5% above CAP Black Book 'Clean', you can reflect this in your estimated residual values
- Subscribe to a publication such as CAP Monitor that predicts residual values – but don't follow it blindly. Even better, subscribe to several of the publications that predict residual values.
- Consider arranging alternative disposal routes for individual vehicles where you face a large residual value loss. For example, market these vehicles strongly among your staff to see if they or members of their families would like to buy them.
- Consider adjusting estimated residual values to reflect vehicle colours and optional extras.
- Review estimated residual values frequently.
- Consider whether there are going to be any special events that will be occurring at the end of the lease that may affect sale patterns, for example the World Cup, Christmas or some other event that will distract buyer attention.

- Establish a residual value committee to approve changes to estimated residual values.
- Adjust estimated residual values to reflect the circumstances in which the vehicle is to be driven. Published residual value estimates assume average driving conditions.
- Produce reports showing how you have arrived at your residual values estimates (at least for benchmark vehicles).
- Revalue your entire residual value portfolio regularly in the light of the latest information and make provisions for future losses if necessary.

Bad practice:

- Allowing any one person to dominate the residual value setting process.
- Relying too heavily on any one publication.

DURING THE LIFE OF THE VEHICLE

Good practice:

- Produce a monthly report for each vehicle added to the fleet in that month, comparing the estimated residual values you have set and those that CAP Monitor has set. CAP Monitor is just one organisation's view; it might be right or wrong but you should consider the reasons for any major differences.
- When you buy a new vehicle you intend to keep for three years, consider what you believe it will be worth after 6, 12, 18, 24 and 30 months. At the end of each of these periods, check your original estimates against the current market value. If it becomes apparent that residual values are deviating widely from your expected levels, try to pinpoint why and modify your assumptions. For example, if you thought interest rates would be around 6% and they have since grown to 9%, this might explain the reduction in demand. (If you see such a wide deviation you may decide to provide additional depreciation in this year's accounts to reflect this).

AFTER SALE OF THE VEHICLE

Good practice:

- Monitor sales performance against *CAP Black Book*. If you are consistently selling vehicles at a figure above (or below) *CAP Black Book* 'average', you can take this into account when setting residual values.
- Produce reports showing sale performance relative to *CAP Black Book* 'average' and 'clean'.

5.13 MAINTENANCE RISK

5.13.1 BACKGROUND

Vehicles are complex pieces of machinery with many components and moving parts. Like all such equipment they require regular servicing and maintenance. And like all such equipment, occasionally they go wrong.

The cost can be modest or high, though a regularly serviced vehicle is likely to need fewer expensive repairs than a vehicle where servicing has been skipped.

If you own a vehicle or are buying it on hire purchase, finance lease, conditional sale or a similar product, you have to bear all of the cost of servicing, maintenance and repair. If the vehicle is expensive to service, has expensive parts or has more than its fair share of problems, you have to bear the cost.

In the parlance of the industry, in this situation you are bearing the 'maintenance risk'.

5.13.2 HOW TO PROTECT AGAINST MAINTENANCE RISK

If you wish to take this risk you will want to obtain information about the likely cost to maintain your vehicles. This is available from a variety of independent sources or you can look at the rates quoted by contract hire companies to see how much they are charging for maintenance within their rentals.

It is surprisingly easy to quantify service and maintenance costs, as they arise with known regularity and cost. Around 75% of the cost of maintaining a vehicle is made up of standard manufacturer-scheduled servicing, maintenance, tyres and replacement of worn parts (such as brake pads).

The frequency of component failure is well known too, by make and model. However, models change frequently, so just as a few years' data has been accumulated and conclusions about reliability have been arrived at, the manufacturer comes along with a new model and you have to start again gathering data again from scratch.

If you arrange your own maintenance you will need to have in-house maintenance control skills.[185] Without these you will not know what to authorise and how much to pay.

The alternative to doing it yourself is getting a contract hire or fleet management company to maintain your vehicles and take the maintenance risk. In exchange for a flat monthly charge, included in the contract hire company's rental or the fleet manager's charges, they will pay for all of the service maintenance and repair work on the vehicle. If their estimates of the cost of running the vehicle are incorrect, they bear the loss (or indeed the profit).

---

185 See 5.3.

In either event, you get peace of mind from knowing that you have to pay only a fixed amount and that the risk is no longer yours.

5.13.3 EXERCISES

What is maintenance risk?

How might you protect against it?

What is residual value risk?

What is the difference between residual value and estimated residual value?

What vehicle finance products give you the residual value risk?

What products (vehicle finance or otherwise) take the residual value risk from you?

What factors do contract hire companies assess in setting residual values?

A contract hire company has total assets of £300,000,000. It is geared 7:1. Its average estimated residual value is 50% of purchase price. All of the vehicles are financed over three years. Making whatever simplifying assumptions you wish, what is the company's likely loss over three years if they sell their cars for an average of only 40% of purchase price?

6 RENTALS, INTEREST

6.1 LIST PRICE, ON THE ROAD PRICE AND CAPITAL COST

Before considering rental and interest calculations, we need to define the above terms.

6.1.1 LIST PRICE

The list price of a vehicle is the price the manufacturer quotes in its publications. Dealers use the list price as the starting point for calculating the price you pay, then tell you the discount they will offer (if any).

6.1.2 ON THE ROAD PRICE

The price you pay to drive the car away, including road tax and dealer discount but before any deposit or part-exchange value. It does not include petrol.[186]

6.1.3 CAPITAL COST

This is an expression used by a finance company, lessor or contract hire company to describe the amount it will be financing.

It will be less than the list price or the on the road price, because they may get volume related bonuses, input VAT recovery, a deposit or equivalent payment.[187]

Lessors and lenders have a paradox: they want a high deposit to reduce their credit risk, but a low deposit to maximise the amount they advance, as this is the amount on which they earn their margin.

All of their interest calculations are based on the capital cost.

---

186 So presumably this is the price for placing the car on the road, rather than getting it moving on the road.

187 See 6.2.

6.2 RENTAL PATTERNS

A variety of rental patterns (or 'payment profiles') are available. These can be split into four classes:

- high initial rental
- regular initial rental
- spread rental
- all in advance.

6.2.1 HIGH INITIAL RENTAL

High initial rentals normally involve the payment of three or sometimes six rentals on delivery of the vehicle. This creates a 'terminal pause'. If rentals are pre-paid at the start of the contract there is no need to pay them at the end of the contract.

A typical payment profile is 3+33. You pay two extra rentals on delivery so you don't need to pay any rentals at the start of months 35 and 36. Four-year business is often transacted with a 3+45 payment profile.

High initial rental payment profiles are usually offered to private individuals, smaller fleets and SMEs (small and medium size enterprises).

The high initial payment gives the lessor an additional measure of protection should the client default on their payment obligations and the car have to be repossessed. The balance outstanding in the lessor's books will be that much lower and they will make a smaller loss when they sell the vehicle.

A high initial rental is usually called a deposit in agreements where the customer has the ability to buy the vehicle, for example contract purchase and hire purchase.

6.2.2 REGULAR RENTALS

Regular rental profiles require equal monthly, quarterly or annual payments to be made throughout the contract.

Typical profiles are 1+35 or 1+47. These are normally offered to public sector bodies and large companies, where the lessor believes there is less credit risk.

6.2.3 SPREAD RENTALS

We have seen so far that if you want to lease a vehicle for three years you can pay monthly rentals on a 3+33 or 1+35 basis. A further possibility exists; 3+35.

Under this arrangement you pay a high initial payment (the initial three) followed by 35 monthly payments. These rentals are lower than would have been paid under a 3+33 arrangement and the lessor receives a large payment on delivery to reduce their exposure.

This arrangement is called 'spread rentals', presumably because it spreads the rentals over another two months.

Spread rentals have developed from the desire of smaller companies to have the lowest rentals possible, notwithstanding the fact that they have paid a high initial rental. They increase the lessor's credit risk slightly compared with 3+33.

6.2.4 ALL IN ADVANCE

Some hirers ask to pay all of their rentals in advance.

This would make no sense at all on a hire purchase agreement as this is a full payout finance agreement. If you can afford to pay for the vehicle up front there is no reason for you to set up a finance agreement and pay for the vehicle in advance.

However, on contract hire agreements it is not unusual for cash-rich companies to ask for all rentals to be paid up front. They do this to take advantage of the lessor's ability to recover input VAT on the purchase price of the vehicle.[188] This reduces the overall cost of the transaction to the client. As the lessor is just funding the residual value, the interest cost borne by the client is low, too.

There is nothing odd or underhand going on here. As contract hire is an operating lease – in other words, a simple rental agreement – there is no reason why rentals should not be paid in advance if both parties agree. After all, if an equipment hire shop can ask for payment in advance if you hire a piece of equipment, why not pre-pay for a car if you have the cash?

6.2.5 PAYMENT IN ADVANCE OR ARREARS

In the majority of cases rentals are paid in advance; i.e. at the start of the month to which they relate (or quarter, where the rentals are payable quarterly).

Lessors prefer this as it reduces their credit exposure more rapidly.

Nonetheless, it is not unusual to see larger companies negotiating payment in arrears. They do this for cash flow reasons and they pay a little more interest for the privilege.

6.3 INTEREST RATES

6.3.1 SIMPLE INTEREST

A lender agrees to lend you £100 and you agree to pay them back £110 in one year. You both understand that this represents 10% interest payable in one year, so the interest is 10% per annum.

Now imagine you borrow £100 and agree to repay £110 in six months' time. The lender tells you that this is 10% interest but you feel uncomfortable about this. Surely if it was 10% interest you should to repay only £105, not £110? 'Ah yes', the lender says, 'but that would be on the assumption that I was charging you 10% per annum interest, whereas in fact I am just charging 10% interest.'

188 See 17.1.4.

This is simple interest, a rate of interest that ignores the period over which the money is borrowed or the frequency with which payments are made.

It is easy to see why it can cause confusion.

6.3.2 FLAT RATES

Flat rates of interest are calculated by taking the total amount of interest payable, dividing this by the number of years of the loan, dividing the result by the amount advanced and multiplying by 100.

If you borrow £100 repayable in thirty-six equal monthly repayments of £3.61 over three years, with a total repayment of £130, the flat rate will be calculated as follows:[189]

> £130 – £100 = £30, the total amount of interest payable.
>
> £30 ÷ 3 = £10, the total interest divided by the number of years.
>
> £10 ÷ £100 x 100 = 10% per annum flat

This is a slightly more sophisticated method of expressing an interest rate than simple interest because it takes into account the period over which the money is borrowed.

Nonetheless, don't you feel uncomfortable that this interest rate ignores the fact you are making monthly payments? The interest rate on this loan would be 10% per annum even if you made all of the repayments on the third anniversary of the granting of the loan. In that situation the money would have been sitting in your bank account rather than the lessor's and you could have used it or earned interest on it.

So flat rates are not particularly helpful either. They also have the potential to deceive the unwary, as we will see below.

The Consumer Credit Act makes it illegal for consumers, including sole traders and partnerships, to be quoted simple or flat rates of interest, so clearly the legislators felt that these are unsatisfactory methods of describing interest rates.

6.3.3 COMPOUND INTEREST

Now that we have considered two methods of calculating interest that ignore the amount and timings of your repayments, we need to look at a method that takes both of these into account.

Compound interest calculations recognise that every time you make a loan repayment it reduces the amount you owe the lender. It is therefore a fairer and more honest system of quoting interest rates. It also allows you to compare interest rates offered by a lender over a period of time, and also to compare the different ways to repay (monthly, quarterly, with or without a deposit, in advance or arrears, with or without a terminal lump sum payment, etc).

---

189 Ignores 4p rounding error

Compound interest is straightforward but seems to cause enormous confusion because you cannot use mental arithmetic to see how the compound interest rate has been calculated.

We need to consider three different types of compound interest: nominal rates, true rates and annual percentage rates (APRs).

6.3.4   NOMINAL RATE OF INTEREST

A nominal rate of interest is one that takes the annual interest rate, based on the amount of interest to be paid in the year, and divides it by 12 to reflect monthly payments.

Many mortgages and business loans are expressed as nominal rates.

As the compounding is not done monthly it allows the lender to show a lower rate of interest than the client is paying.

If you borrow £100 repayable in 12 equal repayments[190] of £8.88 over twelve months, with a total repayment of £106.62, the nominal rate will be 1% per month. And 1% per month multiplied by 12 is 12% per annum.

This chart shows the loan being repaid:

Period	Balance at start of period	Interest at 1% per month	Repayment	Balance at end of period
	£	£	£	£
1	100.00	1.00	8.88	92.12
2	92.12	0.92	8.88	84.15
3	84.15	0.84	8.88	76.11
4	76.11	0.76	8.88	67.98
5	67.98	0.68	8.88	59.78
6	59.78	0.60	8.88	51.49
7	51.49	0.51	8.88	43.12
8	43.12	0.43	8.88	34.67
9	34.67	0.35	8.88	26.13
10	26.13	0.26	8.88	17.51
11	17.51	0.18	8.88	8.80
12	8.80	0.09	8.88	0.00
Total		6.62	106.62	

190 It's actually slightly more than £8.88 per month but we'll assume it's exactly this amount to keep the example simple.

The chart is quite straightforward. You can see how 1% per month is being charged and how £8.88 per month repays this loan in full.

The lender tells you this is 12% per annum and this seems reasonable, as 1% per month multiplied by 12 is definitely 12%. Isn't it?

Well, actually it isn't but we need now to consider true rates of interest to prove this.

6.3.5 TRUE RATE OF INTEREST

This is an interest rate reflecting every cash flow that takes place during the life of the agreement and the timing of that cash flow. It uses the monthly interest rate and then compounds this to arrive at the annual rate.

So 1% per month would be 12.68% per annum, calculated as follows:

1% = 0.01

Add 1 to this and it becomes 1.01

Raise this by the power of 12, that is, compound it twelve times and you get 1.01^{12}

$1.01^{12} = 1.1268$

$1.1268 - 1 = 0.1268$

$0.1268 \times 100 = 12.68\%$

So somehow 1% per month becomes 12.68% per annum. Can this be correct?

Yes, it is and the example below shows how this happens. To make this clear we have to simplify the loan calculation. We will assume that repayments are made monthly, that interest accrues monthly and that the loan is repayable at the end of the year.

In the following situation, you borrow £100 and will be charged 1% per month interest.

When we were looking at nominal rates we saw that 1% per month equals 12% per annum. If that is the case for a loan repaid monthly it must also be the case for a loan where interest is charged monthly and the whole debt is repaid at the end of the year. We will assume that the loan stays in place for 12 months and is then repaid in full.

That must mean that you should make a repayment of £112.00 at the end of the year, right?

Let's see.

Month	Start	Interest	End
	£	£	£
1	100.00	1.00	101.00
2	101.00	1.01	102.01
3	102.01	1.02	103.03
4	103.03	1.03	104.06
5	104.06	1.04	105.10
6	105.10	1.05	106.15
7	106.15	1.06	107.21
8	107.21	1.07	108.29
9	108.29	1.08	109.37
10	109.37	1.09	110.46
11	110.46	1.10	111.57
12	111.57	1.12	112.68

So what has happened here? 1% per month has not created a debt of £112.00 at the end of the year but £112.68. Why is this?

It is because the 1% interest charged every month was itself accruing interest in subsequent months. As that interest on interest grew, you were charged an extra £0.68 by the end of the year. So 1% per month is not the same as 12% per annum, it is actually 1% per annum compounded 12 times, or 12.68% per annum.

The number of compounding periods in the year changes the true interest rate but keeps the nominal interest rate unchanged.

If you were charged 1% per month it could be described as either 12.0% per annum nominal interest or 12.68% per annum true interest. If you were charged 3% per quarter this would be 12% per annum nominal interest but only 12.55% per annum true, as this example shows:

Quarter	Start	Interest	End
	£	£	£
1	100.00	3.00	103.00
2	103.00	3.09	106.09
3	106.09	3.18	109.27
4	109.27	3.28	112.55

Doesn't the nominal rate begin to look rather pointless in this situation? It gives you no real idea of the true interest cost you will incur. It would be better if you could be quoted just the true rate, as this is what you will be paying.

Flat rates can easily cause confusion. Nominal rates are better, but only tell half the story and they always show a smaller figure than the true interest rate.

All banks quote nominal rates to business borrowers and some lenders still quote flat rates.

A borrower quoted a 6.62% interest rate with monthly repayments will think it compares favourably to a 4.5% bank base rate[191].

However, if the 6.62% is a flat rate it represents a 12.0% nominal rate, far higher than the 4.5% bank base rate. And it represents a 12.68% true rate.

In my view flat rates should be made illegal for all transactions and only true rates should be quoted.

6.3.6 Annual percentage rates (APRs)

Whilst we could discuss at length the 'best' interest rate to use in business-to-business transactions, in consumer lending it has already been that decided that flat rates and nominal rates are inappropriate measures of the amount of interest a consumer pays on a loan.

The Consumer Credit Act 1974, as amended, sets out only one acceptable interest rate, the annual percentage rate, or APR.

The APR is the true rate of interest on the amount borrowed, taking into account any fees or other amounts payable by the borrower to the lender. Once the true rate has been calculated it has to be rounded to the nearest decimal point to arrive at the APR.

In the example in 6.3.5 we saw that 1% per month gives a true rate of 12.68% per annum. If you simply had to repay £112.68 at the end of the year, the APR would be 12.68% rounded to the nearest one decimal point, ie12.7%.

The lender has to ensure that the APR is given prominence in any advert or quotation.

If the lender charges you a fee this must be included in the APR calculation.

Continuing the above example, let us assume they charge an arrangement fee of £10. This makes the total amount repayable £122.68. Hence the charge for credit (interest and fee) is £22.68. This is 22.68% of the amount borrowed. Rounded to the nearest decimal point, this becomes 22.7% APR.

The regulations state that when carrying out the rounding, if the second figure behind the decimal point is 5 or above, the first figure behind the decimal point

---

191 See 6.3.12.

should be increased by one and the second and any subsequent figures behind the decimal point should be disregarded. Where the second figure behind the decimal point is 4 or lower, it and any subsequent figures behind the decimal point should be disregarded and the first figure after the decimal point should remain unchanged.

Which is a rather verbose way of saying:

If the interest calculation delivers a result of say

- 10.01%, 10.02%, 10.03% or 10.04%, the APR is 10.0%.
- 10.05%, 10.06%, 10.07%, 10.08% or 10.09%, the APR is 10.1%.
- And any numbers after the first decimal point are always discarded

6.3.7 FIXED AND VARIABLE RATE TRANSACTIONS

In the UK, most leases and hire purchase agreements require you to make payments that remain static regardless of changes in market interest rates. Thus these are 'fixed rate' borrowings.

You can contrast this with borrowing by way of, say, a bank overdraft, where the amount payable changes whenever market interest rates (in this case bank base rates) change. Transactions that have this variability of payment are usually called variable rate or floating rate transactions.

Most financial products described in this book can be offered at either fixed or variable rates.

If you enter into a fixed rate lease you are certain how much you will have to pay over the lease period. Thus with a fixed rate contract you have no 'interest rate risk'.

If you opt for a variable rate contract you take the full market interest rate risk.

You may be keen to pay a variable rate of interest, perhaps because you believe market interest rates are likely to fall and you want to take advantage of this.

Fixed rate contracts are easy to administer and they make planning simple. With variable rates you'll never be sure how much you have to pay and you will have to check every charge, as it will differ from the previous one. Taking cars on fixed rate deals makes it easier to budget and to keep track of repayments.

Before opting for a variable rate transaction, consider the replacement pattern of your fleet. Are your replacements spread fairly evenly over the next few years? If you replace these vehicles on fixed rate contracts, the rate you pay will effectively be the average of the interest rates that apply during that period. This will be close to the rate you would have paid had you taken all of the cars on floating rate deals.

If all of your cars fall due for replacement at the same time and you think interest rates will fall soon, it makes sense to take a variable rate deal rather than to fix your payments for the next three or four years.

6.3.8 Market interest rates

In variable rate transactions, the amount you repay is varied according to the behaviour of market interest rates during the period of the contract.

The contract will specify a market rate indicator or benchmark to use in the variable rate calculation. There are many such indicators to choose from but Finance House Base Rate, bank base rate and London Interbank Offered Rate are the most commonly used.

6.3.9 Bank base rate

There is no one 'bank base rate'. Every bank publishes its own base rate. While all of the major clearing banks tend to move theirs in unison, many of the smaller banks keep their base rates higher than the clearers, often reflecting their higher borrowing costs. So variable rate contracts need to state which bank's base rate is to be used in the payment calculations.

6.3.10 London Interbank Offered Rate (LIBOR)

LIBOR is the benchmark rate used by banks to borrow money from each other.

If a major bank wishes to borrow from another major bank, it will pay the LIBOR rate plus a very small margin.

LIBOR moves frequently, often several times a minute and the traders in bank dealing rooms track this during the day.

Therefore, if LIBOR is used in a vehicle finance contract as the basis for a variable rate calculation, the timing of the LIBOR quoted in the market is important. It is not unusual to see agreements referring to 'LIBOR quoted at 10.00 am'.

There are many Sterling LIBOR rates, reflecting the different periods for which the money can be borrowed. Hence, the market quotes Sterling LIBOR 'overnight', 'one-month', 'three-month' and so on. If a vehicle finance agreement calls for the rate of interest to be set and adjusted once a quarter, it is likely that the three-month LIBOR rate will be used, as this will roughly equate to the lender's borrowing costs for that period.

6.3.11 Finance House Base Rate (FHBR)

Finance House Base Rate (FHBR) is a rate published monthly by the Finance & Leasing Association (FLA).[192] It is calculated by averaging the three-month Sterling LIBOR rates in the money market over the previous eight weeks and rounding the result up to the next half point. This is meant to approximate to the short term borrowing costs of the companies in the finance industry.

FHBR is published daily in the Financial Times and is shown on the FLA website www.fla.org.uk.

192 See 19.6.4.

As an example of the use of FHBR, your vehicle finance hire purchase agreement might be priced at FHBR +3%. The agreement sets out how changes in the rate of FHBR will affect the repayments you have to make.

As LIBOR is a nominal rate[193] so is FHBR.

6.3.12   Short and long term interest rates

It is worthwhile considering here the difference between base rates and long term interest rates.

Bank base rates reflect short term money market considerations. They can change frequently according to macro-economic pressures. If the government announces a change in levels in public spending, or if there are concerns about the exchange rate, the government, as the biggest borrower in the market, will alter the price at which it is prepared to borrow money and bank base rates will almost definitely come into line.

Longer term interest rates, for example one-year LIBOR, reflect what lenders and borrowers think market rates will be doing in the longer term. If they think that short term interest rates are high and are likely to fall, long term rates today will be lower than short term rates. And vice versa if they think rates are likely to rise.

A leasing company offering you a fixed rate transaction over three years will normally borrow the money over the same period in order to lock-in its cost of money over that period.[194] The cost of money over three years will often be quite different from short term money costs and therefore there will be no direct relationship between bank base rates and the lessor's cost of funds for a particular transaction.

So if bank base rates rise or fall by, say, 1% there is no particular reason to expect leasing rates to rise or fall by 1%.

If you enter into a variable rate lease, one of three methods will normally be used to calculate the payments that you will make:

a)   Fixed capital plus variable interest

Under this arrangement you will make a fixed monthly repayment against the capital balance you owe to the lender. In addition, you will make a monthly or quarterly interest payment, based on the then-current market interest rates.

An example may help here. To keep it simple we will ignore VAT and assume that no balloon rental applies.

> You agree to enter into a finance lease on a £36,000 vehicle over a thirty-six month period at FHBR +4%. You will make thirty-six monthly payments in advance of £1,000. In addition, at the end of every month, you will pay interest.
>
> During the first month you owed £36,000 – £1,000 = £35,000. FHBR for that month was 8%, so FHBR +4% equals 12% per annum, or 1% per

---

193 See 6.3.4.

194 This is a simplification. Many financial institutions can and do mismatch their lending and borrowings, depending on how they think interest rates will change.

month. 1% x £35,000 = £350. So you will pay £350 interest at the end of the first month as well as making the second capital repayment of £1,000.

b) Fixed rentals plus annual adjustment

With this method, at the start of a lease the rental will be calculated based on then-current market interest rates. This rental will remain unchanged throughout the period of the lease. At the end of each year, the lessor will calculate an annual adjustment to bring the amount you have paid into line with the actual performance of an interest rate index during the year. This is sometimes called the 'notional' basis.

So for example, using the details in the example above, if you had chosen the fixed rentals plus annual adjustment method, you might pay £1,200 per month for thirty-six months. If FHBR fell gradually during the lease period, this £1,200 would represent a higher payment than was necessary. In the background the lessor would be tracking the actual amount of interest that should have been paid. Once a year they would repay you the amount you had overpaid. If FHBR had risen, you would have underpaid and would be charged the difference.

As market interest rates fluctuate all the time, in some months you may owe money to the lessor and in others they may owe you but by making the adjustment only once a year they reduce the administration for both parties.

c) Fixed capital and interest payments with a terminal adjustment

This is a variation on the above method, the only adjustment being made once at the end of the lease. While this reduces administration for both parties, the disadvantage is that it can lead to a very large payment being made by one party at the end of the lease.

If it is a large payment due to you, it can mean that the lessor has been sitting on your funds for a considerable period of time. On the other hand, if a large payment is due from you to the lessor, this can come as a nasty surprise to you and also gives them an additional credit risk – maybe you will be unable (or unwilling) to make this payment at the end of the lease. For these reasons, this method of calculation is rare.

All variable rate methods of rental calculation give you the risks and rewards of interest rate movements. If rates increase you will lose money compared with having taken out a fixed rate lease. However, if you think that today's market interest rates are high and you expect them to fall, variable rates may be attractive to you.

6.3.13 A AND B FACTORS

Most corporate lessors and private individuals will never come across this method of calculating finance agreement payments but it is included here for the sake of completeness.

When a contract hire company buys a car to lease to a customer, it needs to fund the car. Nowadays, many contract hire companies are owned by banks and the methods of funding they use can be quite sophisticated, involving swaps and money market borrowing[195]

Many small and medium size contract hire companies finance their car purchases using bank facilities. In most cases they use back-to-back finance or undisclosed agency arrangements to finance their cars on a deal-by-deal basis.[196]

As they may be financing several hundred cars each month, it is not practical for them to ask the bank to quote the repayment required on each car.

So a practical problem arises; how does the contract hire company know, on a car-by-car basis, how much it will cost to finance the vehicles it buys?

The banks could simply quote an interest rate and leave it to the contract hire company to calculate the repayment. However, as we have already seen there are many different types of interest rate and there is therefore scope here for confusion.

They could also quote the amount that would be repayable for each £1,000 financed. So taking the example in 6.3.4, and multiplying up the numbers by 10, we can see that the repayments on a £1000 loan[197] at an interest rate of 1% per month would be £88.85 per month:

Period	Balance at start of period £	Interest at 1% per month £	Repayment £	Balance at end of period £
1	1000.00	10.00	88.85	921.15
2	921.15	9.21	88.85	841.51
3	841.51	8.42	88.85	761.08
4	761.08	7.61	88.85	679.84
5	679.84	6.80	88.85	597.79
6	597.79	5.98	88.85	514.92
7	514.92	5.15	88.85	431.22
8	431.22	4.31	88.85	346.68
9	346.68	3.47	88.85	261.30
10	261.30	2.61	88.85	175.07
11	175.07	1.75	88.85	87.97
12	87.97	0.88	88.85	0.00
Total		66.19	1066.19	

195 See 19.4.8.

196 See 19.4.8.

197 The word 'loan' is used here as shorthand; a contract hire company could use loans, bank-to-back hire purchase, back to back lease purchase, operating lease or undisclosed agency to fund its vehicles and the arithmetic would be the same in all cases.

This deals with the fact that the capital cost of the vehicle is a variable in each calculation; in other words, that it can change from car to car.

The problem here is that a rate per thousand is based on the purchase price of a car and does not take into account the fact that the repayment will also change if the balloon repayment of the loan changes. Contract hire companies will want to set a balloon repayment equal to the estimated residual value of each car. Each make and model of car will have a different residual value and these will change over time. In other words, the balloon repayment is a variable too.

Some banks solve this problem by providing their rate charts to contract hire companies showing A and B factors (sometimes called Positive and Negative factors).

1. The A factor is similar to the rate per thousand shown above. It is the amount by which the capital cost should be multiplied as step one of the repayment calculation.

2. The B factor is the amount by which the residual value/balloon rental should be multiplied as step two of the repayment calculation.

The result of step two is deducted from the result of step one and the net result is the repayment that should be made to the bank.

6.3.14 EXERCISES

What is the difference between on the road price and capital cost?

What is a terminal pause?

What is a spread rental?

What is a rental profile?

Name the different types of rental profile.

Why might a company wish to pay all rentals in advance?

What is the difference between simple and compound interest?

What is the difference between a flat rate and a nominal rate of interest?

What is compound interest?

Why does it cause confusion?

If you borrow £100 repayable in 12 equal repayments of £10 over twelve months, with a total repayment of £120, what is the nominal rate of interest? What is the true rate of interest here? What would the APR be if this was a consumer transaction?

What is 1.5% per month as a nominal rate? What is it as a true rate?

Why does a transaction showing a 20% nominal rate give different true rates if the interest compounding periods are changed from monthly to quarterly?

What are A and B factors?

Are the interest rates that banks quote to businesses flat rates, nominal rates, true rates or APRs?

What is the definition of an APR?

How do fees affect it?

What is the difference between a fixed and a floating rate transaction?

Why might you prefer a variable rate deal to a fixed rate one?

How is FHBR calculated?

What is LIBOR and how often is it calculated?

Bank base rates fell today by 1% but your leasing company tells you its rentals for new business are not changing. Is it being unreasonable?

What are the methods of calculating variable rate finance lease interest?

6.4 RESIDUAL VALUES AND BALLOON RENTALS

Residual value risk has already been discussed.[198] In this section we discuss its impact on rental calculations.

By building a residual value or balloon rental into a finance agreement, the lender can reduce your regular monthly payments and still earn the return they require.

In the cash flow on the next page, the lender finances a £14,000 vehicle over twenty-four months. Payments are monthly in arrears. The nominal interest rate is 12% per annum or 1% per month.

---

198 See 5.12.

Month	Opening balance £	Interest £	Payment £	Closing balance £
1	14,000.00	140.00	659.03	13,480.97
2	13,480.97	134.81	659.03	12,956.75
3	12,956.75	129.57	659.03	12,427.29
4	12,427.29	124.27	659.03	11,892.54
5	11,892.54	118.93	659.03	11,352.43
6	11,352.43	113.52	659.03	10,806.93
7	10,806.93	108.07	659.03	10,255.97
8	10,255.97	102.56	659.03	9,699.50
9	9,699.50	96.99	659.03	9,137.47
10	9,137.47	91.37	659.03	8,569.81
11	8,569.81	85.70	659.03	7,996.48
12	7,996.48	79.96	659.03	7,417.42
13	7,417.42	74.17	659.03	6,832.56
14	6,832.56	68.33	659.03	6,241.86
15	6,241.86	62.42	659.03	5,645.25
16	5,645.25	56.45	659.03	5,042.67
17	5,042.67	50.43	659.03	4,434.07
18	4,434.07	44.34	659.03	3,819.38
19	3,819.38	38.19	659.03	3,198.55
20	3,198.55	31.99	659.03	2,571.51
21	2,571.51	25.72	659.03	1,938.19
22	1,938.19	19.38	659.03	1,298.55
23	1,298.55	12.99	659.03	652.50
24	652.50	6.53	659.03	0.00

Note how the equal monthly repayments of £659.03 reduce the balance outstanding in the lender's books to zero after the final payment has been made.

This cash flow could relate to a conditional sale agreement, where you pay £659.03 for twenty-four months then you become the owner of the vehicle.

Let us now assume instead that you want to take the vehicle on contract hire. This means you will hand it back to the lessor at the end of the agreement and that they will have to sell it to recover the balance of their investment. In this example they estimate the car will be worth £8,000 on disposal, so they build this amount into the rental calculation.

The cash flow now looks like this:

Month	Opening balance £	Interest £	Payment £	Closing balance £
1	14,000.00	140.00	362.44	13,777.56
2	13,777.56	137.78	362.44	13,552.89
3	13,552.89	135.53	362.44	13,325.98
4	13,325.98	133.26	362.44	13,096.80
5	13,096.80	130.97	362.44	12,865.33
6	12,865.33	128.65	362.44	12,631.54
7	12,631.54	126.32	362.44	12,395.42
8	12,395.42	123.95	362.44	12,156.93
9	12,156.93	121.57	362.44	11,916.06
10	11,916.06	119.16	362.44	11,672.78
11	11,672.78	116.73	362.44	11,427.06
12	11,427.06	114.27	362.44	11,178.89
13	11,178.89	111.79	362.44	10,928.24
14	10,928.24	109.28	362.44	10,675.08
15	10,675.08	106.75	362.44	10,419.39
16	10,419.39	104.19	362.44	10,161.15
17	10,161.15	101.61	362.44	9,900.32
18	9,900.32	99.00	362.44	9,636.88
19	9,636.88	96.37	362.44	9,370.81
20	9,370.81	93.71	362.44	9,102.07
21	9,102.07	91.02	362.44	8,830.65
22	8,830.65	88.31	362.44	8,556.52
23	8,556.52	85.57	362.44	8,279.64
24	8,279.64	82.80	362.44	8,000.00

The lessor only needs to receive a rental of £362.44 to repay their capital investment and interest in this transaction. Note how the interest rate is still 12% per annum nominal, or 1% per month. They are making the return they need to make over their cost of funds while receiving a much smaller rental.

The rental will be even lower if the lessor believes that the car will sell for more than £8,000 and higher if they believe it will sell for less.

Here is the same example showing that, with an £11,000 estimated residual value, the rental reduces to £251.22.

Month	Opening balance £	Interest £	Payment £	Closing balance £
1	14,000.00	140.00	251.22	13,888.78
2	13,888.78	138.89	251.22	13,776.45
3	13,776.45	137.76	251.22	13,662.99
4	13,662.99	136.63	251.22	13,548.40
5	13,548.40	135.48	251.22	13,432.66
6	13,432.66	134.33	251.22	13,315.77
7	13,315.77	133.16	251.22	13,197.71
8	13,197.71	131.98	251.22	13,078.46
9	13,078.46	130.78	251.22	12,958.03
10	12,958.03	129.58	251.22	12,836.39
11	12,836.39	128.36	251.22	12,713.53
12	12,713.53	127.14	251.22	12,589.45
13	12,589.45	125.89	251.22	12,464.12
14	12,464.12	124.64	251.22	12,337.54
15	12,337.54	123.38	251.22	12,209.70
16	12,209.70	122.10	251.22	12,080.57
17	12,080.57	120.81	251.22	11,950.16
18	11,950.16	119.50	251.22	11,818.44
19	11,818.44	118.18	251.22	11,685.40
20	11,685.40	116.85	251.22	11,551.04
21	11,551.04	115.51	251.22	11,415.33
22	11,415.33	114.15	251.22	11,278.26
23	11,278.26	112.78	251.22	11,139.82
24	11,139.82	111.40	251.22	11,000.00

A word of caution is needed here. If you take a car on contract hire, the lessor takes residual value risk and you can compare quotes between different suppliers and take the cheapest. You don't need to be concerned with the estimated residual value that each lessor has included in its calculations. That's their worry, not yours.

If you are unsure whether to take contract hire or hire purchase, and get quotes on both, it may be quite misleading to compare quotes just on the basis of the monthly payments. In the hire purchase transaction, you will be taking the residual value risk and the funder may offer you low rentals followed by a high balloon payment that you are obliged to pay.[199]

Continuing the above example, let us imagine that several contract hire companies have quoted you rentals for a particular car on non-maintenance contract hire and that the quoted rentals average £251.22 per month. A finance company suggests that you take the same car on hire purchase at £214.55 per month.

As you can see from the following cash flow, you will have to pay a balloon payment of £12,000.

Month	Opening balance £	Interest £	Payment £	Closing balance £
1	14,000.00	140.00	214.15	13,925.85
2	13,925.85	139.26	214.15	13,850.96
3	13,850.96	138.51	214.15	13,775.33
4	13,775.33	137.75	214.15	13,698.93
5	13,698.93	136.99	214.15	13,621.78
6	13,621.78	136.22	214.15	13,543.85
7	13,543.85	135.44	214.15	13,465.14
8	13,465.14	134.65	214.15	13,385.64
9	13,385.64	133.86	214.15	13,305.35
10	13,305.35	133.05	214.15	13,224.26
11	13,224.26	132.24	214.15	13,142.35
12	13,142.35	131.42	214.15	13,059.63
13	13,059.63	130.60	214.15	12,976.08
14	12,976.08	129.76	214.15	12,891.69
15	12,891.69	128.92	214.15	12,806.46
16	12,806.46	128.06	214.15	12,720.38
17	12,720.38	127.20	214.15	12,633.44
18	12,633.44	126.33	214.15	12,545.63
19	12,545.63	125.46	214.15	12,456.94
20	12,456.94	124.57	214.15	12,367.36
21	12,367.36	123.67	214.15	12,276.88
22	12,276.88	122.77	214.15	12,185.51
23	12,185.51	121.86	214.15	12,093.21
24	12,093.21	120.93	214.15	12,000.00

199 There is a limit to the amount that a lender can stretch this in order to offer you a low-sounding monthly payment. If he makes it too low and leaves you having to pay a large balloon payment, he runs the credit risk that you may be unable to make this payment and the further risk that if he repossesses the car it may not fetch this amount on resale.

It is clear that all of the contract hire companies that have provided quotes believe the car will be worth £11,000 at the end of the contract. You may pay less per month under the hire purchase arrangement, but if the contract hire companies are right and you take the HP deal, you will be £1,000 out of pocket when you sell the car after three years.

6.5 EARLY TERMINATION ARITHMETIC

If you wish to terminate the agreement early, one of several methods of calculation may be specified in the agreement.[200] The 'percentage of future rentals' and 'sliding scale based on time of the early termination' methods have already been discussed under Contract Hire.[201]

In this section we will discuss annuities and the 'sum of the digits' method.

6.5.1   ANNUITIES

Most people are familiar with the way a repayment mortgage works. You borrow a sum of money over a long period, make monthly repayments that only change if interest rates change, and at the end of the contract the mortgage has been fully repaid.

At the end of the first year the mortgage statement arrives and you are horrified to learn that, of the thousands of pounds repaid during the year, most have gone to repay interest and this has left only a tiny amount to repay the capital borrowed. The reassuring explanation is given by the lender: 'Don't worry, we have not made a mistake, this is perfectly normal, you owe more in the early years so most of the repayment is interest but in later years this will reverse and most of your repayment will be capital.'

The same principle works with any hire purchase agreement. In the early months the repayments are mainly interest, in the later months mainly capital.

Here is an example:

> A vehicle costs £10,000. The hire purchase agreement is for thirty-six months and calls for thirty-six equal monthly repayments, each being made at the start of the month, the first being made on delivery of the vehicle. The interest rate is 12% per annum nominal[202] which equates to 1% per month. The repayments are £328.85 per month.

---

200 If the agreement is silent on the method to be used, ask for written details.
201 See 1.2.9.
202 See 6.3.4.

	Opening balance £	Payment £	Interest £	Capital £	Closing balance £
1	10,000.00	328.85	96.71	232.14	9,767.86
2	9,767.86	328.85	94.39	234.46	9,533.39
3	9,533.39	328.85	92.05	236.81	9,296.58
4	9,296.58	328.85	89.68	239.18	9,057.41
5	9,057.41	328.85	87.29	241.57	8,815.84
6	8,815.84	328.85	84.87	243.98	8,571.85
7	8,571.85	328.85	82.43	246.42	8,325.43
8	8,325.43	328.85	79.97	248.89	8,076.54
9	8,076.54	328.85	77.48	251.38	7,825.16
10	7,825.16	328.85	74.96	253.89	7,571.27
11	7,571.27	328.85	72.42	256.43	7,314.84
12	7,314.84	328.85	69.86	258.99	7,055.84
13	7,055.84	328.85	67.27	261.58	6,794.26
14	6,794.26	328.85	64.65	264.20	6,530.06
15	6,530.06	328.85	62.01	266.84	6,263.22
16	6,263.22	328.85	59.34	269.51	5,993.71
17	5,993.71	328.85	56.65	272.21	5,721.50
18	5,721.50	328.85	53.93	274.93	5,446.57
19	5,446.57	328.85	51.18	277.68	5,168.89
20	5,168.89	328.85	48.40	280.45	4,888.44
21	4,888.44	328.85	45.60	283.26	4,605.18
22	4,605.18	328.85	42.76	286.09	4,319.09
23	4,319.09	328.85	39.90	288.95	4,030.14
24	4,030.14	328.85	37.01	291.84	3,738.30
25	3,738.30	328.85	34.09	294.76	3,443.54
26	3,443.54	328.85	31.15	297.71	3,145.83
27	3,145.83	328.85	28.17	300.68	2,845.14
28	2,845.14	328.85	25.16	303.69	2,541.45
29	2,541.45	328.85	22.13	306.73	2,234.72
30	2,234.72	328.85	19.06	309.80	1,924.93
31	1,924.93	328.85	15.96	312.89	1,612.03
32	1,612.03	328.85	12.83	316.02	1,296.01
33	1,296.01	328.85	9.67	319.18	976.83
34	976.83	328.85	6.48	322.37	654.45
35	654.45	328.85	3.26	325.60	328.85
36	328.85	328.85	0.00	328.85	0.00

This calculation[203] is called an annuity or an actuarial calculation. Note how the interest amount is higher in early months, lower in later months.

The fact that repayments are split between interest and capital is an economic fact of life and occurs regardless of the way that the funder has chosen to record the loan or lease in its books. The funder will have borrowed money to finance your contract and its borrowings will be working in exactly the same way. As you make your repayments to the funder, it will make repayments on its own borrowings.

An early termination will usually leave a balance outstanding in the funder's books that is larger than the then-current value of the vehicle being financed. The only exceptions are where you have paid a large initial deposit or the vehicle has retained its value remarkably well or a combination of the two.

This means that the amount the funder needs simply to break even on an early termination may come as a surprise to you.

6.5.2 The sum of the digits method

Clearly, the average borrower needs a simple method to help him work out how much interest is due each month. If he could work this out he could calculate how much of each payment goes to reduce the capital balance and therefore the outstanding balance he would be due to pay in the event of early termination.

The simple method that has developed over the years is called the sum of the digits method, which is also called the Rule of 78. It works as a good substitute for the more complex but more accurate, actuarial calculation.

Rather than charging interest on the balance outstanding during each a month, it takes the whole interest charge for the contract and spreads it across all of the months using a weighting system.

Once again, it's best to illustrate this with an example.

> We will use the same facts as in the above example. Note that the client borrowed £10,000 and has to repay £328.85 x 36 that is, a total of £11,838.76. Therefore the interest he is paying totals £1,838.76.
>
> Now we will do something strange and add up 1 + 2 + 3 + 4 and so on up to 36. The sum of numbers 1 to 36 is 666.[204]
>
> The first payment repays £99.39 of interest under the Rule of 78. That's calculated as 36 ÷ 666 x £1,838.76. The second payment repays 35 ÷ 666 x £1,838.76, that is, £96.36.
>
> The full schedule for this example is:

---

203 This schedule was calculated using the 'goal seek' function in Excel, though it could also have been calculated using the annuity function on a financial calculator. Many years ago we would have used something called annuity tables, which are long lists of numbers that show the split between interest and capital in a standard annuity. You may still be able to find annuity tables online or in some bookshops.

204 Which some may find a little spooky.

Payment No.	Rule of 78 Calculation		£
1	36	÷ 666 x £1,838.76 =	99.39
2	35	÷ 666 x £1,838.76 =	96.63
3	34	÷ 666 x £1,838.76 =	93.87
4	33	÷ 666 x £1,838.76 =	91.11
5	32	÷ 666 x £1,838.76 =	88.35
6	31	÷ 666 x £1,838.76 =	85.59
7	30	÷ 666 x £1,838.76 =	82.83
8	29	÷ 666 x £1,838.76 =	80.07
9	28	÷ 666 x £1,838.76 =	77.31
10	27	÷ 666 x £1,838.76 =	74.54
11	26	÷ 666 x £1,838.76 =	71.78
12	25	÷ 666 x £1,838.76 =	69.02
13	24	÷ 666 x £1,838.76 =	66.26
14	23	÷ 666 x £1,838.76 =	63.50
15	22	÷ 666 x £1,838.76 =	60.74
16	21	÷ 666 x £1,838.76 =	57.98
17	20	÷ 666 x £1,838.76 =	55.22
18	19	÷ 666 x £1,838.76 =	52.46
19	18	÷ 666 x £1,838.76 =	49.70
20	17	÷ 666 x £1,838.76 =	46.94
21	16	÷ 666 x £1,838.76 =	44.17
22	15	÷ 666 x £1,838.76 =	41.41
23	14	÷ 666 x £1,838.76 =	38.65
24	13	÷ 666 x £1,838.76 =	35.89
25	12	÷ 666 x £1,838.76 =	33.13
26	11	÷ 666 x £1,838.76 =	30.37
27	10	÷ 666 x £1,838.76 =	27.61
28	9	÷ 666 x £1,838.76 =	24.85
29	8	÷ 666 x £1,838.76 =	22.09
30	7	÷ 666 x £1,838.76 =	19.33
31	6	÷ 666 x £1,838.76 =	16.57
32	5	÷ 666 x £1,838.76 =	13.80
33	4	÷ 666 x £1,838.76 =	11.04
34	3	÷ 666 x £1,838.76 =	8.28
35	2	÷ 666 x £1,838.76 =	5.52
36	1	÷ 666 x £1,838.76 =	2.76

Compare the actuarial calculation with the Rule of 78 calculation and you will note that the latter gives us a pretty close approximation of the more accurate actuarial figures.

The difference is shown on the chart opposite.

To determine a Rule of 78 early termination figure, we can use the Rule of 78 interest figures to replace the balances shown in the first chart, to produce the chart shown on page 262.

Payment No.	Actuarial £	Rule of 78 £	Difference £
1	96.71	99.39	2.68
2	94.39	96.63	2.24
3	92.05	93.87	1.83
4	89.68	91.11	1.43
5	87.29	88.35	1.06
6	84.87	85.59	0.72
7	82.43	82.83	0.40
8	79.97	80.07	0.10
9	77.48	77.31	-0.17
10	74.96	74.54	-0.42
11	72.42	71.78	-0.64
12	69.86	69.02	-0.84
13	67.27	66.26	-1.01
14	64.65	63.50	-1.15
15	62.01	60.74	-1.27
16	59.34	57.98	-1.36
17	56.65	55.22	-1.43
18	53.93	52.46	-1.47
19	51.18	49.70	-1.48
20	48.40	46.94	-1.47
21	45.60	44.17	-1.42
22	42.76	41.41	-1.35
23	39.90	38.65	-1.25
24	37.01	35.89	-1.12
25	34.09	33.13	-0.96
26	31.15	30.37	-0.78
27	28.17	27.61	-0.56
28	25.16	24.85	-0.31
29	22.13	22.09	-0.04
30	19.06	19.33	0.27
31	15.96	16.57	0.60
32	12.83	13.80	0.97
33	9.67	11.04	1.37
34	6.48	8.28	1.80
35	3.26	5.52	2.27
36	0.00	2.76	2.76

Payment No.	Opening balance £	Payment £	Rule of 78 Interest £	Capital Repayment £	Closing balance £
1	10,000.00	328.85	99.39	229.46	9,770.54
2	9,770.54	328.85	96.63	232.22	9,538.31
3	9,538.31	328.85	93.87	234.98	9,303.33
4	9,303.33	328.85	91.11	237.74	9,065.59
5	9,065.59	328.85	88.35	240.51	8,825.08
6	8,825.08	328.85	85.59	243.27	8,581.81
7	8,581.81	328.85	82.83	246.03	8,335.79
8	8,335.79	328.85	80.07	248.79	8,087.00
9	8,087.00	328.85	77.31	251.55	7,835.45
10	7,835.45	328.85	74.54	254.31	7,581.14
11	7,581.14	328.85	71.78	257.07	7,324.07
12	7,324.07	328.85	69.02	259.83	7,064.24
13	7,064.24	328.85	66.26	262.59	6,801.64
14	6,801.64	328.85	63.50	265.35	6,536.29
15	6,536.29	328.85	60.74	268.11	6,268.17
16	6,268.17	328.85	57.98	270.88	5,997.30
17	5,997.30	328.85	55.22	273.64	5,723.66
18	5,723.66	328.85	52.46	276.40	5,447.26
19	5,447.26	328.85	49.70	279.16	5,168.11
20	5,168.11	328.85	46.94	281.92	4,886.19
21	4,886.19	328.85	44.17	284.68	4,601.51
22	4,601.51	328.85	41.41	287.44	4,314.07
23	4,314.07	328.85	38.65	290.20	4,023.86
24	4,023.86	328.85	35.89	292.96	3,730.90
25	3,730.90	328.85	33.13	295.72	3,435.18
26	3,435.18	328.85	30.37	298.48	3,136.69
27	3,136.69	328.85	27.61	301.25	2,835.45
28	2,835.45	328.85	24.85	304.01	2,531.44
29	2,531.44	328.85	22.09	306.77	2,224.67
30	2,224.67	328.85	19.33	309.53	1,915.14
31	1,915.14	328.85	16.57	312.29	1,602.86
32	1,602.86	328.85	13.80	315.05	1,287.81
33	1,287.81	328.85	11.04	317.81	969.99
34	969.99	328.85	8.28	320.57	649.42
35	649.42	328.85	5.52	323.33	326.09
36	326.09	328.85	2.76	326.09	0.00

So under Rule of 78, the balances at the end of each month would not differ significantly from those under the actuarial method.

The Rule of 78 gets its name from the fact that it represents the sum of the numbers from 1 to 12. So, in calculating a Rule of 78 settlement in a one-year contract, the denominator in the formula would be 78, not 666.

The contract may specify that one, two or more months' interest have to be added when calculating the actual settlement amount.

If you decide that you wish to hand back the vehicle (and if the lessor agrees to take it back and sell it) these early termination settlement amounts will be reduced by the actual or projected sale proceeds of the vehicle.

7 LEASE v BUY

7.1 DISCOUNTED CASH FLOW

Should you buy a vehicle or should you lease it?

In answering this question you need to consider whether you want to take the residual value risk, the tax effect if you buy rather than lease, and balance sheet issues.[206] You will need also to carry out a financial evaluation of the lease v buy decision. That is what this chapter will be focusing on.

You are about to acquire a new car. It costs £10,000. You expect to sell it in three years' time for £3,000. You had expected to buy it for cash but the salesman is offering you a non-maintenance contract hire deal at £2,800 per annum, payable annually in advance.[206]

You had planned to buy it using your bank overdraft on which you currently pay interest at 10% per annum

You have to decide whether to lease or buy. What are the thoughts that run through your mind?[207]

> 'Three times £2,800 is £8,400. The car will be worth, say, £3,000 at the end. Am I better off (a) paying three rentals at £2,800, or (b) paying £10,000 now, paying the interest on my overdraft and getting back £3,000 when I sell the car at the end of three years?'

You need a tool to be able to make these comparisons and the best tool that we have is called discounted cash flow analysis (DCF).

DCF is a method of comparing alternative business decisions based on the cash flows they will produce and expressing these in today's money terms, also called present value (PV).

DCF is used in investment appraisal and analysis. You can use it for lease v contract hire v contract purchase v hire purchase v lease purchase v buy decisions, in fact for any situation where you have choices to make that will involve different cash flows.

---

205 See 5.12, 17.1.2-4 and 8.4 respectively.

206 A bit unusual but bear with this as it makes the maths easier later.

207 "I've got space on my overdraft, leasing is going to be complicated, he's asking me to fill in all of these forms, I bet he earns more commission if I take it on contract hire."

An employee deciding whether to take a company car or a cash option can also use DCF to establish the cheapest option.

DCF uses the idea of the time value of money. This is the concept that says £1 received in one year's time is worth less than £1 received today. This is because you could invest £1 today to generate more over the year and also because inflation will reduce the value of that £1 over the year.

It uses interest rates to 'discount' (that is, to reduce) future cash flows to 'today's' value (present value) so that they can be added up or deducted as if they were all happening today. Then the present value of all of the cash flows of two competing options is compared and the option showing the highest present value (or the lowest negative present value) is the winner.

Let's look again at the assumptions we made above:

You are considering whether to lease or buy a £10,000 car. You expect to sell it in three years for £3,000. Your normal borrowing cost is 10% per annum You are being offered a non-maintenance contract at £2,800 per annum, payable in advance. You have to decide whether to lease or buy.

Option one is to buy the car and sell it in three years.

£10,000 paid today is £10,000 in today's money (present value).

Next you need to determine the present value of the £3,000 receivable in three years' time. We do this by adjusting the £3,000 by an interest rate, 10% per annum, using compound interest. This is known as 'discounting'.

A simple way to think of this is to ask 'how much would I have to invest today to give me £3,000 in three years if I earn 10% per annum interest?

The answer is £2,253.94

This spreadsheet proves that this figure is correct.

Year	Start balance £	Interest £	End balance £
1	2,253.94	225.39	2,479.34
2	2,479.34	247.93	2,727.27
3	2,727.27	272.73	3,000.00

You could calculate this using trial and error or using the Excel 'goal seek' function.

An easier way to do it would be to use a calculator to work out the value of the formula:

$1 \div (1.1)^3$.

That is, one divided by 1.1 and raised to the power of 3.

The steps here are as follows:

Work out 1.1 to the power of 3.

i.e. 1.1 x 1.1 x 1.1 = 1.331

Then divide 1.331 into 1, i.e. 1 ÷ 1.331

The answer is 0.751315. This is called the discount factor.

Then multiply the discount factor by £3,000.

The answer is £2,253.94 (actually £2,253.944 before rounding)

This is the present value of £3,000 received in three years time at a discount rate of 10% per annum.

The reason you needed to work first with 1.1 is that 0.1 is 10% and for the discounting arithmetic to work you have to place the 10% after the number 1 in DCF calculations. So, for example, if you were about to work out the discount factor for 8% over 4 years, you would use $1 \div (1.08)^4$.

If you buy the car you will pay £10,000 today and receive £3,000 in three years' time. That £3,000 in three years' time is worth £2,253.94 to you today.

So, if you buy, you will pay out £10,000 and receive £2,253.94 in "today's money", so the net cost to you today is £7,746.06. (This is the net cost to you but not necessarily to someone else. If their borrowing rate is 12% they will arrive at a different answer.)

Option two is to lease the vehicle for three years.

As each rental falls due at a different time you have to do three discounting calculations; after one, two and three years. You will need different discount factors for each of these payments to reduce (that is, discount) the value of the rental to present value terms.

We saw that solving $1 \div (1.1)^3$ gave us the discount factor for a cash flow arising in three years' time. Similarly, $1 \div (1.1)^2$ is the discount factor for a cash flow arising in two years' time and this is the date when the last rental would be payable under the leasing option.

$1 \div (1.1)^1$, that is, $1 \div 1.1$, is the discount factor for the first rental and $1 \div (1.1)^0$ is the discount factor for any payment on day one. However, $1 \div (1.1)^0 = 1$, reflecting the fact that there is no need to discount a cash flow that occurs on day one.[208]

We then add up the three present values of the three discounted rentals and see that they total £7,659.50.

The chart shows how we can then compare the two options.

Option 1: PURCHASE			
Buy for 10k today and receive £3,000 in three years			
Step 1; determine value of £3,000 in three years at today's value (present value)			
The discount rate is	$1 \div (1.1)^3 = 0.751315$		
So	£3,000 x 0.751315 =		£ 2,253.94
Less: Outlay today			£10,000.00
Present value			-£ 7,746.06
Option 2: LEASE			
Pay £2,800pa starting today, for three years			
First rental (This occurs today so there is no need to discount it)			-£2,800.00
2nd rental	£2,800 ÷ 1.1	0.909091 =	-£2,545.45
3rd rental	£2,800 ÷ 1.12	0.826446 =	-£2,314.05
			-£7,659.50
So contract hire is cheaper than purchase by			£86.55

So now we have our two options:

- buy for a PV of £7,746.06 or
- lease for a PV of £7,659.50

If you lease you will save £86.55 in present value terms. If there are no other factors that you need to consider, this analysis shows that you should opt for the lease and save £86.55.

---

208 Any number raised to the power of nought is 1.

This has been a very simple example. You can use DCF techniques to decide between any two series of cash flows, however complex. For example, you might wish to consider payments that are to be made monthly, on specific days of the month, or an irregular payment pattern, or you might include the tax effects of the options you are considering.

We have ignored VAT, corporation (or income tax) and expenses in these examples but in a real evaluation these should be included.

7.2 EXERCISES

What is the difference between a residual value and a balloon rental?

How do they affect HP and lease calculations?

What happens to a rental if a residual value is increased?

What happens to an HP repayment if a balloon rental is reduced?

If the monthly payments on a non-maintenance contract hire deal are higher than on an HP deal for the same car, should you take the HP deal?

What is DCF?

You normally borrow money at 8% per annum You are offered two deals; a three-year HP agreement at £2,900 per annum payable in advance with a £3,300 balloon payment, or a non-maintenance contract hire at £3,000 per annum. Which is cheaper for you?

Other than rentals and HP repayments, what other cash flows might you bring into a lease v buy DCF calculation?

8 LEASE ACCOUNTING

8.1 ON OR OFF BALANCE SHEET?

8.1.1 THE BALANCE SHEET TREATMENT OF LEASES

Accountants and auditors are concerned to ensure that a true and fair view is shown in the financial results that a business reports to its shareholders, creditors, employees, other stakeholders and the public. For this to happen, all businesses need to report similar transactions in a consistent manner.

Most business transactions are quite straightforward and it is unlikely that any two accountants would record them differently. However, there are many areas where two accountants could hold varying views on how a particular transaction should be recorded. Add in a little bit of pressure from the management or owner of the business for the accountant to come up with some 'creative accounting' and hey presto, identical businesses can end up reporting widely differing results.

Hence in the late 1960s the Accounting Standards Steering Committee (ASSC) was formed by the UK accountancy bodies, to produce 'best practice' rules for recording and reporting business transactions.

The ASSC issued Statements of Standard Accounting Practice (SSAPs) with the intention of standardising accounting practice. They had a hit-list of topics requiring standardisation and over the years they made good progress through this list: how to account for VAT, depreciation, stock and work in progress, earnings per share – all of these they dealt with without a hitch. They stumbled a bit on SSAP7 accounting for inflation, later withdrawing completely that accounting standard.[209]

In 1990 the ASSC was renamed the Accounting Standards Committee (ASC) and its role was taken over by the Accounting Standards Board.

---

209 It was only issued as a 'provisional' standard, called Provisional Statement of Standard Accounting Practice (PSSAP) 7, reflecting how difficult it is to account for inflation and how controversial this issue was at the time. They had another go at it some years later but that was not too successful either. Fortunately, the low inflation of the 1990s arrived just in time to save the accounting profession from having to adopt an agreed method of inflation accounting.

The ASB issues Financial Reporting Standards (FRSs). It is mandatory for accountants to implement SSAPs and FRSs when preparing financial statements that are to be released to the general public. Effectively, SSAPs and FRSs are accounting law in the UK for small and medium size companies that are not publicly quoted and therefore don't have to report financial results under International Accounting Standards.[210] There is some push to make all businesses company with international standards but that is unlikely to happen for some years.

8.1.2 SSAP21

In 1984 the ASSC issued Statement of Standard Accounting Practice 21, 'Accounting for leases and hire purchase transactions'. (This was amended in 1997).

SSAP21 took a decade to produce, longer than any previous accounting standard. It was also the lengthiest standard to date and it was accompanied by an even larger set of guidance notes that explained how to implement the recommendations of the standard.

When SSAP21 first saw the light of day it was as an 'exposure draft', that is, a draft standard issued for discussion purposes. It was called ED29 and it caused uproar. A big industry had grown up offering finance leases[211] to UK companies and a major selling point was that the assets did not have to appear on the balance sheets of the lessees – that is, they did not have to be 'capitalised' – because the lessees did not own the assets.

The leasing industry argued that as they, rather than their client, owned the asset, it should appear on their balance sheets rather than the client's. They said that lessees should account for the lease rentals as revenue expenditure and charge them directly to their profit and loss accounts.

The industry lost its argument with the standard-setters and SSAP21 was published requiring capitalisation of finance leases.

Why did this happen? Why did the 'ownership' argument fail? It was because accounting academics had moved away from the idea that the balance sheet should reflect just the assets a company owns. Instead, they had warmed to the idea that it should show all of the assets employed in a business, regardless of how they were obtained or financed. So it was the right to use the vehicle in the business that was the asset, rather than the ownership of the asset itself.

There is some similarity with property accounting in this thinking. If you buy a twenty-five year lease on a commercial property and take a bank loan to do so, you know you have to hand the property back at the end of the lease period to the freeholder, or other landlord. They own the property, not you. You just own a right to use it for twenty-five years and have an obligation to the bank. Yet no one would

---

210 See 8.3

211 See 1.6.

say you should keep that investment off your balance sheet. It is a substantial business asset that you have paid for and it would distort the reported results of the business if you just charged the annual loan repayments to your profit and loss account.

8.1.3 FRS 5

 The Accounting Standards Board issued Financial Reporting Standard 5, 'Reflecting the substance of transactions in assets and liabilities' in 1994 and has been amended several times. It was designed to move accounting on a further step.

It requires that in their accounts companies should show the financial consequences of transactions regardless of the financial structures that are used. This upholds the long-standing accounting principle of 'substance over form', which says that it does not matter what the documents say the transaction is, it's the effect of the transaction that is the key.

FRS5 applies to all transactions, rather than just being targeted at leasing. It helps to resolve one of the long-standing problems with the implementation of SSAP21.

SSAP21 defines a finance lease as one where substantially all of the risks and rewards of ownership of an asset are transferred to the lessee. This begs the question – what is meant by 'substantially' and how should it be measured?

SSAP21 offered some help here; it said:

> 'It should be presumed that … a transfer of risks and rewards occurs if … the present value of the minimum lease payment … amounts to substantially all (normally 90% or more) of the fair value of the leased asset'.

It says that if this applies to a lease it should be treated as a finance lease and capitalised.

The leasing industry rode a coach and horses through the intentions of the standard by shouting the mantra 'If the residual value is more than 10% of the price of the asset you can leave it off your balance sheet'.

We'll ignore here the fact that the clause referred to 'present value', thereby requiring a discounted cash flow calculation to be carried out before the decision could be made on the size of the residual that is required to keep an asset off the lessee's balance sheet.

The main point is that the reference to 90% was only meant to be a guide to decision-making. The key step in deciding the accounting treatment was to decide whether the real risk of ownership had passed to the lessee. And in many of the deals that were struck the real risk of the sale proceeds remained with the lessee and only in remote circumstances would the lessor bear a loss. Nonetheless, citing the 90% of present value 'rule', many companies managed to keep these assets off their balance sheets.

Many funders and lessors managed to stretch the interpretation of SSAP 21 to allow finance leases to be 'on balance sheet'. The ASC saw that this was happening and tried to outlaw it through Technical Release 664 in 1987. It called for the risks and rewards of the transaction to be looked at closely in determining whether a lease was a finance or operating lease, rather than looking at just the 90% test. This release did not have the hoped-for impact and many finance leases continued to be accounted for as operating leases. It took the publication of FRS5 to stop the practice of wrongly accounting for the borderline cases.

FRS 5 says:

> 'A reporting entity's financial statements should report the substance of the transactions into which it has entered. In determining the substance of a transaction, all of its aspects and implications should be identified and greater weight given to those more likely to have a commercial effect in practice. To determine the substance of a transaction it is necessary to determine whether [it] has given rise to new assets or liabilities. Evidence that [it] has ... an asset is given if [it] is exposed to the risks inherent in the benefits. Where a transaction [creates] an asset, the item should be recognised on the balance sheet if ... a future inflow or outflow will occur and the item can be measured at a monetary amount with sufficient reliability.'

While the accounting language may be slightly impenetrable, the message is pretty clear: if you have any residual value risk the lease has to go on your balance sheet.

FRS5 helped to do away with artificial structures, because it is much more prescriptive.

8.2 SO WHY IS CAPITALISATION AN IMPORTANT ISSUE?

Whether or not an item appears on the balance sheet can have a material effect on the published results of a business and particularly its return on assets (RoA).

RoA is a ratio much favoured by financial analysts as it shows how well a company is using its assets. It is calculated as pre-tax profits divided by total assets multiplied by 100 and is therefore expressed as a percentage.

'A' Plc and 'B' Plc are both in the same industry. Both make £1,000,000 profit. A Plc employs £10,000,000 of assets while B Plc employs £12,000,000. Therefore A is making a 10% return on assets, while B is making only 8.33%.

If B were to lease £2,000,000 of vehicles under, say, contract hire, rather than buying them outright, it could remove the £2,000,000 of assets from its balance sheet and show the same return on assets as A.

8.3 INTERNATIONAL ACCOUNTING STANDARD 17 (IAS17)

The International Accounting Standards Committee (IASC) was formed in 1973 to co-ordinate all accounting standards around the world, an ambitious project given the widely differing business practices in different countries. Its approach has been to set standards that make good accounting sense.

The IASC issued International Accounting Standard 17 (IAS 17) in 1982, which for all material purposes permits leases to be accounted for either as set out in the American lease accounting standard Financial Accounting Standard 13 (FAS 13) or as set out in SSAP21.

From 1993 to 2001 the major accounting bodies in the UK, Canada, Australia, the USA and New Zealand, together with representatives of the IASC, had a working group called the G4+1[212]. In 1999 the G4+1 issued a discussion paper *Accounting for Leases: A New Approach* proposing that all leases should be disclosed on the balance sheets of lessees, including contract hire. This did not mean the cost of the vehicle would have to appear on the balance sheet of the lessee, only the discounted value (the 'present 'value') of the minimum rental payments that the lessee was contractually obliged to pay. This amount would be substantially less than the capital cost of the vehicle as it would ignore the residual value.

This G4+1 paper did not create as much excitement as might have been expected. The technical press reported on it but the fleet press largely ignored it. It is fair to say that most of the leasing industry would have preferred it to go away. In any event, the proposal made slow progress.

The G4+1 disbanded in 2001. It felt that it had no further function because a new International Accounting Standards Board (IASB) had been formed. It issues International Financial Reporting Standards.

The IASB has asked the UK Accounting Standards Board to review lease accounting. On the formation of the new IASB and lease accounting has been designated 'non priority' status by the IASB.

In 2002 the IASB published a consultation paper setting out draft revisions of IAS17.

International accounting standards have not been mandatory to date. However, that's all about to change.

In 2000 the European Commission issued a report[213] advising that before the end of the year they would formally propose that all consolidated accounts be produced in accordance with International Accounting Standards with effect from 2005. The proposal was issued in 2001 and related to listed companies only.

---

212 Yes, I know that this makes five countries so it should be the G5+1. Originally there were only four nations and they kept that name when the committee grew.

213 'EU Financial Reporting Strategy: The way forward'

On 7 June 2002 the European Council of Ministers approved a regulation that required all listed companies to comply with International Accounting Standards with effect from 1 January 2005. On 19 July 2002 this was approved by the European Parliament[214] On 29 September 2003 the European Commission approved all existing international accounting standards.[215]

The UK Department of Trade and Industry has announced that International Accounting Standards will also apply to unlisted UK companies.

In 2004 the Accounting Standards Board issued *UK Accounting Standards: A Strategy for Convergence with International Financial Reporting Standards.* It says that there is no sense in using two different sets of accounting standards in the UK and that convergence of UK accounting standards to International Financial Reporting Standards is a foregone conclusion. It therefore proposed a speedy but phased transition to one set of standards that will replace UK standards.

The move to IAS17 has little impact on the lease accounting method used by lessees in the UK because IAS17 is similar to SSAP21 for lessees. However, it had a significant effect on the way lessors account for some types of lease. See 19.4.13.

Throughout the last decade it has been widely expected that IAS17 would be replaced at some stage with an accounting method that reflects the thinking of the G4+1 group.

8.4 LESSEE ACCOUNTING

8.4.1 Operating lease accounting

Operating leases include contract hire, daily hire, rental agreements and leases of any other description where the risks and rewards of ownership do not transfer to the lessee.

SSAP21 says that rental agreements and operating leases should be kept off the balance sheet of the lessee and treated as revenue expenditure.

The industry has always considered that this is eminently sensible; when you rent something from a contract hire company and have every intention of handing it back at some stage it makes sense that the asset should not appear on your balance sheet. You just want to use the asset, pay the rentals and show these in your profit and loss account.

Operating lease rentals should be accounted for as expenses in the profit and loss account on a straight-line basis, even if the payments are not made on this basis.

Under SSAP21 you are required to include an accounting policy note in your annual financial report stating that operating lease rentals have been accounted for

---

214 Regulation (EC) No 1606/2002 of the European Parliament.

215 Except IAS 32 and IAS39 which were being reviewed by the IASC at the time and are not relevant to vehicle management.

in this way. The note must split the operating lease costs between plant and machinery and other operating lease rentals.

You must also show future commitments under operating leases, split between those payable in less than one year, 1–5 years and more than five years.

The note will look like this:

Future commitments under operating leases:

Expiring	Land	Other
Under one year	£x,xxx	£x,xxx
1–5 years	£x,xxx	£x,xxx
Over five years	£x,xxx	£x,xxx

8.4.2 FINANCE LEASE ACCOUNTING

What then of finance leases, where you pay for the asset and the lessor's finance charges in full, then get to keep the majority of the sale proceeds?

SSAP21 provided the first official definition of a finance lease and said it was a lease that transfers "substantially all of the risks and rewards of ownership of the asset to the lessee". It also said that these should be shown on the balance sheet of the lessee.

The way that this should happen was by recording an asset and a liability.

On day one of the lease, the following entry will be made in the company's books:

- **Debit:** Fixed Assets account with the present value of the minimum lease payments[216]
- **Credit:** Lease Obligations account (a creditor in the balance sheet)

The minimum lease payments are those to which the lessee is committed. So, if there is an optional secondary rental period those rentals will be excluded from the calculation.

The interest rate used for the discounting period will be the rate used by the lessor in calculating the lease rental. If this is not known, a reasonable estimate may be made.

The fixed asset figure and the lease obligation figure are, by definition, equal on the day they are first entered into the books. From that day on they will be treated differently and it is unlikely they will remain the same over the period of the lease.

As the rentals are paid, they are normally allocated between the profit and loss account (an interest element) and the balance sheet (reduction in the capital value of the finance lease obligation). It is normal to do this using an actuarial method of calculation that produces a constant interest cost to the business on the declining balance owed under the finance lease. Hence the balance sheet value of the lease obligation always represents the present value of the future payment obligations under the lease.

---

216 See 7.1.

However, this is quite a complex method of calculation, so often the 'sum of the digits' method is used instead.[217]

For small leases of immaterial amount, some companies just allocate the finance element on a straight-line basis over the lease period.

Here is a simple example:

■ You enter into a finance lease with a leasing company.

■ The cost of the vehicle is £10,000

■ The annual rental payable in arrears is £4,021.15.

■ No balloon rental is payable.

■ You are to receive 97% of any sale proceeds.

So the lease type is certainly a finance lease, as the lessor has only a 3% interest in the leased asset.

You know the interest rate in the lease is 10% per annum.

The total payments are £12,063.45. As the capital cost is £10,000, it follows that £2,063.45 of interest is being paid.

First you have to decide how to allocate the £2,063.45.

	Outstanding during the period	Interest charge at end of period	Sub-total	Rental	Carried forward
	£	£	£	£	£
1	10,000.00	1,000.00	11,000.00	4,021.15	6,978.85
2	6,978.85	697.89	7,676.74	4,021.15	3,655.59
3	3,655.59	365.56	4,021.15	4,021.15	-
		2,063.44		12,063.44	

Note: this chart was produced using the 'goal seek' function of a spreadsheet program. Had we not known the cost of the vehicle – which is quite often the case with a finance lease as there is no reason why the lessor should disclose this – we could have entered the monthly rentals and the interest rate and 'solved' for the present value. This would have produced the £10,000.00 figure that needs to be shown in the balance sheet.

In the example, you owe £10,000 for one year. At the end of that year you are 'charged' interest of 10% and simultaneously pay a rental of £4,021.15. That brings the balance of your obligation to £6,978.85 and this amount is outstanding for the whole of year two until, once again, interest is charged, though this time on the reduced balance.

This process continues until you have paid all of the rentals, and nothing remains outstanding.

217 See 6.5.2.

In this example, the finance charges to be allocated between the three years are £1,000.00, £697.89 and £365.56 respectively. (If your financial year does not coincide with the lease payments, these amounts will have to be allocated on a time basis between the different years).

As your three rentals included these interest charges the balance of each rental must have repaid the capital due to the lessor, as follows:

Year	Rental £	Interest charge at end of period £	Capital £
1	4,021.15	1,000.00	3,021.15
2	4,021.15	697.89	3,323.26
3	4,021.15	365.56	3,655.59

Now we can see the amount of capital repayment. Note how it increases over time, just like a mortgage repayment.

For accounting purposes the asset should be depreciated over the shorter of the lease period and the useful economic life of the asset.

Vehicles will almost always have a longer useful economic life than the lease period.

They may be depreciated in any of the ways permitted by FRS15, accounting for depreciation.[218] That means you will depreciate a finance-leased asset in the same way that you would depreciate a similar asset bought outright.

So, continuing the above example, you now have to decide how to depreciate the leased asset.

You know that the vehicle costs £10,000 and your accounting policy for depreciating other vehicles is 25% per annum straight line. So you depreciate at £2,500 per annum, thus:

Year	Cost £	Depreciation £	Carried forward £
1	10,000	2,500	7,500
2	7,500	2,500	5,000
3	5,000	2,500	2,500

218 Financial Reporting Standard 15 'Tangible Fixed Assets' issued by the Accounting Standards Board February 1999.
See www.frc.org.uk/images/uploaded/documents/FRS%2015.pdf

At the end of the third year, the lessor sells the vehicle or else you sell it as their agent.

Let us assume sale proceeds are £3,000. Of these, under the terms of your agreement with the lessor, you will retain £3,000 x 97% = £2,910.

As £2,500 is outstanding in your books, you will record a £410 profit on disposal of the vehicle.

This example has, once again, been kept deliberately simple. Most real-life calculations will involve monthly payments, balloon rentals and payments in advance.

SSAP21 also sets out the disclosure requirements for finance leases.

The financial statements of the business must contain a note showing how finance lease assets are depreciated.

The interest payable should be disclosed separately in the profit and loss account under the heading Interest Payable.

Assets financed on finance leases should be disclosed separately on the balance sheet as part of Fixed Assets.

The finance lease obligations should be disclosed separately as finance lease creditors in the balance sheet, split between those amounts due within one year and those due later.

A note to the accounts should show the gross rentals payable, as follows:

Payable	£
In under 1 year	x,xxx
In 1 – 5 years	x,xxx
In over 5 years	x,xxx
	x,xxx
Less:	
Future finance charges	x,xxx
Total	x,xxx

8.4.3   HIRE PURCHASE ACCOUNTING

SSAP21 says hire purchase and other deferred purchase methods of finance should be 'capitalised', in other words, shown on the balance sheet of the borrower.

This was not a contentious part of SSAP21. Even before the standard had been published, hire purchase agreements had always been capitalised. It is logical to do so because:

■ you are buying an asset

■ you are using hire purchase as a form of borrowing

■ the asset will be yours to sell at the end of the lease

■ the transaction is similar in many respects to taking a loan to buy an asset; a transaction that would always be on your balance sheet.

Hire purchase transactions are normally accounted for in the same way as finance leases, except, of course, that they should be referred to as Hire Purchase in the financial statements.

8.4.4 LOCAL AUTHORITY LEASING

Local authorities are just as concerned about the dividing line between capital and revenue expenditure as quoted companies.

For generations governments have been keen to control local authority capital expenditure, as this is reported as part of the Public Sector Borrowing Requirement, a key economic measure of financial prudence.

Government is less concerned about local authorities using operating leases as the rentals are classed as revenue, rather than capital expenditure. Hence a very large amount of plant, machinery and vehicles is leased to local authorities every year on operating leases and contract hire.

8.5 LESSOR ACCOUNTING

SSAP21 sets out the accounting methods to be used by lessors to record different types of leases in their books.

A detailed explanation of these rules is beyond the scope of this book as it is unlikely to be of interest to fleet managers.

Nonetheless, the introduction of International Financial Reporting Standards brought about a significant change in the way that lessors account for some types of agreement and this is discussed further in 19.4.13.

8.6 FUTURE DEVELOPMENTS IN LEASE ACCOUNTING

At the time of writing (September 2011) lease accounting is a very hot topic.

The IASB published the exposure draft of a new lease accounting standard in 2010[219] and it seems they will modify and reissue this in 2011. The draft reflects the work they have done in conjunction with the US Financial Accounting Standards Board (FASB) and reflects the desire to have one globally accepted standard for lease accounting.

---

219 www.ifrs.org/Current+Projects/IASB+Projects/Leases/Leases.htm

The exposure draft proposes a major change that will affect lessees - operating leases will have to be shown on the balance sheet of lessees.

This represents a further step along the journey started when SSAP21 was published in 1984.

Leases on or off balance sheet (lessee)	Pre-SSAP era (to 1984)	SSAP21 (1984-2012?)	IASB proposals (from 2012?)
Finance leases	Off	On	On
Operating leases	Off	Off	On

Finance leases and operating leases were both off balance sheet until SSAP21. Then it became necessary for lessees to put finance leases on balance sheet. It seems certain that soon it will be necessary for lessees to put operating leases on balance sheet too.

This raises an interesting question; what exactly is it that is being put onto the lessee's balance sheet? It can't be the ownership of the asset, say, the car - the lessee doesn't own the car. And it can't be the purchase or list price of the car – the lessee hasn't paid for that and will not do so.

The accounting standard setters have decided that the lessee does own an asset however; the right to use the vehicle over a period of time. And the lessee has a corresponding liability too; the obligation to pay the lease rentals.

This is called the 'right of use approach'.

SSAP21 and IAS17 categorised leases according to where the risks and reward lay. Broadly, they said that if the hirer took the full residual value risk the asset had to appear on their balance sheet but if they didn't take full RV risk they could leave the asset off their balance sheet. The new exposure draft does away with this type of distinction and will put all leases onto the lessee's balance sheet. The only exceptions would be leases that cannot be extended beyond twelve months.

The rules apply to all organisations that publish accounts under international accounting standards, but not those – generally smaller businesses - that report under UK generally accepted accounting principles (GAAP – which includes SSAP21).

The exposure draft requires lessees to account for the right they have to use the asset (i.e. the vehicle) and the liability to pay lease rentals. They steps lessees would need take are:

ASSETS

- Establish the compulsory payments they are required to make under the lease
- Discount these to present value[220] using the lessees' incremental borrowing rate

---

220 See 7.1.

- Depreciate the asset every year in accordance with their regular accounting policy for the depreciation of such assets. The depreciation method needs to comply with *International Accounting Standard 16 – Depreciation (IAS16)*.

Liabilities

- Establish the compulsory payments they are required to make under the lease.
- Discount these to present value using an appropriate discount rate

    This will give you the same figure used in Assets, above, which means that the balance sheet asset and liability start off at the same figure at the commencement of the lease

- Reduce the liability by the capital (principal) element of each lease payment that is made, by assuming that the lease is an annuity

For this purpose you should separate out any maintenance or service elements included in the lease. These can be written off to profit and loss account as incurred.

You can ignore leases under 12 months. The rentals on these will continue to be expensed on a straight line basis.

As this is only an exposure draft at this stage – and one that has been hotly contested and debated since publication in 2010, no-one yet knows what the final wording will be. It is unlikely to come into effect before 2015 although companies will have to amend their accounting procedures before then so that they are able to include accurate prior year comparative figures in their accounts once the new arrangements become mandatory.

8.7 EXERCISES

What is SSAP21?

Why is it important for lessees and lessors?

Why is lease capitalisation an important issue?

Produce an RoA calculation showing how RoA increases if leases are not capitalised.

How should you account for an operating lease, a finance lease and a hire purchase transaction in your books?

What notes to your accounts are necessary in each case?

What is IAS17?

What are the major changes that are being proposed by the IASC/FASB?

9 INTERNATIONAL LEASING

There are two quite different and unrelated topics to be discussed under this heading:

- 'global' or 'pan-European' leasing deals and
- cross-border leasing.

9.1 'GLOBAL' OR 'PAN-EUROPEAN' LEASING DEALS

One of the major driving forces of the last thirty years has been the globalisation of business. Many brands have become internationally recognised and many of us have found ourselves working for companies with overseas parent companies or subsidiaries.

Before the UK joined the European Economic Community most British workers would not have thought it possible they would have close working relationships with colleagues working in Paris or Dusseldorf but for many this is now a reality.

With the growth of international businesses has come the growth of purchasing power. Most large businesses try hard to use their purchasing clout to deliver cost savings. This involves appointing suppliers that can deliver products or services in all of the countries in which the client operates.

Vehicle leasing is, in theory, a good area for purchasing managers to focus on when looking for cost savings. A business with a big fleet spread across several countries can find that its vehicle leases represent a significant overhead.

So, the argument goes, if you bundle up all of your vehicle leasing into one package, offer it out to tender to a few suppliers, set out the outline terms on which you wish to be supplied and the maximum price you are prepared to pay then, hey presto, you will get one price in all markets and huge cost savings.

Simple, yes? Well, actually, no, because while great in theory, the devil is in the detail.

Let's assume your business operates in five countries within the EU. Not all countries within the EU have joined the Euro, so you will not get common prices across the EU without the lessor taking a currency risk.

Different currencies mean different interest rates. As interest cost is a key element of a leasing company's rental, lessors cannot offer the same interest rates across countries without taking an interest rate risk. Car prices vary across the EU so lease rentals cannot be the same.

Taxation has not been harmonised within the EU, so after tax depreciation allowances[221] the net cost to the lessor of delivering vehicles in each country will be different.

Used car prices vary across the EU so residual values, a key element of rental calculation, are different. Hence lessors cannot offer the same prices in all countries.

Legal systems differ so one contract will not work in all countries.

Need we go on? The point is that it is not possible to offer one lease deal across the EU.

Now imagine your company is a multinational with operations in the USA, Brazil, Portugal, Zaire, Japan and Singapore. If a deal cannot be made to work within the EU it is certainly not going to be possible to put together one agreement that will work in all of those locations.

Notwithstanding this, international deals are being done. Clients opt for the simplicity of doing business with one organisation but the leases are then written in each country in local languages, following local law and custom, with rentals being paid in local currency.

In these situations an agreement may be signed between the leasing company and the client's headquarters, setting out the general principles of the arrangement but this is likely to deal only with administrative and reporting issues (quality, best practice, delivering information and service using e-commerce, etc) rather than pricing or structure. Where the agreement does cover pricing it will only deal with elements of pricing, and principles, rather than trying to set one price across all countries.

ORGANISATIONAL STRUCTURES

Many vehicle leasing companies operate in several countries.

The truly international vehicle leasing businesses own their overseas operations. Others operate within alliances, where different businesses agree to co-operate to meet the needs of their multinational clients.

At best, these arrangements involve integration of the procedures of the 'alliance partners', so that the client receives a seamless service and cannot differentiate between the services from each of these independent businesses.

However some of these are just referral arrangements, where the client is introduced to a local supplier and is left to deal with them as a prospective new client.

---

221 For example, capital allowances in the UK.

9.2 CROSS-BORDER LEASING

As the name suggests, cross-border leasing involves a company in one country buying a vehicle and leasing it to a business in another country.

These transactions are usually entered into for tax reasons, in order to reduce the cost for the client and generate more profit for the lessor at the expense of the tax authorities in one or both countries.

The two areas that are often the focus of cross-border leasing deals are VAT and capital allowances.

Although it is a European tax, VAT is not harmonised across the EU. Individual countries have been left to develop their own flavours of VAT so the rules and the rates differ between the member states. There is therefore plenty of scope for finding a country that treats an 'outbound' cross-border lease in one way and another that treats an 'inbound' cross-border lease differently, so that little or no VAT is payable in either country.

Capital allowances are generally given to purchasers of vehicles. However, different countries have different rules for deciding which party should receive the allowances if an asset is leased. So there may be some scope for finding a jurisdiction in which lessors are given tax allowances for buying vehicles to lease overseas and then finding another jurisdiction that gives capital allowances to lessees. Hence in the one transaction two lots of capital allowances are obtained. This is known as the 'double-dipping' of tax allowances.

It is an area where professional advice is essential for both the lessor and the lessee, as mistakes can be expensive.

Whilst lessors and consultants are always looking for opportunities to reduce fleet costs by using sophisticated solutions such as cross-border leasing, the fact is that these deals are rare and probably account for less than 1% of UK vehicle purchases.

9.3 EXERCISES

Should you expect to pay the same rental for a particular car in several countries? If not, why not?

Where 'global deals' are written, what contractual arrangement is normally adopted?

What is a cross-border lease?

What is 'double-dipping'?

COLIN TOURICK INTERVIEWS ALD INTERNATIONAL EXECUTIVES

MARC VAN ECK (REGIONAL SALES MANAGER) AND

STÉPHANE RENIE (SALES & BUSINESS DEVELOPMENT DIRECTOR)

Q. I suppose we need to start out by defining what we mean by an International deal. Presumably, at one extreme, it can mean as little as looking after the local needs of one multinational client in a couple of countries, and at the other end of the spectrum can involve a client having one deal applied across dozens of countries?

A. An international deal can be defined as one where a customer appoints a leasing company as its sole or preferred supplier through an international agreement covering several countries and having a potential of anything from several hundred to thousands of vehicles. The international deal will also imply that there is an international key account management structure in place on the supplier side to manage the vehicles covered by the agreement.

However, international deals can vary just like local deals can, and there can be a segmented approach to managing such an international customer. And similarly to a local deal, but with even greater acuity, key issues have to be addressed prior to choosing an international approach to fleet.

THE MANDATE

The issue of an internal mandate is of paramount importance, as without it, any international fleet project is doomed to fail almost from the outset. Having a clear mandate is one of the biggest challenges faced by the international fleet manager today. Without a clear and strong mandate, buy-in will have to be achieved during the fleet project, which will slow down the process and inevitably limit the scope for success.

So the key question is how to go about obtaining a mandate, ideally supported by senior management within the fleet manager's company. The approach depends to a great extent on the nature and structure of the company the fleet manager is working for. A clear view of the internal decision making structure (and players) is needed in order to "sell" the project internally and obtain the level of support needed to drive the international fleet project forward.

A company with a very decentralised structure is less likely to participate in an international fleet project. On the other hand, a company with a centralised structure, possibly with category management already in place, will have a greater chance of success.

THE GOALS

A few initial questions need to be answered:

■ What role does the fleet play in the company's business model?

■ What are the objectives of an international fleet deal?

■ What are the expected benefits and deliverables of an international fleet leasing approach?

■ Is the fleet project led/sponsored by procurement, human resources, finance?

The answer to these questions will "naturally" lead to strategic choices on the key components of the fleet policy. For example, this is how we think that the primary goals impact on the key components of an international fleet project:

	Goal: Cost Reduction	Goal: Control Maximization	Goal: Reduce Admin	Goal: Driver productivity & satisfaction
Lessor Sourcing	Single source or big multi-supply	Single lessor accountable	Single Goal supplier	Selection based on strong SLA
Manufacturers	Limited/Single	Exclude some	Restrictions	Few restrictions
Vehicle Choice	Specified: No choices	Limited selector	Limited selector	User chooser
Car Policy	Strict: defined by cost	Strictly defined and monitored	Guidelines and suggestions	Locally defined
Lifecycle	Flexible: adjust to market dynamics	Strictly defined, few exceptions	Strictly defined and implemented	Equitable across country/region
Outsourcing	Selective	In-house managed	Full outsourcing	VIP outsourcing
Road Safety	Share costs with drivers	Rigorous training with in-vehicle telematics	Few exceptions	User-friendly training programme

THE GEOGRAPHICAL SCOPE

International fleet managers typically select the region within the scope of their responsibilities where they have the greatest opportunity for a successful implementation. This means that the scope could be international, but the approach could be to focus on an EMEA region, and then possibly drilling down to smaller regions e.g. CEE; Nordic; Baltic; Mediterranean; etc.

Fleet managers realise that if they can include more countries they will increase their purchasing and leveraging capabilities with the suppliers. Being part of an international deal is also likely to generate more savings for a smaller country than for an established, bigger fleet where local leverage is already significant. Including more countries means realising greater savings for the Group, thereby helping the fleet manager meet their targets and boosting their remuneration packages. So there is a strong temptation to consult suppliers and aim to assemble the maximum number of countries possible, but this has to be balanced against the issue of mandate: trying to include countries where there is only a weak mandate to do an international deal can slow down the process and compromise the overall outcome.

THE SUPPLIER SETUP

Once senior management have provided a mandate the international fleet manager needs to decide how many suppliers to include (sole / dual / multi supplier) and the type of suppliers (international and/or local heroes).

This will result in a number of different possibilities, including:

▪ Finding international leasing provider(s) with a matching or greater geographical coverage

▪ Selecting a best-in-country provider (and accepting that this may result in working with many different leasing providers)

▪ Selecting regional leasing provider(s)

Aiming for one setup or the other is not a neutral decision that can be taken out quickly and out of the blue. The following factors will have an influence:

▪ the company decision-making structure (a very decentralised company with strong local decision makers will be inclined to opt for local heroes).

▪ the fleet size: the larger the fleet in a country, the greater the necessity to benchmark between 2 or 3 suppliers. On the other hand, fleets with fewer than 150-200 vehicles will be more open to sole supply since the cost of managing several suppliers will surpass the expected savings of permanent competition between two or three players.

▪ the level of expectations from the supplier: an international setup arrived at by cherry-picking the best local bids will result in a large supplier base and will be effective in delivering short term savings. Conversely, reducing the supplier base to one or two preferred international suppliers will move the relationship to a different level, where other sources of value can be expected, as illustrated by the graph below.

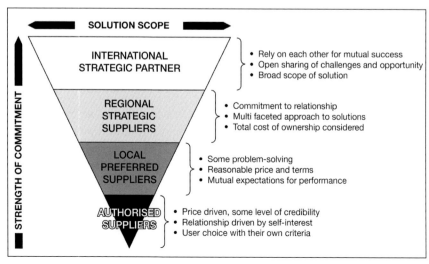

Q. It must be relatively easy if the purchasing manager of a large multinational wants to have one supplier of, say, photocopiers. One price can be agreed centrally and the product can then be rolled out locally. However, it must be a lot more difficult with vehicle leasing and management; new cars sell for different prices in different countries, there are currency differences, different interest rates, different tax regimes, different customers and fashions, different residual values and different legal systems. How do you begin to do a deal that allows a multinational to leverage their buying power in this market?

A. Full service leasing is indeed far from being a commodity. It might be easier to look first at the objectives an international deal will not be able to achieve, in order to better understand what is actually achievable. These myths include:

- Getting the same price everywhere: for the obvious reasons you mentioned regarding differences in car prices, taxation, residual values etc.

- Getting the best price anywhere, anytime: when a non-authorised supplier comes in with a very aggressive one-shot offer, is it worthwhile accepting and are you comparing apples with apples?

- Getting exactly the same product and level of service throughout the world. Market practices and structure vary a lot country to country. Take the example of fuel cards and you will soon come to the conclusion that one size (provider) does not fit all.

- Getting one international framework agreement that will cover all issues and replace local agreements (see below).

In order to leverage your purchasing power, with a product as complex as full service leasing and / or fleet management, indeed requires much preparation and thought.

First of all, the fleet manager needs to establish a **baseline** in order to determine if cost savings can be achieved, and to make them measurable. This is quite a complex exercise, considering the fact that there can be several countries in scope, each with their own taxation; legislation; geographical limitations; etc.

Ideally the baseline needs to be established by comparing the current fleet to a similar new fleet. However, cars currently being leased are essentially costs from the "past" so comparing them to new quotations would mean looking at "future costs". This would not be an accurate approach as the comparison would not be on a like for like basis. So where does that leave us?

The fleet manager ideally needs to start by having an overview of the current fleet, where it is located, the most commonly leased vehicle models, etc. It is also essential to have a clear idea of the current spend of the fleet, including fuel and miscellaneous fleet-related costs. Indirect costs, such as overhead can also be included, depending on the scope of the fleet project. Having an overview of the fleet spend will enable the fleet manager to compare the cost of running the current fleet against a leasing provider's proposal.

Once the baseline has been established, the **areas where buying power can be leveraged** need to be identified. These can be as follows:

- Management fee
- Interest uplift / commercial margin
- Vehicle discounts
- Insurance terms & conditions
- Relief vehicles
- Volume incentive / bonus
- Payment terms
- Etc

Having identified the areas for possible buying power leverage, it has to be understood that these are fairly common to all the markets in scope of an international deal. Further areas for leverage will depend largely on the markets involved. In other words, are these mature, emerging or exotic markets in terms of fleet leasing?

At a certain point, the areas that can be leveraged with the customer's buying power should be listed accordingly in an **International Agreement** / Statement of Principles / Statement of Work / etc. This captures the commercial conditions that can be applied to all the countries in scope of the agreement. The agreement provides a framework for the management of the customer's fleet on an international basis. It will not be possible to have one international agreement that replaces the need for country local master lease agreements (MLAs).

Local MLAs will always have to be signed because they contain the terms and conditions relevant to providing fleet management products and services in the markets in which they apply. Different countries have their own legislation, taxation, liabilities, etc. Therefore the international agreement functions as an umbrella agreement under which the local MLAs operate. Local MLAs usually have to be signed in the local language, even if an English translation is made available.

The international agreement will form the basis of the relationship between the leasing supplier and the customer, containing qualitative aspects as well as the quantitative aspects previously mentioned. Qualitative aspects can include Service Level Agreements (SLAs); escalation procedures, Key Performance Indicators (KPIs) that are used to measure the performance of the leasing supplier, the international key account management structure, etc.

Q. Purchasing managers enter into international deals in order to reduce their total cost of ownership. Please explain how leasing companies go about delivering these savings.

A. Total cost of ownership (TCO) can mean different things to different people, so the following definition could be useful:

Ideally a TCO assessment offers a final statement reflecting not only the cost of purchase but all aspects in the further use and maintenance of the equipment, device or system. This includes the costs of training support personnel and the users of the system, costs associated with failure or outage (planned and unplanned), diminished performance (i.e. if users are kept waiting), costs of security breaches (in loss of reputation and recovery costs), costs of disaster preparedness and recovery, floor space, electricity, development expenses, testing infrastructure and expenses, quality assurance, boot image control, marginal incremental growth, decommissioning, e-waste handling and more.

To reduce TCO and therefore obtain cost savings, purchasing managers need to concentrate on the following:

- Identify the scope of the fleet project
- Establish the baseline (to compare current and future costs based on received proposals)
- Obtain a clear mandate (with senior management support)
- Involve the country fleet management teams in order to ensure a successful implementation and limit push-back during this process
- Decide on sourcing model (sole / dual / multi supply)
- Identify areas where buying power can be leveraged (as explained previously), which are then captured in an international agreement
- Agree timelines for implementation with the leasing supplier
- Agree a cost saving methodology with the leasing provider in order to achieve ongoing TCO reduction, by identifying and targeting areas for potential savings (which needs to be measurable). Work on all the different components of TCO and track them over time.

The latest study conducted by ALD at international level on a basket of international customers shows the following breakdown.

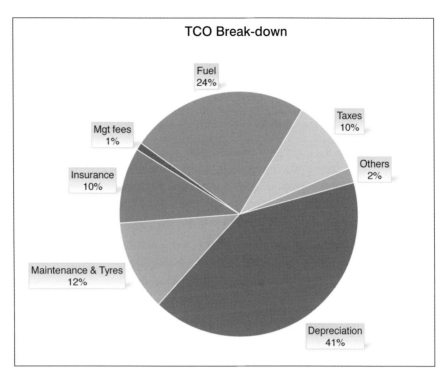

TCO Break-down

Fuel 24%

Taxes 10%

Mgt fees 1%

Others 2%

Insurance 10%

Maintenance & Tyres 12%

Depreciation 41%

Some of these TCO components are predictable because they are typically included in the monthly rentals.

Other expenses such as fuel, body repairs and end of contract damages are out of scope of the monthly rental but operationally they can be quite significant. They are more difficult to tackle because they cover areas difficult to negotiate internationally (e.g. fuel), more complex to monitor (all the more so at an international level) and often require in-depth work on driver behaviour (e.g. fuel consumption, road risk management).

Fleet managers often start by optimising the upfront "predictable" costs, i.e. the monthly rental. To do that, they need to carefully design the car policy and negotiate good terms from both the OEMs and the leasing companies… that's why more and more multinationals go through a tender process in order to deliver savings internationally.

Q. So what should fleet managers consider when writing tender documents? How can they create the 'perfect' tender?

A. There are obvious topics that have to be addressed in detail if companies want to successfully implement an international fleet approach:

■ the funding method (ideally a closed-end full service lease with an open-view on cost components)

■ the scope of services to be included

■ the car policy (from a user-chooser model to a restrictive list)

■ the supplier base strategy (car manufacturers and lessors) and

■ the type of suppliers targeted (international or local).

These issues are all strategic, and quite complex. But if companies want a successful tender, they should, firstly, look into the less glamorous subject of **process and methodology.**

While the number of international tenders has increased significantly over the last five years, the percentage of tenders officially or unofficially cancelled has remained stable at around 25%, which means that one tender out of four never reaches the decision making stage, let alone the finalised tenders producing a result that is partially diminished for the very same reasons.

The reasons for these failures are numerous and generally relate to tender methodology rather than content. Therefore, we will focus on what is, according to us, the most critical element in an international fleet strategy: the preparation of the tender.

Step 1: Purchasing team selection and defining the objectives of the tender

■ Select an experienced international team with the support of regional/local stakeholders. Discuss with the end-users and agree the key elements involved in the process.

■ Define roles and responsibilities of all levels involved.

■ If the project is driven centrally make sure the international team has the mandate from all the entities involved.

■ Appoint a sponsor at executive level.

■ Define clear and internally agreed targets: savings, process optimisations, supplier base consolidation, etc.

Step 2: Process definition

■ Define the most suitable format to be used, i.e. Request for Information (RFI), Request for Proposal (RFP), Request for Quotations (RFQ).

■ Select the criteria and evaluation process.

■ Decide which vendors have to be included/excluded.

■ Define the minimum requirements.

■ Create the documents, keeping in mind the objectives of the tender.

■ Define a reasonable time frame (4 to 6 months for Step 3 to Step 5).

Step 3: Tender issue

Step 4: Response analysis – negotiation round

Step 5: Decision and contract signature

Step 6: Implementation

It usually takes **one year** between the selection of the team and the signature of an international agreement with the selected vendor(s). Before investing time and resources in such an ambitious project it is crucial to make sure that it has good chances to deliver tangible results. The key to success is in the preparation phase and in a constant and transparent communication with the internal stakeholders and possible vendors.

Q. Most multinationals are now taking note of the need to reduce carbon emissions. How can an international fleet management deal help them achieve this objective?

A. The 3 main reasons fleet clients and lease drivers choose a more 'environmentally-friendly' car are as follows:

1. HSE / CSR reasons: From an environmental and sustainability / green fleet policy point of view, fleet clients seek to reduce their CO_2 footprint.

2. Cost reduction reasons: Fleet clients realise that reducing their CO_2 also results in a lower TCO through for example lower fuel consumption, lower taxation and improved residual values. Also, with rising fuel costs over the recent years, lower CO_2 vehicles use less fuel, thus stabilising the average fuel costs when being offset against increasing fuel costs.

3. Lease drivers are also choosing more environmentally friendly cars in order to pay less tax / benefit-in-kind (BIK) taxation for the private use of the vehicle. A typical example is the high penetration of hybrid vehicles in The Netherlands due to lower BIK.

Where are we today? The current picture on CO_2 will vary from one country to the other. As an example, the current CO_2 emissions of the whole ALD fleet stands at 150.8 g/km across all 37 countries. Strong disparities appear between countries, with our fleet in Turkey averaging 134g/km due to the particular profile of the local fleet and our fleet in China and Mexico showing vehicle CO_2 averages above 175g/km. Most European countries stand between 140g/km (e.g. France and Belgium) and 150g/km (Italy and UK). Our fleet in Spain and Germany, respectively, show 156g/km and 158g/km averages.

In terms of variation between 2007 and 2010, the highest CO_2 reduction has been seen within the Nordic countries with a 16% reduction in Sweden, 13% in Finland and 12% in Denmark. Netherlands and Belgium also show a positive trend with a reduction of 10% and 7% respectively. On a global basis, within our fleet, CO_2 emission reduction is accelerating with a1% reduction between 2007 and 2008, a 1.4% fall between 2008 and 2009 and a 2.3% reduction between 2009 and 2010. These figures, of course, do not reflect a more significant reduction in CO_2 of new vehicle deliveries, as they replace vehicles delivered 3 or 4 years ago that had inherently higher carbon emissions.

The acceleration in the CO_2 decrease is primarily due to the tremendous efforts made by car manufacturers. Thanks to strong R&D investment, in 2009 they reached the European 2012 target. The trend should continue to accelerate over the next 2-3 years, mainly driven by the CO_2 reduction from OEMs and vehicles being renewed with more efficient models. After 3 years, the trend is likely to decelerate until electric vehicles arrive in any volume, which we don't forecast before 2015.

Hence the need to complement this positive "external" push by internal work on the fleet policy. Having an international deal in place helps companies reduce carbon emissions in many different ways:

■ Consultancy in car policy design: during the vehicle and model selection process the average CO_2 emissions can be identified, as well as the targeted average CO_2 emissions.

■ Reporting: CO_2 emissions, both theoretical (OEM official data) and real (actual consumption) can be monitored on an on-going basis through international reporting tools.

■ Governance: an international supplier can be made accountable for CO_2 achievements.

■ Knowledge and Benchmarking: on an international fleet, the CO_2 picture is still very diverse and international leasing companies have a great deal of benchmarking information available. It can be invaluable for an international fleet manager to share best practice across markets within their group or compare a company to a sector average. This is all the more important in emerging markets, which are representing an expanding share of the fleet and where CO_2 emissions tend to be much higher.

■ Solutions: leasing companies have already released some green initiatives that may not impact directly on the fleet's average CO_2 emissions but which will impact the mobility footprint of their customers. For example, car sharing solutions are likely to expand and will allow our customers to take the right car for the right purpose, introducing electric or downsized vehicles for city usage.

In the same vein, mobility solutions will help people choosing complementary transportation such as train, scooters or EVs instead of their regular car. By keeping their everyday car, such a mobility programme will not lower the fleet's CO_2 average but will lower the most polluting mileage in favour of a well-adapted solution.

All these hard and soft factors can contribute to controlling and improving the carbon footprint of the company on a global basis.

Q. What tools can suppliers offer fleet managers to help them run their fleet internationally?

A. All international leasing suppliers can provide access to a global reporting tool via a dedicated homepage, with data in the global reporting application customised to the user's preferred currency, units of measure and date formats. All data can be exported using Excel and can also be reviewed online in a graphic, table or tree view, and can easily be attached to an email.

In addition, the tool is programmed to enable external data uploads which can be done either by the customer or by the leasing provider.

The information provided by international reporting tools are updated regularly, and reports can be exported in PDF, Excel® or CSV formats to offer customers the flexibility needed when looking at consolidated international reporting.

As a minimum the following reports are usually available:

- Expenses by vehicle
- Lease and mileage analysis
- Inventory by manufacturer
- Vehicles on order
- Fleet evolution
- Product evolution
- Mileage deviation
- CO_2 emissions

In addition, at local level, detailed reports are available, depending on local markets. The exact format and frequency of this reporting will often be agreed on local business level but will include such data as:

Fleet evolution:	Outstanding orders:
Number of contracts at beginning of the period	Order reference
Number of terminations during the period	Vehicle description
Number of deliveries during the period	Estimated delivery date
Number of contracts at the end of the period	If available, contract reference of the existing vehicle

Deliveries report	Mileage deviation report
Order/Contract reference	Contract reference
Vehicle description	Registration number
Delivery date	Vehicle description
Registration number	Contract duration and mileage
Chassis number	Last known mileage
Delivery agent/dealer	Contract end date
	Estimated end mileage and deviation
Fleet overview	**Upcoming terminations report**
Contract reference	Contract reference
Registration number	Registration number
Vehicle description	Vehicle description
Contract duration and mileage	Contract end date
Estimated end date	If available, order reference of the renewing contract

In most countries these reports should be available through an online reporting tool generally updated on a daily basis.

Besides international online reporting tools, international leasing suppliers often offer the possibility to receive email newsletters containing industry news (taxation and legislation, used vehicles market, insurance, fuel, manufacturer and leasing company news, etc) that may have a direct impact on local fleets.

Q. Please explain how the various suppliers of international leasing and fleet management services are organised.

A. There are a number of international leasing providers today, however, the distinction should be made between those providers which are corporately owned and those that work through partnerships.

At present, there are only a handful of leasing providers that are corporately owned that have significant geographical coverage, whilst others operate through partnerships. Having an extensive coverage means that the leasing provider is much better positioned to offer a comprehensive proposal, with in-depth knowledge of the markets covered by their geographical network. It also means that the provider is able to dictate to its subsidiaries the strategy regarding pricing levels, service offering, etc from a central perspective.

In the case of an association or partnership of leasing providers, it is often down to "good intentions" and it is very difficult to dictate to the various partners what their pricing strategy should be. During a long (and increasingly longer) tender process, it is common to find such partnerships eliminated at an early stage.

The nature of the partnership tends to determine the level of success which can be achieved. There are several partnerships such as Global Fleet Services (GFS), which is comprised of ARI, Oryx, and some others.

According to the latest release of the company profiles in Fleet Europe (June 2011 edition), the coverage of the major leasing players is the following:

Leasing Company	Number of countries
ALD International	27 (Europe) + 11 (ROW)
Alphabet International	13
Arval	19 in Europe
Athlon Car Lease International	9 subsidiaries, 18 incl. partners
Citroën Business Finance	23
Daimler Financial Services	n/a
Directlease	3
Fiat Group Automobiles Capital	14
GE Financial Services	19
KBC Autolease	6
ING Car Lease International	8 subsidiaries, 13 incl. partners
Leaseplan International	30
Peugeot Finance International	23
Sixt Leasing	44
RCI Banque	39

In the case of ALD Automotive, activities are coordinated by ALD International based in Paris. ALD International is the holding company for its 37 corporate subsidiaries throughout the world, and is responsible for the development and oversight of Group business. ALD offers the widest corporate coverage of any fleet leasing company worldwide. Furthermore, ALD entered a global partnership with Wheels Inc. in 2009, to strengthen coverage in the United States and Canada, and enable customers to go global in their fleet management strategy.

Q. Do multinationals use any particular structures to reduce tax in their international leasing requirements?

A. A cross-border acquisition solution is currently not viable due to the high cost of transportation and importation between the different countries, even within the EU. However, international leasing providers are continuously evaluating this opportunity, as well as others, to offer their customers the most cost effective fleet management solution.

In addition, extended warranties applicable in the local service networks are only valid if the vehicles are purchased through local channels, hence increasing the operational cost of these vehicles and increasing their total cost of ownership.

Finally, several practical issues in such a scheme will demand a much higher overhead investment due to the differences in specifications between the markets, hence taking away any possibility of direct driver management during the quotation and order procedure.

Due to new EU regulations in 2010, taxation takes place in the country where the car is used, therefore negating any tax advantage.

Q. What developments have there been in the international leasing and fleet management market in the last few years that have been particularly valuable to fleet managers in multinational companies?

A. First of all, it is fair to say that the full operational leasing product itself has not changed dramatically over the last few years. However the industry and the product have matured, in a number of directions.

Overall, the quality of service provided has improved both at an operational level across countries and, at more strategic level, with international account managing teams available from OEMs and leasing companies.

The product has become much more transparent, with a more open view on cost components and considerable improvements in the reporting systems. Online reporting capabilities have grown considerably in recent years, with a greater focus on CO_2 and fuel consumption reporting, as well as TCO-related reporting.

For multinational companies there is also more choice in the number of international leasing providers compared to 8 or 9 years ago. Previously, there were only one or two major players able to provide an international offering, but this has now changed.

The potential geographical scope of leasing providers has also enlarged: leasing companies are looking for growth potential in emerging countries, starting the local business with international key accounts who want to consolidate their supplier base and improve control and governance of local operations.

On the customer side, a number of significant trends have impacted the life of international fleet managers.

We have seen a more centralised approach to the fleet from the customer's side. This is in part due to continuing trends in globalisation and therefore a more centralised role for procurement. These trends were accelerated and accentuated by the financial crisis, which placed a greater emphasis on cost saving. The decision making criteria have become more complex. With more focus and a better understanding of what TCO is really made up of, this has resulted in more decisions being based on TCO methodology. Before this it was often based on pricing at a "moment in time" which did not take account of the fact that the "entry-level" pricing offered would almost certainly be different 6 to 12 months later. Also, and very importantly, carbon footprint has emerged as an important factor within company strategy on a global basis, sometimes on a par with Total Cost of Ownership.

Q. Is anything happening now, or will anything be happening soon, that is likely to change the landscape for fleet managers in multinational companies?

A. In the coming years, we can see a number of significant but progressive shifts happening in the life of fleet managers.

The first shift is "**functional**" and relates to their scope of responsibilities beyond the subject of the car fleet. With a continuing and increasing focus on sustainability and CSR measures, the need to reduce companies' carbon footprint is starting to change the way we view company vehicles. We are seeing a drive towards reducing emissions, thus reducing TCO, against a background of an increase in CO_2-related taxation which makes company vehicles more costly to operate. So the search is on for optimising the way we use company vehicles.

We expect to see a development in the area of mobility solutions, whereby the company vehicle is no longer the primary form of mobility, but only a part of it. This means that mobility solutions are starting to be offered, whereby the driver's journey is determined by the most cost-effective and sustainable modes of transportation. This may include a combination of company vehicle, train, plane, bus, taxi, EV, car-sharing, etc. Multinational companies may move towards offering mobility budgets to drivers, enabling the driver to use specially-developed software to determine the most cost-effective and sustainable way to travel.

Working with a mobility solution will require a new approach by fleet managers. Their current role could well evolve to that of a mobility manager, in the broadest sense. The challenge will be to become an "expert" in this field. In turn, international leasing providers have the challenge, and also at the same time a considerable opportunity, to fill the role of full mobility provider.

The other shift is likely to be **geographical**. In a quest for growth the reach of multinationals is forever growing and expanding into emerging markets. This creates a need for locally-based staff who require mobility solutions. If we take the example of the BRIC countries (Brazil, Russia, India and China) or countries like Mexico and Turkey, we would historically find a mix of either:

■ Very large locally-run fleets, with internal fleet management (in Russia, Brazil or Mexico for instance)

■ Very small car fleets relative to the country potential in India and especially China. These vehicles, previously limited to top management, are likely to trickle down to the workforce because letting employees take care of their own mobility raises some obvious questions in terms of governance and corporate responsibility.

This situation is likely to change: the centre of gravity of international fleet is going to shift, with stabilising or downsizing fleets in mature countries and rapidly growing fleets in emerging markets. So the scope of fleet managers' jobs will broaden. This will certainly make the job even more interesting but also more challenging as these new horizons are unfamiliar, the market practices and actors are significantly different and respect for corporate standards is often a challenge.

Q. If you were to advise a fleet manager on the best practice when it comes to multinational leasing and fleet management, what would that advice be?

A. A short answer would be, of course, to appoint ALD Automotive to manage your fleet at an international level! But, joking apart it is vital to keep the two following ideas in mind:

■ keep a pragmatic and **focused approach**: too many tenders go for a holistic approach and ask for hundreds of quotations that are never analysed, rather than focusing on the key areas

■ put a strong emphasis on local **implementation**: a lot of energy goes into striking good deals at a tender phase which are then not (or not sufficiently) implemented due to a wide array of reasons, starting with a lack of internal communication and local buy-in.

In a longer answer, based on our experience of best practice with many multinational companies that have successfully implemented an international fleet approach, the following recommendations would be made:

FUNDING METHOD

In Europe, and in line with IAS 17, we would strongly recommend a closed-end full operating lease set-up, with an open view on the cost components. This method is now widely offered throughout Europe and is clearly the leading financing method for corporate fleets. In a nutshell, it offers the following advantages compared to finance leases or outright purchase:

■ Less administration for your entities

■ Cash-beneficial solution

■ Elimination of operational risk

■ Accurate knowledge of TCO when designing car policy and ordering individual vehicles

■ Overall cost reduction through use of lease partner's expertise (e.g. residual values, tax beneficial vehicles, SMR, fuel efficiency)

In some of the less mature markets, the advantages of this method compared to an in-house managed and purchased fleet are not so well-known yet but should be constantly under study.

Services to be included

Ideally, a standard package of services needs to be defined at corporate level, then applied in-country, to optimise the client's overall costs, taking into account administrative work, operational risk and a high level service to their drivers.

Depending on the country availability or maturity, these can be fine-tuned at local country level. The services we normally recommend include:

■ Financing (see above)

■ Maintenance & service: in Europe, this includes standard service as well as technical repairs due to normal wear and tear

■ Tyres: actual number of tyres will depend on annual mileage of the individual drivers

■ Consultancy & advice on car policy and taxation, best-buy models per country, optimum renewal cycles, environmental aspects

■ Reporting: both at local country and international level

■ Road and registration taxes, according to local legislation

■ Fuel card management: actual choice of the fuel provider can vary between countries but the card handling and invoicing should be centralised to the client's lease service provider

■ Replacement car (pay on use) and pre-contract vehicles

■ Accident management, with an insurance package arranged through the lease service provider, which will be more cost-effective than working directly through local brokers

■ A single-point-of-contact approach for client drivers and fleet administrators

Car policy

In recent years, Europe has seen a strong evolution from 'user chooser' car policies based on monthly rentals or even list prices, towards more restrictive policies with a limited number of models available per category. In the client's case, and due to the different entities per country, this means applying some standard rules which then need to be adapted to the local market or entity flavours:

■ define a number of categories (4-6) according to job level and car need (e.g. junior sales/job need, sales, senior sales, middle management, senior management)

■ for each category, every country or entity will define a choice of 2-3 vehicle models which reflect the best-buys for that category in that market, taking into account the importance of HR related criteria versus sourcing in each country/entity

■ try to limit as far as possible the number of manufacturers selected per country, to increase the negotiating power at local country level (additional discounts can be negotiated up to 4-5% on the list price when concentrating client volumes with limited number of OEMs). The selection of manufacturers can be looked at from an international level, with a potential additional saving through volume related bonuses at European level

■ new starters do not necessarily receive a new car but might receive an existing car from someone who has left the company. With a restrictive car policy choice this will be much easier to realise than with a user-chooser policy.

■ model selection to be based on a Total Cost of Ownership approach, based on monthly rental cost, including fuel costs, environmental taxes, insurance, etc, rather than just being based on list price of the vehicle

Supplier base

The strategy on the number of suppliers needs to be looked at from two perspectives:

Manufacturers: see above. In a perfect world, 2-3 manufacturers should be selected at a European level, possibly allowing individual countries to replace one of the European manufacturers with a local one

Lease service suppliers: the fewer suppliers, the easier it will be for the client to gain rapid control of their fleet costs and strategy, with minimum administrative costs. However this will of course be more difficult to implement in the local entities, as they will probably all want to convince their Head Office that their supplier is the best one. For this reason, several companies have started by implementing 2-3 lease suppliers at international level, from which the countries can choose, with a clear strategy to reduce this over time to 1-2 suppliers based on regular quality and cost performance evaluations. In such a set-up, it is probably best to ask the smaller countries to select one of the preferred ones for their country, while some of the bigger ones might prefer to select 2 of the preferred ones at local level.

Advantages and added value of selecting an international lease supplier

In order to put in place strategic cost reduction plans, the first step is to define the baseline and keep a comprehensive and transparent view of what is happening in the different countries. This will only be possible when partnering with suppliers who can offer the client such a view and who have the experience of international fleet management projects. Based on the objectives and reactions of our customers, some of the main advantages of selecting an international program can be summarised as follows:

■ Leveraged negotiation power by consolidating their volumes across all countries

- Consolidated reporting, giving the client a full insight into local market situations

- Seamless information flow and escalation process thanks to a solid account management structure, at both an international, regional, and local level. This will ensure an efficient implementation, and ongoing account management services.

- Transparency on the contracts set-up, as well as transparency and continuity in pricing, through a common open view quotation template, based on centrally agreed pricing terms (management fees, interest margins, reference interest rates)

- Ensuring high level service across all markets, supported by an international Service Level Agreement, which is adapted locally to match the market maturity and expectations. In many cases, customers find they start enjoying better service than before because they are working with international players rather than local ones.

- Realisation of strategic cost reduction programs, driven and monitored centrally through a common methodology

- Objective advice on best practices, in line with local markets but with an international and expert view on current and future market trends. International leasing providers have a lot of experience and in depth knowledge of the markets in which they operate, especially when it comes to less mature leasing markets. We would advise fleet managers to make use of this knowledge, and also to utilise the consulting services of the international providers.

- Strong support from the lease service supplier in the negotiations with the manufacturers, both at national and international level

- Sustainability of the strategy by selecting a strong lease partner, backed up by a strong shareholder. Choosing a leasing provider is not an easy task, but an important point which arose during the financial crisis was the issue of sustainability with regards to the supplier. Is your international leasing provider a sustainable company? During the crisis, the market saw some players withdrawing (albeit temporarily in some cases) from the market, and thereby causing some multinational companies to be left without supply from some leasing providers.

In our experience of dealing with international accounts, clients recognise that international leasing companies provide value, coverage, and a much needed insight into the operating fleet of the multinational companies. They provide a consolidated view, and the mechanisms to identify areas for potential cost savings and fleet harmonisation.

10 TELEMATICS

Telematics is the name given to the combination of telecommunications and computing.[222]

Over the past fifteen years we have seen a sharp increase in the number of telematics devices installed in motor vehicles. The earliest of these were location-tracking devices that could be switched on to alert the police if your car was stolen.

Mobile phone companies know where you are at any time. Your phone logs in to the closest cell. With the widespread use of mobiles, suppliers now use this feature to provide real-time traffic reports that can be delivered to you through your mobile phone, based on where you are at the time and the traffic conditions as reported by local roadside monitors.

Satellite navigation, using the US global positioning satellite system developed for military use, is now commonplace. 'Satnav' takes away the need to carry maps and allows the driver to concentrate on the road rather than on the route. Using moving electronic maps, pointing devices and voice instructions, the device directs the driver step by step to his destination.

Telematics systems can now hold an archive of all of a vehicle's movements and allow these to be played back as journey reports in your office. Some systems allow you to see where all of your company's vehicles are located, in real-time. You can also get reports of fuel usage and consumption, the current and average speed of the vehicle, when the doors were opened and closed and the G-force that was being experienced when the car drove too fast round a corner or braked sharply just before an accident.

The emergency services can be summoned automatically if an airbag is activated or at the touch of a button you can be connected to a live emergency services operator.

Drivers can log their mileage as either business or personal at the press of a button when they start each journey and the log can then be used to submit business mileage expense claims into your office.

---

222 A brief note for lovers of the English language. There is a tendency for advertisers to say things like "Telematics are changing the face of fleet management". However, despite the fact that it ends in the letter 's', the word 'telematics' is singular rather than plural. So we should say *telematics is* not *telematics are*, though it is correct to say *telematics devices are*. In this regard telematics is similar to the words physics or optics.

There has been at least one case where an in-car telematics system has saved a life. A driver reported severe chest pain as he was driving. The company was able to pinpoint his location through his in-car telematics system and call an ambulance. He had a collapsed lung, a life-threatening condition.

The possible uses of these systems are endless. If, for example, you have a team of service engineers or delivery drivers who spend all day on the road, you can quickly check their location if a client calls to ask how long it will take before the driver arrives. Rather than calling the driver to find out where they are, you can have a quick look at a screen and pass the information to the customer. There is no need to phone the driver and risk distracting them from the road whilst they are driving.

The telematics market has grown rapidly. Initial progress was hampered by a lack of agreed protocols but these have been standardised, so manufacturers are producing devices confident they will be compatible with other parts of the network.

10.1 THE NEAR FUTURE

Telematics systems are slowly beginning to revolutionise the way we use our vehicles.

As cars become more technologically advanced and use software to manage key processes, manufacturers will send software updates directly to the engine using telematics, rather than asking you to call into the dealership. This will happen without your knowledge or involvement.

Manufacturers or dealers will send messages to your car advising you that a service is due. You will be able to book a service directly from your car into the dealer's servicing diary without phoning.

If you have locked yourself out of the car the system will help you regain access. Get an electrical fault and it will talk you through the procedure to isolate and repair the problem. If you are parked and have left the car, it will notify you if your alarm has been activated.

We have become used to telematics features being delivered via a special box but increasingly they will arrive via a mobile phone, personal digital assistant or laptop PC.

Soon we will get to the stage where the car will prompt you that it has discovered a fault that requires attention. It will tell you it has checked the parts system at all of the nearby dealers to see which has the parts for the job and selected a particular one as it is on your normal route home and because their rates are the cheapest. It will say that it has provisionally booked the car into the workshop in thirty minutes for the fault to be seen to and that Alan Jones the service manager is looking forward to seeing you. It will tell you it is a twenty-minute job costing £125. It will also tell you that if you do not have it done, there is a 53% probability a major component failure will occur within the next 1,300 miles, which would cost £650 to repair. If you accept the system's suggestion to get it seen to right away, you will just say "Yes" and the satnav will direct you there. All of this will be voice-activated.

10.2 TELEMATICS AND FLEET MANAGEMENT

Telematics systems stop fleets from being beyond the control of the fleet manager. The ability to store journey, route, speed, mileage, g-force and fuel consumption details allows you to pinpoint problems. You can see if your delivery drivers are speeding or driving aggressively, spending too long over lunch or stopping to do some personal shopping.

You can now have real-time cost control over your fleet.

Telematics helps with route planning and this is particularly useful if you have delivery drivers who are calling at several addresses a day. The system calculates the optimum route in advance and modifies this during the day as real-time traffic information is received, or updated orders or instructions are received from customers. This saves money and reduces driver frustration.

If one of your vehicles is involved in an accident the system can accurately identify its location, the speed and direction of travel prior to the accident and the precise time of the accident.

These systems can deliver real benefits for drivers, providing them with information to help them do their jobs more effectively, saving them time, reducing paperwork and form-filling and providing feedback to help them drive more safely.

You should decide what features you need from a telematics system and buy a system that delivers these. If you don't need the "bells and whistles" of the most complex new system, don't buy the system, however interesting it may be to see the system at work.

Researchers are developing 'head-up' displays similar to those used in military aircraft. These will allow the driver to read the information without looking away from the road.

Some people have expressed surprised that there has not been a public outcry, or even a public debate, about the invasion of privacy these devices can involve, especially the ability to monitor the drivers' movements outside business hours.

You may be able to give your staff the ability to switch off the telematics device at such times, whilst still keeping open the ability to locate the vehicle if stolen.

No doubt some fleet drivers will complain about privacy issues. The Data Protection Act is important here. It only permits companies to hold data on private individuals if they have agreed to that data being held and if they have received an explanation of the use to which it will be put. Fleet managers should consider obtaining signed declarations from their drivers consenting to their movements being tracked and this data then being held on computer for analysis.

Each company needs to have an agreed policy on how to deal with these issues.

10.3 EXERCISES

What is telematics?

What functionality is available now?

How can telematics help you to run your fleet?

AN INTERVIEW WITH DAVID YATES,
UK MARKETING DIRECTOR OF ALD AUTOMOTIVE

Q. Your company has been a major exponent of the benefits of using telematics systems to manage vehicle fleets. How long have you been doing this and why have you pushed this so heavily?

A. We've been involved with the fleet telematics sector for 10 years, having launched an initial pilot programme with our customers as far back as 2001. For two years we worked with a major technology partner to develop a system that could integrate with our core fleet management software. This early experience proved invaluable in gaining a thorough understanding of the benefits of telematics within the fleet market. Following this trial we formally launched our ProFleet2 telematics product in 2004.

Back then, telematics was still very much in its infancy and our focus was more on our own internal control and asset management. We managed 30,000 vehicles at the time and, with the exception of an occasional odometer reading whilst a vehicle was in for a service, neither ALD nor our customers ever had any accurate, up to date record of its mileage or how it was faring against its contract.

Neither could we ever be sure the vehicles would be serviced on time; since a vehicle being returned without a full service history would have a major impact on its resale value – and lead to a potential customer recharge – our aim was, obviously, to prevent this from happening in the first place.

It was originally developed, therefore, as a way of reminding drivers to service their vehicles on time and improve the service booking process. As the telematics proposition has evolved, however, so too have the benefits now offered and these are now being appreciated by a wider audience of fleet managers, drivers and leasing companies.

Telematics has now become an all encompassing fleet management solution, meeting a wide variety of needs. Whereas it may have been perceived by many as an unnecessary 'gadget' just a few years ago, the feature rich systems of today are now at the forefront of helping companies to cut fleet operating costs, enhance CSR credentials, assist with legislative compliance and improve business efficiency.

What ALD has succeeded in doing with our own product offer, ProFleet2, is offer a cost effective solution to meet today's market needs that is functional, simple to install and ready to use 'day one'. It is not trying to be something overtly complicated or 'uber clever' for the sake of it. What's important is that it gives customers – both fleet managers **and** drivers – clear information that helps them do their job more efficiently and within a sensible budget.

Q. For a fleet manager who is familiar with satnavs but unfamiliar with modern telematics systems, how would you explain what these systems do?

A. There are a lot of misconceptions about what telematics is and what the various systems can do. One definition is "the integration of wireless communications, vehicle monitoring systems and location devices" but as that, perhaps, is still a mouthful I'd see it, simply, as technology which can help a company improve the efficiency of its fleet by accessing key information on vehicle location and performance, including driver behavior. In saying this however, without caveats to protect the sensitivities of the driver, even this explanation can still give rise to misunderstanding.

> "CO_2 data for every journey is required by our parent company. ALD's ProFleet2 system enables us to capture that data with minimal effort."
> **Transport Manager**

Where telematics has occasionally received 'bad press' it is because of a negative perception of 'big brother' and this has, quite understandably, caused many companies to dismiss the benefits of telematics without further investigation. So we acknowledged these potential concerns very early and created an online consent process to ensure the only driver information their fleet manager can see is data they are happy to 'release' e.g. business journeys rather than private ones outside office hours. What's important to the successful implementation of telematics is the buy-in of drivers whether the company's key motivator is cost, legal or moral.

Q. Legal and moral issues?

A. The legal obligations for businesses to manage their duty of care are well documented but companies have a moral duty to ensure the health and safety of their employees too. And if there's a cost effective solution that can help employees drive more smoothly and safely, leading to fewer injuries and fatalities, surely we're morally bound to investigate it further?

It's only in recent years that we've seen fleets carry out a thorough process of checking driver licences as standard and, yet, even this most basic of checks is still not carried out by thousands of companies throughout the UK. Even if we were to accept that a business **has** carried out such a check, and that appropriate insurance is in place giving them the *legal* entitlement to drive, few then have any idea how their employees **actually** drive once they leave the office car park.

Workplace banter about 'boy-racers' or 'aggressive drivers' or about a colleague who appears always to be 'half asleep' may be dismissed as office humour but what would happen if one of those traits resulted in an accident, a potentially fatal one? Who's to blame? The driver is, obviously, but the business can also be culpable for allowing that individual to drive on company business in the first place, without having any proper processes in place to ensure their safety.

Companies have a moral obligation to ensure the well being of their employees – and all other persons, potentially, affected by them – whilst driving on business. Senior management can't simply walk away from their responsibilities once the keys are handed over to a driver for their new vehicle.

Monitoring activity in an office work place is common practice, of course – especially where employees are given a £20,000 piece of machinery to use – and whilst there's obviously more of a logistical difficulty in doing likewise with an employee 'on the road', companies still need to look beyond 'sales figures' or 'call out' statistics when reviewing the performance of their fleet drivers.

By using telematics, fleet decision-makers can ensure 'smarter driving' does not drop off their radar. Drilling down on any journey undertaken and accessing data such as vehicle speed, acceleration and braking habits can give clear information on where a potential risk might lie, allowing them to take pro-active, corrective action – before it's too late.

To comply with legislative requirements too, companies must demonstrate not only that they have implemented an occupational road risk policy but also that they pro-actively monitor the performance of work related road safety at regular and frequent intervals.

By having auditable records proving that staff are not being asked to undertake unreasonable business journeys, that they do have adequate breaks, that vehicles are regularly serviced and roadworthy and that 'high risk' driving behaviour is acted upon early, telematics can reduce the very real risk of prosecution.

In addition, fleets have a duty to their shareholder, too. It's important that businesses avoid any negative media coverage resulting from a work-related road crash. Such an event could prove disastrous for an organisation and its future trading, with a corporate brand being severely or permanently damaged.

Q. Fleet managers are especially keen to reduce fleet costs at present. How can these systems help?

A. Fleet management specialists like ALD can assist in creating cost efficient fleet policies and determining an optimum funding route, but the need to manage the costs 'on the road' remains. So more and more forward thinking companies are now turning to telematics, recognising the crucial role it can play in cutting operating cost. And, of all these costs, fuel spend is the one that can deliver the greatest savings.

According to the Fleet 200 Report published by Sewells the largest 200 fleets in the UK across 10 industry sectors spend £1.2bn p.a. What that figure might be in 12 months time is anybody's guess but one thing is for sure, if a fleet can achieve a fuel saving of 10%, that's a huge figure in anyone's budget.

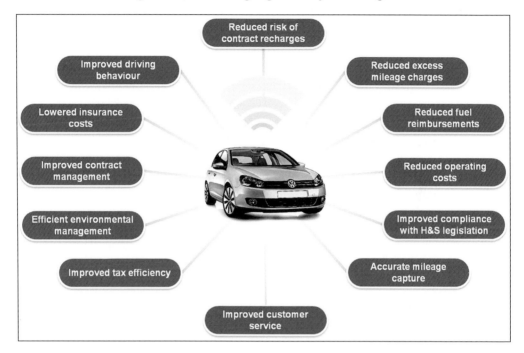

REDUCED MILEAGE REIMBURSEMENT

In an article appearing in Personnel Today in February 2008 ('False expense claims cost UK employers more than £1bn a year') it was estimated UK businesses pay out approximately £5.8b p.a. in employee expenses with over £1b estimated to be false or 'out-of-policy' claims. In a separate article published in Director of Finance Online in June 2009 ('Not just MPs on the fiddle') 20% of employees admitted to having exaggerated claims and13% would be likely to do so in the future if they found themselves in economic difficulty and thought they could get away with it.

In Personnel Today in December 2010, a survey from employee expenses management company, GlobalExpense claimed that 25% of UK staff that had ever claimed expenses admitted to exaggerating them, with business mileage the most likely to be exaggerated. This compared with only 15% in a similar survey in 2009. This was supported by a survey of 3000 UK employees conducted by Travelodge which found that the second most common expense 'scam' was adding mileage to a claim.

Given these alarming statistics it's hardly surprising that accurate mileage capture is so important and this is backed up by research which highlighted mileage bills dropped by 25% when organisations introduced measures to capture and audit their drivers' mileage reports.

Mileage capture, historically, has been achieved by drivers recording business mileage on a paper-based log. However, such systems rely on the integrity of

> 66 The Fuel Management System via ProFleet2 provided savings of £90,000 in fuel submissions for private useage in its first year, as well as accurately reporting the reduction in our Carbon Output. In addition, over £100,000 of vehicles were recovered using its tracker capability 99
>
> *Fleet Manager*

employees for their accuracy, are open to widespread abuse and are administratively cumbersome for both employees and employers.

An auditable mileage trail, clearly identifying work-related trips and private mileage is, therefore, essential to avoid journeys being exaggerated, duplicated (claiming for a journey shared with a colleague) or completely fabricated.

If a mileage over-estimate of 10% sounds like an unrealistic figure plucked out of the air, it's worth asking how unrealistic a mileage claim of 125 miles from London to Bristol sounds? Very plausible but if the actual mileage was 113, a round trip would 'cost' your business 250 miles rather than the actual figure of 226. A small sum in itself but multiplied over several trips – either by accident, rough estimates or deliberate action – and by several drivers and the cost soon mounts up. Such an error could easily cost a business more than £700 per driver over 3 years, based on 20,000 business miles p.a. paid back at 12ppm. Over a fleet of 50 cars this would total over £36k in excess fuel claims alone.

With telematics, odometer readings from journey reporting can be relied upon. They aren't calculated on the back of a 'fag packet' and, as yet, I've not yet heard of one that knowingly adds a few miles 'to be on the safe side'! By simply asking employees to attach their 'telematics' mileage report to their expenses sheet, this not only avoids mistakes but it'll save them from the drudgery of manually completing mileage returns every month too!

Within ALD's ProFleet2 system we've also successfully trialled mileage reporting that is integrated direct into payroll through an approval workflow process. Line managers can automatically authorise a driver's mileage report (or question, as appropriate) and this feeds directly into payroll, thereby ensuring the whole claims process is administered quickly and efficiently. And where a claim is not submitted on time, HR deducts the whole of the driver's fuel card expense that month from their salary – private and business. If an employee needed any more motivation to complete their submission on a timely basis I've not yet come across it!

REDUCING UNAUTHORISED JOURNEYS

With remote mileage capture and journey reporting, telematics can also help improve control over pool car and commercial vehicle use by identifying unauthorised journeys (e.g. 'out of hours' activity) and any excessive private mileage. And, as telematics is embraced by a company there is also less likelihood of similar journeys being undertaken in the first place, resulting in lower mileage abuse and reduced fuel and rental costs. If this saved just fifty miles being driven each week, over 3 years this could save a business over £1200 on fuel and £500 in contract hire rental costs alone, a saving of £85k for a fleet of fifty vehicles, without even trying!

Fleet Cost League Table

The table below summarises all the total events that contribute to your overall fleet cost by driver (Harsh Acceleration, Excessive Idling, Excessive Speed and Over-Revving). This allows you to see your "best" and "worst" performing drivers in order that you can review driving styles and therefore reduce costs to your business.

The "Fuel Cost" column shows the approximate fuel cost of business journeys for the selected period, based on a nominal of £1.26 per litre for diesel and £1.22 per litre for petrol.

Note: The MPG figure is the manufacturers published figure and NOT the MPG average achieved by the driver.

Driver Name	Registration	Make	Model	MPG	Duration	Distance	Fuel Cost ▼	Accel	Braking	Idling	Speed	RPM	Total
Driver3	Reg3	Vauxhall	Combo Van	41.5	01:02:58	1126.9	£155.55	13	81	14	43	47	198
Driver18	Reg18	Vauxhall	Vivaro	40.5	01:03:40	904.1	£127.88	12	47	11	0	87	157
Driver9	Reg9	Vauxhall	Insignia 5 Door Hatch	37.2	00:22:48	820.3	£122.31	1	25	11	4	12	53
Driver8	Reg8	Vauxhall	Astra Hatch	39.8	01:01:09	856.9	£119.42	1	60	15	0	52	128
Driver12	Reg12	Vauxhall	Vivaro	40.5	01:02:01	759	£107.35	0	16	22	0	12	50
Driver16	Reg16	Vauxhall	Vivaro	41.5	01:08:15	773	£106.70	1	27	49	0	47	124
Driver6	Reg6	Vauxhall	Vivaro	41.5	00:21:37	769	£106.15	0	51	7	0	7	65
Driver2	Reg2	Vauxhall	Vivaro	41.5	00:18:35	663.1	£91.53	0	6	5	0	41	52
Driver5	Reg5	Vauxhall	Combo Van	41.5	00:21:16	630.2	£86.99	4	4	5	0	8	21
Driver10	Reg10	Vauxhall	Astra 5 Door Hatch	46.3	00:15:40	516.3	£61.85	1	14	13	0	27	55
Driver7	Reg7	Vauxhall	Vivaro	41.5	00:13:31	444	£61.29	1	8	3	2	46	60
Driver1	Reg1	Vauxhall	Astra Hatch	39.8	00:21:59	433.1	£60.36	0	1	19	0	18	38
Driver17	Reg17	Vauxhall	Vivaro	37.2	00:12:03	336.7	£51.85	1	6	6	0	20	33
Driver13	Reg13	Vauxhall	Vivaro	40.5	00:12:41	303	£42.86	0	4	18	0	29	51
Driver15	Reg15	Vauxhall	Vivaro	41.5	01:02:49	286.6	£39.55	0	0	0	0	0	0
Driver14	Reg14	Vauxhall	Vivaro	40.5	00:09:55	245.4	£34.71	0	2	12	0	8	22
Driver11	Reg11	Vauxhall	Vivaro	40.5	00:08:18	208.7	£29.52	0	3	5	0	19	27
Driver7	Reg7	Vauxhall	Vivaro	41.5	00:00:00	0	£0.00	0	0	0	0	0	0

IMPROVING FUEL CONSUMPTION

Whilst the above has focused on 'mileage management', a vital area of cost control which is often neglected is 'driver management'. A fleet may be funded in the most cost efficient manner; its policy may have been constructed in the 'greenest' of fashions but that counts for little if drivers have no regard to fleet budgets with their inconsiderate driving.

We all know that fast driving and heavy acceleration reduce fuel consumption. Harsh braking is also a waste of fuel as, too, is needless vehicle idling. But how does a fleet manager know if he's running a tight ship or his fleet is burning cash?

With very little effort drivers can easily cut fuel bills by 5-10% and, as we have found through our involvement in the annual MPG Marathon, with some careful driving, fuel consumption can actually be improved up to 50% compared with the manufacturer approved figures.

- Drivers who reduce their speed from 85mph to 70mph will save nearly half a litre of petrol every 10 miles (IAM)

- Driving at 70mph uses up to 9% more fuel than at 60mph and up to 15% more fuel than at 50mph (Act on CO_2)

- Cruising at 80mph can use up to 25% more fuel than at 70mph (AA)

But without sitting beside your driver every day, how else can you monitor their driving styles and encourage them to adopt a smarter driving approach? Telematics provide an ideal solution with fleet managers alerted quickly to any potentially costly driving behaviour, which can then be addressed swiftly and correctly in a targeted fashion.

And even when a vehicle's stationary, telematics data can identify how long an engine is left idling. Armed with such information, fleet decision-makers can then

"Having worked with ALD for over 10 years I have always been impressed by their innovative approach to fleet management and ProFleet2 has, certainly, ticked all the boxes for us."

Operations Manager

start encouraging employees to turn their engine off, which delivers financial savings and environmental benefits, and is safer for the driver too.

One interesting fact is that, even where driving behaviour is not necessarily specifically reviewed, where telematics systems are adopted it is human nature that employees are likely to drive more responsibly and operate within 'best practice' guidelines. Independent research supports this, highlighting that drivers will often change behavior on their own without requiring intervention from HR or Fleet, who are therefore able to focus their time on more pressing issues.

Using league tables to benchmark drivers, fleets can identify drivers more prone to 'costly' driving behavior and ensure valuable training resource is focused on activity most likely to have a beneficial impact. This can also encourage friendly competition among employees to become 'the best driver' and some fleets use this data to reward smarter driving too.

Whilst fleets can always fall back on new engine technologies to show improvements in fuel efficiency, the reality is that the it will take a company years to reap these rewards with a change cycle every three or four years. Using telematics, however, is a far more effective option, with just a small investment in a telematics system bringing a potential reduction in costs immediately.

Lower insurance premiums

The relationship between insurance and telematics is continually strengthening. Increasingly, insurers are realising the value of telematics, with their fleet risk being far more measureable given the journey and driver management data being made available. With some insurers stipulating 'tracking' devices are fitted as standard to individual high performance vehicles it is not long before fleet insurance premiums are heavily influenced by the fitment of telematics across a fleet.

Fleet management

Telematics alone will not reduce costs or accidents but it does provide key management information to help fleets make accurate and informed decisions that manage such issues; allowing fleets to identify the significance of any risks and react quickly. For any business serious about controlling cost, telematics is certainly an option to consider.

Having access to this data, however, will have little impact if there's no commitment to act upon it and it has to be remembered it's only one tool in the fleet armory. It shouldn't, therefore, be seen as the silver bullet; the culture of the company has to be ready for change too!

Q. Are there any other costs telematics can help reduce?

A. Yes, definitely!

With service intervals being extended and vehicles regularly reallocated it's easy to see how services can be missed. Drivers are, no doubt, very busy and, even if they do know when their next service is due, it is probably not convenient having their vehicle off the road for any time. With lengthy servicing lead-times, too, it could be several weeks before a service is possible. The consequence?

■ Future resale values are affected from a poor service history

■ Routine repairs can become more complex and costly after a missed service

■ Warranty programmes can be invalidated

■ A missed service can cause a component failure with catastrophic consequences

This, of course, could lead to costly re-charges being passed on, both to the company and the driver.

With remote odometer readings and pre-defined preference settings, however, telematics can automatically remind drivers to service their vehicle allowing work to be carried out in a timely manner and alerting fleet managers should a request not be actioned.

The reduced resale value of a 3 year old car with 30,000 miles and a missed service could be c.£250-£500; the cost of repairing or replacing a gearbox following a missed service might be c.£2,500; an invalidated warranty repair such as a starter motor or new engine could cost £250 and £3,500 respectively. All needless recharges, which could be prevented by using telematics systems such as those provided by ALD.

On the back of such service reminders, fleets could also benefit from a reduction in hire car costs. With proactive service reminders resulting in advance service bookings, fleets should see their hire car costs reduce with the greater availability of courtesy cars, which are generally unavailable with late booking. Over the life of a typical contract this could save maybe £150 per vehicle; multiplied over a fleet the costs increase significantly.

Historically, leasing companies have relied upon servicing garages phoning through mileage readings and the keying-in of data, often incorrectly, causing fleets to regularly face unbudgeted excess mileage fees at end of contract. With automated mileage capture, however, account reviews can be carried out in an informed and structured manner, bringing greater transparency to contract management and reducing the likelihood of problems.

Q. And presumably they also help detect stolen vehicles?

A. With GPS functionality the chances of a stolen vehicle being recovered are increased significantly with 'track and trace' functionality provided as standard. In the early days, however, when our vehicles were fitted with non GPS telematics technology we still managed to help police recover a number of stolen vehicles and make a number of arrests. Essentially, this was achieved as a result of cell-site triangulation giving the police a target area in which the stolen vehicle could be found. In the last two years alone, sixty stolen vehicles have been recovered, valued at £1.3m, as a direct result of vehicles having ProFleet2 fitted. One customer has even had sixteen vehicles recovered to date.

> "We use ProFleet2 to ensure our vehicles are serviced on schedule, which is important from both a duty of care viewpoint and ensuring costs are controlled. The fact that it has helped police recover our leased vehicles when they've been stolen has been an added value benefit."
>
> **HR Manager**

If a vehicle is stolen this will obviously have an adverse affect on future insurance premiums. Having a car off the road for three months whilst a new one is ordered could cost more than £2,500 in hire car costs alone for self-insured fleets. For insured fleets this would inflate the claim which would then impact on the renewal premium. Insurers generally leave claims for 6 weeks before any pay out so six weeks' car hire is a minimum and correspondence and any agreement on valuation can often take three-to-four weeks to settle.

Q. Can they help reduce tax?

A. Less obvious, perhaps, but of significant value is where telematics can help reduce potential taxation too. A private use benefit will not arise if a van is used only for work journeys and where private use is commuting, or there is 'insignificant' private mileage. However, where a private use benefit is identified, the annual benefit value is currently £3,000 for the van and £500 for any free or subsidised private fuel provided. Clearly, a significant liability can arise, especially if previous tax years are included.

Companies and drivers are much less likely to get caught out by this if there is an auditable record of 'out of hours' use. We're aware that HMRC are currently investigating the private use of commercial vehicles in a number of fleets to ensure there are proper processes in place to reduce unauthorised driving. Telematics provides the ideal audit control.

For fleets operating ECO schemes, it is critical to have mileage records submitted on time every month, as ECO fleets move from annual to monthly reconciliation. Without business mileage data, the company should assume 100% private mileage, resulting in the grossing up of the monthly allowance. e.g. 1,000 business miles at 40p = £400 tax-free but grossed up for tax and NI, in the event of zero business mileage, is £690 (40% tax & 2% NI from April 2011). The cost would be £290 per car or c£29,000 for a fleet of 100 cars.

Q. What are the benefits to drivers? Don't they resent the 'spy in the car'?

A. A motivated employee is the most valuable asset any organisation has, so before introducing telematics, it is best practice to consult with any staff affected. Any benefits telematics might bring could easily be diluted by any HR fallout if it is clumsily implemented as part of company-wide clamp down on cost.

Adopting telematics for the wrong reasons is a sure-fire way to fail. If it's proposed as a way of monitoring employee behaviour to highlight poor driving, drivers will soon resent this which will immediately create barriers and be demotivating and not conducive to creating a productive and co-operative workforce!

However, if it's communicated positively and seen as a tool to help drivers pro-actively, improve safety and reduce accidents it will be seen as a much more

> **❝** By introducing ProFleet2, having the ability to monitor vehicle movements, identify unnecessary journeys, idling times and erratic driving behaviours, a 37% reduction on fuel spend was achieved **❞**
>
> Fleet Manager

positive measure and there should be no such concerns. From the outset ALD has always respected the views of drivers and seen them as a key stakeholder in the whole telematics debate. This is why we build in 'driver consent' functionality so that fleet managers can only see journey data their drivers are happy to release. The drivers, therefore, remain 'in control'.

The objective has to be to create a climate where all parties can embrace telematics as a tool to help achieve shared objectives and if fleets can communicate the benefits in a positive way there is less likely to be any resistance. Drivers need to see the wider benefits of telematics rather than seeing it as a trigger for punitive action

As well as service reminders, drivers can obtain journey reporting via their own unique web-site to help them manage their business mileage claims. For example, our ProFleet2 system records everything accurately and automatically and meets HMRC guidelines on expenses claims and submissions, saving everyone time and energy. Reports also highlight issues that might contribute to driver fatigue, thereby encouraging drivers to change their driving behaviour – before it's too late.

Employees who think they are driving for too long should be advised to speak to their employer, who are responsible under road traffic and health and safety law to avoid setting unrealistic schedules and must not put employees at risk through work-related activities. Having a stolen vehicle recovered quickly also reduces the stress which any victim would, naturally, feel and increase the likelihood of any personal possessions being recovered too

And with driver access to their own telematics reporting, research suggests they will be less inclined to speed meaning they'll keep their licences a while longer!

So there shouldn't be any resentment and, had the telematics industry adopted a more 'inclusive' stance and recognised the driver's view more pro-actively, telematics adoption amongst fleets would be several years further down the road!

Q. Are there any statistics on the overall benefits of in-vehicle telematics systems?

A. There is significant research and numerous case studies with statistics to support the benefits of telematics.

Frost & Sullivan research has reported fuel savings of 15% being achieved from companies that have successfully implemented a telematics solution, and other research has suggested this figure could be as high as 20%. It's well documented that Tesco saw an immediate reduction in fuel spend of 12%, too, as well as a 6% reduction in vehicle damage since telematics was introduced. From ALD's own findings customers have reported reductions of 11-15% in business mileage expenses simply by asking drivers to add ProFleet2 'journey reports' to their own expense reports.

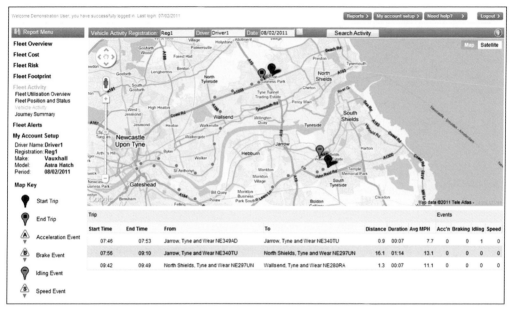

Zurich estimates that telematics could improve fuel consumption by 11% and reduce the number of vehicle collisions by 20%, in addition to the benefit of recovering stolen vehicles. ALD has even seen one self insured fleet save over £350k from the recovery of stolen vehicles in the last 18 months alone.

According to a survey by Digicore in 2010, 77% of those companies that had fitted telematics claimed they'd reduced their costs, 64% saw an increase in productivity, 52% felt there'd been an improvement in security and 51% said they'd experienced enhanced fleet and employee performance.

The statistics supporting telematics are, therefore, substantial but one common factor behind all successful telematics implementations is an ongoing management commitment to a change in culture: not just to reduce operating costs but to improve the safety of their employees and all other road users.

Irrespective of the statistics above, however, the questions still remain; without effective technology such as telematics, how else can you:

- Record accurate business mileage?
- Monitor excessive private mileage?
- Reduce unauthorized driving?
- Recover a stolen vehicle?
- Measure fleet utilisation?
- Tell where your vehicles are?
- Identify costly or risky driving behaviour?
- Accurately record overtime claims?
- Provide auditable health & safety records?
- Measure the success of eco-driving training?

Q. So in conclusion, you're really confident that telematics can help fleet managers manage their vehicles?

A. Definitely. With vehicle costs rising, fuel at record prices and higher taxation increasingly eating into everything we do, unsurprisingly, **cost control** is the number one priority for fleet managers. And whilst the focus on **risk management** may have taken a slight step backwards as companies battened down their hatches during the recession, it's clear that health and safety legislation is still high on the fleet agenda. **Environmental issues**, too, are a major consideration albeit the green agenda has probably moved away from 'conscience' to being a 'cost issue'. It's still on the radar but principally because lower CO_2 vehicles save money … rather than the planet.

State of the art telematics systems such as ProFleet2 utilise in-vehicle telematics in which key vehicle management and driver performance data is remotely accessed allowing the supplier, fleet contacts and drivers to benefit from a wide range of in-built features.

The most modern systems incorporate GPS functionality so customers can now gain a unique insight into the inner workings of their fleet, which can be managed in a more cost effective, safer and greener way than ever before, at minimal cost.

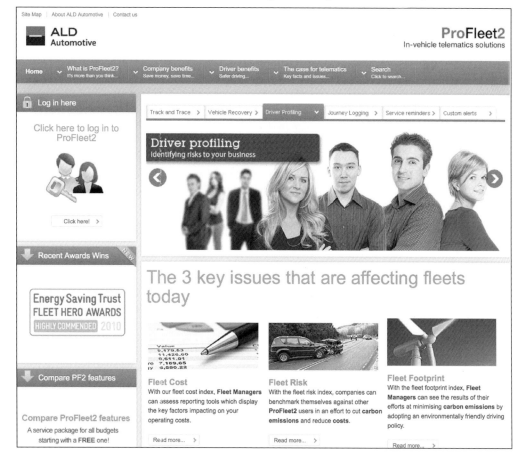

On our website www.profleet2.com fleet managers and drivers can learn more about the service and better understand the benefits of ProFleet2, helping them present the case for introducing this technology. Fleets can then select one or more of a combination of 4 product options depending upon their specific needs:

1. Standard (Driver View):

This is provided as a no cost option within fully maintained contract hire agreements. Individual vehicle journeys are automatically recorded and are made available to drivers, exclusively, via a password protected website that also gives them a comprehensive reporting suite.

Key journey data is recorded with start and end locations and times, odometer reading, distance travelled and a customisable 'journey type' field. We are also about to add actual MPG and CO_2 emissions per journey based on the performance of the vehicle and the driving style of the driver. With download options into CSV, Excel or PDF formats – over a date range specified by the driver – these reports provide all the information needed when submitting expense claims for business mileage or overtime.

Another key benefit is that ProFleet2 automatically reminds drivers by email to service their vehicle and alerts fleet managers should a request not be actioned. Whilst not replacing their obligations, ProFleet2 does at least provide added peace of mind when drivers are not as conscientious as they should be!

2. Standard (Fleet Manager view)

Fleet managers do not have access to the Standard (Driver View) site but, should they wish to view this, the Standard (Fleet Manager view) provides the same reporting information listed above for all vehicles on their fleet. However, they can only do so once drivers have given consent via a user set-up feature on the driver site. Fleets can then set their own specific reporting criteria, thereby providing them with exception reporting relevant to their occupational road risk policy. A 'custom alert' facility can also give fleet managers a warning via email, allowing them to maintain control even without needing to be logged on.

3. Premium

Fleets that need more detailed management information can opt for the Premium Plus package. In addition to the above reporting suite, fleet managers also have access to driver profiling information such as excessive speed, harsh acceleration, hard braking, excess idling and over-revving.

As with the Standard View the reporting menu structure is divided into Fleet Cost, Fleet Risk and Fleet Footprint sections. Depending upon which product option has been requested – and any custom criteria entered – specific journey data and driving behaviour 'events' relating to these 3 key issues are displayed in tables and easy-view graphs.

> **"** ALD Automotive's PF2 technology has helped us reduce the fuel bill attributed to our fleet of seventy vehicles by 20% since its inception in August 2010. The 20% saving has been achieved by using the 'fleet league table', which shows which drivers are braking and accelerating harshly, idling for long periods of time, over-revving or speeding **"**
>
> Fleet Manager

To highlight the relevance of each report, brief information is also provided e.g. *"idling for 30 minutes can consume 1 litre of fuel which will create 2.5kg of CO_2", "Motorway driving at 70mph can bring savings of around 10% for your fuel bill compared to driving at 80mph"*

One of the most useful features within the reporting suite are the league tables which quickly identify drivers who are either driving poorly or, more positively, those drivers who should, potentially, be rewarded for their 'smarter' driving habits. Whether a fleet operates a 'stick or carrot' approach, they can help highlight risks and opportunities, which is especially useful in identifying not just who may need training but also in what areas e.g. speed awareness, eco-driving, etc. Should the driver then follow a course of training fleets have a completely independent and auditable record of the number of 'events' pre and post training to measure its success (or otherwise!).

4. Premium Plus

With Premium Plus, ProFleet2 offers an even greater insight into the inner workings of a fleet with vehicle position and status and journey routing shown 'real-time', which is especially useful for fleets where regular customer service calls are made and where response time SLAs need to be adhered to. This information is also critical for the speedy recovery of stolen vehicles. Track and trace reporting is provided as standard allowing fleets to monitor the effectiveness of journey scheduling.

As for the future, as a company that has long recognised the value of telematics, ALD is well aware of the pace of change in technology and is continually working on more added value functionality to maintain ProFleet2's leading edge.

The bottom line is that 'you can only manage what you can measure' and ProFleet2 provides a tool to do this, not only identifying 'where' the fleet is – and has been – but 'how' the vehicles have been driven too.

It is a proven, cost effective and practical fleet management tool that can be implemented with minimal effort, delivering a key set of management information to help fleets reduce cost, reduce risk and manage their carbon footprint.

For any company serious about managing its fleet, telematics is no longer a side-line activity; it's centre spot!

ENVIRONMENTAL ISSUES

INTERNATIONAL

For decades scientists have been debating the reasons why the planet is getting hotter.

This argument is complicated by the fact that the planet has heated and cooled many times over the millennia for quite natural reasons. However, there is now remarkable unanimity between most of the world's scientists: they believe the main reason for global warming is the rising concentration of greenhouse gases in the earth's atmosphere – the 'greenhouse effect'.

In response to growing concern, the government established the Royal Commission on Environmental Pollution to take evidence and examine this problem. In its report in June 2000 it said, 'Human-induced factors are having a discernible effect on climate'.

In 1992 most of the world's governments met at a conference in Kyoto, Japan, and agreed to take steps to reduce the emissions that cause the greenhouse effect. This landmark convention and protocol were heralded as bringing a new approach to environmental management that would arrest the damage we have done to the planet.[223] The agreement included an undertaking to reduce average levels of carbon dioxide emissions per vehicle to 140g/km by 2008.

While many governments agreed to this step, before the convention could enter into force it required it needed to be approved by at least 55 countries, and they needed to account for at least 55% of the total carbon dioxide emissions[224] from that group.

By 2001 dozens of countries had ratified the agreement but they had not reached the 55% threshold required for the protocol to have legal effect. When George W Bush was elected President of the USA in 2001, one of his government's first acts was to say it would not be bound by the agreement.

---

223 You can read the full transcript of the Kyoto protocol at
     www.unfccc.de/resouces/convkp.html This site also contains an excellent
     beginner's guide to the protocol.
224 At 1990 levels.

Therefore, even though 122 countries ratified the agreement, these only accounted for about 44% of the relevant total CO_2 emissions.

In July 2001 a new treaty signed by 178 governments in Bonn effectively replaced the Kyoto treaty. It watered down the commitments given at Kyoto.

Rather than simply requiring governments to reduce carbon dioxide emissions by 5.2% from their 1990 levels, as required by the Kyoto accord, countries were to be given credit for their properly managed farmland and forests. These so called carbon dioxide 'sinks' absorb carbon dioxide, so countries such as the USA and Canada that have large areas of forest would not have to reduce their carbon dioxide output from industrial processes and transport as much as they would have under the Kyoto accord.

Environmental groups believed that this would lead to only a tiny reduction in carbon dioxide output.

The 2009 Copenhagen conference on climate change ended without agreement, leading many to wonder whether it was going to be possible to reach a global binding agreement on climate change. Some poorer countries wanted the richer countries to do more, so they blocked progress.

The next major climate change conference took place in Cancun in 2010, where some progress was made. The conference agreed to a 50% reduction of CO_2 emissions by 2050 and that they would aim to restrict global warming to an average of 2 degrees Celsius above pre-industrial times. The wealthiest nations have committed that by 2020 they will reduce their CO_2 emissions by 25-40 percent below 1990 levels. Scientists believe this is the minimum required in order to avert the worst effects of global warming.

They also agreed to establish a US$100bn Green Climate Fund to help poorer nations play their part in carbon reductions. A further scheme will provide cash for poorer countries who agree to curtail deforestation programmes.

So there has been progress but currently the Kyoto agreement remains the only legally binding agreement on carbon reduction between nations. It expires in 2012. Several large nations never signed it and others have said they will not renew it.

EUROPEAN UNION

The EU is making real efforts to reduce its greenhouse gas emissions. EU carbon emissions have fallen 16% in the last two decades against a background of 40% economic growth. The plan is to reduce total emissions in 2020 by 20% below 1990 levels, with renewables accounting for 20% of energy production.

Looking specifically at vans (up to 3.5 tonnes), the commission wants CO_2 emissions to reach 175g/km by 2016 and 135g/km by 2020. In addition, manufacturers are expected to ensure that by 2014 the CO emissions of three quarters of the vans they manufacture must not exceed 175g/km CO_2. Two years later the commission expects that no new van's emissions will exceed this level. Many believe this target is overambitious and will not be achieved.

Further information is available from the Commission's Climate Action web pages.[225]

These changes are part of the Commission's plan to reduce all of the EU's domestic emissions by 80 to 95% by 2050.

Transport is expected to deliver a significant proportion of this reduction. The plan shows that, compared to 1990, the total emissions from all transport (other than marine transport) has risen by 30%, and that the Commission believes this could be reduced by 10% - 39% by 2030 and by 84% - 97% by 2050.

In 2005 the EU introduced an Emissions Trading System (EU ETS) to allow businesses to trade greenhouse gas emission allowances. It covers some 11,000 industrial plants in 30 countries and will soon be extended to cover airlines, pharmaceutical companies and other high-emissions businesses. The system sets limits ("caps") on the greenhouse gases that can be emitted by these plants, and the companies receive tradable emissions allowances based on these limits. Each year a company must surrender sufficient allowances to cover its emissions. If it fails to do so it pays a fine. However, if it reduces its emissions it will have spare allowances that it can either carry over into a future period or sell to a less efficient organisation that needs more allowances. This encourages participants an enormous incentive to cut emissions. Allowances will be reduced over time – by 21% between 2005 and 2020 – so companies will either have to cut emissions or buy allowances in the market.

The EU ETS seems to be working. Emissions from these organisations are falling and over time it is hoped that the system will be adopted elsewhere and become global.

Fleet managers in these businesses are already being asked to contribute their efforts to reducing their organisations' greenhouse gas emissions.

UK

The key piece of legislation relating to atmospheric warming is the Climate Change Act 2008, which requires UK emissions of greenhouse gases (GHGs) to fall by at least 80% by 2050, compared to 1990 levels. To achieve this the Act introduced carbon budgets, which are legal caps on the total amount of greenhouse gases produced in the UK. Performance against this limit is measured after deducting any allowances that have been purchased under the EU ETS.

The Act set up the Committee on Climate Change (CCC), an independent body whose remit is to advise the government on setting "and meeting carbon budgets and on preparing for the impacts of climate change".

225 ec.europa.eu/clima/policies/transport/vehicles/index_en.htm

The carbon budgeting process sets targets and measures performance for periods of five years, and in 2011 the government accepted the CCC's recommendation in relation to the fourth carbon budgeting period, which will run from 2023-2027. If the UK achieves this target it will means that between 1990 and 2027, total UK carbon emissions will have fallen by 50%. At the time of writing the government had yet to publish a plan showing how it expects to achieve this reduction.

The automotive sector has been praised by the CCC for its CO_2 reduction efforts. Average new car CO_2 emissions in 2010 were 144.2g/km, representing a 20% reduction in a decade. It is difficult to picture what a measure like 144.2g/km actually means. This statistic may help: a car emitting this amount of CO_2 produces its own weight in CO_2 every 5,200 miles.

More information on the UK's efforts to reduce greenhouse gasses can be found at the CCC's website: www.theccc.org.uk.

11.1 GREENHOUSE GASES

There are four main greenhouse gases; carbon dioxide (CO_2), chlorofluorocarbons (CFCs), nitrous oxide (N_2O) and methane (CH_4).

11.1.1 CARBON DIOXIDE (CO_2)

95% of carbon dioxide occurs naturally. The remaining 5% is man-made, of which 60% comes from deforestation and energy generation. A further 20% comes from industrial processes unconnected with road transport. That leaves 20% from road transport.[226]

So, of the total CO_2 in the atmosphere, only 20% of 5%, that is 1%, comes from road transport. This statistic explains some of the frustrations that the motor manufacturers express when talking about this topic. If they reduce the CO_2 output of all road vehicles by 20% it will make only 0.2% difference to the quantity of carbon dioxide being emitted into the atmosphere.

The UK car benefit tax regime offers a lower level of vehicle excise duty and car benefit tax on cars that emit less CO_2.[227] This is a good example of government action to reduce greenhouse gases.

The UK benefit in kind tax regime encourages drivers to trade down the CO_2 scale to reduce the tax they pay. Most fleet managers have long-since recognised the value of adding diesel cars to their fleets.

When a new vehicle is type-approved its CO_2 output is established, and this remains unchanged unless the vehicle's fuel type is changed.

---

226 Source: SMMT.

227 See 17.2.1.

In deciding which vehicles to acquire, you and your drivers will need lists showing the CO_2 of various makes and models of car. There are several sources of this data.

- Your contract hire company should be able to provide this.

- The Vehicle Certification Agency (VCA) publishes this information and it is available online from http://carfueldata.direct.gov.uk

- The Society of Motor Manufacturers and Traders also provides this information on its website www.smmt.co.uk.

- Individual manufacturers publish fuel consumption and CO_2 data in their marketing material and on their websites.

- All new V5s issued after 1 March 2001 show CO_2 data. For older vehicles the data should be available from the manufacturer, if available. If a vehicle was registered before 1 Jan 1998, it may not have a published CO_2 figure. In this case it will be taxed on engine size based on the following scale, without the 3% diesel supplement.

Under 1401 cc	15% of list price
1401 – 2000 cc	22% of list price
Over 2000 cc	32% of list price

11.1.2 CHLOROFLUOROCARBONS (CFCs)

CFCs are chemicals used in the manufacture of refrigeration units. When refrigerators leak, or when they are destroyed after use, these chemicals escape into the atmosphere.

CFCs are very strong greenhouse gases but as there are less of them in the atmosphere than carbon dioxide, nitrous oxide and methane they do less damage.

They tend to attract more interest for the damage they cause to the ozone layer, the protective layer in the ionosphere that shields the earth from most of the sun's ultra violet rays. It is damaged by CFCs and the effect is believed to have caused the 'holes in the ozone layer' that have appeared over the north and south poles in the last twenty-five years. This has led to an increase in skin cancers, especially in Australasia.

So CFCs are mainly a skin cancer issue, not a global warming issue.

In his book 'A Short History of Nearly Everything', Bill Bryson wrote the best description of CFCs I have read.[228] This is a précis:

> "Ozone is a form of oxygen. It is a bit of a chemical oddity in that at ground level it is a pollutant, while way up in the stratosphere it is beneficial since it soaks up dangerous ultraviolet radiation. Beneficial ozone is not terribly abundant, however. If it were distributed evenly

228 Published by Black Swan. ISBN 0 552 99704 8.

throughout the stratosphere, it would form a layer just 2 millimetres or so thick.

"Chlorofluorocarbons are also not very abundant but they are extravagantly destructive. A single kilogram of CFCs can capture and annihilate 70,000 kilogrammes of atmospheric ozone. CFCs also hang around for a long while – about a century on average – wreaking havoc all the while. And they are great heat sponges. A single CFC molecule is about ten thousand times more efficient at exacerbating greenhouse effects than a molecule of carbon dioxide – and carbon dioxide of course is no slouch itself as a greenhouse gas. In short, chlorofluorocarbons may ultimately prove to be just about the worst invention of the twentieth century."

The level of CFCs in the atmosphere has been slowly reducing following the Montreal Protocol.

Just when scientists thought they had fully understood the effect of greenhouse gases and CFCs, researchers[229] have begun to draw attention to the action of hydroxyls in the atmosphere.

Hydroxyls are molecules that clean up atmospheric pollutant gases such as nitrous oxides, sulphur dioxide and carbon monoxide. The bad news is that they require ultra violet light to work effectively. Reducing the level of CFCs in the atmosphere will close the hole in the ozone layer and reduce the amount of ultra violet light in the atmosphere, which will in turn affect the efficiency of hydroxyls. Thus, it is argued, more pollutants will build up in the atmosphere.

Could this be the next big environmental scare?

11.1.3 NITROUS OXIDE

Nitrous oxide is a greenhouse gas but is probably best known as 'laughing gas'. It has a variety of uses, including as an anaesthetic for operations and to boost the performance of racing cars.

Most environmental emissions of nitrous oxide come from the manufacture of an acid used in the manufacturing of nylon. It also comes from agricultural soil, fertilisers and coal-fired power stations. Road transport produces only a small percentage of the nitrous oxide released into the atmosphere, though this percentage trebled in the 1990s as nitrous oxide is also produced by catalytic converters.

11.1.4 METHANE

Methane is the fourth of the major greenhouse gases that cause global warming. It is a naturally occurring gas emitted by coal and other mines, farm animals and drying peat bogs.

229 US National Center for Atmospheric Research, Boulder, Colorado.

11.2 PARTICULATES

Particulates are small soot-like particles emitted into the atmosphere when any carbon-based fuel is burned. These emissions are especially high in diesel fuel. They are not greenhouse gases but environmental pollutants.

It is believed that particulates cause a variety of health problems. They are blamed for the rise in child asthma cases and have been cited as a carcinogen responsible for causing a variety of different cancers.

In 1998 the government's Committee on Medical Effects of Air Pollutants (COMEAP) suggested that each year particulates are responsible for respiratory problems that cause the early death of 8,100 vulnerable people and 10,500 hospital admissions in the UK. These fatalities are among people who are already very ill and their deaths are likely to be brought forward by a few weeks.

The government adds a 3% surcharge to car benefit tax when a company car driver chooses a diesel-engined car, reflecting its concerns over particulate emissions.

11.3 CLEAN AIR ENFORCEMENT

The Vehicle & Operator Services Agency[230] carries out spot checks on vehicle emissions. They check tens of thousands of vehicles each year and issue prohibition notices banning around 4% of these.

In most cases the drivers are given twenty-four hours to fix the problem, though in the worst cases the emissions from some cars are so bad the inspectors immediately impound the cars.

The standard MoT test measures the vehicle's emissions. However, it does not test the emissions when the car is at full throttle, which is the time when they are at their highest level.

The government is considering the introduction of roadside pollution monitoring devices that use lasers to measure certain pollutants in exhaust fumes. As a vehicle passes the monitor, a laser checks the exhaust fumes for pollutants. Then second and third lasers check the speed of the car. This is necessary because slower vehicles emit thicker exhaust fumes than faster ones.

The monitoring devices would be placed on hills to ensure the vehicle was travelling at full throttle. The test would either be automatic, with the vehicles that fail being photographed (in the same way as speed cameras work today), or manual, with Vehicle & Operator Services Agency officers on hand to stop the offending vehicles.

---

230 VOSA is a government agency formed by the merger of the Vehicle Inspectorate (VI) and the Traffic Area Network (TAN) division of the Department for Transport (DfT). See 19.6.10

11.4 CONGESTION

11.4.1 THE PROBLEM

The first post-war government investigation into the use of pricing to alleviate road congestion was the *Smeed Report* written by Professor Reuben Smeed in 1964.[231]

It recognised that through road and petrol taxes we pay a great deal for the use of our vehicles. However, the marginal cost of deciding to take a particular journey is low, as we don't pay for the use of the roads.

The report predicted that road traffic would continue to grow simply because it costs so little to take each journey. It recommended the introduction of a series of roadside beacons to log car use.

The government ignored the report.

In the intervening decades road traffic has risen sharply. According to the SMMT's *Motor Industry Facts 2011*, we drive 31.3 million cars, 3.6m light commercial vehicles, 560,000 heavy goods vehicles and 91,000 buses.[232] That's a total of 36.5m vehicles, before adding in around 40,000 taxis, 1.2m motorbikes, 320,000 agricultural vehicles and 90,000 special purpose vehicles. So the total is over 38m vehicles.

We drive our cars around 250 billion miles p.a., a number that rises around 10% every decade, only slowing when there is a recession.

It is no wonder our roads are congested.

According to the Commission for Integrated Transport[233] 24% of UK trunk roads are congested for at least an hour each day. That's the highest level in Europe. In Spain the figure is 18%, The Netherlands 14%, Italy 9%, Germany 7% and France 4%.

The British government commissioned Sir Rod Eddington, a former chief executive of British Airways, to examine how the UK's economic development was being impacted by its transport system. He delivered his report, the Eddington Transport Study[234] in 2006, and pointed out that we take 61 billion journeys a year and that some parts of the system are under severe strain. He said "If left unchecked 13 per

---

231 There is a good academic paper on this at
   www2.cege.ucl.ac.uk/cts/tsu/papers/pbginau.htm

232 www.smmt.co.uk/wp-content/uploads/SMMT-Motor-Industry-Facts-2011.pdf

233 The Commission for Integrated Transport (CfIT) was abolished on 14 October 2010 as part of the government cuts.

234 Downloadable from
   www.thepep.org/ClearingHouse/docfiles/Eddington.Transport.Study%20-%20Rod.pdf

cent of traffic will be subject to stop-start travel conditions by 2025. He expressed strong backing for congestion-targeted road pricing and said it was the best alternative to introducing a massive road-building programme.

According to the government, an estimated 1.6bn working hours are lost in the UK every year through delays caused by traffic congestion. That's 1.6 *billion*, not 1.6 million.

It costs your business a great deal to have a driver and his car sitting in traffic.

There seems to be a general political consensus that congestion cannot be allowed to increase forever. The motorways were built to move freight traffic efficiently. It was never expected that they would become clogged with commuter cars.

The government wants to encourage a move from cars to public transport, with more use of rail transport for both passengers and freight. Provision for cyclists has increased enormously in recent years, with local authorities laying down thousands of miles of cycle lanes.

We have seen more steps that put public transport before private transport, such as 'smart bollards' that block entrance to city centres for cars but slide away to allow buses and emergency vehicles to pass. We can expect more such schemes.

The Transport Act 2000 allows local authorities to devise road user charging schemes, which can involve payment by cash, paper voucher or electronic means. Drivers can be charged on any of the following bases:

- For entering an area
- For being present in an area
- For driving a certain distance
- For passing a certain point

There are no stipulations as to whether drivers should be charged for using the road at a particular time of day or for driving on a particular type of road or when driving a particular type of vehicle.

The Act gives national exemption for the emergency services and the disabled. Local authorities are allowed to exempt more groups.

These schemes have to be part of a local integrated transport scheme. In a highly unusual departure from most tax-raising legislation, the revenue from these schemes is hypothecated. This means it is 'ring-fenced' for use only for a specified purpose to fund local transport improvements. The legislation ensures that these funds will remain hypothecated for at least ten years. This will allow local authorities to plan long term without the fear that they will invest now in anticipation of future revenues, only to find the revenue stops because the government changes the rules in a few years' time.

Local authorities have to send their congestion-charging proposals to the Secretary of State for approval. A scheme will only be approved if he or she is convinced that it will lead to public transport being improved and that the proceeds will go to create real transport improvements and reduced congestion. Local people have to be consulted before approval is granted.

We already have one major congestion-busting scheme. When it opened in 2004 the 27 mile long Birmingham Northern Relief Road - the 'M6 Toll' - became the UK's first tolled motorway. It provides much-needed relief to the congested M6 in Birmingham, which was designed to carry 72,000 vehicles per day and was carrying 160,000. Tolls are payable by cash or credit cards at toll booths, and fleets can obtain electronic payment tags to display on windscreens. More information is available from www.m6toll.co.uk.

11.4.2 WORKPLACE PARKING LEVY

The Transport Act 2000 allows local authorities to levy charges on workplace parking spaces.

Employers will have to buy a licence according to the number of parking spaces used. The licence will authorise a certain maximum number of vehicles to park in a particular workplace at any one time.

The Act exempts parking spaces used by customers at retail outlets or leisure sites.

Even though they have these new powers, local authorities have been slow to introduce these schemes. Nottingham will be introducing their scheme in 2012, and proposals are actively being investigated by other cities including Manchester, Bristol, Newcastle, Leeds, Birmingham and Sheffield.

11.4.3 CLEAR ZONES

This scheme, launched by the government in 2001, was designed to improve the quality of life for city residents. Local authorities were encouraged to devise schemes to reduce urban traffic congestion and pollution. The schemes could include restricting access to the city centre, traffic management measures or only allowing access to city centres for those vehicles meeting emissions standards.

Several cities and regions set up clear zone schemes before the funding dried up in 2005 and the schemes ended. Nonetheless the baton was taken up in London by the councils in Camden, City of London and City of Westminster. These councils aim to introduce new technologies and measures to improve the 'live-ability' of their areas, and to act as a test-bed for measures that will reduce congestion and pollution.

We can expect to see more from this initiative and you can follow developments on Clear Zone's website.[235]

11.4.4 LONDON

From its inception the Greater London Authority has taken seriously the reduction in road congestion and the improvement in London's environment, through

235 www.clearzones.org

investment in the public transport network, congestion charging, appropriate planning and other mechanisms. It aims to reduce emissions from vehicles by targeting the most polluting vehicles (mainly heavier diesel vehicles); increasing the take-up of newer, cleaner vehicles and fuels; introducing low emission zones in London and increasing the take-up of 'zero emission' forms of transport.

It launched London's congestion charging scheme in February 2003 and this has led to a significant reduction in traffic entering and moving in the zone, and a reduction of congestion in zone, whilst traffic immediately outside the zone did not materially increase. There has also been a significant increase in the number of passengers travelling by bus. The zone was extended west in 2007 but in 2011 the western extension was abolished.

Under the congestion charging scheme, drivers pay £10 to drive in the centre of London from 7am to 6.00 pm, Monday to Friday (but not bank and public holidays or from 25 December - 1 January inclusive). Payment can be made by phone, text message, in some shops and on the internet.[236]

Residents get a 90% discount.

You can pay the charge at Post Offices, petrol stations, by phone (0845 900 1234), by text message, on the internet or by automated phone message.

There are exemptions for emergency vehicles, licensed taxis, buses, public transport, coaches, motorbikes, mopeds, bicycles, NHS staff carrying drugs or patients' information and disabled badge holders.

There is a 100% Congestion Charge discount[237] for vehicles meeting Euro V emissions standards[238] and emitting less than 100g/km of CO_2, electric and plug-in hybrid electric vehicles, vehicles with more than nine seats, roadside recovery vehicles and tricycles that are one metre or less wide, and two metres or less long.

You need to register for discounts. The charge is £10 per vehicle.

To encourage early payment an additional £2 surcharge applies for paying the charge on the day following the day of travel.

There are no toll booths or barriers. To enforce the scheme, fixed cameras have been installed at the perimeter of the zone and mobile camera units are parked within the charging zone.

---

236 www.tfl.gov.uk/roadusers/congestioncharging/6743.aspx

237 If your fleet includes alternatively-fuelled vehicles that operate in central London, you should note the distinction between an exemption and a 100% discount. They cost the same but the latter allows the Mayor to reduce the discount at any time. Of the groups of vehicles obtaining the 100% discount it's unlikely he would ever start charging the disabled or breakdown vehicles. But alternatively-fuelled vehicles? Maybe.

238 Any car first registered on or after 1 January 2011 is automatically deemed to have met this standard.

There is a penalty charge of £120. This is reduced to £60 for payment within 14 days.

To save time and cost you can register your vehicles on a Transport for London (TfL) database. You can then use one of two schemes to pay the congestion charge.

THE CC AUTO PAY SCHEME

■ Register up to 5 vehicles.

■ TfL automatically logs when your vehicles enter the congestion zone.

■ Automatic month-end charge to your credit or debit card

■ Congestion charge is £9 per day

THE CC FLEET AUTO PAY SCHEME

As Auto Pay Scheme except

■ For 6 or more vehicles

■ TfL take payment by direct debit

■ Dedicated Fleet Helpline: 020 7649 9860, open 8.00am and 6.00pm, Monday to Friday

■ Online facility allows you to change registered vehicles and register ad hoc vehicles such as courtesy cars

The advantage of these schemes is that you avoid being charged a penalty.

The fleet industry has had a series of meetings with TfL about the operation of the congestion charging scheme, following many reports by fleet operators of charges being levied incorrectly and TfL failing to deal with matters promptly. TfL formally apologised to fleet operators in 2010 and promised to get matters under control.

Information about congestion charging can be obtained from www.london.gov.uk.

While London is often mentioned as the first location where road user charging was introduced, in fact Durham beat the capital to it. Motorists pay £2 to drive into the historic town centre – a World Heritage site – from 10am to 4pm, Monday to Saturday (excluding bank holidays). An automatic number plate recognition system logs vehicles entering the zone, and drivers are required to pay at the Parking Shop by 6pm the following day.[239] There are a number of exemptions from the charge.[240]

The Durham scheme has been particularly effective. Traffic has fallen by more than 90%.

Dozens of other local authorities have looked at introducing congestion charging. Schemes in Manchester, Edinburgh, Birmingham, Coventry, Nottingham, Cambridge and other cities have been considered and rejected.

239 Parking Shop, 56 North Road, Durham, DH1 4SF
240 See www.durham.gov.uk

London Low Emission Zone (LEZ)

Transport for London operates the London LEZ, which is designed to encourage vehicle operators to operate only low pollution vehicles in Greater London.

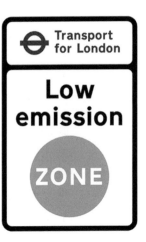

The scheme rules are changing from 3 January 2012 and this book ignores the rules applying before that date. (You can find them on the TfL website[241])

The scheme targets vehicles emitting large amounts of particulate matter[242] and from 3 January 2012 vehicles will need to meet the Euro IV standard for particulate emissions to avoid the daily charge.

The following vehicles will be the subject of the daily charge from 3 January 2012:

- Vehicles weighing more than 3.5 tonnes gwv and registered before 1 October 2006
- Lorries
- Motor caravans
- Motorised horseboxes
- Breakdown and recovery vehicles
- Snow ploughs
- Gritters
- Refuse collection vehicles
- Road sweepers
- Concrete mixers
- Fire engines
- Tippers
- Removal lorries
- Some specialist vehicles
- Vehicles weighing more than 5 tonnes gwv and registered before 1 October 2006
- Buses
- Coaches

The LEZ operates 24 hours per day, 365 days a year.

The charge is payable per day and the charging day ends at midnight, so you'd need to pay for two days if the vehicle was within the LEZ over midnight. If a vehicle is parked throughout a day there is no need to pay the LEZ charge for that day.

---

241 www.tfl.gov.uk/roadusers/lez/default.aspx

242 See 11.2

If a vehicle does not meet the above standards you can fit an approved filter (which then has to be inspected and certified by VOSA[243]), replace the vehicle, organise your fleet so that that vehicle does not operate in greater London, convert the vehicle to run on gas or pay a daily charge.

If you drive a vehicle into or around the LEZ the registration number will be read by one of the many roadside cameras operated by TfL and checked against the central database. If your vehicle does not meet the emission standard and you have not paid the daily charge, you will be charged a penalty charge.

The charges are shown on page 336.

The charge applies to all vehicles, wherever registered, so you should advise TfL if you plan to operate a non-GB vehicle within the LEZ, including one registered in Northern Ireland.

Further information is available from Transport for London.[244]

11.5 MOTORVATE

This government-sponsored and underwritten membership scheme is operated by the Energy Saving Trust. It is designed to encourage firms to reduce CO_2 emissions from their car fleets.

Motorvate provides advice, auditing and verification of fleet emissions and the opportunity to network and share best practice with other fleet managers.

Motorvate will help you gather your emissions data and build a business case to present to management. Member benefits include a regular newsletter, members' conference, the right to use the Energy Saving Trust Motorvate logo and evidence to support your ISO 14001 certification. (ISO 14001 is the international standard designed to ensure your company manages its environmental performance.)

You can join Motorvate on the Energy Saving Trust website:

www.energysavingtrust.org.uk

---

243 See 19.6.10.
244 www.tfl.gov.uk/roadusers/lez/

LONDON LOW EMISSION ZONE CHARGES

Vehicle	Weight	Daily Charge	Penalty Charge	If paid within 14 days
Larger vans Motorised horseboxes 4x4 light utility vehicles Pick-ups Other specialist vehicles	1.205 tonnes unladen - 3.5 tonnes gvw	£100	£500	£250
Motor caravans Ambulances	2.5 - 3.5 tonnes gvw	£100	£500	£250
Minibuses (with more than 8 passenger seats)	Up to 5 tonnes gvw	£100	£500	£250
Lorries Goods vehicles Motor caravans Motorised horseboxes Breakdown and recovery vehicles Snow ploughs Gritters Refuse collection vehicles Road sweepers Concrete mixers Tippers Fire engines Removals lorries Other specialist vehicles	More than 3.5 tonnes gvw	£200	£1000	£500
Buses Coaches (with more than 8 passenger seats)	More than 5 tonnes gvw	£200	£1000	£500

11.6 EXERCISES

What were the Kyoto accord and the Cancun conference?

What are the four greenhouse gases?

Where does carbon dioxide come from?

Why will your drivers need information about the CO_2 output of their company vehicles?

What are CFCs?

Why did the government introduce the 3% diesel surcharge?

How will the workplace parking levy work?

12 FLEET POLICY

12.1 DEFINITION

In its narrowest sense, 'fleet policy' means the list of vehicles you give to your staff from which they can choose their company vehicle. Many fleet managers and people in the vehicle leasing industry use the expression 'fleet policy' in this way.

However, it also has a wider meaning. In its broadest sense, it means everything that your company defines as your standard way of running your car fleet, including:

- The vehicles you select
- Whether you allow users to choose their vehicles
- Whether they are allowed to contribute extra ('trade up') to get a better car
- Your policies for dealing with driver safety
- Advice you give drivers on the safe use of their vehicles
- What happens if a driver returns a vehicle and it is found to have been damaged

Another way of expressing this is the 'company car policy'.

Generally in this book the wider definition has been used. It is more appropriate as it reminds us all that there is much more to running a fleet than just deciding what vehicles should be selected.

12.2 FLEET LIST

12.2.1 VEHICLE SELECTION

Every vehicle your company uses should be fit for the tasks it will be required to do.

If the vehicle is to be used by a sales engineer to carry heavy loads, the maximum load weight, carrying capacity and sill height will be important.

If it is to be used for long-distance motorway driving by a sales manager, a larger engine and longer wheelbase will be important, as these will make the journey more comfortable.

In some industries it is tempting to offer sports cars or performance cars to young graduates, in order to recruit the best talent. Fleet managers have learned the hard way to resist this temptation as inexperienced drivers and high performance cars are a dangerous mixture that can lead to expensive mistakes or worse.

Some city centres will soon ban high-emission vehicles. If your drivers need access to one of these cities they should be allocated low-emission vehicles.

You will need to consider the type of fuel, number of doors and whether the vehicle transmission needs to be manual or automatic.

Some companies allow employees to select optional extras. Some extras will enhance resale values while others will not. For example, leather seating will enhance value in high-value cars but not on basic models. Alloy wheels can cost more to buy and to run: if they are in good condition they will enhance the resale value but if damaged they can cause the resale value to fall by hundreds of pounds.

The vehicles you select should reflect your company's image and the industry in which you operate. If you sell luxury goods to the landed gentry, arriving in a small basic fleet car may not project the right image; if your company's image is 'green', your fleet should reflect this.

Almost every fleet uses vehicle cost information to decide which vehicles to include on the fleet. However, there are a variety of ways that they can calculate this cost, as follows:

- The list price of the vehicle
- The actual cost of the vehicle, i.e. the list price less any discounts
- The contract hire rental
- Whole life costs, including fuel and insurance costs
- Total cost of ownership (TCO), i.e. whole life cost plus taxation

Each approach is an improvement on the ones listed before, with TCO being the best option by far.

12.2.2 ALLOCATION POLICY

Having considered the most appropriate vehicles for the job, you will also have to set an allocation policy – deciding who gets what.

Most organisations allocate vehicles according to staff grade. However, in recent years many companies have offered their employees more flexibility to choose vehicles that reflect their private as well as their business needs.

So, for example, if a service engineer has young children she may prefer to have an estate car instead of a van.

Flexibility is good for staff motivation and morale but if you offer too much flexibility the costs can begin to rise.

A good approach is to select a benchmark car for each group of drivers (sales representatives, middle management, senior management, directors, others) and build the list from there, using whole-life costs[245] rather than list price.

In this age of sex equality is important to remember to allocate cars without discriminating between men and women. In 2003 a group of women successfully won a case at Industrial Tribunal where their male colleagues were allocated better cars than they were allowed under the company's car scheme.

Some companies allow employees to contribute to the cost of a more expensive vehicle ('trade up'). This can either be paid for by monthly deduction from salary or as a lump sum on delivery of the vehicle – each of which can have a different benefit in kind income tax effect.[246]

Some also allow employees to trade down, which can be quite useful for a perk car driver if their partner already has a car.

If used cars are allocated, the policy should specify how long they will be kept.

Your vehicle allocation policy should be changed from time to time when models are discontinued, new cars are released or car prices change.

12.3 FIXED ALLOCATION LISTS

You can publish a fixed list that sets out all of the vehicles available for each grade of driver, or you can allow drivers to choose their own cars.

The advantage of a fixed list is that it gives you certainty and control. Fewer anomalies will arise and your staff will easily understand the system.

The disadvantage of a fixed list is that vehicle costs change frequently and the list will need to change too. You will need to decide how often to make this change. If you do so infrequently you may find that the business bears the increased cost of cars as prices rise but you cannot remove them from the list until the next review date. If you change the list frequently a vehicle available to a group of drivers last month may suddenly be unavailable to them this month if a price rise has moved the car out of their range.

Fixed lists tend to be poor for employee morale.

If you use a fixed allocation list you should consider the CO_2 emissions of the vehicles. A fixed list containing only high-emission vehicles will be a cause of employee dissatisfaction; effectively you will be forcing your drivers to pay high levels of personal tax on their vehicles.[247]

---

245 See 12.4.

246 See 17.2.1.

247 See 17.2.1.

12.4 USER CHOOSER

This is the alternative to the fixed list. The driver chooses a vehicle based on their seniority and the cost of the vehicle.

Some companies allow their drivers to select vehicles based on the manufacturers' published list prices. However, this approach is inadvisable, as list price does not reflect the discounts you can obtain on different makes and models.

Alternatively you can allow drivers to choose any car up to a limit, based on the invoice price of the vehicle to the business; that is, the cost after discounts. This is better than basing selection on list price. The trouble is that invoice price does not reflect fully the whole-life cost of the vehicle to your business over the period in which you will use it.

Allowing drivers to select cars up to the value of the contract hire rental of a particular benchmark car represents a further improvement. It has the advantage that the rental automatically reflects purchase discounts, depreciation and interest costs, though it excludes insurance and fuel costs.

WHOLE-LIFE COST

Whole-life cost reflects the total cost of using the car over the period in which it will be retained by the business. It therefore includes depreciation, interest, fuel, servicing, maintenance and repairs.

It is generally agreed that whole-life cost represents the best form of allocation policy.

If you decide to base your fleet allocation policy on whole-life cost you will need to assemble whole-life cost data. There are several sources, including magazines, fleet management and contract hire companies, motoring organisations and specialist publishers.

12.5 DRIVER INFORMATION

It is good fleet management practice to put a driver handbook or instruction card into each car giving clear instructions on issues likely to arise when the car is on the road. This can be a condensed version of the instructions set out in the company car policy.[248]

The driver handbook should include information on:

■ What to do in the event of an accident or breakdown[249]

■ Where to get the vehicle serviced

---

248 See 5.3.4.

249 See 1.19.

- Where to obtain tyres, brakes, exhausts
- What to do in the event of glass breakage
- What to do if a new tax disc or MoT certificate has not arrived by the due date
- What to do if a rental car is required

In all cases the names and phone numbers of the contracted suppliers should be included.

12.6 DAMAGED VEHICLES

A driver has returned one of your vehicles and you are not happy with the condition. It may or may not be a leased vehicle.

What should you do about it?

Should you charge the driver for the damage and, if so, how much?

The BVRLA *Fair Wear and Tear Guide* discusses the dividing line between acceptable wear and tear to a vehicle, given its age and mileage, and unacceptable damage.[250] As this document is an industry standard, it provides a good starting point for determining whether the condition of the vehicle is acceptable. If the vehicle is leased and its condition is unacceptable it is likely that the contract hire company will recharge you for the damage when they collect the vehicle. Then at least you will have an idea of the cost of the damage.

If the car is not leased no one will send you an invoice for the cost of the damage; you will just receive less when the car is sold.

As with all matters relating to fleet vehicles, if you have a clear company policy at the outset and everyone knows what this is, you will have fewer problems later.

In setting up your policy it may help you to know that 25% of companies do nothing if the driver returns a car in unacceptable condition, 40% recharge the cost of restitution to the driver, 40% recharge the cost to the cost centre and 30% take disciplinary action against the driver. These add up to more than 100% because some companies take more than one of these actions.

A reasonable policy might be:

- Advise your drivers they have to look after their company vehicles and that they will be penalised for keeping them in an unsatisfactory condition
- Issue them with a copy of the BVRLA *Fair Wear and Tear Guide* (it is available by post from the BVRLA[251]) or a similar home-produced document
- Advise them they will be recharged the cost the company incurs as a result of the unreasonable condition of the car, whether this arises through a recharge from a leasing company or a reduction in sale proceeds

250 See 1.2.13.

251 See 20.0, Sources of Information

- Make it clear that failure to maintain the vehicle in proper order may lead to disciplinary action being taken, which in turn may lead to the withdrawal of the vehicle without compensation or its replacement with a smaller or cheaper model.
- Say that repeated damage to the vehicle may lead to disciplinary proceedings including, in an extreme case, dismissal for damaging company property.

Instruct drivers to report all damage to you as soon as it occurs.

Advise them that if they damage a vehicle they may have to undergo a course of driver training before being allowed to drive a company vehicle again.

You policy should fit in with your fleet objectives and company culture.

12.7 COST-REDUCTION STRATEGIES

There are many strategies you can employ to reduce your fleet costs. They are listed here in no particular order. Different companies with different fleets will derive different levels of benefit from employing these strategies.

12.7.1 FOR EMPLOYERS

- Stop providing free private fuel[252]
- Choose the right financial product[253] for your fleet, bearing in mind that different funding methods will have different costs
- Move to a fixed list not a user chooser policy[254]
- Use total cost of ownership or whole-life costs to select vehicles for your fleet list[255]
- Remember that it is the weight of a car rather than its engine size that normally has the highest impact on mileage per gallon
- Make sure cars are serviced regularly. This will ensure fuel efficiency and identify vehicle problems before they become expensive to repair.
- Use demonstrator cars where available[256]
- Only allocate company cars to employees that actually need them
- Encourage drivers to minimise business travel
- Consider taking cars on daily hire rather than using employees' cars and paying them a mileage allowance[257]

---

252 See 17.2.8.
253 See 1.1-17.
254 See 12.3.
255 See 12.4.
256 See 16.13.
257 See 5.9.

- Consider having pool cars available for occasional journeys[258]
- Ensure the early termination clause in your contract hire agreement is as good as you can negotiate[259]
- Avoid early terminating leased vehicles: redeploy them within the business
- Renegotiate contract hire agreements mid-term rather than building up big excess mileage charges[260]
- If you have a large fleet, consider taking third party motor insurance and self-insuring the comprehensive risk[261]
- Consider introducing a cash-for-car scheme[262]
- Use journey-planning tools[263]
- Consider introducing an ECO scheme[264] or a salary sacrifice scheme[265]

12.7.2 FOR EMPLOYEES

- Consider taking a cash option if it is offered
- Choose a low CO_2 vehicle, perhaps a diesel[266]
- Consider giving up free private fuel.[267]
- Consider a salary sacrifice scheme[268]

12.8 STAFF MOTIVATION

Books have been written on staff motivation so in the next few paragraphs we can barely hope to do more than touch the surface of this complex topic.

Research over the last thirty years has consistently shown that company cars are a most valued and prized employment benefit amongst UK employees, second only to pension benefits.

Our love affair with the company car is deeply entrenched and has survived the efforts of many Chancellors of The Exchequer who have tried to tax us out of them.

---

258 See 16.12.
259 See 1.2.9.
260 See 1.2.6.
261 See 1.21.20.
262 See Chapter 3.
263 See 16.11.
264 See 3.7.
265 See 3.8.
266 See 17.2.1.
267 See 17.2.8.
268 See 3.8.

While there are no reports of people leaving their jobs in order to get a better car, many employees have chosen between two prospective employers on the basis of the quality and status of company car on offer.

It is clear that you can easily de-motivate your staff by trying to remove cars or watering down the status of the cars on offer.

There is good evidence that staff enjoy having the flexibility to choose their own car.

Some companies have successfully introduced 'cafeteria-style' flexible benefits systems that allow employees to choose their own benefits.

Employees like having the flexibility to contribute towards the cost of a more expensive car, or to trade down to a smaller car and either pocket the savings or spend them on enhancing another benefit.

Research suggests up to half of UK companies give their employees the option to take extra salary instead of having a company car – cash-for-car.[269]

Where the schemes are voluntary the take-up of the cash option has been low, usually less than 10%. Where the company car scheme has been scrapped and employees have been forced to take cash and use their own cars for business, often this has led to employee resentment. Employees do not like having to assume risks they did not take before they and they feel the loss of valuable staff benefits.

It is important to note that you cannot force an employee to use their private car on company business.

12.9 EMPLOYMENT CONTRACT

Employment contracts govern the relationship between employers and employees. Every employee has to be given a statement of his or her terms and conditions of employment – their employment contract.[270]

The contract becomes relevant when you decide to change company car policy, for example, by moving away from company cars to cash allowances.

You need to check whether the employment contract allows you to do this unilaterally. If you try to force people into a cash-for-car or ECO scheme when they have a contractual entitlement to a company car, you are breaching their contracts of employment. If they have been continuously employed for over a year an

---

269 See Chapter 3.

270 *Employment Rights Act 1996.* If you do not keep these up to date these an industrial tribunal may award 25% extra compensation to your employee. (*Employment Act 2002*).

employee could sue for breach of contract and unfair dismissal. Several groups of employees have engaged solicitors to act for them against their employers on precisely this issue – not a great way to motivate staff.

The maximum compensation payment an Industrial Tribunal will award for unfair dismissal is £80,400 (from 1st February 2011).[271]

If there is no right in the employment contract for you to vary the contract, you will need to get the employee's agreement to vary it to allow a cash-for-car scheme to be introduced.

Even if there is a right for the employer to vary the contract this right should be exercised reasonably. 'Reasonably' here means that it should be reasonable from the employee's rather than the employer's perspective.

If you have a contractual right to alter the contract and decide to exercise this right by introducing a cash-for-car scheme that is fair and reasonable, the employee must go along with it or they can face the possibility of disciplinary action.

If an employee refuses a reasonable request to change his employment contract they can be dismissed and offered re-employment on revised terms.

12.10 THE GREY FLEET

First, a definition.

1 A company car is a vehicle that an organisation makes available to their employee.

2 A cash allowance car is a car that is bought by (or leased to) an employee who uses funds provided by their employer. Usually, this allowance is made available under a cash-for-car arrangement, where the employer has stopped providing company cars but gives their employee an allowance to pay for mobility.

   Sometimes the car is provided through an arrangement the employer has made with a fleet management company and is 'fully managed', might like a company car would be. The employer almost always sets out rules the employee must comply with; the age and type of car that should be used on company business, perhaps a list of cars that should not be used, stipulations regarding insuring the car and having it regularly serviced, and so on.

3 A grey fleet car fits into a third category; it is any car owned by an employee that is used for work-related journeys. Historically fleet managers were not interested in these vehicles, because they were not 'on the fleet'. The employee simply used their car for business mileage and claimed an allowance for each mile driven.

---

271 Employment Rights (Revision of Limits) Order 2009, SI 2009/3274. This limit is changed annually.

When the second edition of this book was published in early 2005 it did not contain any reference to the grey fleet because this expression did not exist at that time. There can be few fleet managers who are unfamiliar with this term now; it has shot to the top of the list of many fleet managers' concerns. The reason? Health and safety.

In the last few years employers have had the crashing realisation that their employees were using private cars for business mileage and that, in many cases, the employer had no idea:

- what car was being driven
- whether it was being regularly serviced – indeed, whether it was even roadworthy
- whether it had an up-to-date MOT
- whether the car was insured for business use

Corporate manslaughter legislation carried the threat that employers could be found responsible for any at-work fatality, regardless of who owned the car. Many fleet managers were given responsibility for grey fleet issues for the first time. They realised that there were large numbers of employees using their personal cars for work travel and that the employer did not have even the most basic information about those vehicles. In many cases they didn't even know whether the drivers were licensed to drive.

And in many cases they discovered that these drivers had not opted to take out 'business use' cover when insuring their cars, and were therefore uninsured for these journeys.

Once employers had woken up to the grey fleet issue they realised that there was another angle they needed to consider; the CO_2 emissions of those cars. In most cases grey fleet vehicles are older and more highly polluting than company cars. If a company wanted to reduce its carbon footprint it could not ignore the grey fleet.

These issues have encouraged many organisations to tackle the issue of the grey fleet. Some have issued drivers with company cars; others have increased the use of rental cars and others have introduced the same sort of controls on grey fleet drivers and cars as they had already operated on company cars.

Fleet companies now offer a raft of services for companies that operate grey fleet vehicles, including regularly checking drivers' licences and insurances.

One advantage of encouraging drivers to stop using grey fleet cars is that the mileage reimbursement rates for these cars have traditionally been quite high, because employers have paid mileage reimbursement rates that would be appropriate for nearly-new cars whereas their employees were driving much older cars. Many organisations have found that by discouraging the use of grey fleet cars, encouraging the use of rental cars and promoting the use of videoconferencing they have cut their costs quite significantly.

12.11 DISABLED DRIVERS

Disabled employees have rights under the Equality Act and it is illegal for their employer to discriminate against them.

This legislation, which replaced Disability Discrimination Act, defines a disabled person as someone with a physical or mental impairment that has a substantial and adverse effect on their ability to perform normal day-to-day activities and that has lasted or is likely to last for more than 12 months. "Normal day to day activities" include walking and driving. The Act also applies to an employee who met this definition in the past but no longer meets it or who has just been diagnosed with a serious illness (such as cancer or multiple sclerosis) that is likely to become progressively more serious.

When a disabled employee joins is recruited into a role in which an able-bodied employee would have a company car, you have an obligation to provide one to them too, adapted as necessary so that it can be driven safely and comfortably.

If the driver has had an assessment at one of the seventeen UK centres run by the Forum of Mobility[272] they will be able to give you a report showing the adaptions they require.

12.12 EXERCISES

What does 'fleet policy' mean in its narrow and wide senses?

What should you consider when setting up your allocation policy?

What is 'trading up'?

What are the advantages and disadvantages of (a) fixed lists and (b) user chooser?

What might you put in a driver handbook?

How might you save money on your company car fleet?

What are the rules surrounding changing employees' employment contracts?

Why might you need to know about the Disability Discrimination Act?

---

272 www.mobility-centres.org.uk

13 HEALTH AND SAFETY

13.1 BACKGROUND

Road safety in Britain is good by international standards though there are still over 208,000 reported driving accidents involving personal injury.

According to Department for Transport figures, the key statistics for 2010 were:

- People killed in road accidents reported to the police 1,857 (the lowest since national records began in 1926).

- 24,517 people were reported killed or seriously injured in 2010 (9% lower than 2009)

According to the government, 'for the majority of people, the most dangerous thing they do while at work is drive on the public highway'.[273]

If you drive 25,000 miles each year you are as likely to die on the road as a coal industry worker is whilst in a mine, and more likely to die than a construction worker on a building site.[274] A sobering thought, given that these are generally considered to be two of the highest risk occupations.

13.2 HEALTH AND SAFETY LEGISLATION

Section 2 of *The Health and Safety at Work Act 1974*, gives employers a 'duty to ensure so far as is reasonably practicable the health, safety and welfare at work of all employees.'

It is important to note the words 'at work'. Driving 'for work' is 'at work' for this purpose and so is driving between offices or from home to a work-related course. Commuting to work in the employee's own car is not 'at work' but a detour to a client en route to work is 'at work'.

Therefore, your health and safety policy has to cover car use regardless of how you acquire your cars. If an employee uses their own car for work, you as employer are

---

273 Source: Health and Safety Executive
274 Source: Health and Safety Executive

liable for the health and safety of the driver and other road users arising from that use.

You cannot avoid your health and safety responsibilities by moving from company cars to a cash-for-car or ECO scheme. In fact, a significant number of fleets that have moved to cash options have had to call in health and safety consultants to look at the new risks that this creates.

The *Management of Health and Safety at Work Regulations 1992* Section 3(1) requires that you assess the risks your employees are exposed to at work and examine how these can be reduced. If you have more than five employees you must keep a record of this assessment and advise employees on the risks and how to reduce them. If a group of employees is at particularly high risk you must identify this group and record the details.

A 'competent person' needs to assess and implement any steps that need to be taken to reduce the risks. You must plan, organise and control the risks. You risk prosecution if you fail to do so. If you don't carry out a risk assessment you could be prosecuted, even without an accident having occurred.

The Health and Safety Executive (HSE) is the government department responsible for promoting safe working practices, as well as investigating accidents and launching safety-related prosecutions. It can provide guidance on all health and safety issues, including driving related safety issues. Its website www.hse.gov.uk is a valuable resource.

Under section 4(1) of *The Provision and Use of Work Equipment Regulations 1998*, equipment used at work must be suitable for the task. Legal experts believe that this definition includes employee-owned vehicles used on the employer's business.

Let us assume you have a cash-for-car scheme under which your employees can choose their own vehicles. Mr X chooses a vehicle that is unsuitable for his particular job. Perhaps he is using a small hatchback to transport a heavy load that should be carried in a van. Let us now assume that while driving along a winding road he loses control and the vehicle is involved in an accident in which someone is injured.

In this situation, the employer is likely to be held responsible for the injury.

13.3 CORPORATE MANSLAUGHTER AND CORPORATE HOMICIDE

Despite the provisions of *The Health and Safety at Work Act 1974*, many in legal circles felt that businesses were not being held accountable for the deaths of their drivers and other road users when company vehicles were being used. There had been very successful prosecutions for corporate manslaughter.

In one case the directors of a haulage company were found guilty of manslaughter after one of their drivers fell asleep at the wheel of a lorry. Two people died and the directors of the company were given suspended prison sentences.

However, lawmakers still believed the legislation was weak and that more could be done. After some years of deliberation the *Corporate Manslaughter and Corporate Homicide Act 2007* was introduced, and it became law in April 2008.

Under the new law companies, partnerships, organisations and government bodies face a criminal offence and large fines if they are found to have caused death due to gross corporate health and safety failures.

Legislators and the HSE have made it clear that businesses with effective systems for managing health and safety have nothing to fear from the Act; it is targeted at the worst cases of corporate negligence and is designed to ensure that organisations take health and safety seriously.

The Act does not introduce new standards. It just makes it easier to prosecute when gross health and safety failures lead to death. The legislation targets organisations rather than individuals within organisations, because individuals can already be prosecuted for gross negligence manslaughter and for health and safety offences.

Government departments and other Crown bodies are now liable to prosecution for the first time.

Many employers do a very good job when it comes to managing the risks their company car drivers are exposed to - ensuring these drivers have up-to-date driving licences and that all of these cars are insured, regularly serviced, have MoTs and so on.

A smaller number of employers do a similarly good job when managing the driving risks their cash allowance takers are exposed to. And fewer still do a good job when it comes to managing the risks amongst employees who drive their own cars for business purposes.

It is good fleet management practice to apply the same risk management procedures and techniques to every employee who drives a vehicle on company business, even if they only use their car for a work-related journey once a year. The Health and Safety Executive would be as interested in a driving-for-work fatal accident caused by one of these cars as it would if the accident was caused by a company car.

The Institute of Directors and Health and Safety Commission[275] have issued *Leading Health and Safety at Work*, a guide for business leaders and company directors. It sets out an action plan for embedding health and safety principles, a summary of the legal position, a checklist of key questions for business leaders and a list of resources and references for implementing the guidance in detail. It is available for free from the Health and Safety Executive website.[276]

---

275 The Commission merged with the Health and Safety Executive on 1 April 2008.
276 www.hse.gov.uk/pubns/indg417.pdf

13.4 WORK RELATED ROAD SAFETY TASK GROUP (WRRSTG)

The government established this group to examine the safety of business drivers and establish a blueprint for reducing work-related road accidents.[277]

They published an influential discussion document, *Preventing At-Work Traffic Accidents*[278], which said that one third of the fatal road accidents each year in the UK are work-related. Whilst we may think there are many more dangerous jobs than driving, only 600 people die in all other work-related accidents each year.

Whilst the document is now some years old it is worthwhile mentioning here as it held valuable information for fleet managers. It investigated the causes of accidents and proposed long term solutions to work-related road safety problems.

The report encouraged fleet managers to:

■ Reduce the number and length of road journeys their drivers take

■ Plan routes

■ Work to reduce long hours spent driving

■ Assess drivers' capabilities and take precautions

■ Check drivers' licences

■ Consider whether the employees need glasses

■ Look at their drivers' accident histories and motoring convictions.

If fleet managers are unable to assess these, it suggested they should get help.

It also focused on the size and comfort of car seats and proposed that this area be taken as seriously as the comfort of employees at computer workstations.

The group did not place all of the responsibility on employers. They said that drivers share responsibility, must take care of themselves and must comply with traffic laws.

The WRRSTG said the business case for better work-related road safety is overwhelming. Although safety costs money, this should be regarded as an investment bringing the long term benefits of reduced accidents, downtime, insurance costs and repair bills, and increased fuel efficiency and staff morale.

The Royal Society for the Prevention of Accidents (RoSPA)[279] produces many helpful booklets for employers on reducing on road accidents. www.rospa.co.uk/roadsafety

---

277 This was sponsored by the Department for Transport and the Health and Safety Commission.

278 www.hse.gov.uk/roadsafety/experience/traffic1.pdf

279 Further information from RoSPA, 28 Calthorpe Road, Birmingham, B15 1RP. Phone: +44 (0)121 248 2000 Fax: +44 (0)121 248 2001 www.rospa.com

A valuable resource for employers wishing to learn more about occupational road safety is The Occupational Road Safety Alliance (ORSA).[280] ORSA brings together employers, trade unions, local authorities, police forces, safety organisations and professional and trade associations. It aims to raise awareness of work related road safety and to encourage businesses to manage at-work road risk more effectively.

A number of employers have moved drivers back from cash schemes into company cars, for fear that the employer would otherwise be responsible for at-work accidents occurring in cars over which they have no control (size, suitability, quality, servicing, etc).

13.5 "DRIVING AT WORK – MANAGING WORK RELATED ROAD SAFETY"

The Health and Safety Executive and Department of Transport published this 24-page guide. It an important document as it is the government's considered response for calls for legislation to be extended to cover driving for business purposes.

The report says that existing legislation is adequate but businesses need to realise that existing health and safety legislation imposes general duties that have to be met by businesses at all times.

The report covers:

■ Employers' responsibilities for work-related road safety

■ How businesses can benefit from taking these responsibilities seriously

■ How to manage work-related road safety and

■ How to assess the risks involved in work-related motoring

It says that businesses must have in place effective systems to manage safety.

It is necessary to carry out risk assessments and to check drivers, vehicles and their licences.

The report is available from www.hse.gov.uk/pubns.

The HSE has issued 'Investigating accidents – a workbook for employers, unions, safety representatives and safety professionals' to help businesses investigate accidents.

---

280 See 19.6.11.

13.6 ROAD SAFETY ACT 2006

This Act introduced new offences, stiffer penalties and provisions whereby offenders can attend courses rather than have points on their licences.

A full copy of the Act is available on the government's Legislation website.[281]

Some of the major issues it covers are:

■ New offences of causing death (a) by careless or inconsiderate driving or (b) while unlicensed, disqualified or uninsured or (c) while using a mobile phone.

■ Being the registered keeper of an uninsured vehicle.

■ Radar and some other speed detection devices are banned. Devices that simply tell the driver the location of a speed camera are still legal.

■ A six point penalty for failing to provide information on the driver of a vehicle that has been photographed by a safety camera.

■ A sliding scale of penalties according to whether the speeding offence was minor or severe.

■ The Act authorises the use of alcohol sensors to stop a driver starting the car.

13.7 TIREDNESS

Ten people were killed at the Selby rail crash, which was caused when a motorist fell asleep at the wheel of his car, which left the road and drove into the path of a train. The motorist was convicted and jailed for five years.

In response to that accident, when investigating at-work road accidents the police now try to find the real reason behind the accident. This will include looking at the full service history of the vehicle to ensure that it was properly maintained, and the arrangements made by the company to ensure that drivers do not have to speed to appointments or drive for too long without a break.

Researchers at Loughborough Sleep Research Centre, part of Loughborough University, have carried out research into the risk of driver fatigue.[282] They have discovered that drivers – particularly young men - are aware they are falling asleep but ignore the warnings and carry on driving regardless. They also point out that it is dangerous to have even one alcoholic drink at lunchtime because the body has a natural mid-afternoon dip in alertness.

Their advice is to stop driving, have a caffeinated drink and wait 30 minutes for the caffeine to kick in before driving off.

---

281 www.legislation.gov.uk/ukpga/2006/49/contents
282 www.lboro.ac.uk

According to the government-backed THINK! campaign, almost 20% of accidents on major roads are sleep-related and these are the most likely accidents to end in serious injury or death. Peak times for accidents are in the early hours and after lunch with men under 30 having the highest risk of falling asleep at the wheel.[283]

Their advice is to have 15-minute break every two hours, don't start a long trip when tired, avoid long trips at night, stop in a safe place if sleepy, then have a high-caffeine drink and a rest for 15 minutes to allow time for the caffeine to kick in.

The Department for Transport is looking at ways to reduce at-work driving and they commissioned research into a new approach to the management of fatigue, called a fatigue risk management system (FRMS)[284]. They define a FRMS as:

> a scientifically-based, data-driven addition or alternative to prescriptive hours of work limitations which manages employee fatigue in a flexible manner appropriate to the level of risk exposure and the nature of the operation

They conclude that:

> In theory, a risk-based and systematic approach to fatigue management is more effective and the trials of FRMS that have been conducted have provided encouraging, albeit mainly subjective, results.

> The next stage in the project will involve interviewing regulators, operators and other relevant groups with experience of FRMS in order to collect candid information on how FRMS has fared in practice; how best to realise the potential benefits for safety of FRMS; and how to avoid problems with its implementation.

13.8 HEALTH AND SAFETY POLICY

As we have seen, there is a legal requirement for every company to assess the risks its employees are exposed to and to put in place measures to reduce these risks.

The first step for most organisations is to produce a formal Health and Safety Policy document that sets out, at a high level, the company's commitment to safety at work and the rules they expect their staff to follow. The managing director or owner should sign the policy.

There is little point in producing such a document and holding a meeting to launch it to the employees if the director who signed the document does not attend. This sends out the message 'We have produced this document because we had to, we are paying lip service to it and you might as well do so too'.

---

283 think.direct.gov.uk/fatigue.html

284 www2.dft.gov.uk/pgr/roadsafety/research/rsrr/theme3/literaturereview/pdf/ rsrr110.pdf

A useful document on workplace safety is available from the Health and Safety Executive – HS (G) 136 *'Workplace Transport Safety'*[285]

The British Safety Council provides a wealth of resources for organisations wishing to adopt the best practices in health and safety management.

Website: www.britsafe.org

If you operate light commercial vehicles fitted with mobile elevating work platforms, you should be aware that the HSE has issued a guide to operating them safely. This is available from the HSE on 0845 3009923[286]

BRAKE

Brake is a charity that works to stop unnecessary road accident death, injury, trauma and expense, and to create roads that are safe for everybody – motorists, cyclists, pedestrians, truck and bus drivers, motorcyclists and horses. They promote the safe use of roads by addressing the skills and attitudes of road users, enforcement of traffic rules and appropriate punishment and education of road users who break the law.[287]

They produce guidance on these topics and advise policy makers, the media, professional transport companies and all road users about the importance of prioritising safety on the road. They organise a Road Safety Week[288] and actively support traumatised road accident victims.

Brake is a non-profit making organisation funded by donations.

They run the *Pledge to Drive Safely* campaign, designed to stop deaths on roads by improving the safety of drivers. Drivers are asked to:

BELT UP   front and back and ensure children are correctly restrained

SLOW UP   abide by limits and only overtake if totally safe

BUCK UP   calm yourself before driving if stressed, angry or excited

SOBER UP   'just say no' to alcohol or drugs if driving

WAKE UP   take breaks every two hours on long journeys, never drive on if you are tired

SHUT UP   put your phone on message service and well out of reach

CHECK UP   check brakes, tyres, lights, mirrors, and windows

This is good advice to give your drivers. They can sign the pledge at www.fleetsafetyforum.org/pledgeform.aspx

---

285 www.hse.gov.uk/pubns/indg199.pdf

286 'Preventing Falls From Boom-Type Mobile Elevating Work Platforms', HSE 2003

287 Material in these paragraphs was written by Brake for this book, for which I am grateful.

288 See www.roadsafetyweek.org.uk

One of Brake's divisions is the Fleet Safety Forum, which provides guidance and tools to tackle road risk within your company.[289]

Brake can be contacted at brake@brake.org.uk or fleetsafetyforum@brake.org.uk

13.9 IMPLEMENTING A HEALTH AND SAFETY REVIEW OF WORKPLACE DRIVING

This section sets out the procedures you might follow in assessing the risk of road accidents in your business and the steps you might then decide to implement to manage those risks.

Some words of caution are necessary here. You can buy some excellent textbooks that show how to carry out a safety risk assessment. The next few paragraphs contain only a thumbnail sketch of this complex area and should be considered as guidance only, not definitive or prescriptive.

Furthermore, as we have already seen, *The Management of Health and Safety at Work Regulations* require that a competent person must carry out your risk assessment. You should consider carefully whether to engage an expert to assess the risks your drivers are taking and how these can be reduced.

The steps in the risk assessment should be:
- Collect data
- Analyse the data
- Consider risk reduction strategies
- Present your recommendations to senior management
- Implement your road safety plan
- Evaluate the effects of the changes

13.9.1 COLLECT DATA

You need to establish what has happened in the recent past. You will need to collect accident data though but you may be surprised at how little data you have to hand.

Tucked away in files there may be details of the accidents that have been reported to the insurer but it is quite possible you will have no record at all of the minor accidents that did not cause an injury or an insurance claim. These accidents are important though; if several vehicles have been several minor collisions when cars have driven out of your car park, it may be time to alter the exit arrangements (layout, obstacles, signage, bushes, etc) to the car park before a more serious accident occurs.

289 See 19.6.14

Assemble a list of all of the accidents that have occurred in the last five years, showing:

- Name and address of the driver
- Their normal office or depot location
- Driver's age and sex
- Time of day of the accident
- How long they had worked for the company
- Date of their last eye test
- Information on any health problems reported
- Their manager's name
- Whether the driver was at fault
- The make, model, mileage and age of the vehicle
- Whether the vehicle servicing was up to date at the time of the accident
- Damage to own vehicle caused by the accident
- Damage to third party vehicle caused by the accident
- Injury caused by the accident
- Location of the accident
- Distance from the driver's home and normal place of work
- Whether the driver had been speeding
- Road and weather conditions
- The type of vehicle driven by the third party
- The nature of the collision (head on, hit while parking, etc)
- The manoeuvre that your driver was doing (reversing, turning, etc)
- The manoeuvre that the other vehicle was doing (reversing, turning, etc)
- The nature of any injuries to the driver and third parties
- Any defects reported on your vehicle
- The cost of the incident
- The cause of the accident
- The action that was taken after the accident (driver training, disciplinary action, dismissal)

13.9.2 ANALYSE THE DATA

You should look for trends or patterns in the report.

Consider carefully how you will measure the data. The absolute number of incidents may be too a blunt a measure. It may be better to consider the number of accidents, write-offs, and injuries per thousand miles driven.

Try to establish the true cost to the business of road accidents. Bear in mind that repair and excess charges are the tip of the iceberg. The real cost includes downtime, time off work, administration and increased insurance premiums.[290]

Benchmark your data with other companies. Your insurer will normally be happy to provide this information.

By comparing your accident record with other firms and reviewing your accident history, you may be able to see if specific areas need attention.

For example:

- If new drivers are having accidents, do you need a better induction system for them?

- If accidents are occurring when your employees' family members are driving the company's cars, what can you do to reduce the incidence of these? Train them, too? Change the policy to ban driving by family members aged under a certain age?

- Did a number of the accidents take place when the drivers were using mobile phones? If you have not already implemented a total ban on their use, now may be the time to do it. To make this complete, instruct your office-based staff not to speak to your drivers while they are on the road.

- Is one manager's area having more accidents per business mile than others? If so, this may be evidence that the manager is pressuring the drivers to do too much in the day.

- Is there evidence that drivers are not taking road safety seriously? If so, show them road safety videos, put safety reminder stickers in vehicles and use other devices to help to remind the drivers that safety is of paramount importance.

- Is there evidence that driver training may be necessary? As already discussed in section 1.20, driver training is a good thing and is to be encouraged. However, if your company has had a spate of accidents that occurred during long journeys, there may be no point in sending the drivers on a training scheme to improve their driving skills. It would be better to alter work rosters to remove the need for long journeys.

---

290 There is a useful device for getting management to focus on road safety issues. Don't just tell them that road safety cost the company £27,000 last year. Tell them instead that, as the company makes 10% profit on the items it sells, it had to sell £270,000 of goods or services last year just to cover the costs of accidents.

13.9.3   CONSIDER RISK REDUCTION STRATEGIES

As well as identifying the causes of past problems, these are some general strategies that you can consider to reduce the likelihood of accidents.

- Reduce the overall level of driving for work, through the use of videoconferencing or telephone conferencing, and through better planning of work journeys.
- Reduce the number of hours that can be driven in a day.
- Limit the time that can be spent driving without a break.
- Use telematics to measure the hours driven, hours driven without breaks, excessive journey lengths, the average and maximum speed, harsh acceleration and braking, etc.
- Limit distances being driven in any day.
- Alter the specification of the vehicles on your fleet allocation list. Include as standard safety items such as side airbags, anti-lock braking systems, electronic stability programs (ESP) and high-visibility brake lights. Top-of-the-range executive cars now include intelligent cruise control that monitors the progress of the car in front and automatically applies the brakes as the car in front slows. This is an excellent tool, particularly for motorway driving.
- Alter the colour of the vehicles being selected so that only bright colours are chosen.
- Attach reflective decals the vehicles to make them more visible.
- Issue drivers with a checklist of the vehicle safety checks they should carry out every day, week and month. Their mileage or expenses claim should include a certificate signed by the driver confirming they have carried out these checks.
- Only select cars that get high marks in Euro NCAP tests.[291]
- Ensure vehicles are serviced at their due times and mileages. If the driver misses a service, an office-based system should identify this and notify him or her of the need to book in the vehicle for servicing.
- Insist only manufacturer-approved consumables and spare parts are used on your cars when they are serviced or repaired.
- Require drivers to notify you as soon as any fault occurs on the vehicle that may prejudice road safety.
- Inspect drivers' licences when they join the company or whether they are given the right to drive company vehicles for the first time. Check these again every six months.[292]
- Include a safety pack in the car and train drivers on how to use the contents.[293]
- Ensure that drivers know the loading capacity of their vehicles and instruct them never to overload a vehicle.

---

291 See 13.11.
292 See 5.11.3.
293 See 13.16.

- Explain to drivers that they must refuse any request from a manager to drive in a manner, or on a journey, or in a vehicle they consider unsafe or where doing so would increase the risk of an accident. Give them a name and a phone number of the person to contact (probably the health and safety officer or the fleet manager) if they do not believe their manager is taking their concerns seriously.

- Require all drivers to have their eyesight tested regularly and to report the date and outcome of the test to the company, – even if they do not wear spectacles. (You can buy vouchers to give to employees that can only be redeemed towards the cost of an eye test and a pair of spectacles).

- Require all drivers to sign the health and safety policy annually to reaffirm their commitment to the company's safety standards. This should include a policy on the use of mobile phones in cars and a section on driving when drowsy.

- Appoint a road safety improvement committee, drawn from around the business, to meet regularly, review accidents and develop procedures.

- Consider charging the driver if they have an accident. Many companies do this. Typically, they charge the excess amount on their insurance policy and many increase this if the individual is involved in several accidents in one period.[294]

- Consider an incentive scheme to reward careful driving. These have been successful, but can also create a culture where minor accidents are not reported.

- Employ an accident management company.[295] They will collate information on your accidents, analyse the data and give recommendations.

- Fit speed limiters to your cars. These will give you fuel savings as well as reducing the severity of speed-related accidents.

13.9.4 Present your recommendations to senior management

- It is important that senior management 'buys into' the findings.

- Agree an action plan that shows which managers are responsible for implementing the various recommendations.

- It is normal for several departments to be involved in implementing such plans.

13.9.5 Implement your road safety plan

- Launch your changes with as much publicity as possible within the organisation. Get the managing director to address all staff on the changes. Issue revised driver handbooks.

- Consider whether a change in your employment contracts or the company car policy would help reduce accidents. Many companies make it clear in these documents that every road accident will be investigated and that if the

---

294 See 12.6.

295 See 1.19.

employee is at fault he or she may be required to attend additional driver training before being allowed to drive again for the company. Repeat 'offenders' may have their company vehicle removed. Other disciplinary measures may be taken, including dismissal.

13.9.6 EVALUATE THE EFFECTS OF THE CHANGES

■ Every three months, review the changes you have made and their effectiveness. Consider whether further changes are necessary and, if so, propose these to senior management.

13.10 THE USE OF MOBILE PHONES

According to the government you are four times more likely to have an accident when using a mobile phone and reaction times are around 30% slower when using a mobile phone, slower in fact than if someone has been drinking alcohol and is at the legal limit. Research in the USA showed that being distracted on a mobile phone call had caused almost one in five road deaths.

Advice from their THINK! Road safety campaign is that drivers should not make or answer calls when driving, never use a hand-held mobile when driving even when at traffic lights or in a traffic jam, park safely before using a mobile phone (not on the hard shoulder of the motorway) and don't call people when they're driving.

If you expect drivers to use mobile phones when driving for work and they then have an accident, the employer and the directors of the company may both be held responsible.

A hands-free phone may be slightly safer than a hand-held one, because at least both of the driver's hands can be used for driving the vehicle. But what happens when they dial a number?

Research in Germany showed that dialling a number when driving means travelling 150 metres blindly. And once the call has been dialled, even the use of a hands-free phone can still cause distraction.

When the use of mobile phones was made illegal in Japan, the number of mobile phone-related accidents halved.

We all know that when we use a mobile phone, or indeed any phone, we enter a parallel universe where we become less aware of the things around us.

The Department of Transport introduced a partial ban on the use of mobile phones while driving in 2003. The regulations ban drivers from speaking, sending or receiving a call with a hand-held phone, except when calling the emergency services.

296 Road Vehicles (Construction and Use) (Amendment) (No 4) Regulations 2003

The precise wording of the legislation is:

> 'No person shall drive a motor vehicle on a road if he or she is using a hand-held mobile telephone. A mobile telephone is to be treated as hand-held if it is, or must be, held at some point during the course of making or receiving a call.' [296]

There was early speculation that the ban might cover the use of loudspeaker system and hands'-free earpieces but the government decided not to ban these as they present enforcement difficulties. Therefore drivers can still press a button to receive a call so long as the phone is not held.

A driver can still use a mobile phone to dial 999 if there is a genuine emergency and it isn't safe or practicable to stop or are safely parked.

This chart explains the rules.

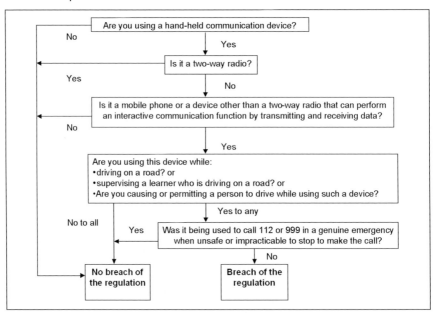

The rules don't just cover mobile phones. They also extend to any hand-held device that can be used to send or receive spoken or written messages or still or moving images or can access the internet.

Since February 2007 the offence has carried a minimum £60 fine and 3 penalty points, with fines of up to £1,000 and 6 points on conviction. If the vehicle is a goods vehicles or any vehicle that can carry more than eight passengers, the maximum fine is £2,500.

Even before the new regulations were announced, employers could be prosecuted if they were to 'cause or permit' their employees to use a hand-held mobile phone for work when driving.[297] These regulations remain in force, so employers as well as drivers have responsibilities in this area.

---

297 Reg. 104 Road Vehicles (Construction and Use) Regulations 1986.

If an employee has an accident when driving and using a hand-held mobile phone, and is convicted, their use of the phone will be taken into consideration when they are being sentenced.

Hence in one case a fleet van driver was jailed for three years for causing death by dangerous driving whilst using a hand-held mobile phone. The court heard that the van was driven onto the wrong side of the road and crashed into a pick-up truck being driven by a pensioner. The police obtained evidence from the mobile phone company to confirm that the van driver had been speaking on his mobile phone at the time of the accident.

The driver's employer had a policy banning the use of hand-held mobile phones when driving, and the driver had signed confirming receipt of the handbook.

From comments in court during the case, it was apparent that the police would have prosecuted the driver's employer had it not been for this policy.

In another case heard at Newcastle Crown Court, a delivery driver pleaded guilty to causing death by dangerous driving while driving for work. He had been using a hand-held mobile phone at the time of the accident. His employer prohibited the use of hand-held mobile phones in the company's vehicles. This was clearly set out in the driver handbook that had been issued to the driver and that he had signed for. In court the Crown Prosecution Service said that it was not planning to prosecute the employer in this case, because it had a robust policy.

The message here is clear; a well-written driver handbook reflecting best practice can save your company from prosecution.

It's a good idea is set up a message that says 'I am driving and cannot take your call. Please leave a message and I will call you back when it is safe to do so'.

More information on the regulations is available from the government's Directgov website.[298]

It is worthwhile considering having a company policy on other distractions while driving, such as eating and drinking.

13.11 EURO NCAP TESTS

Euro NCAP stands for the European New Car Assessment Programme. It is an independent body that tests cars to determine how they would perform in different types of crash.

It has been testing vehicles since 1997 and is now backed by five European governments, the European Commission, many consumer organisations and motoring organisations in every European country.

---

298 www.direct.gov.uk/en/TravelAndTransport/roadsafetyadvice/DG_188761

According to Euro NCAP, while all governments enforce safety standards in car manufacture, these are only minimum standards that don't tell you what would happen in the event of a crash or encourage manufacturers to improve their safety standards.

Euro NCAP subjects vehicles to a variety of tests:

- **Standardised simulated accidents** – front impact, side impact and pedestrian impact – to show how the various parts of the body of each occupant would be affected. It uses a starring system to rate each vehicle that it tests.

- **The ability of the car to avoid accidents** – focussing on a vehicle's handling, visibility, ergonomics and lighting

- **Child protection** – showing how different cars and child seats perform in road accidents

- **The safety benefits of new technology** – showing how features such as lane departure alarms and blind spot monitoring will help the driver avoid accidents

The Euro NCAP website lists all the vehicles tested to date and shows how they have scored. This can be found at www.euroncap.com.

Only a few vehicles were awarded Euro NCAP's maximum 4 Star award in the early years of its testing procedures and many popular fleet cars received low marks. Car manufacturers now take crash safety much more seriously. Euro NCAP raised the ceiling and created a 5 Star award and an increasing number of vehicles are achieving this standard.

13.12 USE OF INTERNAL SAFETY FEATURES

13.12.1 HEAD RESTRAINTS

Most modern vehicles are fitted with some form of head restraint. They protect against neck and back injuries caused by whiplash – the injury that occurs when the head is thrown back if the vehicle is hit from behind.

Surprisingly few drivers know how to adjust head restraints for maximum safety. The hardest part of the restraint should be level with the driver's ears and as close to the head as possible. It should never be used as a headrest.[299]

---

299 See 1.21.10.

13.12.2 SEAT BELTS

The law states that seat belts must be worn when they are fitted to the vehicle.

There are some exemptions:

- Drivers of emergency services vehicles
- Service engineers taking vehicles on test-drives under trade plates for maintenance purposes
- A passenger in a trade vehicle who is investigating a fault in the vehicle
- Licensed taxi drivers plying for hire or carrying passengers
- Drivers of private hire vehicles that are for hire or carrying passengers
- During a driving test, driving test examiners who believe that wearing a seat belt could cause an increased level of danger
- Delivery and collection drivers on local rounds where they are required to stop at least every 50 metres
- Any driver when reversing a vehicle (or an instructor with a learner driver who is reversing a vehicle)
- People holding medical exemption certificates (these are awarded if a doctor believes your medical condition makes it inadvisable for you to wear a seat belt). The exemption certificate must be kept in the vehicle and you will need to advise your insurer that you are driving without a seat belt. Pregnant women are not exempt from wearing a seat belt unless they hold a medical exemption certificate.

Everyone in the vehicle must wear a seat belt. A child under 14 may wear an approved restraint instead.

If an adult passenger refuses to wear a seat belt, they are personally responsible. If a child under 14 refuses to wear one, the driver is responsible.

There have been some ill-advised suggestions that seat belts are no longer the best form of restraint and that vehicle occupants can rely on the airbag alone. However, where airbags are fitted it is vitally important that seat belts be worn too. Airbags are designed to deploy with a slight delay to allow the seat belt to do its job of restraining the passenger or driver. If seat belts are not worn the airbag will deploy too late and will not be effective. There should be a gap of at least 25cm between the driver's breastbone and the steering wheel.

13.12.3 CHILD RESTRAINTS

Most fleets allow their staff to fit child restraints to company vehicles. If these are fitted, the driver must ensure that the manufacturer's instructions are closely followed, that the right restraint is selected for the car, and the age and size of the child, and that rearwards-facing restraints are not used in the front passenger seats.

The Department for Transport's website provides a helpful chart, shown on the next page:

Person	Front seat	Back seat
Child up to 3 years old	Correct child restraint must be used	Correct child restraint must be used if fitted. If not available in licensed taxi or private hire car, child may travel unrestrained
Child from 3rd birthday to 12th birthday, or 135cm tall, whichever comes sooner	Correct child restraint must be used	Correct child restraint must be used if fitted. Child must use adult seat belt if correct child restraint is not fitted, either in a licensed taxi/private hire car, or for short journeys in an unexpected necessity or if two occupied child restraints prevent fitting of a third. If no seat belts are fitted in the read a child age over 3 may travel unrestrained.
Child 12 or 13, or over 135cm tall	Seat belt must be used if fitted	Seat belt must be used if fitted
Any passenger age over 13	Seat belt must be used if fitted	Seat belt must be used if fitted

13.13 SAFE BRAKING DISTANCES

Advise your drivers to keep their distance, as shown in the Highway Code. Most rear-end accidents are caused by motorists driving too close to the car in front.

Some police forces police train their drivers to think of their car as being in the centre of a safety bubble. The bubble comes quite close to the sides of the car, but projects a good distance away from the car to the front and the rear.

The idea is quite simple; you are not going to collide with another vehicle unless you allow it to enter your safety bubble. So you should position your car at a sufficient distance from other cars so that you will be less likely to collide with them.

Another good piece of advice to drivers is to have in mind the need for an escape route. When driving on the inside lane of a motorway they can use the hard shoulder as an escape route if the road in front of them is suddenly blocked by, for example, a car swerving in front of them. However, no escape route is available if

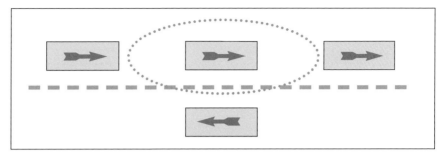

they are in the outside lane of a motorway overtaking a truck, so they should only overtake when they are certain that the manoeuvre is completely safe.

Many drivers, especially heavy vehicle goods drivers, drive close to the vehicle in front in order to travel in its slipstream and therefore reduce drag and increase fuel efficiency. As a fuel efficiency measure this is quite effective. As a road safety measure it is potentially disastrous. Drivers should be instructed not to do this. It costs lives.

13.14 CARAVANS AND TRAILERS

If an employee tells you she wants to use her company car to tow a caravan on holiday, what should you do? You need a policy on this.

There is nothing wrong in allowing drivers to use a company car to tow a caravan. However, it is not a good idea if the car is small and the caravan is heavy. The handbook of the car will set out its towing capability and the caravan's handbook will set out its weight. It is worthwhile bearing in mind that the caravan's weight will be quoted unladen; it may weigh much more when filled with suitcases, crockery, bicycles and the like.

When filling the caravan, most weight should be placed over the caravan's axle. If the load is put too far forward it will place strain on the car and make it difficult to control. If the load is placed too far back it will cause the caravan to sway, particularly on bends.

It is hard to reverse a vehicle that is towing a caravan or a trailer. You should ensure the driver is competent to do this before they hitch a caravan to your company's property.

The driver should be reminded not to slip the clutch of the car, as it could easily overheat with the extra load, and they should follow the caravan and the car manufacturers' recommendations for tyre pressures.

Towing a caravan significantly reduces acceleration and markedly affects the handling and braking characteristics of the vehicle.

The legal speed limit reduces by 10mph when towing a trailer on a road with a 60mph or 70mph speed limit.

13.15 THE HIGHWAY CODE

The Highway Code is one of the most widely recognised books in the country. It lists everything that we must and must not do when driving a car. It also lists best practice in driving behaviour in areas where the government has decided not to legislate.

We all read it when preparing for our driving tests but most of us never pick it up again.

Every driver should be familiar with *The Highway Code*. It is good fleet management practice to provide a copy to all drivers and require they abide by it. The Stationery Office publishes it, and it is available from the Department for Transport or www.direct.gov.uk.

The Driving Standards Agency publishes an excellent book on driving skills, *The Official Driving Manual*. It is a guide to safe driving written by the experts who set the driving test standards. It covers topics such as manoeuvring, defensive driving, all-weather driving, breakdowns, towing and European driving.

These books are available from bookshops and can be ordered from The Stationery Office on 0870 600 5522 or www.hmso.gov.uk.

If some of your drivers have reading difficulties, or if English is not their first language, you may be interested in the Interactive Highway Code.[300] Produced under licence from The Stationery Office, the images from the book have become animations and the written text is now narrated.

13.16 SAFETY PACKS

It is good fleet management practice to ensure that every company vehicle is supplied with a safety pack. The better fleet management and contract hire companies supply these with every vehicle they deliver, sometimes for free, sometimes for a small charge

A good safety pack will contain the following items:
- Fire extinguisher
- Jump leads
- Window hammer to break the window in the event of an accident
- Yellow reflective jacket for use in breakdowns at night, particularly on motorways
- Torch
- Flashing warning lamp

300 See www.highwaycode.net

- De-icer
- Screen wash fluid
- Warning triangle (this is required in many EU countries and should be placed 100 metres behind the vehicle in the event of a breakdown)
- Spare bulbs (these must be carried in some EU countries)
- Spare fuses (these must be carried in some EU countries)
- First Aid kit

You should ensure your drivers know how to use of all items you provide, such as jump leads or a first aid kit. Health and safety legislation requires this.

ACCIDENT PACK

As well as the above safety-related items, it is good practice to have a sealed pack in each company car containing accident record forms, pen and witness detail sheets. It used to be advisable to include a disposable camera and a film processing envelope but perhaps this is now unnecessary as so many phones include a camera.

WINTER DRIVING

It is good fleet management practice to advise drivers to prepare their vehicles for the onset of winter. They should take their vehicles for a winter check-up at a fast-fit outlet or their normal servicing dealer. Most will provide this service for free.

Drivers should check their vehicle servicing is up-to-date.

They should check brakes, lights, indicators, steering and tyres before setting off on any journey.

If the vehicle is likely to be used in a remote part of the country where severe weather routinely strikes in winter, they should carry spare warm clothes, some food and drink and a shovel in the boot.

On the continent it is normal for leasing arrangement to include the supply, fitting and seasonal storage of winter tyres. This practice has not reached the UK although a number of contract hire companies report that they are receiving enquiries about this.

13.17 DANGEROUS GOODS

If your vehicles carry dangerous items you need to register with the Environment Agency.

For this purpose, dangerous items include:

- Toxic gases
- Butane gas
- Propane gas
- Explosives
- Fireworks
- Other flammable items
- Strong acids
- Radioactive materials

You must register if you carry more than certain prescribed quantities of these items and if you fail to register you face a fine of up to £5,000.[301]

If you are registered your vehicles must display the relevant orange sticker or stickers listing the nature of the danger.

The regulations[302] require you to appoint a Dangerous Goods Safety Adviser.[303] This is a person who has passed an approved course of instruction. You need not employ them, they can be a consultant.

Further information is available from the Health and Safety Executive.[304]

301 Carriage of Dangerous Goods by Road Regulations 1996 amended 1999, 2007 and 2009

302 Transport of Dangerous Goods (Safety Advisers) Regulations 1999

303 See www.businesslink.gov.uk/bdotg/action/detail?itemId=1078039058&type= RESOURCES

304 www.hse.gov.uk

13.18 INTERNAL DRIVING LICENCES

Consider this scenario.

> A manager asks his assistant to drive to a branch office to pick up some files. He hands the keys to his company car to the assistant, so that the assistant will not have to use his own car.

> This seems reasonable to the manager.

> 'Clearly', he thinks, 'I am using a business asset for a business purpose, my assistant has a driving licence so there can be nothing wrong in allowing him to drive my company car'.

Now consider another scenario.

> A company car driver has two minor accidents in a short period of time. You want to impose some sort of sanction upon him but don't know what to do. The sanction has to be serious enough to encourage the driver to modify his driving habits so that there are no more accidents. On the other hand you don't want the sanction to be too draconian, like removing the car or downgrading the car the driver is allocated: these sanctions would be demotivating and therefore might be counter-productive.

A number of companies have introduced a novel tool that helps in both of these situations; the internal driving licence.

The company issues one of these licences to all authorised drivers. It confirms their right to drive for a fixed period. At the end of that period they apply for a new internal driving licence, by delivering their old one to the fleet manager together with their official UK driving licence.

The internal driving licence can work in much the same way as a UK driving licence: if you tot up more than 12 penalty points you lose the licence and therefore lose the right to drive a company vehicle.

Penalty points can be awarded on a more draconian basis than the government employs. So, for example, if the driver is involved in an accident that is his fault, this will attract points. Similarly, penalty points can be awarded if the driver abuses the vehicle, does not have it serviced when due, does not return it in a proper condition, allows it to be used by unauthorised drivers, etc.

The company can produce a schedule of penalty points covering all eventualities and distribute these to all drivers. A fair, visible, well thought out system is likely to win acceptance from drivers and is likely to be a constant reminder to them to drive safely.

13.19 SMOKING IN COMPANY CARS

The UK-wide ban on smoking in public places was completed on 1 July 2007, making it illegal to smoke in almost all 'enclosed' and 'substantially enclosed' public places and workplaces. This definition includes business vehicles used by more than one person.

The laws in England,[305] Northern Ireland,[306] Wales[307] and Scotland[308] make it illegal to smoke in company cars used by more than one person but in Scotland the law is different, banning smoking only in company vans and lorries but not company cars.

No-smoking signs must be displayed in business vehicles and managers are obliged to prevent people from smoking in these vehicles.

Local authorities enforce the new law. Smoking in a company vehicle used by more than one person is a criminal offence carrying a fixed penalty of £50 (£30 if paid within 15 days). If it does to court the maximum fine is £200.

Company vehicles used by more than one person must display no-smoking signs. Penalty for non-compliance is a fixed penalty notice of £200 (reduced to £150 if paid within 15 days). A court can fine a maximum £1000.

There is no fixed penalty option for a manager who fails to prevent smoking in a company car. On conviction a court can impose a fine up to £2500

"Driving At Work – Managing Work Related Road Safety" (published by the Health and Safety Executive and Department of Transport[309] says "Many incidents happen due to inattention and distraction". The legislation on the use of mobile phones while driving was designed to prevent drivers being distracted.

Which begs the question: is lighting and smoking a cigarette an activity that distracts the driver? The answer is probably yes, though I am sure that smokers would disagree.

A number of companies ban their employees from smoking at all in company vehicles, even when the driver is travelling alone. They believe – correctly – that a smelly car will be worth less when the time comes to sell the car.

Few have considered whether smoking when driving distracts the driver. Given the general thrust of recent health and safety pronouncements relating to driving for work, it is probably worthwhile for every company to carry out a risk assessment and have a policy on smoking in company cars.

---

305 Health Act 2006
306 Smoking (Northern Ireland) Order 2006
307 Health Act 2007
308 Smoking, Health and Social Care Act 2006
309 www.hse.gov.uk/pubns/indg382.pdf

13.20 THE BVRLA GUIDE TO DRIVING AT WORK

The BVRLA has produced a comprehensive guide[310] that aims to present the risks associated with driving at work and what can be done to minimise them.

It covers:

- The legal framework
- Selection of the vehicle
- Safety technology within the vehicle
- Vehicle record keeping
- Vehicle load and equipment
- Grey fleet advice
- Breakdown
- Pool vehicles
- Insurances
- The driver
- Driver qualification
- Driver familiarity with the vehicle
- Driver fitness
- Drugs and alcohol
- Driver training and assessment programmes
- Mobile phones
- Smoking
- Speeding and traffic offences
- Vehicle accidents and breakdowns
- The journey
- Driving schedules
- Route planning
- Telematics
- Alternatives to driving
- Weather conditions

It also includes four valuable annexes to help BVRLA members and their customers/drivers with vehicle selection and maintenance. There is also a pre-employment check list and an accident an incident report card.

These annexes are reproduced here in full:[311]

---

310 www.bvrla.co.uk/Advice_and_Guidance/Driving_at_work.aspx
311 © BVRLA

the BVRLA guide to
driving at work

Annex A - vehicle selection check list

Below is a helpful checklist for you to use to assess which type of vehicle is best suited for your needs.

How will you mainly use the vehicle; for short, start/stop trips, long journeys on trunk roads and motorways, for carrying children, adult passengers or lots of luggage or equipment? The answers to this question may point you towards a particular type of car or specific safety features.

EURO NCAP
What is the EURO NCAP rating of the vehicle? _____ stars
The European New Car Assessment Programme (EURO NCAP) conducts crash tests with specific models of new cars and grades their performance according to how well they protect the occupants and the severity of injuries to a pedestrian struck by the vehicle. Initial research has shown that each EURO NCAP star reduces the risk of fatal or serious injury for occupants by 12%. EURO NCAP reports details of how the vehicle performed in each test the results of which are published widely and can also be viewed at: www.euroncap.com.

Anti-lock braking system (ABS)
If the front wheels lock during severe braking the driver is likely to lose control of the vehicle. Anti-lock braking systems prevent the wheels locking, and in adverse driving conditions can minimise stopping distances while still allowing the driver to steer around obstacles.

To be fully effective, ABS needs to be used correctly and many drivers would benefit from specific training.

| ABS fitted? | Yes ☐ | No ☐ |
| Training required? | Yes ☐ | No ☐ |

Brake lights
Separate brake and rear lights have proven more effective than those which are integrated and a third, central brake light mounted fairly high up and away from the other lights provides extra warning to following drivers, especially in heavy traffic.

| Separate brake and rear lights? | Yes ☐ | No ☐ |
| High level brake lights? | Yes ☐ | No ☐ |

Head restraints
Properly adjusted head restraints help to reduce or prevent whiplash injuries which can occur even in minor impacts. They are common for front seats but less so on rear seats. Adjustable head restraints can be raised or lowered although they may need regular re-adjustment. Fixed head restraints cannot be adjusted but check that they are the right height for the occupants - the top of the head restraint should be at eye level. Rear head restraints may reduce visibility to the rear.

| Head restraints on front seats? | Yes, fixed ☐ | Yes, adjustable ☐ | No ☐ |
| Head restraints on rear seats? | Yes, fixed ☐ | Yes, adjustable ☐ | No ☐ |

Seat belts
Modern cars have inertia-reel seat belts on the four outer seats which automatically lock the belt during hard braking or cornering. Many models have seat belt pretensioners and/or webbing grabbers. Pre-tensioners tighten the belt during the first milliseconds of crash and webbing grabbers clamp the belt just outside the reel.

Some cars equpped with air bags may have load limiters on the front seat belts which allow some forward movement and limit the forces on the chest during an impact.

Seat belts on all seats?	Yes ☐	No ☐
Central three-point seat belt in rear?	Yes ☐	No ☐
Inertia-reel seat belts on outer seats	Yes ☐	No ☐
Seat belt pre-tensioners	Yes ☐	No ☐
Seat belt webbing grabbers	Yes ☐	No ☐
Seat belt load limiters	Yes ☐	No ☐

the BVRLA guide to
driving at work

Annex A - vehicle selection check list (continued)

Airbag information

There is a risk of injury if an airbag hits a driver or passenger while it is inflating, although this can only happen if the occupant is sitting too close to the airbag.

Check that you do not have to sit too close to the steering wheel in order to properly manage the controls. Advice in the USA is that the distance between the centre of the steering wheel and the driver's breastbone should be at least 10 inches. However, airbags differ from car to car, so always follow the manufacturer's advice. If you are sitting too close, check whether the manufacturer can adjust the foot pedals so you can sit further away (avoid fitting pedal extensions). Otherwise, consider looking for an alternative vehicle.

Some cars have a switch which enables the airbag to be turned off. However, this means that the protection offered by the airbag is lost, and there are concerns that such devices may not work properly.

Airbag fitment

Driver Airbag	Yes	☐	No	☐
Passenger Airbag	Yes	☐	No	☐
Side Airbags	Yes	☐	No	☐

Rearward-facing child seats should never be fitted in the front seat if there is a passenger airbag.

Load Restraint.

Loads and luggage in the rear of cars need to be properly restrained to prevent them from moving and injuring the occupants in a crash or under emergency braking. Heavy loads may affect the vehicle's handling, and the tyre pressures may need to be adjusted - check the vehicle handbook. Folding rear seats, especially split seats, may be weaker than fixed seats. Some may be unable to restrain heavy loads in severe frontal collisions. Many cars have anchor-points and/or straps in the boot for restraining heavy objects.

Seats

Folding seats	Yes	☐	No	☐
Split rear seats	Yes	☐	No	☐
Anchor-points/straps	Yes	☐	No	☐

the BVRLA guide to
driving at work

Annex B - maintenance check list

Example of a safety inspection record (to be conducted once a month)

Vehicle registration number   Recorded mileage
Make, model and derivative
Date of inspection   Operator
Serviceable - please enter the appropriate code: S - serviceable, R - repair required, X - safety item defect, N/A not applicable

A: Inside vehicle				
Item	Serviceable	Defect found		
Driver's seat				
Seat belts				
Mirrors				
Glass and view of the road				
Windscreen wipers and washers				
Driving controls				
Steering control				
Tax disc				
Satellite navigation system				
Interior general				
B: Exterior of vehicle				
Exterior of body				
Exhaust emissions				
Road wheels and hubs				
Tyre tread depth	NSF	OSF	NSR	OSR
Tyre defects	NSF	OSF	NSR	OSR
Tyre pressures	NSF	OSF	NSR	OSR
Spare wheel and carrier				
Wings and wheel arches				
Oil and waste leaks				
Fuel tanks and system				
Rear markings and reflectors				
Lamps				
Direction indicators				
Hazard warning lamps				
Headlamp aim				
C: Fluid levels				
Brake/clutch fluid levels				
Engine oil level				
Radiator coolant level				
Windscreen washer level				

The BVRLA Guide to Driving at Work

the BVRLA guide to
driving at work

Annex C - pre-employment check list

Please Print	Surname	First name(s)
Address		
	Post Code	Phone
Date of birth	National Insurance number	Driver number

I hold the following driving licence(s)

Type (car/LGV/PSV)	Licence/permit no.	Issued by:	Expiry date

In the past five years I have been involved in the following motor accidents and / or received the following traffic violations

Date	Accident / traffic violation	Location	Penalty

Medical	Do you have a DVLA notifiable medical condition?	Yes	No

Permission is granted to: _____ to refer to the appropriate licensing authority and / or to my previous employer(s)

Date: /   /20   Signature of applicant:

The following must be completed by the interviewer

I have examined the the applicant's medical history and driving licence(s) as noted above and confirm:

The applicant does NOT have a DVLA notifiable medical condition ☐
All licences are in the name of the applicant ☐
All licences are valid for the country in which the applicant is resident ☐
All licences are valid for the group(s) stated ☐
A copy has been made and is attached ☐
Each licence has the following restrictions:

Remarks	

Date: Signature of interviewer

The BVRLA Guide to Driving at Work

the BVRLA guide to
driving at work

Annex D - incident report card

Company information

Vehicle make, model and derivative

Vehicle registration number/fleet number   Depot

Your full name   Phone

Your home address

                                                        Postcode

Description of damage to other vehicle/property

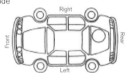

If an agency driver, state agency name

Your signature   Date   mark damaged areas with an 'x'

Other notes - including details of any injuries

Dear third party

The driver of this vhicle does not admit any liability, whether written, spoken or implied. If you consider our driver to be at fault, however, please phone (name)   on (phone number)   during office hours (9.00am - 5.00pm).

All correspondance should be sent to the address below.

Insurer   Policy number

Address

We would politely remind you that it is a Common Law duty to keep your losses to a minimum.

Incident report card

You should complete this card for all incidents, however minor. IF YOU HAVE AN INCIDENT

1. STOP.

2. Remain calm, even if provoked by other parties. Do not argue or show aggression.

3. Call the emergency services if anyone is injured or there is serious damage to vehicles or property. If the police attend the scene, note the reporting officer's name, number and station.

4. Use this incident card to record information about the accident, exchange details with third parties and take thename and address of witnesses. PLEASE COMPLETE IN BLOCK CAPITALS.

5. Third parties are obliged to give you their name, address, registration number and insurance details under section 154 of the Road Traffic Act 1988.

6. If a camera is available, discreetly photograph the scene from different angles. Include vehicles in their impact position, damage to your own and third party vehicles/property, skid marks and signposts.

7. Contact your depot supervisor and/or the insurance department as soon as it is practical to do so, using the following telephone number . . . .

The BVRLA Guide to Driving at Work

13.21 EXERCISES

Which piece of legislation makes it mandatory to ensure health and safety of employees at work?

Is a car driven for work 'at work' for health and safety purposes?

What is the Health and Safety Executive and why is it important?

What is the British Safety Council?

What are the items in the Brake Pledge to Drive Safely?

What fleet data should you collect for a health and safety review?

How might you analyse the data?

What steps should you take to implement your plan?

Is it legal to use a mobile phone when driving?

What is Euro NCAP?

Should caravans be fitted to company cars?

What might you put into a safety pack and an accident pack?

What is a Dangerous Goods Safety Adviser?

14 VANS AND COMMERCIAL VEHICLES

Most of the topics covered in this book apply to cars, vans and light commercial vehicles (LCVs). This chapter deals with some areas where LCVs differ from cars.

Light commercial vehicles (also called light goods vehicles) are defined as having two axles, weighing up to 3.5 tonnes and having no rear side windows.

Lorries (or trucks) are outside the scope of this book.

14.1 VAN AND LCV SELECTION, DISPOSAL AND USE

There are eight different categories of vans:

MICROVANS

These are small vans, ideally suited to city centres. They are often used by sandwich vendors who call on several office blocks every lunchtime.

PICK-UPS

These are flat-bed, single- or double-cab vehicles. They have a large open load area (though hard and soft covers are available for these). Until a few years ago most British people would have been more familiar with these from American movies rather than from seeing them on British roads, though they have become more popular here because they have enjoyed benefit in kind income tax breaks.

4X4 VANS

By removing the rear seats from a conventional 4x4 car, and adding two rear doors, manufacturers have produced tough vehicles capable of carrying heavy loads over rough terrain. They can be quite heavy on fuel consumption compared with car derived vans.

CAR-DERIVED VANS

These are mainly regular passenger hatchback vehicles that have been converted into vans by blocking off the rear windows and adding a rear door. They are more comfortable to drive than other vans and have good fuel economy. Load-carrying capacity is restricted, though.

COMPACT PANEL VANS

These are a medium size vans that offer a relatively good balance of load handling, driving refinement and fuel economy. Typical users might be a retail outlet that needs to deliver white goods (washing machines, etc) to local customers.

LARGE PANEL VANS

These are larger vans, capable of moving larger loads over long distances in reasonable comfort. They come in short and long wheelbase versions. It is hard to generalise about the typical user, as they will be valuable to so many different businesses.

LIGHT VANS

These vans take up the same amount of road space as a car, but have high roofs so they can carry more than a car-derived van.

CHASSIS CABS

These are flatbed heavy-duty vehicles, often used by builders to carry building materials. They are ideally suited for carrying heavy loads over shorter journeys.

White is the most highly prized colour for a used van and achieves the best resale price. Yellow and black are not popular colours amongst used van buyers and sale prices reflect this.

Unlike cars, metallic paint does not increase the resale value of vans; in fact it is likely to reduce it. Flat colours do much better.

Air-conditioning can add to the resale value of a car but it has no effect on the resale value of a van. It also adds from 5-10% to the fuel consumption of the vehicle.

If your vans need to display your company logo or advert, use removable vinyl decals rather than painting directly onto the vehicle. If decals do not allow light to pass through, the paintwork will fade unevenly and this will show when the decals are removed. All signage should be removed before you sell your vans: buyers will pay less where they have to do this. Perhaps more importantly, they may use your vehicles to carry out fraudulent activities.

A plywood or custom-made lining should be fitted as standard to all vans. This costs little and affords excellent protection against internal damage.

When selling vans at auction, it is best to choose an auction specifically targeted at buyers of LCVs, rather than cars. The right buyers will be in the audience and when bidding they will be far more understanding if your vans have high mileage.

When operating vans, drivers should be made aware that there are additional health and safety risks over and above those that arise when using a car.

Consider any manual handling risk. Be careful to select a van that is appropriate to the job and that allows easy loading and unloading of the type of goods you carry.

If there is a tail lift or a refrigeration unit, the driver will need to be trained to use them. The driver should be made aware of the van's payload limit and if special equipment is fitted this should be taken into account in calculating the remaining allowable payload. If you overload a van you may bring its weight into the category requiring heavy goods vehicle operator licensing.

The maximum speed for vans on most roads is 10 mph lower than for cars. The same rule applies to car derived vans weighing more than 2 tonnes (incl the weight of the payload).

It is illegal to overload a vehicle. If you have an accident and your vehicle is overloaded, this may invalidate your insurance.

The Vehicle and Operator Services Agency (VOSA)[312] stops and weighs over 30,000 buses, trucks and vans/car-derived vans each year. Of these roughly 10%, 30% and 67% respectively are overloaded.[313]

VOSA produces a useful document *Vehicle safety: the dangers of overloading*, which provides good advice on how to avoid your vehicle being overloaded.[314]

14.2 TOWING A TRAILER

If a van has a gross weight of less than 3.5 tonnes it can be used to tow a trailer up to 7 metres long and 2.3 metres wide. The length of the van and the trailer must not exceed 18 metres.

It is permissible to use a van to tow a longer trailer so long at the trailer has been specifically designed to carry its load: for example, the trailers that are used to carry gliders.

If you plan to tow a trailer behind dual purpose vehicle (one that can be used for carrying both goods and passengers, such as a 4 x 4 or pickup) and the combined weight exceeds 3.5 tonnes, you may need to fit a tachograph and comply with the EU drivers' hours rules. This topic is outside the scope of this book. You can find details on the Department for Transport website.[315]

---

312 See 19.6.10.

313 www.dft.gov.uk/vosa/repository/09%20296.pdf

314 www.dvani.gov.uk/uploads/compliance/
VOSA_VehicleSafety_DangersofOverloading.pdf

315 www.dft.gov.uk/vosa/repository/
Quick%20guide%20to%20towing%20small%20trailers.pdf

14.3 VAN BEST PRACTICE

The Department for Transport has established a Best Practice programme for van fleet operators, designed to help you cut costs and reduce CO_2 emissions. It provides free information on many topics that will interest van operators, such as fuel efficiency, driver safety, choosing the appropriate vehicle and managing fuel costs.

More information is available from 0300 123 1133 or the Business Link website.[316]

The SMMT, VCA and DFT have jointly produced a free guide for van operators.[317] It covers:

- ■ Choose the van size that best suits the job
- ■ Consider what engine you need
- ■ Check tyre pressures regularly
- ■ Change your vehicle's oils according to servicing schedules
- ■ Replace blocked air filters
- ■ Keep your speed to a minimum to save fuel
- ■ Improve your driving technique
- ■ Use technology such as Satnav to minimise travel

---

316 www.businesslink.gov.uk/bdotg/action/
    detail?itemId=1083690132&type=CAMPAIGN
317 Right Van Man. www.smmt.co.uk/shop/right-van-man-february-2009/

15 MINIBUSES

A minibus is defined as a motor vehicle designed to carry 8-16 people and the driver.

There are strict rules covering their use for business, including a requirement that they should be tested annually.

15.1 DRIVING LICENCE

There are complex rules covering the driving of minibuses, reflecting the fact that they are driven by disparate groups with different needs, for example:

- An employer who needs to transport people within the UK,
- A company that needs a relatively large vehicle to transport goods and people abroad
- A community organisation that delivers low-cost local transport to local residents
- A scout group where the 18 year old leaders need to transport children on outward bound trips.

This chapter contains an outline of the rules to give you some familiarity with the issues, but if you plan to operate a minibus you should check the rules carefully on the DVLA website.[318]

Your entitlement to drive a minibus depends on whether you passed your driving test before 1 January 1997. If you are entitled to drive a minibus on your UK licence you'll be entitled to do so elsewhere in the EU on temporary visits.

15.1.1 DRIVING TEST PASSED BEFORE 1 JANUARY 1997

If you passed your driving test before 1 January 1997 you will have automatically been given D1 (minibus) or A (licences issued before 1990) entitlement to drive a minibus so long as:

- You are over age 20
- The minibus has no more than 17 seats (including the driver's seat)

---

318 www.direct.gov.uk/prod_consum_dg/groups/dg_digitalassets/
@dg/@en/@motor/documents/digitalasset/dg_4011275.pdf

■ It is not being used for hire or reward (this only applies if your driver's licence is marked with category D1 code 101).

However, you can still drive a minibus at age 18 if you are:

■ Not carrying passengers *or*

■ Driving distances not exceeding 50km on a regular service *or*

■ Driving a vehicle designed for a maximum 16 passengers within the UK *or*

■ Driving a vehicle with up to 16 passengers under either an s19 or s22 permit (see below).

15.1.2 DRIVING TEST PASSED AFTER 1 JANUARY 1997

Your licence does not automatically give you an entitlement to drive a minibus. You are only allowed to drive category B vehicles, which are those with up to eight passenger seats.

However, there are exceptions to this rule. If you are a volunteer unpaid driver you can drive vehicles with up to 16 passenger seats within the UK for social purposes only, so long as all these conditions are met:

■ You are age 21 or older

■ You are driving under the auspices of a non-commercial body

■ You have held a driving licence for at least two years and

■ Maximum gross weight of the vehicle does not exceed 3.5 tonnes.

15.2 MINIBUSES DRIVEN FOR HIRE AND REWARD

'Hire or reward' means carrying passengers who pay a fare or who contribute to the cost of the vehicle. This definition includes minibuses used by airlines or hotels as courtesy vehicles.

There are special rules for minibuses used for hire or reward.

If you passed your driving test in a car your licence does not allow you to drive a 9-16 seater minibus for hire or reward. Furthermore, if the licence was awarded after 1 January 1997 the driver has to be over 21 to drive for hire or reward.

There are a number of exceptions to these rules:

SECTION 19 PERMIT HOLDER

A section 19 permit can be issued by the Department for Transport to educational, religious, social, cultural and other such organisations.

The permit allows these organisations to charge for use of the minibus without having to comply with normal public service vehicle licensing requirements and without the drivers needing to pass the 'public carrying vehicle' test.

The organisation must only offer the service to its members rather than the general public and it is not allowed to make a profit from the service.

A vehicle driven under a section 19 permit may not be taken abroad.

SECTION 22 PERMIT HOLDER

These are community bus permits, issued by the Department for Transport, allowing local bus services to be operated on a voluntary, non-profit basis using volunteer drivers.

PUBLIC SERVICE OPERATOR LICENSING

If a driver holding only a car licence wishes to drive a minibus for hire or reward without section 19 or a section 22 permit, he has to apply to the Department for Transport for a category D licence. This is the successor to the old Public Service Vehicle licence.

A category D licence allows the driver to drive any minibus carrying more than eight passengers.

15.3 SEAT BELTS AND MINIBUSES

Passengers in the rear seats of large minibuses (over 2,540kg) are not legally required to wear seat belts.

When travelling in small minibuses, all passengers are required to wear seat belts (where fitted).

If the passenger is under 14, the driver is responsible if a passenger is not wearing a seat belt. Above this age the passenger is responsible.

15.4 TAKING A MINIBUS ABROAD

If you wish to take a minibus abroad, it must be fitted with a tachograph.[319] (This is not necessary when travelling to the Republic of Ireland). This is required on all vehicles capable of carrying more than eight passengers.

In addition, you will need to carry the following documents:

a) **An 'own account' certificate**

This shows that the vehicle is not being used for transporting goods and is being driven by an employee of the company to transport the company's staff. This exempts the driver from the local licensing rules abroad. It can be obtained from VOSA.

319 See 15.6

b) VE103

A VE103 is required if the minibus is leased.[320] This replaces the V5C and confirms that the vehicle is on hire and that the registered keeper has consented to the vehicle being taken abroad. It is an essential document.

c) Proof of insurance

A 'green card' is not compulsory in the EU but it is elsewhere. At the minimum, you need to hold written evidence that the minibus is covered by third party insurance.

d) A driver's licence

This must show D or D1 entitlement. If it does not do so, you should apply using form INTP4, available from the local traffic office.   You will need to show that the driver has at least one year's minibus driving experience.

If you hold an older-style paper driving licence you are advised to take an official translation or an international driving permit.

15.5 SPEED LIMITERS

If your business operates a minibus that was first registered between 1 October 2001 and 31 December 2004, which has a Euro III engine and is used in the UK, its speed must be restricted to 56mph.

This legislation also applies to goods vehicles between 3.5 and 7.5 tonnes.

No vehicle fitted with a speed limiter can use the outside lane of a motorway with three or more lanes.

15.6 TACHOGRAPHS

A tachograph must be fitted and operated in any minibuses with more than eight seats that is being driven for commercial purposes or taken abroad. The tachograph records the driver's hours and ensures compliance with driving hours regulations.

This rule does not apply if the minibus is being driven for private purposes or by s19 or s21 permit holders.

Most tachographs nowadays are digital. You will need to register your company at the DVLA to obtain a company card, and the driver will need to register to obtain a driver smart card.

The company card allows to you turn the tachograph on and off and to download the information stored on the tachograph.

---

320 See 16.5.5.

The driver card is plugged into the tachograph when the vehicle is running and stores details of the driver's hours and journey information.

The driving hours regulations say that driver should drive for no more than nine hours a day, and should have a break of at least 45 minutes every 4-5 hours.,

See the DVLA website for more information.[321]

15.7 EXERCISES

What is an LCV?

How are van drivers taxed?

What licences are required by minibus drivers?

What are the rules for taking a minibus abroad?

What are the rules about use of seat belts in minibuses?

---

321 www.businesslink.gov.uk/bdotg/action/detail?r.s=sl&r.lc=en&type= RESOURCES&itemId=1082073307

16 FLEET ADMINISTRATION

This chapter deals with issues that arise in the day-to-day running of a fleet department.

16.1 VEHICLE EXCISE DUTY (VED)

Considering that it is only one tax, this duty has a number of names.

It is still commonly called the road fund tax or road fund licence although these names technically disappeared years ago. Some call it 'car tax', as in 'I have to get my car taxed', yet it has never officially been given this name.

The general public often calls it simply 'the tax disc', reflecting the simple logic that it is a tax and you have to buy a paper disc.

The correct name is vehicle excise duty (VED).

The registered keeper of a vehicle must ensure it is properly and continuously taxed if it is used or kept on a public road. This means that you must have a valid tax disc even if you keep your vehicle on a public road but don't drive it.

If your vehicles are on contract hire the contract hire company will send you a new tax disc about a week before the old one expires.

The registered keeper of the vehicle normally receives a VED renewal reminder form V11 during the month before the old tax disc expires. The form has to be taken to a Post Office with a valid motor insurance certificate and MoT certificate and a cheque for the amount payable.

Tax discs can be purchased for periods of six or twelve months (although the government is considering extending this to two or possibly three years).

If you have a large fleet and you are the registered keeper of the vehicles, going to the local Post Office to buy tax discs can be a chore. This is one task that is worth outsourcing to a fleet management company. They use data links with the DVLA to renew tax discs and can add this to their service for a small fee.

If you sell a car and wish to apply for a tax refund, you can apply in writing to the licence issuing authority or vehicle registration office (not the DVLA). You can obtain a form V14 for this purpose from the Post Office. The amount refunded will reflect the number of full months unexpired on the tax disc at the time you post it to the DVLA.

Since 1 March 2001, VED rates have been graduated, based on the vehicle's CO_2 emissions.

The amount payable depends on the date when the vehicle was first registered. If this was before 1 March 2001 VED is payable by reference to engine size: up to or over 1549 cc. If it was registered on or after 1 March 2001 it is payable by reference to thirteen CO_2 bands A-M, as shown below.

Rates of VED in 2011/12, for cars first registered on or after 1 March 2001:

Band	CO_2 emissions g/km	Standard rate £	First year rate £
A	Up to 100	0	0
B	101-110	20	0
C	111-120	30	0
D	121-130	95	0
E	131-140	115	115
F	141-150	130	130
G	151-165	165	165
H	166-175	190	265
I	176-185	210	315
J	186-200	245	445
K	201-225	260	580
L	226-255	445	790
M	Over 255	460	1,000

These rates apply for both petrol and diesel cars.

Band K includes cars emitting more than 225g/km first registered before 23 March 2006.

There is a discount of £10 for all alternatively-fuelled cars, which applies to both the standard and the first year rate.

Rates of VED in 2011/12, for vans:

Van category	£
Vans registered before 1 March 2001 - up to 1,549cc	130
Vans registered before 1 March 2001 - over 1,549cc	215
Vans registered on or after 1 March 2001 not exceeding 3.5 tonnes	210
Euro IV vans registered 1 March 2003 - 31 December 2006 not exceeding 3.5 tonnes	130
Euro V vans registered 1 January 2009 - 31 December 2010 not exceeding 3.5 tonnes	130
Standard rate	205

Rates of VED in 2011/12, for motorcycles

Engine size	£
Not exceeding 150cc	16.00
151-140cc	35.00
401-600cc	53.00
Above 600cc	74.00

It costs a lot for the government to collect VED. Over the years there have been occasional calls from the fleet industry and others for it to be scrapped and for the extra tax to be collected simply by adding an amount to the price of petrol.

It is doubtful whether this will ever happen. It would disadvantage people living in rural areas who have no alternative than to use their cars. In addition, road tax renewal gives the government an annual opportunity to check that each car on the road has valid car insurance and an MoT. Even in these days when the DVLA, car insurance and MoT databases are connected, and police cars have automatic number plate recognition cameras to catch offenders, is hard to see them giving up this important safety check.

16.2 STATUTORY OFF ROAD NOTIFICATION (SORN)

If you intend to keep a vehicle off the road you don't need to apply for or renew the VED.

Sadly, over the years many people evaded payment of this duty by making the excuse that the vehicle was off the road.

To reduce the number of tax dodgers the government introduced SORN.

If the DVLA discover you do not have a tax disc and you have not submitted a SORN declaration in which you confirm the vehicle is off the road, (that is, 'declared SORN' in DVLA terminology) they can fine you a minimum fine of £1000 and your vehicle could be clamped, impounded or crushed.

They can fine you even if they have not received a report that your vehicle is on the road without a tax disc.

So doing nothing is no longer an option when a tax disc expires. The DVLA has enforced 100% registration since 2004.

So, if you plan to keep a vehicle off the road for a period, perhaps because the driver is abroad and the vehicle is not being used, or because it is being repaired, you must immediately submit a SORN.

You can only obtain a refund on a tax disc if a vehicle is off the road if you have first submitted a SORN.

The road fund licence renewal contains a SORN declaration notice and instructions on how and when it should be completed.

Alternatively you can declare SORN using form V890 from a Post Office that issues tax discs or a DVLA Local Office.[322] Otherwise you can contact the DVLA Customer Enquiry Unit on 0300 790 6801 or 01792 786369.

If you are applying for a refund of tax you can declare SORN on the refund application form V14 or V33.

If you make a false SORN declaration when the vehicle is used on a public road you can be fined a maximum of £5,000 and imprisonment.

The problem with the SORN regulation is that it does not fully meet the needs of business fleets. Generally speaking, if you lease a car you will keep it until the anniversary of the purchase date (which is likely to be the first registration date) and then arrange for the leasing company to collect it. In practice, collection takes time and the leasing company runs the risk of keeping the vehicle on the road after the tax disc has expired.

The regulations have recognised this problem. The DVLA has approved special arrangements when leasing companies de-fleet cars at the end of a lease when the VED expires.

In this situation, if the leasing company plans to sell the vehicle within fourteen days, and sale actually takes place within this period, they do not need to make a SORN declaration so long as the vehicle is not driven on the road in that period.

If the vehicle is used in this period when untaxed, it will be subject to a fixed penalty charge unless it is displaying trade plates.

If the leasing company knows that the vehicle will be unsold by the end of this period, they must make a SORN declaration. If the car is actually used after this period they must make a backdated tax disc application.

So when your contract hire company seems very keen to collect your vehicle at the end of the lease, now you know why.

16.3 MINISTRY OF TRANSPORT TEST (MoT)

This test was established to ensure that all vehicles on the road meet a minimum standard of safety. By law,[323] cars and vans are required to undergo the test at a Department for Transport-approved testing station before the third anniversary of their registration date and annually thereafter.

The test covers lighting, steering, suspension, brakes, tyres, wheels, seat belts, exhaust system, exhaust emissions and other safety-related aspects of the vehicle. It does not cover engine, clutch or gearbox condition.

322 In the phone book under 'Department for Transport'.
323 *Road Traffic Act 1988* s45 and s46.

If you get a new MoT no earlier than a month before the old one expires, the new MoT will be post-dated to commence when the old one expires. However, the MoT test station will only do this if you produce your old MoT certificate at the time of the test.

If you lose a certificate the testing station will issue a duplicate. If they have closed down, the local office of the Vehicle & Operator Services Agency will supply one, for a small fee.

The rules are slightly different for a minibus or any vehicle designed to carry more than eight people. The front of the MoT certificate contains boxes on which the test station must confirm the number of seat belts fitted and whether a seat belt test has been carried out. The old MoT certificate for a minibus always has to be given to the MoT test station when a new MoT test is carried out.

If you have a problem with an MoT certificate (for example, you are buying a car and believe you are being offered a forged MoT certificate), you can get advice from Vehicle & Operator Services Agency's MoT Enquiry Line on 08703 300 444.

Since 2003 all MoT testing stations have been linked by computer system. Certificates are printed out rather than handwritten and records are stored electronically, including records of vehicle mileages.

The government is considering reducing the frequency of MoT tests, reflecting the fact that modern cars are more reliable than in the past.

16.4 VEHICLE REGISTRATION

16.4.1 VEHICLE REGISTRATION DOCUMENT (V5C)

The DVLA issues a vehicle registration document for every vehicle sold or imported into Great Britain. This is called a form V5C but many members of the public still describe it as the 'logbook'.

The old style vehicle registration document – the V5C – was phased out a few years ago and the V5C was redesigned in 2010 as a crime prevention measure. The new version is red (it used to be blue).

The vehicle registration document shows the registered keeper of the vehicle. This need not be the same person as the owner of the vehicle.

The form is essentially an extract of information held on the Register of Vehicles at the DVLA.

There is a legal obligation to advise the DVLA if the registered keeper's name or address changes or if there are changes to the vehicle that make its description as shown on the vehicle registration document inaccurate. For example, if you replace an engine the new engine number will not match the number on the V5C, or if the vehicle is resprayed the colour shown on the V5C may be incorrect.

Failure to notify the DVLA of such changes can lead to a £1,000 fine or a fine of £5,000 plus imprisonment for knowingly giving false information to the DVLA.

If you sell a vehicle or transfer it to another person, you must notify the DVLA by following the instructions shown on the V5C. Under EU regulations the V5C (or a VE103)[324] has to be carried in the vehicle when driving anywhere within the EU.

In 2003 the law was changed regarding tax discs. Since that date it is has been mandatory to present either a V11 or a vehicle registration document to obtain a tax disc.

16.4.2 NEW VEHICLE REGISTRATION CERTIFICATE (V5C)

The old V5 form was phased out in 2005 and was replaced with a Vehicle Registration Certificate (V5C).

The registration certificate complies with European Directive 1999/37/EC and has been introduced across the EU.

16.4.3 CLOCKED CARS

You are encouraged but not legally required to enter your VAT number and the mileage of the vehicle onto the V5C when selling it to a motor trader. If you fill these in it helps to prevent the 'clocking' of vehicles – turning back the mileage to increase the vehicle's value.

It is estimated that one in four cars is clocked at some stage in its life and that the aggregate cost to consumers exceeds £580 million each year.[325] This type of crime is on the increase. VOSA reports that the MOT mileage of nearly 700,000 cars a year is less than the mileage the previous year.

Buyers believe they are getting relatively low-mileage cars that are safe. The reality is that in many cases they are buying high-mileage clocked cars that may be unsafe.

It is illegal to sell a clocked car. By law a dealer is required to properly describe a vehicle. If it is described as having a lower mileage than it has travelled, the dealer is committing an offence.

Interestingly, at present it is not illegal to clock a vehicle. There is pressure for this aspect of the law to be amended, as the person who clocks the vehicle is surely as guilty as the person who then sells it – and is often the same person.

16.4.4 CARS DECLARED A TOTAL LOSS

If you have comprehensive motor insurance and your vehicle is written off as a total loss, the chances are that's the last time you will think about it. The insurance company makes a payment to you or your leasing company and you concentrate on

---

324 See 16.5.5.
325 Source: OFT.

replacing the vehicle. The business of disposing of the vehicle is left to the insurance company.

However, if you self-insure the comprehensive part of your motor cover and only buy third party, or third party fire and theft cover, you have to worry about vehicle disposal.[326]

There is a danger that a car declared a total loss by the insurer will be bolted back together again by a back-street repair shop and sold on to an unsuspecting member of the public. To ensure this does not happen, insurers report total loss vehicles to the DVLA using form V23.

They also advise the Motor Insurance Anti-Fraud & Theft Register (MIAFTR), an organisation run by The Association of British Insurers. MIAFTR keeps a list of all vehicles subject of total loss claims.

When motor insurers issue a new policy they check with MIAFTR to ensure the vehicle is not on the register.[327]

If you run a big self-insured fleet and one of your vehicles is so badly damaged in an accident that it is beyond economic repair, you should use form V23 to advise the DVLA.

If you wish to be public-spirited and ensure that such a vehicle does not end up being recycled back onto the road by back-street repairers, you may wish to register details of the vehicle with MIAFTR. Their address is MIAFTR, Association of British Insurers, Dolphin House, New Street, Salisbury, SP1 2PH. Phone: +44 (0)1722 435579 www.miaftr-hpi.info

MIAFTR defines four categories of vehicles:

Category A. Scrap value only. No economically salvageable parts. Only value is as scrap metal. This may be the result of the vehicle being burnt out

Category B. Can be broken up for spare parts

Category C. Repairable total loss vehicles but repair costs will exceed the value of the car before the accident

Category D. Repairable total loss vehicles where repair costs will not exceed the value of the car before the accident. . These may include vehicles that would have taken so long to repair and involved the insurer in such high hire vehicle costs that they decided to declare them a total loss to save time and costs. In other words, the vehicle could have been economically repaired but the insurer chose not to do so

Salvage disposers are required to use their best endeavours to ensure that Category A and B vehicles are never returned to the road.

---

326 See 1.21.20.

327 This is only one of MIAFTR's functions. It also acts as a register of fraudulent and repeated insurance claims and thereby helps to protect the insurance industry against fraud.

If you self-insure you must notify the DVLA on form V23 as soon as you have identified that you have a Category A, B or C vehicle.

If you are the registered keeper and an insurer makes a total loss payment to you, you must notify the DVLA (unless the insurer does so for you) by using the red section of the V5C. You must then destroy the rest of the V5C.

If you self-insure and sell a Category A, B or C vehicle to a salvage company you are advised to give them a photocopy of the V5C and not the original. If anyone tries to re-register a Category A, B or C vehicle the DVLA will advise the police, who will investigate.

MIAFTR passes information on all Category A, B, C and D vehicles to the credit agencies Equifax HPI and Experian. If any future purchaser of such a vehicle tries to buy it on finance, the finance company will be alerted to its 'total loss claim' history.

Under the terms of the Code of Practice, all Category A vehicles must be crushed. Once any salvageable components have been removed the shell, frame and chassis of Category B vehicles have to be crushed. Category C and D vehicles can be sold on for repair.

If you self-insure and ask a salvage agent to dispose of a vehicle, you should ensure the vehicle is disposed of correctly. *The Environmental Protection Act 1990* provides for fines up to £5,000 if you send the vehicle to an unlicensed site or up to £20,000 and six months' imprisonment for dumping by the roadside. Such penalties would only be issued in an extreme case. It is more likely that for one offence you would receive a £300 fixed penalty notice issued under s 2A (1) Refuse Disposal (Amenity) Act 1978 for abandoning a vehicle.

You should only use a salvage agent that can guarantee it complies with the terms of the Act. The legal obligation is yours and you cannot delegate it to a third party.

The insurance industry, motor salvage industry, Home Office and Department of Transport have drawn up the *Code of Practice for the Disposal of Motor Vehicle Salvage*. It sets out the steps to be followed if a vehicle is declared a total loss. A copy is available from www.abi.org.uk/Information/Codes_and_Guidance_Notes/40510.pdf.

16.4.5   VEHICLE IDENTITY CHECK

If a vehicle is written off as a total loss and is subsequently repaired, it must be inspected by the Vehicle & Operator Services Agency before it can be returned to the road. The purpose of the check is not to inspect it mechanically, merely to confirm its identity.

This is a crime-reduction measure.

Each year the identities of thousands of written-off cars are transferred to cars that have been stolen by thieves. They pass off these cars to innocent buyers as accident-damaged cars that have been repaired.

The V5C for the vehicle is marked to note that it has passed the identity test.

16.5 VEHICLES TAKEN ABROAD

While every effort has been taken to ensure the information in this book is correct, regulations in different countries change frequently so it is important to re-check this information before you travel.

The motoring organisations' websites include a comprehensive list of the things you need to be aware of when driving in different European counties.

16.5.1 DRIVERS LICENCE

You must have a full driver's licence to drive in most EU countries. It must be produced on demand, unlike in the UK where the police allow some 'days of grace' before you have to produce it.

The minimum driving age is 18 in most European countries, 17 in Ireland and Iceland and 16 in the Isle of Man.

16.5.2 PASSPORTS

If you are travelling on business your passport must not expire during your visit. Some countries require the expiry date to be some date after your planned return to the UK, in some cases at least six months after.

16.5.3 INTERNATIONAL DRIVING PERMIT

Many countries require you to hold an international driving permit before you can drive there. This is not required if you are driving within the EU. An international driving permit can be obtained from the AA, RAC and some post offices.

16.5.4 GB STICKER

A GB sticker is compulsory in all European countries, unless your number plate includes the EU symbol. If you drive outside the EU (including Switzerland) you must show a GB sticker. This may be a separate sticker or it may form part of the licence plate.

If you are using the familiar white GB sticker it should be stuck as close as possible to the rear number plate of the car and any trailer.

16.5.5 VE103 – VEHICLE ON HIRE CERTIFICATE

In 1963 the EU passed a resolution requiring a driver to hold a form VE103 if they wish to take their leased vehicle across borders within the EU. This is a short form that confirms that the driver has the owner's permission to take the vehicle overseas. It therefore replaces the V5C for overseas travel and is accepted in all the EU countries.

It is important to note that the VE103 is the only document that the authorities will recognise as evidence of the owner's consent to take the vehicle abroad. A letter of authority from the owner is insufficient for this purpose.

Without an original V103 the vehicle can be impounded and the driver can be fined.

There are several organisations in the UK that are authorised to issue VE103 forms, including the BVRLA.

16.5.6 SAFETY WHEN DRIVING ABROAD

One of the problems with road safety is that the government and road safety campaigners lecture us so much about road dangers that we end up believing that British roads are dangerous places. The fact is that road deaths have been falling and are now at an all-time low of 'only' around two thousand each year. Of course, that's 2,000 too many.

However, the bad news is that the roads abroad are usually worse.

Compared with the UK, road users are five times as likely to be involved in a fatal accident in Greece or Portugal and three times as likely in France or Spain.

These are not nice statistics, made worse by the fact that, as someone who normally drives on the left-hand side of the road, your risk while driving in these countries is even higher. If your drivers are travelling abroad, it is worthwhile briefing them on this extra level of risk.

In all European countries it is mandatory to wear a motorcycle crash helmet when in control of a motorcycle.

In most European countries it is mandatory to carry warning triangles, in many it is mandatory to carry light bulbs and fuses and in a few it is mandatory to carry a fire extinguisher and a first aid kit.

In some countries drivers must wear reflective jackets if they step out of their vehicle after a breakdown at night or at times of poor visibility.

In some countries it is illegal to have a mobile phone switched on when driving.

These rules change frequently so we will not list here the items that must be carried in each country. See the motoring organisations' websites.

16.5.7 HEADLAMPS

In most European countries it is mandatory to drive on dipped headlights.

If you are driving a right-hand drive car, you will need to adjust your headlights when travelling elsewhere in Europe to ensure you do not dazzle oncoming drivers. The easiest way to do this is to buy stickers from motor spares shops to place in front of the headlight lenses to alter their beam. Many vehicle headlights show the area that has to be 'blacked out' in order to alter the beam pattern but it is probably best to buy a kit and follow the instructions, rather than producing your own home-made ones.

16.5.8 SNOW CHAINS

In many European countries it is a legal requirement to fit snow chains to your vehicle when driving during winter. Do bear in mind that these should only be used on snow and that prolonged use on hard surfaces will damage the tyres.

If you plan to use snow chains for the first time, it is a good idea to try to fit and remove them first in dry, warm, light conditions. It is not much fun trying to do this for the first time at night in sub-zero conditions, with snow on the ground.

16.5.9   SPARE CLUTCH AND ACCELERATOR CABLES

One of the most common causes for vehicles to break down is when clutch or accelerator cables snap. While many components a particular model of car are identical regardless of whether it is a left-hand or right-hand drive, it is often the case that the cables fitted to left-hand drive cars are of a different length to those fitted on right-hand drive cars. Hence it is less likely that a motor repairer in, say, Belgium will carry the right cable: the cable may have to be ordered and this can cause delay.

So it may be worthwhile carrying spare clutch and accelerator cables. They cost very little and the saving in time can be considerable.

16.5.10   CHILDREN

Many countries do not allow children to sit in the front seat of a moving vehicle.

16.5.11   ILLEGAL IMMIGRANTS

Every so often the TV news shows images of refugees trying to make their way across the Channel. While most of the media attention has focused on freight trains and the heavy trucks carried on shuttle trains, illegal immigrants also try to gain entry in the boots of cars and the back of vans.

It is a criminal offence to bring an illegal immigrant into the UK.

The *Immigration and Asylum Act 1999* gives both the driver and the owner of the vehicle an obligation to detect an illegal immigrant who enters using their vehicle. The driver is criminally liable and can be fined or imprisoned. Variable penalties now apply, taking account of the degree of care exercised by motorists and truck drivers to ensure that clandestine entrants were not carried in their vehicles. In assessing whether a penalty should be charged, and the amount of the penalty, HM Customs consider:

■ Whether the vehicle had good security

■ Whether drivers checked the vehicle for clandestine entrants before leaving for Britain

■ Whether the driver and the owner of the vehicle have a good previous record in this regard

■ Whether the driver co-operated and brought the clandestine entrant to the attention of the authorities

HM Customs' policy is not to randomly stop and search vehicles but only to do so when it has reasonable suspicions that illegal acts are being carried out.

If you rent a vehicle, you may discover the rental company refuses to issue a form VE103 because they do not wish to give authority for the vehicle to be driven abroad. A number of BVRLA rental members have made this decision as they do not wish to risk their vehicles being involved in illegal immigration or bootlegging.[328]

16.5.12 INTERNATIONAL MOTOR INSURANCE

All UK motor insurance policies provide the minimum cover required in the EU and some other European countries.[329] However, this is only third party cover, so it does not cover the cost of damage to your vehicle.

If you have comprehensive motor insurance cover and wish to drive abroad, you must ask the insurer to extend the policy to cover Continental motoring. If you do not do so and have an accident, you are likely to find that you only have third party cover.

In most countries you must carry a copy of your motor insurance certificate in the vehicle.

Some rental companies issue International Motor Insurance Certificates ('green cards') to prove the vehicle is comprehensively insured. This is not compulsory in the EU (except Romania and Bulgaria) but is required in many non-EU countries.

16.5.13 BAIL BONDS

A bail bond is a guarantee that an amount of money will be paid to a court as security for bail. They are of interest here as they are useful in some non-EU countries for security in the event of a road accident. If you are driving a car involved in a road accident you can be detained and the car can be impounded.

A bail bond can be obtained when you apply for a green card from either your rental company, your motor insurer, the AA or the RAC.

16.5.14 BOOTLEGGING

You may ask: 'What has this to do with company vehicles?'

Do any of your drivers pop over to Calais to stock up on cheap cigarettes and drink? Yes, no, or don't know?

If you answered yes or don't know, this section is for you. HM Revenue and Customs has impounded many company cars where the drivers have been caught importing more goods than permitted, especially cigarettes and alcohol.

If the driver is using a vehicle supplied on rental or contract hire, it is likely that the hire agreement will make you liable for costs or losses that the rental or contract hire company suffers if the car is impounded.

328 See 16.5.14.
329 See 1.21.6.

The first time someone is caught bootlegging in a rented or leased vehicle, the vehicle will be taken away from him or her and they will be fined. HM Customs will notify the rental or leasing company ('the owner') that the vehicle has been involved in bootlegging and will arrange to return it direct to the owner.

If the driver is bootlegging again and the vehicle is seized a second time it will be restored to the owner on payment of a larger fine.

Rental companies are becoming particularly vigilant about hiring out vehicles that may be used for bootlegging and the BVRLA maintains a register[330] showing the names of hirers who have had rental cars impounded. BVRLA members usually check this register before hiring vehicles and will normally deny rental to these people.

HM Customs can prosecute rental companies if bootleggers persistently use their cars: hence the rental companies need to be vigilant.

In July 2000 HM Customs changed its policy and decided to use its powers[331] to confiscate any vehicle involved in smuggling. However, in February 2002 the Court of Appeal condemned this policy and said that confiscation can only be used in the most serious cases, where forfeiture of the vehicle will allow Customs to recover any lost taxes or duty.

In 2002 HM Customs announced that they would no longer carry out random searches on cars but would stop and search cars where they had specific reasons for doing so. An example would be a car known to have made several trips across the Channel in a reasonably short period of time.

They also announced that the burden of proof that bootlegging was taking place would be placed on HM Customs rather than the alleged bootlegger. So the driver no longer has to prove the items are for personal use, HM Customs has to prove that they are not.

16.5.15 EUROPEAN HEALTH INSURANCE CARD

You can get free or low cost emergency medical treatment elsewhere in the EU and in Switzerland if you carry a European Health Insurance Card. You can apply for one at Post Offices.

There is a mounting body of evidence that these cards are not as helpful as might have been expected. Many travellers report that they have gone to a doctor's surgery on the continent and offered their European Health Insurance Card, only to be asked for their credit cards instead. On asking they are told that it takes too long for the doctor to recover the costs via the bureaucracy.

---

330 See 19.4.3.

331 *Customs and Excise Management Act 1979* s14(1).

16.5.16 LOW EMISSION ZONES

In much the same way that London has a low emission zone, other countries are in the process of considering these.

In Germany you can only drive into a major city if your vehicle bears a windshield sticker confirming your entitlement. Forty-six cities have already introduced the scheme and more are planning to follow. You can obtain a sticker from www.umwelt-plakette.de. If you fail to show the sticker on your windscreen you face a €40 fine, though some cities allow you a period of grace before penalising you.

16.6 DRIVING LICENCES

It is absolutely essential that drivers' licences should be checked regularly and frequently to ensure that the driver is still licensed to drive and has not accumulated penalty points without advising the company.

This applies to all employees who are driving on company business, whether they are driving company cars, cars acquired with cash allowances or their own cars (grey fleet cars).

You need to have a company policy setting out what will happen should a driver be banned from driving or accumulate a number of penalty points.

It is important to remember that motor insurances are invalidated if an unlicensed driver (e.g. a banned driver) is at the wheel.

Driver licence checking is something you can do in-house or outsource to your contract hire company or a specialist suppliers.

16.6.1 TYPES OF LICENCE

Drivers' licences have to be renewed every ten years until the driver is 70. The new style 'photocard' licence was introduced in 2001, which means that a growing number of these licences are now beginning to expire.

The driving licence has two parts; a plastic photocard and a paper 'counterpart' document.

The plastic photocard is issued in provisional and full forms. The provisional licence is green, looks like the full licence and is clearly marked 'provisional'. The full licence is pink and shows the categories of vehicle for which the driver is licensed.

The counterpart driving licence is a paper document that is issued with the photocard. It shows whether the driver holds any provisional entitlements to drive vehicles other than those for which the full licence is valid. It also shows any endorsements, court-imposed sentences and disqualifications. If there are too many endorsements for full details to be shown, the counterpart will be marked 'continuation sheet to follow' and the information will be listed on a continuation sheet.

If you change your address you must notify the DVLA by completing the relevant section on the counterpart and submitting it with the photocard to the DVLA. If you fail to advise a change of address you can be fined.

The issue number on the licence is important. This is made up of two numbers plus an alphabetic character. The alphabetic character identifies the latest counterpart issued for that photocard.

The counterpart and the photocard are both bar-coded to ensure they are matched up during the production process. In Wales, the counterpart is printed in both English and Welsh.

You may obtain further information about driving licences on forms INF60, INF61 and INF60/2 available from the DVLA. www.DVLA.gov.uk.

The photocard and the counterpart must both be produced when taking a driving test, hiring a vehicle or producing your licence at the request of the police.

It is good fleet management policy to inspect both the photocard and the counterpart for all drivers periodically. If one of your employees drives without a licence the vehicle is automatically uninsured. A good approach is to inspect licences when new employees join the company, then every six months thereafter.[332]

Drivers who passed their standard driving test before 1 January 1997 can drive vehicles up to 7.5 tonnes without restriction on the weight being towed (if any).

However, drivers passing after this date are only allowed to drive vehicles up to 3.5 tonnes that are not being used to tow more than 750kg.

16.6.2 DISABILITY[333]

There are a number of disabilities that must be notified to the DVLA, to allow it to determine whether a driver should retain their licence and continue to drive on the roads. The DVLA publishes a long list[334] of the disabilities that must be notified, which include epilepsy, strokes, other neurological conditions, mental health problems, physical disabilities and visual impairments.

If you report a disability to the DVLA they will send you a form asking for further information and asking for consent to contact your doctor. A medical assessor working for DVLA will then decide whether you will be allowed to drive.

---

332 See 5.11.3.

333 See also 12.11.

334 www.direct.gov.uk/en/Motoring/DriverLicensing/MedicalRulesForDrivers/
MedicalA-Z/index.htm

The charity Ricability produces guidance for motorists who have specific disabilities.[335]

The organisation Disabled Motoring UK can provide further information about DVLA procedures. This charity (formerly Mobilise) was formed by the merger of two long-standing charities, the Disabled Drivers` Association and the Disabled Drivers` Motor Club.

Website: www.disabledmotoring.org

16.6.3 DRIVERS FROM OTHER COUNTRIES

A visitor to the UK with a valid full driving licence issued in any of the following countries can drive any type of vehicle listed on their licence.

Austria	Belgium	Bulgaria	Czech Republic
Republic of Cyprus	Denmark	Estonia	Finland
France	Germany	Greece	Hungary
Iceland	Ireland	Italy	Latvia
Liechtenstein	Lithuania	Luxembourg	Malta
Netherlands	Northern Ireland	Norway	Poland
Portugal	Romania	Slovenia	Slovakia
Spain	Sweden	United Kingdom	

If their licence was issued in Jersey, Guernsey or the Isle of Man they can drive any car and motorcycles listed on their full and valid licence for 12 months, or a larger vehicle (e.g. a truck or bus) listed on your licence that they drive into the UK.

If their licence was issued in any other country they can drive any cars and motorcycles shown on their full and valid driving licence for 12 months.

These rules change from time to time so it is always best to refer to the interactive tool shown on the directgov website for the latest information.[336]

16.7 MANAGEMENT REPORTS

Even if your fleet comprises only a handful of cars you will still need to have information to allow you to manage them as efficiently and effectively as possible.

---

335 www.ricability.org.uk/consumer_reports/mobility_reports

336 www.direct.gov.uk/en/Motoring/DriverLicensing/
   DrivingInGbOnAForeignLicence/DG_4022561

The nature and scope of the reports you obtain will largely be determined by your own needs but the following will be indispensable to most fleet managers:

■ List of makes, models, registration numbers and drivers of all vehicles in the fleet

■ List showing when vehicles are due to be replaced, in replacement date order

■ List of vehicles due to terminate soon (this is usually supplied by the contract hire company)

■ List of cars operating over or under the expected mileage. This is usually supplied by the contract hire company and is important as it gives an early warning of possible excess mileage charges and allows you to take remedial action. If you fund the vehicles by outright purchase this is still a useful report as it allows you to consider whether any action is required, for example, swapping a high-mileage car with a low mileage car to even up the mileage so no vehicle with excessive mileage is offered for sale.

■ Cars that have passed the original lease termination date. Again your contract hire company will usually supply this if the vehicles are on contract hire. Do you have an agreement with them to allow you to extend the vehicle lease?   If not, you may be incurring penalties under the contract.

■ P46 report, to allow you to complete the P46 tax form as required by law.[337]

■ Actual running costs to date compared with estimates. This allows you to pinpoint issues and problems.

■ Actual fuel consumption to date compared with estimates. Once again this allows you to spot problems.[338]

16.8 FLEET MANAGEMENT SOFTWARE

If you are running your own fleet of vehicles, and in particular if you are funding or managing them yourself rather than using a contract hire or fleet management company, it is essential to keep on top of your fleet information.

You need a good diary system (to remind you when to replace vehicles, renew vehicle excise duty, motor insurance and MoTs), a system that captures service histories, a way of capturing fuel consumption information and so on.

The system should allow you to compare the running costs of different vehicles and the motoring costs incurred by different drivers.

A good system will help you to identify abuse by drivers and garages, make it easier to make warranty claims and identify when a vehicle needs servicing.

You can keep this information in a manual filing system and much of it is already captured in your accounting system.

---

337 See 16.15.

338 Such as heavy use of the driver's right foot.

If your fleet is small you can probably hold the rest of this information on simple record cards for each vehicle. However, manual systems are not ideal for collating, comparing or rapidly accessing large quantities of data, and accounting systems do not hold information in ways that are useful to a fleet manager.

At some point it will become useful for you to use fleet software to help you run the fleet.

There are many types of fleet software available. At the lowest end of the market you will find packages for a few hundred pounds that are designed to help the busy manager of a small fleet to organise his or her day. At the top end, you can spend hundreds of thousands of pounds on a system that will help run a large, complex fleet.

At least one of the software suppliers can also provide you with useful vehicle data such as new and used vehicle prices and predicted maintenance costs.

You can find the suppliers of these systems through adverts placed in fleet publications or by attending fleet industry events and seminars.

There is a whole industry built around helping businesses to decide what software to buy. There are a variety of methodologies available to help you to make your selection. Most of these are expensive, involve the use of consultants and are beyond the scope of smaller businesses.

So for this latter group, here are a few things to consider:

■ Decide what you need before you start talking to possible suppliers

■ Check their offerings against your 'needs' list

■ Make sure you distinguish between the things that you need and those that would just be nice to have.

■ Make sure that there are no misunderstandings between you and the supplier as to the meaning of technical words

■ Consider sending out an invitation to tender, describing your requirements and asking them to respond point by point. Make it clear that these responses will form part of any contract you may enter into with them at a later date

■ Check their references. Speak to existing clients – are they happy?

■ Check their financial clout. They may have great software but if they are unlikely to be around to support you or develop the software you would be better off looking elsewhere

■ Meet their staff. You will be relying on them, possibly for many years. How experienced are they?

■ Involve your users in the selection process

■ Make sure the system will cope with your growth plans

■ If you operate in several countries, consider whether you need the system to handle several currencies and, if so, make sure it can do so

■ Consider whether you like the technology they are using.

For many years Microsoft® has been the pre-eminent supplier of desktop operating systems. Hence much modern software has been written to run in a Windows®[339] environment.

Similarly, the most successful database product is made by Oracle®[340] and there are many thousands of programmers able to support your system if it is written on an Oracle database.

Does this mean you should only consider buying a product based on Windows or Oracle? Not at all. There are many excellent products in the market that have a strong user following that use neither of these products.

Look beyond the functionality of the package (what it does) and look at the underlying technology as well.

Try to get a performance guarantee. If the supplier says that the system will handle your 800 vehicles and that response times using a networked PC with a 4Mbit processor will be under 0.01 seconds, it should be willing to back that up with a guarantee.

Ignore any marketing hype you may receive. You will be using this software for many years, long after the salesman has spent his commission. You need the substance, not the spin.

Consider how far the supplier has developed the product, how many companies have bought it and the supplier's future development plans. If you are being sold version 5.6 of a product that has been in the market for five years and version 6.0 is due out in six months, you may feel some degree of comfort. Many users will have contributed to the development of the product, it is likely (but by no means certain) that most of the bugs will have been eliminated and the company is still investing in developing the product. These are all good signs and much better than buying Version 1.0 from a new entrant to the market, however interesting its product.

If you take your vehicles on contract hire, or engage a fleet management company, you may be able to get much of the functionality you need through online access to their systems. Most of the bigger players now give clients direct access to a range of fleet management tools.

However, do bear in mind that this is their system, not yours. So if you have several different suppliers your information will be scattered over several systems.

And if you change fleet supplier you will lose access to these tools.

---

339 Microsoft and Windows are trading styles owned by Microsoft Inc.
340 Oracle Inc.

16.9 E-COMMERCE

The next step in the development of your relationship with your contract hire or fleet management company is to use their web-based e-commerce system.

These may include quoting, management reporting, vehicle ordering and disposal, extension processing, changing driver details and more.

16.10 IN-HOUSE LEASING COMPANY

For decades many large diversified groups operated in-house leasing companies. They bought vehicles and leased them to other divisions.

By concentrating vehicle management expertise in one place these groups have benefited from economies of scale, know-how and efficiencies. Some of the biggest fleets in the UK have been operated in this way. They are useful for groups wanting central fleet control.

The VAT regulations add an extra dimension to these businesses. As long as they deal at arm's length with their intra-group 'customers', in-house leasing companies can recover 100% of the input VAT on the purchase of cars. This is because the in-house leasing company is using the vehicles solely for the business purpose of leasing to another business.

This puts them in the same position as regular contract hire and leasing companies and this VAT saving gives them is a significant benefit.

To recover this input VAT the in-house leasing company must have its own VAT registration.

If there is any private use of the vehicle in the in-house lessee can only recover 50% of the input VAT paid on rentals they pay, or even less if the lessee is partially exempt for VAT purposes.

They also suffer the normal partial corporation tax disallowance on the rentals paid on vehicle emitting more than 160g/km.[341]

Nonetheless, there can still a tax benefit to the group overall from operating an in-house leasing company. Against this benefit has to be set the cost of setting up and running the in-house leasing company.

16.11 JOURNEY PLANNING

If you only have perk cars in your fleet, you can comfortably skip this section.

On the other hand, if your business fleet is involved in distribution, journey planning is already a central part of the management of your fleet and you are likely to be an expert in the subject.

341 See 17.1.3.

The majority of vehicle fleets fit somewhere between these two extremes.

Most vehicle running costs relate to the mileage a vehicle covers. Fuel cost, depreciation, tyres, servicing, repairs, component failure and even the number of accidents are all mileage-related.

So if mileage costs money, how do you go about minimising it?

The easiest approach is to eliminate the need for the journey in the first place or to reduce the amount of driving that takes place. Video-conferencing companies make their living from this idea.

But if a journey has to happen, the next step is to try to minimise the number of miles that are driven. That's where journey planning comes in.

If your business has service engineers or salesmen on the road, you can plan their days to minimise mileage. It should be easy to devise a simple route that allows them to move from one call to another, without zigzagging backwards and forwards around the country

There are a number of tools available to help you plan their routes. The simplest tools are the internet-based websites such as Google Maps or Bing Maps (formerly Multimap). These allow you to enter your start point and destination, decide whether you want the quickest or shortest journey and in a few seconds they calculate the best route and deliver step-by-step instructions and a route map.

Another approach is to use one of the many CD-based mapping systems sold in the high street or available from some motoring organisations. These work in the same way and, although you have to pay to buy them, the cost is modest if you are going to plan a lot of routes.

The next step is to put the technology in the vehicle for the driver to use, as discussed in chapter 10.

16.12 POOL CARS

If you have a number of employees who only use a car for business occasionally, you might like to consider keeping a few pool cars on your fleet rather than providing them with dedicated company cars.

As employees do not consider that the pool car is 'theirs', you will not need to buy high-specification cars to meet their needs. A pool car can often be a low-specification, smaller-engined vehicle that does the job and no more.

However, it can be quite difficult to manage pool cars.

Demand for them within your organisation is unlikely to be constant so your cars may sit idle for several days and then you may find that you need more cars than you have got.

The best approach is probably to have enough pool cars to ensure that they are in near-constant use and to use daily hire cars to meet any extra demand.

The other problem is that pool cars tend to be treated poorly by drivers. As no one driver feels any 'ownership' of a pool car, they are unlikely to keep it clean or worry about checking oil, tyres etc.

Generally though, pool cars are a good flexible resource. They can be acquired in the same way that you acquire the remainder of your fleet; for example, outright purchase or contract hire.

Pool cars do not attract car benefit tax.[342]

In the past few years quite a lot of work has been done to introduce modern technology to the management of pool cars.

Electronic boxes can be fitted to pool vehicles to allow authorised drivers to book the vehicle electronically (via text message or over the internet), gain access by using a smart card and deactivate the immobiliser by keying in a PIN number. The vehicle keys are securely stored in the vehicle.

A number of contract hire companies have cars that they can make available for use as pool cars.

16.13 DEMONSTRATORS

Manufacturers know that you are more likely to buy a vehicle, particularly a new model, if you are given a reasonable period in which to test-drive it. Therefore they operate quite large fleets of demonstrator vehicles.

If your fleet is large and you have a direct relationship with a manufacturer they will supply you with demonstrators direct. Otherwise, your contract hire or fleet management company should be able to organise the use of demonstrators for you.

The manufacturer's local franchised dealer may also arrange this for you, though you may find they are reluctant to help if the order is likely to be placed with a contract hire company that will buy the vehicle elsewhere.

16.14 COMMUNICATING WITH DRIVERS

There is quite a lot of information that you need to provide to, or receive from, your drivers. Let's assume a new employee joins the company and you will be giving them a company vehicle.

---

342 See 17.2.1 Pool Cars.

You may need to provide them with:

- A copy of the latest fleet policy
- A list of the vehicles they can choose from
- A fuel card
- An expenses claim form and instructions on how to use it
- A form that allows them to list their business mileage – essential if you are paying for all fuel using a fuel card and recovering the non-business fuel cost via a deduction from payroll[343]
- And possibly a form on which they list information required by your insurers

In the old days you would have kept a thick manual containing this information and issued it to each new joiner. Today's web-enabled companies hold all of this information on their intranets, direct their driver to the relevant intranet pages and simply obtain a note signed by the driver confirming they have read this information.

Once the new driver has his car you will need to keep in touch. You will have to send reminders when a service or MoT is due or overdue and when the vehicle is due for replacement. Much of this is now done by email.

A simple way to record these events is to keep an email folder for each driver. By holding sent emails in your Sent Mail folder until the driver has responded as required, you will be certain that you have not missed anything.

Even when email is not appropriate, such as when a tax disc is to be sent to the driver, it is still useful to email the driver to confirm the tax disc has been sent and to ask for an email confirming receipt.

Many of the fleet software packages allow emails to be sent directly from the package to the driver and log the fact that these have been sent.

16.15 FORMS P11D AND P46 (CAR)

The form P11D is an annual return of benefits-in-kind provided to directors or employees earning more than £8,500 per year. You, as employer, have to submit it to HM Revenue and Customs and the employee by July 6 after the year-end to which it relates.

The form shows the travel, entertainment and other benefits given to the employee or paid for by the employer on the employee's behalf.

---

343 See 5.8.2.

It includes details of all company cars driven, dates of use, their engine sizes, list prices and CO_2 emissions, whether private fuel has been provided and whether the ownership of any car has been transferred to the employee.

The form P46 (Car) is a more detailed form, listing the engine type (petrol, diesel, hybrid, electric, bi-fuel), level of CO_2 emission, price paid, capital contribution, employee name and other information required by HM Revenue and Customs to allow them to assess the correct tax liability for an employee who receives a company car.

It only has to be completed when there has been a change and it has to be sent to HM Revenue and Customs quarterly, 28 days after the end of each tax quarter (that is, 28 days after 5 July, 5 October, 5 January or 5 April).

There is no particular reason to wait until the end of the quarter to submit this form. It is a good idea to submit it when the change occurs and the information is at hand and fresh in your mind, rather than running the risk of forgetting to submit it.

The employer is liable for a penalty of £3,000 for submitting incorrect information on a form P11D or P46 (Car). In addition there is a penalty of £300 plus £60 per day if the form is sent late to HM Revenue and Customs or the employee.

Form P11D (b) is a further annual return that you have to complete in respect of company vehicles. In this case it relates to National Insurance contributions and shows the Class 1A NIC due from the employer. It has to be sent by July 6 after the tax year to which it relates and there is a penalty of £100 per month for each fifty employees. If the form is more than twelve months late, the maximum penalty is 100% of the National Insurance contributions due.

It is a good idea to give employees copies of all tax forms before they are submitted to HM Revenue and Customs.

If you pay your employees a mileage rate that exceeds HM Revenue and Customs Approved Mileage Allowance Payments (AMAP[344]) for the use of their private cars on company business, you must advise your employees the total amount paid, the total miles this relates to and the rate per mile at which payment was made. This must be done before July 6 after the tax year to which it relates.

344 See 17.3.6.

16.16 MOTOR INSURANCE DATABASE

There has always been a problem with uninsured vehicles operating on Britain's roads. They cause significant problems and expense for drivers of other vehicles when there is an accident and the police find it very difficult to trace such vehicles.

It is estimated that the cost of uninsured vehicles in Britain exceeds £380m, and this cost is borne by honest motorists paying higher insurance premiums.

Under the terms of the EU Forth Motor Insurance Directive all vehicles have had to be registered on the Motor Insurance Database since 20 January 2003.

The Motor Insurers Bureau operates the database and their website gives details of the registration procedure: www.mib.org.uk.

The obligation to register your cars on the database is yours. However, you should ask your insurer or broker whether they plan to do this for you. If they are not going to do this for you they will advise you how to go about it.

You will need to submit the required data, either to your broker or direct to the database, and whenever you change your vehicles you must update the database.

Cars that are to be held by fleets for less than 14 days do not need to be registered.

If you fail to register a vehicle you will be liable to a £5,000 fine.

16.17 INITIAL VEHICLE REGISTRATION FEE (IVR)

This £55 fee is payable when a new car is registered in the UK.

Some vehicles are exempt from the fee.[345]

---

345 See www.direct.gov.uk/en/Motoring/BuyingAndSellingAVehicle/
    RegisteringAVehicle/DG_4022317

16.18 TRANSFER OF VEHICLE REGISTRATION NUMBERS

16.18.1 CHERISHED NUMBERS

The DVLA provides a Cherished Transfer Facility that allows a registration number to be moved directly from one vehicle to another subject to certain conditions.

Both vehicles must be currently licensed, subject to annual testing and available for inspection. However, unlicensed donor vehicles will still be considered if the licence for the donor vehicle expired no more than six months prior to the date of the application; or if the donor vehicle is less than 3 years old (less than 1 year old for HGVs).

Recipient vehicles must be currently licensed in order to participate in the number transfer arrangements.

To transfer a registration number, use a V317 transfer application form that is available from your nearest DVLA Local Office or from DVLA Swansea.

16.18.2 REGISTRATION NUMBER RETENTION FACILITY

If you wish to retain the use of a registration number but do not have a vehicle on which to use it, you can apply to retain the number using the DVLA Retention Facility. This situation could arise, for example, when you have just sold the vehicle bearing your cherished number and have yet to buy a new vehicle.

This facility allows the registered keeper to remove the registration number from a vehicle and to hold it for up to twelve months before allocating it to another vehicle. This period can be extended annually provided it is not allowed to lapse. Only the registered keeper of a vehicle is entitled to apply to retain its registration number.

Only vehicles meeting the conditions set out in 16.18.1, above, are eligible for this facility.

To retain a registration number, apply using a V778/1 retention application form that is available from your nearest DVLA Local Office or from DVLA Swansea.

16.19 DRIVER AND VEHICLE LICENSING IN NORTHERN IRELAND

The DVLA is responsible for driver and vehicle licensing in Great Britain. In Northern Ireland, Driver and Vehicle Licensing Northern Ireland (DVLNI) handle these responsibilities.

The DVLNI is accountable to ministers, parliament and the Northern Ireland Assembly.

The work of DVLNI is broadly equivalent to that carried out by the Driver and Vehicle Licensing Agency (DVLA) and Transport Area Networks (TAN) and local authorities in Great Britain. It provides a variety of testing and licensing services, and operates vehicle licensing (motor tax) offices in Armagh, Ballymena, Belfast, Coleraine, Downpatrick, Enniskillen, Londonderry and Omagh.

Website: www.dvani.gov.uk

16.20 COMPENSATION RECOVERY UNIT (CRU)

Road accidents cost the NHS hundreds of millions of pounds a year.

In 1999 the government introduced legislation[346] allowing the Department of Work and Pensions to recover NHS costs wherever possible.

The CRU makes enquiries after an accident to see who has been held responsible for the accident. If the driver is a company car driver and his or her employer has comprehensive cover, the CRU will claim from the insurer.

If the employer self-insures the fleet, the CRU will claim from the employer.

So one of the unexpected side effects of self-insuring your company car fleet is that you could start receiving charges from the CRU.

---

346 *Road Traffic (NHS Charges) Act 1999,* now amended by the *Health and Social Care (Community Health and Standards) Act 2003*

16.21 EXERCISES

What is a form V11?

What difference does it make to VED if a car was first registered before 1 March 2001?

What is SORN?

What is covered by an MoT test on a car and a minibus?

What form should you use to notify the DVLA if you sell a car?

How is the BVRLA mileage database used?

What is MIAFTR?

When do you need an international driving permit?

What is a VE103?

When might you need a bail bond?

Why should you be concerned about bootlegging?

What disabilities have to be notified to the DVLA?

Which fleet management reports might you need to help you run the fleet?

What are the advantages of an in-house leasing company?

How can you reduce the work-related mileage driven by your staff?

What is a P46 (Car)?

What is the IVR fee?

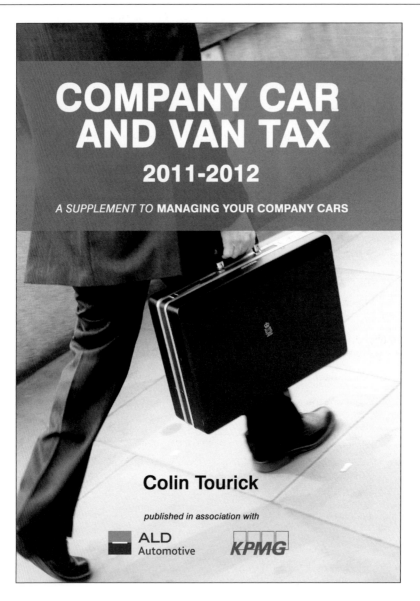

17 TAXATION

This chapter has been produced in association with **KPMG**

The tax rules in this chapter were accurate at the date of publication. Tax rules tend to remain unchanged for several years whereas tax rates, benefits, allowances and so on tend to change annually. To ensure that this book remains relevant for as long as possible, this chapter deals with this topic in a general way but does not include tax rates, benefits, allowances or examples for any specific tax year.

Company Car and Van Tax[347] *is a companion edition to this book. It is similar to this chapter but also includes tax rates, benefits, allowances and examples for the year in which it is published.*

*We plan to publish **Company Car and Van Tax** annually and you can get a copy from either www.aldnews.co.uk/tax, www.tourick.com or good bookshops.*

Taxation – it's everywhere.

Just about every decision you make about your fleet – the cars you choose, the method of finance you use and the way you pay for fuel and services – has a tax impact. There are several taxes at work here:

- VAT
- income tax
- corporation tax
- fuel and vehicle excise duties and
- national insurance contributions.

This chapter looks first at the employer's tax position. Historically, that has been the first priority for a fleet manager.

We will then go on to look at the employee's position.

As car benefit tax rates have changed, particularly since the CO_2-based car benefit tax regime was introduced, fleet managers have needed to understand the employee's tax position in order to make fleet policy decisions their employees will accept.

347 Published by Eyelevel Books in association with ALD Automotive and KPMG.

THE EMPLOYER'S TAX POSITION

17.1.1 MOTOR EXPENSES

Typically, your company can obtain corporation tax relief on motoring expenses as it incurs them. This includes motor insurance, road tax, servicing, maintenance and repair costs.

Tax relief for motoring expenses is given on the normal accounting basis. The expenditure has to be allocated to the period to which it relates and it is dealt with on an 'accruals' rather than a 'paid' basis.

Hence if a motor insurance premium relates to the year commencing 1 December and the company has a 31 December year-end and the bill has not been paid by that date, one twelfth of the premium will be allowable for corporation tax (or income tax for a partnership or sole trader) regardless of the fact that the premium has yet to be paid.

17.1.2 CAPITAL ALLOWANCES

BACKGROUND

Companies pay corporation tax on their profits. However, before applying this year's corporation tax rate to this year's profits to determine the corporation tax liability, some adjustments need to be made. The one that concerns us here is the adjustment for depreciation.

Which takes us to the question; what is depreciation?

Depreciation can be defined as the amount of the value of an asset (in this case a vehicle) that has been used up in a particular period. An example may help:

> You buy a car on the first day of the company's financial year for £15,000 and plan to keep it for three years.
>
> You expect that at the end of the third year, you will sell it for £6,000.

If you put the car in your books at £15,000 and simply do nothing for three years you will show a loss in your books ('depreciation') of £9,000 on sale.

This does not feel comfortable or right. This is mainly because, in the interim, you will have shown two years of profits that have not reflected the fact that the vehicle was in use and that you 'used up' part of the vehicle's value in creating that profit.

So clearly you need to show that you used up some of the vehicle's value in years one and two (or, in accounting parlance, you need to 'provide for depreciation' in these years). The question is, how much?

One approach would be to say that you expect to 'lose' £9,000 of value over three years so you should set aside £3,000 each year. Nice and simple.

Another approach would be to say that the vehicle's market value will be £11,000 at the end of year one, £8,500 at the end of year two and £6,000 at the end of year three so you should set aside £4,000, £2,500 and £2,500 respectively.

There are other amounts that could be proposed but we need not go into these here. The key point is that if companies were allowed to deduct depreciation from their profits before their tax liability was calculated, it would mean they would have a hand in determining their own tax liabilities. Parliament doesn't like the idea that every company could adopt different depreciation policies and could therefore arrive at different amounts of tax payable. So they do not allow companies to include any depreciation whatsoever in their tax calculations.

Therefore, if depreciation has been provided in your company's accounts in arriving at the year's profit, it has to be added back to the profits before the corporation tax liability is calculated. Instead, HM Revenue and Customs allows you to provide for depreciation for tax purposes using a standard method of depreciation that is called 'capital allowances'.

Capital allowances are deducted from profits before arriving at taxable profit, rather than depreciation.

Capital allowances were first introduced in the *Income Tax Act 1945*. Successive governments have used them to encourage investment in manufacturing industry and today the government uses them to encourage companies to reduce the emissions of their company car fleets.

For capital allowances purposes[348] a car is defined as a mechanically propelled vehicle except a vehicle:

- constructed in such a way that it is primarily suited for transporting goods of any sort, or
- of a type which is not commonly used as a private vehicle and is not suitable for use as a private vehicle.

There are a number of vehicles that fall outside this definition and that therefore are not treated as cars for capital allowance purposes but may still be treated elsewhere within the plant and machinery allowance rules. They include motorcycles, driving school cars fitted with dual controls, 'blue light' fire and police emergency vehicles, traditional London black taxis and double cab pick-ups capable of carrying a payload of one tonne or more.

Quadbikes are treated as cars for capital allowance purposes because they are not primarily suited for transporting goods and are suitable for use as private vehicles and commonly used as such.

The cost of buying personalised car registrations does not qualify for capital allowances, although the small cost incurred in buying the physical number plate itself does qualify.

FIRST YEAR ALLOWANCES

Most assets can attract one of two types of capital allowance; first year allowances (FYAs) and writing down allowances. It is the first year allowances that are usually altered by government to encourage a particular type of investment. Most cars are specifically excluded from first year allowances, however the government is currently using FYAs to encourage businesses to buy very low emission or electric cars.

A business that has the right to claim first year allowances may decide not to do so, perhaps because they don't have enough profits against which to offset the allowances. In this case, any balance of unclaimed first year allowance should be transferred to the main plant and machinery capital allowance pool where it will attract writing down allowances.

WRITING DOWN ALLOWANCES

Writing down allowances (WDAs) on cars are available to businesses carrying out a trade and incurring capital expenditure. The car must be used for the purpose of the trade.

For a lease of less than five years where the car cannot become the property of the lessee (i.e. where the lessee cannot take title to the car), the owner/lessor and not the lessee should be able to claim capital allowances. Leases normally include a clause that makes it clear when the owner/lessor, rather than the lessee, will claim the capital allowances.

---

348 S268A CAA2001 – note, there is a Glossary at the end of this chapter.

The writing down allowance rules for cars changed in April 2009. As the majority of cars acquired by fleets before that date have already been (or will soon be) defleeted, the old rules are ignored here. They can be found on the HMRC website.[349]

Since April 2009, writing down allowances on cars have been calculated by reference to their CO_2 emissions.

You can find a car's CO_2 emissions on its V5C certificate or at http://carfueldata.dft.gov.uk.

Cars emitting between a lower threshold and 160g/km of CO_2 attract writing down allowances on a reducing balance basis. These cars go into the main plant and machinery capital allowance 'pool', rather than being accounted for as individual assets. Therefore the purchase prices of all cars and most other plant and machinery are accounted for together, with a standard 20% writing down allowance being calculated on the total balance that is in the pool at the year end.

Cars emitting over 160g/km attract a 10% writing down allowance on a reducing balance basis and go into a separate pool.

Writing down allowances are calculated on a 'reducing balance' basis, meaning that the WDA percentage is applied to the original capital cost of the vehicle, then the 'unrelieved balance' is carried forward to the next year, then the WDA percentage is applied to the balance brought forward and so on. So you receive less writing down allowance each year.

When assets are sold the proceeds are deducted from the total balance of the pool, leaving a smaller amount of 'unrelieved balance' on which to calculate writing down allowances at the year end. If the disposal proceeds are greater than the 'unrelieved balance' of the pool then the excess amount will give rise to a taxable 'balancing charge'.

In other words, the fact that the business has sold the car does not necessarily mean it stops receiving writing down allowances. What actually happens depends on the overall behaviour of the pool.

The rules do not include the concept of a 'balancing allowance' or 'balancing charge' on a particular car (unless the vehicle is in a single asset pool because it is being driven by a sole trader or a partner in a partnership and there is an element of private use – see below). If the sale proceeds are less than the unrelieved balance, the car will continue to be depreciated on a reducing balance basis and it will take many years for the business to receive full tax relief on the depreciation. If the car is the only asset in the pool, there would then be a balancing charge or allowance on disposal.

When carrying out leasing calculations – for example, tax-based lease v buy discounted cash flow (DCF) calculations – you need to look at the whole behaviour of the pool to determine the cash flows that will actually arise on a particular car.

---

349 HMRC Manual CA23500 – Plant & Machinery Allowances (PMA): Cars.

Private use by a sole trader or partner

Under the income tax rules, if a car is not used exclusively for business purposes – perhaps because the proprietor of the business or partner in the partnership uses it for commuting – the first year allowance or writing down allowance that may be claimed must be reduced in proportion to the amount of private use.

If the car qualifies for first year allowances the amount claimed in the year of purchase will simply be reduced by the proportion of private use.

If the car qualifies for writing down allowances, it will go into its own single-asset special pool. The initial capital allowance calculation will be identical to the one discussed above but the actual WDA claim will be restricted to the business-use proportion.

This example assumes the car is subject to 50% private use:

	£	Disallowed %	WDA Claim £
Year 1			
Cost	10,000		
WDA 20%	2,000	50%	1,000
Carried forward	8,000		
Year 2			
WDA 20%	1,600	50%	800
Carried forward	6,400		
Year 3			
Sale proceeds	2,900		
Sub-total	3,500		
WDA 20%	700	50%	350
Carried forward	2,800		

Under the corporation tax rules, if a car is not used exclusively for business purposes – perhaps because the company car driver uses it for commuting – the company can still claim the full amount of capital allowance as if there was no private use.

Periods less than or greater than one year

If trade starts or stops part way through an accounting year, the writing down allowances are reduced pro-rata to the period of trade.

If the accounting period for a company is more than twelve months it will be divided for writing down allowance purposes into two accounting periods, each of a maximum of twelve months. However, if the business is a partnership or a sole trader, the accounting period can exceed twelve months for capital allowance purposes and the writing down allowance will be increased pro rata.

ANNUAL INVESTMENT ALLOWANCE

All businesses can claim an Annual Investment Allowance on expenditure on plant, machinery, bikes, vans and trucks – but not cars – up to an annual limit.

VERY EXPENSIVE CARS

As we have seen, capital allowances are a method whereby your business can obtain tax relief for the capital expenditure it incurs on assets that are to be used in the business.

If you buy an expensive car that blatantly exceeds the type of vehicle needed by the business, HM Revenue and Customs will seek to reduce the level of capital allowances. They may argue the choice of car has more to do with the personal choice of the driver (usually the owner of the business) than the needs of the business itself. They have case law to support this approach.[350]

In determining whether to allow the business to claim full capital allowances on such a vehicle, HMRC will consider:

■ the size and type of car;
■ the nature of the business;
■ the extent to which the car is used for business purposes;
■ the relationship between the cost of the car and the turnover of the business.

A very expensive car that is bought 'on the business' but rarely used for the purposes of the business is likely to be denied full capital allowances. On the other hand, if the same vehicle is used for a substantial level of business mileage you are likely to be granted full capital allowances without restriction.

17.1.3 IF THE EMPLOYER LEASES A VEHICLE

CARS

As with other motoring expenses,[351] tax relief on contract hire and operating lease rentals is given on the 'accruals basis'.

Many leases require that you make a lump sum payment on inception of the contract. This protects the lessor against your default. Rather than allowing you tax relief on the lump sum payment when it is paid, HM Revenue and Customs requires that for tax purposes the lease rentals should be spread evenly over the period of the lease. This will normally match your accounting treatment.

---

350 G H Chambers (Northiam Farms) Ltd vs Watmough, 36TC711
351 See 17.1.1.

The Revenue published *Statement of Practice 3 (SP3/91)* in 1991. This statutory provision says that when determining how tax relief will be given for finance lease rentals, uneven rentals must be spread evenly over the period of the lease and then split into interest and capital repayment elements. To calculate the interest element you may use the Rule of 78, the actuarial method or, for small leases, the straight-line method.[352]

If you use the Rule of 78 or the actuarial method, interest costs will be higher in the earlier part of the lease, so you will receive more tax relief on interest in this period.

Significant corporation tax changes[353] for leased vehicles came into effect for limited companies from 1 April 2009 (6 April 2009 for sole traders or partnerships).[354] Under the new rules, where a company car's CO_2 emissions exceed 160g/km, 15% of the lease rental is disallowed. Below this threshold the rental is fully tax-deductible.

If the lessee is unable to recover input VAT in full (perhaps because they are an insurance company or bank and are partially-exempt for VAT purposes[355]), the 15% restriction will apply to the total cost they incur, including any irrecoverable VAT.

Maintenance expenditure included in the rental is always fully tax-deductible so long as it is shown separately on the rental agreement.

It is not unusual for there to be a chain of leases between the owner of a vehicle and the end-user that actually drives and operates the car. For example, a bank may lease a car to a contract hire company that then leases it on to a company for use as a company car. In these situations, the 15% restriction only applies to the last lease in the chain and the rental is fully tax-deductible for any intermediate parties.

If a daily hire (car rental) company leases a car from a lessor and hires it out on short term hire, the rental paid to that lessor is fully tax-deductible.

If a lessee hires a car for a short period (not more than 45 days) for use in their own business, the rental they pay is fully tax deductible.

These rules apply to all types of leased car but don't apply to electric cars or to any car first registered before 1 March 2001.[356]

If a leased car is off the road (perhaps because of an accident) and the lessor provides a replacement for a period, the replacement is treated as if it was the lessee's main car when determining whether the 15% restriction should apply. So, for example, if the lessee's main car has CO_2 emissions at a level where the rent would be fully tax-deductible and replaces the car for a short period with a car that

---

352 See 6.5.2 and 8.4
353 ITTOIA 2005/S48, CTA 2009/ S56 and 1251 and ICTA 1988/S76ZN
354 The old rules – based on the 'half the excess' rule – are ignored in this book.
355 See 17.1.4
356 ITTOIA 2005 / S48 & CTA 2009/S56

has emissions where only 85% of the rent would normally be tax-deductible, the 15% restriction will not apply and the lease rentals will continue to be fully tax-deductible.[357]

The legislation contains anti-avoidance provisions to ensure that lessees do not deliberately hire cars in 'creative' ways to try to avoid the 15% restriction.[358]

MOTOR CYCLES

The rental payable on any motorcycle[359] leased after 1 April 2009 (by companies) or 6 April 2009 (by sole traders and partnerships) is fully tax deductible.

17.1.4 VAT

VAT ON PURCHASE AND SALE OF VEHICLES[360]

For VAT purposes a car is a motor vehicle:

- with more than three wheels; *and*
- is of a kind normally used on the roads; *and*
- is built or adapted for the carriage of passengers; *or*
- has rear roofed accommodation and side windows.

This excludes caravans, ambulances, mobile shops, breakdown recovery vehicles, prison vans, vehicles designed to carry only one or more than 12 people in total, and vehicles weighing 3 tonnes or more (unladen) or with a payload capacity of 1 tonne or more of cargo.

VAT QUALIFYING AND VAT BLOCKED CARS

If you buy a car for business use you can recover 100% of the VAT paid on the purchase (the input VAT) so long as the vehicle is not available for private use. For this purpose, 'private use' includes any arrangement whereby the vehicle could be used for commuting or could be parked at home overnight.

A car on which VAT has been so recovered is described as a 'VAT qualifying' car. A car on which recovery has been 'blocked' is subsequently described as a 'VAT non-qualifying' car. Once a car has become non-qualifying it retains this status forever.

When a VAT qualifying car is sold the vendor has to charge VAT (output tax) on the sale price and has to account for this to HM Revenue and Customs.

Buyers do not pay more for VAT qualifying cars so sellers have to pay part of the gross selling price of the car to HMRC.

---

357 ITTOIA 2005/ S50A (8) and CTA 2009 / S 58A (8)

358 ITTOIA/S 50A (5) & CTA 2009/ S 58A (5)

359 Definition: s185 (1) Road Traffic Act 1988

360 The starting point for anyone wanting clarification on the VAT rules is 'The VAT Guide' Notice 700 issued by HM Revenue and Customs.

In practice, input VAT can only be recovered on the purchase of a car when the primary use of the vehicle is:

■ for self-drive hire; *or*

■ as a taxi; *or*

■ for driving instruction; *or*

■ when it is used exclusively for business purposes, for example by a leasing company or by a corporate fleet as a pool car. A pool car is one that is not allocated to any individual and is normally kept at the company's place of business rather than an employee's home (i.e. it is unavailable for private use).

In any other circumstances the car will be treated as available for private purposes and therefore VAT incurred on its purchase cannot be recovered (i.e. it is 'blocked'). Typically most company cars are VAT blocked.

You cannot recover VAT on the cost of accessories when they are supplied as part of a single supply of a VAT blocked car, even if these accessories are invoiced separately.

When you sell a car on which you have incurred VAT that you have been unable to recover (because it was 'blocked' from recovery), the sale proceeds will be exempt for VAT purposes and any VAT you incurred on collection, delivery, auction fees, smart repairs or other disposal costs will not be recoverable.

If you lease or purchase a car where there is to be no private use (i.e. a car where the VAT incurred on the purchase is recoverable) and you receive a volume related bonus or a payment direct from the manufacturer or dealer, the credit note accompanying the bonus will reduce the amount of input VAT you can recover on the purchase. Input VAT recovery will be reduced by the VAT on the bonus received. Generally this will only apply to pool cars bought by large fleets, or cars bought by rental or leasing companies.

It sometimes happens that there is a change in the use of a VAT qualifying car and it starts to be used for private mileage. If this happens you must account for output VAT as soon as the change of use occurs by making a 'self supply charge'. The output VAT on this 'self-supply' charge has to be calculated on the then-current market value of the car. Even though output tax has been accounted for the recovery of the input tax is blocked. This situation might arise, for example, when you buy a pool car then subsequently issue it to a driver as their company car and allow them private use. The car then becomes a VAT non-qualifying car.

Partial exemption

VAT exempt sales can cause a nasty problem for companies - partial exemption.

Trading companies with a turnover exceeding the VAT registration threshold, selling most types of goods and services, have to charge output VAT on their sales and are able to recover all of the input tax they pay when buying goods and services. The costs the company incurs (and on which VAT is incurred) are 'used' entirely in making onward taxable supplies.

Partly VAT-exempt companies cannot recover all of the input VAT on their purchases because not all of their onward supplies are taxable. Instead, partially exempt business can only recover a proportion of VAT incurred on overheads (often referred to as residual costs) and those costs that can be wholly and directly linked to making taxable onward supplies.

The standard method for determining the recoverable proportion of VAT on overheads is to:

- add together the total standard, reduced rate and zero-rated sales; and
- divide the result by total sales (excluding certain categories of non-business and incidental sales income); then
- multiply the result by 100.

This is an example of the 'standard' partial exemption method:

> A fleet operator has VAT exempt insurance commission income of £4 million and taxable leasing income of £10 million.
>
> It buys goods and services which cannot be 'directly attributed' to the taxable or exempt sales (e.g. it pays general overheads) totalling £2 million per year on which it pays VAT.
>
> The VAT incurred on these 'non-attributable' costs can only be recovered in the same proportion as the proportion of the taxable to total income of the business, in this case:
> 10,000,000 ÷ 14,000,000 x 100 = 72%.

Partial exemption is a complex area of VAT. For further details, a good starting point is to refer to HMRC Reference: Notice 706 'Partial Exemption'.

VANS

If you buy a van for business use, the input VAT on purchase is fully recoverable.

When you sell a van on which VAT has been recovered, VAT must be charged on the full selling price. The agreed sale price for cars and vans is a gross (VAT inclusive) value.

Most businesses are unable to recover the input VAT they incur when buying a car but can reclaim the input VAT on commercial vehicles. Legislation in 1992 defined the dividing line between cars and commercial vehicles for VAT purposes.[361] Sometimes it is difficult to ascertain whether a van should be treated as a car or a commercial vehicle, so HMRC has issued guidance on the dividing line between cars and vans.[362]

Most vans are clearly commercial vehicles for VAT purposes, in that they have metal side panels behind the front seats, a load area that is unsuitable for carrying

---

361 Value Added Tax (Cars) Order 1992

362 www.hmrc.gov.uk/VAT/sectors/motors/what-is-car.htm

passengers and no rear seats. However, some vehicles – '**car-derived vans**' – look like cars but they have been converted into vans. For example their rear seats have been removed, a load area has been created and the rear windows have been blocked out.

HMRC will view such a vehicle as a van if, after conversion, it meets their technical specification of a van, can function as a commercial vehicle (though just removing the rear seat would not be adequate) and the load space is unsuitable for carrying passengers.

If you are uncertain whether you can recover VAT on a car-derived van, you should ask the supplier to confirm that the vehicle meets HMRC's technical criteria. If the car-derived van was first registered before 1 October 2003 it is unlikely that it will satisfy all the criteria set out in HMRC's guidance, but if it looks like a car-derived van as set out above HMRC will allow the vehicle to be treated as a van for VAT purposes. The HMRC website contains a list of 'borderline' vehicles where there might otherwise be some doubt and shows whether HMRC categorises these as cars or vans for VAT purposes.

HMRC also issues guidance on the VAT treatment of '**combination vans**'. These look like vans but have (or can have) rear passenger seats fitted. They are treated as cars for VAT purposes unless:

- they have a payload of more than one tonne; *or*

- the load area after the fitting of rear seats is larger than the passenger area so that the load area is large enough for the predominant use of the vehicle to be the carriage of goods.

Light commercial vehicles with double-cabs (four-door pick-up trucks) have a second row of seats, can seat four passengers and the driver and have an uncovered area behind the cab. They are suitable for private use but that doesn't automatically mean they are taxed the same way as company cars. Indeed there was initially much discussion about whether these were cars or vans for income tax and VAT purposes.

HMRC acknowledge that these vehicles present them with a challenge when establishing the predominant purpose of construction because on the surface many double-cabs appear to be equally suited to convey passengers or goods. Hence HMRC cannot come up with a single categorisation for all double cab pick-ups or give a blanket ruling on any particular model, as the standard vehicle may have been adapted in the factory, by the dealer or after purchase. So each case depends on the facts and the exact specification of the vehicle.

Generally, if a double cab pick-up has a payload of 1 tonne (1,000kg) or more it is accepted as a van for VAT and also for benefit in kind tax purposes. Payload means gross vehicle weight (or design weight) less unoccupied kerb weight. (Care is needed when looking at manufacturers' brochures as they sometimes define payload differently).

Under a separate agreement between HMRC and the Society of Motor Manufacturers and Traders (SMMT), a hard top consisting of metal, fibre glass or similar material, with or without windows, is deemed to weigh 45kg. Under this agreement, the weight of all other optional accessories is disregarded. This approach applies for both VAT and benefit in kind tax purposes.

Potential purchasers can obtain advice about the payload of a particular model from the manufacturer or dealer.

VAT ON MOTOR EXPENSES[363]

VAT is fully recoverable on any vehicle running costs paid by a business, including servicing, repair, maintenance and petrol, even if there has been some private use.

If you reimburse your employees for fuel costs (and other expenses) they have incurred for business purposes, you can recover the input tax paid so long as you reimburse them no more than the actual business-related expenditure they incurred. If they don't buy the fuel using a fuel card, debit card or credit card provided by their employer – which create a direct contractual relationship between the employer and the supplier – you will need to retain invoices or receipts covering the cost of all of the fuel that has been bought for business purposes.

HMRC accepts that there may be a mismatch between the business fuel reimbursement claimed by an employee in one month and the actual petrol receipts for that month, because, for example, the driver may have filled up the tank just before the month end. But they do expect that where reimbursement claims are made, these will be supported by receipts dated before the business mileage was actually driven. Where a company does not issue fuel cards, the best option is probably to ask the driver to submit all their fuel receipts, covering both business and private mileage, because this will ensure that there are sufficient invoices to cover all business mileage in the period.

FREE PRIVATE FUEL

If your business pays for the fuel for a vehicle you can recover the input VAT in full so long as there is no private use of the vehicles. However, if there is any private use you can only recover the business element of the total input VAT you pay.

To calculate the amount of input tax you can recover you may choose to keep detailed records of the business and private mileage driven, calculate the percentage of business mileage and recover that proportion of the total input tax you have paid on the fuel.

Alternatively, if you prefer, you may recover all of the input tax and account to HMRC for output VAT on the fuel as if it was being sold to the employee. Rather than perform any complex calculations splitting the total mileage between business and private, this charge is based on a scale related to the vehicle's CO_2

---

363 See HM Revenue and Customs VAT Notice 700/64

emissions.[364] The charge is paid on each VAT return and the amount payable depends on whether the company submits a VAT return annually, quarterly or monthly.

Dual fuel vehicles that can operate on, for example, LPG and petrol, have two published CO_2 emission figures. In this case the lower one should be used.

If all of the fuel is used for business purposes the scale charge will not apply.

As fuel is normally a general overhead cost of the business, if your business is 'partially exempt', only a proportion of the VAT incurred on fuel will be recoverable as input tax. However, the full scale charge (and output tax thereon) is payable, so the irrecoverable element of the VAT incurred on fuel will be a cost to the business.

As long as the VAT scale charges are applied, then, subject to the partial exemption comments above, you can recover 100% of the VAT paid on the purchase of vehicle fuel, without adjusting for any private use.

Even though the scale charge simplifies the VAT calculation you must still record details of the cars for which free or cheap fuel has been supplied, the CO_2 emissions of those cars and the type of fuel they use (petrol, diesel, etc).

MILEAGE ALLOWANCE PAYMENTS

If you pay a mileage allowance to an employee for the business miles they drive, you can recover part of this as input VAT so long as you only pay a 'reasonable amount'. For this purpose, the motoring cost tables published by motoring organisations are considered reasonable.

You need to keep records to substantiate this claim, including details of the vehicle, engine size, miles travelled and how you calculated the VAT recovery.

To simplify this calculation you can use the advisory fuel rates published by HM Revenue and Customs.[365]

VAT ON FINANCE PAYMENTS

No VAT is charged on the instalments payable under hire purchase, lease purchase, contract purchase or conditional sale agreements. This is because the 'supply' of the vehicle for VAT purposes occurs at the time when the contract is entered into. The supplier issues a VAT invoice at the start of the agreement to account for output tax on the whole value of the goods. The purchaser recovers the VAT on this invoice (subject to the partial exemption and 'blocking' rules already discussed), rather than during the period of the agreement when the instalments are actually paid.

If the car is returned to the supplier under a hire purchase, lease purchase, contract purchase, conditional sale or PCP arrangement the original price the car was sold

---

364 See *Company Car and Van Tax* for the current scale of charges.
365 See 17.2.7.

for is adjusted for VAT purposes by the amount credited to the customer's account (generally the outstanding capital value on the agreement).

When this happens, the supplier will issue a credit note to the customer for this price adjustment. If the customer was able to recover the VAT incurred on the original purchase of the car, the credit note will result in an adjustment to the customer's input VAT recovery, giving rise to a repayment of the VAT on the credit note to HMRC. Where the VAT was blocked from recovery for the customer, the credit note is also effectively 'blocked' in that there is no need to make a corresponding adjustment to the level of input VAT recovered on the agreement.

All VAT registered lessors must charge output VAT on their lease rentals and must show whether the car is VAT qualifying. This includes finance lease, contract hire, operating lease and personal contract hire agreements.

If you are a VAT-registered lessee the input VAT you pay on the cars you hire on contract hire, operating lease or finance lease is fully recoverable so long as there is no private use.

If there is any element of private use you can recover only 50% of the input VAT on the lease rental and any excess mileage charges relating to the supply of the leased vehicle (though see below regarding maintenance). This amount of recoverable VAT will be shown on the leasing company's invoices for qualifying cars.

If you hire a car to temporarily replace a company car that is off the road, you can only recover 50% of the input tax shown on the rental. However, if you take cars on daily rental for other reasons you can recover 100% of the input VAT so long as the rental period does not exceed ten days.

If you lease a van you can recover the input VAT payable on the rentals in full: the 50% disallowance only applies to cars.

If your contract hire agreement contains a maintenance package covering servicing, repairs, maintenance etc, you can fully recover the input tax on this element of the rental regardless of whether there is any private use. For this reason all contract hire companies show their clients how the contract hire rental splits between the maintenance and finance elements. The contract hire company's profit margin, overhead recovery and excess mileage charges have to be split between these elements pro rata.

Motor insurances, including creditor insurance and gap insurance, are subject to insurance premium tax (IPT), not VAT. IPT is not recoverable for VAT purposes but is tax deductible for corporation tax purposes.

If a lease or contract hire agreement is terminated early, the leasing company has two options. If it wishes it can treat any early termination payment and rebate of rental as being fully taxable, in which case it will normally offset one against the other and raise a VAT invoice for the net amount. If this results in a charge to the lessee the 50% VAT block will not apply. However, if the rebate of rentals exceeds the termination amount chargeable and the lease had been the subject of a 50% VAT block, the lessee needs to account in their VAT return for 50% of the VAT on the credit note.

Alternatively, if it prefers, the leasing company can regard any early termination payment and rebate of rental as being totally outside the scope of VAT.

No VAT charge arises on any payment made by an employee for the private use of a company car where the employer has suffered a 50% input VAT restriction or where input VAT recovery was denied on the purchase of the car. If the employer recovered VAT on the purchase of the vehicle, or recovered 100% of the VAT on the lease rental, it follows that there is no private use.

However, if the use of the vehicle changes and the employee starts to be charged for private use, the employer has to account for output VAT on the purchase price of the car (if bought) or must stop recovering 50% of the input VAT on the rental (if leased).

17.1.5 CLASS 1A NATIONAL INSURANCE CONTRIBUTIONS

An employee who receives a company car is taxed on the 'cash equivalent value' of the car.[366] The employer must pay Class 1A national insurance contributions on these benefits, taking into account the car's CO_2 emissions, the fact that it may not be available for the whole year and the other adjustments described in 17.2.1.

Class 1A contributions are also payable if the employee receives free fuel and is taxed on the fuel scale charges.[367]

17.1.6 ROAD FUEL DUTY

Road fuel duty has to be reviewed annually by the government as it is an 'ad valorem' tax. That is, the value is fixed in pence per litre rather than as a percentage of sale prices. If inflation were to soar away the government would still collect a fixed percentage (the standard VAT percentage) of the value of most sales through VAT. But its tax–take on road fuel duty would remain the same in pence per litre unless it increased it annually.

17.2 THE EMPLOYEE'S TAX POSITION

17.2.1 CARBON DIOXIDE BASED CAR BENEFIT TAX

Car benefit tax is payable by directors or employees earning over £8,500 (including the value of any benefits-in-kind) who drive company cars that are made available for their private use so long as there is no transfer of ownership of the vehicle to the employee.

For the tax to arise the car has to be made available 'by reason of their employment' so it does not matter if the car is owned, leased or supplied by someone else.

---

366 See 17.2.1.
367 See 17.2.8.

The tax also applies if the car is made available to a member of the employee's family or household, including their spouse, parents, children (and their children's spouses) and guests.

If the car is simply given to the employee (i.e. there is a transfer of ownership) as a gift or sold to them, no car benefit arises. It is this provision for the transfer of ownership in the tax law that Employee Car Ownership Schemes[368] rely on. If the car is a gift or is sold at undervalue the employee will be taxed on the 'money's worth' they receive, which usually means the second hand market value less any amount they pay for the car.

Car benefit tax is payable in full even if the employee part-owns the car.

No car benefit tax arises if the employee is specifically prohibited from using (and does not use) the car for private purposes or the car is a pool car (the rules for pool cars are explained below).

There is also no charge to tax if the employee is employed in the emergency services (police, fire, fire and rescue, ambulance or paramedic) and the car or van is an emergency services vehicle used for emergency response and it is fitted with a blue flashing light (or the only reason why it isn't fitted with one is to protect the security of the driver). To be exempt from car benefit tax even when using the car for private mileage, the employee must be liable to respond to emergencies as part of their normal duties and must not use the car privately except when commuting or on call (and even then the vehicle must not be used beyond the locality of the employee's home and work).

The purpose of this legislation[369] is to improve emergency vehicle response times rather than confer a benefit on public sector employees.

No charge arises if any car is being driven by a disabled employee and:

■ it has been adapted for the employee's special needs (or it is an automatic and their disabilities do not allow them to drive any other car); and

■ the employee is prohibited for using the car for any purpose other than:

■ their business travel; or

  ◆ ordinary commuting; or

  ◆ travel between any two places that is for practical purposes substantially ordinary commuting; or

  ◆ travel to a place of training; and

■ the car has only been used in accordance with these provisions.

---

368 See 17.2.13.

369 S248A ITEPA 2003

THE CASH EQUIVALENT

The taxable benefit of a company car is calculated by reference to the 'cash equivalent'. This is derived by multiplying its list price (including VAT, delivery costs and all extras fitted before the vehicle is delivered) by an 'appropriate percentage' which relates to the CO_2 emission level of the car.

To determine the appropriate percentage of list price for a specific vehicle the exact CO_2 figure of the vehicle should be rounded down to the nearest 5g/km.

Broadly, the steps to be followed are: [370]

1. Find the price of the car. This is normally the list price including any charges for delivery and relevant taxes (such as VAT or VED). If the car does not have a list price, perhaps because it is a special import or left hand drive, use the price the manufacturer, distributor or importer might reasonably have set for the car.

2. Add the list price of any accessories initially supplied with the car, even if these were bought for less than list price or have subsequently been removed from the car. Also add the full value of any accessories that were subsequently fitted to the car, for each year or part year that the accessory was available to the employee, even if it was removed part way through the year. There is no need to include accessories with a value of under £100. If an accessory is replaced like for like with another accessory, it is treated as if there was no replacement. But if it is replaced by an accessory of superior quality (e.g. a better sound system), add the value of the new item and deduct the value of the old one.

3. Make any required deductions for capital contributions by the employee (max. £5,000), as shown in Capital Contribution below.

4. Make an adjustment if a car is a classic car. Classic cars tend to have a market price that exceeds their original purchase price, so you need to make an adjustment (see below) for a classic car. For the purposes of this clause a classic car is one that is more than 15 years old, worth more than £15,000 at the end of the tax year and has a market value higher than the amount that would otherwise be arrived at after step 2, above. The market value is defined[371] as the price the car might reasonably have been expected to fetch on a sale in the open market on the last day of the tax year (or the last day it was available to the employee).

5. Find the appropriate percentage for the car, based on the car's CO_2 emissions (rounded down to the nearest 0 or 5g/km), as shown on the HMRC website.

6. Multiply the figure after Step 4 by the appropriate percentage at Step 5.

7. Make any required deduction for periods when the car was unavailable for at least 30 consecutive days in the tax year. (See detail on unavailability below).

8. And finally, make any required deduction for payments made by the employee for private use of the car.

---

370 S121-124 ITEPA 2003

371 S147 ITEPA 2003

Example:

List price of the car	£22,000
List price of the accessories	£2,000
Capital contribution	£(4,000)
Classic car adjustment	0
Sub-total	£20,000
Appropriate percentage	25%
Car benefit	£5,000
Car unavailable for half of the year; £5,000 x 50%	£(2,500)
Paid for private use; 6 months @ £30 per month	£(180)
Car benefit subject to tax at marginal rate	£2,320

EMISSIONS-BASED 'APPROPRIATE PERCENTAGE'

Since 1 January 1998 every new car sold in the UK has had an approved CO_2 emission figure for tax purposes. This book ignores the tax rules that applied before April 2002, which were based on engine size and business mileage rather than emissions. The published CO_2 figure is derived during the UK or EU Type Approval process, is set for the car's life and is not altered even if the car is modified or accessories are added.

You can obtain the appropriate percentage to use in car benefit calculations from the HMRC website.

The government wants to encourage the use of road fuel gas cars (LPG and CNG) so instead of using the list price of a road fuel gas in step 1 above you may use the manufacturer's list price for the equivalent petrol-engined car, which will normally be lower. In addition, if a petrol-engined car is converted to run on gas, the conversion cost should be ignored when calculating the step 1 price.

DIESEL CARS

A 3% supplement is added to the percentage of list price if the vehicle is diesel powered. From 2011-12 this applies to all diesel cars, including those that comply with Euro IV emission standards. This reflects government concerns about the fact that diesel fuel contains 'particulates', small solid soot-like particles that are deposited locally when diesel is burned. While these do not affect the ozone layer and are not greenhouse gases, they may be carcinogenic and they do affect local air quality.

OTHER FUEL TYPES

Vehicles of all other fuel types (hybrid, bi-fuel, LPG and bioethanol) receive the same appropriate percentage figure as a petrol vehicle that has the same level of emissions (i.e. there is no difference).

CLASSIC CARS

To determine the value of a classic car in step 4, above, you should determine a reasonable open market valuation of the car at the end of the year (or the last date the car was available to the employee) and deduct any capital contributions made by the employee.

If a car does not have an approved CO_2 figure (perhaps it was a grey import), the following percentages apply in step 5 above for cars first registered after 1 January 1998.

Engine size	Appropriate %
≤1400	15%
>1400 and ≤2000	25%
>2000	35%

CPAITAL CONTRIBUTION

If the employee makes a contribution of up to £5,000 towards the purchase price of the car (a 'capital contribution') this can be deducted from the list price before starting to calculate the car benefit tax, for the year the capital contribution was made and for subsequent years. A capital contribution can only relate to one car and cannot be carried forward to the employee's next car.

If an employee's company car is given to another employee the recipient doesn't derive any tax benefit from the original capital contribution.

The contribution from the employee to the employer must meet certain tests before any capital contribution deduction can be allowed. If the payment is simply a loan to be returned to the employee in full on the sale of the car, or is a payment for the private use of the car, it cannot be deducted from the list price for car benefit tax purposes.

If the employee forfeits the £5,000 after it has been paid, or only receives back a proportion of it on sale of the vehicle (no more than the proportion that the sale proceeds represents compared with list price), the capital contribution can be deducted from list price.

DISABLED DRIVERS

If a disabled driver needs an automatic transmission car you can use the cost of an equivalent manual car in step 1 if it is less than the cost of the automatic. 'Equivalent' here means that the manual car must have been registered around the same time as the automatic car and must be the closest variant available. This concession is only available if the driver holds a blue disabled badge.

In step 2 you can also ignore the cost of any accessories, adaptations or disability equipment that needed to be fitted to allow the employee to use the car.

If the CO_2 emissions of the equivalent manual car were lower than the emissions of the automatic car, you can use the emission level of the manual car in step 5 above.

The normal rule is that if a driver is given a company car and is prohibited from driving any private mileage (including commuting) for the whole tax year, they are exempt from car benefit tax. However, if the driver is disabled and the car has been specially adapted to their needs, the legislation[372] exempts them from car benefit tax even if they use the car for regular commuting, provided there is no additional private use.

LIST PRICE

When calculating the cash equivalent value of the car you should use the list price published by the manufacturer on the day before the car was first registered. The inspector of taxes checks your returns against Glass's Guide to check their accuracy.

Then you must add the cost of delivery, VAT, number plates and accessories fitted when new, but not VED or the initial registration fee. It does not matter whether you bought the vehicle new or secondhand.

If you subsequently attach an accessory costing more than £100, this increases the list price to be used when calculating the cash equivalent from that year onwards.

CAR NOT AVAILABLE

If the company car is not available to the employee (or his family or household) for a minimum of 30 consecutive days, car benefit tax can be reduced pro-rata on a time basis.[373]

For this purpose, 'unavailable' includes the car being off the road as a result of a breakdown or accident, the car being inaccessible to the employee, the keys not being available and so on. However, if it is just parked at home because the driver is unable to drive or is abroad for several weeks, the car is still deemed to be 'available' because in these cases it is the driver who is unavailable.

HMRC won't accept that the car is unavailable if the driver is banned from driving or ill, or if the car has no road tax, MOT or car insurance. However, if the employer withdraws the car because of one of these reasons, HMRC will accept that the car is genuinely unavailable.

If the company car is not available and the employee is provided with a replacement, there will be no extra car benefit tax payable unless the replacement car is materially superior to the regular car in quality or list price. However, if the main intention was not to provide a superior car (e.g., perhaps that was the only car available), no extra car benefit tax will be payable.

When claiming a reduction in car benefit tax because a car is unavailable you have to supply HMRC with evidence that the car was unavailable.

372 S247 ITEPA 2003
373 S143 ITEPA 2003

EMPLOYEE PRIVATE USE CONTRIBUTIONS

If the employee is required to make payments to the company in consideration of being allowed to use the vehicle privately (a private use contribution) their tax liability will be reduced by the amount of this payment, pound for pound.[374] However, they must have been required to pay this as a condition of the car being made available and they must actually have made the payment. If the employer charges the employee VAT on these contributions, this can be deducted too.

If the amount the employee actually pays exceeds the amount of the chargeable benefit, no car benefit charge will arise. Otherwise the car benefit charge is reduced by the amount actually paid.

If the employee pays for specific items such as petrol or insurance, these don't qualify as deductions even if the employer requires the employee to pay these amounts.

If you give a cash refund to an employee for taking a car of lower value than they were entitled to under your fleet policy, the employee has to pay income tax on the refund at their marginal rate and your business can receive tax relief on the payment. National insurance is payable by both employer and employee as if this was simply an extra salary payment.

TRANSACTIONS AT UNDERVALUE

If the employee buys a car from their employer for less than its market value, the difference between the price paid and the market value is taxable at the employee's marginal rate of tax.

NO PRIVATE USE

If an employee uses a company vehicle for business use only - that is, they do not drive any private mileage, use it for commuting or park it at home overnight - they are not liable for car benefit tax.

However, if the vehicle is 'available for private use' a tax charge will arise – whether or not the employee actually uses the vehicle.

POOL CARS AND VANS

If an employee drives a pool car or pool van there is no benefit-in-kind charge.[375]

HM Revenue and Customs is very keen to ensure that employees do not use pool cars and vans as their regular company vehicles in order to avoid tax. Therefore, to be treated as a pool car or van the vehicle has to be:

- available by reason of employment to more than one driver;
- actually used by more than one driver; *and*
- it must not 'normally' be kept overnight at one employee's home.

374 S144 ITEPA 2003
375 S167/8 ITEPA 2003

Some modest private use is allowed if it is 'incidental' to the business use. An example would be if the car or van were to be taken home to allow an early start on a business trip, though if this happens frequently it would be treated as a company car or van.

IF CARS ARE SHARED BY SEVERAL DRIVERS

In some organisations a few employees share the use of one car. The legislation[376] sets out rules to ensure that each employee only pays tax on their usage of the vehicle.

In this case you need to calculate the cash equivalent of the car as if each of the drivers had exclusive use and then reduce this on a 'just and reasonable' basis. You can exclude lower paid workers (earning under £8,500 p.a.) from these calculations, i.e. you can assume they don't exist. You can similarly exclude directors with low pay if they do not own or control directly or indirectly a material interest in the shares of the company or if the company doesn't exist to trade and make a profit (e.g. it exists for charitable purposes).

The law is silent on how to do the calculations. HMRC will accept any split of the benefit agreed between the employer and the employees, so long as it does not artificially reduce the overall amount of tax payable. One logical way to split the benefit is pro-rata to the number of days when each employee was the sole or main driver or took the car home overnight.

If the employer pays for fuel and allows the vehicle to be used by the drivers for private use (including commuting), the employees share should the tax liability for the free fuel in the same proportions as they share the car benefit liability.

IF MANY CARS ARE DRIVEN BY ONE DRIVER

If you are in the motor industry your employees may drive many cars every year. In this situation it could be incredibly burdensome for employees to log every time they use a car for private mileage.

Nonetheless, if a driver wishes to log the private use of all of the cars they have driven – detailing the type of car, the list price, the dates, the CO_2 emissions of those cars, etc. – they are permitted to do so.

As an alternative, if the employer is in the business of motor manufacturing, new or used car sales, car leasing, daily hire or fleet operations they are permitted to use an 'averaging' method to simplify the calculation of the benefit charge. This involves allocating an employee to a 'group' according to the cars that were available to that group for a sample period of the year - a night of the employer's choice during the period 17-31 January in the previous tax year. The car benefit is based on the average list price and CO_2 emissions of a notional car in that group.

---

376 S148 ITEPA 2003

The steps to calculate a group average are:
1. Identify the cars to be averaged.
2. Separate the cars into groups (e.g. local, regional or national).
3. Calculate the average price of the notional car in each group.
4. Calculate the average CO_2 emissions and, therefore, appropriate percentage of the notional car in each group.
5. Determine the benefit charge for the notional car in each group.
6. Identify employees within these arrangements.
7. Allocate these employees to groups.

Each employee is therefore taxed according to the average price and CO_2 levels for the notional car in each group rather than the actual cars they drove.

This approach is only available where employees are allowed to take cars home but aren't allocated a specific vehicle.

The employer is required to retain detailed information on the cars and drivers showing how the averaging calculations were carried out.

Employees can be allocated to one group for a period but if their jobs change they can be moved to another group and pay a different amount of car benefit tax.

Many of the cars being driven by motor industry employees are awaiting sale so it is normal for these to be filled with petrol at the employer's expense. When employees use these for private journeys they must pay tax on the benefit of the free fuel. The taxable fuel benefit is calculated using the appropriate percentage for the notional car, as calculated in the averaging procedure.

If the employer doesn't provide free private fuel they will have to prove to HMRC either that there was no private use or, if there was, that the employee paid for this fuel in full.

DEMONSTRATOR AND COURTESY CARS

If a motor-industry employee takes a car home at night for the specific purpose of taking it to a customer, the whole journey is deemed to be a business journey and no car or fuel benefit arises.

CHAUFFEURS

If an employee is provided with the services of a chauffeur, this expense is a taxable benefit. The employee pays income tax at their marginal rate on the full cost their employer incurred in providing the chauffeur.[377]

WHAT IS A CAR?

For the purposes of the car benefit legislation[378] a car is a mechanically propelled road vehicle that is not a motorcycle or invalid carriage or of a construction

377 P3 Ch 10 and s239 (4 and 5) ITEPA 2003
378 S115(1) ITEPA 2003

primarily suited to be a goods vehicle or not commonly used as a private vehicle and unsuitable to be so used (e.g. a bus). It doesn't matter how the vehicle is actually being used; the key thing is the purpose for which it was constructed.

If a vehicle has side windows behind the driver and passenger doors, or additional seats are (or could be) fitted in the row behind the driver, it is likely to be treated as a car for car benefit purposes.

The tax treatment of vans is discussed in 17.2.4.

Luxury off-road vehicles and MPVs are always treated as cars because they can be used privately and are not designed for carrying goods.

17.2.2 FREE PARKING

If you provide free car parking to your employees at or near the main place of work or as a result of business travel, this is not taxable. However, if you reimburse your employees' private parking costs, both income tax and national insurance contributions are due on these payments.

17.2.3 THE SELF-EMPLOYED

It is important to know whether a person who works for you is employed or self-employed. The 'consultant' who has worked for you full time for the last two years and whose invoices have been submitted monthly may say they are self-employed but they may well be your employee for legal and tax purposes.

If you classify them incorrectly you will be liable to pay PAYE and national insurance contributions on their income. If you allow them the use of a company car, even only occasionally, you need to be aware of possible tax consequences if their tax status is challenged.

Unfortunately, the dividing line between employment and self-employment is not defined in law, though HM Revenue and Customs' *Employed or Self Employed* publication provides some guidance.

Broadly, a person is likely to be self-employed if they:

- don't have to work a set number of hours;
- can choose when, where and how to do the work;
- can't be moved from task to task;
- aren't paid by the hour, week or month but agree a fixed price regardless of how long the job may take;
- don't receive overtime or bonus payments;
- can sub-contract the work to someone else;
- must use their own tools and equipment;
- do not enjoy employment-type benefits;
- have the risk in their own business;

■ regularly work for a number of different people;

■ can refuse to do particular tasks.

If a person is self-employed none of the company car benefit tax rules applies to them.

17.2.4 TAX ON PRIVATE USE OF VANS

VAN BENEFIT

Benefit in kind tax is payable by a director, or an employee earning more than £8,500 per year, who is provided with the use of a company van (up to 3.5 tonnes) that is available for private use by them or a member of their family or household.[379]

If you provide a company van to an employee it is always treated as being available for private use for tax purposes, unless no private mileage is allowed and none is driven (both tests have to be met). If there is any private use it must be 'insignificant' to avoid the van tax charge.

A van driver who enjoys unrestricted private use of a company van is taxed on a benefit for the use of the van. A taxable amount is added to the employee's salary and taxed at their marginal rate.

If an employee is required to pay a personal contribution to the business for the private use of the van, and actually does pay this, the amount they pay will be deducted from this charge. The payment must have been made because the employee is enjoying private use of the van and not because they decided to upgrade the van above their normal entitlement.

In addition, if the van is only available for part of the year, the charge will be pro-rated.

Unlike the situation with company cars, no tax relief is available if the employee makes a capital contribution.

If a van is a true pool van, no tax will arise on private use. The rules for pool vans are broadly similar to those for pool cars.[380]

When a company car driver takes his or her vehicle home, this is deemed to be private mileage for tax purposes. Most company van drivers take their vans home overnight because they are required to do so for the efficient operation of the business. It would be impractical to require them to drive their private cars to work in order to collect their vans before starting their day's work. Therefore 'commuting' by van drivers is not considered to be private use, and if this is the only non-business mileage they drive they will not be charged any van benefit tax.

Similarly, if a van is deemed to have 'insignificant' private use (defined as 'too small or unimportant to be worth consideration' and if this is the only non-business mileage the employee drives they will not be charged any van benefit tax.

---

379 S114-154 ITEPA 2003
380 See 17.2.1.

VAN FUEL BENEFIT

If an employee is provided with free fuel for the private use of a company van they will be taxed on this benefit. A taxable amount is added to the employee's salary and taxed at their marginal rate. This is payable in addition to the company van tax.

If free fuel is provided for a company van and the employee (and members of their family or household) are prohibited from driving any private mileage – and actually don't drive any – this fuel charge will not arise. For the purpose of this clause you can ignore commuting to work and any insignificant amounts of private use.

The employer is also required to pay Class 1A national insurance on van fuel benefit.

It is good fleet management practice to ensure that the employee's contract of employment sets out the rules for the private use of a company van and to actively ensure that no significant private use takes place.

17.2.5 TAX ON PRIVATE USE OF OTHER FORMS OF COMPANY TRANSPORT

There is no tax payable for the private use of a heavy goods vehicle so long as title in the vehicle is not transferred to the employee and the vehicle is not wholly or mainly used for private purposes. 'Private' here excludes commuting, so tax will be payable if the vehicle is regularly used for commuting, though in practice an employee would need to drive substantial levels of private mileage in an HGV before HMRC would seek to tax this as a benefit in kind.

If an HGV is mainly used for private purposes it will be taxed each year at 20% of the cost of the vehicle (if provided to the driver from new) or its market value as at the date it was first provided as a benefit. If the vehicle is leased to the employer the employee will be taxed on the lease rentals if these exceed 20% of the cost of the HGV. The employee also has to pay tax on any costs incurred by the employer in providing the vehicle.

Similar rules apply to the provision of other forms of transport such as motorbikes and motor vessels. They are taxed at 20% of the cost of the asset or the lease rentals, whichever is more.

17.2.6 HMRC APPROVED MILEAGE ALLOWANCE PAYMENTS (AMAP)

If an employee uses their own car on company business, you can pay them an amount not exceeding the HMRC Approved Mileage Allowance Payment rate without the employee bearing any tax or national insurance liability. The legislation[381] also says that so long as the payment does not exceed the AMAP amount neither the employer not the employee need to report it to HMRC.

If an employer pays a mileage rate that exceeds the AMAP rate, the excess has to be reported on the employee's P11D and will be taxable.

---

381 S230(2) ITEPA 2003

AMAP rates are higher for the first 10,000 business miles and lower thereafter.

The higher amount may be paid NIC-free irrespective of the level of business mileage.

These two rates reflect the fact that some motoring costs are fixed (road tax, insurance, depreciation, etc.) whereas others vary according to the mileage driven (fuel, servicing, etc.).

These rates are payable regardless of engine size or CO_2 emissions.

AMAP rates are quite generous for drivers of smaller cars though often they do not cover the full costs of running bigger cars. This is a deliberate government step to encourage the move to smaller cars for environmental reasons.

As long as an employer pays no more than the AMAP rate, neither they nor their employees need to record the actual costs of business mileage, just the mileage itself.

Many employees are unaware of a tax-efficient aspect of the AMAP rules. If you reimburse them at a rate that is lower than the AMAP rate they can claim tax relief on the difference.[382]

Employers can also make tax-free payments to employees for business mileage travelled using their own motorbikes and pedal bikes. See HMRC website for rates.

17.2.7 TAX ON BUSINESS FUEL

If you pay for the business mileage driven by your employees in company cars, no income tax or Class 1 or 1A national insurance contribution arises so long as the payments do not exceed the **advisory fuel rates**. If you can demonstrate that the actual cost was higher than the advisory rate you may ask HMRC to agree a higher amount but there is no guarantee they will accept this.

The rates are reviewed by the government every year on the first of March, June, September and December. Employers can check the latest advisory fuel rate figures on the HMRC website.

If you pay a driver more than these amounts, the surplus will be taxable and subject to NIC.

HM Revenue and Customs will also accept these rates for VAT purposes. It is important for employers to retain actual fuel receipts paid for by the employees to prove that this VAT was actually incurred.[383]

382 S231 ITEPA 2003
383 See 17.1.4 VAT on Motor Expenses

17.2.8 TAX ON FREE PRIVATE FUEL IN CARS

If you pay for the private mileage driven by an employee (or a member of their family or household) in a **company car** on which a car benefit charge arises,[384] they will have to pay tax on the benefit.[385] This applies regardless of whether the fuel is paid for by credit card, voucher or cash. For this purpose 'private mileage' includes commuting to and from work.

The tax is payable in addition to any car benefit tax on the car itself and is payable in full irrespective of the period of time during which free fuel is available. However, the charge may be pro-rated if the vehicle is unavailable for a period during the year, or the benefit is withdrawn part way through the year and is not reinstated. Pro-rating is not available if the employee already has a company car and is provided with free private fuel for that vehicle part way through the tax year.

If the employee is required to make good (and actually does make good) the full cost of the free fuel used for private mileage, this tax is not payable. If they make good only part of the cost, the full charge is payable.

When ensuring that the cost of this private fuel has been fully reimbursed to the employer, HMRC will accept either of the following calculation methods:

- The actual cost of the private fuel, calculated by reference to the actual mileage driven and the actual fuel bills; *or*

- The cost calculated by reference to the HMRC advisory fuel rates.[386] The advisory fuel rates were designed to be used by an employer wishing to reimburse an employee for business mileage driven in a private car but they can also be used to calculate the amount the employee should reimburse the employer for fuel provided for the private use of a company car.

This reimbursement by the employee should be made no later than 30 days after the end of the tax year to which it relates.

The free fuel charge arises whether the employer owns the car or leases it.

If an employee uses their own car and is reimbursed the cost of business mileage, tax on private fuel benefit does not arise and the Approved Mileage Allowance Payment (AMAP) rules apply.[387]

If any free private fuel is supplied to an employee for use **in their own car**, the employee will be subject to tax on the total value of private fuel supplied, including VAT.

---

384 See 17.2.1.
385 S149-153 ITEPA 2003.
386 See 17.2.7.
387 See 17.2.6.

CALCULATING THE FUEL CHARGE ON A COMPANY CAR

The actual cost of the fuel is ignored when calculating the taxable benefit.

Instead the benefit is based on the car's CO_2 emissions and a flat rate set by the government for the tax year. The amount of the benefit changes annually.[388]

The steps involved in calculating the fuel charge are:

1. Determine the 'appropriate percentage' for the car, following the rules that apply when calculating the car benefit (see Emissions-based 'appropriate percentage' in 17.2.1 above).

For electric vehicles there is no fuel benefit. If a car is unavailable for part of the year the fuel charge is reduced pro-rata. Similarly if free private fuel is withdrawn and not reinstated or if the car is shared.

2. Multiply the appropriate percentage by the flat rate fuel charge set for that year.

This gives you the fuel charge that will be added to the employee's salary and be taxed at his or her marginal tax rate.

Example:

Hilary is a higher rate taxpayer

She checks her car's CO_2 on the HMRC website and discovers that its taxable percentage is 10%

She multiplies the flat rate fuel charge for the year by 10% and then (as she is a 40% taxpayer) she multiples the result by 40% to arrive at the benefit in kind tax she must pay.

If she fully reimburses her employer, no fuel charge will arise.

Many firms have stopped providing employees with free private fuel because the tax payable by the individual exceeds the benefit received.

CALCULATING WHETHER YOU BENEFIT FROM TAKING FREE FUEL

Work out how much you would spend if you bought the fuel yourself by multiplying the private mileage you drive in the tax year by the average cost of fuel per gallon and the mpg of your car.

Calculate the fuel charge for the car, by multiplying the 'appropriate percentage' by the flat rate fuel charge[389] for the year.

Multiply the fuel charge by your marginal rate of tax.

If the cost of buying the fuel yourself exceeds the tax payable on the fuel charge, you are benefiting from having it paid for by the company.

388 S150(1) ITEPA 2003 and SI 406, 2010
389 S248 (3) ITEPA 2003

If the tax payable on the fuel charge is more than you would spend buying the fuel yourself, you would be better off paying for it yourself.

If the fuel benefit charge is higher than the cost of the fuel, you would be better off paying for all private fuel yourself.

Even if a driver is benefiting from receiving free private fuel, it is worthwhile checking how much it is costing the company to provide this benefit. Both parties may be better off if the company gives the driver an increase in salary and stops providing him with free private fuel.

17.2.9   Car sharing

You can pay employees an allowance of up to 5p per additional employee per business mile if they carry fellow employees on business journeys. Advise your drivers to check that their insurer does not categorise this as 'hire and reward' driving, otherwise this arrangement may nullify their cover.

Car sharing is becoming more popular as employers try to encourage their employees to reduce CO_2 emissions by sharing journeys to work and to work-related off-site meetings.

If your employees are part of a commuting car sharing arrangement and their car share breaks down on a particular day (perhaps the car physically breaks down or the driver just does not show up) you can make tax free payments to them to pay for their journey to or from home. These payments can only be made tax free when the share arrangement breaks down as a result of an emergency or for some other reason for a short period.[390]

17.2.10   Minibuses

Input VAT is recoverable in full on the purchase of a minibus.

If you provide a minibus or a bus to allow your employees to go to work or to go shopping at lunchtime, no car benefit tax charge arises as long as the vehicle has more than nine seats fitted by the manufacturer.

You can pay a bus company to carry your employees to and from work without any national insurance or income tax liability arising. However, caution is necessary here. If you simply buy the employees a zone ticket they could use for travel to and from work and also for purely private travel, a tax liability might arise.

17.2.11   Congestion charging

If one of your employees drives a company car into a congestion charging zone and pays the charge, you can reimburse them and they will have no liability to income tax. Similarly, if you meet the cost directly there will also be no income tax.

---

390 See.1.10.

This is because the benefit in kind tax payable by an employee on a company car is deemed to cover all of the costs involved in running that car – including servicing, repairs, maintenance, vehicle excise duty (VED), insurance and congestion charging. Hence no separate income tax liability arises if you reimburse the congestion charges they incur when driving a company car for private purposes.

For employees who use their own vehicles, tax relief for congestion charges is available only for business travel or where it is necessary to travel to a temporary workplace, but not for ordinary commuting or private travel.

If a **self-employed person** pays the congestion charge the cost will normally be tax deductible if the journey was for business purposes but not if it was a personal or commuting journey.

17.2.12 TAXATION OF EMPLOYEE CAR OWNERSHIP SCHEMES (ECOS)

ECO schemes have been around for about 20 years and are used by a number of larger businesses to reduce the cost of cars for employees undertaking business journeys. See 3.7.

In essence, ECO schemes are designed to provide all of the benefits of a traditional leased company car, for both the employer and the employee, but the underlying financing agreement is not a lease but a credit sale agreement.[391] This agreement transfers title to the vehicle to the employee from day 1.

This takes the employee out of the company car benefit taxation rules, because in order to be taxed as a benefit in kind a car must be made available for private use by an employee, director, or member of their family or household, by reason of employment, *without title in it transferring to them*.[392] ECO schemes achieve their tax objectives by giving the employee title in the car from day one via the credit sale agreement.

HMRC will usually want to review all of the documentation and rules of an ECO scheme before determining how it should be treated for tax and national insurance purposes, even if you use an 'off the shelf' scheme provided by a firm of accountants. It is in your interests to provide all of the documentation to HMRC before you launch the scheme to receive their 'clearance' (though there have been occasions where they have declined to comment until after a scheme has been launched). If you change any of the scheme documents or rules, you will need to go back to HMRC to get these signed off.

TAX AND NIC CONSEQUENCES OF ECOS

When an employee pays tax on a company car the tax charge covers most of the costs the employer has incurred including depreciation, maintenance, road tax, etc. There are no other car-related costs that can be liable to a separate charge, other than the cost of any chauffeur.

---

391 Section 114 ITEPA 2003
392 Section 203 ITEPA 2003

However, ECO schemes don't work the same way so HMRC will be interested in every cost the employer has incurred on providing the car, including the price the employee pays for the car (the 'headline' amount in the credit sale agreement), the guaranteed future price (the price at which the employee agrees to sell back the car to the leasing company), as well as road tax, servicing and so on.

As an example, HMRC will want to ensure that the guaranteed future price, mileage allowance payments or other payments to the employee are not so high that the employee ends up making a profit. If such a profit does arise, this will be taxed because it arises *by reason of the employee's employment.*[393]

Under an ECO scheme, the employee is responsible for meeting the costs of owning and running the car. Their employer provides them with a combination of:

■ a mileage allowance for business travel (which is tax and NIC-free so long as it does not exceed the AMAP rate); and

■ a cash allowance to cover the finance payments (due under the credit sale agreement), motor insurance premiums and maintenance and repair costs (which is taxable and subject to NIC).

The employee is no longer liable to benefit in kind tax as they no longer have a company car.

The payments and deductions are generally processed through the employer's monthly payroll process.

It is normal for ECO schemes to provide that the employee will receive the maximum amount payable under the AMAP rules, because this then gives the employee the maximum tax- and NIC-free benefit.

Under an ECO scheme the employee cannot receive capital allowances on the vehicle or tax relief for interest paid on the credit sale agreement.

The national insurance rules[394] say that if an employee is paid more than the AMAP rate for the use of their privately owned vehicle ("Relevant Motoring Expenditure") they will be liable to Class 1 NIC on the excess.

For tax purposes, if the employee is paid less than the AMAP rate they can carry this forward to set against excess payments until the end of the tax year. However they cannot carry it forward into a subsequent tax year. The difference is lost.

EMPLOYERS' PAYE RESPONSIBILITIES

Where an employer makes payments to employees relating to the purchase or running of a private car, and those payments are liable to PAYE and Class 1 NIC, these must be put through the employee's payroll immediately and cannot be carried forward to be dealt with as a lump sum at a future date.

---

393 Reg 22A (4) SSCR 2001 as amended by as SI 770, 2004
394 Regulation 66(2) of the ITPR 2003 (SI 2003/2682)

Normally the leasing company that arranges the ECO scheme will calculate the amount the employer has to put through the payroll but this does not absolve the employer of responsibility for recording the amounts of PAYE and NIC payable and paying this to HMRC.[395]

PAYE SETTLEMENT AGREEMENTS

HMRC operates PAYE 'settlement agreements', a special scheme that allows employers to account for PAYE and NICs on minor or irregular taxable benefits, or benefits that can be difficult to calculate in order to process them via the company's payroll. In addition, HMRC tends not to allow liabilities relating to cars to be included within PAYE settlement agreements.

The system allows the employer to calculate the amount of the benefit, gross it up for income tax and NIC purposes and simply pay over the tax and NI to HMRC.

Under some earlier ECO schemes, payments to employees were settled and taxed using PAYE settlement agreements but HMRC won't now allow this. These payments have to be dealt with via the payroll.

17.2.13   TAXATION OF SALARY SACRIFICE SCHEMES

Salary sacrifice is a formal agreement whereby an employee agrees to accept a lower salary and in return receives a benefit from their employer.

These schemes[396] have been around for years. You may be familiar with schemes in which employees forego part of their salary and receive benefits such as childcare vouchers and free health screening. These arrangements are worthwhile if the employee pays a lower rate of income tax on the benefit than they would have paid if they had taken the salary.

Under a salary sacrifice scheme for cars the employee gives up a part of their salary, so their employer saves the sacrificed salary and Class 1 NIC. The employer then pays to lease the car and pays Class 1A NIC on the benefit in kind. The employee pays car benefit tax but this will be low if they choose a car with a relatively low level of CO_2.

Once the car has been delivered the employer will deduct the salary sacrifice amount from the employee's gross salary. This amount is generally set up by the employer to cover the cost of providing the vehicle (including rental, maintenance, admin, insurance etc). The employee is allowed to sacrifice however much salary they desire, so long as this does not bring their gross salary below the national minimum wage levels.

The employee saves income tax and primary Class 1 NIC on the salary they have sacrificed. They have to pay benefit in kind tax but they can keep this low by choosing a low-emission car. So the employee is encouraged to give up an older car for a newer, low-emission one.

---

395 See 14.2.

396 Heaton v Bell, House of Lords (46TC211)

The employer has to pay Class 1A NIC on the value of the benefit, instead of Class 1 NIC on the salary but this normally provides a significant saving to the company because Class 1A NIC is based on the CO_2 emissions of the car. Some companies choose to pass the Class 1A NIC charge back to the employee by increasing the salary sacrifice amount.

Whenever an employee opts into or out of a salary sacrifice scheme, HMRC expects the arrangement to be properly documented with a legally enforceable agreement recording the new terms and conditions of employment, so that the employee's entitlement is clear.

There is case law[397] that says that if the employment contract allows the employee to forego the car and revert to taking their regular salary at any time, the salary sacrifice scheme will fail and the employee will pay income tax as if they were still receiving their full salary, rather than paying car benefits tax on the company car (though their national insurance liability will still be based on what they actually receive).

However, if the employment contract confers the right to switch out of the leased car and revert to salary in the event of a major unforeseen life event such as redundancy of a partner, pregnancy, marriage or divorce, the salary sacrifice scheme will not fail.

A well-designed salary sacrifice scheme needs to anticipate all of the situations that might arise. For example, if an employee goes on maternity leave they are entitled to continue to receive their employment benefits even if they are on Statutory Maternity Pay or indeed are receiving no pay, and therefore have little or no salary to sacrifice. This is potentially a large cost for a company.

In addition, when an employee receives Statutory Maternity Pay, Statutory Adoption Pay or Statutory Sick Pay, these benefits are based on the actual amount of the employee's salary. The fact that the employee receives a lease car under a salary sacrifice scheme is ignored, so they may end up receiving a lower level of SMP, SAP or SSP than would otherwise have been the case, or none at all. Whilst the employer can choose to pay SSP or SMP at a higher level they will only be able to recover the lower amount from HMRC.

There are some other situations where the reduction of gross salary – a key feature of salary sacrifice schemes – might affect the payment of some earnings-related state benefits, but these are beyond the scope of this book.

When operating salary sacrifice schemes, employers must collect the correct amount of PAYE and NICs for the employee's cash salary and must correctly handle the tax and NIC issues and reporting relating to the non-cash benefits.

It is advisable, but not essential, for employers to obtain approval for salary sacrifice schemes from the HMRC Clearances Team.[399] HMRC's view is that salaries and benefits are a matter between employers and employees (a matter of employment law not tax) and therefore the role for HMRC is more limited here, but they will provide comment and clearance if asked.

17.2.14   CYCLISTS MEALS ON 'CYCLE TO WORK' DAYS

Generally, if an employer provides free meals to employees, these are treated as a benefit and are taxable. However, if these are provided by an employer a few times each year in order to encourage employees to cycle to work, they are exempt from tax.[398]

17.3 EXERCISES

Why do capital allowances exist?

What levels of capital allowance are payable on company cars, bikes, vans and trucks?

What is depreciation?

What does 'pooling' mean?

What does 'VAT blocked' mean?

What extra VAT is payable if you give an employee free private fuel?

What VAT is payable on finance payments?

How does the CO_2-based car benefit tax system work?

What is the 3% diesel surcharge?

Explain how capital contributions are treated.

How are vans treated for benefit-in-kind purposes?

Explain AMAP.

What are cyclists' breakfasts?

How is the reimbursement of congestion charges taxed?

How do ECO schemes deliver tax savings?

What are the key tax issues arising with salary sacrifice schemes?

---

398 SI 205, 2002

17.4 GLOSSARY

Abbreviation	Legislation
CAA 2001	Capital Allowances Act 2001
CTA 2009	Corporation Tax Act 2009
ICTA 1988	Income and Corporation Taxes Act 1988
ITEPA 2003	Income Tax (Pensions and Earnings) Act 2003
ITPR 2003	The Income Tax (Pay As You Earn) Regulations 2003
ITTOIA 2005	Income Tax (Trading and Other Income) Act 2005
SI 205, 2002	Statutory Instrument 205, The Income Tax (Exemption of Minor Benefits) Regulations 2002
SI 406, 2010	The Car and Van Fuel Benefit Statutory Order No. 406, 2010
SI 770, 2004	Social Security (Contributions, Categorisation of Earners and Intermediaries) (Amendment) Regulations 2004
SSCR 2001	Regulation 22A (4) of the Social Security (Contributions) Regulations 2001

18 THE PHYSICAL VEHICLE

18.1 ENGINES

18.1.1 PETROL

With all of the talk of emission levels and the rise of diesel and alternative fuels, we should not forget that the majority of the cars on our roads are fuelled by conventional petrol and that this situation is likely to continue for many years.

Some commentators believe the petrol engine is nearing the end of its development potential. However, some progress in petrol engine technology is on the horizon.

Petrol has been cleaned up considerably over the years. We are all now used to unleaded petrol and despite the early protests that unleaded would bring lots of nasty consequence, the transition went well though some have been shocked by the very high cost of replacing catalytic converters.

Another development was the introduction of ultra low sulphur (ULS) in 2005, as required by the European Union Emissions Auto Oil Programme. ULS fuel reduces nitrous oxide emissions, extends the life of catalytic converters and will allow new petrol engine technology to be introduced, such as gasoline direct-injection technology. This will take us only a small step away from zero sulphur content petrol, which will allow a further reduction in CO_2 emissions from engines.[399]

At some stage new 'variable motion' petrol engines will be developed, which will automatically adapt the cubic capacity of the engine to the current driving conditions. For example, when the car is driving normally the engine will reduce its own cubic capacity by altering its pistons so that the car runs like it has a small engine. At speed or under heavy acceleration the engine will 'grow' to provide additional power.

The implications for fleets are considerable. Few fleet vehicles are only driven in town, in suburbs or on motorways. Most fleet vehicles cover a combination of these. So a vehicle with a large engine that would be comfortable cruising at 70mph on the motorway may often have to be driven through town centre rush hours at speeds of under 10mph. If the engine could adjust its own capacity to accommodate this, the cost savings could be very significant.

---

399 It will also stop catalytic converters emitting a smell of rotten eggs.

18.1.2 DIESEL

Rudolph Diesel invented the diesel engine in the 19th century. He realised that if diesel fuel was introduced to an engine at the same time as hot compressed air, the fuel would ignite without the need for a conventional ignition. So there would be no need for the sparking mechanisms that petrol engines required.

Most heavy goods vehicles today are powered by diesel engines. Diesel powered cars had been very popular in many countries but until recently they had not caught the imagination of the British car-buying public. There are probably four reasons for this; image, smell, availability of the fuel and vehicle handling.

The image problem was not helped by the fact that diesel pumps at most fuel stations were to be found in the bays reserved for trucks. And then there was the smell of the fuel and the fact that it stuck to your skin if it splashed when you were filling up. Altogether, this was not a pleasant experience.

Petrol retailers eventually redesigned their filling stations, putting diesel pumps alongside petrol pumps and providing plastic gloves for those who wanted to avoid being splashed.

That dealt with some of the perceived problems but not with the fact that diesel engine cars sound different, especially at low speed, ('like a bus or a taxi') and that they feel odd if you have only driven a petrol engine before.

There is a good reason for this. They *are* different.

Diesel engines tend to generate less power than petrol engines but more torque. Torque is the force that makes a car go faster and is more important in moving a car forward than raw power. As diesels have greater torque they can be more highly geared. Hence they can be more relaxing to drive and more energy efficient on motorways.

Unfortunately diesel engines take time to generate the torque necessary for full output. If you are trying to accelerate a diesel-powered car from a standing start, it feels sluggish, then as speed increases the power kicks in and you accelerate rapidly. 'Flooring' the accelerator at low speeds does not produce extra acceleration, it just wastes fuel.

Diesel engine technology has been developing over the years.

'Common rail' technology is replacing the older 'indirect' system. With the direct system the fuel was pumped into the combustion chamber at a pressure determined by the speed of the engine and was delivered through separate fuel lines to each cylinder. In common rail engines all of the injectors get their fuel from one rail (fuel feed line) at a constant high speed and pressure regardless of engine speed. So the fuel atomises better, fuel efficiency increases and the engine provides a smoother, quieter ride.

Diesel vehicles generally cost more than a similar size petrol engined vehicle. There are several reasons for this but the upsurge in demand over the past few years has probably contributed to this price difference.

The good news is common rail vehicles have depreciated more slowly than equivalent petrol engined cars. Buyers of these vehicles know that diesel engines tend to be very reliable, even with high mileage. So when you come to sell the car you may get back some of the premium you had to pay when you bought it.

Diesels give much better fuel consumption and common rail diesel engines give at least 10mpg more than similar power petrol engines.

Diesel engines burn less fuel and therefore produce fewer emissions. However, they produce higher nitrous oxide emissions and more smoke and are noisier than petrol cars. They also emit particulates that are said to cause cancer.[400]

The current generation of diesel engines is type-approved to Euro V emission standard. The earlier standard, Euro IV, required particle filters to be fitted to reduce carbon monoxide, nitrous oxide and hydrocarbon emissions.

The new standard applies to all new vans (up to 2.5 tonnes gross weight) and minibuses sold in the EU from 1 January 2011, and to heavier vans a year later. The new standard reduces the acceptable levels of carbon monoxide, nitrous oxide and hydrocarbon emissions but does not specify how manufacturers should go about meeting the standards.

Manufacturers are adopting one of two approaches to meet the targets. Some are introducing a new stage in the management of exhaust gases – they are injecting urea into the exhaust gasses before they pass into a catalytic converter. Others are cooling the exhaust gases and then passing them back into the engine where they are burned again.

Diesel engined cars have become much more popular with fleet drivers since the introduction of the CO_2-based car benefit tax regime.

It used to be necessary to service diesel engines frequently but this is no longer the case. It is now quite normal for diesel service intervals to be 12,000 miles and even longer if the engine is lubricated with fully synthetic oil.

With the rise in the number of diesel vehicles many people have been driving diesels for the first time. Every year more than ten thousand drivers fill up their cars with the wrong fuel. Old habits, it seems, die hard, and if you have been filling up with petrol for decades it is easy enough to fill up your new diesel-engined company car with petrol too.

These fuels work on a completely different basis to petrol cars (ignition for the petrol, compression for the diesel) so it is not possible to drive one type of car if the tank is filled with the wrong the wrong fuel. It has to be pumped out. This is an expensive option that usually requires the car to be towed to a garage.

Fleet managers should warn their drivers about filling up with the wrong fuel and make it clear that the cost of rectifying this problem will have to be borne by the driver.

---

400 See 11.2.

They should also be warned not to try to drive a vehicle with the wrong fuel as this will lead to engine damage. Pumping out the fuel tank might cost £100.[401] Repairing a damaged engine could cost thousands.

Image, it seems, is almost everything to the British motorist. For many years diesel was seen as an industrial fuel used for trains and heavy goods vehicles rather than as a serious alternative for cars. Only 7% of new cars sold in 1990 were diesel engined. This rose to 25% by 1994 as drivers became attracted to the high levels of fuel-efficiency that diesel engines offer. Demand then fell, down below 15% by 1999 but since then diesel has grown strongly and by 201 it accounted for more than 46% of new car sales.

There are a number of reasons for this:

- The tax system encourages fleet drivers to select low-emission cars and diesels certainly emit less CO_2 than equivalent petrol-engined cars
- Companies keen to project a green image have encouraged their fleet drivers to drive diesel cars
- Diesel engines have become much more refined
- MPVs and 4x4s have become more popular and a high proportion of these have diesel engines
- The government's scrappage scheme brought forward the purchase of large numbers of smaller cars, which tended to be petrol engined

18.1.3 COMPRESSED NATURAL GAS (CNG)

Compressed natural gas, or CNG, is an alternative fuel that is already offered as a dual-fuel option by some vehicle manufacturers. This gas is in abundant supply – it is the gas that comes into our homes. It is also considered by some experts to be the cleanest fuel in terms of total emissions (especially local air pollutants).[402]

CNG cannot currently be bought at retail petrol stations so only those fleets that have installed their own CNG tanks are using it. Because of this, it is only suitable for vehicles that return to base several times a day, or overnight, such as those operated by distribution or engineering businesses.

CNG has a lower calorific value than petrol and therefore gives fewer miles to the gallon.

There are plans to produce domestic CNG compressors for home users to use in their garages. The idea is that you would fill up your car overnight from your normal household gas supply and drive off in the morning with a full tank of CNG. Domestic natural gas costs a fraction of the price of petrol.

If domestic compressors are introduced there is a risk that the government would lose huge petrol tax revenues. It will be interesting to see how they deal with this

401 That's what it cost me… ☹
402 According to the Environment Agency: phone 03708 506 506

possible leakage of tax revenues. One option will be for them to instruct the gas companies to find a way to bill householders separately for gas destined for use in the home and the car.

18.1.4 LIQUEFIED PETROLEUM GAS (LPG)

Liquefied petroleum gas, or LPG, has been available as an alternative fuel for decades. Some 150,000 vehicles run on LPG in the UK and 7 million in Europe.

LPG engines are considered relatively clean, because they emit less hydrocarbons and carbon monoxide than petrol engines and less nitrous oxide and particulate matter than diesel engines.

LPG is available from around 1,400 of the 14,000 retail fuel sites in the UK.

Like CNG, LPG tanks are stronger than petrol tanks. In fact they are made of steel that is thicker than a Land Rover's chassis. They include many safety features including an electronic device that cuts off the flow of fuel in any of the following situations:

- The ignition is turned off
- The car stalls
- The car hits another object
- Excess flow of fuel is detected

They are therefore considered safer than petrol tanks.

All LPG cars are bi-fuelled; that is, they are fitted with LPG tanks and petrol tanks, and the driver can switch between these.

LPG costs less per litre than diesel and you can save even more if you buy it in bulk and bunker it. However, like CNG, LPG has a lower calorific value than petrol so you will not achieve the same number of miles per litre.

Experts believe that running a fleet on LPG is 35% cheaper than petrol and 20% cheaper than diesel.

New LPG cars and vans cost around £1,500+ VAT more than their petrol-engined equivalents, or you can pay a similar amount to have a car converted to run on LPG. You will pay a little more if you opt to have the LPG tank fitted into the well where the spare wheel is usually stored.

Further information is available from the UKLPG, the LPG trade association. Website: www.uklpg.org

18.1.5 ELECTRIC VEHICLES (EVs)

The world's oil stocks could be depleted within forty years. Clearly, we need to find other ways to power our mobility than fossil fuels. Electricity could be the answer, so long as it can be produced using renewable energy sources such as wind or wave power.

It used to be that just milk floats were powered by electricity, but car manufacturers have been working for years to produce viable EVs and several are now available on the market.

The range of such vehicles is an issue; it might be safe to use them in a city, or short trips away from a base, but it is clearly essential to be able to recharge the vehicle before the battery goes flat.

The cost of the battery packs has also become a major talking point. These are very expensive and have a limited life – less than the life of the car – so they will have to be replaced at some stage.

Nobody actually knows what electric vehicles will be worth in three or four years. These are relatively new cars and few have been sold so far. Therefore, setting residuals for these cars is a matter of educated guesswork.

It is interesting to look at other markets for insights into what might happen to electric RVs, and to some extent it is possible to draw parallels between electric vehicle RVs and a much more mature market – the housing market. Both markets have a mainstream product: internal combustion and electric power in the motor market, mainstream and retirement property in housing market. Retirement homes and mainstream homes can look the same and do exactly the same job, but there are far fewer buyers of retirement homes than mainstream homes so demand is much lower. A quick look at estate agent's window will show that retirement homes sell for much less than identical mainstream homes.

The motor manufacturers believe there is a market for electric vehicles and they're definitely right, but no-one really knows how much demand there will for used EVs. It's likely that used car buyers will welcome these cars because the cost-per-mile is so low, but no-one is certain. And once we add in the potentially huge cost of replacing the battery packs, it is no surprise that some lessors have been setting 20% RVs on EVs, making lease rentals very expensive.

And these cars have tended to be rather expensive compared to say diesel cars, though the government provides a £5,000 grant for cars with CO_2 below 75g/km, which helps bring the cost down.

In June 2011 the government published its Plug-In Vehicle Infrastructure Strategy paper setting out how it plans to encourage the public to buy and use electric vehicles.[403] It plans a series of regulatory measures to encourage the installation of more charging points and make it easier for people to charge their cars at home.

---

403 www.dft.gov.uk/publications/plug-in-vehicle-infrastructure-strategy

It is clear that there we will see a lot of investment in electric vehicle charging points in the next few years.

Source London plans to install 1,300 electric vehicle charging points across London by 2013.

One company plans to install a network of charging points at motorway service stations, powered by energy produced by wind power and solar panel parks.

About 1,000 charging points have already been installed in the UK through the government-backed Plugged-In Places programme, which provides 50% grants for local authorities and others towards the cost of installing recharging points. Currently the programme only operates in London, Milton Keynes and the North East but this is being extended to other regions of the UK.

Under most recharging schemes the user registers and pays a monthly fee and a small usage charge.

ELECTRIC VEHICLE GRANTS

The government has set aside £400m to encourage the development and purchase of low-emission vehicles. This programme is being run by The Office for Low Emission Vehicles (OLEV) which comprises officials from three government departments: (1) Transport, (2) Business, Innovation and Skills and (3) Energy and Climate Change.

OLEV provides a grant of £5000 (or 25% of the cost of the car, whichever is lower) towards the purchase price of plug-in electric cars. The discount is available to anyone and is automatically deducted from the purchase price by the manufacturer, who then claims the grant from OLEV.

The cars that qualify must be designed and constructed for the carriage of passengers, comprising no more than eight seats in addition to the driver's seat,[404] have CO_2 emissions no greater than 75g/km, be able to travel 70 miles on a charge (or if a hybrid must be able to travel at least 10 miles on electric-only power, have a maximum speed exceeding 60mph, have a warranty of at least 3 years or 60,000 miles and the consumer must be offered a further two year warranty on the battery and drive train, battery performance still has to be reasonable after three years and to meet certain minimum crash test standards.

More information is available from the Department for Transport website.[405]

---

404 M1 category under Directive 2007/46/EC of European Parliament and Council. See eur-lex.europa.eu/LexUriServ/LexUriServ.do?uri=OJ:L:2007:263:0001:0001:EN:PDF

405 dft.gov.uk/topics/sustainable/olev/plug-in-car-grant/

18.1.6 HYBRID ELECTRIC VEHICLES

A plug-in-and-drive vehicle is not practical for most fleet drivers but hybrid petrol/electric vehicles offer a good solution. They work by marrying a conventional petrol engine, an electric motor, a lot of batteries and a sophisticated computerised management system to control the process. They don't need to be plugged in to recharge the batteries either.

As these cars pull away from the kerb they are powered by the battery. When the accelerator pedal is pressed more heavily the petrol engine switches in and delivers more power to the wheels. At slow cruising speed the car reverts to battery power, and when cruising at high speed it uses the petrol engine.

When the petrol engine is working and spare power is available, this is directed to the batteries and is used to charge them. When you take your foot off the accelerator and began to decelerate, the latent power still available in the forward movement of the car is used to charge the batteries. The car needs neither battery nor petrol engine power at that stage.

The best way to describe this is to think of a bicycle with a dynamo lighting system. As you pedal, the movement of the wheels is used to power the lights. As you decelerate, the lights stay on because the wheel is still moving; your leg power is no longer being used but the momentum of the bike is still enough to power the lights.

You cannot plug a hybrid car into a wall socket. It gets all of its power from deceleration or the spare power left in the petrol engine as you are driving, though plug-in hybrid engines are on the way.

Apart from the technological wizardry that you see on the instrument panel - showing where the power is coming from and going to at any particular moment - hybrid cars behave like normal cars and the driver soon forgets about the technology and just concentrates on driving.

Hybrid cars offer high fuel efficiency. In one test, both cars delivered more than 50mpg driving through congested suburban roads in Manchester during the rush hour.

The United States Department of Energy has one of the most useful resource centres on alternative fuels to be found on the web, the Alternative Fuels and Advanced Vehicles Data Center (AFDC). Its website is at www.afdc.energy.gov/afdc/

18.1.7 HYDROGEN

Hydrogen fuel has been identified as the cleanest fuel to power a motor vehicle.

Most industry experts believe hydrogen will replace fossil fuels such as petrol and diesel in the long term future (about 20 years' time). Several manufacturers have developed prototype vehicles that use hydrogen to power either fuel cells or conventional engines.

Hydrogen in fuel cells can be used to power an electric motor. In its cleanest guise, called direct hydrogen, the only emission is steam.

Fuel cells are a good replacement for batteries– they are smaller and lighter and allow greater vehicle range.

The government issued this statement in 2001:

> 'The government's commitment to delivering both air quality and climate change benefits through increased use of environmentally friendly alternative fuels in the UK supports the early steps towards a hydrogen-based economy'[406]

LPG tanks are pressured to 7 times normal atmospheric pressure (7 Bar), roughly the same pressure as the tyre of a sports bicycle. CNG tanks are pressurised to 200 Bar and hydrogen tanks to a massive 700 Bar. Because of this, hydrogen fuel tanks in cars and light commercial vehicles are likely to be much more expensive than conventional fuel tanks.

Despite these challenges, some commentators believe that direct hydrogen would be the best hydrogen fuelling system for Britain to adopt.

Another challenge is that the process for manufacturing hydrogen requires significant amounts of power. If that power came from fossil fuels the CO_2 emissions problem would not be solved – it would simply be shifted upstream from the car to the production facility. However, if wind or wave power could be used to power these factories, we would have an emissions-free manufacturing process that produces an emissions-free vehicle fuel.

And the good news is that Britain has more potential to generate wind and wave power than any other European country.

Another way to produce hydrogen is to use methanol as the fuel source for vehicles. Methanol has a very high hydrogen content. The hydrogen is extracted from methanol 'on board' the vehicle through a reformer system. It can use existing logistics and filling station networks without the need for major adaptations.

The downside to this onboard methanol process is that it creates some CO_2 and it is only about 10% more energy-efficient that the best modern diesels.

The Department of Energy and Climate Change website gives up-to-date insights into developments in moving towards a hydrogen economy.[407]

The have been various trials of hydrogen-powered vehicles and hydrogen-powered buses appeared on London streets some years ago.

However, it is not expected that commercially viable hydrogen powered vehicles (i.e. cheap and flexible enough for wide business use) will become a reality in the next few years.

We should expect hydrogen to be the fuel of the future, not just an alternative fuel curiosity.

---

406 From Gordon Brown's Budget speech 7 March 2001.

407 hwww.decc.gov.uk/en/content/cms/meeting_energy/h2_fuel_cells/h2_fuel_cells.aspx

18.1.8 BIODIESEL

This is the fuel that occasionally provokes tabloid newspaper articles along the lines of 'Cars to be powered by used oil from burger bars.'

Biodiesel is a type of fuel that can power a vehicle. It is produced from renewable sources such as vegetable or animal oils, including recycled cooking oils. Rapeseed oil, recycled cooking oils and conventional diesel fuel can all be used to power vehicles.

Biodiesel fuel emits no sulphur, and lower levels of particulates and less nitrous oxide than diesel. It is also biodegradable; that is, it breaks down in the atmosphere after use.

Users of biodiesel report little difference in performance over conventional diesel fuel.

Biodiesel is now available at a small but growing number of UK filling stations, and it is mixed with conventional diesel in some outlets.

The British Association for Bio Fuels and Oils (now merged into Renewable Energy Association),[408] says that biodiesel produces between 50% and 70% less carbon dioxide emissions than petrol, and some 30% less than LPG or CNG. It believes that biodiesel will be a major green fuel in the future.

People producing up to 2500 litres of biodiesel per year for personal use do not have to register or pay duty. If you buy biodiesel fuel for your vehicle make sure it comes from a reputable source. HMRC have powers to fine companies that use fuel on which duty has not been paid. In extreme cases they can impound the vehicles.

If you plan to alter your vehicles to run on biodiesel you should talk to the manufacturer to ensure that you do not invalidate their warranty.

18.2 MATS AND FLAPS

Most contract hire and leasing companies fit these as standard on the vehicles they supply – and with good cause. If you don't fit a mat to your vehicle the damage to the carpet will significantly reduce the value of the car at resale.

Not fitting mats to a car is a false economy: they cost so little that it is best to make them standard on all of your cars.

Similarly, mud flaps are simple inexpensive accessories but they reduce significantly the damage caused by stones being thrown up by the tyres. They also reduce the chance of stones flying up into the windscreens of other vehicles.

---

408 Renewable Energy Association 7th Floor, Capital Tower, 91 Waterloo Road, London SE1 8RT Phone: +44 (0) 20 7925 3570 www.r-e-a.net

18.3 LICENCE PLATE

Before 1998 licence plates changed annually in August, which caused a huge boom in new car sales in August with up to 25% of each year's new registrations being delivered in one month, right in the middle of the peak holiday period.

No one gained from this system and the extra cost of having so many vehicles manufactured, stored and delivered in a short period of time was ultimately borne by the consumer, so it was replaced by the current system of six-monthly plate changes in March and September.

The new pattern of letters and numbers is:

AB12 CDE

In this system, **A** denotes the registration region and **B** the local office.

If an X is shown as the first letter, the vehicle is a direct or personal import or has come into the country under a VAT free scheme. If the first letter is Q the vehicle is of uncertain origin.

The **third character** designates the month of registration.

0 stood for March and 5 for September for the first decade and has now been replaced by 1 and 6 which will last for a further decade. In later decades, 2, 3 and 4 will stand for March, and 7, 8 and 9 for September.

The **fourth character** is a month indicator.

1 denotes 2011, 2 denotes 2012, etc.

So, 12,13, 14 … etc denote March 2012, 2013, 2014 … etc and 61,62, 63… etc denote September 2012, 2013, 2014 … etc.

The remaining letters, **CDE**, are selected randomly.

Because 0 and 5 were used as the starting points for March and September. This system will last for 49 years without requiring a change.

Many new registration plates now sport the EU emblem and the national identifier ('GB'), though the inclusion of these is optional.

Number plates have to comply with British Standard AU 145d.

The name of the number-plate supplier now has to be shown on the plate.

A section at the bottom centre of the plate is available to use if you wish to personalise the registration plate, for example, by inclusion of an advert. Dealers and leasing companies use this to splash their names on your cars but there is no reason why your company's name should not be shown there. The area available for personalisation is 178mm wide by 13mm high.

Letter	Region	Local Office	Local Office Identifier
A	Anglia	Peterborough, Norwich, Ipswich	AA-AY (not AI, AQ)
B	Birmingham	Birmingham	BA-BY
C	Cymru	Cardiff, Swansea, Bangor	CA-CY (not CI, CQ)
D	Deeside to Shrewsbury	Chester, Shrewsbury	DA-DY (not DI, DQ)
E	Essex	Chelmsford	EA-EY
F	Forest & Fens	Nottingham, Lincoln	FA-FY (not FI, FO, FQ, FU)
G	Garden of England	Maidstone, Brighton	GA-GY (not GI, GQ)
H	Hampshire & Dorset	Bournemouth, Portsmouth Isle of Wight	HA-HY (not HI, HQ) HW
K	Unnamed	Luton, Northampton	KA-KY (not KI, KQ)
L	London	Wimbledon, Stanmore, Sidcup	LA-LY (not LI, LQ)
M	Manchester & Merseyside	Manchester	MA-MY
N	North	Newcastle, Stockton	NA-NY (not NF, NI, NQ)
O	Oxford	Oxford	OA-OY
P	Preston	Preston, Carlisle	PA-PY (not PI, PQ)
R	Reading	Reading	RA-RY
S	Scotland	Glasgow, Edinburgh, Dundee, Aberdeen, Inverness	SA-SY (not SI, SQ)
V	Severn Valley	Worcester	VA-VY
W	West of England	Exeter, Truro, Bristol	WA-WY (not WI, WQ)
Y	Yorkshire	Leeds, Sheffield, Beverley	YA-YY (not YI, YQ)

Year/month designators for the first 15 years of the new system are:

Date	Code	Date	Code
		Sep 2001 - Feb 2002	51
March 2002 - Aug 2002	02	Sep 2002 - Feb 2003	52
March 2003 - Aug 2003	03	Sep 2003 - Feb 2004	53
March 2004 - Aug 2004	04	Sep 2004 - Feb 2005	54
March 2005 - Aug 2005	05	Sep 2005 - Feb 2006	55
March 2006 - Aug 2006	06	Sep 2006 - Feb 2007	56
March 2007 - Aug 2007	07	Sep 2007 - Feb 2008	57
March 2008 - Aug 2008	08	Sep 2008 - Feb 2009	58
March 2009 - Aug 2009	09	Sep 2009 - Feb 2010	59
March 2010 - Aug 2010	10	Sep 2010 - Feb 2011	60
March 2011 - Aug 2011	11	Sep 2011 - Feb 2012	61
March 2012 - Aug 2012	12	Sep 2012 - Feb 2013	62
March 2013 - Aug 2013	13	Sep 2013 - Feb 2014	63
March 2014 - Aug 2014	14	Sep 2014 - Feb 2015	64
March 2015 - Aug 2015	15	Sep 2015 - Feb 2016	65
March 2016 - Aug 2016	16	Sep 2016 - Feb 2017	66

It is mandatory to use only the approved typeface.

If you need a replacement number plate (e.g. because yours has been lost, stolen or damaged) you have to go to a registered supplier and provide them with one of the following documents to prove you are entitled to it:

■ Vehicle Registration Document (V5C)

■ Certificate of entitlement (V750)

■ Vehicle Retention Document (V778)

The supplier has to record information about the registered keeper and the vehicle.

The scheme has been designed to reduce the practice of 'ringing' whereby car thieves use the identity of a scrapped vehicle to disguise one that has been stolen. Tens of thousands of vehicles are stolen and 'ringed' each year and all of them require a new number plate, so this system makes it more difficult for thieves to sell stolen cars.

It is important not to use any registration plate other than the 'standard' design. Plates must be secure and visible. MOT testers are required to check that the plate confirms with the regulations and the lettering has not been altered to make it less legible or less easy to establish the true identity of the car.

18.4 CLASSES OF VEHICLE

The motor industry divides car types into a number of classes. These are useful as they allow you to compare a vehicle with the other vehicles in the same class on the basis of price, performance, etc.

There is some correlation between the depreciation rates of cars in the same class so even when selecting a brand new model you can start to estimate its residual value by looking at the residual performance of vehicles in the same class.

The classes are:
- City car
- Small car
- Lower medium
- Upper medium
- Junior executive
- Executive
- Luxury
- Performance
- Compact or mini-MPV
- MPV
- 4x4 lifestyle
- Convertible

18.5 DAYTIME RUNNING LIGHT (DRL)

These lights are automatically switched on when the engine is started.

Under EU law they became mandatory for all new types of passenger car and small vans vehicles from February 2011, and will become mandatory for trucks and buses in August 2012.

18.6 RADIOS

Most people are aware that the government plans to turn off analogue broadcasts and make us a digital-only nation in 2015. All new vehicles sold in the UK by 31 December 2013 are required to be fitted with digital radios. In fact many manufacturers are already fitting digital radios though in some cases these come at an additional cost.

This topic is of interest to fleet managers because it raises the question: if fleets buy vehicles fitted with analogue radios in 2012 or 2013, will these radios be obsolete when the vehicles come to be sold in or after 2015?

The answer is yes. It's surprising there has not been more discussion in fleet circles on this topic because it is quite possible that these vehicles will be worth less in the used vehicle market than if they were fitted with digital radios.

The good news is that it should be possible to buy plug-in analogue-to-digital adaptors that will keep these radios working once the digital switchover is complete. However, no-one knows whether a car fitted with an adaptor will sell for the same price as a car fitted with a digital radio. Probably not.

18.7 THE NEAR FUTURE

The motor vehicles of thirty years ago are very different to those we are driving today. While we cannot know what vehicles will look like in thirty years' time, we have a good idea of the changes that will arrive in the next decade.

Some manufacturers are researching so-called 'drive-by-wire' systems where hydraulic and mechanical connections between mechanical 'hard' parts are replaced or reduced by electronics. Some cars already use an 'electronic accelerator' instead of a hydraulic throttle cable. The current Mercedes E-class features a brake-by-wire system.

Such electronic systems – already used on airliners - could be used to steer vehicles in a few years' time. Instead of a mechanical steering wheel attached directly to a steering column that moves the wheels, the driver could move a control column that sends electric signals to change wheel direction. These systems save weight and will cause less injury to the driver in the event of an accident.

Sophisticated electronic devices are being introduced that sense when an accident is about to take place, tighten the seat belts and increase the power of the brakes when the pedal is depressed.

Suspension systems are likely to become more dynamic. Computer-controlled electronic adjusters will alter the springs and the dampers in milliseconds according to the vehicle's body roll, steering angle, velocity, braking action and acceleration.

Headlights are likely to be modified so that they aim where the front wheels are pointing.

The European Union has shown itself to be a powerful force for the introduction of safer vehicles by mandating the introduction of a number of safety-related features:

- Electronic Stability Control (ESC)

  This helps a driver keep control of their skidding car. There has been a consensus in fleet circles for some time that this should be fitted as standard in business vehicles to ensure the safety of drivers. Mandatory in all new cars by 2014.

- Tyre pressure sensors

  They are already to be found in some cars. They work by integrating small transmitters into tyre valves and they offer a real increase in safety. Mandatory from 2014.

- Advanced emergency braking systems (AEBS)

  These systems provide additional braking power in emergency situations. Mandatory for new models by November 2013 and for all models by November 2015. Only applies to some classes of vehicle.

- Lane departure warning systems (LDWS)

  These warn the driver when their vehicle veers out of its lane. Mandatory for new models by November 2013 and for all models by November 2015. Only applies to some classes of vehicle.

18.8 EXERCISES

What are the advantages of ultra low sulphur petrol?

What is biodiesel?

Who invented diesel?

What is torque?

How does common rail work?

What are the advantages of (a) LPG and (b) CNG?

What is the difference between hybrid and dual-fuel?

Why is hydrogen considered the fuel of the future?

What are the eleven classes of motor vehicle?

What is the legal minimum tyre tread depth?

What are the rules for mixing radial and cross-ply tyres?

19 VEHICLE FINANCE AND MANAGEMENT INDUSTRY

19.1 AN EXPLANATION OF THE STRUCTURE

The vehicle finance and management industry is made up of contract hire, leasing and fleet management companies and brokers.

There are several hundred suppliers offering contract hire so it is as well to know what type of business you are dealing with.

19.1.1 CONTRACT HIRE COMPANIES

The expression 'contract hire company' is often used as a shorthand generic term covering all vehicle financing and management companies. The fact that this has become a generic term is due to the success of contract hire as a product in the UK market over the past three decades. However, many of these companies offer much more than just contract hire. Indeed some offer all of the vehicle finance, insurance and management products listed in Chapter 1.

Many contract hire companies are now owned by banks. These companies are all 'prime funders' in this market; that is, they use their own money to fund the vehicles they buy to lease to you. Unless you have gone to them via a broker there is no middleman so you are getting direct access to those players in the market who have the cheapest money cost possible. Money cost is a key element in calculating a contract hire rental, so dealing direct can often be the cheapest way to obtain a car on contract hire.

Some small contract hire companies (and also a few bigger ones) finance their contract hire businesses by entering into 'back to back' finance agreements. They obtain their vehicle on finance (hire purchase or finance lease) from a finance company or bank and they then enter into a contract hire agreement with you. You pay the contract hire company and need never know that someone else owns the vehicle.

The funder will usually have some type of security interest in the lease you have entered into with the contract hire company. Therefore, if your contract hire company fails to meet its obligations to the funder, the funder will enforce its security by writing to advise you that you have to pay them in future.

19.1.2   LEASING COMPANIES

Contract hire is a lease, so it stands to reason that many people call contract hire companies 'leasing companies'.

However, some leasing companies do not offer to supply the car or provide any fleet services.[409] If you find the car, they will fund it.

They do not take residual value risk and their finance packages reflect this.

They offer finance lease, loans, hire purchase and lease purchase, rather than contract hire, contract purchase or operating leases.

19.1.3   FLEET MANAGEMENT COMPANIES

Fleet management companies buy, maintain, sell, administer and carry out various other management functions for their clients' vehicle fleets.

Many fleet management companies sell contract hire and other vehicle finance products, too. In some cases, a management's decision to call their business a fleet management company, as opposed to a contract hire company, has more to do with the way they wish to position themselves in the market rather than the fact that they specialise in fleet management.

19.1.4   FINANCE AND LEASING BROKERS

There are more than a thousand car finance and contract hire brokers in the UK. Some specialise in providing vehicle loans, some only offer contract hire and others use a funder to supply the finance while they supply, maintain and manage the vehicle.

It used to be very easy to set up in business as a contract hire broker but with the arrival of the credit crunch a lot of leasing companies decided to stop taking business from brokers so perhaps it's now somewhat more difficult than before.

Some brokers are one-man-bands whilst others are big businesses arranging finance for more than a thousand cars a year.

Many brokers present you the funder's agreement to sign. You therefore enter into a direct contractual relationship with the funder. The broker may then offer you their own maintenance package or that too may come direct from a contract hire company.

Some players in the market will offer you their own contract hire agreement to sign. It is clear to you when you sign that you are entering into an agreement with a contract hire company and you have dealt with the representative of the contract hire company. However, many contract hire companies are in fact brokers acting as undisclosed agents for a contract hire company. In this situation the agreement you have signed is not with the agent at all but with the contract hire company that stands behind them that is providing the finance.

---

409 Such as servicing, maintenance, repair and re-licensing.

There can be advantages in doing business through a contract hire broker. There is no need to shop around for the cheapest quote – the broker will do this for you.

If your business is not financially strong a broker is likely to be able to find a company willing to lease vehicles to you, whereas you might otherwise spend ages trying to find someone.

And a local broker who gets to know you and your business may be able to offer a more tailored and intimate service for you than a large contract hire company could provide.

The main disadvantage in doing business via a broker is that you are introducing a third party to the transaction and they have to live, too. Brokers earn fees for introducing business to contract hire companies, hundreds and sometimes over a thousand pounds per vehicle. You will be paying for this through your rentals so you need to ensure you are getting good value for money.

It is a sign of the increasing importance of brokers in this market that the BVRLA[410] has allowed brokers to become members. There are now over 100 BVRLA Leasing Broker Members and they are required to comply with a strict code of conduct covering issues such as:

- A requirement to operate at the highest level of integrity
- The need to issue clear quotations
- Vehicles must be described accurately
- The broker must not make misleading statements or misrepresentations
- The need to obtain a written agreement (a mandate) from the client prior to acting on their behalf
- The broker must advise the client on the most suitable product
- Procedures for handling client monies
- The client's right to cancel an agreement
- Staff training
- Efficient and professional operations
- Complaint handling procedures

A copy of the code is available from the BVRLA.[411]

19.1.5   TOP 50 CONTRACT HIRE COMPANIES

In the 1980s private individuals, dealers and vehicle manufacturers owned the majority of the top fifty contract hire companies. During the 1990s the industry underwent significant changes so financial institutions now own more than 60% of the top 50 contract hire companies (by fleet size), leaving just 20% owned by vehicle manufacturers. Independents and dealers now own less than 20%.

---

410 See 19.6.3.

411 See 20.0 for contact details.

The pace of change among the bigger players has been even more rapid. Few of the 20 largest contract hire companies have avoided name changes, take-overs or mergers. The trade press have called the largest companies the 'superleague'.

It is worthwhile looking at the reasons for these changes.

Before financial institutions began buying up contract hire companies, many of them were active lenders to those same contract hire companies. They discovered this market to be a safe place for their money.

Vehicles are excellent assets for banks to finance; they are tangible, moveable and easily identified. There is an efficient market for the sale of used vehicles and vehicles tend to hold their value well compared with some other types of asset.

Compare this with other assets that the banks were being asked to finance in the 1990s:

■ Computer hardware that could not be identified once it had been installed and which in any event became obsolete soon after it had been bought

■ Computer software that had little or no value to a bank if it 'repossesses' it

■ Other hi-tech equipment with a limited resale market.

Yes, the contract hire vehicle market looked like a very safe place for the banks to put their money. And the contract hire companies took the residual value risk, so the banks just had to offer full-pay-out funding through a finance lease or hire purchase.

Many banks began to realise the contract hire companies were making good profits, using the banks' money as their prime source of raw material, while the banks were making very slim margins indeed on providing their funds to such companies.

Worse still, many of the contract hire companies were relatively undercapitalised,[412] so if the used vehicle market turned down sharply they would be unable to sustain heavy losses. That would leave the banks having to step in and take over the businesses. 'Much better', so the banks' argument went, 'that we just buy into these companies and get all of the risks and rewards, rather than staying in the background and getting a slim margin when things go well and losing heavily when things go badly'.

So the banks started buying contract hire companies, particularly the independents and the dealer-owned companies. The prices they paid for some of their acquisitions were staggering; up to £2,500 per vehicle in excess of the balance sheet value of the companies' assets at the top of the market, i.e. £2,500 of goodwill per vehicle. This is much more than a contract hire company expects to make on an average three-year contract hire deal. The banks were willing to pay these high levels of goodwill because they believed these businesses would continue to make strong profits, particularly from the sale of used vehicles and their clients would come back and replace these vehicles at the end of the lease.

---

412 They had a great deal of borrowings but little capital of their own. Hence their capital could be wiped out if the value of their assets declined sharply. See 5.12.4.

Some of these buyers were very disappointed to discover that neither of these assumptions proved to be correct.

As the financial institutions moved into the market, they brought with them a key competitive advantage; their low money cost. This converts into lower rentals for clients, and many smaller contract hire companies found they could not compete. This hastened the scramble to sell out to the new entrants.

Some contract hire companies have sought to become global or pan-European players to meet the needs of international businesses that will demand sole-supply arrangements with one supplier across all of the countries in which they operate.[413]

19.1.6 COMPETITION

There is a very healthy market for contract hire and indeed all forms of vehicle finance. You can choose from many suppliers offering similar products and you should be able to find the organisation that best meets your needs on service and price.

You need to decide whether to deal with just one contract hire company (sole supply), or whether you prefer dual or multi-supply.

There are advantages and disadvantages to each of these.

Sole supply gives you the benefit of a close relationship with a company that will take your business seriously – they have a lot to lose if you go elsewhere. You will only be able to benefit from pooled mileage arrangements across all of your vehicles if you are on a sole supply arrangement,[414] and this only sole supply gives you the opportunity to get consolidated management reports covering the whole of your fleet.

However, you may prefer to have two or more suppliers and get them to quote for each vehicle, so that you can choose the cheapest on the day.

Even though they may buy cars for the same price and have very low money costs, it is quite normal for contract hire companies to offer different rentals on the same vehicle, simply because their views on the residual values and maintenance costs of the vehicle differ.[415]

---

413 See 9.1.
414 See 2.6.1.
415 See 5.12-13.

19.2 EXERCISES

What is the difference between contract hire and fleet management companies?

How are contract hire companies financed?

How do brokers operate?

Why have banks taken over contract hire companies?

19.3 COMPLAINTS AGAINST FLEET COMPANIES

Companies in the fleet industry pride themselves on providing a good service. Nonetheless, from time to time things do go wrong, which is perhaps understandable given the many transactions that they handle on behalf of their clients.

Many disputes arise simply through the client's lack of understanding of the agreement that has been entered into. This is also understandable; a quick look at the contents pages of this book shows the complexity of this industry and its products so there are bound to be occasions where clients find that they don't get what they thought they were getting.

If this happens, the supplier has not done its job properly and they should be happy to explain what has happened and work to resolve the issue. The key message, therefore, is to read the contract.

If you have a complaint with the service you receive from a fleet company, in the first instance it is best to try to resolve it with the person you normally deal with. If you are unsatisfied with the response, ask to speak to their manager.

If you are still not happy after you have elevated the complaint up to a higher authority, it is time to get formal. Write to the company setting out the problem and your complaint. Address it to the managing director if you wish but send a copy to the most senior manager that you have spoken to. If your problem is still not resolved, you may wish to check if your supplier is a member of the British Vehicle Rental and Leasing Association.

The BVRLA has a code of conduct and every member undertakes to uphold and abide by it. If your supplier is a BVRLA member and you believe they have failed to comply with the code of conduct, you can make a formal complaint to the BVRLA. It will investigate the complaint on your behalf and if necessary you may use its conciliation service to resolve the problem.

BVRLA code of conduct[416]

What customers can expect

A MANDATORY CODE OF CONDUCT FOR MEMBERS OF THE BRITISH VEHICLE RENTAL AND LEASING ASSOCIATION

INTRODUCTION

The BVRLA is the trade body for companies engaged in the leasing, rental and fleet management of cars and commercial vehicles for both corporate and consumer users.

This Code of Conduct sets out the standards which the BVRLA expects its members to achieve in all aspects of their business. BVRLA membership assures the customer that they should expect the highest levels of professionalism and integrity when renting or leasing vehicles from a BVRLA member.

The BVRLA promotes ethical trading, clear pricing, transparent terms and conditions and high-quality vehicles and customer service standards through the auditing of its members. This auditing covers vehicles, branches, vehicle inspection records and customer service standards.

The association operates a conciliation service for its members and their customers to help resolve disputes.

Adherence to this Code of Conduct is a condition of membership and serious breaches of the code will result in expulsion from the BVRLA.

OUR STANDARDS

By signing up to the Code of Conduct BVRLA members agree to abide by the following standards:

1   Transparent pricing for all products and services both on printed media and all websites which promote a member's products.

2   Not to misrepresent any facts concerning their products or services.

3   Behave at all times with integrity and ensure that all other persons or agents appointed by the member also follow the standards set out in the Code of Conduct.

4   Comply with and understand all related statutory controls and regulations relating to the service or product provided.

5   Provide advice as necessary to help customers make an informed choice based on the customer's identified needs.

6   Operate from an established commercial place of business which is maintained to a professional standard.

7   Not to use any advertising material containing misleading or inaccurate statements. Members will comply with the codes and standards set by the regulators for the broadcast (Ofcom) and non-broadcast (Advertising Standards Authority) media.

---

416 Reproduced here by kind permission of the British Vehicle Rental and Leasing Association.

8   Provide safe and roadworthy vehicles, which as a minimum will be maintained in accordance with the law and manufacturers' servicing requirements (where members retain the responsibility to maintain the vehicle).

9   To resolve customer complaints according to the standards set out in the BVRLA Code of Conduct.

Rental: Specific Terms

The following core principles apply to all rental cars and vans.

There is additional information for customers leasing or renting a commercial vehicle over 3.5 tonnes, and on the leasing and fleet management of cars and vans.

- SHORT-TERM RENTAL – CARS AND VANS

VEHICLE SUITABILITY, MAINTENANCE AND SAFETY

Cars and vans should, where possible, not be older than three years from the date of first registration or have more than 60,000 miles on the odometer. Where advised, members should assess the customers' requirements for the vehicle, for example, number of passengers or load details, to help determine the most suitable vehicle for their needs.

All members will undertake to maintain, inspect and operate cars and vans to at least the standard of the BVRLA's Quality Assurance programme. As part of this programme members must permit the association or its appointed agents to carry out unannounced independent inspections of the vehicles available for immediate rent and maintenance records.

Members will adhere to manufacturers' recommended routine maintenance and servicing arrangements and will inspect all vehicles prior to the commencement of each rental to ensure they are safe and roadworthy.

MOTOR VEHICLE INSURANCE

Where the vehicle is on rent members must carry insurance provided by an authorised UK motor insurer to the following minimum levels at all times:

- Unlimited third party liability for bodily injury.

- Third party liability for property damage for a minimum of £1 million.

The member shall always specify in the rental agreement the extent of the customer's financial responsibility if the vehicle is damaged or lost/stolen and in the event of third party claims.

If the customer's own motor insurance is used, the member shall check that suitable vehicle insurance is in force at the time the vehicle becomes the responsibility of the customer. The responsibility for the continuance of the motor insurance rests with the customer. The customer should be asked to complete a third party indemnity form or equivalent which provides full details of the insurance cover in place and indemnifies the member against claims, liabilities, losses (including loss of use), damages and expenses due to the failing of the customer's own insurance policy. Members may obtain a copy of this form from the BVRLA website.

Members should ensure the customer is made aware of their obligations to insure the vehicle and update the Motor Insurance Database with all vehicles that will be covered by their own insurance policy for more than 14 days.

RESERVATION AND BOOKING

Where members accept a reservation or booking for a car or van rental, they must clearly advise exactly what is included in the price quoted, details of any excess payments, location charges or other products/services which may be applicable. If the booking is made via a website the full terms and conditions should be clearly available to the customer to download and review prior to confirming the booking.

Members must advise customers at the reservation stage of any requirements for them to have a minimum level of driving experience and if there are any restrictions on the type of vehicle which can be rented due to experience. Members should also make it clear what identification requirements are required to collect the vehicle and what payment methods are acceptable.

Where a reservation/booking is made directly with the member but cannot be fulfilled by the member, the third party providing the vehicle must be a BVRLA member.

Members must make customers fully aware of their cancellation and no-show policy when confirming a reservation or booking. This information must include details of any cancellation periods, the amount for which the customer will be held responsible and how the customer is required to communicate the cancellation.

RENTAL AGREEMENT

Customers must always receive a copy of the agreement and the terms and conditions applicable to their rental. Members should take necessary steps to ensure that the customer reads and understands the key terms of the agreement, and help clarify any items as requested, before the agreement is entered into. All key terms should be provided in a summary form for the customer, especially those in relation to contractual waiver restrictions and exclusions.

PRICING, INCLUDING FUEL OR BATTERY RECHARGING POLICY

Members will provide clear and transparent information on how all charges are calculated, including all additional charges which are not optional at point of rental.

If a member requires an excess mileage charge to be made, then the policy relating to limited mileage tariffs and the daily mileage allowance must be explained clearly. Members must also ensure that they clearly explain the basis on which any excess mileage charge will be calculated.

Prior to the commencement of the rental, the customer must be informed of the fuel return policy and the options available, together with the basis on which any refuelling charges will be raised. Where the customer is required under the agreement to purchase fuel at the beginning of the rental, the terms of the fuel purchase and the basis of the charges should be clear.

The member must make a written note of the rental vehicle's fuel levels at both the start and end of the rental. The levels of any other fluids required in the vehicle, such as AdBlue, should also be noted.

Where an electric vehicle is provided, the member will clearly state what the battery charge policy is. This should include: the charge level the vehicle should be returned with, the basis on which any recharging charges will be raised and whether fast charging of the battery is not permitted. The battery charge level should be agreed at both the start and end of the rental.

DAMAGE AND THEFT PROTECTION PROGRAMME

Where members offer a damage and theft protection programme, the customer should be made fully aware of the fixed sum they will be liable for, when this will become due for payment and all exceptions which are not covered by the damage and theft protection programme.

This is also applicable to any additional products, normally purchased at the rental desk, such as an excess reduction product, which reduces a customer's liability further or in some cases reduces it to zero.

METHOD OF PAYMENT

The member will state, prior to the commencement of the rental, the basis for any deposit required, including any mandatory damage excess, and the options for payment by the customer when the vehicle is returned.

PRE-RENTAL INSPECTION

Vehicles that are ready to rent must have undergone a pre-rental inspection to ensure that they are in a clean and roadworthy condition in accordance with the BVRLA Ready to Rent Checklist or another similar standard which reflects this requirement.

Members must ensure that all damage, such as scratches, dents and the vehicle condition both inside and out, is clearly indicated on the inspection report or rental agreement. Prior to a rental commencing, the customer must be given the opportunity to check and agree both the interior and exterior condition of the vehicle before signing the rental agreement or any other inspection report.

Members should, where requested, help the customer become familiar with the basic operation and use of the vehicle. They should also provide the vehicle handbook – or relevant extracts of it – together with instruction as to the type of fuel that should be used in the vehicle and advice on charging the battery if the vehicle is powered in part or whole by electricity.

POST-RENTAL INSPECTION

A representative of the member and the customer themselves should check the vehicle as soon as possible after the end of the rental. Members should ensure that the vehicle is inspected with the customer present and any damage not previously recorded on the inspection report/rental agreement must be noted and signed for by both parties on all the copies of the rental agreement/inspection report.

If an inspection is not possible, this should be agreed in writing by both parties with a clear explanation as to the reason for non-inspection. In such circumstances, both parties must agree that any damage subsequently found but not noted on the pre-rental inspection form will be charged to the customer.

VEHICLES RETURNED OUT OF OFFICE HOURS

If a customer is permitted to return a vehicle outside normal opening hours they must be provided with clear procedures for doing so. The customer should be advised of their responsibility for motor insurance, post-rental damage, road traffic offences and parking the vehicle in a secure and safe location.

End-of-rental charges

If the customer is not present during the post-rental inspection process, the member will issue a written notification to the customer to advise of any end-of-rental charges that become due. The notice will include the reasons why the charge has been raised, together with summary details of how the charge(s) has been calculated and when the charge will be taken by the nominated method of payment agreed by the customer on the rental agreement.

Customers will be advised of the steps they should take should they wish to query the charges and, when requested, the member will provide all necessary documents to help substantiate end-of-rental charges.

• FREQUENT RENTERS AND RENTING BY THE HOUR

Members may offer a rental product where the customer has entered into terms and conditions in advance of a booking being made. This could be in circumstances where the customer is registered with the member as a regular customer or where members offer a rent-by-the-hour service. Subject to the following requirements being fully met, a member representative does not have to be in attendance prior to each and every rental.

Pre- and post-rental inspections

Members will instruct the customer to carry out visual checks on the condition of the vehicle immediately before and after the rental takes place. The visual check should not include any mechanical or technical checks of the vehicle but should ensure the vehicle is safe to operate.

The customer must be given clear instructions on how to confirm and record the condition of the vehicle and damage to the vehicle, together with any other details which the customer may be required to record, such as fuel level, odometer reading, accessories and battery charge. Such written record should be signed by the customer and clearly indicate the date and time the inspection was undertaken.

There should be clear instructions given to customers on what to do if the vehicle does not match the last condition report, if available.

Roadworthiness inspections

Members are responsible at all times for ensuring that their vehicles are roadworthy and safe to use. All such vehicles shall undergo a roadworthiness check every 1,000 miles or every fortnight, whichever comes sooner. The roadworthiness inspection will be in accordance with the motor manufacturer's recommendations and adhere to the BVRLA's Quality Assurance programme.

Driver licence checking

The member must, in their pre-agreed rental terms and conditions, make it clear that the customer is responsible for confirming that they have a legal entitlement to drive the class of vehicle being rented. The member should ensure that customers are clearly advised that they should immediately notify the member of any driving endorsements received since the entitlement to drive notification was provided, along with medical conditions which may affect the validity of the driving entitlement.

Driver licence checks should be conducted prior to an agreement being signed and on an annual basis thereafter.

Leasing and Fleet Management: Specific Terms

The following core principles apply to all leased and fleet managed vehicles, and related maintenance services.

STATUTORY CONTROLS AND REGULATIONS

Members should comply with all relevant legislation. Members must, where appropriate, hold all necessary licences and registration to trade lawfully, including a valid consumer credit licence and data protection registration.

CONTRACTS

Customers must be supplied with copies of all the contracts they enter into. Contracts may be supplied in printed or electronic formats.

QUOTATION AND PAYMENT TERMS

Members will provide clear pricing, including the number of advance payments/deposit and subsequent frequency of payments. Details of any circumstances under which the rental charges might change prior to delivery of the vehicle should be included.

Members will include details of the point at which the customer will be in breach of the contract due to late payment.

VEHICLE SUITABILITY

Where possible, members will assess and advise on the most appropriate vehicle based on the requirements of the customer. All vehicles provided to customers should be to the current manufacturer specification.

DUTY OF CARE

Members will ensure that, where possible, they assist customers with their duty of care responsibilities by providing the latest specification vehicles and advice on maintenance to ensure vehicles being driven are well maintained.

INSURANCE

Members will check at the beginning of a contract that the customer has steps in place to update the motor insurance database with all new vehicles added to the fleet and provide assistance where required.

ROAD TAX

Where the member has responsibility for taxing the vehicle, they will ensure it is renewed in good time before the existing road tax expires.

EARLY OR VOLUNTARY TERMINATION OF CONTRACT

Members will clearly define their policy regarding the early termination of a contract. Such a policy and relevant legal requirements may include the following items:

- The recovery of loss of value.
- The handling of maintenance payments.
- Excess mileage charges.

- Any adjustments to finance charges.
- The method of settlement in the event of the total loss of the leased vehicle.
- Charges for unreasonable wear and tear.

CONTRACT EXTENSION

Members will define the policy in relation to:

- any change to the services provided in the event of formal or informal contract extension.
- circumstances in which the vehicle might be recovered by the member during any extension period.

EXCESS MILEAGE

Members will explain their policy on:

- any requirement to return the vehicle at an agreed mileage.
- any circumstances relating to mileage which would require rewriting of the contract, and any charges associated with such contract rewriting.
- details of any increase or decrease of permitted mileage during formal or informal contract extensions.
- mechanisms for charging or allowing for over or under mileage at contract end or any other period during the contract.
- any charges associated with excessive battery degradation due to fast charging or excess mileage at contract end.

END OF CONTRACT AND RESTORATION CHARGES

Prior to the end of the contract, members will clearly explain:

- the end-of-lease vehicle return standard, including: vehicle condition, service and maintenance, vehicle accessories and MOT (if appropriate).
- the collection process and inspection procedure.
- the customer's rights relating to disputes over the collection process and inspection procedure.

THE END-OF-CONTRACT PROCESS

A representative of the member and the customer must check and agree on the vehicle's condition when the vehicle is collected. All readily apparent vehicle damage will be noted and signed for by both parties on the collection sheet. If, for whatever reason, an inspection is not possible, then this should be agreed in writing, with a clear explanation of the reason for non-inspection. The member must ensure that the customer has been advised that after the vehicle has been collected it will undergo an inspection in line with the agreed fair wear and tear policy.

In the event of a dispute concerning the condition of the vehicle, the customer will pay for an examination/review of the evidence by an independent qualified engineer, e.g. an engineer unrelated to the original inspection, agreed by both parties. The engineer's decision will be binding on both the customer and member. If the engineer's decision is in favour of the customer, the member will refund the reasonable cost of the inspection to the customer.

MAINTENANCE STANDARDS

Where members are responsible for servicing and maintaining the leased vehicle, they must ensure that all such activities are carried out at accredited outlets,[417] unless agreed otherwise with the customer. If the customer has agreed to be responsible for servicing and maintaining the vehicle, then the agreement with the customer should specify that this is carried out in line with manufacturers' guidelines and specifications. Members may have a written agreement which states that the repair outlet will repair the vehicle in accordance with manufacturers' standards and guidelines.

By meeting these obligations, members will help to demonstrate their commitment to delivering and operating to high standards that are set and regulated by a recognised industry trade body and guarantee the safe operation of their vehicles.

CUSTOMER INFORMATION

In the event of the termination of a fleet management contract, members should ensure that all fleet data held on behalf of the customer, such as service history, vehicle documentation, etc, is transferred in a timely and efficient manner upon request. The transfer of any commercially sensitive information is excluded from this obligation. Members are encouraged to follow the spirit of good business practice in the case of lease agreements.

Commercial Vehicle and Minibus: Specific Terms

In addition to the preceding terms applicable to rental and leasing, the following terms apply specifically to the rental and leasing of commercial vehicles and minibuses.

MAINTENANCE AND SAFETY

All members will undertake to maintain, inspect and operate vehicles to at least the minimum standard of the BVRLA's Commercial Vehicle Quality Assurance Programme (CVQA Programme). The programme permits the association to carry out independent checks of vehicle inspection and maintenance records and vehicles available for immediate rent to ensure they are maintained to at least the manufacturers' recommended standards and the BVRLA's CVQA standards. These are based on the Department for Transport's Operator and Passenger Service Vehicle Licence Regulations.

In addition to the manufacturers' recommended routine maintenance and drivers' reports[418], arrangements should be made for vehicles and their equipment to be inspected at appropriate intervals to determine the condition of those items which make a significant contribution to their safe and legal operation. The BVRLA recommends members adhere to the Department for Transport's guidelines

---

417 Accredited outlets must adhere to the standards set by regulatory bodies, and/or be a member of a recognised industry trade body (such as the Retail Motor Industry Federation, Independent Automotive Aftermarket Federation or Society of Motor Manufacturers and Traders) and be authorised by motor manufacturers. They may be either franchised or independent organisations.

418 Drivers' walkaround inspections of vehicles, which should take place before a vehicle is driven for that working day.

published in the *Guide to Maintaining Road Worthiness* for vehicles over 3.5 tonnes gross vehicle weight and for vehicles with more than eight passenger seats.

RECORD KEEPING

Members should ensure that inspection records for vehicles are kept for at least 15 months and that they are available to customers, the BVRLA and the Vehicle and Operator Services Agency when requested.

VEHICLE SUITABILITY

Members should assess the needs of the customer based on their advised use of the vehicle to help determine the most suitable vehicle for the job.

This could include identifying an appropriate vehicle specification and protective equipment for the driver and passenger(s), taking into account any requirements for load restraint equipment, vehicle racking and bulkheads.

SAFETY OF LOADS

Members should be familiar with the recommendations of the *Code of Practice: Safety of Loads on Vehicles*, produced by the Department for Transport. In addition, members must point out to customers the dangers of overloading the vehicle generally, or on individual axles, as well as the need to comply with all current legislation.

TOWING TRAILERS

Towing a trailer puts greater demand on the vehicle and the driver. It can also bring the vehicle into scope of the EU Drivers' Hours Rules and change the driving licence required. Information on acceptable trailer-towing weights can be found in vehicle handbooks. Customers should be encouraged to notify the member when they intend to tow a trailer. Customers intending to tow should be advised that:

- the vehicle must not exceed either its Gross Vehicle Weight (GVW) or the Gross Train Weight (GTW).
- the dimensions of a trailer being towed by a vehicle with a GVW over 3.5 tonnes should not exceed 2.55m in width or 12m in length.
- care should be taken to ensure even distribution of loads to avoid overloading of individual axles.

ADVICE TO THE CUSTOMER

Information relating to the vehicle's safe operation and use, its dimensions, payload and weight restrictions should be provided prior to each rental. In particular, information on the height of the vehicle must be provided in the vehicle cab.

OPERATOR LICENCE CHECKS

Although there is no legal obligation on members to check that a customer has a valid operator licence, consideration should be given to the benefits of ensuring that a valid O-licence is in place, where appropriate.

TACHOGRAPHS

Members should, if possible, ensure the customer is familiar with the type of tachograph in the vehicle and its basic operation. Customers should be alerted to the importance of locking-in their personal data so that it cannot be accessed by other customers.

MINIBUSES

Members should make sure the customer is familiar with the safe operation of minibuses and the legislation which surrounds them, including the requirements to record and observe EU drivers' hours rules and have a PSV operator's licence.

Complaint Handling

BVRLA members should aim to deliver a high level of service.

Complaints should be resolved quickly and amicably.

All staff should be aware of the company's complaint-handling procedures and staff dealing with complaints should respond swiftly, paying particular attention to:

*   advising customers of the complaints procedure, how to use it and what additional options are available to them.

*   treating complaints seriously and dealing with them in a positive and friendly manner.

*   issuing an acknowledgement to any complaint, regardless of how it is received, within five working days of receipt, with the objective of resolving the dispute within 15 working days.

*   learning from all complaints and responding proactively to prevent similar incidents from occurring.

*   maintaining a complete record of all complaints.

A small number of complaints may remain unresolved. The BVRLA Conciliation Service exists to help resolve those disputes that cannot be resolved between the parties by the method described above. The service levels for members whose complaints are referred to the BVRLA are set out below.

CONCILIATION PROCEDURE

Unresolved complaints can be referred to the association by either the customer or the member involved.

Details should be submitted in writing or by email to: Chief Executive, British Vehicle Rental and Leasing Association, River Lodge, Badminton Court, Amersham, HP7 0DD. complaint@bvrla.co.uk

Stage 1 Informal Conciliation Service

In the first instance, the BVRLA will aim to resolve the matter on an informal basis using the information presented by both parties. Where any information is requested from the member this should be sent within five working days. Based on the information available the BVRLA will provide both parties with its initial findings and recommendations. If either party disagrees with the outcome of the informal conciliation service, a formal conciliation procedure can be invoked.

The BVRLA aims to resolve complaints through the informal conciliation service within 30 days.

Stage 2 Formal Conciliation Service

If either party has asked for the matter to be escalated to the formal conciliation service, all relevant details will be promptly forwarded to the Conciliation Committee, a body whose members are appointed by the BVRLA Board.

CONCILIATION COMMITTEE

Disputes referred to the Conciliation Committee shall be actioned and a decision notified to the customer within 30 working days from referral.

WHAT IS COVERED UNDER THE CONCILIATION SERVICE?

Conciliation procedures shall apply solely to disputes arising from the vehicle rental and leasing activities of members.

COMPENSATION

The Conciliation Service is unable to award any form of indirect compensatory payments in relation to alleged financial losses arising from a breach of the rental or leasing agreement by either party to the dispute.

REFUNDS

The Conciliation Service will only have jurisdiction to consider matters relating to charges linked to the rental or lease that have been requested by the member.

NO RESTRICTION OF RIGHTS

Nothing in this code restricts, nor is intended to restrict, the rights of a complainant or a member, to pursue remedies through the courts.

MONITORING AND COMPLIANCE

The BVRLA's continual monitoring and internal procedures are aimed at ensuring that members meet and comply with this Code. It is a condition of membership that members comply with this Code.

Rental Charter

The BVRLA's Rental Charter applies to all members involved in the short-term rental of cars and commercial vehicles and forms a brief summary of the specific terms found in this Code of Conduct.

As a member of the British Vehicle Rental and Leasing Association we pledge to provide for our customers:

- a vehicle which is suited to your needs and maintained to the manufacturer's recommended standards, which has been cleaned and thoroughly checked.
- complete details of pricing, fuel/battery policies and any excess mileage charges.
- an overview of our damage and theft protection options, including excess levels and exceptions to the protection.

- the opportunity to inspect the interior and exterior of the vehicle prior to the rental to ensure it is line with the condition stated on the inspection report or rental agreement.

- the opportunity to inspect the vehicle when it is returned at the end of rental and agree on the condition. If this is not possible then we will agree this with you in writing and any additional damage found will be charged to you.

- a commitment to the British Vehicle Rental and Leasing Association's Code of Conduct.

- an effective complaints procedure with access to the Conciliation Service administered by the British Vehicle Rental and Leasing Association.

Leasing & Fleet Management Charter

The BVRLA's Leasing and Fleet Management Charter applies to all members involved in the leasing and fleet management of cars and commercial vehicles and forms a brief summary of the specific terms found in this Code of Conduct.

As a member of the British Vehicle Rental and Leasing Association we pledge to provide for our customers:

- advice on the most appropriate vehicle based on the requirements of the customer and assistance with duty of care responsibilities by providing the latest specification vehicles and advice on maintenance.

- transparent pricing for all charges and a clear statement of the total number of payments required under the contract and their frequency.

- servicing and maintenance of vehicles at accredited outlets in line with the manufacturers' guidelines.

- a clear statement of our policy for the early termination of a contract, extension of contract, or mileage or other limitations.

- information on the end-of-lease vehicle return standard, the collection and inspection procedure, and a dispute resolution process.

- commitment to the British Vehicle Rental and Leasing Association's Code of Conduct.

- an effective complaints procedure with access to the Conciliation Service administered by the British Vehicle Rental and Leasing Association.

FINANCE & LEASING ASSOCIATION CODE OF PRACTICE

A number of contract hire and leasing companies are members of the Finance & Leasing Association (FLA). It too has rules by which its members are required to abide.

The business finance code is set out on the following pages. Some sections are not relevant to vehicle finance so these have been removed.

FLA BUSINESS FINANCE CODE

Guidance to members

June 2011

INTRODUCTION

This Code sets out the standards that FLA members will meet when providing asset finance to businesses and the public sector. Compliance with the Code is a condition of FLA membership. Members' compliance with the Code is governed by the FLA's Business Code Group. In the event of continued or repeated non-compliance, the FLA will take action, including a warning or expulsion from FLA membership. The FLA operates a conciliation procedure for customer complaints that cannot be resolved by members, and also offers an independent mediation scheme.

THE FLA BUSINESS FINANCE CODE

COMMITMENTS

1   FLA members will abide by the Code and all relevant laws and regulations, will trade fairly and responsibly with customers, and will promote responsible trading between intermediaries and customers.

2   Before a business finance agreement is contracted, FLA members will provide customers with appropriate information.

3   FLA members will make business finance agreements that are clear and fair.

4   FLA Members will provide effective customer service.

5   FLA Members will clearly explain the options available to customers at the expiry or termination of business finance agreements.

6   Members will operate appropriate complaints procedures.

GUIDANCE NOTES

Commitment 1: FLA members will abide by the Code and all relevant laws and regulations, will trade fairly and responsibly with Customers, and will promote responsible trading between intermediaries and customers

ABIDING BY THE CODE

1.1   Providing adequate training for staff, bringing this Code to their attention as relevant to them, and requiring them to carry out their duties in accordance with it.

1.2 Following the Code throughout the course of the company's business finance activities, including in respect of assigned agreements, from the date of assignment.

1.3 Encouraging businesses who introduce customers to them to meet any relevant parts of this Code.

MAINTAINING GENERAL STANDARDS OF PROFESSIONAL CONDUCT

1.4 Respecting the confidentiality of information supplied by customers.

1.5 Not knowingly misrepresenting facts to customers.

1.6 Considering cases of financial difficulty reasonably in light of the customer's circumstances.

1.7 Avoiding contributing to conflicts of interests by disclosing any fees paid by FLA members to customers' retained advisers in the public sector.

MAKING AGREEMENTS THAT ARE APPROPRIATE TO THE ASSETS BEING FINANCED

1.9 Ensuring that minimum periods of hire are no longer than a period reasonable in relation to the expected working life of the assets financed, provided the assets are maintained in accordance with the manufacturer's recommendations. Members should use judgement in assessing the reasonable period of hire. All periods should be consistent with the commitment to trade fairly and responsibly. Regardless of whether the customer has signed a declaration accepting responsibility for the life of the equipment, the members should judge that the minimum period of hire is reasonable in relation to the expected working life.

1.10 For new operating lease business finance agreements with the public sector, basing the agreement on residual values that are appropriate to the asset being financed.

PROTECTING THE REPUTATION OF THE INDUSTRY

1.11 Notifying the FLA of any matters which might adversely affect the reputation of the industry or the FLA, whilst protecting client confidentiality.

1.12 Reviewing annually compliance with the Code, and confirming to the FLA that the Code has been followed.

Commitment 2: Before a business finance agreement is contracted, FLA members will provide customers with appropriate information.

FLA members will meet the Commitment by:

PROVIDING INFORMATION ON THE COST AND DURATION OF THE AGREEMENT

2.1 Providing relevant information on the payments to be made and the duration of the agreement.

PROVIDING INFORMATION ON SERVICES PROVIDED DURING THE AGREEMENT

2.3 Providing relevant information on services to be provided, including:

- The amount of rental payments attributable to charges for services, except where it is clearly stated that the business finance agreement is inclusive of services, (for example a "bundled agreement" with a captive finance company).

- The period during which the supply of services will continue, if that period is different from the minimum period of hire, and the cost of the supply of services after the end of that period.

- Any limitation on the amount or volume of services provided, and the cost of the supply of services after any such limitation has been exceeded.

- Any increase in the amount of any charges for services which will occur without any action or notice by the member or supplier, other than changes in VAT.

PROVIDING INFORMATION ON WHAT HAPPENS AT THE END OF THE AGREEMENT

2.4 Providing information on:

- Any period of notice required in order for the customer to terminate the agreement.

- Any payments or charges payable by the customer upon early termination of the agreement.

MAKING CLEAR WITH WHOM THE BUSINESS FINANCE AGREEMENT WILL BE AGREED

2.5 Making clear when a business finance agreement, other than an undisclosed agreement, is designed for placement with one of a number of potential alternative lessors.

2.6 Making clear whether the business finance agreement is being made with the supplier/manufacturer, or a separate company.

2.7 Making clear who will provide any services included in the agreement.

PROVIDING ADDITIONAL INFORMATION FOR PUBLIC SECTOR CUSTOMERS

2.8 Providing information to public sector customers on:

- Any commission, fee or other payment that the member will pay to an advisor acting on behalf of an NHS Trust or Foundation Trust.

- Any arrangement with a third party covering the member's exposure to the residual value of the equipment.

- Where the member is acting as a broker, the nature of any mandates or agency agreements entered into between the member and the lessor which relate to the transaction.

Commitment 3: FLA members will make business finance agreements that are clear and fair

FLA members will meet the Commitment by:

3.1 When a business finance agreement continues without amendment, beyond a minimum/initial period of hire, giving the customer the right to terminate the agreement at any time by giving not more than 3 months notice.

3.2   Including a discount in the termination figure to reflect accelerated receipt of future rental payments, excluding any part of such rentals attributable to charges for services.

3.3   Excluding from the termination figure the price of any services which will not be required following termination, if a contract for support services has already finished.

Commitment 4: FLA Members will provide effective customer service

FLA members will meet the Commitment by:

4.1   Having effective procedures in place for responding to customer enquiries or problems throughout the life of the agreement.

4.2   Notifying customers in advance of fees that are payable for ad hoc services.

Commitment 5: FLA Members will clearly explain the options available to customers at the expiry or termination of business finance agreements

FLA members will meet the Commitment by:

5.1   Supplying to a customer an early termination figure upon their request.

5.2   Providing a reminder to customers, setting out the options available, when the customer is required to give notice to terminate at the expiry of a minimum/initial period of hire, between three months and one month before the last date on which the customer can give notice.

5.3   At the expiry of every public sector business finance agreement under which the member retains residual value rights, considering any reasonable requests by the customer to retain possession/use of the asset for an appropriate period, and agreeing a new business finance agreement at a fair market rate. If residual value rights are sold to another member, that member should also consider such requests.

Commitment 6: Members will operate appropriate complaints procedures

FLA members will meet the Commitment by:

6.1   Having in place appropriate procedures for addressing complaints.

6.2   Providing details of the FLA's conciliation and mediation schemes to customers making complaints.

PARTICIPATION IN FLA CONCILIATION SCHEME

6.3   On receipt of a complaint referred from the FLA, instigating an investigation and sending an initial response to the complainant within ten business days.

19.4   HOW CAR LEASING AND CONTRACT HIRE COMPANIES RUN THEIR BUSINESSES

Contract hire is the main UK fleet finance and service product and from the client's point of view it is very straightforward. You pay the rentals and the leasing company supplies, maintains and disposes of the vehicle, and takes the RV and SMR risks.

Whilst this might be a simple product from the client's perspective it requires a great deal of effort for the contract hire company to deliver this product and service.

This section is included to give you an insight into the multitude of things a contract hire company has to do.

If you visit the offices of a vehicle leasing or contract hire company you may find it difficult to tell that it is involved in motor finance and management. All you will see are people sitting at desks, talking on the phone and gazing at their computer screens. You could be in a call centre, stock broker or an investment bank.

Scratch below the surface and you will be very surprised indeed by the number of things going on.

These will include:

- Purchasing cars
- Approving and paying maintenance invoices
- Selling cars
- Issuing contracts
- Credit checking new and existing clients
- Issuing quotes
- Handling a variety of insurances (motor, gap, creditor protection, keyman)
- Product development
- Monitoring legislation
- Calculating residual values, maintenance budgets and rentals
- Monitoring interest costs
- Managing cash
- Advising clients on fleet policy and taxation (of many types)
- Buying and issuing tax discs
- Claiming government grants.

Then there are the normal things most companies do such as:

- Marketing
- Selling
- Accounting

- Collecting debts
- Paying bills
- Planning
- Financial reporting
- Managing quality systems
- Managing computer systems
- Housekeeping
- Dealing with premises issues
- Managing health and safety issues

In fact, the list is endless.

This chapter does not look at most of these items because general business management issues are covered in hundreds of other books. It also does not focus on the generic fleet management processes such as purchasing, maintenance control, vehicle disposal and so on – these are dealt with elsewhere in this book.

Instead, it looks at just a few topics that are specific to the fleet leasing industry.

19.4.1 Credit management

When a leasing company buys a £20,000 vehicle for a client and delivers it to their office or home, they need to be confident that the client will keep their side of the bargain; make payments on time, look after the vehicle and return it as agreed at the end of the contract. Before they get too far down the process of establishing a relationship with a client they carry out a credit assessment.

They obtain basic information from the client such as business name, address and type and ask for a copy of their latest audited accounts. They review these and look at four main elements; profitability, liquidity, growth and the market sector in which the business operates.

If a company is profitable it is more likely to be able to meet its obligations as they fall due than if it is loss-making.

Trends are important in this analysis. Many companies have the occasional bad year in which they make an exceptional loss but this may not affect the long term viability of the business.

However, a downward trend in profitability over several years is worrying and may be a precursor to financial collapse.

Liquidity can be defined in many ways but for our purposes it can be described as the ability of a company to pay its debts as they fall due. A common measure of liquidity is the 'current ratio' – the ratio of current assets to current liabilities in the balance sheet.

Current assets are those assets - that is, those things that the company owns - that can be turned into cash quickly, usually within one year. So current assets include stock, work in progress, debtors, cash at the bank and so on.

Current liabilities are those liabilities – that is, those things that the business owes to others – that will fall due in the short term, again normally within one year. If a company has more current assets than current liabilities it should always be able to pay its debts as they fall due by converting those assets into cash in order to meet the liabilities.

In many ways liquidity is more important than profitability. It may be a truism but the fact is that companies do not call in the administrators on a Friday morning because they are unprofitable. They call them in because they cannot pay that month's wages.

If the company's accounts are out of date the client may be asked for a copy of their latest management accounts. If the accounts are old and the company has not submitted accounts to Companies House within the statutory period, or if the company do not have – or will not provide – up to date management accounts, the leasing company will begin to get worried. If a company cannot keep its house in order it may be a sign that it cannot keep its commercial relationships in order either.

Some contract hire, motor finance and leasing companies will look at 'collateral gap' as part of their credit and risk management procedures. Collateral gap is the difference between the balance that will be outstanding in their books over the course of the financing and the value of the vehicle.[419]

This is useful information given that the size of any loss the lessor will make on default is directly related to the value of the vehicle in the used car market at that time. Lessors are happier financing vehicles that depreciate slowly than those that depreciate more rapidly.

As well as obtaining information from the prospective client, leasing companies will also obtain report from a credit reference agency. There are several agencies that will provide a report containing the type of information that leasing companies are interested to see.

The report will include analysed financial statements going back over several years, allowing the leasing company to see the trend of the company's financial performance. It will also include basic information on the company's name, address, officers and market sector, and these can be checked against the information that the prospective client has supplied.

None of this will tell whether the prospective client actually pays its bills on time, so the credit agencies carry out surveys among suppliers to check this and include this information in their report.

Finally, the report will show if there are any mortgages, judgements or winding up orders recorded against the company.

Credit assessment is both a science and an art. Each contract hire or leasing company has its own view of what is and is not a creditworthy business. Some of

---

419 See graph 1.22.6.

them create financial models (formulae) to help them determine whether a particular company is the right sort of them to deal with.

For example, a particular lessor may decide to reject any company that has not been in business for at least three years, has not made a profit for the last two years, and does not have a current ratio of more than 1:1 or net worth of more than £400,000.

An experienced credit manager might look at a company that has failed such a test, realise that it is in a sector of the economy that is growing strongly, see that it has just signed a long term government contract to deliver something that it is capable of delivering and therefore approve rather than reject the prospective client.

When the applicant is a private individual, lessors gather information about them from the form that they complete, and carry out a search at a credit reference agency. The agency report will show, among other things, whether the applicant lives where they claim to live, using information obtained from the electoral roll.

The consumer credit industry was alarmed by the judgment in the case of Robertson v City of Wakefield in 2001.

Brian Robertson, a retired accountant, sued Wakefield Council and the government. He argued he was required by law to register to vote, that the electoral roll was routinely sold to direct marketing companies, and therefore his right to privacy under the Human Rights Act was undermined. The court agreed and said human rights considerations meant the electoral roll should not be sold for any purpose.

In 2002, after several months of confusion, the government announced that full access to the electoral roll would still be available for the purposes of checking credit and fraud prevention. It said:

> 'There is a clear public interest in there being a… prudent availability of credit [and] it is the government's view that there would be a real risk [to this] if the full register were no longer available for assessing credit applications.'

It went on to say this was more important than any loss of individual privacy.

Prudent lenders must ensure they know their customers. So when leasing to private individuals they have to check their identity. Inspecting an applicant's driving licence is an important part of this check and with the driver's permission a lessor can check this at the DVLA. Daily hire companies are major users of this service.

Each vehicle leasing and contract hire company tends to specialise in one or more particular client group, such as

- ECOs
- Salary sacrifice schemes
- Small and medium size enterprises
- UK Plc
- Public sector bodies.

■ Sub-prime (i.e. people or small businesses that would generally find it difficult to get leasing facilities elsewhere)

The use of credit assessment tools helps each of these businesses to ensure they only take the credit risks that meet their chosen risk profile and allows them to reject deals that they consider to be too risky.

19.4.2 CIFAS – THE UK'S FRAUD PREVENTION SERVICE

You may think that the consumer credit industry – the banks, building societies, finance companies, leasing companies and so on – are arch competitors who are at each other's throats all the time.

And you would be right.

There has never been more choice for consumers who are searching for credit.

But at least in one area the credit industry is totally united – its desire to reduce fraud.

In 1988 the major UK consumer credit lenders established CIFAS, the credit industry fraud avoidance system. It was the world's first not-for-profit credit industry fraud avoidance system. Its name was changed in 2000 to 'CIFAS – the fraud avoidance system' and again in 2002 to 'CIFAS – the UK's fraud prevention service'.

It protects its members by pooling information about criminals. Members notify CIFAS about fraud and this is stored on the CIFAS database. If another member then searches on that consumer's address CIFAS notifies it there is a fraud registered against that person or address. The two lenders are then able to speak direct to confirm details.

So this is a system that gives benefits to members and also gives them the responsibility of notifying fraud and speaking to a competitor who may be about to be defrauded.

It is a system that has worked very well.

Each year CIFAS logs around 50,000 cases of consumers trying to obtain credit by adopting false identities. Clearly, there is a need for CIFAS and it is doing a good job.

CIFAS now has over 250 member companies drawn from all areas of consumer-focused and financing businesses, including factoring, insurance, share dealing, commercial credit, banks, building societies, leasing companies, discounters, retailers, telecoms and mail order companies.

CIFAS is an independent company limited by guarantee. The police and the national consumer council have observer status within CIFAS.

CIFAS provides a useful service to consumers. Individuals who have been the victims of theft or burglary in which their personal documents have been stolen can register the theft at CIFAS to protect themselves against impersonation attempts.

The CIFAS website contains advice on fraud and scam prevention. See www.cifas.org.uk.

19.4.3 BVRLA RENTAL INDUSTRY SECURE CUSTOMER SYSTEM (RISC)

The BVRLA maintains an online database of thousands of 'bad hirers'.

These may be:

- Car thieves
- Fraudsters who rent cars and disappear
- People involved in smuggling or in conveying clandestine immigrants
- Hirers who extend a vehicle rental without authorisation
- People who have returned vehicles in bad condition.

When a new hirer makes an enquiry to a BVRLA rental company that has subscribed to the system the rental company can quickly discover if any other BVRLA rental member has had problems with the hirer. This is invaluable information in helping the rental company decide whether to rent to that customer.

RISC is another example of an industry uniting to fight fraud for the common good.

19.4.4 PORTS ANTI THEFT SYSTEM

The size of the UK car theft 'industry' is massive. Many cars are stolen when on hire purchase, lease or hire from motor finance, leasing or daily hire companies. Many of these cars are then exported.

To try to reduce the risk that stolen cars will be exported, vehicles are detected using automatic number plate recognition equipment at ports and the Channel Tunnel.

The stolen vehicle database is dated by the police following information from leasing and asset finance companies. Any 'hits' represent stolen vehicles and these are stopped by the police at the port and the driver is questioned. This scheme has been very successful, having caught stolen cars worth millions of pounds since it was introduced in 2000.

The police have been particularly pleased with this collaboration with the credit industry because stolen cars are often linked to other crimes such as smuggling and drug trafficking. So arrests for vehicle theft have led to further arrests for a wide variety of crimes.

19.4.5 VEHICLE FRAUD UNIT

The Vehicle Fraud Unit is a joint venture between the police and credit industry that is designed to reduce motor fraud.

If you see a thief breaking into a car and trying to drive it off, phone the police and they will race to the scene to try to catch the offender. If the same thief fraudulently fills in a credit application form and manages to get a finance or leasing company to hand over a car, and then refuses to pay, the police have historically been more reluctant to act. They tended to the view that this is a normal commercial transaction that had gone wrong and left the lender to pursue its remedies through the courts.

The police always accepted this was not ideal but were constrained by limited resources. After talks with the Home Office, the credit industry agreed to contribute towards the cost of a small team of officers in Merseyside Police who would be dedicated to fighting motor vehicle fraud.

That project – Operation Pimpernel – ran throughout the late 1990s and was a success, with millions of pounds of vehicles being recovered. These arrests often led to other charges being laid for unrelated crimes.

In 2001 the Metropolitan Police adopted this model and set up a dedicated team of officers based at the Vehicle Fraud Unit, funded by the credit industry. In 2007 it became part of the ACPO Vehicle Crime Intelligence Service (AVCIS), a national police unit dedicated to investigating and recovering fraudulently-obtained vehicles and prosecuting offenders. The FLA has sponsored the Vehicle Fraud Unit of AVCIS since September 2007. So far the Unit has so far recovered over 1,000 vehicles worth £16m.

The AVCIS website[420] contains useful information on vehicle crime, including answers to questions such as:

■ I think my car has been stolen. What should I do?

■ I think I might have bought a stolen car. What should I do?

■ My number plates have been stolen from my car. What should I do?

■ How can I avoid buying a stolen vehicle?

■ I think my car has been cloned. What should I do?

Some critics have said that arresting fraudsters is core police work and that it should not have to be paid for by the victims of the crime. However, the reality is that the police do not have unlimited resources and the credit industry has found that this partnership is cost-effective and brings valuable results.

There is an interesting precedent here.[421] During the 1921 coal strike there were violent pickets outside English coal mines. The police attended, but in the view of one mine owner they did not provide enough officers. A compromise was reached – the police would provide seventy extra police officers and the mine owner would pay the council for this. After the strike had ended the owner refused to pay and a court case ensued. The court decided that it was wrong for a public authority to demand payment for normal services. But if the public authority went further than was necessary, in return for a promise of payment, then it could recover the cost.

420 avcis.police.uk
421 Glasbrook Bros Ltd v Glamorgan County Council, 1925 AC 270, House of Lords (HH 200)

19.4.6 ACPO/BVRLA Stolen Vehicle Reporting Agreement

Operation Pimpernel has not been the only collaborative venture between the finance industry and the police. The ACPO/BVRLA Stolen Vehicle initiative is another.

If a BVRLA member completes a witness statement, provides a vehicle description and follows certain prescribed procedures the police will treat vehicle fraud as theft. The vehicle will be logged as stolen on the Police National Computer.

If the vehicle is spotted the police will arrest the driver.

19.4.7 Insurance Fraud

According to the Association of British Insurers, bogus insurance claims doubled between 2005 and 2010.

There were 40,000 cases detected in 2010, which may just be the tip of the iceberg.

From 2012 the industry is setting up national Insurance Fraud Register to bring all fraud details into one database. The police are also setting up a national police unit to investigate insurance fraud.

There has been a rise in the number of insurance claims being made after 'bogus' accidents, where criminals make fraudulent insurance claims following staged accidents. According to the Insurance Fraud Bureau[422] there are at least 30,000 of these 'cash for crash' accidents every year. If you believe your fleet has been the victim of one of these fraudsters, notify your insurer, the police and the Insurance Fraud Bureau.

19.4.8 Treasury management

Money is the most important raw material of a contract hire or leasing company. Money, as my Mum always told me, does not grow on trees. It comes from somewhere and it needs to come in large quantities to allow lessors to buy the vehicles in the numbers their clients require.

Lessors use one or more of the following methods to fund their businesses:

Back to back finance

Under this arrangement a lessor obtains a vehicle under a contract hire, finance lease or hire purchase agreement with a third party funder, then 'sub-lease' the vehicle to you.

Undisclosed Agency

Here the lessor acts as agent of the funder to buy the vehicle, lease it to you and collect the rentals. This agency arrangement may be disclosed to you or totally undisclosed.

422 See 19.6.2

Only if there was a problem – perhaps the lessor fails to pay the rentals to the funder, or you go into default and they wish to manage the contact with you thereafter – would the identity of the funder or the existence of the agency arrangement be disclosed to you.

Third party funding

Under this arrangement a contract hire company acts as agent of the funder to buy the vehicle. They give you the funder's leasing agreement to sign and you pay rentals direct to the funder. When the funder receives these they pay part of the rental to the contract hire company that introduced the business to them. This may simply be a commission payment.

Alternatively, if the contract hire company has agreed to provide maintenance services as part of the deal, the funder will pay over the maintenance element of the rental you pay them.

Parent funding

This involves the use of funds provided from within a lessor's group to finance their vehicle leasing business. Parent company funding is sometimes carried out without match funding, leaving the lessor exposed to interest rate risk.

Match-funding

Match funding is the process whereby a lessor's cash inflows and outflows are matched, thereby ensuring their interest costs match their revenues. Another way of describing this is to say that the maturities of their assets and liabilities are matched.

Neither of these descriptions is particularly helpful, so here is an example:

> Jones is a one-man contract hire business. He has no cars under lease and no clients. He decides that you will be his first client. He will lease you one car, on 1 August 2012, at a monthly rental of £500 payable for thirty-six months. He calculates this rental will give him a 12% interest return on his money. He goes out and buys the car.
>
> How will he finance it? He could use his bank overdraft. If he does so he will owe the bank the price of the car and you will owe him some rentals. His bank charges him interest of base rate plus 3%. Let's assume bank base rate is 5%, so he is going to make a 4% margin over his cost of funds in leasing the car to you. On 1 November 2012 bank base rates rise by 1%. Now his overdraft is costing him 9% and his margin is reduced to 3%. At a stroke, the increase in bank base rate has wiped 25% off his margin.
>
> The lease has still got 33 months to run. If base rates rise again he could lose even more of his margin or even start making a loss.

How could he avoid this problem? The only way is to match-fund, which means locking in the cost of his borrowings for the duration of the contract.

There are several ways that he can do this and back to back funding is just one of them.

If he had 10,000 vehicles under lease, rather than one, he would be borrowing tens of millions of pounds rather than a few thousand pounds. And at this level of operation he can directly access the money markets for his funding, borrowing at a margin over London Interbank Offered Rate (LIBOR) to finance his business.

The only problem with the money market is that it prefers to lend lump sums that are all repayable on maturity of the loan. This is called a bullet repayment. There is not much point in Jones borrowing all of the money for three years and being unable to repay the loan during that period. What will he do with the rentals that arrive from his clients in that period? He could put them on deposit but that exposes him to another risk – the volatility of the deposits market.

One approach would be to borrow a series of loans maturing at different dates to finance his portfolio of leases.

He could borrow an amount for one month, another for two months, another for three months and so on up to thirty-six months. Then, as the rentals arrive each month he could use them to repay the loan.

This is sometimes called 'strip funding' and it is a common way of financing lending businesses.

Another approach would be for Jones to borrow short term all the monies that he needs to finance the fleet. As rentals start rolling in they would be used to repay this debt. As he buys more vehicles he would borrow more cash.

This arrangement would ensure that Jones always has the cash to buy the cars his clients require. However, so far, he still has an interest rate risk. In order to eliminate this and match his interest costs to his revenues he could enter into 'swap' arrangements.

A swap is a financial instrument under which one party (with short term borrowings but needing long term borrowings) swaps its obligation to pay interest with another party (with long term borrowings but wanting short term borrowings). The effect is that the party holding short term borrowings pays interest as if it had long term borrowings.

This sounds more complex than it is in real life.

To enter into a swap to lock in the interest costs, Jones would ask a bank to sell him a series of swaps of different maturities and he would pay them the interest in the same way as if he had borrowed long term funds.

Leases do not always run for thirty-six months. Sometimes Jones's clients might ask him to terminate a lease early, other times they may ask to extend it and occasionally they will wrap cars around trees so there is little to be done other than to end the lease.

So a portfolio of leases is a rather dynamic thing and the funding arrangement that lessors set up one day may become unbalanced after a few months of trading.

They can find themselves with a car coming off lease but having to keep their own funding in place for the rest of the loan period. To adjust for this, they carry out a periodic calculation showing how closely the borrowings in their loan portfolio match the assets they are funding.[423] This will reveal the 'gap' that exists and show how much they have to borrow and for what periods, to rebalance the maturity of their assets and liabilities.

19.4.9 ENTERPRISE ACT 2002

This allows the Office of Fair Trading, trading standards offices and other bodies nominated by the Secretary of State to stop a course of business simply if unfair conduct has occurred or is likely to occur.

The agency wishing to take enforcement action must first give notice to the business that it believes is infringing the regulations. This gives the business the opportunity to change its behaviour and to give undertakings to the agency that the unfair behaviour will not be repeated.

If agreement cannot be reached, and the activity continues, the agency can seek a court order to stop the unfair activity.

If a provider of consumer credit or hire were to trade in a way that was unfair to its customers, each customer would have the right under the Consumer Credit Act to apply to the court to rectify the situation. However, if the OFT were to learn that the provider was behaving so unfairly that the rights of many people were being harmed, the OFT could use its powers under the Enterprise Act to require the provider to stop the unfair behaviour.

19.4.10 V5C - END OF CONTRACT

As already mentioned in 16.4, a tax disc cannot be issued unless a V5C or V11 is produced. This can cause some difficulties for car leasing and finance companies offering PCP[424] and hire purchase agreements.

When these products are sold without a maintenance package, it is normal for the vehicle to be registered in the client's name and for the client to buy the annual vehicle excise duty. The clients hold the V5Cs and the V11s are sent direct to them.

At the end of these agreements it is sometimes difficult to get the V5C returned by the client. Where there has been a default and the vehicle has been repossessed it is even more difficult.

As it is not possible to obtain a new tax disc without a V5C or V11, lessors and finance companies have found difficulty in selling these vehicles for their full market value.

---

423 Or, put another way, they can check how the cash flows of the loans match the cash flows of the leases.

424 See 1.18.1.

It is possible to obtain a new V5C but, as a crime-prevention measure, the DVLA will not issue one until they have sent a V712 letter to the registered keeper. This tells the registered keeper that someone has applied for a V5C for their vehicle and asks for their permission to issue a new V5C.

If the registered keeper consents to this the DVLA will issue the new V5C to the finance company.

This process can take up to six weeks.

If the client refuses to give this permission the only option available is for the finance company to re-register the vehicle in its own name. This increases the number of registered keepers of the vehicle and reduces the market value of the vehicle.

The DVLA has been sympathetic to the problems this has caused to the industry but so far has been unable to offer any alternative solution.

19.4.11   BVRLA ILLEGAL IMMIGRATION PENALTY PROCEDURE

Where a vehicle is found to be carrying an illegal immigrant, the driver can be fined for separately for each clandestine entrant and the vehicle can be impounded until the fine is paid.

The government has recognized that it is unfair to penalise a leasing company if one of its vehicles is impounded in this way: after all, the leasing company does not have day-to-day control of the vehicle.

The BVRLA has negotiated a special agreement with the Home Office to allow these vehicles to be released quickly and at no charge to the leasing company. The arrangement is only available to BVRLA member companies if they sign up to a special code of practice.

More information is available from the BVRLA.

19.4.12   REPOSSESSIONS

The vast majority of leases and car finance agreements run their full term without difficulty.

Some clients do not pay their rentals or other charges on time, occasionally because they are unable to pay but more often because they raise a legitimate query over a particular invoice.

In a small number of cases the agreement goes into default and the vehicle has to be repossessed.

If the agreement is a conditional sale agreement, hire purchase agreement or any type of lease, the legal position is that the finance company/lessor remains the owner of the vehicle and has a right to repossess and sell it.[425]

---

425 See chapter 1

However, if the agreement is a credit sale agreement there will be no such right, as title to (ownership in) the vehicle will have passed to the borrower at the start of the agreement. In these situations the lender will have to rely on some other form of security.

Normally, these agreements are only seen as part of employee car ownership schemes[426] in which the lender gets security from the borrower's employer in the form of a guarantee, and they can claim on this if the borrower is in default.

If the car has been sold by the borrower/lessee without the consent of the lender/lessor, the rules are complicated.

If the asset is a car and was bought by a private individual acting in good faith (i.e. they fully believed they were buying a car from someone who had the right to sell it), the buyer gets good title to the car. The finance company/lessor has to pursue their client for repayment.

If the asset was a car and was bought by a private individual who was not acting in good faith (i.e. they knew or should reasonably have been expected to know that the seller had no right to sell the car), the buyer does not get good title to the car. The finance company/lessor has the right to repossess it from the buyer and the buyer can pursue the seller for recovery of any amounts he paid him for the car.

These rules only apply if the asset is a car. For any other asset further factors are taken into consideration:

■ Whether the buyer was aware the asset was subject to a hire purchase or conditional sale agreement

■ Whether the buyer physically took control of the asset

■ Whether the original finance/lease agreement was subject to the Consumer Credit Act.

These are mentioned here for completeness though these rules are beyond the scope of this book.

19.4.13   LESSOR ACCOUNTING

SSAP21 sets out the accounting methods to be used by both lessors and lessees to record lease, hire purchase and similar transactions.

Lessee accounting is dealt with in 8.4.

The introduction of International Financial Reporting Standards into the UK had a significant impact on some lessors, who had to change from accounting under SSAP21 to IAS17.

IAS17 requires:

■ Finance leases to be accounted for on a pre-tax basis. Under SSAP21 it was common for UK lessors to account for them on a post-tax basis, utilising the net cash investment method of accounting.

---

426 See 3.7.

■ Operating leases to be accounted for using one of the depreciation methods used in international standards, such as straight line depreciation. Some UK lessors had accounted for depreciation using an annuity basis or reverse rule of 78, and these are no longer available.

At the time of writing it is uncertain what the new lease accounting standard[427] will look like. We know that the IASB intends to issue a new exposure draft soon. The lessor accounting rules in any new standard is likely to be significantly different to either SSAP21 or ISA17.

We also do not know when it will be introduced. Even if it is delayed for a few years lessors will have to change their systems before then because whenever a new accounting treatment is required the prior year comparative numbers have to shown according to the new treatment.

You can get up-to-date information on the progress of this new standard from the IFRS website: www.ifrs.org

19.4.14 BVRLA DATA SURVEY

BVRLA members are able to subscribe to this survey that allows them to compare the residual values that they are setting with those being set by other members.

Members submit details of the residual values they are setting on all model derivatives that are available in the UK, over a range of periods and mileages. They can then access information online that shows their RV on each vehicle and its position in the market.

The identities of the other respondents is not disclosed, so this information, whilst of general assistance to the member, cannot be used tactically to undermine another contract hire company that is quoting for a particular vehicle on a particular day.

19.4.15 BVRLA VEHICLE MILEAGE DATABASE

The BVRLA maintains a mileage database with the specific aim of reducing the clocking of vehicles.

The database records vehicle mileages and disposal dates. BVRLA members submit this data to the BVRLA when their vehicles are serviced or sold. It is then sent to credit agencies and made available to the general public.

Dealers, traders and garages check the database to verify that the mileage reading on a car is accurate. Dealers know they have a legal obligation to properly describe the cars they are selling so this is a valuable tool for them. Trading standards officers also have direct access.

The BVRLA set up this consumer-protection system after discussion with the Office of Fair Trading. The BVRLA recognised that, as its members were disposing of a

---

427 See 8.6.

significant percentage of all used cars in the UK, it was well placed to provide this service to its members, the motor trade and the general public.

The data that members have to submit is:

- Vehicle registration number
- VIN number
- Vehicle make and model
- Disposal date
- Disposal mileage
- BVRLA member code

Many members submit additional data: colour, registration date, fuel type, body damage, odometer changed, engine damaged.

The database contains data on millions of vehicles.

19.5 SELECTING A FLEET COMPANY

Contract hire, fleet management and leasing companies should supply the vehicles you want for the periods you require, whilst making your business life easier and helping reduce costs.

As in all sectors of the economy, there are horses for courses. Some suppliers offer cheap-and-cheerful cut-down services, others offer full service and advice, whilst others sit somewhere in the middle.

The full service companies should provide you with:

- Assistance in selecting your funding policy (e.g. contract hire, contract purchase or a combination of methods)
- Assistance with your fleet allocation policy (which cars you should have on your fleet list, which groups of drivers should be entitled to which cars, etc)
- Assistance in monitoring vehicle usage and driver behaviour
- Fast response times for quotes, enquiries and reports (Their response should arrive in hours, not days.)

You will choose whichever supplier you think best meets your needs but, as in all sectors, don't expect to get full service and advice at pile-'em-high-sell-'em-cheap prices.

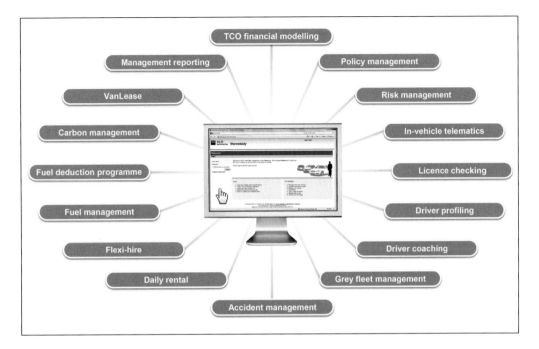

19.6 ORGANISATIONS

This chapter gives a thumbnail sketch of some of the organisations relevant to fleet managers or fleet companies.

19.6.1 ASSOCIATION OF CAR FLEET OPERATORS (ACFO)

Many fleet managers value having contact with other fleet managers.

This was the guiding thought behind the establishment of the Association of Car Fleet Operators. Their regional structure offers the opportunity to network with other fleet managers locally. They hold frequent meetings with speakers who are experts in their fields.

ACFO has a campaigning role and represents over 700 members (running over 400,000 cars and vans) in discussions with government departments.

They also provide fleet information, advice on legislation, training, a weekly email news sheet and the bi-monthly magazine Fleet Operator.

ACFO website: www.acfo.org

19.6.2 INSTITUTE OF CAR FLEET MANAGEMENT (ICFM)

The ICFM was founded in 1992. It is an independent body that provides training and education to car fleet managers, administrators, fleet service providers and those whose job responsibilities include fleet. Its courses lead to recognised vocational qualifications.

It is keen to foster and promote best practice in all aspects of car fleet management and to advance the professionalism of its members in all their undertakings, encouraging success for them as individuals and delivering real value to their employers.

Membership is open to all people involved in the fleet industry. The benefits of membership are:

- A valuable network of contacts.
- Opportunities for personal development.
- Access to information designed to enhance role performance and support the application of best practice.
- Professional recognition through certification, designatory letters after your name, award presentation and, where appropriate, press exposure.
- Opportunity to sharpen professional skills through enrolment on ICFM education and training programmes.
- Access, via the website, to the Interactive Guide to Car Fleet Management.
- Eligibility to attend the annual national members' conference.
- Access to the Member Advice Service for specific advice or guidance on policy, operational or strategic matters.
- Opportunities to publish professional articles or exchange ideas and concepts through the website.
- Network of contacts and access to information.
- Discounts on a range of services.

There are four levels of membership spanning the different levels of experience and qualification in vehicle fleet management:

AFFILIATE – AffICFM

For those about to enter the profession or having less than six months' experience in any role associated with fleet administration, fleet service support provision or employee mobility management.

ASSOCIATE – AICFM

For those with more than six months' experience in any role associated with fleet administration, fleet management, fleet service support provision or employee mobility management. Holders of the Introductory Certificate in Car Fleet Management.

MEMBER – MICFM

For those who can demonstrate, by reference to their record of success and other professional qualifications, that they are totally conversant with all aspects of the five units of competence covered in the Certificate in Car Fleet Management syllabus and who have proven ability in the operational management of a substantial company car fleet. Holders of the Certificate in Car Fleet Management.

FELLOW – FICFM

For full Members of the Institute who have successfully completed the advanced course of study leading to the Diploma in Car Fleet Management and have spent an established period in the strategic management of a vehicle fleet (normally for five years).

The ICFM's courses are combined with job-based assignments or projects designed to show that the student has understood the theoretical training and can apply it in their own business. Programmes are externally moderated and endorsed by the Institute of Leadership & Management (ILM), part of the City & Guilds Group.

Website: www.icfm.com

19.6.3   BRITISH VEHICLE RENTAL AND LEASING ASSOCIATION (BVRLA)

PURPOSE AND MEMBERSHIP

The BVRLA is the trade association of the UK vehicle leasing, rental and fleet management industry. Formed in 1967, its members represent more than 85% of the car and commercial vehicle leasing and contract hire industry by fleet size.

It is a member of Leaseurope, an umbrella body that represents the interests of national associations of 16 European countries.

Its mission is to represent its members on major policy issues, raise standards of operation and service and promote and protect members' interests.

Its aims and objectives say that it represents members' interests by educating and informing government about the industry's importance, ensuring that government and the EU takes the industry's views into account when framing impending legislation.

It provides members with a wide range of services, promotes the expansion of the market for the industry's services, develops and implements training programmes, stimulates improvements in vehicle design, maintains close links with overseas counterparts, provides members with market information and reacts rapidly to members' needs for new initiatives.

The BVRLA has over 400 members – leasing and rental companies – who own and operate around 2.5m cars, vans and trucks. This represents nearly half of all company cars in the UK.

They buy nearly half of all new vehicles sold in the UK. Together they manage 65% of all company cars in the UK.

Members spend approximately £16 billion each year on vehicles and £4 billion on support services.

Membership of the BVRLA is only granted to applicants that meet the organisation's strict standards and agree to abide by the BVRLA Code of Conduct.[428] A growing number of brokers have become members in recent years.

BVRLA members are required to give their clients the best quality of service that is fair to the client and the member, without hidden pricing. Members provide a service that is 'Quality Assured' by the association.

The BVRLA *Fair Wear and Tear Guide* is the industry standard for determining whether a vehicle has been returned at the end of a lease in fair condition.[429]

BVRLA TRAINING

The BVRLA offers training courses for employees in member companies, details of which are included here because this book is read by many people in BVRLA member companies.

Certificate in Fleet Consultancy

This is designed to align the rental/leasing sales function much more closely with the role, responsibilities and requirements of a typical fleet manager. Successful participants gain a professional qualification which has been externally accredited by the Institute of Leadership and Management.

ATA Technical Customer Service Advisor Programme

The BVRLA offers the ATA (automotive technician accreditation) Technical Customer Service Advisor (Rental & Leasing) programme to those working in technical services departments within the fleet industry.

Leasing Broker Sales Accreditation

The BVRLA offers Leasing Broker Sales Accreditation for sales staff within its leasing broker members. This is just one of a series of measures aimed at raising standards within the sector.

Fair Wear and Tear Standards Training

Delegates gain an understanding of the key principles influencing vehicle resale so they may be able to demonstrate practical knowledge of the BVRLA Fair Wear and Tear condition standards when talking to customers.

Selling Contract Hire

Designed to give delegates a greater understanding of areas such as finance, taxation, competitive contracts, margins and underwriting considerations. The aim is to make more confident, knowledgeable and effective.

Introduction to the Fleet Industry

Delegates receive an overview of the industry (size, growth potential, and competitor analysis), vehicle acquisition methods, the concept of whole life costs and the advantages of contract hire.

BVRLA website: www.bvrla.co.uk.

---

428 See 19.3.
429 See 1.2.13.

19.6.4 FINANCE & LEASING ASSOCIATION (FLA)

The FLA is a trade association that was formed through the merger of the Finance Houses Association (representing finance companies, mainly bank-owned) and the Equipment Leasing Association (representing leasing companies).

The facilities its members provide include finance leasing, operating leasing, hire purchase, conditional sale, personal contract purchase plans, personal lease plans, secured and unsecured personal loans, credit cards and store card facilities.

FLA has three areas of focus; asset finance, consumer credit and motor finance.

- The **Asset Finance** division serves finance houses, the finance arms of product manufacturers, merchant and investment bank subsidiaries and small niche finance providers. Members of this division provide over £20bn p.a. of asset finance.

- The **Consumer Credit** division serves the needs of the wide range of organisations involved in the provision of consumer credit, including banks and retailers, Members of this division provide over £53bn p.a. of credit.

- The **Motor Finance** division serves the needs of organisations that offer motor finance, including banks, contract hire companies and motor manufacturers' finance companies. FLA motor finance members provide £15-20bn of motor finance p.a., covering at least half of all new car registrations. They finance over 1.5m new and used car each year.

The FLA represents the views of its members to the government and other bodies. It runs courses and conferences and provides statistics and market information

A number of contract hire and leasing companies are members of the FLA, usually because they are part of groups that have wider asset finance interests.

FLA members have to comply with either a business or consumer code of practice[430] and there is a dispute resolution service for FLA members and their clients.

At the start of every month the FLA publishes the Finance House Base Rate, reflecting money market interest rates. [431]

19.6.5 SOCIETY OF MOTOR MANUFACTURERS AND TRADERS (SMMT)

The Society of Motor Manufacturers and Traders (SMMT) exists to support and promote the interests of the UK automotive industry at home and abroad. It acts as the voice of the motor industry, promoting its position to government, stakeholders and the media.

It publishes a range of reports on the UK automotive sector, many of which are available for free download. Of particular interest is Motor Industry Facts, an annual review of facts and figures about vehicle registration, production data and innovations.[432]

430 See 19.3.
431 See 6.3.11.
432 www.smmt.co.uk/reports-publications/industry-data

19.6.6 The Institute of the Motor Industry (IMI)

Formed in 1920, the IMI is the professional body for people employed in the motor industry.

It is the Sector Skills Council for the automotive retail industry and the governing body for the Automotive Technician Accreditation (ATA) scheme. Its offers a wide range of education and training programmes, with topics covering technical, management, sales, customer service, administration and training and development.

All of the IMI's 25,000 members agree to adhere by its code of conduct.

The IMI publishes *Motor Industry* magazine.

Website: www.motor.org.uk.

19.6.7 The Chartered Institute of Logistics and Transport in the UK

The Institute of Logistics and Transport was formed in 1999 with the merger of the Institute of Logistics and The Chartered Institute of Transport.

Its mission is to facilitate the development of personal and professional excellence, to encourage the development of leading-edge thinking and best practice in logistics, supply-chains and all transport and to provide relevant and valued services to members and employers.

Their 20,000 members work in transport, vehicle management and logistics and are generally responsible for the movement of people and goods. The institute advises the government on transport policy and publishes the monthly journal *Logistics & Transport Focus* and a wide range of papers on transport and logistics. They run training and development courses including an introductory certificate, certificate in professional competence, advanced diploma and MSc.

The Institute has local branches throughout the country.

Website: www.ciltuk.org.uk

19.6.8 Financial Services Authority (FSA)

The FSA is the body that regulates the financial services industry. It was established by *Financial Services and Markets Act 2000*, in which its objectives were defined as maintaining market confidence, promoting public understanding of the financial system, consumer protection and fighting financial crime.

It is an independent, non-government body that exercises statutory powers set out in various acts of parliament, including the *Financial Services Act 1986*, the *Banking Act 1987* and the *Financial Services and Markets Act 2000*.

Many lessors are owned by banks and are therefore regulated by the FSA. Bank regulation by the FSA includes reviews of banks' capital adequacy, protection of depositors' monies and the management of risk.

Should you believe that a financial institution is conducting business in a manner that may be illegal or damaging to the well-being of its customers or depositors, you may wish to contact the FSA to report your concerns.

The FSA levies fines of more than £2,000,000 on regulated businesses each year. Most are due to the mis-selling of financial products to consumers. This is a regulator with real teeth.

Website: www.fsa.gov.uk.

19.6.9 ENERGY SAVINGS TRUST (EST)

The Energy Saving Trust was set up after the 1992 Earth Summit in Rio de Janeiro, to help reduce carbon dioxide emissions in the UK. It is of interest to us because it provides fleet managers with a range of transport advice services that could save your organisation money, improve your environmental impact and help you meet your organisation's corporate social responsibility targets. The EST is funded by government and can deliver advice in England, Scotland and Wales.

They can provide advice for fleets of any size. If you have a small fleet you can email them a question and they'll let you have the answer. If you have between 10 and 100 vehicles you can sign up for their free monthly fleet briefings email.

If you have more than 20 vehicles they will carry out a free Fleet Health Check to calculate your carbon footprint and highlight opportunities for you to reduce emissions and costs.

If you have more than 50 vehicles (20 In Scotland) the EST will carry out a free and detailed environmental review of your fleet.

Website: www.energysavingtrust.org.uk.

19.6.10 VEHICLE & OPERATOR SERVICES AGENCY (VOSA)

This government agency was formed by the merger of the Vehicle Inspectorate (VI) and the Traffic Area Network (TAN) division of the Department for Transport (DfT).

The agency aims to improve road safety and environmental standards, and reduce vehicle crime.

VOSA:

- Promotes and enforces compliance with commercial operator licensing requirements
- Processes applications lorry and bus licences
- Registers bus services
- Operates and administers all vehicle testing schemes
- Supervises the MOT Testing Scheme
- Enforces the law on vehicles to ensure they comply with legal standards and regulations

■ Enforces drivers' hours and licensing requirements

■ Provides training and advice for commercial operators

■ Investigates vehicle accidents, defects and recalls

VOSA staff have the power to stop vehicles for roadside checks. If a vehicle exceeds the emissions limits

■ by less than 10%, the driver will be told the test results advised that the engine requires servicing.

■ by more than 10%, the driver will be told that an offence has been committed and will be given a Fixed Penalty Notice.

Website: www.vosa.gov.uk

19.6.11   THE OCCUPATIONAL ROAD SAFETY ALLIANCE (ORSA)[433]

The Occupational Road Safety Alliance (ORSA) brings together employers, trade unions, local authorities, police forces, safety organisations and professional and trade associations. It believes, in common with the Government and the Health and Safety Commission, that employers should manage at-work road risk within the framework that they should already have in place for managing all other occupational health and safety risks.

Its aims are to:

■ Facilitate networking between key stakeholders

■ Encourage joint working to raise awareness in organisations of the need for action on work related road safety

■ Promote the exchange of information on new initiatives and best practice

■ Establish a statement of common goals

■ Organise events

■ Establish technical co-operation

ORSA believes that all employers, large or small, private or public, should seek to develop a systematic approach to managing occupational road risk that is appropriate to their business, for example by:

■ Gathering and analysing key safety and risk data on their vehicles, journeys, drivers, crashes, causes and costs

■ Setting and communicating clear corporate road safety objectives

■ Ensuring everyone understands their role in achieving them

■ Introducing targeted safety measures based on suitable risk assessment (backed by standards, targets and timescales)

■ Monitoring performance and learning from accidents and incidents

■ Carrying out periodic performance reviews in order to feed back lessons learned

---

433 This section was produced by ORSA and is reproduced here with their permission.

ORSA encourages employers to commit themselves to achieving a cycle of continuous improvement in road safety performance, ensuring that this approach is underpinned by a proactive, positive road safety culture lead by all senior managers with full workforce consultation and participation.

It urges employers to sign up to this challenge to improve safety on our roads and to share their good practice with all other organisations that share the same vision.

Their website, www.orsa.org.uk, contains resources that will be useful to you in developing an action plan to improve the safety of your employees on the road.

19.6.12 THE INSURANCE FRAUD BUREAU (IFB)

The IFB was formed by the insurance industry in 2006 to detect and prevent insurance fraud. It shares information across insurers and has been responsible for the arrest of hundreds of arrests.

If you suspect insurance fraud you can report this to the IFB on 0800 328 2550 or via www.insurancefraudbureau.org. They will identify the insurer that has been affected and will work with them to ensure the fraud is detected, investigated and if possible prevented.

19.6.13 VEHICLE REMARKETING ASSOCIATION (VRA)[434]

The VRA was established in 2010 by a group of like-minded individuals from companies involved in all aspects of remarketing who handle, sell, inspect, transport or manage more than 1.5 million used vehicles p.a.

Its objectives are to:

- create better awareness of the activities of professional remarketing
- raise standards and generate an accepted 'best practice' across the industry for key disciplines like vehicle inspection
- provide a much needed voice to represent the sector in the trade and consumer media on issues which affect remarketing suppliers and customers
- provide an effective focal point through which major matters concerning those involved in remarketing can be addressed
- raise the profile and professionalism of the industry to ensure recruiting good quality people becomes much easier
- generate views and opinions of the industry for use in lobbying for the greater good of the remarketing sector
- create a forum where members can network, exchange views, debate key topics and share Best Practice

Full membership is available to those companies such as auctions, contract hire and leasing companies, manufacturers and dealer groups that directly work in the remarketing industry

---

434 This material was produced by the VRA and is included here with their kind permission.

Associate membership is available to those companies who do not work directly in the remarketing industry such as those from marketing, accountants, lawyers, transport, inspection and logistics.

Member benefits include:

- Free access to VRA's annual remarketing seminar
- Help shape and develop an industry-wide inspection standard for used vehicles
- Gain access to exclusive training courses
- Provide high level industry feedback to the used vehicle guide
- Use the VRA website to advertise job vacancies, free for the first 2 weeks
- Use the VRA website and regular networking sessions to share tips and advice with other remarketing professionals
- Support VRA in lobbying the government to ensure remarketing is represented on key issues
- Let the VRA help you recruit new remarketing staff

You can contact the VRA via their website www.vehicle-remarketing.co.uk

19.6.14 FLEET SAFETY FORUM

The Fleet Safety Forum provides guidance and tools to tackle road risk within your company. It is a division of Brake.

For an annual subscription you can get access to the Forum's website, which provides:

- Reports on how to tackle road risk. Topics include driver eyesight, vehicle maintenance systems and the recording and analysis of crash data.
- Case studies of companies that have significantly reduced their road risk through a variety of management methods.
- A database of research by road safety academics around the globe.
- Pledge2DriveSafely campaign toolkit that enables at-work drivers to make a professional promise to comply with the most critical safety rules. The Pledge2DriveSafely campaign tool kit includes resources video clips, presentations, games and quizzes suitable for driver induction programmes or on-going educational and remedial programmes.

Subscribers also receive a fortnightly email bulletin of the latest news on road risk management and discounts to Fleet Safety Forum events (including their workshop and annual conference), the opportunity to enter and attend the annual Fleet Safety Forum awards and to engage in Brake's wider programme of community events.

19.6.15 BRAKE

Brake is a charity that works to stop unnecessary road accident death, injury, trauma and expense, and to create roads that are safe for everybody. See 13.8 for more details

19.6.16 RETREAD MANUFACTURERS ASSOCIATION (RMA)

The RMA is the trade association for UK manufacturers of retreaded tyres. It lobbies government on matters which can affect the retreading industry and is a member of BIPAVER (The European Association for Tyre Retailers and Retreaders).

The RMA promotes the safety, economic and environmental benefits of retreaded tyres.

Website: www.retreaders.org.uk

19.6.17 VEHICLE BUILDERS AND REPAIRERS ASSOCIATION (VBRA)

VBRA is the trade association for vehicle body builders and repairers. It is very keen to remind consumers that they can choose where to have their vehicles repaired and don't have to accept the "threats and coercion"[435] of the insurer.

Website: www.vbra.co.uk

19.7 EXERCISES

List the different ways you might make a complaint against a fleet company.

What are the key elements of the BVRLA code of conduct?

What are the key elements of the FLA code of practice?

How does credit management work?

What is CIFAS and what does it do?

How does match-funding work?

Explain deferred tax.

What is VOSA?

435 Sic – VBRA website

A

ALD Automotive Limited
Oakwood Park
Lodge Causeway
Fishponds
Bristol
BS16 3JA
Website: www.aldautomotive.co.uk

Association of Car Fleet Operators
Membership Coordinator
35 Lavant Street
Petersfield
GU32 3EL
Phone 01730 260162
Website: www.acfo.org

B

British Independent Motor Traders
Association (BIMTA)
One Media
Kenwood House
1 Upper Grosvenor
Tunbridge Wells
Kent
TN1 2EL
Website: www.bimta.org.

The British Safety Council
Email: ask@britsafe.org
Phone: +44 (0)20 8741 1231
Website: www.britsafe.org

British Vehicle Rental and Leasing Association
River Lodge
Badminton Court
Amersham
Buckinghamshire
HP7 0DD
Phone: +44 (0)1494 434747
Fax: +44 (0)1494 434499
info@bvrla.co.uk
Website: www.bvrla.co.uk

Brake
PO Box 548
Huddersfield
HD1 2XZ.
Phone: +44 (0)1484 559909.
Fax: +44 (0)1484 559983.
Email: brake@brake.org.uk or
fleetsafetyforum@brake.org.uk

Business Car magazine
Progressive House
2 Maidstone Road
Foots Cray
DA14 5HZ
E-mail: editorial@businesscar.co.uk
Website: www.businesscar.co.uk
Tel: +44 (0)20 8269 7741

Business Car Manager Ltd
95 Station Road
Hampton
Middlesex
TW12 2BD
Phone: +44 (0)208 783 0999
Email: editor@businesscarmanager.co.uk

C

CAP Motor Research Limited
Capitol House
Bond Court
Leeds
West Yorkshire
LS1 5EZ
Email: marketing@cap.co.uk
Website: www.cap.co.uk
Phone: +44 (0)113 222 2000
Fax: +44 (0)113 222 2001

carbon heroes ltd.
2 Lake End Court
Taplow Road
Taplow
Maidenhead
Berkshire
SL6 0JQ
Phone: +44 (0) 843 290 3800
Website: www.carbonheroes.com

The Chartered Institute of Logistics and
Transport in the UK
Earlstrees Court
Earlstrees Road
Corby, Northants
NN17 4AX
Website: www.ciltuk.org.uk

CIFAS
6th Floor, Lynton House
7-12 Tavistock Square
London
WC1 9LT
Email: cifas@cifas.org.uk
Website: www.cifas.org.uk

Consumer Credit Trade Association
The Wave
1 Viewcroft Road
Shipley
West Yorkshire
BD17 7DU
Phone: 01274 714959
Fax: 0845 257 1199
Email: info @ccta.co.uk
Website: www.ccta.co.uk

Criminal Injuries Compensation Authority
Tay House
300 Bath Street
Glasgow
G2 4LN
Phone: 0300 003 3601
Fax: +44 (0)141 331 2287
Website: www.cica.gov.uk

D

Department for Transport
Great Minster House
76 Marsham Street
London
SW1P 4DR
Phone: 0300 330 3000
Fax: 020 7944 9643
Email FAX9643@dft.gsi.gov.uk
Website: www.dft.gov.uk/

Disabled Motoring UK
Ashwellthorpe
Norwich
NR16 1EX
Phone: 01508 489449
Email: info@disabledmotoring.org
Website: www.disabledmotoring.org

Driver and Vehicle Licensing Agency (DVLA)
Swansea
SA6 7JL
Phone: 0300 790 6801
Website: www.dvla.gov.uk

Driver and Vehicle Licensing Northern Ireland
Chief Executive's Office
County Hall, Castlerock Road
Coleraine
Co. Londonderry
BT51 3TA
Phone 0845 402 4000
FAX :- (028) 7034 1398
Minicom :- (028) 7034 1380
Website: www.dvani.gov.uk

E

The Energy Saving Trust
Phone 0845 602 1425.
www.energysavingtrust.org.uk.

Euro NCAP
2 Place du Luxembourg
1050 Brussels
BELGIUM
Tel: +32 2 400 77 40
Fax: +32 2 400 77 41
Website: www.euroncap.com

F

Finance & Leasing Association
Imperial House
15-19 Kingsway
London
WC2B 6UN.
Phone: +44 (0)20 20 7836 6511
Helpline: 0800 023 4567 (free)
Fax: +44 (0)20 7420 9600
Email: info@fla.org.uk
Website: www.fla.org.uk

Financial Ombudsman Service
South Quay Plaza
183 Marsh Wall
London
E14 9SR
Phone: +44 (0)20 7964 1000
Email: enquiries@financial-ombudsman.org.uk
Website: www.financial-ombudsman.org.uk

The Financial Services Authority
25 The North Colonnade
Canary Wharf
London
E14 5HS
Phone: +44 (0)20 7066 1000
Website: www.fsa.gov.uk

Fleet Safety Forum
PO Box 548
Huddersfield
HD1 2XZ
Phone: +44 (0)1480 559909
Fax: +44 (0)1480 559983
Email: brake@brake.org.uk

G

Glass's Information Services Ltd
1 Princes Road
Weybridge.
Surrey
KT13 9TU
Phone +44 (0)1932 823 802
Fax +44 (0)1932 849 299
Email: Customer Services -
customer@eurotaxglass.co.uk
Website: www.glass.co.uk

Greater London Authority
City Hall
The Queens Walk
London SE1 2AA
Phone: +44 (0)20 7983 4000
Fax: +44 (0)20 7983 4057
Email: mayor@london.gov.uk
Website: www.london.gov.uk

H

The Health and Safety Executive
Website: www.hse.gov.uk

HM Revenue and Customs
Local VAT offices – see phone book
Website: www.hmrc.gov.uk

HM Stationery Office
The National Archives
102 Petty France
London
SW1H 9AJ
Phone 0870 600 5522
Website: www.hmso.gov.uk

HPI Limited
Dolphin House
New Street
Salisbury
SP1 2PH
Website: www.hpi.co.uk
Phone: +44 (0)1722 413 434
Fax: +44 (0)1722 412164

I

Institute of Car Fleet Management
Administration Centre
P.O. Box 314
Chichester
PO20 9WZ
Phone: +44 (0)1462 744914
Fax: +44 (0)1243 607591
Email: administration@icfm.com
Website: www.icfm.com

The Institute of the Motor Industry
Fanshaws
Brickendon
Hertford
SG13 8PQ
Phone: +44 (0)1992 511 521
Fax: +44 (0)1992 511 548
Email: imi@motor.org.uk
Website: www.motor.org.uk

The Insurance Fraud Bureau (IFB)
Phone 0800 328 2550
Website: www.insurancefraudbureau.org

L

London Congestion Charging
PO Box 4782
Worthing
BN11 9PS
Phone: 0845 900 1234
Website: www.cclondon.com

UKLPG
Camden House
Warwick Road
Kenilworth
Warwickshire
CV8 1TH
Email: autogas@uklpg.org
Website: www.uklpg.org

M

MIAFTR
HPI Limited
Dolphin House
New Street
Salisbury
SP1 2PH
Email: questions@miaftr.hpi.co.uk
Phone: 01722 435579
Website: www.miaftr-hpi.info

The Motor Insurers' Bureau
Linford Wood House
6-12 Capital Drive
Linford Wood
Milton Keynes
MK14 6XT
Phone: +44 (0)1908 830001
Website: www.mib.org.uk
Email: Enquiries@mib.org.uk

Motorvate
www.energysavingtrust.org.uk

Bing Maps internet-based map site
Website: www.bing.com/maps

O

Office of Fair Trading
Fleetbank House
2-6 Salisbury Square
London
EC4Y 8JX
Phone: +44 (0)20 7211 8000
Fax: +44 (0)20 7211 8800
Email: enquiries@oft.gsi.gov.uk
Website: www.oft.gov.uk

Office of the Information Commissioner
Wycliffe House
Water Lane
Wilmslow
Cheshire
SK9 5AF
Phone: 0303 123 1113
Fax: +44 (0)1625 524510
Website: www.ico.gov.uk

The Occupational Road Safety Alliance
(ORSA)
Email: furtherinfo@orsa.org.uk
Website: www.orsa.org.uk

R

Renewable Energy Association
7th Floor, Capital Tower
91 Waterloo Road
London
SE1 8RT
Phone: +44 (0) 20 7925 3570
website: www.r-e-a.net

Retread Manufacturers Association
PO Box 320
Crewe
Cheshire CW2 6WY
e-mail: rma@greentyres.com
Phone +44(0) 01270 561014
Fax: +44 (0)1270 668801
Website: www.retreaders.org.uk

S

The Society of Motor Manufacturers and
Traders Limited
71 Great Peter Street, London SW1P 2BN,
United Kingdom
Phone: +44 (0)20 7235 7000
Fax: +44 (0)20 7235 7112
Email: smmt@smmt.co.uk
Website: www.smmt.co.uk

T

Thatcham
The Motor Insurance Repair Research Centre
Colthrop Way
Thatcham
Berks
RG19 4NR
Phone: +44 (0)1635 868855
Fax: +44 (0)1635 871346
Email: enquiries@thatcham.org
Website: www.thatcham.org

Tyresafe
5 Berewyk Court
White Colne
Colchester
Essex
Tele:- 01787 226995
Fax:- 0845 301 6853
Website: www.tyresafe.org,.uk
Email:tic@tyresafe.org.uk

U

UK government
You can search the UK government's
websites via www.direct.gov.uk

V

Vehicle & Operator Services Agency
Berkeley House,
Croydon Street,
Bristol BS5 ODA
Email: enquiries@vosa.gov.uk
Website: www.vosa.gov.uk

Vehicle Builders and Repairers Association
(VBRA)
Belmont House
Gildersome
Leeds
LS27 7TW.
Phone +44 (0)113 253 8333.
Fax +44 (0)113 238 0496.
Email: vbra@vbra.co.uk
Website: www.vbra.co.uk

Vehicle Certification Agency
The Eastgate Office Centre
Eastgate Road
Bristol
BS5 6XX
Phone: +44 (0)117 951 5151
Fax: +44 (0)117 952 4103
Website: www.vca.gov.uk

Vehicle Remarketing Association
Phone: steve@nobull-communications.co.uk
Email: 01628 526208
Website: www.vehicle-remarketing.co.uk

TABLE OF AUTHORITIES

INDEX

Have you found this book valuable?

Could we have presented the information
in a better way?

Is there something you would have
liked to learn more about?

Did we omit any part of the fleet industry?

If we produce a 4th edition of this book,
how could we make it even better?

We would like to hear from you!

Please send us feedback via

www.tourick.com

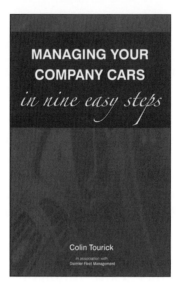

Managing Your Company Cars in Nine Easy Steps

ISBN 978 1902528243, Eyelevel Books, 2008. List price £15

Available in hard copy from good bookshops, amazon.co.uk and www.tourick.com

Also available as pdf download fromwww.tourick.com

In many areas of business – human resources, property management, manufacturing, IT and so on – there are thousands of books to help company managers make the right decisions, reduce costs and manage risks.

However, even though most new cars are bought by businesses, and the cost of the car fleet can be a very significant business expense, there were almost no textbooks on this important subject. Colin Tourick wrote Managing Your Company Cars to fill this gap. Now in its second edition, it continues to sell around the world.

In this new book, Managing Your Company Cars in Nine Easy Steps, he takes the most essential material from Managing Your Company Cars and condenses it into a much slimmer volume, making it an excellent introduction to this specialist topic.

Thank you for buying Managing Your Company Cars.
We hope that this book will help you manage your fleet effectively.

However this book can only offer general information.
There is no substitute for professional advice tailored to your specific needs.

Are you sure your fleet costs are under control?

There are many ways to reduce your costs without reducing
the quality of the cars you offer your drivers.

Are you sure you are using the best method to fund your fleet vehicles?

No one method is right for every company.
You may need to use different methods for different cars to minimise your costs.

Are you worried about your duty of care to your company car drivers?

You have to minimise the risks.
You may need to carry out a comprehensive risk review.

We are impartial and independent fleet management consultants.

We would be delighted to discuss any aspect of the management of your fleet.

There is no substitute for tailor made advice
from an impartial, independent source.

CT&A

Building Profit, Developing People

Colin Tourick and Associates Limited is a management consultancy specialising in the leasing and fleet management market.

We help leasing and finance companies boost revenues, reduce costs, increase profits and develop new products.

We help fleet managers cut costs, manage their fleets more effectively and save tax.

We help leasing and finance companies outside the UK apply UK know-how to develop their businesses.

We help all manner of businesses improve their pricing and develop their people.

The business was formed by Colin Tourick in 1992. Colin has 32 years' experience in vehicle management and asset finance.

Hilary Davis is a management coach with 15 years' professional experience working with senior management teams in Top 100 companies.

CT&A
Management Consultants
Colin Tourick and Associates Limited
London
postmaster@tourick.com
www.tourick.com